AUTHORITY, STATE AND NATIONAL CHARACTER

Authority, State and National Character

The Civilizing Process in Austria and England, 1700–1900

Helmut Kuzmics
University of Graz, Austria

and

Roland Axtmann
University of Wales Swansea, UK

Studies in European Cultural Transition

Volume Thirty Six

General Editors: Martin Stannard and Greg Walker

Routledge
Taylor & Francis Group
LONDON AND NEW YORK

First published 2007 by Ashgate Publishing

2 Park Square, Milton Park, Abingdon, Oxon OX14 4RN
711 Third Avenue, New York, NY 10017, USA

Routledge is an imprint of the Taylor & Francis Group, an informa business

First issued in paperback 2016

British Library Cataloguing in Publication Data
Kuzmics, Helmut, 1949-
Authority, state and national character : the civilizing process in Austria and England, 1700-1900. - (Studies in European cultural transition)
1.Authority 2.Power (Social sciences) 3.National characteristics, Austrian – History 4.National characteristics, English – History 5.Austria – History – 18th century 6.Austria – History – 1789-1900 7.Great Britain – History – 18th century 8.Great Britain - History – 19th century
I.Title II.Axtmann, Roland
303.3'6

Library of Congress Cataloging-in-Publication Data
Kuzmics, Helmut, 1949-
[Autorität, Staat und Nationalcharakter. English]
Authority, state and national character : the civilizing process in Austria and England, 1700-1900 / by Helmut Kuzmics and Roland Axtmann.
p. cm. — (Studies in European cultural transition)
Includes bibliographical references and index.
ISBN 0-7546-3560-0 (alk. paper)
1. Authority. 2. Power (Social sciences) 3. Literature and society—Austria. 4. Literature and society—England. 5. National characteristics, Austrian—History. 6. National characteristics, English—History. 7. Austria—Civilization—17th century. 8. Austria—Civilization—18th century. 9. England—Civilization—17th century. 10. England—Civilization—18th century. I. Axtmann, Roland. II. Title. III. Series.

HM1251.K8913 2000
303.3'6—dc22

2006006946

The authors would like to thank the Austrian Ministry of Education, Science and Culture; the Province of Styria, Department for Science and Research; and the University of Graz/Austria for supporting the translation of this book.

First published in German as: Helmut Kuzmics/Roland Axtmann, *Autorität, Staat und Nationalcharakter. Der Zivilisationsprozeß in Österreich und England 1700 – 1900.* Leske + Budrich: Opladen 2000.

Bruce Allen and Alex Skinner provided excellent translation services.

ISBN 13: 978-0-7546-3560-4 (hbk)
ISBN 13: 978-1-138-27348-1 (pbk)

Contents

General Editor's Preface ix
List of Tables x
Acknowledgements xi

1 Introduction 1

Authority and affect-modelling 1
National habitus 5
The argument in overview 14

2 The Formation of the English State and the Sociogenesis of Political Authority 25

Preliminary remarks 25
Historical changes in the balance of power between Crown and Parliament in England 27
Elements in the pacification and disciplining of English society 42
Aspects of the formation of the English fiscal state 59

3 The Formation of the Austrian State and the Sociogenesis of Political Authority 69

Confessional absolutism in Austria 76
Reform absolutism 83
Constitutionalism, parliamentarization and the struggle of the nationalities 98

4 Feudal Patrimonialism and Ecclesiastical Coercion of Conscience in Austria 115

Literary examples from the end of the era 115
Development of ecclesiastical authority and its imprint on the Austrian habitus 121
Peasant attitudes to feudal-patrimonial authority: Some literary examples 128
The feudal warrior code in Austria: Some reflections and a first comparison with England 131
Authority in the dock: the experience of the Great War 137

5 Feudal Paternalism in England: Developments Within the Gentleman Canon 145

A literary example from the end of the era 145
The gentleman canon and Puritanism: Pathways to the English character 151
Literary examples of how the gentleman canon evolved in the 18th century 156
The gentleman canon and parliamentarianism in Trollope's *Can You Forgive Her?* 164

6 The Courtly Element in the Austrian Character: Authority, Pretence and Servility 179

An example from the end of the era 179
The Austrian mode of interaction with authority as exemplified by Viennese popular comedy 183
The courtly pattern and Vienna's urban middle classes in Nestroy's reception 188
The courtly element in Habsburg bureaucracy parodied: The case of Herzmanovsky-Orlando 198
Authoritarianism and self-irony in the Austrian habitus: Some remarks on the literary examples in Herzmanovsky-Orlando and Nestroy 203

7 Proud Detachment as an Element of English Authority Relationships: 'Indirect Rule' 215

An example from the end of the era 215
Defoe's Robinson and his servant Friday 218
Authority, proud reserve and English character in Jane Austen's *Pride and Prejudice* 221
Digression: Ships, discipline and English character as exemplified in the Hornblower novels of C.S. Forester 233
Reflections on the examples dealt with thus far, and on comparison with Austria's courtly model 239

8 Bureaucratization as an Austrian Civilizing Process 245

Examples from the end of the era 245
From Josephinist officialdom to the *Vormärz* police state: Reflections in bourgeois literature 251
Karl Postl's (Charles Sealsfield's) *Austria, As It Is* as an analysis of the *Vormärz* authoritarian state: Authority and Austrian national character in the early 19th century 258
Grillparzer: Patrimonial authority and bureaucratic timidity as Austrian character traits 265

The official through parody: Herzmanovsky-Orlando 284
A comparison with England: The 'civil servant' in Trollope 288

9 Puritanism, Book-Keeping and the Moralization of Authority in the English Habitus 293

Examples from the end of the era 293
Defoe's *Moll Flanders* and the anonymous authority of the market 298
Dickens' *Oliver Twist* and the morality of pitilessness 307
Evangelicalism and the rise of a new middle-class morality: Jane Eyre and St John Rivers 310
A comparison with Austria: Nation and patrimonial authority in Joseph Roth 314

Bibliography *325*
Index *351*

General Editors' Preface

The European dimension of research in the humanities has come into sharp focus over recent years, producing scholarship which ranges across disciplines and national boundaries. Until now there has been no major channel for such work. This series aims to provide one, and to unite the fields of cultural studies and traditional scholarship. It will publish the most exciting new writing in areas such as European history and literature, art history, archaeology, language and translation studies, political, cultural and gay studies, music, psychology, sociology and philosophy. The emphasis will be explicitly European and interdisciplinary, concentrating attention on the relativity of cultural perspectives, with a particular interest in issues of cultural transition.

Martin Stannard
Greg Walker
University of Leicester

List of Tables

2.1 National revenue, 1558–1688 at current prices 60

2.2 National revenue, 1559–1688 at constant prices 60

2.3 National revenue, 1689–1715 at current prices 61

2.4 Government expenditure as a percentage of gross national product, 1820–1910 (current prices) 65

2.5 National revenue per capita of population in £, 1822 to 1903–1904 66

2.6 Selected types of income as a percentage of total revenue, 1843–1913 66

Acknowledgements

Writing this book has been a lengthy and complicated journey that began in the early 1990s. It started with a grant of the Austrian *Fonds zur Förderung der wissenschaftlichen Forschung* enabling one of us, Helmut Kuzmics, to spend a year (1990–91) in Cambridge and thus, to start a project that should later turn into this book. Between 1990 and the publishing date of the German version of it, many years have passed, years, in which we received a great deal of help from a substantial number of helpful colleagues, through comments, extensive discussion or important hints: Karl Acham, Graz; Reinhard Blomert, Berlin; Leslie Bodi, Melbourne; Stephan Böhm, Graz; Rainer Czaputa, Graz; Eric Dunning, Leicester; Peter R. Gleichmann (†), Hannover; Franz Höllinger, Graz; Gernot Lauffer, Graz; Jacques Le Rider, Paris; Gerald Mozetič, Graz; Maggie O'Neill, Staffordshire; Gregor Pozniak, Vienna; Heiner Rutte, Graz; Ralph Schroeder, Oxford; Michael Schröter, Berlin; Steve Sharot, Bersheba; Annette Treibel, Bochum/Karlsruhe; Efrat Tseëlon, Leeds/Dublin; Richard Wall, Cambridge; Cas Wouters, Utrecht; Jörg Zilian (†), Graz. Gerald Mozetič, Heiner Rutte and Jörg Zilian (†) read various drafts of this book and helped to eliminate errors of all kind. We are also grateful for the ideas and contributions of some excellent students in graduate courses at the University of Graz – Barbara Hönig, Ruth Kümmel and Dieter Reicher. The lengthy and certainly very demanding task of translating an enormously tricky German text was more than satisfactorily performed by Bruce Allen, Heidelberg (Chapters 1, 4–6) and Alex Skinner (Chapters 2–3, 7–9). The translation was only made possible by the financial assistance of the Austrian Ministry for Education, Science and Culture, the Government of the Province of Styria, and the University of Graz. We wish to thank them all. During the time-consuming process of translation, we have also received invaluable help from Eric Dunning, Leicester; Jonathan Fletcher, Singapore; Steven Loyal and Steven Quilley, both Dublin, and Brigitte Steingruber, Graz. Many thanks! Regina Fritzsche assisted in preparing the Index. Particular mention, finally, deserves Gertrude Selbitschka, who wrote and formatted the final version of this book. Without her skill and patience this book would not have been published.

Graz, Swansea
December 2006

Chapter 1

Introduction

Authority and affect-modelling

A number of films well evoke the spirit and existential certainties of the departed British Empire and its even more utterly vanished pendant, the Habsburg Monarchy. There is, for example, *Chariots of Fire* (1981), an epic film of now iconic stature, which follows the making of British athletes through to Olympic triumph in the middle-distance track events. A numinous 'Englishness' that fairly evades the sociologist's net shines through this saga of enterprise and fair play, of altercations with college authorities set against the spirit of commercialization, down to the final sporting breakthrough, as sensational as it is hard-won. Just such a tussle between university authorities and headstrong students, waged *sotto voce* but no less boisterously for all that, marked also by elements of great mutual respect and enacted in scenes of subtly deployed bodily language against the backdrop of an instantly recognizable college landscape, strikes the Continental observer as 'typically English', though she might be unable to say exactly why this is so. Altogether different is the impression made by grumpy privy councillors and fetching chamber maids (equally familiar fare to Austrian cinema-goers) in films starring the 'people's actor' himself, Hans Moser: somehow we know stories like this could never have happened in London or Cambridge. But how *do* we know? What is it that makes these slightly absurd portrayals of moaning subalterns, ready to burst into song at the drop of a hat, so unmistakeably and so utterly Austrian? In this book we assume that such sociologically vexed questions will yield only, if at all, to a multi-layered analysis of authority and co-incident patterns of psychic sedimentation.

'Authority' covers an exceptionally broad spectrum. Essentially, we shall proceed from two different angles. One is to analyze the balance of forces within the respective societies as manifested in struggles between major social groups since early modern times, a balance that had acquired clear contours by the First World War, the caesura that would see off Habsburg Monarchy and English global hegemony alike. The clearest expression of this balance of forces is the strength and status of the organs of state control – the police, the military and the administration. The other angle is to analyze the psychic structures whereby power is internalized in inculcation, deployment and toleration. We shall assume that the structures of (legitimate) authority and emotions associated with deployment and also toleration of power can indeed vary greatly. Taking our cue from Norbert

Elias, we postulate a social 'habitus' (Elias 1996), explicable in terms of the 'biography of state societies'. Not only social macro-structures such as states or markets, but 'inner' psychic structures for modelling emotions and affects, show an astonishing degree of stability. Despite undergoing slow transformation from generation to generation, they still manage to reproduce themselves. Here it is important to isolate the formative settings for the imprinting of human emotions and relationships. The social character of the courtier, merchant or soldier also specifies, at least in part, the character of the French, Dutch or Prussians. This dimension of how power and powerlessness is experienced is usually hard to probe historiographically. In order to analyze the link between developmental structures and the formation of 'national character' or 'state character', we explore belletristic literature that flourished in Austria and England between the early 18th and early 20th centuries.

Different mentalities in different cultures can never be a mere reflex of state formation processes; they can derive equally well from environmental factors like the climate or social processes prior to state formation – such as ethnogenesis. Much of all this would likely yield to scholarly or scientific scrutiny; much, to be sure, would continue to elude our gaze. In any event, it is a useful heuristic device to begin by asking: what can we say in light of what is known about the state and state-formation processes?

Certainly in central and northwestern Europe these diverged as widely as can be. In England and Austria we have two of the longest-lasting European great powers (along with France, Russia, Prussia and the Ottoman Empire, later joined by the new nation-states of Italy and Germany – the latter taking over from Prussia). Their comparison alone suffices to justify the present study, particularly as the contrast could hardly be greater between the island state, which was unified at a comparatively early date, and the multi-national patchwork state situated at the junction of diverse civilizational roads between East and West, North and South. The collapse of the Habsburg Monarchy at the end of the First World War may therefore be seen as a natural caesura – after which something new was embarked on, though the old would long continue to impact on the new. Comparisons of Austria with England are not exactly thick on the ground, even in the macro-sociological literature. This stands in marked contrast to the well-researched variations between France, Germany and England. Though the state-formation processes of the two have been comparatively treated – for example, by Parsons (1970), Anderson (1974) and M. Mann (1988) – the aspect of how these processes impacted on the respective mentalities remains, however, unchartered territory. The Baroque bulbous spires – the 'onion domes' – of Catholic Austria were no less alien to English travellers as the understated greys of English churches and churchyards were to itinerant Austrians. No less alien to each visitor were the political cultures, the rules of etiquette in public spaces, the sporting cultures, etc. Impressions of this kind – which can also be gleaned from how individuals related to the state authority – belie touted clichés of a uniform Western modernity. Thus, a not unimportant point of departure for this work is to demonstrate just how different these societies were on the affective level of emotions and imprinting of experience. Our book studies a period terminating at that caesura that was to bathe the 20th century (so hopefully begun) in the lurid and red colour of blood now inseparable from how we think of it. Naturally, it is clear that each history is written from the vantage of a discrete present and its problems. But it is no disservice to point out that the differential civilizational processes in England and Austria (countries which found themselves in 1914 on opposing sides in a war neither wanted – they were the last of the major belligerents to declare war on each other, yet they almost never met on the field of battle) helped shape their respective destinies in the 20th century. The Austria of former times has gone; England still holds on as a great power, albeit on a reduced scale.

To what extent did habituations developed by 1914 influence the further domestic and foreign policy fortunes of England and the Central European states that succeeded the Dual Monarchy? Interesting as the question is, we must leave its resolution to others. We attempt in this book to get beyond bald assertions to the effect that Austria was an authoritarian system with an inchoate parliamentary presence, while England was a paragon of democracy and parliamentary bourgeois society – assertions that have much to do with the *legenda negra*, the 'black legend' of Habsburg, as described by Friedrich Heer. This begins with the image of a repressive Catholic Spain (Habsburg being seen in Protestant-Anglo-Dutch perspective); proceeds via the notion of the 'dungeon of the peoples' as developed in the 19th century on the basis of identification with Hungarian, Czech and Italian national movements; and culminates in the derisory appraisals of the truncated republic heard at the dying days of the 20th century (cf. Heer 1981: 344–5; Bruckmüller 1996: 132–3). Turning to England, there has been – presumably no new development this – a 'Central European' perception of England oscillating between the poles of 'bulwark of freedom' (as in reports by Germanophone visitors: see Maurer 1992) and 'perfidious Albion' (especially common before, during and after the Great War). These images vent observations and appraisals of perturbing – in an Austrian perspective! – encounters with parliamentary rule and the unbridled sway of the marketplace, neither of these two institutions being well understood at home.

We build upon the sociology of Norbert Elias, whose leading idea (Elias 2000) itself comes from Freud's psycho-analytic theory of culture. The enculturation process consists, for Freud, in an incremental steering, or repression, of 'drives' (lumped together as the 'id') by a 'super-ego' (which internalizes external constraints) and a controlling 'ego' (which delimits itself energetically from its amorphous initial state to a greater or lesser degree). This process, which is repeated in every individual, gives rise to denials and conflicts, many of which cannot be accessible to ego control and so are discharged, poorly processed, into the neurotic substrate of the cultural social order. Elias has historicized and empiricized this line of thought, plausibly suggesting that the European upper classes, as they passed from being savage warriors to refined courtiers, have all undergone just such a 'civilizing' process.

According to Elias, humans are exposed to acute 'external' constraints – either natural or human. Harsh nature does this by deficiencies and shortfalls of all kinds – a cold or hot climate or inadequacies in the food supply, for instance. 'External' constraints (or, as Elias also calls it, 'constraints by others') of human provenance might be bloody wars or the overseer's whip or the daily burdens of social communication, things humans are given to inflicting on their fellows. These all model the 'plastic psychic apparatus' of humans (Freud) and pave the way for non-uniform 'apparatuses of self-constraint', sharply regimented in their individual dimensions and able freely to unfold in others. If human growth is associated with severe and sudden fluctuations in external constraints on behaviour and if, as a result, social and naturally induced insecurity is great (as when contagious disease rapidly brings about death), then the human self is hard put to know what pre-emptive stance to adopt. The challenge facing the human self is to learn, despite fluctuations and incivilities of social development, to maintain some sense of *joie de vivre* and to achieve such stability as serves this end. But what if the social pressure which emanates from without (or from nature) becomes more equitable, predictable or calculable? What if eruptions of physical violence by stronger against weaker become rare or are eliminated almost entirely? Then the modelling of the 'affective household' (as Elias calls it, in the sense of a 'drive economy') becomes more equitable. Constraints become easier to foresee, and are foreseen. Deliberate self-control becomes easier; at the same time the individual has implanted in him or her an automatically (i.e., blindly) functioning apparatus of self-control. The stability and peacefulness of the social processes without are matched by enhanced stability and peacefulness of the psychic processes within.

According to Elias, there arose a general constraint for foresight and for planned behaviour that spread as Western civilization evolved. This also applies to what he calls a social constraint for self-constraint (Elias 2000: 365). What does this mean for the individual affective household? What Freud calls 'sublimation', Elias calls a muting of drives, that is, the diminishing of psychic contrasts, which in turn is accompanied by more ways in which to satisfy needs. Life becomes richer in nuances, if less colourful. Life psychologizes and rationalizes itself. A key role is played here by shame-related anxieties. Shame is a fear of social degradation, occurring even when there are no physical constraints and chiefly dependent on one's super-ego; and it tends to accompany relationships of authority. To cite Elias:

> The conflict expressed in shame-fear is not merely a conflict of the individual with prevalent social opinion; the individual's behaviour has brought him into conflict with the part of himself that represents this social opinion. It is a conflict within his own personality; he himself recognizes himself as inferior. (Elias 2000: 415)

The shame and embarrassment threshold for a whole series of vital bodily needs has been lowered, even as the number of rules and situations where we are expected to keep our affects on a tight leash has grown. So it is that in our bureaucratized and marketed worlds a decidedly fine-meshed network of invisible social constraints has accreted, making all talk of 'spontaneity', of fully embracing the here-and-now, seem doomed in advance.

The gradual spread of functional democratization during the civilizing process has a dampening effect on the affective household, in conjunction with an overall lengthening of action chains that impells to greater rationality and foresight. Given a crass disparity of power, A can live at B's cost virtually unchecked. Rules of etiquette rise to the fore as power is distributed more equitably, which happens as parties are drawn increasingly into a denser 'network of interdependencies'. Thus the larger princely courts were generally pacific and rich in human relationships, as compared with castles where minor knights presided over local society. And today's bureaucratic settings are less authoritarian than the hierarchical orders of the 19th century had ever been.

National habitus

In his seminal work of 1939, Norbert Elias set out the conceptual approach associated with his name.

> The social units that we call nations differ widely in the affect-economies of their members, in the schemata through which the emotional life of the individuals is moulded under the pressure of institutionalized tradition and of the present situation. (Elias 2000: 29)

This statement adumbrates what Elias would later come to refer to as 'national habitus'. Elias still uses the term 'national character', which he drops as 'pre-scientific' later on in *The Germans* (Elias 1996). However, it is roughly coterminous with 'national habitus'. Moreover, in his *Process* book we already find him talking of a 'psychic habitus', especially in the final section of the second volume. Not that the term 'national character', in the context of the above statement, is used randomly or just in passing; indeed, the opposition between 'civilization' (with its French courtly connotations) and 'culture' (of middle-class German provenance) was Elias's point of departure for mounting his own notion of 'civilization', so much so that comparing France and Germany became one of the core themes of *The Civilizing Process*. Here too we find the idea advanced that 'national characters' arose from 'social characters'. In the French case, for example, the social character of a courtly class underwent slow transformation in what he terms an ever-widening movement (Elias 2000: 32), yielding the French national character as we know it. Compared to either France or England, the German national character, when it crystallized, was much more exclusively bourgeois since the German middle-class intelligentsia of the 18th century remained separate from the nobility.

For Elias, the 'national character' or 'habitus' must be construed in terms of a relatively permanent imprinting of emotions and affects, or, to be more precise, in terms of the entire 'affective household' of nations. Even on a 'pre-scientific' level, that is, in day-to-day interactions, members of different nations usually have little trouble recognizing each other. We thus have the 'typical Italian' or the 'typical German', who are readily discernible no matter what that person's individual traits may be. Yet when one attempts to perceive oneself as a typical representative of a nation, this proves much more difficult. Success here presupposes 'self-distancing', as Elias argues in *The Germans* (Elias 1996). Typical, and therefore recurrent, behavioural patterns (such as the pliant courtier that is never far below the surface in many a Frenchman; the German who cannot forbear dispensing advice to all and sundry, whose remote ancestor was a professor or bureaucrat in the 18th century) can be observed immediately and correspond to typical modes of feeling and experiencing. By 'habitus' Elias essentially means something akin to 'second nature' or social learning that has become embodied (cf. Dunning/Mennell 1996: IX). In this context, 'affect modelling' refers to emotions whose expression is communicated socially to others, as part of an older emotional system of self-control, of regulating group relationships as well as relationships between group and individual. It is more rigid than the language-mediated control system of the neo-cortex. Elias (1987) distinguishes three components of this emotional system: an emotional component (pleasure or aversion) in the narrow sense; a somatic component (a palpitating heart, for instance); and also a behavioural component (flight or attack), which includes too the expression of emotions that have signal character for group members (laughter or weeping, etc.). According to distinctions made in social psychology, we can discriminate mimicry, gesticulation, acoustic signals, physical appearance and comportment, or how one approaches or withdraws from others, as expressions of affects (cf. Argyle 1972). This means that members of different nations can tell themselves apart in terms of all these dimensions. For example, older Continental Europeans distinguish themselves from older middle-class Americans by their facial expressions, by their bodily comportment, and (of course) by their clothes: evidently, clothes can be changed, the former presumably can not. In some cultures people speak louder than in others, or they gesticulate more, and so on and so forth; yet these cultural imprints are scarcely expressions of our genes. These imprints reflect the fact that self-regulation and individualization are mirrored in a social habitus as well as in a national habitus.

Concomitantly with the development of societies from 'survival units' of band, village or tribe into towns or states, there occurs the development of personality structure in the direction of greater individualization. This process of individualization is owed to the affiliation of individuals to larger survival units and the corresponding need to face up to the complex demands of denser webs of social interdependence.

> In less differentiated societies, such as the Stone Age hunter-gatherer groups, the social habitus may have had a single layer. In more complex societies it has many layers. [...] It depends on the number of interlocking planes in his society how many layers are

> interwoven in the social habitus of a person. Among them, a particular layer usually has special prominence. It is the layer characteristic of membership of a particular social survival group, for example, a tribe or state. In members of a society at the developmental stage of a modern state this is referred to by the expression 'national character'. (Elias 1991b: 183)

Since Austria was a multi-national state with as many languages as nations (and even more dialects, each one manifesting regional diversity), this problem becomes extremely virulent (not least in practical terms). But in the English case too we can assume multiple infolded loyalties and a similar profusion of layers of habitual imprints.

In his treatise on the ethnic origins of nations, Anthony Smith (1986) developed an extremely rich casuistry of ethnic and national societies. This he did from a process-sensitive perspective. Recognition of the relative permanence of such processes brings him to religion, tradition, language, indeed to all semi-enduring institutions capable of conferring identity and continuity on an ethnic group or a nation. Especially in the case of Austria, but also to a considerable extent in the case of England with its Celtic fringe, it is necessary to distinguish analytically between ethno-linguistic layers of social habitus on the one side, and layers where the state has influenced the social habitus on the other. There are German theorists who are not at all keen to release Austria from the German fold. In particular, those theorists who take their cue from Elias should know what a central role the state-formation process plays for him in terms of habitus formation. While on the one hand today's Rump Austrians are linguistically close to Bavarians (and in the Vorarlberg to Alemanns) and even share with them a taste for certain dishes and traditions, like celebrating the Baby Jesus rather than Father Christmas, Austrians differ from Bavarians and Swabians, on the other hand, because, for example, of the great-power status of their monarchy, the complex way in which their bureaucracy was structured, and the many wars fought on their southern flanks. We shall discuss the significance of these factors later on. To take the English case, it is a fact that many of that country's competitive team sports have Celtic roots, which opens up the possibility that the spirit of fair play might be ethnically derived as well. Nevertheless, we focus as far as possible on the state-formation process and its aftermath. But since the English influence on the British state formation was preponderant since at least the time of union with Scotland (1707), it is legitimate, to argue that English state character constitutes the 'national character'. With regard to the Austrian part of the Habsburg Monarchy as it was in 1914, we do not find a similar convergence between state and nation. Quite the contrary. It was the forces of nationalism that finally ripped apart the multi-national state; therefore, in this work, it will make more sense to posit for Austria a 'state habitus' or 'state character'. For as far as the influence of the central state extended, as well as that of its sustaining institutions and class structure, one can discern a uniform feature of behavioural imprinting even in the many other peoples of the monarchy – that is, it is not confined to the so-called 'state people', the German-Austrians. A simple image may help show what was specific to such a 'state character'. Imagine, if you will, a darkened room with a Christmas tree in it, decorated with lots and lots of pine-cones, silver tinsel and chocolate hangings. Imagine now the light is turned on, illuminating from the side this gaudy profusion of disparate decorations – the lighting is such that though all do not exactly look alike, all are bathed in a single hue, that is, they can be seen under a unitary 'aspect'. So ethnic 'characters' can certainly be said to exist. Instructive in the given context for many reasons is Smith's contribution to the debate (which goes even further than Elias does). First, he pays particular attention to the 'proto-national phase' of ethnic groups and to group emotions attributable to these, thus helping to resolve an enigma we find, to an extent, in Elias too. The enigma is this. How is it that the German national character, for example, formed in stages that are miles – or rather centuries – removed from the formation of a German nation-state? Elias hints at a possible answer in his *Symbol Theory* (Elias 1991a), in which he recognizes the importance of language in the imprinting of habitus – by sharing a language that is incomprehensible to outsiders, a people erects walls around itself; humans hand down from generation to generation experiences idiosyncratic of their culture thus defined. Language opens, and simultaneously restricts entry to, gateways to certain experiences proto-typical of a culture. Hence the emotional charge that certain linguistic expressions have. Austrian *Gemütlichkeit* and English 'fairness' (or 'fair play') are terms that do not travel well in translation. In Smith's perspective, however, this ethno-linguistic transition in the 'genealogy of nations' is not that rare; here the typological-comparative method has the advantage that it can delimit fairly well a frame of reference in which highly diverse forms of ethnic community are accommodated (extending from city-state loyalties to diaspora situations and the like). Lateral-aristocratic types (Poland, Hungary) are ranged against vertical-urban 'demotic' ones (which correspond to classically bureaucratized nation-states). For them to survive requires an ethnic core – or else they are driven to invent one. All are in search of a homeland – often mystical sites of the ancestors. All have their heroic epoch, their golden age in the remote past. (Smith is less cynical on this score than Hobsbawm (1990), who is prepared to label just about everything an arbitrary invention.) If Elias invokes what he calls the 'German nostalgia for empire', and the gloomy German songs that extol heroic death, as answering to a quite unique attitude to destiny, one deeply ingrained in the German habitus (with 'self-fulfilling' consequences?), Smith's eight 'myths of descent" are not less insightful. Turning on the when and where of origins, there are myths of genealogy, wandering, liberation, a golden age, decline and defeat (or exile) and restoration to former glory.

Central to how Elias construes 'national habitus' is certainly the long-term character of the causal processes involved, but also the relative 'stability' of the habitus itself. In contra-distinction to a cultural-comparative sociology or to national character studies based on surveys, Elias does not freeze 'habitus' in the manner of an anatomical cross-section; instead he refers each isolated trait to its discrete genesis and duration. Though there are patterns that span many generations, there are also those spanning only three. This is precisely what distinguishes any uncovered layers (always plentiful!) of a 'national habitus' from 'stereotypes' of the kind peddled by spiteful neighbours or by peoples in thrall to an ideal 'we'. They conserve a cross-section of features over long tracts of time for what might have been realistic only at a very specific moment. To be sure, recent years have seen a revival within sociology of the historical perspective (cf. on this point Abrams 1982; D. Smith 1991). Yet Elias is most certainly opposed to the bulk of modernization theorists, technological optimists and 'post-modernists', for whom everything that divides the present of a (post-) industrial society from its feudal past matters far more for how a society experiences itself than a history deemed to be 'dead'. Elias's assertion that the character of Germans is still influenced to an extent by the failure of the Hohenstauffen emperors in the High Middle Ages is unlikely to be found in mainstream sociology textbooks (cf. Elias 1996: 5). And who today would be bold enough to claim that the Thirty Years War still casts its long shadows over Germans? Or that the English still owe their democratic habitus to political developments in the aftermath of the Civil War back in the 17th century (cf. Elias/Dunning 1986)?

The train of thought, as common in everyday life as it is in sociology, that prevents recognition of habituation processes that operate over the long term, might be described as follows. The overwhelming present of modern technology and industry, of new communication techniques and an urbanized life-style, makes the distance to the pre-industrial world seem immense. That no corner of the globe remains immune from the tendencies towards standardization has the effect of pushing national and cultural differences into the background, stripping them of significance for the 'Western' world. A prominent representative of the view of modernity that stresses discontinuities – and hence an opponent of such a 'gradualist' stance – is A. Giddens (cf. Giddens 1990). However, standards of affect modelling change less from generation to generation than do technical and instrumental rationality. Humans are the chief sources of fear and satisfaction for their fellows – and it is through largely unplanned fear that humans are shackled rigidly to the reality principle. Great fear passed down the generations also marks the limits of human inventiveness. How else can one explain the stability of Puritan sexual fears across the centuries?

There is abundant evidence supporting the view that historically embedded differences among nations are of significant explanatory importance. The evidence ranges from stable differences in suicide rates, through diverging responses when asked to estimate one's personal happiness (Inkeles 1997[1]), to differential rates of murder and manslaughter. Yet these rates seem stable enough on the national level. Recognition of such diversity naturally does not mean that any given instance is due to a basic set of nation-specific 'personality structures' – quite superficial conventions may well be at work. Also, to recognize the existence of substantial differences between nations and other social units at any point in time is not to say that they will stay so for ever. Time may bring about change. A convergence theory of modernization (Yang 1988) is not necessarily doomed by such findings, because the onset and duration of such a process, which is likely to achieve global spread, would still be highly uncertain.

Scholarly study of national characters and/or nationally imprinted forms of a social habitus therefore faces in empirical terms a battery of questions requiring positive answers. To what extent is it ever justified to talk of a more or less stable 'habitus' or habitual trait?[2] What are the modalities of cultural reproduction, and how and by what means does such a 'habitus' alter? How do the following interlink: cognitive and affective components, language-mediated noetic components and affect-based memories; also, situational and personality-related items involving both institutional and 'inner' aspects of psychic *experience*?

Probably one of the most frequent category errors found in everyday discourse of 'national character' is to confuse 'situation' and 'person'. No one in their right mind would attribute, say, North German or English predilection for building with bricks to a psychic disposition manifested in a deep-seated need for red tiles – that a material culture reproduces itself not entirely by psychic mechanisms is beyond doubt. But those who charge Germans with ingrained fascist leanings often skirt over the fact that Germans have found themselves in other historical situations too, and continue also to be shaped by these. The political structure of a society, its social stratification, its legal system, and its economy, first of all create *stable situations* that generate behavioural conformity which are relatively independent of popular attitudes, emotions and habits. Thus, for example, Germany remained a country with a strong rural presence well into the 20th century; we should therefore not be surprised to find in Germany a greater longing for community than in countries where the peasantry is but a distant memory. While we probably must concede to Elias that psyche and society are two sides of one coin, this does not entitle us, without further inquiry, to invoke mentalities as explanations, given that social institutions, simply by existing and having the defining power they do, are perfectly able to compel the behaviour in question. Especially the label 'uncivilized' is liable to be trotted out as a knee-jerk reaction, along with a brace of moral judgements. Elias's twin concepts of 'civilization' and 'decivilization' have received much attention (cf. Kuzmics 1989; Mennell 1989; Fletcher 1997). To be sure, the semantic core is basically identical in both concepts. Elias (2000), on the one hand, distinguishes analysis of the linguistic use of terms like 'civilizing' or 'civilization', as in the mentality of the French upper classes of the 19th century, with their demonstrative staking out of maximal distance from savages and peasants. On the other hand, he filters out the semantic components of refinement, of growing inhibition and peaceableness. A third, more technical, form of the concept is then worked up within the frame of macro- or micro-theory, in which a finer enmeshment and more equitable distribution is postulated for external constraints and self-constraints. Normative connotations rarely feature in Elias, but they are not unknown: in particular they appear when he analyzes how Germans drifted into the embrace of the Nazi dictatorship. Given Elias's biography, such normative questions should not come as a surprise. The moral question – why was it that so many made no attempt to check the downward spiral into savagery? – is very much at the forefront of his normative queries. Yet, it must be analytically possible to discriminate catastrophes from slow structural processes that result in the production of salient personality dispositions. There is also the impact of situations where change proceeds at dramatic pace. In the history of the early 20th century major catastrophes, of which many were connected, issued in powerful *new situations.* In his book on *Modernity and the Holocaust* (1989), Bauman goes even further: he makes the *situation* of modernity itself responsible for civilization becoming derailed, rather than any civilizational shortcomings of the Germans themselves.

In any event, for analytical purposes there are three aspects of a 'national habitus' [*Volkscharakter*, national or ethnic character]: there is a core domain, in which the external constraints and self-constraints that are specific to a culture are inducted in the early years of life (say, by age six) and are 'built into' the affective household; then there is a transitional zone, in which the stability of individual behaviour and social figurations into which human beings are embedded depend upon each other; lastly, there is a peripheral zone of possibly weak internalizations but with stable situational constraints that are clear and unequivocal which may express a culture's uniqueness just as well.

How does all of this bear on our project? One of our chief aims is to delineate the very different paths by which in Austria and England alike social institutions (particularly institutions of state) affected the experiential worlds of those whose lives they touched. In order to avoid category errors such as knee-jerk moralizing, it is important not to lose sight of situational constraints such as those which have led in one society to bureaucratic statism and in the other to a stronger unfolding of markets and parliament. That is, we should not always, and as a matter of course, try to explain processes of 'systemic differentiation' in terms of affective states. This would be to tread a downward path into reductionism.

Another point to note is that affects are generally rather more rigid than are cognitively based forms of behavioural control. And yet the high degree to which human affects are cognitively permeated is manifested in how we express them. Take laughter, for example – here the bandwidth of mimetic forms of expression reaches all the way from apologetic grins to bitter hoots to derisive cackles, while the great plasticity of our facial muscles ensures that there are as many expressions of social mimicry as there are cultures. Thus we see that the empirical questions arising in any analysis of national character are extremely complex. But this we can say with certainty: to range cognition (rationality) against emotion (affects) is to embrace a sterile dichotomy. Affects and their cognitive integration into lengthy action chains, the extent of our capacity for long-term action, are to be thought of as continuously sited along a continuum. Elias (1987) was convinced that no sharp dichotomy can long be sustained. Empirically, of course, the degree of rational distancing from one's emotions can vary. It is of great importance to take stock of how cognition and emotion interrelate, especially when attempting to explain the persistence of 'ultra-stable' structures in times of rapid (even ultra-rapid) change on the part of core social institutions. Here we cannot escape postulating deep-seated emotional needs that have undergone cultural shaping.

Finally, a key distinction must be adumbrated. According to Elias, only nation-states have achieved a level of integration that, more than any other level of group belonging, underpins a special 'we-identity' even as it generates a special emotional intensity. This we-identity, however, should not be confused with the social – or national – habitus. 'National identity', national feeling or 'patriotism', loyalty to the nation or nationalism (the latter often enough accompanied – rightly or wrongly – by 'genuine' or 'false' pride in one's nation) may seem parallel terms, yet they refer to quite different things. Hidden away are two quite different issues: (a) the existence of national feelings, which can range from a vague sense of belonging all the way to crude nationalism; and (b) the imprinting of the affective household, inasmuch as this is explicable within the compass of a 'biography of national state societies' (Elias). In terms of conceptual logic, we are dealing with two different levels – national feelings can be spontaneous and simply arise in a particular situation; they need not be deeply rooted in the past. Empirically, though, very often there will be a link: thus, for example, it is one of the idiosyncrasies of English national pride that it is first encountered very early, namely in the Late Middle Ages – its remarkable continuity may even be deemed constitutive (cf. for relevant observations by Germanophone visitors to England Robson-Scott 1953: 16). National identity in turn is linked to awareness of being part of a nation, conceived as a community of descent or perhaps thrown together by destiny; it has everything to do with historical memory (or a carefully edited version thereof). Imprinting of the 'affective household' and the 'habitus', on the other hand, is predicated often, indeed usually, on unconscious states – social and psychic 'deep structures' – and these are, as a rule, too self-evident ever to be called in doubt.

To repeat, the analyses put forward in this book move within the horizon of a specific sociological theory, that is, Elias's theory of the civilizing process. The starting point of our discussion is Elias's insight that institutionalized political collectives have a unique affective economy, a 'national habitus' or 'national character', which sets 'nations' apart. According to Elias, the historically specific process of state building is the key causal factor in the formation of a national character. We show how differences in the power configuration and the institutionalization of political authority in England and Austria, respectively, resulted in different types of national character. In this book, then, we combine a 'thick description' of the English and Austrian 'national habitus' with an analysis of macro-political change, that is, of state formation. We address both the question of the stability and the cultural reproduction of a national habitus and that of changes in its constituent features over time. The acceptance of the longevity of collective habitualized psychic dispositions necessarily raises the question as to the causal significance of national character regarding institutional political change: 'national character' may hence be considered as both *explanandum* and *explanans*. To put it in a terminology that sits somewhat uneasily with Elias's methodology:

we shall analyze 'national character' both as a 'dependent' and 'independent' variable.

Not every reader of this book will approach its analysis on the basis of a familiarity with the sociological theory of Norbert Elias. An English reader, in particular, may well have expected yet another long entreaty on the peculiarities of the English or on English identity and Englishness. There is a substantial literature along these lines. Roger Scruton's recent 'elegiac' reflections on England (2001) are a 'classical' exemplar. Paul Langford's endeavour to identify Englishness by recounting English manners and character on the basis of observations made by foreigners (many of them Continental Europeans) between 1650 and 1850 is yet another 'characteristic' treatment. His book has an almost lexical nature. He 'identifies' six (supposed) major traits of Englishness – energy, candour, decency, taciturnity, reserve, and eccentricity – and then pours the rich content of his reading notes into each of these categories. It is an engrossing read, but the reader is given neither an explanation for the emergence of this cluster of traits, nor its cultural reproduction over time.

As discussed above, we hold fast to an analytical distinction between a 'we-identity' and a 'national habitus' – without wishing to deny that traits of the 'national habitus' may become an intricate element of a 'we-identity' – a discursive, rhetorical, or symbolic invocation of certain features with highly valued moral qualities – 'Play up! play up! and play the game!' We do, however, wish to dissociate our approach from those endeavours, going back in the English case well into the 19th century, that link the notion of 'national character' to moral theories and moral sensibilities in the light of which certain of its features are then praised or condemned, or policies are evaluated on the basis of whether or not they are likely to bring up morally valued character traits or are in accordance with those traits (Collini 1991: 91–118). Still, we are sympathetic to John Stuart Mill's attempt to formulate a 'theory of the causes which determine the type of character belonging to a people or to an age', with character being defined as 'the opinions, feelings, and habits of the people'. Mill argued that such a 'political ethology', 'the science of the formation of character', should analyze 'the effect of institutions or social arrangements upon the character of the people', but also address the question as to what kind of national character was congenial (or even necessary) for representative government (Mill 1974: 861–74, 904–7; Romani 2002; Varouxakis 1998; Varouxakis 2002).

Let us now turn to an overview of the substantial arguments which we are putting forward in our study.

The argument in overview

Let us now apply Elias's arguments concerning national habitus to England and Austria. The first point to note is that the paths by which force is rendered incorporeal and invisible have diverged widely in each case. The English national character has long been attributed traits answering either to the 'gentlemanly ideal' or to middle-class 'Puritanism' (Peabody 1985: 95–108). The typical Englishman is said to be cold and reserved; he is said to value his privacy above all else; he expects not to be interfered with in his private affairs, but has sufficient self-control to grant to others the same freedom from interference he claims for himself. Related to this, so it is said, is a more general control over his feelings, in which excessive displays are avoided and thought embarrassing – letting off steam is deemed a weakness, as is any demonstrative parading of strength. Chivalrous, aristocratic reserve for one thing, and individualism aligned to the marketplace for another, seem inextricably interwoven, giving us that high degree of affective control often seen as 'typically English'.

Analytical treatments of the English novel show, from the early 18th century (Defoe, Smollett, Richardson), an intensifying of *civilizational* constraints against a backdrop of the 'gentlemanly' ideal – the origins of which were pan-European and aristocratic – in the direction of greater control chiefly over aggressive impulses, but also over all emotions that might be regarded importuning or molesting others. The English civilizing process appears to have gone very far indeed, as compared with other European societies, and can be seen as evolving towards a situation where only a quite small gap separates formal and informal behaviour as understood by Elias (Elias 1996: 28; Wouters 1979). Relative continuity and linearity are also evident (by Austrian standards). The Austrian civilizing trajectory leads to a greater disparity between affects that are given free rein in private, or towards subordinates, and the formal comportment that is required towards superiors and in 'official' situations. Austrian submissive friendliness and *Gemütlichkeit* – a constant theme of Viennese popular comedy – were cultivated especially in domestic settings with high-ranking masters, settings in which the feudal-caste, patrimonial life-style yields slowly to that of the bureaucrat. Thus this particular civilizing process, in which growing restraint characterizes the expression of feeling, takes place under a patrimonial-bureaucratic aegis. The liberal-bourgeois trajectory here has left few traces only.

The 'typical Austrian' is said to be amiable and charming, indecisive and emollient (Hofmannsthal 1957), and is unable to deny anything to other people. On the down side, he is bureaucratic and pedantic, and has a fetish about duly constituted authority (Magris 1988: 7–22; Lhotsky 1974: 321). He inclines to exuberance of feeling (Bassett 1988: 37), is polite but with a tendency to grovel, to bow and scrape like a courtier; at the same time, though, as asserted by Claudio Magris in the *Habsburg Myth*, he has a streak of stoical resignation and believes in even-handedness; he perennially longs for a strong and benign father figure who can curb perennial bickering and feuding. Here we also encounter two images: that of a hedonistic and ostentatious – one might say Phaeacian! – Austrian Catholicism with its penchant for easy-going ways (however skin-deep they often are!), and that of the seignorial bureaucrat with an almost tragic devotion to duty, for whom the ticking-over of administration matters more than any decision-taking, for whom order is decency and good manners and vice versa and whose life-style is as modest as it is moderate.

Nowhere perhaps are the disparities more striking than in what might, broadly speaking, be called 'political socialization'. On superficial inspection, in both Austria and England 'feudal' groups were slowly replaced by middle-class and later 'workerly' groups (Elias 1996: 470, fn. 56) who took control of key monopolies (i.e., taxation and the use of force), whereupon the party state and parliamentarianism commenced their triumphal march. But by 1914, Austria (*Cis-Leithania*) was of course anything but a mature constitutional-parliamentary system: authoritarian traits remained dominant. As pointed out already by Elias/Dunning (1986) and also by Dahrendorf (1969, 1982), England had witnessed at an early date (and certainly no later than the Restoration of Charles II) a process whereby the relatively homogeneous class of estate owners (which included some middle-class elements) were reconciled to a peaceable transition to parliamentary rule. This incremental move, evolutionary in spirit rather than revolutionary, to a more broadly based power-sharing (even if the outcome was, as Laslett claims (1989), still very much a 'one-class society') went hand in hand with discovery of the so-called public virtues – to wit, a sense of 'fairness', loyalty to the sociopolitical order, a readiness to compromise, to name but a few. In contrast, Austria was at the start of this period an extremely heterogeneous, great-power state, with its landed hierarchy still largely feudal in its make-up. Neither had it achieved a classical 'courtly society' in the French mould (cf. Evans 1979; Bruckmüller 1985). The pivot on which the civilizing process turned was the reforms of Maria Theresa and Joseph II (Bodi 1995a) in which values of rationalization and 'humanization' were pushed through from the 'top'. If Austria's contribution to modernity was an easy-going patrimonial order-cum-authoritarian-bureaucracy, then England's was the achievement of a civil, middle-class society. This explains some deep-seated traits in the Austrian character – the conviction, for instance, that all blessings come from on high, a dread of running afoul of authority, a need for harmony, proneness to apathy, but also a readiness to make demands of the state. Often mercy matters more than justice.

The present work proceeds according to a simple scheme. First, we analyze the rise of the English (Chapter 2) and Austrian (Chapter 3) states, focusing on the sociogenesis of political authority (monopoly of taxation and the use of force). No attempt is made, however, at this stage, systematically to compare the two societies. To achieve a firmer grasp of the ultra-stable elements of power-sharing between princely central power and aristocratic (later middle-class) groups, as well as between nobility and lower classes, it soon became clear that our study needed to be broadened so as to incorporate the feudal run-up, in both countries, to the period under examination. In the Austrian case, we consider 'manorial absolutism' to have been a formative influence on 'confessional absolutism' (sprung from the Catholic Counter-Reformation) and, by derivation, on the 'reform absolutism' of the 18th century. In the English case, we found a matching trajectory in the feudalism of an England united quite early on, then overlaid by a Norman veneer (but where the nobility had to make do with significantly fewer personal prerogatives over their subjects and where aristocratic-republican features were long visible); an England that then progressed by way of Tudor quasi-absolutism to parliament's historical victory over the despotic impulses of a centralized monarchy. Here it was imperative to bear in mind at least two sorts of power balances: one between king and nobility, another between nobility and 'the people'. From these different starting points, 'domestic' state development in England and Austria in the 19th century converged only to a small extent. Their respective position within the geopolitical power configuration was equally diverse. Here we focused closely on how the English monopoly of taxation evolved in the 18th century, from which it appears that a fairly broad-based upper and middle class benefited (as it did from acquisition of colonies) while the lower orders bore the cost. This constellation seems to have proved highly congenial to English parliamentary rule, even as it enabled a considerable unfolding of market forces. The Austrian Monarchy of the 19th century could not evade the stormy forces of economic modernization and political democracy either. Yet once again it had to proceed in line with those vertical patterns and that parallelogram of centrifugal tendencies which had long been a datum of Austrian state development, in which, to employ a metaphor, an ultra-powerful heart (the state and its bureaucracy) had to pump blood into an uncooperative periphery of external organs – and with the perennial risk of overreaching itself in the process. While over lengthy tracts of time Hungary, the German Imperial princes and the Habsburg grand nobility were restive, by the 19th century this role had been taken on by the so-called nationalities. This development and an extremely menacing situation (in geopolitical terms) may have been responsible for the Austrian state's feeling that it had to cloak its weakness by a show of strength. The English state, however, could afford to be liberal on the basis of its infrastructural strength (Mann 1993).

After these two macro-structural inquiries, we embark on an analysis that aims to tease out those means by which authority is exercised, ensures but also finds acceptance. For that purpose, institutional history is linked with a psycho-historical approach. In the airy world of generalities, it is too easy to mistake chalk for cheese; only when studied in the particularizing light of literary example do the features we describe take on colour and intensity. The round of detailed psycho-historical studies begins with a chapter (4) on feudal and clerical patterns of the exercise of authority in Austria, with a sidelong glance at the English situation. A perusal of the situation at the end of the era is followed by a sociogenetic sketch (a scheme repeated in the ensuing chapters).

How did the protracted tradition of patterns of personalized, hierarchical dependency affect the imprinting of Austrian 'social characters'? In the empirical analysis, 'Austria' chiefly means the non-Hungarian parts of the monarchy, plus the Slavic territories, even if delved into their experience mainly through literary voices writing in German. This analytical focus is in line with our diffusion model that emphasizes the formative power of the state elites. In our chapter sequence of textual interpretations for the Austrian case, we follow the three-phase scheme implicit in our earlier macro-analysis: from manorial absolutism through to confessional absolutism in the context of the Counter-Reformation to reform absolutism. We assume that, in each of these phases, relatively stable habitus patterns were laid down which continued to shape the affective experience of Austrians until the end of the period under study. In Chapter 4 we treat principally the manorial-cum-warrior nobility aspect, but also the role played by the ecclesiastical power apparatus in its ability to control souls. Chapter 6 takes into account the institutional form through which the power of absolutist ruler and nobility developed: in Austria much more so than in England, yet less than in France, that power was linked to the formation of court society. Chapter 8 treats bureaucratization and officialdom as the Austrian civilizing process *par excellence*, having its starting point in reform absolutism and remaining the backbone of the multi-national and multi-ethnic state in later times, until new forces were starting to work in the 19th century in favour of bourgeois, national and 'working-class' emancipation.

The English pattern of habitus formation can be ordered *mutatis mutandis* in terms of phases of Anglo-British state formation. In stark contrast to the Austrian developmental trajectory, the sociogenesis of feudal paternalism in England (due to a much more evenly balanced division of powers between monarch and a finely graded nobility) went hand in hand with the rise of a 'gentlemanly canon' which was then being modified and refined, not by a court society but rather by a 'parliamentary society' (Chapter 5). Whereas in Austria it was the Catholic Church that imposed hierocratic constraint and policed religious and social morals, in England we find this key role devolving to Puritanism. Despite the early consolidation of an Anglican hierarchy, we repeatedly find Puritanism rising to the fore. Frequently, Puritanism's influence develops in tandem with bouts of market penetration – and this alone constitutes a natural counter-pole to Austrian bureaucratic statism (Chapter 9). In similar opposition to the decided 'orientation to external constraints' (constraints by others) so central to the courtly and bureaucratic power dispensation in Austria, in England a pattern emerges of 'proud distance' and 'indirect rule' between those of unequal rank (Chapter 7). Besides Puritanism with its preponderantly middle-class roots, we suspect that 'proud distance' was a core factor behind the 'moralization of state authority' within and without, in colonial rule and in international relations, that resonated so widely in 19th century England (Chapter 9).

An introduction is not the place to state our findings. Yet it would be remiss, at this point, not to review a number of surprises sprung by our analysis of literary texts from the 18th to the 20th centuries. Often the literary texts are more than mere sources – it is not unusual for them to elaborate insights and descriptions that can, without too much licence, be called sociological. It is striking how often in

Austria authority is experienced as peaceable, how often the resultant bureaucratic habitus appears benign. Literary means also permit depiction of the almost uncanny mechanisms linking the outer show of authority to inner paralysis – as manifested in severe anxieties turning on shame and guilt. To be sure, the English examples hardly reveal a society of cheerful insouciance; what we find is a more reality-driven, a more active and self-confident attitude to authority – from the elites on down, though here too fear of being embarrassed, or otherwise shamed, is manipulated by one's 'peers' to ensure observance of norms. The obverse of notions of authority that are predicated on an addiction to harmony and a hankering for an authoritarian state that result in bureaucratic hesitancy and a politically harmless proclivity to self-irony and self-parody is an Austrian inability to engage with rule-governed and self-responsible political discourse coming from 'below'.

In many respects the English civilizing process, as manifested especially in 'muscular Christianity' whereby humanistic middle-class canons (visible to an extent in the Evangelical movement) are mixed in with an ethos of gentlemanly chivalry, appears very far-reaching, not least in the way in which emotional expressions of the importuning kind are muted reciprocally. And yet this throws up a question: why is it that Austrian feudal-patrimonial authority and patrimonial-bureaucratic rationality turn out, in many respects, to be more civilized (associating this notion with refinement, inhibiting aggressive urges, cultivating peaceable and benign ways, and the like) than the utilitarian marketplace rationality of a country like England, with its vastly more developed economy? How, then, do such notions translate into modes of experience? Which states of emotion and benchmarks of affective regulation correspond to such processes?

In our analyses we have combined cross-sectional (i.e., comparative) with longitudinal (i.e., process-oriented) methods in order to trace aspects of habituation and mentality. In our necessarily detailed and comprehensive analysis of literary passages, we have endeavoured to bring the civilizing structural patterns to imaginative life. Even if we have not fully succeeded in doing so, our goal was to document those social constraints that ensure interactions with state and state-supported authority to become more civilized – though the trajectories followed in Austria and England were very different. The following dimensions emerged as central.

(1) The relation between state authority and subservient attitudes on the one hand, and between state authority and emancipated self-organization within a 'civil society' on the other, clearly wore a different face in Austria and England, even at the turn of the 20th century. Why did parliamentary rule find it harder to take root in Austria than in England, despite its ability to facilitate discourse between persons, parties or 'blocs' with different interests? Here we must take cognisance of the fact that in Austria too there was a great deal of 'institutionalized compromise' (indeed it survives still in the institution of 'social partnership'), but not very much fair-minded, rule-abiding public dispute. Whether the collapse of parliamentary rule in 1934 can be explained

by invoking habituation is hard to say (in any case, by then the entire economic and statist matrix of the Habsburg Monarchy's political culture had broken down). One suspects, anyway, that for a culture of harmony and static grandiosity such as that of Catholic-Habsburg Austria, dramatic change was harder to come to terms with than in the case of a culture where conflict was embraced as normal and unavoidable.

(2) Another dimension is to compare the respective civilizing processes in terms of the cost of frustrations imposed on the individual. Evidently there is an Austrian culture of dutiful subservience and obedience, just as there is an English one of deference and playing by the rules. In each case there is a high degree of affective inhibition involved. One of the points of departure for this book was the observation that suffering from modernity is very strongly filtered through the national character. Even now, as we have moved into the 21st century, it is not so much a diffuse narcissistic anxiety of a late-capitalist and bureaucratized society of mass consumption that shapes relationships with authority, as Lasch (1980) suggested. In line with the core argument that we develop in this book, we claim that authority is affectively experienced as a result of social and cultural constellations that in each instance have had their unique historical imprint.

(3) Therefore, we hope to correct a major deficit in otherwise sound examinations of macro-sociology and institutional history. They fail to show how differential formative processes of state authority actually play out in terms of the psychic experiences of social actors. These are of interest for mainly two reasons: first, because state-formation processes disclose their full social significance only if understood in terms of their psychic meaning. What we get, instead, are vague theories and speculations as to how power and powerlessness are experienced, lifted from everyday life in the national culture in question. Second, because without salient knowledge of mentalities and 'habitus' we are unable fully to explain structural singularities within societies. Without a sound understanding of the formative power of 'habitus', it is hardly possible to grasp the forces of perseverance in times of social change, nor the way in which societies may respond to existential challenges. For instance, it could be argued that the feudal leadership of the Habsburg Monarchy was fatefully entrapped in its warrior ethos of honour when it – in concert with political elites in the other European states – stumbled into the Great War. The same might also be said of the transition from a strongly hierarchical 'authoritarianism' to a constitutional system of parliamentary rule.

By focusing on how national habitus is formed and shaped, our book joins a large number of studies on political culture. This field in its 'classical' form, that is, as originally conceived by Gabriel Almond, understood 'political culture' as subjective orientations within a national collectivity towards politics. In this tradition, political culture was said to contain cognitive, affective and evaluative aspects. Thus 'political culture' drew together knowledge and conceptions relating to political reality, emotions bearing on politics, and acquiescence to political norms and values. The 'content' of political culture, and the extent of its acquisition by the individual, were seen as resulting from such factors as childhood socialization and upbringing, media influence and exposure to state policy in adult years. These subjective orientations on the part of individuals were to be ascertained through surveys. The final task confronting classical politico-cultural research was to ascertain how political culture feeds into the 'political system'. The power of institutions to shape political culture was expressly recognized (cf. Almond 1993).

From the study of political culture, *thus construed*, Norbert Elias is poles apart. To the extent that the classical approach analyses the individual's 'psychic' dispositions at all, they are derived from his or her immediate experience or else from experience relayed by the 'media' in the context of such 'political socialization' as the individual has taken from his or her social and political milieu. Over and against such a focus on the present moment (which Elias dismisses as 'presentism'), Elias stresses the long, deep breath of history and the need for a historical-comparative approach. Elias is not centrally concerned with analyzing how individuals feel towards the state or other political 'authorities'. Rather, what is original in Elias is his focus on the state's own role in imprinting affects and on the psychic sedimentation of authority in individuals and collectivities alike. Finally, Elias opens our eyes to action-relevant habituations rooted in psychic structures that are themselves shaped by (even as they help shape) authority structures. He argues that from such long-term reciprocities arise nation-specific patterns of habituation. Thus Elias paves the way for linking up political psychology and the study of political culture within a comparative-historical perspective.

In addition to a political and institutional analysis, this study applies the analytic lens of a 'sociology of emotions' (cf. Scheff/Retzinger 1991) in its interpretation of key novels, and, occasionally, plays. This inevitably raises the question of how reliable literature is for sociological analysis, that is, the extent to which it is grounded in reality. Clearly all genres of literature must, as a rule of thumb, discharge at least two functions: they entertain, move, even thrill their readers or audiences, or else they seek to vindicate, to counsel or inspire. These functions are largely non- or supra-cognitive, since either they appeal directly to aesthetic and emotional needs or they culminate (ideally) in appropriate action. Yet, moreover, works of literature go beyond just narrating or telling a 'good story' – before the rise of sociology the novel arguably can be seen as a kind of 'proto-sociology' (Lepenies 1988). Even today, the novel sometimes functions as *ersatz* sociology. This function of literature may usefully be labeled 'cognitive-descriptive', because it complements our knowledge of the social world. We suggest that the distinction between sociology and literature is one of degree rather than kind. This claim is borne out by the importance of 'style'. While this yardstick can be neglected in the natural sciences, to do so in the social sciences is risky, a point book reviews never tire of making. The sociological uses to which literature can be put are therefore twofold. The more conventional use treats it as a reservoir of evidence that can be mined by sociology or history. The other one is to accord it the status of a serious contribution to sociology in its own right. Only few would protest against the first use, especially in the toned-down version, in which each cultural product – Baroque music, jazz, architecture, painting, etc. – serves to articulate, or indirectly represent, underlying social processes or structures. But the notion that literature can 'realistically' be read as sociology is refuted by two powerful streams in today's human sciences: one in the social sciences (i.e., in the narrow sense), the other in traditional literary criticism.

A weighty voice comes from the ranks of quantitative social history – more precisely, from the social history of the family (and so from the British empiricist tradition). P. Laslett called his essay on the literature-science interface 'The Wrong Way through the Telescope' (Laslett 1976). In it he drew up a short list of criteria for accepting literary sources as informative of, and valid for, social reality. A sociology of literary expression is desirable, Laslett tells us, in which the following question is addressed: for which audience is which message intended? Since exaggeration, colouring, understatement and invention are common weapons in the literary arsenal (poetic truth, after all, differs from real-world truth), this means that any social scientist who would draw on literature must first have a theory about this relationship. But even the claim to depict 'inner data' (if we may thus term information concerning attitudes and feelings) should be greeted with general scepticism, as Laslett sees it. Everywhere allowances have to be made because literary texts are closer to commentary rather than description; they bring out tendencies rather than correctly reproduce reality; they offer reflection rather than mirroring; they persuade, accuse and attempt to shock rather than to provide a neutral depiction; they are selective rather than comprehensive when it comes to reproducing social reality, though it is impossible to know what the author has omitted.

Laslett's empirically grounded scepticism would therefore invite us not to use literature sociologically, although he does indicate a possible escape route. We may attempt patiently to reconstruct, through a sociologist's lens, the complex communicative processes within which literature takes place. We need to be on the look out for 'genre' and 'formulaic writing', that is, those aspects of literature that literary critics might pick up on as well – text, narratives, traditions and the like. We must pick up on features that have less of a cognitive-descriptive than an extra-cognitive function.

Scepticism of the feasibility of realistic textual interpretation is as old as the study of literature itself. 'Literary theory' has taken giant strides in recent decades, pushed forward by Marxism, structuralism, hermeneutics, phenomenology and Psychoanalysis. What, then, have these attacks meant for older understandings of literary criticism? At one end of this development we find so-called deconstructionism, in which all claim to truthful depiction of reality is dismissed as a bad joke (cf. on this point Eagleton 1983; Hodge 1990). In a certain respect, too, there has been a remarkable convergence between Laslett's measurement-oriented critique and new streams from within 'literary theory' which itself disputes the 'realism' of literature. Both stress the strategic detail, the meaning of which it is sociology's task to reconstruct; both stress especially literature's pragmatic functions that detract from its descriptive realism; both are pre-disposed to attach great importance to genres that do, in fact, make little claim to realistic observation. But both ignore the promise that lies in interpreting literary works along holistic, synthesizing lines, provided this track addresses the typical in society in a way similar to sociology. For novels have, as we have seen, an irreducibly dual nature – to entertain and to inform.

Our use of novels and dramatic literature assumes that literature indeed does tender valid descriptions and interpretations of social phenomena. We have, as a rule, tried to isolate factors impacting negatively on the veridicality of literary insights and findings. In the bulk of the authors considered we made allowance for their social vantage-point, for where they were sited in the literary-cum-social process of communication, for how this citing may have affected their perspective. However, we are offering an interpretation of literary texts from the point of view of sociology rather than from literary theory. Our selected texts fall under two categories: the first contains accounts of psychic states and experiences of persons in their group relationships (let us call them psychic processes in interaction) – accounts that outstrip what professional sociologists can normally manage in terms of exactitude or proficiency. Prototypes are Charles Dickens and Johann Nestroy, each of whom possessed an uncanny ear, as it were, for the speech of the common people. A second body of texts has a more indirect – a more strongly synthesizing – access to social reality, in the sense that the spotlight is no longer on particular interactions that can be pinned down directly in space and time; instead the authors have classified and typologized their own theory-based observations. This applies chiefly to self-professed parodists and typifying ironists, such as Doderer and Herzmanovsky, but also to the likes of Kafka, whose bleak inner world eventuated in a world-model of peerless consistency. The first two writers had their own mental map of Austria, pointing their social observations in certain directions; Kafka's texts defy all spatio-temporal ordering; they seem plucked from the human dungeon itself. Here too we have attempted to allow for the citing and perspective of these authors. To the above-mentioned classes of literary examples can be added a third: best described as a loosely strung-together bundle of texts already discussed elsewhere, texts that are semi-fictional and autobiographical and have undergone secondary interpretation. To the extent they were included at all, we were persuaded of their value; to have omitted them would have been costly: what our account gained in dogmatic correctness, it would have forfeited in fullness.

A final word on our *modus operandi* in selecting literary sources and interpretations. That our choice of authors from Defoe to Sassoon, from Nestroy to Musil, can lay no claim to representativeness is self-evident. The number of Austrian authors not included on our list is impressive enough; in the English case, it is hair-raising in the extreme. That we have, as a rule, passed over trivial or inferior texts in favour of texts of some literary merit has everything to do with the acuteness of the writer's descriptive and observational powers. Were an alternative selection to throw a quite different light on the English or the Austrian habitus, that would naturally tell against us. But in any event that would first have to be shown.

Notes

1 According to Inkeles, in 1979 some 47 per cent of the population of Britain stated that they were *very happy* with their lives; by contrast, only 12 per cent of West Germans agreed and only 10 per cent of Italians. Thus the British head the field for a broad sweep of countries, outstripping even Americans (42 per cent) who came in third (Inkeles: 370).

2 'It takes three generations to make a gentleman' – this sentence earned time and again Elias's enthusiastic plaudits (Elias 1996: 459, fn 16).

Chapter 2

The Formation of the English State and the Sociogenesis of Political Authority

Preliminary remarks

Norbert Elias, as is well known, developed his 'theory of civilization' on the basis of a detailed empirical analysis of French political, social and cultural history. When analyzing the civilizing and de-civilizing processes in Germany in his *The Germans* (1996), Elias deploys a narrower temporal framework than in his work on France, concentrating on historical developments since the Wilhelminian Empire. His work on Germany lacks the observations, rooted in the sociology of literature, that played a key role in his understanding of, for example, changes in the French court and the modulation of affect among the French upper classes. Elias's treatment of English history also lacks the breadth and depth of his analysis of France. Nonetheless, in examining *Sport and Leisure in the Civilizing Process*, the subtitle of their *Quest for Excitement* (1986), Elias and Eric Dunning furnish us with suggestive observations on English developmental history. While we can, therefore, draw on Elias's and Dunning's assertions in our analysis of England, which is anchored in civilization theory, we are unable to take the same approach in our second case study, of the Habsburg Monarchy. Elias did not explore this particular power configuration in any great detail. We thus adopt of necessity differing approaches to the analysis of each case. Our examination of English history begins with Elias's thesis that England experienced a 'civilizing spurt' in the 18th century (Elias/Dunning 1986: 33). We shed light on this 'spurt' by linking it with processes of state formation. This strategy also seems justified by the fact that the history of England is one of the most solidly grounded historiographically; without a clear focus, the available material would overwhelm our account. We do not intend to provide a condensed version of English history. We can, however, identify those aspects of English history that lend empirical weight to Elias's civilization theory. We present the history of state formation in Austria, less well known by readers with social scientific leanings, in rather more detail and through a more conventional chronological approach, in part because Elias, as mentioned above, did not analyze the subject. We nonetheless devote particular attention to those aspects of Austrian history that are of central significance to our interpretation of Elias's civilization theory.

For Elias, the gradual establishment of a parliamentary regime in England over the course of the 18th century represents a distinct pacifying and civilizing 'spurt' (Elias/Dunning 1986: 26–40, 172–4). A similar 'spurt' took place in 17th century France. There, the royal court acted as the central civilizing authority. After the violent and bloody discord that marked the 16th century, the King and his representatives pursued the pacification of French society. The courtization of the aristocracy within French courtly society was an expression of the King's towering position within the absolutist power structure. The pacification of 18th century England, in contrast, was anchored in a matrix of power in which neither the King and his representatives nor the landowning upper classes – not even in alliance with the urban middle classes – were able to achieve a monopoly on power. The dynamics embedded in this balance of power hindered the establishment of an autocratic regime, while the equilibrium within the aristocratic upper class, which still featured bloody inter-factional clashes during the revolutionary turbulence of the 17th century, facilitated the parliamentarization of political life within the framework of a constitutional monarchy. In England, parliament, rather than the court, as in France, became the key civilizing force and thus – according to Elias – the key institution moulding habitus:

> The transformation of the traditional estate assemblies of England into Houses of Parliament in the modern sense of the word denoted not only an institutional change, but also a change in the personality structure of the English upper class ... Social survival and most certainly social success in a parliamentary society depended on a capacity to fight, but to fight, not with dagger or sword, but with the power of argument, the skill of persuasion, the art of compromise. However strong the temptation in electioneering battles or parliamentary contests, gentlemen were supposed never to lose their temper unintentionally and never to resort to violence among equals. (Elias/Dunning 1986: 37)

Here Elias and Dunning argue, correctly, that parliamentarism requires a specific modulation of affect, namely its mastery, which renders possible the non-violent regulation of conflict by means of discourse. At the same time, such modulation of affect is (or can be) the outcome of processes of socialization that are embedded in parliamentary structures, and are in fact essential if parliament is to endure as an institution.

In the following analysis, we attempt to trace the historical formation of the power configuration that led to this 18th century civilizing spurt of such momentous significance to England. This requires us to determine which factors enabled the institutionalization of Crown–upper class interaction in parliament, which featured both conflict and consensus. We must also identify the interdependencies that came to shape behaviour and habitus in the 18th and 19th century. The commercialization of English society and the significance of religion and religious mobilization are among the key factors here. These points are integrated into an analysis of the sociogenesis of the English state, which takes into account the development of the monopoly of taxation and of violence.

Consideration of the 'character' of the English state, as this appears in the fiscal domain, enables us to extend our study into the beginning of the 20th century. Bearing in mind that Elias thought the 'monopoly of taxation' of key importance to the structure of domination, we also provide a brief overview of English financial history.

Historical changes in the balance of power between Crown and Parliament in England

The conquest of England in 1066 by the Norman knightly aristocracy under William 'the Conqueror' led to the establishment of a highly centralized feudal monarchy. The Crown laid claim to ownership of all land and made its supporters 'tenants-in-chief'. These were obliged in return to perform military service for the Crown and furnish it with financial support. Cooperation between the Crown and its vassals was institutionalized – as in other countries – in the Grand Council of the Crown's vassals, the 'Curia Regis.' Again as in other places, this cooperation entailed the ever-present potential for conflict; relations were marked by the efforts of each of the two power groups to increase its power at the expense of the other. The Magna Carta of 1215 was an early attempt constitutionally to divide power (Sayles 1975: 398–408). Three aspects of this agreement are of particular significance. First, the Magna Carta formalized the aristocracy's right to resist any unlawful deployment of the power of domination by the King. Second, it confirmed that matters of taxation could be decided only in collaboration with the aristocratic lords. Finally, it was agreed that a committee consisting of twenty-five lords should be appointed to ensure that the agreement was upheld. A political body independent of the Crown was thus established (Kluxen 1987: 48–63). It was placed on a more permanent footing during the reign of Edward I (1272–1307) as a Parliament (Sayles 1975: ch. 5; Sayles 1950: ch. 27).

Edward's 'Model Parliament' of 1295 summoned all secular and religious lords through a personal message from the King and, through a general writ by the Lord Chancellor to the sheriffs, also the knights, burgesses and the diocesan clergy. The boroughs sent high-ranking magistrates, the counties landowners. Knights and representatives of the urban settlements and villages henceforth formed the 'Commons.' Parliament was then divided into the 'Lords' and 'Commons' during the 14th century. This institutional division showed in the merging of the knights of the shires with the burgesses in the 1340s, the election of a Speaker for the Commons and the introduction in 1376 of 'Impeachment', through which the Commons could censure ministers or servants of the Crown, with the House of Lords functioning as High Court (Kluxen 1987: 75–85, 92–102). The King also recognized Parliament's right to make decisions on the extraordinary income of the Crown during this period (Kluxen 1987: 105–12). The need for such income resulted, above all, from military demands. The Crown's financial dire straits, particularly during the long period of armed conflict with France between 1337 and

1453 (the 'Hundred Years War') over English possessions on the continent – but also as a result of military clashes with Scotland – strengthened Parliament's position. While there was agreement that direct taxation required parliamentary approval, there were persistent disputes over the Crown's right to raise indirect taxes such as customs duty and establish import monopolies, until Parliament's fiscal monopoly was established after the Glorious Revolution of 1688. Yet this right of the Crown was also repeatedly recognized through judicial rulings precisely during the period of 'revolutionary' discord in the 17th century (Loewenstein 1967: 64). In the 14th century, however, Parliament not only established the right to approve (direct) taxes; its increasing power also showed clearly in the development of legislative authority from around 1340. Parliament used this authority first by means of Petitions, then in the 15th century under Henry VI, through Bills. It was frequently able to use its fiscal powers to get the Crown to refrain from using its constitutionally enshrined right of veto over such parliamentary resolutions (Loewenstein 1967: 8; Kluxen 1987: 123–7, 205–7 ['Petition']; Sayles 1975: ch. 7).

England's defeat in the Hundred Years War also altered the domestic balance of power. Defeat weakened the English aristocracy's loyalty to the monarchy: 'Once a victorious royal authority no longer held the higher nobility together, the late-mediaeval machinery of war turned inwards, as brutalized retainers and indentured gangs were unleashed across the countryside by magnate feuds, and rival usurpers clawed for the succession' (Anderson 1974: 118; Kluxen 1987: 138–44). The Wars of the Roses between the Houses of Lancaster and York in the years between 1455 and 1485 culminated in the foundation of a new Tudor dynasty. As Anderson explains, a 'new monarchy' arose in which the power and significance of Parliament declined:

> Before the War of the Roses, Parliaments were virtually annual, and during the first decade of reconstruction ... they became so again. But once internal security improved and Tudor power was consolidated, Henry VII discarded the institution: from 1497 to 1509 ... it only assembled once again. Centralized royal government was exercised through a small coterie of personal advisers and henchmen of the monarch. Its primary objective was the subjugation of the rampant magnate power of the preceding period, with its liveried gangs of armed retainers, systematic embracery of juries, and constant private warfare. (Anderson 1974: 118–19)

The marginalization of Parliament was, however, overcome as a result of Henry VIII's reformation of the church: '[E]specially after 1529, Parliament became a more dynamic and a still less dispensable part of English government than it had been before' (Williams 1979: 35). The Reformation Parliament (1529–36) met for eight sessions, the Commons in particular advocating anticlerical positions, obliging Henry's political intentions regarding state and church. The Commons' position was strengthened as the Crown sought to legitimize for its reformation policy through acts of Parliament. The Commons' sphere of action, the special case of Statute Law, became thus the most important means of advancing state policy. This led to a qualitative change in the nature of parliamentarism. In earlier times, the Commons had to be present in Parliament only on exceptional occasions such as the raising of general taxes or the decree of new statutes. It now had to convene on a regular basis. Since 1531, Parliament had, moreover, increasingly dealt with bills put forward by the Crown, whereas it had previously dealt mainly with its members' draft bills. A partnership thus developed between Crown and Commons, which was to find constitutional expression in the 'King-in-Parliament' formulation. This conception, according to which national legislative authority rested solely with the King, Lords and Commons, who, together, were understood to represent the entire Realm in the 'most High Court of Parliament', was first clearly enunciated in 1534 in the 'Dispensation Act.' Through this formula, all three institutions were legally sanctioned as indispensable and equal participants in the legislative process (Elton (ed.) 1960: 351–3 ['An act for the exoneration of exactions paid to the see of Rome']; Kluxen 1983: 42–5; Guy 1990: 124–39).

Kluxen (1983: 47) argues that the Commons ensured the governability of the nation during this period. Arguably, there also develops a distinct English political 'nation' and English national consciousness during this historical phase. We do not wish primarily to refer to the political and cultural significance of the English Reformation – although the establishment of the Anglican state church shaped mentality and consciousness into the 20th century, and the English Reformation did indeed lead to a dramatic religious mobilization and the development of a large number of different denominations. Admittedly, religious disputes led to political conflicts for almost two centuries after the Reformation, which found their clearest expression in the revolutionary dislocations of the 17th century. In the context of the present discussion, however, we wish to emphasize more narrowly the importance of the interweaving of institutions in the political sphere:

> Ever since the time of Henry VIII, it had been obvious that the king was the ruler of the entire English nation, and not just the head of an aristocratic faction ... And then there was Parliament, in which the unity of the kingdom and the nation was also manifested ... It was agreed that everything Parliament did enjoyed the approval of the whole country. Parliament, for a long time to come, was acting purely in the interest of the crown, passing laws for the whole kingdom and endorsing taxation by the monarch, but it was reckoned to be a political body in which the country's vested interests came together and – at least in theory – were resolved in compromises for the common good. Parliament was the concrete proof that the English nation really existed. (Schulze 1996: 124)

We must, however, keep in mind that during this period the Crown retained the authority to summon or dissolve Parliament as it saw fit. When government and administration again took precedence over legislation under Elizabeth I – not least because the Reformation had now been placed on a firm constitutional footing, but also because of persistent religious difficulties that caused political instability, and because of political disputes with Spain – her Parliament acted more as high court than legislative assembly. It was convened only 13 times in the 45 years of her reign (Kluxen 1983: 48–9). The 17th century, politically speaking, was marked by conflicts between Crown and Parliament over their rights and competencies, and thus over the balance of power within the state as a whole.

The King's prerogatives as the bearer of governmental power formed a central bone of contention in the political disputes of the first half of the 17th century. The King enjoyed the right to summon, adjourn and dissolve Parliament and veto draft bills put forward by Parliament. Royal prerogatives included appointment and dismissal of government officials and supreme command of the armed forces (including the militia) and sole authority in matters of war and peace along with the right of coinage, control of foreign trade and church jurisdiction. Contemporary opinion held that the royal prerogative included the Crown's right to supplement existing law through proclamations, as long as this did not injure Common Law or parliamentary law. The royal prerogatives were increasingly the subject of discord, particularly during the reign of Charles I. The Commons claimed in December 1621, 'that the arduous and urgent affairs concerning the King, state and defence of the realm, and of the Church of England, and the maintenance and making of laws, and redress of mischiefs and grievances which daily happen within the realm, are proper subjects and matters of counsel and debate in Parliament' (quoted in Kenyon (ed.) 1966: 47). With this revolutionary demand, Parliament laid claim to the right to intervene in the sphere of government, traditionally the preserve of the King alone. The political context of this 'protestation' was the financial plight of James I. The continental disputes of the Thirty Years War had not left England untouched. After the defeat of Frederick, son-in-law of James I, at the Battle of the White Mountain in 1620 – a defeat whose implications for the Habsburg Monarchy we shall analyze in the following chapter – and the subsequent occupation of the Electoral Palatinate by Spanish troops, England prepared for war against Spain. Parliament alone possessed the legal right to grant the necessary means to pursue this course of action. The Crown's dependence on Parliament, which first arose in 1621, was again apparent in 1624, when the Commons, through the 'Subsidies Act', legally stipulated that the funds it had granted be used for a specific purpose, in order thus to promote its foreign policy views – and, moreover, even appointed a commission to supervise the use of these funds (cf. Kenyon (ed.) 1966: 76–80).

Parliament again made use of the institution of 'impeachment' to take legal action against politically disagreeable civil servants, loosening the connection between the King and his officials. Impeachment was, from the standpoint of Parliament, an embryonic form of ensuring ministerial responsibility to Parliament, as it later developed. For the King, it represented an attack on his right to appoint his officials and advisors as he saw fit. When Parliament prepared a bill of impeachment against one of the King's closest confidantes, the Duke of Buckingham, Charles I dissolved it. This dissolution also meant that the King now had no legally procured funds at his disposal successfully to pursue his military objectives against France. After the La Rochelle disaster of autumn 1627, when the King failed to support the French Huguenots who faced persecution in France, the

Crown attempted to put the treasury back on its feet by means of a 'forced loan', thus evading Parliament's right to approve taxes. The forced loan was a political disaster. Subjects who refused to pay were arrested; across the country a large number of justices of the peace and some lord lieutenants were dismissed for opposing this policy (cf. Kenyon (ed.) 1966: 106–9). The Parliament of 1628 was summoned against a background of political and legal disputes over the forced loan (cf. Kenyon (ed.) 1966: 80–81). This Parliament now guaranteed the King financial support, but passed the 'Petition of Right' as a counter-move, intended to shackle the King. In this petition, Parliament demanded protection from arbitrary arrest; from taxation without parliamentary approval; from billeting of troops in private houses without financial compensation; and from imposition of martial law on the civilian population – all of which had become problems during the preceding years, when the Crown obtained the forced loan, and in the wake of the war against Spain and France (cf. Kenyon (ed.) 1966: 82–5).

In view of these intensifying disputes between Crown and Parliament, Charles I refrained from summoning Parliament between 1629 and 1640. Yet, once again financial troubles forced the King to summon Parliament. This time around it was a conflict with Scotland, rather than military embroilment on the continent, that laid bare the Crown's dependence on Parliament. Since 1637, the King had been trying to strengthen the secular power of the Scottish Kirk – a policy that provoked resistance from large swathes of the Scottish nobility who managed secularized church estates. At the same time, the Crown was trying to promulgate in Scotland an Arminian liturgical reform and the Episcopal constitution of the English state church. This English intervention triggered the formation, in February 1638, of the Scottish National Covenant, which opposed the church policy and the rule of Charles I in general. Armed conflict led to occupation of large tracts of the north of England by Scottish troops. The Treaty of Ripon in 1640 established a cease-fire and obliged the King, among other things, to pay for the upkeep of the Scottish troops. This he could do only if Parliament granted him the necessary financial means.

We cannot hope to portray here the protracted course of the political crisis as it gradually came to a head. The key point is that the 'Long Parliament', formally in existence from 1640 to 1660, significantly strengthened the position of Parliament as an institution through a series of far-reaching resolutions. In 1641 it passed the 'Triennial Bill', obliging the King to summon Parliament at least once for a 50-day session within a three-year period (cf. Kenyon (ed.) 1966: 219–22). It also voted into law a ban on postponing, adjourning and dissolving Parliament without its agreement. By dissolving the special courts of the Star Chamber – the legal authority charged, among other things, with maintaining the King's peace – and the Courts of High Commission – the royal legal body responsible for the state church – restricting church jurisdiction to spiritual matters and declaring that all acts of government must be subject to the highest Common Law courts, Parliament tried to deprive the King of important rights (cf. Kenyon (ed.) 1966: 223–6). This policy culminated in the 'Nineteen Propositions' of June 1642. Parliament demanded that in future, all advisors to the King and all judges be appointed with its approval, that the King's offspring be raised under its supervision and that it have the right to approve royal marriages. It further demanded the right to an advisory role in matters of war and peace and asserted its total control of the militia. Finally, it declared that it possessed joint responsibility for issues of church reform (cf. Kenyon (ed.) 1966: 244–7). The response of Charles I made it clear that a compromise between Crown and Parliament was unlikely:

> The government ... is (en)trusted to the King; power of treaties of war and peace, of making Peers, of choosing officers and councillors for state, judges for law, commanders for forts and castles, giving commission for raising men, to make war abroad, or to prevent or provide against invasions or insurrections at home, benefit of confiscations, power of pardoning, and some more of the like are placed in the King. (Quoted in Kenyon (ed.) 1966: 21)

It was clear to Charles that acceptance of the 'Nineteen Propositions' could end only 'in a dark, equal chaos of confusion' (quoted in Kenyon (ed.) 1966: 23). Civil war was now a distinct possibility.

Was the wrangling between Crown and Parliament, during the reign of Charles I, over the appropriate use of the royal prerogatives, an expression of a political and constitutional conflict stretching back to the 16th century that peaked in the 1640s and ended in civil war, Charles's beheading in 1649 and thus victory for Parliament? This long-dominant perspective has been 'revised' over the last two decades in a tempestuous debate. This 'revisionism' has generated a new 'orthodoxy' declaring the doctrine of continually escalating constitutional conflict between Crown and Parliament to be obsolete. This view highlights the cooperation between Crown and Parliament, which was generally harmonious. Parliament is here conceptualized as a transmission belt within the state legislative machinery – not only during Elizabeth's rule, but also under James I, and indeed into the 1630s (Wende 1988: 89–95; Greyerz 1994: 14–33). Wende (1988: 94) succinctly sums up the results of the 'revisionist' history in respect to the role of Parliament: 'Wherever and whenever opposition stirred in the English lower house, its aim was not the systematic expansion of Parliament's position at the expense of the Crown ... Constitutional history can no longer refer to a "High Road", that is, a one-way street of historical development leading up to the Revolution.'

According to the 'revisionist' reading, this political consensus can also be demonstrated in the 'ideological' domain. Burgess (1992; 1996) and Kishlansky (1996: 35–9) claim that consensus existed between the Crown and the political nation that crystallized in Parliament in the acceptance of the notion of 'the divine right of kings.' Monarchical power was at the same time viewed as *de facto* limited: 'However divine its origins and God-like its authority, successive monarchs had granted privileges and yielded to principles that established a balance between the prerogatives of the princes and the liberties of subjects. Those privileges had been confirmed in charters, elucidated in statutes, and established by custom. What they were, and what they meant, like the Common Law itself, was not always easy to determine. But that they existed was indisputable and undisputed' (Kishlansky 1996: 37–8). The monarch, after all, swore in the coronation oath 'to confirm to the people of England the laws and customs to them granted' (Kishlansky 1996: 36). This, according to opinion at the time, protected the property rights of the subjects. These rights may not be injured by royal prerogatives. Ritter (1972: 27–31) has stressed that the prerogatives of the King, as bearer of the power of government, extended to all those issues of national life, which did 'not affect the concrete rights of a subject':

> According to contemporary terminology, this domain of 'Government', in which the rights of the King were absolute, was opposed to the sphere of 'Property.' This was understood to mean not only property as such, but the rights of subjects *in toto* ... The House of Commons was considered the chief representative of the interests of Property; it was not, according to opinion at the time, an instrument for controlling the government. (Ritter 1972: 30)

Arguably, a notion of balance between Government and Property obtained. Within the actual sphere of government, however, this balance of power was not supposed to exist, only the 'absolute' power of the Crown: 'The Parliament ... within the overall structure of the constitution, was the institution in which the King and the representatives of the subjects coordinated the interests of Government and Property and in which the power and authority of the King and of the state culminated in the cooperation of all the forces of the polity' (Ritter 1972: 31–2). The conflict between Charles I and Parliament was not initially a dispute over the King's prerogatives, but rather over their application considered by the parliamentary opposition injurious to the 'property rights' of subjects. Nonetheless, the dynamics of the civil war situation led Parliament to assert that it, and not the King, ultimately represented the 'commonweal', the welfare of the 'People', and that not only the royal prerogatives, but also the Crown itself, was surplus to requirements (Burgess 1992: 212–31).

These constitutional antagonisms, which took shape in the context of the taxation policy of Charles I, represented an important dimension in the history leading up to the English Civil War. Charles's policy towards religion and the church contributed to the radicalization of political disputes in the 1630s, by mobilizing anti-Catholic resentment which extended far beyond the circle of pious, puritanically-minded Protestants. We have already referred to the significance of the attempt to anglicanize the Scottish Kirk in 1637 for the destabilization of Charles's system of domination. This way of putting things may be somewhat misleading, however, in that the Anglican Church itself had been subject to a transformation. Since the Elizabethan Settlement in 1559, the Anglican state church had combined a Zwinglian-Calvinist dogmatic orientation and liturgical style with an Episcopal constitution (cf. Elton (ed.) 1960: 400–404). From the 1570s on, Puritanism had developed as a movement for renewal within the state church opposed to Episcopalianism. Organizationally, its reform efforts revolved around the introduction of a Presbyterian constitution on the Genevan model of the Reformed Church, and thus around strengthening the position of the laity within the church, particularly with regard to church discipline (Axtmann 1996). At the Hampton Court Conference of 1604, James I expressed his opposition to this attempt to introduce a Presbyterian constitution, but re-affirmed the church's Calvinist doctrinal orientation (cf. Kenyon (ed.) 1966: 126–7).

Charles's approach represented an attempt to reform the state church – but not in a Puritan direction. On the contrary, English Arminians sponsored by Charles followed the reform movement of Dutch theologian Jakob Arminius and broke away from the traditional Calvinist doctrine of predestination, instead advocating the universality of divine mercy and of free will (Tyacke 1987). At the same time, through changes in ritual and liturgy, the clergy's status was bolstered; priests' role as spiritual mediators, for example, was emphasized. The Anglican Church moved closer to Catholic forms of service. For example, 'the laity was encouraged to kneel during Communion … Communion tables were removed from the nave and again made to serve as alters, and organ playing was integrated into the service' (Greyerz 1994: 93). Greyerz argues that these attempts at liturgical reform mobilized the deep-rooted anti-Catholicism in England. Greyerz's claim that 'every generation between 1588 and 1641 ... had lived through a quite real threat to English Protestantism' is convincing:

> Pope Pious V's excommunication of Queen Elizabeth in 1570, the ominous expedition of the Spanish armada against England in 1588 and not least the Gunpowder Plot of 1605, that is, Guy Fawkes's Catholic conspiracy against James I and Parliament, the general dismay at the royal dynasty's Spanish marriage plans in the early 1620s, the persistent fear of a Catholic invasion in the same decade and finally the outbreak of the Irish Rebellion (1641) [by Irish Catholics] were milestones on the way to the deep-rooted anti-Catholic sentiment that came to mark the consciousness of contemporaries. (Greyerz 1994: 94)

We could add to the list of threats by mentioning, for example, the Crown's foreign policy, initially pro-Spanish and then predominantly pro-French in the 1630s, or Charles's marriage to the Catholic Henrietta Maria. Burgess (1992: 170 and 272, n. 110; cf. Greyerz, 1994: 26, 97) argues that the issue of whether England was doing enough for the Protestant side in the Thirty Years War, and indeed whether it was sufficiently Protestant and still aware of its special role in God's plan of salvation, were central aspects of the political disputes from the late 1620s on. Anti-Catholic sentiment was not only expressed in a 'directly' political manner, but also 'indirectly' in the form of apocalyptic fears that the Antichrist would rise to world domination and as Chiliastic expectations of redemption, which spread with renewed vigour in England in the early 1640s. Such beliefs formed part of the ideological and cultural justification for the English Reformation as a battle against the 'Antichrist.' They were a key component of the religious imagination as early as the 1530s (Christianson 1978: ch. 5; Firth 1979; Lamont 1969; Burrell 1964).

Examination of the interplay between these two elements – the political and constitutional conflict and the religious one – suggests that Kishlansky's (1996: 151–2) opinion of the civil war factions is correct. His pithy formulation deserves to be quoted in full:

> Royalists ... believed in bishops and the divine right of kings not so much as intellectual propositions than as the moorings of a hierarchy in church and state. Their fundamental principle was loyalty – an instinct deeply etched in the patriarchal nature of their society. Disloyalty was base – a violation of a code that made oaths as strong as contracts, voluntary obedience more dependable than law, and self-sacrifice a welcomed duty. Devotion was the emotive force behind the King's cause. Parliamentarians fought for true religion and liberty. They too defended an ancient inheritance – a church purified of recent innovations and a government that respected the inviolability of property. They feared for their souls, and felt that salvation was too important an individual matter to be left in the hands of the church. Their fundamental principle was consent – an ingrained belief in the cooperation between subject and sovereign that maintained the delicate balance between prerogatives and liberties. Without consent, monarchy became tyranny and free men became slaves. Their principal emotion was fear: dread at what would happen if they did not make a stand; terror at what would happen if they failed.

The execution of Charles I on 30 January 1649 led to the establishment of the Commonwealth and the Protectorate under Oliver Cromwell. The bloody turbulence and turmoil of this interregnum ended in the restoration of the Stuart monarchy in 1660, when Charles II, son of Charles I, ascended the throne. Our analysis remains restricted to the relationship between Crown and Parliament, particularly the issue of cooperation or conflict in both constitutional and church or religious matters. Most of the legislation of the 'Long Parliament' of 1641–42 remained in force. Given Parliament's experience of wielding executive power under the Commonwealth, the general consensus in 1660 was that it was now out of the question for it to concern itself with everyday administrative matters (Kluxen 1983: 62–3). While the Crown exercised 'government', Parliament engaged in important political manoeuvres that often brought it in conflict with the Crown. The 'Cavalier Parliament', dominated by men, 'who (or whose families) had suffered for their royalism in the preceding years, and who were therefore not simply willing to get down to business, without first settling old scores' (Greyerz 1994: 206), pursued a political approach that reflected this fact, particularly in matters of church policy.

They aimed to restore the state Episcopal Church, as it had developed under Elizabeth. This meant punishing the various Protestant 'sects' and the Presbyterians, expelling them from the church and marginalizing them within state and society. The Corporation Act of 1661, for example, obliged all municipal officers to swear an oath of loyalty to the King and to take communion in the Church of England. The Act of Uniformity of 1662 led to the 'cleansing' of the church, which involved expelling those clergy who refused unconditionally to advocate Church of England doctrine and its liturgical and ritual practices and to renounce the right of resistance (cf. Kenyon (ed.) 1966: 376–82). Yet again, the position of the Protestant 'nonconformists' became a matter of political contestation. A new wave of anti-Catholic agitation, meanwhile, further weakened English Catholics, who were *de facto* excluded from all civil and military offices through the Test Act (1673). This act must be viewed in the context of the Crown's efforts, through the Declaration of Indulgence of 1672, to allow nonconformists to congregate freely for communal services, provided that their place of worship and the priests were registered and officially authorized. At the same time, Catholics were allowed to practice their religion in their own homes (cf. Kenyon (ed.) 1966: 407–8). The background of this policy was England's rapprochement with France under Louis XIV, who demanded improvement in the position of Catholics in England in exchange for financial support for the English King. Charles II also agreed in the secret Treaty of Dover to convert to Catholicism at an opportune moment. James Stuart, brother and heir to Charles II, openly professed his Catholicism – though he was, like Charles himself, already married to a Catholic. This, along with the war against the Protestant Netherlands in alliance with Catholic France, kept church issues highly charged politically.

In 1678, anti-Catholic hysteria triggered claims of a Catholic conspiracy supposedly aiming to murder the King and impose Catholic rule. This 'Popish Plot' formed the immediate background to the 'Exclusion Crisis' of 1679–81. The political instrumentalization of anti-Catholicism led to a crisis of the state, as the parliamentary opposition wished to exclude James Stuart from succeeding to the throne. Constitutionally, the opposition was in effect claiming for itself 'a significant portion of national sovereignty by bypassing the traditional rights of succession practiced by the ruling dynasty' (Greyerz 1994: 216). Considered from a narrower political perspective, this crisis led to the formation of two political parties: the Whigs as champions of 'exclusion' and the Tories as allies of the Crown. The opposition failed to have its way – not least because the King refrained from summoning Parliament between 1681 and 1685. When Charles II died in 1685, his brother James II succeeded him.

James's policy on religion revolved around strengthening Catholicism in England. In 1687 he published a Declaration of Indulgence 'by virtue of our royal prerogative', and thus without a parliamentary resolution or agreement, in which he bestowed the right to religious freedom upon his subjects (quoted in Kenyon (ed.) 1966: 410–13). He accepted the fact that this policy of toleration would also benefit the Protestant sects and free churches; his core motivation was, after all, to undermine Anglicanism. His policy also affected the staffing of public offices. In 1688 almost a quarter of justices of the peace were Catholic; Catholics gained commissions in the county militias; and more Catholics were appointed as officers in the army. In Ireland, the army was largely purged of Protestants. The universities, traditionally devoted to meeting the educational needs of the Anglican

Church, were forced to take in Catholic students (Greyerz 1994: 227; Kishlansky 1996: 272–3).

In the consciousness of the time, Catholicism and 'popery' were connected with arbitrary rule and the assault on 'property.' The expansion of the standing army from a nominal strength of 14,000 men in November 1685 to around 40,000 men in 1688 heightened fears of those within the 'political nation' and broad sections of the population that they were in danger of losing not only their faith, but also their freedoms (Greyerz 1994: 223). The birth of a Catholic heir in June 1688 magnified these fears. The King himself had contributed to the sustained political mobilization caused by the issue of religion, by taking to court seven Anglican bishops who had expressed opposition in a petition to the reading out of the Declaration of Indulgence from the pulpit. They were found not guilty of 'seditious libel', showing how deep-rooted criticism of the King's policy in fact was (cf. Kenyon (ed.) 1966: 441–7). The King's attempts to determine the composition of the next Parliament by manipulating the elections, subsequently contributed further to the formation of an oppositional union of Whigs and Tories, Dissenters and Anglicans (cf. Kenyon (ed.) 1966: 309–10). The 'Glorious Revolution' of 1688–89 was the result. It brought William III of Orange, a grandson of King Charles I and son-in-law of James II, to the English throne.

How did the balance of power between Crown and Parliament change? The 'Bill of Rights' of December 1689 provides the constitutional answer. It annulled the King's right to suspend or dispense laws. Laws could be passed or repealed solely with parliamentary approval. The raising of taxes too required parliamentary consent. Free elections to Parliament, free parliamentary debates and more frequent parliamentary sessions were also stipulated. The parliamentization of political life was also advanced considerably by the Crown's loss of the right to marshal and maintain a standing army in peacetime without a parliamentary resolution. The size of military units on English territory had now to be set annually by Parliament, and the law governing discipline within the armed forces inside England's borders also required confirmation by means of an annual 'Mutiny Act'. This meant that Parliament had to meet at least once a year. In his appraisal of the 'Bill of Rights' Kluxen (1983: 79) concludes that

> from then on, Parliament [determined] the fundamentals of the constitution and ... [claimed] supreme authority, as it would from this point forward decide, together with the courts, the content of the royal prerogatives. It was no longer the King, but his subjects in Parliament, who defined the commonweal. The title of King was based on a general consensus, and pledging to uphold religion and statutes by taking the prescribed oath was a prerequisite for its acquisition.

While the 'Glorious Revolution', through the 'Bill of Rights', affirmed and extended the rights of Parliament from a constitutional point of view, the armed conflicts with France, in which William III embroiled England, brought about a *de facto* expansion of its power. It was once again the Crown's dependence on the provision of the financial means to wage war that caused the balance of power to shift. The Nine Years War, which came to an end through the Peace of Rijswijk in 1697, as well as the War of the Spanish Succession between 1702 und 1713 (Peace of Utrecht) dragged England into Continental conflicts. This was not simply a matter of pursuing a 'balance of powers' approach for geopolitical reasons. The struggle with France was for many Englishmen a battle to secure their Protestant regime. As Brewer (1989: 140) elaborates, most Englishmen were fighting 'neither for a Dutch king nor for a balance of power in Europe. They cared little for either. They fought to preserve the revolution of 1688, to avert the return of James II, whom Louis supported, and to avoid Catholicism and executive intrusion that had been the hallmark of his reign.' The need to expand the army was as plain as the need for adequate financial backing. As we shall see in more detail at a later point, it was during this period that England was restructured as a 'fiscal-military state' (Brewer 1989). A consensus began to form to the effect that 'the fiscal-military state protected Englishmen's liberties as much as it threatened them. This view ... explains why the focus of opposition to the fiscal-military state gradually shifted away from the attempt to secure its abolition to a policy of containment' (Brewer 1989: 142–3). The financial agreements of 1689–90 resulted, on the one hand, in the King receiving insufficient revenue, thus ensuring Parliament's power: '[I]n future the ability of the king's ministers to secure parliamentary consent to additional revenues was to be of vital importance to the monarch' (Brewer 1989: 145). Parliament now possessed 'the power of the purse' in both peacetime and wartime (Roberts 1977: 76). On the other hand, the Commons decided to impose a 'land tax', which made a significant contribution to the payment of war expenses. Nevertheless, we must bear in mind why this tax appealed to a majority of members of Parliament: it allowed them maximum political control. The 'land tax' required annual approval and thus remained in Parliament's gift rather than the Crown's. It was not, moreover, imposed locally by a royal bureaucracy but was administered by the local elite (Beckett 1985: 299–301; Brewer 1989: 147).

By exploiting the Crown's financial dependence, Parliament succeeded in passing three laws in the two decades following the 'Glorious Revolution', which further secured its position. The 'Triennial Act' of 1694 stipulated that a new Parliament must be convened, that is, new elections must be held at least every three years. The Act of Settlement of 1701 enshrined the Protestant succession and declared the granddaughter of James I, Sophia, Electoress of Hanover and her dynasty legitimate heirs to the throne. The Parliament thus made itself sovereign arbitrator in issues of succession. The 'Regency Act' of 1707 ultimately provided that the Privy Council and Parliament should continue to exist even when the monarch died. How could the Crown assert itself politically in light of Parliament's power?

It is first crucial to note that religious politics continued to be beset by conflict. While the 'Act of Toleration' improved the position of the Dissenters, Catholics enjoyed no such advance. The confrontation coming to a head within the Anglican Church, however, now took centre stage. A High Church faction that was unhappy with the constitutional consequences of the 'Glorious Revolution' and disapproved of tolerance of Dissenters, opposed a Low Church faction that sought to come to terms with both developments. This confrontation became politically significant insofar as the factions linked up with political groupings: High Church with the Tories, Low Church with the Whigs. While the Whigs identified themselves with the results of the 'Glorious Revolution', many Tories advocated an approach that sharply conflicted with the ideas and policies of 1688–89. They remained committed to the notion that resisting the Crown was illegitimate; regarded William's ascendance to the throne as a breach of the constitution; and clung to the idea that the Anglican Church should enjoy a religious monopoly. It was from among their ranks that criticism of William's leadership of the war arose, not only because of the financial burdens it had generated, but also because of the expansion of the machinery of state and government bound up with it. This expansion, they believed, in itself represented a danger to the 'English Liberties', but also enabled the King to establish a system of nepotism and favouritism by means of patronage.

These ideological conflicts took the form of fierce inter-party struggles, which marked the period between 1689 and 1714, and turned the elections held during those years into bitter clashes. The Crown attempted to rein in the power of the lower house by influencing the election and elected members. As Greyerz (1994: 248–9) underlines, the frequent elections established by the 'Triennial Act' forced 'members of Parliament or their patrons among the wealthiest families in the country to do what they could, in the constituencies controlled by them, to ensure the ongoing loyalty of their political clientele by means of regular gift-giving, banquets and other favours.' This ideological polarization also meant that voting took place in more constituencies than had hitherto been usual, and indeed than was usual later on in the 18th century. Election campaigns were untypical before 1689. The voters saw the act of voting 'as a symbolic renewal of their obligations to their patron before the Sheriff', rather than an act expressing their political will (Kluxen 1983: 91). The ideological fault lines apparent in the three decades after the 'Glorious Revolution' led to an understanding of the act of voting as a political and programmatic profession of loyalty. The political mobilization that this entailed was expressed in the increasing number of contested constituencies:

> In the general election of 1705, twenty-six out of forty English counties were contested, a record for the century, although that of 1710 came close when twenty-three went to the polls. As late as 1722 there were seventeen county contests. Thereafter the total drops dramatically, down to four in 1741, three in 1747, five in 1754 and four again in 1761. (Speck 1977: 164)

Until the middle of the 19th century, uncontested elections were the norm. As Kluxen (1983: 127) shows, 107 of 707 seats remained 'uncontested' as late as 1918 – with an electorate of 21 million. The three decades following the Glorious Revolution were thus exceptional, and were succeeded by a period of sharply reduced electoral mobilization. A key reason for this was the 'Septennial Act' of

1716, which provided for new elections only every seven years. For Speck (1977: 164) these facts show particularly forcefully 'that the political elites of England fused into a homogeneous ruling class in the central decades of the eighteenth century' – an observation which, as we have seen, Norbert Elias also made. We shall return to this point later on.

These frequent and expensive election campaigns offered the Crown a chance to increase its power. The Crown's influence on the elections rested, according to Ritter (1972: 92), on four factors:

> 1. The determining influence that the government could exercise on the voting of the tenants of the Crown and those working for the Crown, above all for the customs, tax and postal services (there was of course an open ballot). 2. The support provided to candidates through contributions to the prodigious electoral expenses. 3. The tendency of port cities to elect representatives with links to the government in order to attain special rates or orders to build ships. 4. The tendency, still very strong, to vote for candidates recommended by the King's government out of loyalty to the Crown.

The Crown's powers of patronage constituted another key factor. After the Whigs had succeeded in marginalizing the Tories politically by stigmatizing them as Jacobites, that is, as advocates of the restoration of the Stuart Monarchy, the patronage system was expanded into the 'spoils system' under Whig leader Robert Walpole after George I's ascent to the throne (1714–27). In the mid-18th century, around 45 per cent of representatives were linked to the Crown in one way or another through material interests – whether as officials in the army, navy, administration or at Court; as recipients of a state pension; or as traders doing business with the government (Ritter 1972: 99). The government also enjoyed a majority in the House of Lords. In 1714, 67 Peers were either servants of the Crown or received pensions. This had increased to around 90 in 1752. About 60 per cent of Peers active in the House of Lords thus belonged, on an informal basis, to the 'governing party' (Cannon 1984: 95–6).

While the Crown's prerogatives led to fierce ideological and constitutional disputes and campaigns in the 17th century, it was the Crown's and the Executive's powers of patronage that unified the opposition politically and ideologically until far into the second half of the 18th century. This 'country'-based opposition, hostile to the 'Court' and the Executive, demanded above all effective parliamentary control of the government by means of fair and frequent elections, a reduction in the number of royal *protégées* holding public office, a reduction in the size of the army and a policy of lower taxation (Brewer 1980: 326). Under Charles II, the Whigs in particular advocated this, but the Tories, too, embraced it during the reign of Queen Anne (1702–14). As early as the reign of William III, supporters of both parties made common cause to advance this policy. Under the first two Hanoverian kings, George I and George II, the antagonism between 'Court' and 'Country' was superimposed on the confrontation between Tories and Whigs. 'Country' Whigs and Tories allied against 'Court' Whigs and their 'spoils system', which coloured every aspect of political life. As we shall see, the 'Country' position was expanded into a perspective aiming beyond the immediate political sphere, and was thus closely linked to other discourses on the survival of 'political virtue' in post-revolutionary England. Before probing this issue, it is crucial to investigate further how the matrix of political power gradually changed in the 18th century in such a way as to bring about an oligarchic system.

We have seen how the Crown and the Executive succeeded in securing their power. Yet the Peers too anchored themselves more securely and profoundly within the power structure in England. They dominated the Cabinet during the 18th century. Between 1782 and 1820, 65 men held a Cabinet post, of which 43 were Peers and 14 the sons of Peers. The Peers were in the minority for the first time in the Whig Cabinet of 1835. In the case of a 'conservative' Cabinet, such a minority position happened for the first time in 1858. The aristocracy also enjoyed a hegemonic position in the army and navy, with the Peers 'naturally' near-monopolizing the highest ranks. The possibility of buying the rank of an officer up to and including the rank of lieutenant colonel was the key factor ensuring aristocratic dominance. In 1769, for example, of 102 colonels, 54 were Peers or the sons, grandsons or sons-in-law of Peers. As late as 1875, around half of army officers came from noble families, and in 1912 their share was still 40 per cent – though these figures also include landowning 'gentry.'

The Peerage's influence in the House of Commons was of particular significance in securing its position within the overall matrix of power. This influence manifested itself in the control that Peers exercised over constituencies. Between 1715 and 1785 the number of Members of Parliament (MPs) elected through the patronage of Peers increased by a factor of four. In 1715, 68 MPs enjoyed the protection of a Peer; in 1786 the figure had risen to 210. As late as 1831, the figure was 191, with 90 members of the Peerage controlling the election of over a third of all MPs. The influence of the Peers in the House of Commons, however, went beyond this direct patronage. In 1713, a total of 32 members were sons of English Peers, a figure that had increased to 82 in 1796. Adding the Irish Peers, who were entitled to a seat in the lower house, the 'Peerage element' increases from 8 per cent in 1713 to 21 per cent of all members in 1796 (Cannon 1984: ch. 4; Beckett 1988: ch. 12; Rule 1992: 32–4; Colley 1994: 155).

The high degree of familial connections among its members contributed substantially to the cohesion of the House of Commons in the 18th century. In his study of 'the Aristocratic Century', Cannon (1984: 114–15) provides the following figures:

> In 1715, out of 558 members, no fewer than 234 had fathers who had also served in the House: by 1754, the number had grown to 294, well over 50%. Even in 1784 ... it was 214. This ... was by no means the whole story. In 1754, in addition to the 294 referred to, another twenty-nine members of the House had grandfathers who had served. A further forty-two had brothers serving with them or who had already served ... another twenty-two members had uncles or great-uncles who had served, and ten more had

> cousins who were or had been members. [This] ... gives 397 members who had or had had close relatives in the House – well over 70%.

Beckett (1988, 432) also stresses this aspect of familial linkage. He shows that between 1734 and 1832, 60 per cent of all MPs were drawn from a total of 922 families, and 30 per cent from just 247 families. We can readily agree with Elias that processes of pacification were bound up with the parliamentization of the political system in the 18th century. We must, however, also bear in mind that familial connections played a significant role in these developments.

Elements in the pacification and disciplining of English society

There is, nonetheless, more to the pacification to which Elias refers than these familial bonds and the web of clientelism and patronage. Other developments also played a role. Through the Act of Union of 1707, Scotland, frequent source of violent clashes over the centuries, was securely bound within the matrix of political domination. George I's peaceful ascent to the throne in 1714 and the quelling of the Jacobite rebellion in 1715 ended disputes over the succession and destroyed the Tory Party, tainted by association with the uprising. Peace with France in 1713 led to a lowering of taxes, which were based on property. The rug was thus pulled from under the often economic criticism of Crown policy, while the easing of the economic burden was also expressed in the rising prosperity of large numbers of the property-owning class. This renewed prosperity was also due to the fact that the 'landed interest' and the 'monied interest', that is, on the one hand, property owners and, on the other, men who had grown rich by contributing to the financial basis of foreign policy, moved closer to one another. It had become clear that the 'monied interest' could neither dominate nor marginalize the 'landed interest' politically. Landowners proved ever more willing to engage in financial transactions:

> The foundation of the Bank of England in 1694 first drew in a high proportion of the great monied and commercial magnates of London, but later ... it slowly spread its net rather wider across the countryside. This quiet symbiosis of the monied and the landed interests was greatly assisted by social and educational developments, which were providing them with a common cultural background and a common standard of good manners. (Stone 1980: 84)

One aspect of this symbiosis was the development of a service sector, both in the context of the 'commercial revolution' – in the financial sphere or legal system for instance – but also within the state, whose civil and military 'bureaucracy' expanded during these decades:

> Most professions recruited widely – far more widely, indeed, than did the army. They were consequently able to provide invaluable milieux in which thousands of men of

> landed and often armigerous families could find common ground with thousands more from very different backgrounds. Here a community of interest could genuinely be experienced based on mental concerns and respect. Professional status itself became a bond that served more tightly to integrate many units of local society. (Holmes 1981: 20)

'Professionalization' thus contributed to the development of a 'shared identity' within the 'political nation' and thus within the 'ruling class.' As Stone has shown, this class also evolved a 'cultural' identity.

This 'cultural identity' can be placed within a broader cultural context. The restoration of the Stuart Monarchy followed an age in which religious issues had been discussed with exceptional intensity. The decades of the Restoration were a period of reaction against religious fanaticism that had characterized the interregnum and the years of the Commonwealth. Calvinism, the official theology of those years, went into decline after the Restoration. The political and religious excesses of Calvinism had led to its popular marginalization, apparent in deliberate efforts to take a more moderate approach to religious debates. The clearest theological expression of these efforts was the significance attached to the role of reason in religion. The 'Cambridge Platonists' such as Benjamin Whichcote, Ralph Cudworth and Henry More spoke out against an abstract and dogmatic approach to religion and religious issues (Roberts 1968). The individual conscience, insofar as it was guided by reason and illuminated by the Revelation, was for them the highest authority in religious matters. Their call to reason was unambiguous: '[R]eason is the divine governor of man's life; it is the very voice of God' (Benjamin Whichcote, quoted in Cragg 1950: 42). Another grouping within the Anglican Church, the Latitudinarians, such as John Tillotson, Edward Stillingfleet, Simon Patrick and Gilbert Burnet, went out of their way to remove all 'irrational' elements from religion and referred to the potential of reason to shape behaviour. Since reason cast doubt on every assertion, it encouraged wise restraint and modesty in matters of opinion. A temperament free of prejudice and violent, uncontrolled emotions was however a precondition for the application of reason. The Latitudinarians thus clearly opposed the religious fanaticism of radical Puritans. But their plea for the control of feelings did not mean the 'Stoical' rejection of emotions. On the contrary: they promoted the practice of Christian, neighbourly love and charity, anchored in emotional empathy with the fate of one's fellows:

> Not the Senecan wise man, relieving but not pitying, but the tenderhearted Christian, pitying before he relieves, was the ideal which they preached ... and as time went on their emphasis tended more and more to dwell on those elements of 'softness' and quick emotional response to the spectacle of misery which were to constitute for the eighteenth century the peculiar traits of the 'man of feeling.' (Crane 1967: 200; cf. Donaldson 1973)

Loving one's neighbour by modulating and controlling one's feelings was the Latitudinarians' behavioural ideal. 'Tender' empathy replaced Puritan 'enthusiasm'.

These observations demonstrate that an image of a new type of personality was beginning to emerge within religious and theological discourse, an image that fits the intensifying process of pacification of English society to which Elias refers. This construction of a new type of personality also found support from non-religious sources, as Englishmen explored and developed the 'Country' ideology mentioned above. This ideology, fleshed out within the opposition to the oligarchic regime of the 'Court' Whigs, was rooted in the classic conception of the arms-bearing citizen, who, on the basis of ownership of land, shared domination with his fellow citizens in an independent and autonomous manner. The 'virtuous' citizen exercised this domination to the benefit of all, not in pursuit of his own advantage. The representatives of the 'Country' position had come to feel that '[t]he virtuous freeholder and the independent country gentlemen were ... being squeezed out from the interstices of power by financiers, stock-jobbers, and the toadies of a Whig-dominated administration, [while] their importance in the national economy also declined' (Brewer 1980; 325). The 'Country' ideologues feared that, in the developing commercial and capitalist society, the classic virtues that ensured freedom, such as independence, concern for the common good, battle-readiness, frugality and simplicity, were being edged out and replaced by luxury, licentiousness, excess and softness. The 'corruption' of politics and social life was thus inevitable. The 'Country' ideologues claimed that

> [C]orrupt politicians were residing over a corrupt society. The rot at the top was spreading down, infecting the manners of professional and businessmen, and demoralizing the lower orders. The nation's standards had fallen so low that a parliamentary solution was not enough: nothing short of a national revival could avert the wrath to come. Here the Country mentality merged with a whole range of attitudes which diagnosed corruption as the reigning disease of the times and prescribed moral reformation as the cure. (Speck 1977: 5)

The 'Country' ideologues thus radicalized the classic issue of the connection between political 'virtue', corruption and freedom. The question of which virtues were 'appropriate' to an English society undergoing profound economic and social change required an answer. At the turn of the 18th century the process of redefining the 'classic' virtues began by means of the concept of 'politeness'. The notion of the 'cultivation' of the individual, his 'refinement' and 'perfection' was central to this discourse. The coarse and rough should make way for the refined and sensitive. The aim was modulation of the 'self'. This was to be achieved through 'sociability'. 'Politeness' manifested itself in the art of cutting a pleasing figure in 'company', and was the expression of a social competence that involved avoidance of impropriety: 'By observation, conversation, and cultivation, men and women are brought to an awareness of the needs and responses of others and of how they appear in the eyes of others' (Pocock 1985: 236; Klein 1994).

The social setting for practicing these new virtues were the 'clubs ... masonic lodges, tavern meetings, coffee houses and friendly societies [which] flourished in the name of company, fellowship and credit, free republics of rational society' (Porter 1981: 15). The 'urban Renaissance' which Borsay (1989) dates to the period between 1660 and 1770 and which brought a new dynamism not only to London, but above all to the provincial towns, as centres of trade, sociability and also, increasingly, political agitation, formed the wider social framework for practising 'polite manners'. Borsay (1989: 282) interprets the 'urban renaissance' as

> part of an English enlightenment that was determined to deliver the nation from barbarism into the ranks of the civilized world. At the personal level this involved reforming and refining the individual's mental, moral, and emotional capacities; in the collective sphere it required the assiduous cultivation of sociable behaviour. Public affability, though laudable in its own right, was also of critical value to the cohesion of the nation, for it helped to absorb and reconcile the tensions generated within a politically divided, competitive, and expanding élite.

The various institutional forms of sociability within the urban milieu thus represented a controlled space, in which people with different opinions and interests could exchange views through 'chat'. Respectability and reputation were gained in this space, but also lost. The public sphere, conversation and 'civility' formed an indivisible unity. 'Sociability' both required and aimed to produce an individual who could control and modulate his emotions. The 'politeness' discourse aimed to promote and legitimize processes that created 'a more balanced and thoughtful, less prejudiced and quick-tempered individual', an individual 'who was more likely to understand his neighbours and peacefully coexist with them' (Borsay 1989: 279).

The 'politeness' discourse, like the theological discourse outlined above, thus aimed to design and justify a new type of personality. Both discourses revolved around the ideal of an individual capable of controlling and modulating emotions. The 'sentimental' novels of the 18th century popularized this notion of controlled emotions. The 'man of feeling' became a literary hero (Fiering 1976). Such writing ascribed 'civilized' models of gender:

> This fiction initially showed people how to behave, how to express themselves in friendship and how to respond decently to life's experiences. Later, it prided itself more on making its readers weep and in teaching them when and how much to weep. In addition, it delivered the great archetypal victims: the chaste suffering woman, happily rewarded in marriage or elevated into redemptive death, and the sensitive, benevolent man whose feelings are too exquisite for the acquisitiveness, vulgarity and selfishness of his world. (Todd 1986: 4; cf. Ellis 1996).

The tactful, chaste, pure and modest woman became the touchstone of moral decency; the image of the 'sentimental' male hero contrasted with 'vulgar' male culture – he refrained from gaming, swearing, drinking and tormenting animals for fun (Barker–Benfield 1992: 249–51; 293–7; cf. Goldberg 1984). It was the image of the man as 'man of feeling', which appeared in 'sentimental' literature and, as we have seen, can be traced back to theological and 'politeness' discourses and that inspired some to ask whether this 'civilizing process' would feminize men.

This anxiety was apparent in religious discourse, which attempted to link the figure of the 'tenderhearted' Christian man with the notion of a 'muscular Christianity', and determined the discourse of national identity and national character in the second half of the 18th century. Public opinion blamed the foreign policy setbacks suffered by England in its efforts to develop a global empire, particularly between 1754 and 1757, on the ruling class's adoption of French-style morals, manners and cultural activities. This was thought to have weakened and feminized the national character, a view that John Brown, for example, elaborated in his *Estimate of the Manners and Principles of the Times* of 1757 (Newman 1987: 80–84). A vigorous imperial policy should re-emphasize the real English virtues and the English national character: above all, bravery in battle, will to conquer and manliness (Wilson 1995: 185–205). After the French Revolution and the revolutionary wars, the French model ceased to be an option even for the ruling class. The people who were either active within or affected by the 'Evangelical Revival', which we shall examine in more detail soon, abandoned the 'politeness' ideal with its French connotations and came to accept the ideal of 'sincerity', which aimed to bring 'inner' composure into alignment with 'outer' behaviour (Newman 1987, 142–5, 234–40).

The preceding discussion of discourses on a new type of personality in the 18th century is directly related to an observation made by Norbert Elias and Eric Dunning. They point out (Elias/Dunning 1986: 173–4) that in the 17th century 'manners without morals stood on one side, morals without manners on the other. Early in the eighteenth century the two traditions began to move closer to each other.' This rapprochement occurred through the discourse of 'politeness', which involved an attempt to reconcile the two traditions.

Before concluding this discussion, it is vital to look at a process of disciplining and pacification not mediated by ideological discourses. 18th century England was transformed into a market society. As we have known since Max Weber at the latest, the 'appropriate' personality type for social exchange in the marketplace is the self-disciplined individual, capable of rational calculation because he (or she) has internalized the control of affect. Such exchange, in turn, contributes to the creation of that a personality type. Bearing the preceding discussion in mind, we would like to emphasize here that the burgeoning associations and societies of the 18th century also featured a highly significant economic dimension. Membership in an association, particularly for the 'middling sort', a group which came into being with commercialization, was 'instrumentally rational': 'Clubs were a form of social bonding explicitly established to encourage "mutual benevolence and friendship", "union and friendly feeling", and the type of friendship and mutual aid dispensed within the society was often of a very tangible and direct sort' (Brewer 1982: 219). By joining a club, the businessman could extend his circle of acquaintances and meet potential customers, creditors and business partners in a sociable, amicable atmosphere.

Here he could present himself as polite, affable, reliable and upright – as indeed he had to, if he wished to be a successful businessman. It was within this 'sociability' that the market character could take shape. These clubs also contributed to the pacification of society through their relatively open membership: 'Although there were clubs comprised exclusively of a single class, or of only one occupational group, a large number of societies ... boasted of the way in which they united Anglicans and dissenters, men from different trades, merchants and gentlemen, Whigs and Tories, in a common association, promoting unanimity and harmony where only conflict had previously existed' (Brewer 1982: 219).

It is important to remain aware that the behavioural ideal, summarized in the notion of 'polite manners', was not derived from 'courtly society', as it had been in France. It arose rather within the institutional matrix of 'civil society'. In a sense 'polite manners' were 'sociable manners'.

There were a number of reasons for the Court's weakness as an institution that moulded behaviour. Queen Anne attempted to make use of courtly ceremony as an instrument to unite the 'political nation' during the first decades of the 18th century: by participating in royal rituals, the members of the 'political nation' were to commit themselves to the monarchy. Partisan feuding, however, doomed these efforts to failure. Far from the Crown imposing its will on the political factions, the parties instrumentalized the monarchy:

> [P]arties in the ascendant attempted to appropriate royal ceremony and even the royal person for their own partisan ends. Conversely ... the members of parties in decline, such as the Tories at mid-reign, tended to avoid the court's social and ceremonial functions ... the Whigs not only boycotted the court after their fall from power in 1710, they did what they could to spoil its various activities by spreading rumours of royal illness, cancellations, and poor attendance. Indeed, they went further, attempting to set up an alternative political and social calendar, focussing not on the glories of Anne's reign but on those of a Protestant-Whig past. (Bucholz 1991: 307)

The instrumental role of the monarchy in normal, quotidian politics also marked the rule of George I. The Court of Anne failed to furnish the members of the 'political nation' with social and cultural attractions and to nurture a 'glittering' courtly culture with integrative potential – 'Nothing but ceremony, no manner of conversation', as the Countess of Orkney noted (quoted in Bucholz 1991: 312). George I went further, reducing courtly ceremony drastically. In 1716 many were moved to complain 'that the court lacked that certain majesty and nobility which encouraged reverence for the sovereign' (Beattie 1967: 262). Only when a political opposition, including the heir to the throne, gathered steam, did a more splendid courtly culture develop in competition with that of the royal heir for about three years. Yet this courtly culture was unable to obtain undisputed political and social dominance in this competitive context. Following the reorganization of the government and the development of the Whigs' oligarchic system, 'courtly society' again ground to a halt as the system of dominance stabilized. The Crown's entanglement with power struggles inevitably meant that it had to take a political stance and therefore disappoint certain groupings. It thus exposed itself to constant accusations of taking sides, and was unable to function as a nationally unifying force, whose norms, values and behavioural models could have served as a generally accepted standard.

Linda Colley (1994: 199–204) has convincingly argued that the spatial milieu of the Court in London was also detrimental to the development of a hegemonic courtly culture. There was no palace – similar to that in Versailles – large enough to accommodate a royal retinue: 'Lacking enough space to keep the heir apparent and his family close to him and under his surveillance, a Hanoverian king was likely to find them purchasing their own London establishments ... so creating rival centres to the court and potential bases for political opposition' (Colley 1994: 199). This lack of space, of course, also meant that the most influential and powerful courtiers maintained their own households near Whitehall – as miniature 'courts'. The spatially limited royal household was far smaller than, for example, that of the French kings. Around 1740, the French Court in Versailles consisted of somewhere in the order of 10,000 people, that of George I of no more than 1,500. As Colley (1994: 199) argues, the English Court thus lacked 'the human or spatial resources to forge a discrete court culture or generate all of its own large-scale entertainments.' The English Court thus remained always a 'parasite' on London and dependent on the city's 'services' – 'and because it was situated amidst London's theatres, opera houses, pleasure gardens, clubs and the magnificent town houses of the aristocracy, the court was never the only focus for fashionable society, though it was always an important one' (Colley 1994: 199–200).

A rounded discussion of the Court, as an institution shaping behaviour, must however, probe beyond the first half of the eighteenth century. In the 15th and 16th centuries, as in other Renaissance courts of Europe, the image of royal 'majesty' took hold in England. This depicted the King not only as 'chivalrous' warrior, but attributed to him largesse and magnanimity, piety and reverence, justice and benevolence, as well as generosity and greatness. The stage on which he was supposed to present himself in such a way was his Court. Here he could show 'good lordship': 'The monarch was expected to call his leading subjects to counsel, to arbitrate fairly in their quarrels, and to employ (and reward) their services. He was also expected to listen to their intercessions on behalf of their own clients, and, within limits, to recognise their rights of protection and promotion' (Loades 1986: 2). The Court was thus the centre of political domination; it was the machinery through which patronage was both sought and provided; and it was the cultural centre that manifested the ambitions and preferences of the sovereign (Loades 1986: ch. 1; Asch/Birke (eds.) 1991). The Court exerted a magnetic effect on the aristocracy. In the first half of Elizabeth I's reign, around two-thirds of Peers were regularly present at Court. Towards the end of the 16th century, the Court's significance to the aristocracy was consolidated: '[A]t any given time about half the nobility and about a fifth of the major Gentry families could expect to have one or more members serving at court. For lesser Gentry families the proportion would have been much smaller – perhaps three to four per cent' (Loades 1986: 185; see also Stone 1965: ch. 8, esp. 385–403, 476–504).

The power of royal patronage was deployed specifically to intensify political integration and to centralize political power (Peck, 1986). As we have seen, patronage under the Hanoverian Dynasty was used as a means of balancing out the distribution of power between Crown and Parliament. Political integration occurred, to a significant degree, through Parliament, and political dissatisfaction and opposition could be articulated through peaceable parliamentary intrigues. This situation did not apply under the Tudor Monarchy, when political opposition or dissatisfaction was expressed in aristocratic conspiracy and treachery. Patronage was the means of minimizing this tendency by binding potential opposing forces to the monarchy (MacCaffrey 1961; Neale 1958). It was thus a tool of domestic pacification. Patronage contributed significantly to the process of change that brought about a new code of honour. The 'honourable' gentleman of the 15th century was ready and willing to fight, eager to assert himself and his honour, through violence if need be. The 'courtesy' books of the 16th century, conceived as guides to manners and behaviour for the members of the political class, developed another concept of honour (Whigham 1984). Baldassare Castiglione's *The Book of the Courtier*, which first appeared in 1528 and was published in ten editions in English translation between 1561 and 1612, served as a model. *The Book Named the Governor* by Sir Thomas Elyot, which appeared in 1531 and reached its eighth edition in the 16th century, was particularly influential, while other books such as Thomas Wilson's *The Arte of Rhetorique* (1553), *The Institucion of a Gentleman* (anonymous 1555), Roger Ascham's *The Scholemaster* (1570), John Ferne's *The Blazon of Gentrie* (1586), *The Arte of English Poesie* (1589) by George Ruttenham, but also the *Essays* of Francis Bacon (published in 15 editions between 1597 and 1639) contributed to a redefinition of the concept of honour and political virtue. For Elyot, as for the other authors as well, erudition was more important than battle-readiness to a 'gentleman's' honour. 'Literate magistracy', the wise and erudite dispensing of justice, was now the symbol of 'good lordship'. Service for the monarch and on his behalf became an honourable task and duty. The adoption of the moral teachings of Italian humanism and of neo-stoicism, both centrally concerned with the necessity of controlling one's feelings, lent weight to this redefinition of the concept of honour. Elyot's advice in *Governor* on the correct education of members of the ruling class is forthright: 'It is to be noted that to him that is a governor of a public weal belongeth a double governance, that is to say, an interior or inward governance, and an exterior or outward governance. The first is of his affects and passions, which do inhabit within his soul, and be subjects to reason. The other is of his children, his servants and other subjects to his authority' (quoted in Fletcher 1995: 411).

The call to control one's feelings was bound up with the rejection of physical violence as an expression of personal honour and the promotion of an ideal of the gentleman that privileged Cicero rather than Lancelot (James 1986; Whigham 1984: 13). This habitus characterized the 'courtier' as much as the 'Country' gentleman and enabled both to play the role of servant of the Crown assigned to them within the system of patronage. This version of inner self-discipline was understood as a component in the formation of character or personality in the 'courtesy' literature of the 16th century. The 'politeness' discourse of the 18th century, meanwhile, while it also took for granted the need for the habitual control of the emotions, attached more importance to the performative aspect of sociability, the presentation of 'civility' before an audience, than to a sincere internal commitment (Fletcher 1995: 322–36).

Returning to the significance of the Court as a source of authority which sculpted behaviour, it is clear that, in the cult surrounding Elizabeth, the traditional attributes of royal majesty were reflected and at the same time supplemented by the image of the Queen as Defender of the Realm, of English freedoms and of the achievements of the Reformation in the face of Catholic hostilities from within and without (Haller 1963: ch. 3). The notion of military preparedness, combative Protestantism anchored in diplomatic alliances with other Protestant powers against Catholic Spain and France, together with 'good lordship' at home based on harmonious cooperation with Parliament and frugality, was linked with the person of Elizabeth (Smuts 1987: ch. 2). Royalist propaganda through pictures, literature, theatre, parades and processions, as well as lavish public execution of royal rituals spread and consolidated this image among the general population. The perception of the royal cult and the courtly culture of the first two Stuart kings was, however, quite different. Under James I, courtly culture became increasingly urban; the new styles and predilections, which rose to prominence at the Court, were coloured by London and Continental European cities, while developments in the English provinces ceased to have an effect. The extravagance of the Court of James I contrasted sharply with the demonstrative frugality of the Elizabethan Court; James's pro-Spanish policies, embodying his *de facto* acceptance of the Catholic pursuit of power, were compared to the Protestant policies of his predecessor. Palpable tensions were apparent between sections of the 'political nation' and sections of the royal household, as was the undermining of the monarchy's 'popular' foundation, that is, its support among the general population. Arminian church reform, peace with Catholic Europe and autocratic rule without Parliament became symbolic of Charles I's rule. European influences on courtly culture, above all from France, Italy and Spain, increased – and thus generated a cultural gap between Court and 'Country' (cf. the contrasting evaluations of Zagorin 1969: ch. 4; Sharpe 1992: 209–35). Courtly culture, indeed, became more European precisely in the representation of 'courtliness':

> Perhaps the most effective single vehicle for the idealized image of court life ... was the portraiture of Van Dyck. In his work, for the first time in English painting, the court elite is consistently depicted not as a class of warriors, nor even as an aristocracy of service, but as a caste set apart by its intellectual distinction, spiritual refinement, and instinctive elegance ... the tone consists chiefly in an atmosphere of poise, reserve, and psychic balance. (Smuts 1987: 203–4)

The leadership class depicted here had its emotions and passions 'under control', and was entitled to rule others precisely because it 'ruled' itself. The courtly masquerades, through the King's and Queen's actions, presented the image of the taming and fencing in of chaos and passion, and not only contributed to the glorification of the monarchy through this ideology of the monarchical enforcement of order and peace, but also reinforced the spectators at Court in their own role as agents of political pacification (Sharpe 1992: 224, 230–33). The emphatic aesthetic sensitivity that increasingly took hold at Court and the fascination with ritualistic cognitive and behavioural modes heightened receptivity to the visual and ritual splendour of Catholicism and demonstrated a thoroughgoing rejection of 'puritanical' asceticism. In light of this cultural provocation, the Court was unlikely to mould behavioural tendencies – especially since these cultural differences, as discussed above, were imbricated with political differences.

This evolving cultural difference was one reason why many members of the landowning elite failed to embrace courtly and urban styles:

> The court remained suspect because there clientage, conspicuous consumption, and political competition were a way of life. These attitudes survived the interregnum to pass into the mainstream of English political thought. By the reign of Queen Anne the juxtaposition of urban vice to rural virtue had become an automatic reflex among many English gentlemen, as had the assumption that the political factions and commercial affairs were morally debilitating. (Smuts 1987: 98)

Smuts (1987: 67) is surely right that 'most of the parish Gentry, especially, appear to have remained immersed in the affairs of their neighbourhoods and their estates. They most often have regarded the court as a distant and exotic place.' This reflex made it very hard for the Court to shape behavioural patterns throughout society.

It is, once again, crucial to take the measure of the political dynamics animating the structure of domination. The Court had developed into the political nerve centre, through which the King, the 'centre', was linked with the periphery, the 'localities', through the web of patronage. Two factors threatened this linkage. First, influence at Court was a prerequisite for the effective representation of local interests in the 'centre'. In the 1620s the patronage system dominated political life and blocked access to the Court for a large number of 'interests', especially under the Duke of Buckingham. These excluded 'interests' thus took their grievances and requests to Parliament. At the same time, opposition to royal policy decamped from the Court to Parliament. These processes contributed to the 'politicization' of Parliament in the sense that issues of 'government' alongside the protection of 'property', as elaborated above, were now of parliamentary interest. The Court now experienced political competition from Parliament; it was increasingly Parliament rather than the Court that nationalized the local elites (Sharpe 1986: 340–43, 350; Asch 1989: 214–15).

Second, the position of the Lord Lieutenants – usually drawn from the Peerage and appointed by the King – as agents of royal policy in the counties, changed. To secure status and influence, the great aristocratic families had to be present at Court. This often went hand in hand with a loss of power at the local level. Politically efficient supervision of local administration became increasingly tricky, and was increasingly carried out by the representatives of the Lord Lieutenants:

> While the Lord Lieutenants, however, had stood above local factions because of their power base at Court and in the Privy Council, the Deputy Lieutenants [drawn from the ranks of the Gentry] were frequently representatives of these factions and were thus incapable of exerting a moderating influence on the rivalries between these feuding groups. Control over county-level politics thus slipped from the Crown's hands, while the counties increasingly defended themselves against intervention from outside. (Asch 1989: 214)

London's magnetic pull on the Gentry also represented a challenge to the imposition of rule in the 'Country' (Heal/Holmes 1994). It was the Gentry who were responsible for political administration, maintenance of order and the dispensing of justice at the local, 'country' level. The Gentry flocked to the capital to enjoy the social and cultural attractions of the London 'Season'. The Crown feared this would cause them to neglect their duties and tasks in the 'localities' and therefore issued seventeen proclamations between 1596 and 1640, in which the Gentry were ordered to return to their country estates while the courts were in recess (Heal 1988). While enforcement of these orders was poor, they nonetheless provide an insight into the structure and dynamics of domination in England.

The Gentry was a source of order because of its social leadership role 'in the country' (Beckett 1988: ch. 10). Its power and social position was represented and reflected in its often splendid country houses. For the local Gentry the country house was a socially exclusive place of cultivated conversation and social intercourse with social equals. For the village or rural community, on the other hand, it was a centre of consumption and job creation, a place central to overall economic welfare. It was, moreover, a site for managing the social integration and cohesion of the rural community. This was attempted in a number of ways. The general population was, for instance, integrated into events held at the country house. The ritualized festivities marking the coming of age of the eldest son or a birth, marriage or death of a member of the lord of the manor's family are examples of this, as are annual festivals – Harvest Thanksgiving, for example, springs to mind here – that were integral features of rural festive culture. The lord of the manor could also present himself as doer of good deeds and bolster his hegemonic political and social position by building churches, cottages and schools, by procuring and seeing to the upkeep of a village teacher, and providing food and other types of charitable aid. By participating in sporting activities such as cricket, opening the foxhunt to other social classes and accepting the evolution of horse-racing from an aristocratic pleasure to a national sport – and continuing to take part in it despite the loss of social exclusivity – the landowning class proved itself flexible in the face of changing social relations, but also maintained social contact with the 'lower' classes. The practice of paternalistic domination required the establishment of a public space in which the lord of the manor could parade his power and benevolence and in which those dependent on him could practice deference and show respect. Though London was a magnet for the Gentry, they knew that if they failed to show up in their localities, their power and domination would be at risk.

Their domination was not, however, exclusively based on their power over the rural population, which was economically dependent on them, their paternalism or cultural 'hegemony'. It was as Justices of the Peace (JPs) that the Gentry as a class exercised domination. The 'Justices of the Peace Act' of 1361 established this post. It included policing, judicial and administrative functions. The development of this office need concern us no further here. At the end of the 17th century it was firmly under the control of the Gentry. While clergy often became JPs during the course of the 18th century, the vast majority of rural JPs were drawn from the landowning class until the late 19th century. Until 1910, in the counties JPs were *de facto* appointed by the Lord Lieutenant, who, as we have seen, was typically a member of the higher nobility. The social composition of the judiciary reflected the cooptive character of recruitment. In 1842, for example, of the 3,090 office-holders in 52 counties around 8.4 per cent were drawn from the peerage, 77.1 per cent from the gentry, 13.4 per cent from the clergy and merely 1.2 per cent from other social groups (Berghoff 1994: 112). Only with the introduction of elected County Councils in 1888 did the 'period in which nobles as lords of the manor administered the counties and dispensed justice' come to an end (Schröder 1988: 84). Only then did noble self-administration, in reality generated through cooptation, end.

The JP was responsible for prosecuting and trying suspects. He supervised parish government and was responsible for administration at county level. In principle, JPs thus represented the sole authority responsible for state administration at the local level and enjoyed, moreover, far-reaching judicial power. The JPs for the counties and the districts came together regularly at common sessions: the Quarter Sessions became increasingly important. Judicial hearings in the Quarter Sessions were held before a jury; only very serious cases were referred to the 'Assizes'. Judges from London, travelling the provinces to dispense justice in the name of the Crown, convened the criminal courts twice a year. From the late 16th century, they dealt with cases of murder, grand larceny, breaking and entering, arson, rape and witchcraft. At the same time the judges had a duty to keep an eye on JPs to ensure their administration of justice and political administration was satisfactory (Cockburn 1972).

The JPs' increasing workload and duties led, during the 17th century, to the institutionalization of monthly meetings of neighbouring JPs, known as the 'Petty Sessions'. From the late 17th century onwards, these played and increasingly important role in the fight against and suppression of petty crime and 'delinquency'. They dealt, for example, with paternity cases and illegitimacy as well as matters of poor relief, maintenance of roads and bridges and punishment of disturbers of the peace. As Landau (1984: 209) states, in the 18th century the Petty Sessions became the 'prime focus of judicial power'.

They replaced both the ecclesiastical and manorial courts, gaining responsibility for the prosecution and punishment of petty crime and moral offences. Prior to the Restoration, both these courts were an integral part of the administration of criminal law (Briggs et al. 1996: ch. 3). The manorial courts were a kind of tribunal at village community level, in which, above all, cases involving nuisances that disturbed community life – from quarrelsomeness to slander and the residence of vagrants – were heard, but also cases of theft or assault: 'It was there that decisions were made, not only about agrarian organization, but also about wider issues of local government. They ... appointed the local constable and other officers, and were often a place where local by-laws were passed and enforced' (Sharpe 1984: 83). In the mid-17th century, these courts were largely abandoned. A similar fate befell the ecclesiastical courts. Before the Civil War, they dealt primarily with enforcement of official Church doctrine and punishment of moral offences. While issues of religious conformity also fell under their remit after the Restoration, they ceased to function as enforcing authority for issues relating to moral conduct (Sharpe 1984: 82–9).

Thus, from the end of the 17th century, no judicial institutions existed that might have disputed JPs' local authority. The judicial and political-administrative significance of JPs was also apparent in their increase in number from 2,560 in 1680 to 8,400 in 1761. Norma Landau (1984: 2) has compellingly summed up what this meant:

> Only in England did the state not develop into an entity separate from the elite and in conflict with it. In England the landed elite monopolized government, and the justices therefore embodied the peculiarly English union of social and political power. With their Glorious Revolution English landowners indubitably established their dominance of government. At no time, therefore, were the justices more powerful than in the century and a half following the Revolution.

This observation can now be placed in a broader context. As we have seen, the landowning class held a position of dominance within politics and society until the twentieth century. It should be remembered, however, that their position gradually weakened. Around three-quarters of the members of the lower house in the 1840s were from landowning families. In 1868, this still applied to two-thirds of them. In 1886, only around half of MPs were drawn from such a background; the Parliament of 1880 was the first in which businessmen and industrialists were in the majority. In the first decade of the 20th century, landowning families provided only around ten per cent of members. Between 1868 and 1886 two-thirds of Cabinet members still had connections with landowning families, while between 1886 and 1916 only half of all Cabinet members belonged to the aristocracy (Thompson 1977: 24–6). During the course of the 19th century, as a result of the political and social dislocations produced by industrialization and urbanization, the power and influence of the aristocracy in the cities and urban conurbations declined, and was appropriated by the 'business bourgeoisie' as well as members of the 'professional' class. They were however able to maintain their position 'in the country' until the 20th century.

This 'obstinate survival of aristocracy in Victorian England', to which G.M. Young (1966: 83) refers, resulted from a number of factors. The modification of aristocratic and bourgeois values was one of the key developments here. The commercialization of agriculture took hold early in England. In terms of social structure, this involved the formation of a numerically small class of major landowners, tenants whose working methods were imbued with financial rationality, and a large number of rural workers without property. This constellation laid the foundation for the development of a capitalist agricultural system in the 18th century, which not only provided for the needs of industrialization and freed up workers for the factories through 'efficient' farming methods, but also established the economic anchor of the landowners' political power. This precocious orientation towards the market and profit endowed the aristocratic value system with a certain 'bourgeois-capitalist' tenor. It also made aristocrats more 'culturally' open to involvement in non-agricultural commercial spheres. In the course of the 18th century, the English aristocracy thus engaged increasingly in, for example, coal mining and extraction of other minerals, construction of canals and roads and urban development – and made a substantial income from such activities. As Schröder (1988: 53) states, the English nobility gained several advantages from their highly intensive involvement in non-agricultural businesses, which helps explain their long and stable domination: 'This involvement endowed them with a relatively broad economic horizon, reduced the distance from bourgeois values, provided a more diverse range of income sources and eased their dependence on agriculture and the state of the agricultural economy, allowing greater political flexibility.'

Schröder (1988: 49–51) also mentions the alignment with the bourgeoisie apparent in noble adoption of the norms of bourgeois respectability. The 19th century saw a 'moralization' of the nobility; the aristocratic ideal gained a new, specifically Christian accent. The 'Christian gentleman' turned away from the frivolity of the 18th century and began again to contemplate Christian virtues, particularly as defined under the influence of the pietistic, Puritan 'Evangelicalism' (Wolffe 1991 locates this 'Protestant Crusade' within a virulent, anti-Catholic revivalism). This 'Evangelicalism' privileged the doctrine of human redemption through faith in Christ's expiatory sacrifice on the Cross: Christ paid for our sins on the Cross and thus did all that was necessary for our redemption; it is now incumbent upon human beings faithfully to accept this forgiveness of our sins through Christ as an act of mercy. As a 'way of life' this 'Evangelicalism', emanating from the middle classes, emphasized 'seriousness', ceaseless self-inquiry, self-control and hard work (Bradley 1976). Hannah More, one of the most influential representatives of turn-of-the-century 'Evangelicalism', tirelessly promoted the key values that ought to shape behaviour in a large number of treatises: 'Patience, diligence, quiet and unfatigued perseverance, industry, regularity and economy of time – these are the dispositions I would labour to excite'; adolescents should be brought up to develop 'an habitual interior restraint, an early government of the affections, and a course of self-control over those tyrannizing inclinations which have so natural a tendency to enslave the human heart' (quoted in Bradley 1976: 150). Flawless moral comportment became ever more important to defining what a 'gentleman' in fact was. The gentleman of the 18th century, as we have seen, could develop his personality and build his reputation only by cultivating the virtues of 'sociability'. Not so the gentleman of the Victorian age. Lord Shaftesbury formulated the new ideal pithily in 1844: 'We must have nobler, deeper and sterner stuff; less of refinement and more truth; more of the inward, not so much of the outward, gentleman; a rigid sense of duty, not a "delicate sense of honour"' (quoted in Bradley 1976: 153). One aspect of this redefinition was the assessment of work as that domain of human activity in which moral 'value' could best develop and become manifest. This aspect allowed the 'gentleman' concept to be extended to the industrial and professional middle class that was in the making at the time. The revival of a mystically imbued ideal of chivalry was bound up with this redefinition: England was returning to Camelot – as Mark Girouard (1981) put it. Schröder (1988: 50) points out that 'Chivalry, discreet behaviour, tactfulness, and maintaining a distance from vulgar money-making were what mattered.' He suggests that this shift towards a more moral definition of the gentleman in a sense enabled the modernization of aristocratic rule:

> If gentlemen were those morally superior to others, then rule by gentlemen received fresh legitimation ... The paradox was that this modernization or pseudo-modernization came to pass with the help of nothing other than the medieval-feudal ideal of chivalry, propagated so vigorously in literature, an ideal that provided the status of gentleman with moral legitimation. The assimilation of the English aristocracy into the bourgeois world thus took place not only through the adoption of bourgeois values and modes of behaviour, but also through a shift in the concept of the gentleman, which was ironically marked by the anachronistic revival of the old noble ideal of 'chivalry.' (Schröder 1988: 50–51)

This ideal thus united the aristocracy and middle classes ideologically. The 'public schools' and the universities of Oxford and Cambridge, meanwhile, were the key institutions in which this ideal was developed further and in which the comportment it demanded could be practised. The public schools had become a key formative experience by the close of the Victorian age, one shared by most members of the English elite (Wiener 1981: 16). The cult of organized games, spreading since the 1870s, helped anchor the new gentlemanly ideal: the gentleman's qualities were those of a 'sportsman'; the 'sportsman', meanwhile, was a 'gentleman.' The magazine *Punch* summed up the traits of the 'sportsman' as follows:

> He is one who has not merely braced his muscles and developed his endurance by the exercise of some great sport, but has, in the pursuit of that exercise, learnt how to control his anger, to be considerate to his fellow men, to take no mean advantage, to resent as a dishonour the very suspicion of trickery, to bear aloft a cheerful countenance under disappointment, and never own himself defeated until the last breath is out of his body. (Quoted in Girouard 1981: 235)

Sport was conceived, above all, as an activity that contributed to character building (Haley 1978: 260–61). Girouard is surely right to draw attention to the idea of a 'muscular Christianity', upon which this concept of sport rested to a significant degree. Thomas Hughes, one of the key advocates of this idea, expressed it in his novel *Tom Brown at Oxford* in a chapter entitled 'Muscular Christianity':

> [T]he least of the muscular Christians has hold of the old chivalrous and Christian belief, that a man's body is given to him to be trained and brought into subjection and then used for the protection of the weak, the advancement of all righteous causes, and the subduing of the earth which God has given to the children of man. (Quoted in Girouard 1981: 142)

The 'muscular Christian' was physically strong and hardy, yet also opened his heart to the weak and those in need of protection, without exploiting his role as protector: he was 'pure' because he had his passions under control.

Our discussion of the varied efforts to shape character, such that passions were controlled on the basis of religious conviction, would be incomplete without mentioning the particularly zealous attention paid by the Evangelical movement to the 'profligacy' of the lower classes. The Royal Proclamation Against Vice, issued by George III in 1787, led, for example, to the foundation of a Society for the Suppression of Vice, the key concerns of which were sexual behaviour, pornography, blasphemy, keeping Sunday holy, gambling, drunkenness and blood sports. The members of this society took it upon themselves to report these 'moral' offences to the authorities (Innes 1990). In fact, most of the 'charitable' organizations, of which around 500 existed in the mid-19th century and which included hundreds of thousands of members, devoted themselves to religious and humanitarian issues, keen to contribute to a thoroughgoing reform of 'morals.' It should however be borne in mind that these organizations contributed to the political mobilization of large sections of the population. By pointing up problems affecting society and the state as a whole, and putting forward 'national', that is, 'translocal' solutions, they promoted the medium-term democratization of the political system within the framework of the nation state.

The moral-religious reform movement was able to pick up the thread of the efforts to reform morals in the late 17th century. The political upheaval of 1688 and the social and economic dislocation resulting from the war with France had sparked off a kind of 'moral panic'; the efforts one hundred years later should likewise be seen in the context of political upheavals in America and France and dislocations resulting from war. Shortly after assuming the throne, William III wrote to the Bishop of London that 'as our duty requires, we most earnestly desire, and shall endeavour a general reformation of the lives and manners of all our subjects, as being that which must establish our throne, and to secure to our people their religion, happiness, and peace, all which seem to be in great danger at this time, by reason of that overflowing vice, which is too notorious in this as well as other neighbouring countries' (quoted in Isaacs 1982: 392–3). The founding of the Society for Promoting Christian Knowledge was one of the results of such endeavours. 'Moral reform' crystallized in a programme of action intended 'to revive religious observance, combat heterodoxy and eliminate the more pernicious social evils, such as lechery and drunkenness, for fear of divine retribution' (Hayton 1990: 57; Rupp 1986: ch. 19).

The behaviour of the lower classes was of particular concern to reformers. The so-called 'charity schools' were one institutional manifestation of this reformist zeal (Quinlan 1941; Jones 1964). Their 'ethos' and social function emerges clearly from a statement by Isaac Watt, who produced an 'Essay towards the Encouragement of Charity Schools' in 1728:

> I should persuade myself that the masters and mistresses of these schools among us teach the children of the poor which are under their care to know what their station in life is, how mean their circumstances, how necessary 'tis for them to be diligent, humble and submissive, what duties they owe the rest of mankind and particularly to their superiors. (Quoted in Quinlan 1941: 21)

The founding of 'Sunday schools' occurred in the 1780s, within the context of the 'Evangelical revival' of the second half of the 18th century. In the third decade of the 19th century there were more than 5,000 such schools with almost half a million children in attendance. Towards the end of the 19th century, around three quarters of all children between five and 15 years of age in England attended 'Sunday Schools', now offered by all churches and religious communities (Bradley 1976: 44). Laqueur, a historian of these schools, warns against rushing to the conclusion that they were merely an instrument of discipline deployed by the upper classes. For him, working class acceptance of these schools and appropriation of their inherent potential is a significant aspect of their history:

> In their literature and teaching they stressed moral and ethical as against overt social and political values. Honesty, orderliness, punctuality, hard work and refinement of manners

> and morals may all have been congruent with the industrial system and thus in the interest of the bourgeoisie but they were not therefore middle-class values. The great divisions in early nineteenth century society were not between the middle and the working classes but between the idle and the non-idle classes, between the rough and the respectable, between the religious and the non-religious. All of these divisions ran across class lines. The puritan ethic ... was the ideology of those who worked as against those who did not. (Laqueur 1976: 239)

The present discussion does not require us to evaluate this thesis. It is sufficient to point out that a disciplinary spurt occurred that also embraced the 'working class.' Moreover, given that the process of industrial work, for instance, also had disciplinary effects – as we know from sources other than solely Marx's *Capital* (Thompson 1971: 35–66) – and that the development of professional police forces was greatly advanced (Palmer 1988), it seems reasonable to state that, for the individual, the 19th century was not the age of *laissez-faire*, but of the imposition of control on others and the self (Corrigan/Sayer 1985: 114–80).

Aspects of the formation of the English fiscal state

The final section of this chapter provides an overview of the 'character' of the English 'state' by drawing on Elias's insight that the struggle to achieve a monopoly of taxation was of crucial significance to the dynamics of the structure of domination (Elias 2000: 344–62). Elias saw the monopoly of taxation, together with the monopoly of violence, as the decisive mechanism of state formation. How did this issue manifest itself in England? Which financial means did the English state have at its disposal? For which state activities was revenue used? These issues are investigated here for the period from Elizabeth I's assumption of power in 1558 until the outbreak of the First World War in 1914 on the basis of an overview of selected data. It is vital to keep in mind that, as we have seen, a consensus existed between the Crown and the upper class on fiscal matters at an early date – quite unlike, for example, the situation in Austria, as we shall see. It was a characteristic of the English state that the extraction and mobilization of taxes was managed comparatively early and unproblematically as a result of cooperation between the Crown and upper class – though not without friction and, until the 18th century, repeatedly requiring compromises.

Even in the 21st century, national accounts must be analyzed with due caution. This of course applies even more to records stretching back to the 16th century. Nonetheless, the analysis of the financial history of England is better developed than that of other European countries. One reason for this is also of significance to the issue of state formation. Towards the end of the 17th century, the Treasury Board was established as the 'finance ministry' with ultimate authority over state revenue and expenditure; other government departments were accountable to it in fiscal matters. This institutional innovation made Great Britain the first major

European state with comparatively reliable data at its disposal for managing the budget.

Let us look first at state revenue for the period from 1558 to the early 19th century. Braddick provides the following figures for the period to 1688:

Table 2.1 National revenue, 1558–1688 at current prices

Years	Total (in £1000s)	Annual (in £1000s)
1558–1603	18,360	399.13
1604–1625	12,544	570.18
1626–1640	11,996	799.73
1649–1659	18,919	1719.91
1661–1685	41,066	1642.64
1686–1688	5,925	1975.00

Source: Braddick 1996: 10, Table 1.1

The figures clearly show that revenue in the second half of the 17th century increased dramatically. Michael Mann has calculated average state revenue at constant prices (with the 1451–75 period serving as benchmark) and confirms this change:

Table 2.2 National revenue, 1559–1688 at constant prices

Reign	Years	Revenue (in £1000s)
Elizabeth I	1559–70	89.9
	1571–82	69.0
	1583–92	77.9
	1593–1602	99.5
James I	1604–13	121.9
Charles I	1630–40	99.4
Charles II	1660–72	251.1
	1672–85	268.7
James II	1685–88	353.3

Source: Mann 1986: 451, Table 14.1

Revenue from 1685 to 1688 was thus around four and a half times as high as one hundred years before. The period of the Stuart monarchy's restoration thus saw a significant increase in revenue, which climbed further following the Glorious Revolution of 1688 – through which Parliament gained, among other things, a fiscal monopoly:

Table 2.3 National revenue, 1689 – 1715 at current prices

Year	Total Revenue (in £m)
1689	2.87
1695	4.13
1697	3.12
1701	3.46
1707	5.47
1712	5.83
1715	5.26

Source: O'Brien/Hunt 1993: 174–5, Tables 3 and 4.

Schremmer (1994: 6–7, Table 1) has calculated that revenue from taxes and the like amounted to £2.062 billion for the period from 1689 to 1820, of which £1.65 billion was raised during the reign of George III alone (1760–1820). This growth of state revenue over the course of the 18th century allowed England to become a major European power and hegemonic maritime power. O'Brien und Hunt (1993: 155) have compellingly described the dramatic increase in state spending power linked to these developments:

> In the early sixteen-twenties the revenues available to support Charles I and his government amounted in real terms to orders of magnitude that had remained ... roughly constant for some three centuries of English fiscal history. Fifty years later, after the Civil War and Restoration, his son commanded 2.7 times as much revenue as his late father. By the seventeen-twenties revenues of the Hanoverian state had multiplied by a factor of eight, in the seventeen-seventies by a multiplier of eleven and after the wars with Napoleon the Liverpool administration disposed of thirty-six times as much purchasing power as Charles I ... had [at his disposal] two centuries ago.

English financial history reached an important turning point in the 1640s. Before this period, state revenue was in fact increasing, but failed to keep pace with economic growth and was based on the extension of the royal tax prerogatives. Hitherto, the King controlled three-quarters of total revenue. After the 1640s, finances became 'public', based on taxation, and represented an increasingly large proportion of economic growth. After 1660, all tax revenue came under parliamentary control; the proportion of state revenue drawn from non-parliamentary, non-tax income, which the King continued to control, fell between 1661 and 1685 to around 10 per cent, and between 1685 and 1714 to a mere 3 per cent. Braddick (1996: 16) estimates that in 1714 the public revenue depended almost entirely on taxes imposed by Parliament.

Taxation's contribution to national income increased markedly from the Restoration period on. O'Brien and Hunt (1993: 159) have calculated that in the last decade of the 17th century, total revenue made up more than six 6 per cent of national income for the first time in peacetime; it was never again to fall below this level. This development can be illuminated through examination of selected data. O'Brien and Hunt (1993: 174–5) give the following figures for total revenue as a percentage of national income: 1564 – 2.4 per cent; 1618 – 2.1 per cent; 1664 – 3.8 per cent; 1715 – 9.8 per cent; 1762 – 10.51 per cent; and 1810 – 17.68 per cent. Brewer's calculation (1989: 91) shows that at the end of the War of the Spanish Succession in 1713, the state already claimed 9 per cent of national income through taxation. During the American War of Independence, in the second half of the 1770s, this had risen to between 11 and 12 per cent. O'Brien (1988: 3, table 2) has calculated that in 1690, 6.7 per cent of national income was appropriated through taxation. The figure for 1790 was 12.3 per cent and in 1810, during the war with France, it was 18.2 per cent. These figures may be more comprehensible if we mention that the per capita tax burden roughly tripled in the 18th century, and doubled in the second half of the century alone (Schremmer 1994: 13).

Following the Glorious Revolution of 1688, the English system of national finances rested on two major pillars: excise duty and customs duty on the one hand, and public borrowing on the other. Taking the 18th century as a whole, around 70 per cent of state expenditure was financed by taxation and around 30 per cent through borrowing (Schremmer 1994: 6–7, Table 1). The emphasis within the taxation system was clearly on so-called indirect taxes, excise and customs duty. In the 18th century the shares of direct to total taxes fluctuated between 75 per cent and 80 per cent (Schremmer 1994: 13; O'Brien/Hunt 1993: 166). In the decade after the Glorious Revolution, and thus during the Nine Years War, land tax, the most important form of direct taxation, still brought in around 42 per cent of total tax revenue; during the War of the Spanish Succession the figure was 37 per cent. After 1713, however, it was almost never again to contribute more than around 30 per cent of total revenue (Brewer 1989: 95). Between 1485 and 1660, customs duties levied on imports and exports, and thus the taxation of foreign trade, dominated indirect taxation (O'Brien/Hunt 1993: 140–41). After 1714, however, excise dominated not only revenue gleaned through indirect taxes, but state revenue as a whole, and from the third decade of the 18th century onwards regularly yielded more than 40 per cent of total revenue (Beckett 1985: 306, Table 2). The excise system was introduced and developed in 1643 on the Dutch model. Initially, mainly consumer goods such as drinks and foodstuffs, above all beer, spirits, wine, meat, malt, hop, salt and certain colonial produce such as tea, sugar, and later tobacco were taxed. In the 18th century, excise duty was extended to an ever increasing number of capital goods and also applied to unfinished, semi-finished and finished goods (Schremmer 1994: 9).

The comprehensive and efficient imposition of excise duty required a well-organized system of financial administration. It was estimated that in the 1720s there were around 12,000 permanently employed civil servants. For 1726, Brewer (1989: 66–8) suggests a staff of 6,497 in the financial administration, of which 3,466 worked in the administration of excise duty. In other words, 54 per cent of all permanently employed civil servants worked in financial administration, and within this system more than half dealt with the imposition and administration of excise: '[B]etween 1690 and 1782/3 the overall number of revenue officers increased threefold, reaching a total of nearly 8,300 by the end of the American War [of Independence] ... By the end of the American war the excise establishment was almost twice as large as the entire fiscal administration employed at the time of the Glorious Revolution' (Brewer 1989: 67 and 68). At the end of the 18th century there were around 18,000 civil servants, of which more than 70 per cent worked in financial administration (Tilly 1995: 132).

As mentioned above, public borrowing was the state's second important source of revenue. The national debt amounted to around £664,000 in 1689; in 1820, following the Napoleonic wars, the figure was around £848 million! Between 1689 and 1820, borrowing (not including repayment) came to around £865m; during the reign of George III alone the figure was £725 million (Schremmer 1994: 6–7, Table 1). Borrowing allowed the English government, in the last decade of the 17th century, a higher level of expenditure of around 34 per cent and, calculated for the 18th century, of around 40 per cent. As Braddick (1996: 44) states, this allowed the English state, above all, to increase expenditure on the armed forces. Public borrowing thus became an institution central to acquiring and building the British Empire.

Before we turn to expenditure, however, the political aspect of this development must be underlined. The shift from direct to indirect taxation as the main source of revenue paved the way for a long-term, more or less permanent national debt – for the simple reason that ever more indirect taxes were imposed specifically to cover public borrowing. There developed a systematic connection between excise and national debt. The producers and sellers of dutiable goods indeed paid their taxes, but were able to pass them on to consumers by raising prices. At the same time, a wealthy class evolved as early as the 18th century, growing stronger in the 19th century, which was in a position, and prepared, to invest part of its income in securities. In every year after 1707, no less than 30 per cent of state revenue had to be used to pay for public borrowing. This group of people thus received a pension through their lending, 'which grew into a considerable, independent source of income within the economy as a whole. Their income from interest on capital of a rich social stratum was largely paid, via the state budget, with revenue from indirect taxes, the great majority of which were paid by lower income groups' (Schremmer 1994: 5). O'Brien (1988: 17) comes to a similar conclusion: 'the ... shift to excises levied on domestic production and services probably implies that the "middling ranks" in British society paid for foreign and strategic policies from which they derived a disproportionately small share of benefits.' John Brewer (1989: 42), who studied the 18th century 'fiscal-military' English state, sums up that

> the ease with which substantial sums were raised is attributable to three circumstances: the existence of a powerful representative with undisputed powers of national taxation; the presence of a commercialized economy whose structure made it comparatively simple to tax; and the deployment of fiscal expertise that made borrowing against tax income an easy task.

Public borrowing depended on tax revenue that required parliamentary legislation, suggesting how vitally important Parliament was within the English state. It is crucial, in this regard, to take a closer look at expenditure: only if tax revenue and borrowing were indispensable to necessary expenditure was the Parliament's power secured. Total expenditure for the period from 1689 to 1820 came to around £2.93 billion and for the period from 1761 to 1820 alone to around £2.38 billion (Schremmer 1994: 6–7, Table 1). Applying constant prices (on the basis of the 1690–99 period), expenditure in 1815 (wartime) was around seven times higher than in 1695 (also wartime). A comparison with the years of peace 1700 and 1820 shows a ninefold increase in expenditure (Mann 1986: 485, Table 14.3). In the 18th century, expenditure on the armed forces plus debt repayment accounted for a long–term average of 80 per cent to 90 per cent of total state expenditure: wars drove the state into debt. Borrowing during the American War of Independence and the Napoleonic Wars alone amounted to £725 million and thus represented 83 per cent of total borrowing for the period between 1689 and 1820 (Schremmer 1994: 6–7, Table 1). Debts can thus be put down to expenditure on the armed forces. As Brewer (1989: 40) elaborates, even when debt repayments are excluded, expenditure on the armed forces made up between 61 per cent and 74 per cent of total expenditure during the key wars of the 18th century. In terms of expenditure, the English state of the 18th century was a military state.

Light is shed on the overall economic significance of state expenditure by examining it as a proportion of gross national product (GNP). It has been estimated that in 1688 state expenditure accounted for 5.5 per cent of GNP. Two hundred years later this extraction rate was only 1.5 percentage points higher – but still lay below the rate of 9 per cent of GNP in 1720 (Mann 1993: 369). Mann provides the following figures for the 19th century.

Table 2.4 Government expenditure as a percentage of gross national product, 1820–1910 (current prices)

Year	Expenditure as % of GNP
1820	16.8
1830	12
1840	11
1850	10
1860	9
1870	6
1880	6
1890	7
1900	8
1910	7

Source: Mann 1993: 366, Table 11.3

These calculations lead Mann (1993: 368) to remark that 'state activities decreased as a proportion of national economic activity between the mid-eighteenth and the early twentieth century.' As Schremmer concludes (1994: 49): 'In the late 19th century, the state [appropriated] a significantly smaller proportion of GNP via taxes, etc. than it did following the Napoleonic Wars.'

A closer look at expenditure, however, reveals momentous changes. First, expenditure on the armed forces and debt repayment made up the bulk of total expenditure as late as 1913. Nonetheless, these outgoings accounted for only 58 per cent of the total, compared with 93 per cent in 1792 (Schremmer 1994: 49). Mann (1993: 376) compares central government expenditure on the armed forces (excluding debt repayment) with non-military expenditure and concludes that in 1881, for the first time, Great Britain spent more on civilian than military activities. He states that: '[It was] probably the first time in the entire history of organized states that the greatest Power of an era devoted more of its central state finances to peaceful than warlike activity' (Mann 1993: 376–7). Spending on education, transport, postal and telegraph services and, increasingly, old-age pensions and health dominated civilian expenditure. Spending on the civil service and administration made up 7 per cent of total expenditure in 1792, 16 per cent in 1873 and 22 per cent as early as 1883. In 1913 this had risen to 27 per cent. Spending on public education, old-age pensions and health alone reached £36.9 million, or 67 per cent of civilian expenditure in 1913–14, more than was spent on the army, and was equivalent to 43 per cent of the total military budget; this was however still less than debt repayment, which came to £37.3 million, almost 19 per cent of total expenditure (Schremmer 1994: 50).

Examination of the rate of extraction in the 19th century reveals that state revenue per capita in 1816 was £4.16 and £4.38 in 1913/14. The figures for the intervening period are as follows.

Table 2.5 National revenue per capita of population in £, 1822 to 1903–1904

Year	Revenue per Capita
1822	2.95
1832	2.15
1843	1.97
1853	1.99
1863	2.45
1873	2.43
1883	2.50
1893	2.40
1903/04	3.65

Source: Schremmer 1994: 31, Table 7 and 46–7, Table 13

Fiscally speaking, the state cannot be said to have expanded dramatically in terms of revenue or expenditure in the 19th century. This is also apparent in the fact that public debt in 1856 was 10.7 times annual state revenue, compared to only 3.5 in 1913 (Schremmer 1994: 45).

Closer examination of revenue reveals the following picture:

Table 2.6 Selected types of income as percentage of total revenue, 1843–1913

Year	Excise and Customs Duties	Excise	Income Tax	Stamp Duty and Inheritance Tax	Post, Telegraph and Telephone
1843	64.5	25.0	10.0	13.2	1.1
1853	66.6	28.2	10.3	12.8	2.0
1863	58.4	25.2	14.0	13.1	5.4
1873	61.1	33.6	9.8	13.0	6.3
1883	53.3	30.8	13.6	13.6	10.3
1893	49.9	28.1	14.9	15.3	11.5
1903	43.9	21.2	25.6	14.5	12.1
1913	37.9	20.0	24.0	18.8	15.5

Source: Schremmer 1994: 46–7, Table 1.3

The table shows that over the course of the 19th century the significance of indirect taxes decreased, while that of direct taxes increased. At the beginning of the 20th century, the yield from income tax, reintroduced in 1843, was for the first time greater than that of excise duty. The dramatic increase in income tax in this period was rooted in tax policy changes resulting from the Boer War – just as the Crimean War of 1856 had led to a one-off increase in the income tax yield to 22.2 per cent of total revenue. Reforms of inheritance tax rules in the 1880s and in the early 1890s also had an impact on state revenue. The increase in revenue from postal, telegraph and telephone services allowed the share of total revenue met by taxation to fall from around 97 per cent in 1826 to around 82 per cent in 1913–14 (Schremmer 1994: 55). In view of the change in income and inheritance tax and the increasing significance of direct taxation that this entailed, Schremmer (1994: 54) concludes 'that social justice and social issues increasingly penetrated the national budget, if, that is, a growing proportion of direct taxes equals more justice'.

In light of the formation of the state in the 19th century as reflected in these figures, it is vital to bear in mind that a general consensus prevailed within the elite regarding the – for the most part strictly limited – role of the state: the ideal was a self-regulating society of free individuals, whose individualism was based not on avarice and selfishness, but was conditioned – or, at least, ought to be – by values of propriety, self-control, a sense of duty and Christian morality. The central political issue was whether state intervention was necessary to help individuals reach this freedom, within the frame of these ethical guidelines, and to ensure that people stuck to them. The liberal principle of the 'minimal state' was thus, on the one hand, placed in a tense relationship with the notion of the moral 'renewal' and improvement of society, and on the other hand with the 'humanist-utilitarian' idea of the lessening of individual and social misery by striving to achieve the greatest happiness of the greatest number. One result of the implementation of these ideas were the laws regulating factories or the changes made to the Poor Law and Poor Relief in the first half of the 19th century, and legislation on public health and the health service in the second half of the century. The appointment of state inspectors to supervise these regulations was the administrative manifestation of this interventionism (MacDonagh 1977).

It was nonetheless the ideal of the 'minimal state' that defined politics well into the 20th century. As Thane (1990: 33) lays bare, this 'minimal state', as we have seen, was 'premised upon the capacity of a vast network of voluntary organisations, in co-operation with local government, to superintend most moral, charitable, education and welfare service.' In fact, Thane (1990: 36) underlines that, until the outbreak of the First World War, voluntary 'public welfare' organizations spent as much on social goals as did the state. It was the political dislocations resulting from suffrage reform in the second half of the 19th century, class confrontation and the reordering of the party system rooted in disputes over 'home rule' for Ireland, but also an understanding that the development of the industrial-capitalist system would entail growing social and economic problems, along with the military challenges of the last decades of the 19th century, which were to lead to a more interventionist 'welfare state.'

Chapter 3

The Formation of the Austrian State and the Sociogenesis of Political Authority

This chapter outlines the history of state formation in Austria. What, however, and where, is 'Austria'? And when to begin this history? 'Austria' was in fact an assemblage of countries and territories until well into the twentieth century. At the end of the 15th century Emperor Maximilian I's administrative reforms created two main administrative units, Lower and Upper Austria. Lower Austria comprised contemporary Lower and Upper Austria, although only roughly within current borders. It also included Styria, Carinthia and Carniola, which together made up Inner Austria. Upper Austria consisted of Tyrol, Vorarlberg, the Windisch Mark (that is, very roughly, the Slovenian territories between Styria and Carniola), Gorizia, Istria, Trieste and the non-contiguous southwestern German territories, 'Further Austria' [*Vorderösterreich* or the *Vorlande*]. Over the centuries, the borders of these regions changed for administrative reasons, though these changes are peripheral to our analysis.

This complex agglomeration of countries and territories was enlarged in 1526–27, when the lands of the Bohemian Crown (the kingdom of Bohemia, the margravate of Moravia, the duchies of Upper and Lower Silesia and the counties of Upper and Lower Lusatia) and the Hungarian lands fell to the Habsburgs. Constitutionally, these territorial gains were the result of the marriage treaty of 1506 between Maximilian I and the Jagiellon King Wenceslaus of Bohemia and Hungary. This treaty stipulated that Wenceslaus's daughter would marry Maximilian's grandson Ferdinand, and his son Louis the Emperor's granddaughter. When the Turks defeated the Hungarian army in the battle of Mohács in August 1526 and the young Hungarian king was killed, the Habsburgs became kings of Hungary, Croatia-Dalmatia-Slavonia and Bohemia. Because of the Ottoman Empire's military might as well as aristocratic opposition within the Hungarian lands, however, central areas of Hungary remained under Turkish dominion, and Transylvania eventually lost its independence and became an autonomous principality within the Ottoman Empire. The Habsburgs offered unique military and geopolitical resources in the battle against the Turks, and their claims on the three crowns thus found widespread support (Kann 1974: 9–10). Yet, it was only in 1699 that Hungary was brought fully under Austrian control as a result of the treaty of Karlowitz with the Ottoman sultan.

The Austrian Monarchy, constituted as such in the first half of the 16th century, remained a *Staatenverbindung* [a confederation of states] or, as Otto Brunner (1962: 52) put it, 'a monarchical union of kingdoms and countries' until it came to an end in 1918. This confederation was multinational, multicultural, multi-confessional and multilingual in nature and was characterized by a multiplicity of political constitutions, privileges, immunities and traditions. The political integration of these geographically extensive and politically, culturally and economically heterogeneous regions was the great challenge facing the Habsburg rulers. For centuries, the Habsburg Dynasty, whose members ruled in the individual parts of the monarchy as kings, dukes, margraves or counts, formed the only permanent link between the disparate political and geographical units. How was this link to be further anchored institutionally? Should integration be brought about by the centralization of political power in the Imperial or royal court, by means of an Imperial or royal bureaucracy? Or could and should political integration be pursued through a confederal monarchy? Was there enough political room for manoeuvre to turn a monarchical confederation into a federal monarchy? These questions remained central to the political history of the Habsburg Monarchy well into the twentieth century. The 'answers' or 'solutions' to the problem of political and territorial integration, put forward over the course of centuries, depended on the contemporary power structure, the balance of power between king and aristocracy in the various constitutive 'kingdoms and countries', but also, as we shall see, on the ascent or decline of other social classes. Consideration of these intra-societal factors, however, must be supplemented by the study of the causal significance of geopolitical factors. From the 16th century until the second half of the 18th century, the Ottoman Empire constituted the greatest threat to the territorial integrity and political hegemony of the Habsburgs. From the 18th century until 1866, Prussia brought similar pressure to bear on the monarchy, its territorial integrity and internal balance of power. Together, intra-societal and geopolitical power configurations determined the political space for tackling the monarchy's territorial-political integration.

The administrative structures that evolved since the 16th century as part and parcel of the exercise of domination and as a component of political integration strategies, were nothing short of Byzantine. It is not the aim of this chapter to investigate the intricacies of Austrian administrative history. 'Administration', however, is a prerequisite for and implies 'domination', as Max Weber, famously, never tired of arguing. It is therefore vital to provide here a very basic outline of this history, to be supplemented as our account proceeds (Walter 1972; Hellbling 1974; Link 1983; Brauneder/Lachmayer 1992; Baltl/Kocher 1993; Ingrao (ed.) 1994).

As early as 1527, Ferdinand I laid the foundation for a centralized administration, which persisted until the mid-19th century. The lively history of these institutions shows clearly that the function of most government organs changed over the course of time; that they were, for the most part, highly inefficient; and that their claim to exclusive authority in specific fields was often challenged by other institutions. Ferdinand, for instance, created the Privy Council [*Geheime Rat*] as an advisory body, which lacked direct executive power, but was entrusted with policy coordination as the highest Aulic body. In 1669, the Privy Conference [*Geheime Konferenz*] emerged from the Privy Council. The former body's authority was limited to foreign policy, the latter's to legal issues. As the Permanent Conference [*Ständige Konferenz*], this body remained in existence until Maria Theresa's reforms in 1749. The Privy Council lasted, in various mutations, until the revolutionary year of 1848, when it was replaced by a council of ministers [*Ministerkonferenz*]. Several institutions were, moreover, often simultaneously entrusted with the same policy domain. To take one example, the Aulic Council [*Hofrat*], established in 1527, although formally subordinate to the Privy Conference, dealt with the same material. Its remit was restricted to legal issues through the constitution of the Imperial Aulic Council (*Reichshofratsordnung*) of 1559, thus turning it into the highest court of appeal.

The Court Chancellery [*Hofkanzlei*] was also established early in the history of the Austrian Monarchy. As a subordinate and executive body, it was initially tasked with preparing the submissions and records of the Privy Council and other governmental organs and with drawing up and issuing legal documents. In 1620, when the Court Chancellery was detached from the Imperial Chancellery [*Reichskanzlei*], in existence since 1559, it became the Austrian Chancellery [*Österreichische Kanzlei*], a purely political body, which now took over the role of the Privy Council as the coordinator of Austrian policy. At the end of the 17th century, the Austrian Chancellery had mutated into a 'super-ministry' for home affairs, foreign affairs and justice. In 1742, under Maria Theresa, foreign policy was hived off and transferred to the newly created Court and State Chancellery [*Haus-, Hof- und Staatskanzlei*]. The authority of the Austrian Chancellery was now limited – precisely as had already happened with the Bohemian and Hungarian chancelleries – to the *Provincialia*, that is, it became the highest governmental authority for the old Austrian lands [*altösterreichischen Länder*].

Two other early government institutions point up the monarch's two core tasks: waging war and ensuring the fiscal underpinnings thereof. In 1556, Ferdinand I created the Court Council of War [*Hofkriegsrat*], responsible for administration of the armed forces, and with supreme authority over the Imperial army. One of its key strategic tasks was the management of the 'Military Frontier' [*Militärgrenze*], established in 1522 to protect Austria from the Ottoman Empire. Since the Court Council of War was responsible for all the lands of the Habsburg Monarchy, it was one of most important institutions for welding the monarchy together. Finally, there was the Court Chamber [*Hofkammer*], whose task it was to administer royal revenue raised from 'dominial' possessions, privileges and rights: the princely properties, royal income such as customs duty, tolls and mining, together with revenue from sovereign towns and markets. The Court Chamber was thus not responsible for all state revenue. As we shall see, a very significant portion was controlled by the local political class in the 'kingdoms and countries.'

The battle to establish a state monopoly of taxation was an important aspect of the efforts to integrate the monarchy politically. In pre-industrial societies, the state's long-term fiscal needs could only be met if it successfully appropriated a portion of the agrarian product – whether in kind or in monetary form. Access to the agricultural producers and their product was, however, obstructed by the (largely) aristocratic landlords, who held property rights over the farmland, and frequently over the peasants themselves. This economic power, supported by legal title, also gave landlords local political power. Control over economic and political resources in 'their' locality ensured their involvement in the government of the monarchy.

This influence found expression in the establishment of provincial diets [*Ständeversammlungen*] in all the 'kingdoms and lands' of the monarchy (Sturmberger 1963; Sturmberger 1969; Hassinger 1964; Hassinger 1969; Schulze 1983). The clergy, the nobility and the towns were always represented; in Tyrol, Vorarlberg and parts of Further Austria, peasant communities, too, sent representatives. The aristocracy was however everywhere the dominant class, whether as a single, consolidated class of 'lords' and 'knights', or separately – as was more often the case. Until the reforms under Maria Theresa in the mid-18th century, government by Estates paralleled monarchical government and often overlapped with it. Administration of justice and the maintenance of public order were among their responsibilities, as was ensuring public welfare, by means, for example, of economic or health policies. Their political power, however, was based above all on their right to approve taxes and their control of the fiscal administration: they voted on the 'contribution', the direct tax intended to cover expenditure on the armed forces, and they were also responsible for imposing it. In a nutshell: the financial administration was not in the hands of royal central government, but in those of the Estates:

> The imposition of taxes remained tied to the approval of the Estates [*Landstände*] until Joseph II; the Estates had the sovereign issue 'letters of indemnity' until the 18th century every time they approved of a particular tax, in order to prevent temporally limited approval from being interpreted as a permanent sovereign claim. From the 15th century until 1848, this dualism embedded in the raising of taxes led to the division of state finances into the sovereign '*Camerale*' and the Estates' '*Contributionale.*' To simplify, the '*Camerale*' was largely based on indirect taxes (consumption tax and revenue from tolls, customs duty, royal privileges, monopolies and royal estates), while direct taxes formed the core of the tax system dependent on approval by the Estates ('*Contributionale*') ... The Contribution system remained under provincial authority until the mid-18th century. The use to which revenue was put was correspondingly different: that of the '*Camerale*' for royal household and domestic administration, that of the '*Contributionale*' for external matters and the armed forces. (Sandgruber 1995: 138)

The near-constant state of war between the Habsburg Monarchy and the Ottoman Empire in the 16th century enhanced the Estates' political significance: the

Crown's financial dependence led to regular requests for approval of taxes, without which wars could not have been waged. The Estates of Styria, Carinthia and Carniola also participated more immediately in wars by raising their own military forces. Given that the Estates were also responsible for recruiting soldiers and for provisioning troops, they were of central significance to the monarchical government.

As a rule, the Estates gathered only once a year for a brief session. It thus proved necessary to establish permanent Estates bodies to ensure that tasks of government and administration were carried out competently. A standing committee, presided over by a member of the Upper Nobility [*Herrenstand*], took care of business between sessions. The diets also elected well-paid officials who collected taxes, managed the military responsibilities of the Estates and implemented diet resolutions. The Estates also built up their own administrative staff: 'All kinds of experts (especially jurists), servants and concessionaries, customs and excise officials, teachers, doctors, printers and architects, even painters and cooks, were overseen and paid by the Estates. As administration grew more complex and taxation more ingenious, their share of government actually increased' (Evans 1979: 167).

The monarchical rulers, too, established their own governmental bodies in the 'kingdoms and lands'. Here, too, the influence of the Estates was considerable. In the territories of the monarchy, a lord-lieutenant [*Landeshauptmann* or *Landmarschall*] presided over royal government. As the 'local' representative of the monarch, with the help of a deputy, a small group of advisors and the managers of the *regalia*, his mission was to maintain 'good order', which included judicial and policing functions as well as activities related to economic and health policy. His tasks were thus defined in a manner similar to those of the Estates' government. Although the monarch appointed the lord-lieutenant, the Estates enjoyed the right to nominate a candidate and generally proposed a member of the Estate of lords. This right was ignored for the first time under Maria Theresa. The Estates' influence on the appointment of the lord-lieutenant meant that he was accountable to both the ruler and the Estates, and that his 'local' loyalties to the Estates frequently clashed with his loyalty to the monarch (Hassinger 1969: 265; Evans 1979: 165, 167).

Since Emperor Maximilian's reforms in the late 15th century, the provincial governments [*Landesregimente*] were responsible for 'internal' political administration and for dispensing justice. The sovereign's financial affairs were concentrated in the Court Chamber, with the exception of the Contribution, which constituted the most important single financial resource. This division of responsibilities had far-reaching consequences. Since the Estates' rule was legitimized and their privileges justified 'constitutionally' on the basis of the traditional 'law of the land' [*Landrecht*], they had a profound interest in ensuring that the King's representatives upheld this law when they dispensed justice. They backed up their commitment to the 'law of the land' by occasional payments to the royal councillors (Brunner 1973: 449). They paid little attention, meanwhile, to appointments to the Court Chamber, since the key fiscal competency of raising direct taxes rested with them. Once economic change and administrative reforms allowed for indirect taxes to be raised through the royal administration, the Estates realized that they had neglected this part of the fiscal system at their peril. Before turning, however, to this phase of the struggle over the monopoly of taxation, it is vital to explore in more detail the socio-political and socio-economic foundation of noble power: the control of agriculture and over the agricultural producers by means of seigneurial authority [*Grundherrschaft*].

Property rights to agricultural land allowed the landlords to appropriate a portion of the agricultural yield of their tenant farmers and to avail themselves of labour services. This economic power was reinforced by patrimonial jurisdiction, which enabled the manorial lords to cast a tight net of social and judicial control over the lives of the peasants and peasant communities (Harth 1910). Patrimonial jurisdiction endowed them with the power to prosecute, charge and pass sentence on peasants for failure to comply with manorial rules and regulations and for committing criminal offences and misdemeanours. Economic power was thus backed by judicial power. The right of patrimonial jurisdiction was abolished only in the revolutionary year of 1848, when the state took over the monopoly of judicial administration, sentencing and punishment.

Patrimonial jurisdiction was circumscribed in a number of ways. In the first half of the 16th century, the peasants subject to patrimonial jurisdiction were given the right of appeal to the provincial government. There were, moreover, numerous concurrent and competing patrimonial courts demanding mutual immunity: every right to ownership of land, after all, entailed judicial rights. In addition, county courts [*Landgerichte*] rather than the patrimonial courts were responsible for crimes punishable by death or serious corporal punishment. The county courts had to maintain 'public order' and ensure public safety. Success in either task was hampered by the fact that the county courts had to respect the legal immunities and judicial powers of patrimonial authorities as well as the authorities of towns and markets. In order to apprehend criminals the county courts had to seek the cooperation of manorial lords, and with regard to maintaining public order they were confined to those public places and highways over which no patrimonial authority would, or could, claim jurisdiction (Feigl 1964; 1974).

The interactions between manorial lords and dependent peasantry also curtailed patrimonial jurisdiction. In the agrarian crisis of the 14th century, the peasants had succeeded in improving their power position vis-à-vis the manorial lords (Lütge 1950; Bruckmüller 1985: S. 137–45). The decline in population went hand in hand with a decline in rent income, as many farmsteads were uninhabited. The shortage of workers also compelled the landlords to pay farm workers higher wages and improve their working conditions. 15th century inflation further reduced rent income, as the fixed rent could not be adjusted to changed conditions. All these factors helped the peasants shift the balance of power in their favour. They often succeeded in enlarging their farms and reducing manorial demands. They also strengthened their position within the structure of patrimonial jurisdiction.

During the High and Late Middle Ages, the peasants were able institutionally to anchor their participation in the proceedings of the patrimonial courts. They served not only as jury members, but also became authoritative interpreters of the customary manorial law. It was incumbent upon the most respected members of the peasant community to inform those present at court which customary laws applied in any given case. From the 15th century on, these directives [*Weistümer*] were written down. These *Weistümer* came to define the rights and obligations of all members of the manorial community (Baltl 1951; Baltl 1953; Arens 1904; Winter 1913).

While the peasants may have hoped that the setting down in writing of the old law would lead to greater legal security, however, it was the lords of the manor who managed to turn this innovation to their advantage. Now that the law and appropriate rulings had been codified, hearings lost their character as a form of co-operation between the landlord, as the bearer of patrimonial judicial authority, and the jury as 'representatives' of the dependent subjects. The *Weistümer* inevitably reduced juries' interpretive power. The marginalization of the peasants that this involved also found expression in the fact that hearings no longer brought together the entire manorial community in public places at fixed times during the year: administration of justice now took place in the chancery of the manorial lord.

Population growth and the price revolution in the 15th century opened up new economic possibilities for the manorial lords. For those in Upper Austria, for example, Rebel states that

> the threats offered by the inflationary devaluation of fixed rents and the increased costs of conspicuous consumption were more than offset by the decreasing cost of labor; by the increase in the economic rent of the soil; by inflationary profit-taking through large-scale investment in land, credit, and commodity markets; and by exploiting the advantages of having economic, social and political connections that transcended the limits of the local economies ... The Upper Austrian ... magnates were in a particularly favorable position in that they could draw on an expanding labor pool for skilled, diverse, and increasingly cheap labor, an advantage that would distinguish their experience with forced labor and rural industry from developments in Bohemia where labor was scarce. (Rebel 1983: 23)

The manorial lords, however, believed that for them to make the most of the economic opportunities the *Weistümer* had to be reformed root and branch. They therefore tried, within the Austrian Monarchy of the 16th century – with highly variable success – to realize 'a kind of "noble" or "manorial absolutism", intended to facilitate a "commercialization" of their domains and manorial complexes as well as a rigid regulation of "morals" and of the lives of their subjects as a whole ("social disciplining")' (Winkelbauer 1992b: 157–8). As Roman Sandgruber (1995: 57) argues, the major portion of manorial revenue in the Austrian lands came not from the economic activities of the lords themselves but from extractions from the productive output of subjects in the form of fees for administrative and judicial records and documents, yields from monopolies, tithes and, of course, compulsory labour services. Even the safeguarding of morality was made into a good source of income in the form of fines.

The disciplinary power of the manorial lords over their subjects increased dramatically. As Thomas Winkelbauer (1992b) has shown, the marginalization of peasant participation in patrimonial jurisdiction during the 16th century was followed by the criminalization of extra-judicial mechanisms of conflict regulation. He views these as 'part of a comprehensive subjugation of peasant communities under (manorial) authority' (Winkelbauer 1992b: 138). The manorial lords now established an extensive system of 'moral policing'. They regulated church attendance, behaviour in church, the closure of taverns or prohibition of the sale of alcoholic drinks during church services, the lifestyle of pastors, and issued bans on blasphemy and swearing, witchcraft and fortune-telling, drunkenness, gambling, lascivious dancing and pre- and extra-marital sexual contact (Winkelbauer 1992a: 327).

Peasant unrest over the course of the 'long' 16th century accompanied the restructuring of manorial domination and of agriculture (Bruckmüller 1985: 186–214). A coalition between the manorial lords and the sovereign, however, defeated the peasants (Sandgruber 1995: 57–60). These victories enabled the development and entrenchment of 'manorial absolutism', a form of domination which, along with its moral orientation, can be better understood in connection with attempts by the monarchical rulers to establish a system of 'confessional absolutism' within the Habsburg Monarchy. When in the following section we sketch this policy of 're-catholicization', we concentrate on 'top-down' efforts. It bears emphasizing, however, that 'on the ground' the success of Counter-Reformation endeavours was frequently the result of a 'negotiated settlement' (Patrouch 2000) because of the splintered structure of authority. The gaps and overlaps between seigneurial jurisdictions, of which we have spoken above, presented opportunities to subjects for resistance:

> Conflicts between bishops and emperors, abbots and gentry, rich peasants and poor ones, people called Lutherans or people called Catholics, all created an intensely complex and dynamic world of action. In time and over it, traditions could be created, authority asserted, and practices established and legitimated. (Patrouch 2000: 230–31)

The policy of Catholic reformation had to be inserted, and was played out, within this complex web of interactions.

Confessional absolutism in Austria

The successes of Lutheran and Calvinist Protestantism meant that by the 1560s and 1570s, the Catholic Church's sphere of influence was largely limited to Southern Europe. The Catholic Counter-Reformation conquered France, Poland and Austria, and along with the Italian states and those of the Iberian Peninsula, this success ensured the survival of the church. Manifestly, the Counter-Reformation was of the utmost significance for the institutional survival of Catholicism. But in Austria, and in other places too, it also contributed significantly to the consolidation of monarchical rule and led, as we shall see, to the development of a 'confessional absolutism'.

In the era of Reformation and Counter-Reformation, none of the confessional churches was content with simply specifying the religious dogma and spreading knowledge of it amongst the clergy and the faithful. They also aimed at a complete 'reformation of manners' (Axtmann 1996). In the past, the Catholic Church had denounced a wide range of moral offences and had punished any violations by clerics and laymen alike. The punishment and eradication of sins of commission and omission, especially religious offences and personal immorality, remained a major concern of all churches in the age of confessionalization. Apostasy, heresy, sectarianism and (in Protestant churches) idolatry; wilful absence from church, failure to receive communion and neglect of baptism and (above all in Protestant churches) of catechism; the profanation of Sundays and holy days by working, playing games or drinking during time of church service; practising witchcraft and sorcery; scolding and defamation; usury, avarice and gluttony; prostitution, adultery and pre-marital sex; any violations of the state of holy matrimony – all these, and many more forms of social behaviour were targeted for intervention by the churches through the imposition of church discipline.

Church discipline was supported and supplemented by the disciplinary efforts of state bodies. The *cura religionis*, still deeply rooted in medieval tradition, was regarded as one of the sovereign's key tasks. This 'ideological' justification of 'secular' intervention in religious matters was reinforced further by the political territorialization of the church in the course of the 16th century: the churches became state churches, founded, supported or defended by the political sovereign within his territory, whose doctrines were imposed on subjects through state bodies. To carry out a reformation within a particular territory, or to prevent such a reformation from occurring, was always a political act. It meant subjecting the church, including ecclesiastical law and the forms of religious practice, to state control and authority. Church administration became part of state administration and placed at the disposal of the state the means and instruments that enabled it to expand its radius of action. Reformation and Counter-Reformation were thus important aspects of the formation of the modern state.

The state took over, in particular, regulation of the education system, family life and marriage, as well as welfare and care of the poor, from the 'old' church. These were the areas that the state attempted to control through, for example, its 'police legislation' (Axtmann 1992). Urbanization, the expansion of the money economy and the religious controversies of the 16th century had undermined the 'old order.' Ensuring 'good order', according to contemporary notions, required subjects to display religious and moral integrity in their daily lives. The police ordinances of the 16th century thus aimed at religious and moral renewal. Cooperation between state and church was intended to produce subjects whose social behaviour was morally disciplined. As we have already seen in the case of Austria, the manorial lords too were keen to discipline their subjects within the framework of 'manorial absolutism.'

What was the role played by 'confessionalization' in the formation of the Austrian Monarchy in the 16th and 17th centuries?

In the German Empire in the 16th century, religious conflicts were at once political conflicts. The religious settlement which the Catholic Habsburg Emperor Charles V agreed with the Protestant Imperial Estates in the Peace of Augsburg of 1555, allowed the Imperial Estates, and thus also the Austrian princes, the right to choose between Catholicism and the Confession of Augsburg. This right was coupled with the authority to either drive out or forcibly convert subjects of other faiths (Gampl 1984: 2). This idea was later encapsulated in the maxim *cuius regio eius religio.*

As in the German Empire, so also in the Austrian Monarchy: the geopolitical constellations and the differing political interests of sovereign and Estates resulted in religious fragmentation:

> For while the dynasty remained a pillar of the Roman Church and Tridentine orthodoxy, the majority of the nobility in every one of its constituent lands went over to Protestantism. First the bulk of the Czech landowning class, long habituated to local heresy, became Lutheran, then the Magyar gentry adopted Calvinism, and finally the Austrian aristocracy itself, in the heartland of Habsburg power, was won for the Reformed religion. By the 1570s the greatest noble families in the *Erblande* were Protestant: Dietrichstein, Starhemberg, Khevenhueller, Zinzendorf. (Anderson 1974: 305)

The conflict between sovereign and Estates now appeared in the form of profession of Catholicism or Protestantism. The reason why the Estates were able successfully to resist the principle of *cuius regio eius religio* was their indispensability to the struggle against the Turks, dating back to 1526 (Bruckmüller 1984: 172; Heiss 1991: 103).

The argument that 'confessionalization' was important to the political-institutional formation of the Austrian Monarchy can be pinned down more precisely as follows. First, 'confessionalization' led to an expansion of state activity, as 'police legislation' clearly indicates. Second, the movements for religious reformation in Austria, Bohemia and Hungary were closely interwoven with the power struggle between sovereign and Estates, and the suppression of these movements in these countries by the sovereign was thus at once an attack on the power of the Estates and Estates government, and hence also on political-territorial regionalism in general (Link 1983: 492–3; Sandgruber 1995: 130). In Austria, and even more strikingly in the lands of the Bohemian Crown, the Counter-Reformation was a turning point, which, though it did not spell the end of dualistic state development, certainly modified it decisively (Link 1983: 514). A brief look at the uprising against the Crown in Bohemia, whose suppression, together with victory over the nobility, laid the foundation stone for the development of an absolutist regime, is essential to more fully grasping these developments.

Once again, the changes in the intra-societal balance of power must be related to inter-societal dynamics. The war with the Ottoman Empire between 1593 and 1609 had weakened the position of Emperor Rudolf II. The Emperor was dependent on the Imperial Estates' military and financial support to wage war. The political and geostrategic significance of the Hungarian territories of the Austrian Monarchy, however, enabled the Hungarian aristocracy to obtain concessions from the Emperor in religious matters and also to attain greater political autonomy. In the Treaty of Vienna of 1606, the Catholic Church's monopoly in Hungary was broken and the Lutheran and Calvinist faiths were recognized: religious freedom was thus constitutionally anchored. The treaty also reinforced the high degree of political autonomy that Hungary enjoyed within the Austrian Monarchy, by re-institutionalizing the office of palatine. The palatine was to be elected by the Hungarian Estates assembly, preside over the Hungarian government and hold supreme command of the Hungarian army. The Hungarian Estates demanded that the Bohemian and Austrian diets guarantee that the treaty be upheld – a demand which clearly signalled a shift away from the authority of the sovereign. Yet this demand pinpointed an alternative strategy of political integration to the monarchy: the notion of trans-regional cooperation between the Estates for purposes of mutual protection and aid opened up the prospect of the transformation of the Austrian Monarchy into a confederation of aristocratic republics (Schramm 1991: 177; Berenger 1994: 252).

While the compromise with Hungary did much to stabilize the political situation, the Emperor failed to defeat the Turks. In this context of internal and external threats, the unity of the ruling family broke down as 'fraternal discord' flared between Emperor Rudolf and his brother Matthias. In the ensuing power struggle, the archduke sought support from the Estates in Hungary, Lower and Upper Austria, Moravia and Bohemia. The Estates' confederations, formed in 1608–9, offered 'the sensational novelty of a supra-territorial corporative association for the defence of the Protestant cause' (Schramm 1991: 184), although the archduke's decisive role in this development must be borne in mind (Bruckmüller 1984: 173).

The Bohemian Estates, however, eschewed involvement in this trans-regional cooperation and continued to recognize the Emperor as King of Bohemia, though in exchange they demanded unlimited freedom of religion. In the Letter of Majesty of 1609 the Emperor granted their request. Nonetheless, within a decade the Bohemian Estates launched a fundamental assault on royal-imperial authority. In 1617, the Estates still freely and almost unanimously accepted Ferdinand as king. Following the Defenestration of Prague in May 1618, however, the Protestant Estates took over the government, deposed Ferdinand in 1619 and offered the Crown to the Calvinist Frederick of the Palatinate. The background to this revolt was the slow, initially scarcely perceptible, advance of the Catholic party and the Counter-Reformation in Bohemia. Following the Peace of Augsburg, the Habsburg rulers had pursued a very conscious recruitment policy, appointing Catholic nobles to key posts. Jaroslav Pánek (1991: 137–8) underlines that this did not initially present a problem,

> since, even after 1550, the most eminent magnate families still embraced Catholicism. However, a structural transformation of the Bohemian nobility was taking place, caused especially by the extinction or bankruptcy of ancient noble families. By the beginning of the seventeenth century the three richest noblemen were all Protestants; none of them was a member of the royal administration. This profound imbalance between the affluence and ambitions of non-Catholic nobles on the one hand, and the essentially re-Catholicised government on the other, represented (a) serious contradiction within the political system.

From the beginning of the century, moreover, the Bohemian government was increasingly made up of radical or converted nobles, who actively persecuted all non-Catholics. And the exclusion of Protestants from court patronage threatened their dynastic reproduction and thus pitted a section of the Protestant nobility against a small Catholic state elite (MacHardy 2003).

To repeat, the dualism between monarch and Estates in the first two decades of the 17th century was seriously threatened by the politically and religiously motivated establishment of a trans-regional association of Estates. The prospect of a 'confederation of lands dominated by the Estates and the aristocracy' emerged, whose centre would likely have been the lands of the Bohemian Crown (Bruckmüller 1984: 173). The military defeat of the Bohemian uprising by Ferdinand, with the support of Imperial German and Bavarian troops, at the Battle of the White Mountain in 1620, removed this threat to the monarchy and scuppered the possibility of such an alternative integration strategy (MacHardy 1992).

The Estates' defeat led to far-reaching changes in the political structure of the monarchy (Kavke 1964). One immediate consequence was the changed composition of the Bohemian aristocracy. As a result of the expulsion of Protestant nobles, between half and two-thirds of all noble domains in Bohemia and Moravia gained new owners, which spelt ruin for around half of all noble families (Melton 1995: 113). The economic and thus also political power of many old Bohemian families was destroyed. A new political class attained power, though some families such as the Kinskys, the Czernins or the Lobkowiczs were able further to increase their fortunes. The Bohemian aristocracy developed into a cosmopolitan class, including Italians (Piccolomini), Germans (Schwarzenberg), Austrians (Trautsmannsdorff), Slovenians (Auersperg), Walloons (Bucquoy), Lotharingians (Desfours) and even Irish (Taaffe) (Anderson 1974: 307). Possession of enormous domains in Bohemia and Moravia endowed this new 'Austro-Bohemian' aristocracy with a substantial degree of political, economic and social autonomy. Anderson (1974: 308) points out that this cosmopolitan aristocracy attained *de facto* fiscal immunity by shifting its entire tax burden onto its serfs: 'This transfer naturally smoothed the course of deliberations between monarchy and aristocracy in the Estates: henceforward the dynasty merely requested lump sums from the Estates, leaving them to fix and collect taxes to meet its demands.'

The institution of the Diet was abolished neither in Bohemia nor in other parts of the monarchy. The Estates retained their right to approve taxes. They lost, however, their influence on foreign policy and religious issues. Jean Berenger draws our attention to the significant changes in the internal power equilibrium in the Diet affecting the Bohemian Estates:

> numerous knights left the country and those who remained were generally ruined and so found it difficult to defray the expenses of attending a session of the assembly (the cost of travelling and staying at Prague) ... the Diet was in practice a manifestation of the order of the lords ... the Diet of Bohemia became an assembly of great lords who were in principle loyal to the Habsburgs but who were in a position to defend their own interests. It is possible to speak of absolutism in Bohemia only in so far as the knights and urban patriciate ceased to play a political role and dissension was muffled. (Berenger 1994: 267)

Ferdinand had good reasons for not proceeding more aggressively against the Estates. First, he recognized the important role that the Estates had long played in the administration of the monarchy. There existed no sovereign administrative bodies capable of exercising authority as effectively at the 'local' level. Secondly and above all, he was dependent upon their approval of taxation and their relatively competent tax collection. As we have already seen, state revenue primarily depended on a flourishing agriculture – which ultimately required a compliant peasantry. The ruler's 'consent to the magnates' control over the peasants grew out of the desire not only to win their (political, financial and administrative) support, but to make use of an effective instrument for maintaining order among an unruly peasantry' (Bireley 1991: 232). The Crown and the Estates were thus well advised to work together – always, of course, throughout the monarchy, at the peasants' expense. This cooperation was, and remained, a characteristic of Habsburg rule: 'There was no attempt to develop a class of civil servants, judicial or financial officers, as there was in neighbouring Bavaria or in France ... (Ferdinand's) achievement was to retain (the Estates') participation in government after he had tamed them politically and so to integrate them into his form of absolutism' (Bireley 1991: 232).

In Bohemia the 'elective' monarchy was transformed into a 'hereditary' monarchy. The aristocracy made up for losses in governmental power by more strongly emphasizing their privileges as feudal lords and tightening their grip on their peasant subjects. For the Habsburg Monarchy as a whole, the defeat of the Estates had additional consequences. First, the quelling of the Bohemian revolt influenced the royal Court's relationship with the monarchy's ruling elite. As we have pointed out, the elite was increasingly 'Austro-Bohemian',

> in that its individual members owned Estates spread throughout the Monarchy as a whole ... most members of the *Herrenstand* possessed the right of naturalization ... in at least two territories, which allowed one to hold membership and office in the territorial Estates. This 'trans-territoriality' – reinforced by frequent intermarriage within the 'Austro-Bohemian' élite – was an important source of political unity in the Habsburg Monarchy, since it served to integrate the aristocracy geographically and thereby weaken the centrifugal forces of territorial particularism. (Melton 1995: 121–2; Press 1991a: 14)

Members of this elite, which underwent a form of 'courtization', filled the key posts in the administrative system and at Court. Vienna and the royal Court became the key locus of social and cultural attractions. The Austro-Bohemian elite submitted to the rules and rituals at Court and in return enjoyed the political, social and economic privileges in the gift of the monarch (Press 1990; Press 1991b). However, while the Court was thus able to integrate the aristocracy to a certain extent, this strategy was clearly limited: after all, at the local level a powerful aristocracy was still irreplaceable when it came to ensuring the successful completion of administrative and military tasks on which the monarchy's survival depended (Press 1990: 28–9).

Second, the suppression of the Estates' revolt was also a triumph of the Counter-Reformation. After 1620, the Austrian Monarchy was 'the most important example of a confessionally closed state in the empire, an example of confessional absolutism' (Schindling 1994: 60; Bireley 1994). The Austrian Monarchy was, as we elaborated at the beginning of this chapter, a conglomeration of quite different territories and institutions. Since the late 17th century, however, an overarching, uniform culture had been superimposed upon this configuration – the revived 'cosmopolitan' Catholic Church (Evans 1979, part III). The Catholic clergy, particularly the Jesuits, acquired a central position within the cultural institutions of the monarchy, above all in the education system. The Crown did not attempt to impose its hegemony at the lowest, local level by means, for example, of 'financial' or 'judicial' officers, but rather through the Reformation commission and ecclesiastical visitations. Berenger describes this situation in Lower Austria in the 17th century as follows:

> A patent dating from 13 April 1651 repeated the provisions of previous texts (the patents general of 1634, 1638 and 1645), putting a stop to the peasants' practice of Lutheran worship. Non-Catholics were forbidden to go abroad to practice their religion ... to eat meat on the days of abstinence prescribed by the Church, to read books by non-Catholics that had not received the censor's approval and to welcome or give lodgings to Protestant preachers. The first measures were intended to stifle all religious life among the Lutherans, who were deprived of preaching and sermons and similarly the sacraments, without going so far as to oblige them to convert to Catholicism. However, in 1652 the Emperor (Ferdinand III) created a general commission of the Reformation with the avowed goal of obtaining the conversion of non-Catholic subjects. The patent of 1652 in effect closed the frontiers since subjects could not move away without a

> passport issued by the local authorities. The commission sent into each district monks charged with 'instructing', that is to say, converting by persuasion. They stayed for six weeks, after which Lutherans could convert, request a delay for reflection, or emigrate. (Berenger 1994: 307–8)

The 'confessional absolutism' of the Austrian Monarchy in the 17th century meant a symbiosis of Crown and Church. In the 16th century under Ferdinand I, Maximilian II and Rudolf II, the multinational and multilingual Court was cosmopolitan in tenor. There was, moreover, no privileged class that might have determined the atmosphere at Court with its particular cultural or behavioural standards. The aristocracy certainly played a major role, but members of the bourgeoisie could also attain key positions at Court. Given the rulers' meagre interest in military customs and traditions, a military ethos had equally little prospect of taking hold at Court. During the course of the 17th century, however, the horizon narrowed to the same degree that the influence of Counter-Reformation Catholicism increased. The notion gained currency that 'the Habsburg *imperium* must embody the principles of Catholicism: unity, hierarchy, piety, mystery. At its summit stands the orthodox court, the overseer of general purity' (Evans 1977: 136; Ehalt 1980). This close relationship between Crown and Church found sustained artistic expression in Baroque art, in architecture, music and literature, but also in a 'sacralization' of the landscape, through the construction of new churches, abbeys and monasteries, and through erection of religious statues and monuments alongside country roads, on bridges, in fields, villages or town centres. It was reflected in courtly ceremony, which was deeply rooted in religious rituals; in the prominent role played by the Habsburg rulers at church services, processions or pilgrimages; and in legislation on religious matters, numerically outstripping all other areas subjected to regulation until well into the 18th century (Bruckmüller 1984: 74–80; Gampl 1984). This marked the beginning of the *pietas Austriaca.*

This close relationship between Crown and Catholicism remained highly significant until the end of the Habsburg Monarchy during the First World War. Yet the monarchical rulers increasingly attempted to gain legitimacy for their rule that would be less grounded in the Counter-Reformation and thus less dependent on the Catholic Church. Ties to the church were loosened in the 18th century as a result of the transition from 'confessional absolutism' to 'reform absolutism'.

Reform absolutism

As we have seen, the political struggle between monarch and Estates in the 16th and early 17th century was also a religious conflict. When the rulers had attained supremacy over the Estates, they began to build a more centralized state in which the Catholicism of the Counter-Reformation became the state religion. The next significant dispute between Crown and Estates occurred in the mid-18th century. First Maria Theresa and then her son Joseph II made efforts to reform the institutions of the monarchy in order to secure its territorial unity and status as a major European power. Their aim was to create a yet more centralized monarchy, which was to be governed by an administrative body loyal to the monarch.

This reform absolutism did not develop from a religiously determined 'civil war situation' – as in France, whose political evolution is frequently regarded as the ideal typical case of an absolute state. Harm Klueting claims that Austrian reform absolutism represented an attempt to adapt monarchical institutions to a changed situation. This absolutism was rooted

> in the *integration* of the areas gained from 1687 (Mohács) to 1718 (Passarowitz) in Hungary, Serbia and Wallachia and 1713/14 in Belgium and Italy, in the *identification* of the Austrian lands leaving the Holy Roman Empire, which had been developing since the Pragmatic Sanction, as parts of a greater unity, and since 1740/41, in the *resistance* to Prussia ... As these adaptational problems could only be dealt with through reforms, the Austrian absolutism of the 18th century necessarily evolved as reform absolutism. (Klueting 1993: 92, fn. 5)

The initial conditions in which reform absolutism took hold again bring out the significance of geopolitical constellations and inter-state configurations for the intra-societal power balance and the development of political structures and institutions. In 1687, Austria had beaten the Turks at Mohács and conquered Transylvania; the Peace of Utrecht in 1713, which ended the War of Spanish Succession, brought Emperor Charles VI the Spanish (from now on, 'Austrian') Netherlands (until 1792) along with Milan, which had been Spanish since 1526 and which was to remain under Austrian dominion until 1859; and the victory of Passarowitz of 1718, which ended the war, waged anew against the Turks since 1716, brought new territorial gains: the Banat of Temesvar, northern areas of Serbia including Belgrade, as well as parts of Wallachia and Bosnia. These problems of integration made it vital to consider institutional reform of the monarchy; defeats by the Turks between 1737 and 1739 and by Prussia in the Silesian wars from 1740 to 1742, in 1744 and 1756–1763 (the 'Seven Years War') forced Austria to embark on reforms. Through the Peace of Belgrade of 1739, Austria lost not only Belgrade, Serbia and Wallachia, but also suffered a loss of prestige. From now on, it had to compete with Russia as its main rival in the Balkans. The loss of Silesia to Prussia in the 'War of the Austrian Succession' of 1740 – a loss finally confirmed in the Peace of Hubertusburg at the close of the 'Seven Years War' – not only robbed the monarchy of an important source of revenue, the Silesian linen industry, but was also a blow to Austrian hegemony in the Holy Roman Empire as a direct consequence of the rise of Prussia.

In a sense, the loss of its leading role within the empire had a liberating effect on the monarchy. The issue of 'Austrian' identity could now be tackled more forcefully. In the past attempts to propagate a specifically 'Austrian' notion of state had again and again clashed with the universal imperial concept, inevitably bound up with a supra-national, or more precisely, transregional consciousness. Such a notion also conflicted with the (particular) identity of the 'kingdoms and lands.' The 'Imperial' and 'regional' consciousness, which transcended narrow national ideas, hindered the development and propagation of a specifically 'Austrian' notion of state:

> To become a modern state, Austria had first to be 'separated' out from the Holy Roman Empire – a process that progressed decisively at the beginning of the 18th century, when the lands of the Austrian Habsburgs, augmented by Belgian and Italian territories from the Spanish succession and those wrested from the Turks in the east and south-east, attained a new identity and increasingly understood themselves as 'Monarchia austriaca.' (Matis 1981a: 17)

A key aspect of the formation of this identity was church policy, pursued single-mindedly under Maria Theresa and Joseph II. The previous section cast light on the key significance of Counter-Reformation Catholicism for the development of 'confessional absolutism'. In the period of reform absolutism, the state became determined to extend its control over the church and over religious life in general. The consolidation of the Catholic faith and enforcement of a religious and moral way of living were central goals of the state's church policy (Wangermann 1973: 74–88). As early as 1767, all papal and episcopal decrees required Imperial approval. Visitations through papal nuncios were prohibited and censorship of books was extended to all printed works emanating from the church. As *suprema advocata ecclesiarum* Maria Theresa also laid claim to supervision of the administration of church assets as a whole. The clergy's tax-exempt status was removed entirely and ecclesiastical jurisdiction was limited to clergy. The Church's influence on education was also limited: a large number of primary and secondary schools were now run by the state (Link 1983: 529–30). Maria Theresa, for economic reasons, moved to reduce the number of church holidays. This policy was linked with her measures against begging, idleness and vagabondage: 'Since the large number of church holidays encourages idleness and ... impedes economic productivity, Maria Theresa requested and achieved exemption from the ban on working for around half these holidays ...' (Gampl 1984: 59).

Under the government of Joseph II, a large number of decrees affecting the church were issued ('*in Publico-Ecclesiasticis*'). Link sums up the fundamental maxims of the dominant theory of the state as follows: 'The entire "outer" realm including the temporal powers of the church (is subordinate to) the authority of the secular Sovereign ... who of course remains tied to the *ius divinum* of the Church when carrying out his duties. Every spiritual *potestas in temporalibus* can therefore be exercised only with the approval of the power of the state' (Link 1983: 539). Klueting furnishes us with a detailed list of measures directed at the church (1993 65). These began

> in Maria Theresa's time, with plans to 'reduce the numbers of monks' from 1762, limitation on admission of convent members from 1767, closure of monasteries in

> Austrian Lombardy from 1768 and prohibition of pilgrimages lasting several days in 1772 ... Apart from reduction of holidays and similar interference in the baroque piety of the '*Pietas Austriaca*', Josephs II's policy towards the Church following his mother's death consisted first and foremost of: 1. regulation of dioceses, that is, the state's re-division and foundation of new dioceses and thus the creation of Austrian Catholic bishoprics, 2. centralization of priestly education in state controlled general seminaries, 3. prohibition of direct contact between the bishops and the monasteries and the Roman curia and with the heads of religious orders located beyond Austria's borders and 4. closure of numerous monasteries. The toleration of non-Catholic religious communities was then introduced in 1781 through Joseph's Toleration Patent.

The Toleration Patent of 1781 and legislation affecting religious minorities not only ended the era of persecution that was part and parcel of the Counter-Reformation and dismantled numerous discriminatory practices against Jews; but socially important groups were also integrated into the state. A start was also made at realizing equality in the religious field, as 'non-Catholics' [*Akatholiken*] were now able not only to become officers, but also gained the right 'to purchase houses and goods, (enjoyed the rights of) citizenship and becoming the master of a trade, (and could receive) academic honours and posts in the state bureaucracy [*Civilbedienstungen*]', of course, only through dispensation from the state on a case by case basis. In 'all elections and provision of services uprightness and competence ... and the Christian and moral lifestyle of the candidates [*Competenten*] alone ought to' clinch matters (quoted in Link 1983: 542; Barton (ed.) 1981).

Measures affecting the church thus primarily involved 'the levelling out of non-state areas of autonomy' (Klueting 1993: 65). The significance of Catholicism to moral and political order was certainly not ignored. The 'General Penal Law' [*Allgemeine Strafgesetz*] of 1787 considered crimes that 'lead to corruption of morals' as political crimes. This included, among other things, blasphemy: 'Any person that denies reason to the extent of taking the Almighty's name in vain ... in the presence of other people ... should be treated as insane and held in custody in the madhouse until such time as his improvement has been surely established' (quoted in Gampl 1984: 75). The practical take-over of the church made priests, in effect, to local officials of the state: 'Their responsibilities were by no means limited only to moral and civil education. They also had to promulgate all laws and mandates from the pulpit. Pastoral care was to be pursued in the spirit of education. This explains why priests were instructed to preach about fighting fire, growing potatoes and bee-keeping' (Link 1983: 540).

These church policies were significant not only with regard to identity formation but also as part of a comprehensive project aimed at bringing all political and social realms under the authority of the state. The struggle with the Estates was one aspect of this. As (German) emperors, the Austrian monarchs had supported the Estates in the German territories against the reigning princes in order to prevent the development of absolutist rule. Absolutist regimes in the territories belonging to the empire would have threatened Imperial unity and the Imperial constitution. Yet these efforts to protect the Estates' power in the interest of the 'empire' had weakened the monarchy 'domestically': the Austrian monarchs could not legitimately struggle against the power of its own Estates while backing a dualistic constitution in Imperial territories. The weakened position of the Austrian Monarchy in the (Holy Roman) Empire now enabled it to get started on absolutist reforms in a less inhibited, more direct fashion. Defeat by Prussia made such reforms essential.

The loss of Silesia was in itself a heavy blow for the monarchy. The fact that Prussia managed almost to double tax revenue there within a few years, however, also laid bare Austria's relative backwardness. The government was in no doubt that Prussia's success was down to a more effective administration and the Estates' having been deprived of both the right to approve taxes and responsibility for collecting them. Prussia's suppression of the Silesian Estates signalled to the Austrian Estates their own fate should Prussia defeat the Habsburg Monarchy. The defence of the monarchy made institutional reform necessary: on this the monarchical government and the Estates agreed.

We shall not embark on a detailed description of Maria Theresa's and Joseph II's reforms of the state between 1740 and 1790 (Plaschka et al. (eds.) 1985; Scott 1990; Dickson 1987; Klingenstein 1970; Bradler-Rottmann 1976; Ogris 1981). They centrally aimed at limiting the power of the Estates and dismantling manorial authority over the peasants. Efforts at reform were thus largely a matter of centring political power in the monarchical government such that the Estates and their governmental organs became subject to state control or were replaced by state bodies, and of establishing the state's control over 'municipal administration' that would allow the state direct access to its subjects (Beidtel 1851; Beidtel 1898).

During the reign of Maria Theresa, two major efforts were made at reform. The first attempt was undertaken in 1749 under Count Haugwitz, and the second after the Seven Years War under Wenzel Anton von Kaunitz. In the reform of 1749, the Austrian and Bohemian chancelleries were abolished and replaced by the *Directorium in publicis et cameralibus*, into which the Court Chamber [*Hofkammer*] was also incorporated. As its name suggests, the *Directorium* was responsible for both political and fiscal administration and functioned as locus of coordination for the home affairs of Austria and Bohemia. The newly established supreme legal authority, the *Oberste Justizstelle*, formed from the two chancelleries, took over judicial matters and became the highest authority for the administration of justice. As the *Directorium* and the *Oberste Justizstelle* were responsible for the lands of both the Austrian and Bohemian Crown, the constitutional division between the two states was in effect institutionally removed and a new, centrally led 'core state' was created (Walter 1972: 101; Dickson 1987: I, 325–6). In the 'kingdoms and lands', the Estates' governments were limited to legal issues. The *Representationen und Cammern* were established. These, as the local arm of the *Directorium*, were responsible for political and fiscal administration, including the *Contributionale*. The *militaria mixta*, that is, military administration at provincial level, also came within their remit. One outcome of this institutional reform was that from now on state economic policy, 'welfare policy' and tax policy and administration were intertwined (Osterloh 1970: 13; Dickson 1987: I, 271).

As a direct result of the catastrophic defeat in the Seven Years War, the *Directorium* lost control over the administration of finance. Administration of economic and fiscal affairs was now in the hands of three institutions. The Chamber of Accounts [*Hofrechenkammer*] had the authority to supervise state finances, monetary policy and the budget; its executive power entailed administration of tax revenue, borrowing and enhancing the economy. The Court Chamber managed Crown possessions. The *Hofkommerzienrat* was created to lead trade policy. The *Staatswirtschaftsdeputation*, established in 1767, was intended to tackle general economic policy issues. As a result, the fusion of political and fiscal administration was annulled. Political administration was handed over to the Bohemian and Austrian Chancellery [*k.k. vereinigte böhmische und österreichische Hofkanzlei*]. At the same time, at provincial level, the *Justitiali* were incorporated into the remit of the *Mittelstellen*. This nationalization of justice robbed the Estates of their remaining realms of authority (Osterloh 1970: 25; Hellbling 1956: 292). The most important institutional innovation was the creation of the State Council [*Staatsrat*] in 1761. The State Council was not an executive body, but enjoyed a kind of 'policy-making power' – an authority which was, of course, in principle limited by the monarch, although in the 1770s Maria Theresa accepted a majority in the State Council as sufficient to pass resolutions. The State Council under Kaunitz exercised significant influence during the reign of Maria Theresa. Under Joseph II, however, it lost its central role to the *Vereinigte Hofstelle*, which was established in 1782 and united the Bohemian and Austrian Court Chancellery, the Court Chamber and *Ministerialbancodeputation*. The division into political and financial administrative systems, implemented in the 1760s and 1770, was thus again dismantled.

Joseph changed the system of provincial administration by dividing the monarchy into 13 districts. These reforms signalled the monarch's determination to disregard the historically rooted particularities of the constitutive territories of the monarchy. This disregard also found expression in the fact that Joseph was the only ruler not to have the Estates pay him homage. He therefore felt no compunction about ignoring the Estates' privileges, dissolving the Estates' committees in 1783 and dismissing their officials. Two deputies or envoys of the Estates were assigned to the new state authorities at provincial level as advisors with seats and voting rights to ensure some degree of representation of the Estates. The government, however, retained the right to declare them electable and their election itself required confirmation by the government. This meant a further 'nationalization' of Estate administration (Hellbling 1956: 302–303).

At the 'local' level, the state under Maria Theresa set up circle offices [*Kreisämter*] through which central government attempted to gain control over the exercise of manorial power (Stundner 1970). The circle offices operated as a kind of 'moral police', expected to secure position of the church and the Catholic faith through the prosecution of heretics, but also through control of priests' financial conduct and supervision of church welfare institutions. But the circle offices were also responsible for maintaining law and order. This included, among other things, the obligation to protect the peasants. This task was defined ever more precisely in the course of time. A decree from 1769, for example, stated that rulings by patrimonial courts were legally binding only after the case had been submitted to the circle offices and the judgements had been approved by them (Sammlung [*collection*], V, 479). Peasants were allowed to take legal complaints about their manorial lords to the circle offices. The judicial power of the manorial lords was further curtailed through the institution of the 'subjects' advocate' [*Untertansadvokaten*], intended to provide the peasants with legal assistance if they brought an action or appealed against their manorial masters (Matis 1981b: 289). Yet while the peasants were furnished with the right of appeal, the manner in which these appeals were to be lodged was laid down precisely. A decree of 1772, for example, threatened peasants who made appeals in a stubborn, insubordinate, sacrilegious, cocky or even rebellious manner with hefty penalties (Sammlung [*collection*], VIII, 539). As Bruckmüller argues, their appeals had to follow 'a specific institutional route; they could be made only by individuals or small groups and riotousness was out of the question.' In this way, rural subjects were integrated into the developing 'bourgeois society': 'If they conducted themselves according to the norms of bourgeois, civilized society, that is, if they had internalized avoidance of "indecent" speech and seemingly dangerous forms of gathering to such an extent that they were allowed to take legal action in the first place' (Bruckmüller (1986: 117). Nonetheless, with the institution of the circle offices, the *brachium*, the coercive arm of the state, now extended all the way down to the subject. At the same time, the state afforded subjects a certain degree of protection from the authority of their manorial lords (Sturmberger 1969: 88; Liebel-Weckowicz 1985: 345–7).

The powers of the circle offices over manorial domains and communities were extended and manorial officials were subjected to their authority (Brusatti 1958). The Josephine Penal Code of 1781 gave circle officials the right to review the judgements of the patrimonial courts. It also prohibited manorial officials from imposing fines. At the same time, the fees that manorial officials could charge were legally regulated by the state and they increasingly yielded insufficient revenue to cover their wages. With the exercise of patrimonial jurisdiction and policing becoming ever more costly, a growing number of manorial lords accepted the state's attempts to take over these tasks. Patrimonial legal power was further curtailed once it was decreed (in 1787) that a legal education was a prerequisite for the exercise of a judicial function. If the manorial lords lacked such a qualification, they were obliged to entrust this task to qualified officials. Thus, as a result of reforms of the state and administration under Maria Theresa and Joseph II, manorial domains and urban magistrates were no longer independent in their administrative activities: they were reduced to state organs of first instance.

Manorial officials now were charged with carrying out a wide range of tasks on behalf of the state, such as collecting taxes, recruiting soldiers, policing and the upkeep of roads (Liebel-Weckowicz 1985: 348–9).

Institutional reform was accompanied by the creation of a far-flung bureaucracy. At the beginning of Maria Theresa's reign, the number of royal officials in the Austrian, Bohemian and Hungarian lands was around 6,500. In 1762, this had increased to around 10,000, and stood at around 11,000 at the end of her reign (Dickson 1987: I, 305–10). For the reign of Joseph II, Dickson (1995, 335 and 336, table 2) calculates that the number of officials in central government institutions had sunk to around 3,781 in 1781 and around 3,400 in 1789 (the level of 1781 was reached again in 1796 with 3,769). More than half of these officials worked in the administration of finance (Dickson 1995: 337–8). To this must be added the royal officials in the 'kingdoms and lands'. Dickson (1995: 341–3) calculates a staff in administration and the legal system of around 3,402 in 1778 and around 4,625 in 1788–89, towards the end of Joseph II's reign, that is, an increase of around a third. The number of legal officials was about as high as that of administrative ones. There were also around 6,989 officials in the system of financial administration in 1788–89, and public employees in the mines and coinage, around 1,600 in number in 1782. Adding public employees in the postal service, this makes around 9,000 officials, that is, around 14,500 in 1788–1789 in total. These figures demonstrate that the number of officials more than doubled between 1740 and 1790; that the financial administration system played a central role at both central government and provincial level; and that the administration of justice was a very significant task of the provincial governments.

These royal officials intensified state control and the 'disciplining' of the political, social and economic life of the monarchy. This is apparent in the increase in legislation during reform absolutism. Turning again to Dickson (1987: I, 318), we see that in the first decade of Maria Theresa's reign, 1741–50,

> the annual average number of published decrees was only thirty-six, much the same as the average thirty-one of the period between 1731 and 1740. From 1751 to 1760, the annual average was sixty-eight, from 1761 to 1770 100, from 1771 to 1780 ninety-six ... The total number of decrees listed for 1780–9, 6,206, is more than double the 3,017 of 1741–1780. The annual Josephine average is 690.

If we look at the figures up to 1796, we discover a total of 3,888 decrees, the annual average sinking to 555 (Dickson 1995: table 6). Looking at the areas covered by this 'flood of legislation' in the Austrian and Bohemian lands under Joseph II, we find that church issues (1,121 decrees) were quantitatively most significant, issues of the administration of justice (897) and fiscal affairs (728) ranked above military matters (534); and that issues involving the education system (338) were also of key significance (Dickson 1995: 354, table 8).

The bureaucracy, which developed during the period of reform absolutism, developed a specific professional ethos over the course of time. The material basis for the self-understanding of this class of officials was the (moderate) financial security that public employees gradually gained. An important aspect of this security was the linkage of state pensions to rank and length of service. In line with this, officials had an incentive to gain promotion by improving their productivity and to regard their career as a long-term prospect, which promised security in case of illness, old age and – in case of death – for their family. The principle of seniority, introduced in 1786, put decisions on promotion on a less arbitrary footing and reduced nepotism to some degree. Gaining a position in the civil service was also increasingly linked to passing entrance examinations: not only the sons of noble families, but also men from a 'bourgeois' background could now aspire to such positions (Wunder 1984; Heindl 1985).

In his famous 'pastoral letter' [*Hirtenbrief*] to civil servants in 1783, Joseph II tried to formulate the professional ethos of the class of officials (OEZ II/4: 123–32). Each official ought to fulfill his duties conscientiously, always taking the common good into account and feeling a sense of duty to the 'Fatherland' as a whole, and not, for example, to individual nations or provinces. Within officialdom, all prejudices or rivalries based on such particular loyalties had to be abandoned. The monarch conceived the state bureaucracy as a means of integration, whose task it was to overcome the monarchy's national fragmentation and contribute to developing a unitary, centralized state (Bruckmüller 1984: 91–2).

To understand the institutional aspects of reform absolutism, it is crucial to discuss the political project underlying these changes. These reforms, as we have seen, were intended to curtail aristocratic power. The institution of the circle office clearly served this purpose. These developments were however also bound to find expression in policies affecting the peasantry, as well as in fiscal and tax policy.

As has been pointed out, the political power of the aristocracy rested on its manorial power. The monarch could hope to change the balance of power to his advantage only if he succeeded in reducing this power. Policies concerning the peasantry and taxation under Maria Theresa and Joseph II must be seen in this context (Link 1949; Feigl (ed.) 1982). The monarchy regarded the peasantry as the basis and greatest prop of the state. Policies on the peasantry were intended to ensure that the peasants could provide for themselves and their families and pay their taxes. They were also, however, intended to ensure that they were capable and equipped to defend the fatherland. The 'welfare' of the state required the 'welfare' of the peasantry. The property rights and political rights of the lords had to be subordinated to these welfare considerations. Initially, however, Maria Theresa had to refrain from agrarian reform in order to safeguard her rule. In 1742 she was of the opinion that freeing the peasants was unthinkable. After all, as she said, 'given that there exists no country where differences between lords and subjects are absent, to liberate the peasant from his obligation to the former, would make one unrestrained and the other dissatisfied. On all sides, however, it would offend justice' (quoted in Matis 1981b: 287). Once she had consolidated her rule, however, she expressed a different view:

> The peasantry, which constitutes the most numerous class of citizens and the basis, and consequently the greatest strength of the state, must be kept in an upright condition and in such a state that the peasant can feed himself and his family and in addition afford to pay contribution [*Landesumlagen*] in times of peace and war. The rights of manorial domains must give way in light of these considerations. (Quoted in Matis 1981b: 287)

Additional impetus for pro-peasant policies came largely from peasant unrest, such as that of 1755 in Croatia, 1765–66 in Bohemia, Moravia and Hungary and 1775 in Bohemia, and from famines, such as those occurring at the beginning of the 1770s (Grüll 1963). The abolition of serfdom in Bohemia, Moravia and Silesia in 1781, in Austria in 1782 and in Hungary in 1785 represents the most important efforts to improve peasant living conditions (Grünberg 1893–94; Balázs 1956; Patzelt 1950; Stark 1952). The abolition of serfdom gave peasants freedom of movement, and this geographical mobility weakened the power of the manorial lords over them. This policy must also be viewed, however, in its economic dimension. Since the late 17th century, the state had pursued an interventionist and mercantilistic policy (Klíma 1965; Klíma 1974; Klíma 1985; Otruba 1965; Wright 1966). In Bohemia in particular, this policy led to the development of an important manufacturing industry. Aristocrats owned many of these firms, but the number of 'bourgeois' companies increased sharply in the second half of the 18th century. Yet, labour mobility was limited because of serfdom. As a result, these firms found themselves at a competitive disadvantage vis-à-vis the 'noble' firms, which were able to put serfs to work in production. The abolition of serfdom thus also opened up the labour market and enabled urban manufacturing and trading firms to expand their business (Hanke 1973/74: 539–40). The commercialization of the economy thus forms the frame within which the abolition of serfdom can best be understood.

Regulations governing statute labour also slot into this context (Grüll 1952). The legal regulation of *robot*, which the peasants owed their manorial lords, aimed to furnish the peasant with the right to dispose of his own and his children's and servants' labour power, and thus safeguard his capacity to pay taxes and secure his role as producer within commercial agriculture. Disciplining was also important: for the government, *robot* was a school of idleness and truanting, since the person had no interest in discharging the obligations conscientiously and efficiently (Feigl 1985: 53). Legislation that established the right of the peasant to acquire his farm further strengthened the position of the peasantry as did an inheritance law.

The disciplining of the peasants by integrating them into a commercialized economy was thus an important aspect of policies directed at peasants. This should not, however, cause us to neglect the dimension of political power. These laws clearly aimed to improve the peasants' lot vis-à-vis the manorial lords and thus to weaken manorial power. They also contributed to expanding the fiscal basis of the state. In light of the principle that the yield from the manorial economy was tax-free, while peasant farms had to pay tax, the state had an incentive to minimize the transformation of peasant land into manorial land because this would affect revenue. At the same time, the state was motivated to ease the establishment of new peasant farms on manorial land since this would increase state revenue from taxation.

There was also a military dimension to peasant policies. The monarchy tried to curtail the power of the Estates and the aristocracy in military matters (Bruckmüller 1985: 328–30). The system of conscription of 1763 [*Seelenkonskription*] introduced the rounding up of subjects in regimental recruitment districts. This system established direct contact between the state and the rural population liable for military service. It required a population census – to be carried out by priests – as well as the establishment of special 'conscription authorities'. These were mainly seigniorial authorities supervised by the circle offices. This new method of recruitment triggered a concern for agrarian social policy. From now on, the principle of monarchical protection of the peasantry, of the protection of peasant land and the peasants themselves from the danger of absorption by the landed nobility, played an important role in Austria too – not only because of the necessity of maintaining the economic resource base of the state, but also because of the need to ensure a rural population capable of defending the fatherland.

In respect to the administration of taxes, reform absolutism strove to marginalize the Estates in fiscal matters, too:

> The Estates were indeed allowed to retain their right to approve taxes, but the means thus approved were no longer considered the Estates', but sovereign taxes, and should be administered from now on by sovereign, rather than Estates' officials. This not only ended the separation between the monarchical fiscal system and that of the Estates, between *Camerale* and *Contributionale* and the entire imposition and administration of all direct and indirect taxes had become a matter for the state, but, following the Prussian model, the entire 'political' (domestic) and fiscal administration was to be placed in the hands of sovereign authorities. In return for the easing of the administrative burden on the Estates they were required to pay a higher contribution. Only the *Judicialia* remained under their control. (Link 1983: 520)

The right of the Estates to approve taxes was curtailed by means of the 'decennial recess' under Maria Theresa which stipulated that the Estates' approval of taxes had to remain valid for a period of ten years. The state thus clearly strove to achieve a greater degree of fiscal independence from the Estates. This policy was reinforced by the removal of the tax-free status of manorial property and the increasing importance of indirect taxes over direct taxes (Sandgruber 1995: 139).

The tax reform planned by Joseph II would also have significantly weakened the position of the manorial lords (Mikoletzky 1971). The principle underlying this reform was the physiocratic belief that land was the source of the wealth and prosperity in a state. Regardless of who owned it, all land should be taxed equally. This would have meant a drastic increase in the manorial lords' tax burden. To prevent them from making up for their losses by increasing ground rent and peasant payments, the tax reform was accompanied by a reform of estate regulations [*Urbarialreform*]. This reform aimed to ensure that no subject had to pay more than 50 percent of his gross income to cover his obligations to the manorial lord and the state (Rozdolski 1961: 104). The tax and real estate reform of February 1787 finally imposed a tax of 12 2/9 per cent on gross income from landed property. The peasants were to be allowed to retain 70 per cent of this gross income, which meant that the manorial lords were entitled to extract 17 7/9 per cent of their income. All labour services and other manorial fees which peasants were obliged to pay were to be paid off through this contribution. The reform was thus part of the trend towards the monetization of the economy.

Detailed analysis of this reform project would show how it was thwarted through collusion between high-ranking civil servants, employees of the provincial governments and the manorial lords. Since all high-ranking civil servants were also manorial lords, their own economic interests in maintaining the traditional structures corresponded to those of the 'local' manorial lords. It was thus possible to create a 'grand coalition' against the monarch. The success of this coalition should however be placed in a broader context. Once again, the intra-societal balance of power was bound up with 'inter-state' interdependencies.

The withdrawal of this reform following Joseph's death in 1790 was connected with the political crises triggered by the political conflicts in the 'Austrian' Netherlands and Hungary, the geopolitical dislocations resulting from the wars with the Ottoman Empire and the impact of the French Revolution. In the 'Austrian' Netherlands, the attempt to 'nationalize' the church and religion, and the administrative and legal reforms, met with resistance (Arendt 1843; Lorenz 1862; Stradal 1968; Davis 1974). The traditional rulers saw their power undermined by the policies of the monarch while the rising 'bourgeoisie' in the economically developed, 'modern' 'Austrian' Netherlands demanded representation in political bodies. This opposition movement, which was far from unified, gained impetus from the economic crisis of 1786–87 which was caused by the collapse of trade as a consequence of the American War of Independence and a catastrophic harvest. The opposition mobilized militarily, and the Austrian regime failed to hinder its military successes between 1787 and 1790. The 'Austrian' Netherlands' breakaway from the monarchy loomed. The regime's inability successfully to suppress the uprising was due above all to the Josephine policy of conquest in the Balkans, where the coalition with Russia against Turkey rapidly inspired Prussia to get involved. Prussia not only formed an alliance with Turkey, but determinedly supported the anti-Austrian opposition movements in the southern Netherlands, and also in Hungary and Galicia. The regime was able to send in troops to suppress the uprising only when the war with Turkey ended in autumn 1790. By then, however, the opposition movement had already fallen apart due to inherent class-related differences. The 'traditional' elite's aim was to create a constitution which would have invested them with their accustomed rights of domination. 'Popular' sovereignty meant for them the indirect representation of the people through the Estates. For the 'democrats', on the other hand, it meant political rights for all members of the propertied bourgeoisie (Polasky 1987: 150–52; Stradal 1968: 300–

301, 305). The civil war fought out in the summer of 1790 over this issue made it easier for the Austrian regime under the new Emperor Leopold II, who re-endowed the privileged Estates with most of their old rights, to re-conquer the southern Netherlands.

The crisis in Hungary was rooted in Josephs II's refusal to be crowned by the Estates as King of Hungary and thus to take an oath obliging him to maintain the laws and constitution of Hungary (Haselsteiner 1983; Heckenast 1985). As he also failed to convene an Estates' assembly, all his reforms in Hungary were unconstitutional. The agrarian and tax reforms had already turned the Hungarian aristocracy against the monarch. For geostrategic reasons, the war with the Ottoman Empire handed the Hungarian opposition a weapon which it could use against the monarch. At the end of 1789, the danger of a war on two fronts, against the Turks and against Prussia, began to loom. To deal with this contingency, the regime had provided for the withdrawal of troops from Hungary and their stationing in the northwest against Prussia. This meant, however, that the regime would have lacked a means of keeping the restive Hungarian nobility under control. This military dilemma – but also the uncertain situation in the 'Austrian' Netherlands – caused the monarch to withdraw his reforms in Hungary, with the exception of the Toleration Patent and the emancipation of the peasantry (Wangermann 1959: 50–55). This step was however no longer sufficient to appease the nobility. They were now determined to achieve a comprehensive modification of the constitution of the country and thus, above all, unambiguously to subordinate royal power to aristocratic control. To achieve this, the Hungarian aristocracy strove for an alliance with Prussia. The agreement between Prussia and the Austrian Monarchy in July 1790, however, shattered all Hungarian hopes. Leopold II was now able to install the troops stationed on the Silesian border in Hungary. Military resistance to the monarchy was no longer a feasible option for the Hungarian nobility.

The collapse of the aristocratic revolt in Hungary was not, however, due solely to Leopold II's success in destroying the diplomatic strategy of the aristocratic reform party. Support for the monarchy came also from the 'adjunct parts' ('*partes admixtae*') to the Hungarian Crown, above all from Croatia, Transylvania and from the Serbs of the Banat, who believed their interests would be better served by the monarchy than by the Magyar nobility. Hungary's national antagonisms, which were again to hinder resolution of the problem of political-territorial integration of the monarchy and the problem of the constitution in the 19th century, now came to the fore (Benda 1972). Apart from the opposition of the nationalities, the problem of the peasantry impacted on the policies of the Hungarian nobility, too. Not only in Bohemia, but also in Hungary, had peasant rebellions taken place that attacked the power of the manorial lords. The background to these rebellions was the fear that the reforms, which had helped improve the situation of the peasants, would be annulled. A peasants' declaration of May 1790 called for the monarch and the reform policy to be defended, by force if necessary. The peasants demanded further improvements in their lot through complete abolition of remaining labour service obligations and clearly placed themselves in the camp of Leopold II (Kiraly 1969: 241–3; 218–33; Kiraly 1967). This opened up to the nobility the dangerous prospect that the monarch and peasants might form a coalition. In view of this situation, a compromise was struck between Crown and aristocracy. Hungary was recognized as an independent kingdom, whose 'government' was to be carried out in line with the Hungarian constitution. The Habsburgs were recognized as the hereditary kings of Hungary, who 'governed' by means of laws negotiated between Crown and Parliament. Finally, the Hungarian camp recognized the 'inseparability and indivisibility' of the monarchy. With respect to agrarian matters, the provisions that formally abolished serfdom and legally regulated statute labour largely remained intact. Manorial jurisdiction also remained under state control (Rumpler 1997: 26; Csáky 1981: 40–45).

The pragmatic politics of give-and-take between Crown and aristocracy thus occurred for a number of good reasons. These were joined in 1789 by the dangers arising from the French Revolution to the territorial integrity and political constitution of the monarchy as a whole. The ideas of the revolution represented an attack on the ideological legitimacy of the traditional power structure. This in itself made it vital for the Crown and aristocracy to form a united front to ensure their survival. Military factors also played a role: the wars with revolutionary France shook the monarchy to its core. The fiscal problems thrown up by war and also the problems of administration, recruitment and provisioning of the armed forces could be tackled only through cooperation between Crown and aristocracy. This cooperation was not without its conflicts. The Supreme Judiciary [*Oberste Justizstelle*], for example, was still arguing at the end of 1792 in a 'Josephinist' manner against the claims to domination and power of the (Lower Austrian) Estates and their demand for privileged treatment:

> Only the equal treatment of citizens of all classes when matters of law, and rights to honour, freedom and property are at issue; an equality that excludes all privileges, in matters of administration of justice, which ignores all concepts of supremacy when it comes to truth – such equal treatment of the citizens of all classes is one of the rights of humanity which, since the stain of serfdom and monasticism was removed, have already been felt too strongly by the people of all states for them to be suppressed. (Quoted in Bibl 1904: 89)

Nonetheless, to the degree that the threat to the old order increased from within and without, Crown and aristocracy increasingly closed ranks (Levy 1985).

The shift away from state reform policies in the late 1780s also led to the dismissal of many Josephine officials. Increasingly politically alienated from the new regime, these reform-oriented 'enlightened' public servants founded or joined Jacobin associations that formed on the model of the societies in revolutionary France within the Habsburg Monarchy (Körner (ed.) 1972; Reinalter 1980; Reinalter 1981; Reinalter 1988a; Reinalter (ed.) 1993a; Schuh 1983; Tull 1994; Wangermann 1990). In light of the restorative politics of the post-Josephine era, these associations were convinced that a change of regime was necessary to achieve social and economic changes. Many 'Josephines' mutated from reformers interested in change within the system to 'Jacobins' keen to revolutionize it. In Hungary, too, a political opposition was gathering steam. The minor nobility, advocating national independence for Hungary, organized themselves in the 'Society of Reformists'. The aim was the establishment of a political regime under the leadership of the minor nobility, in which the privileges of the upper aristocracy and the Church hierarchy would be abolished and non-aristocratic groups would be allowed fair parliamentary representation. The 'Society of Equality and Freedom' had an even more radical agenda. Following the successful revolt of the minor nobility, the next step in social transformation should entail destruction of the power of the minor nobility through liberation of the peasants from their feudal chains and the bourgeois reordering of the Hungarian nation state (Palmer/Kenez 1961: 423–6; Bödy 1962: 11; Benda 1979: 201–3; Benda 1977; Fodor 1955; Sugar 1958).

Neither in Austria nor Hungary, however, did these conspiratorial circles represent a truly revolutionary danger to the state. The members of these organizations – intellectuals, former civil servants, Freemasons and Illuminati – tended to limit themselves to private social gatherings, reading circles and discussions, as well as the development of scientific societies and educational associations (Dann (ed.) 1981; Reinalter (ed.) 1993b; Rosenstrauch-Königsberg 1992; Schindler/Bonß 1980). There existed no 'bourgeois' class in the Habsburg Monarchy, which might have formed the mass basis for revolutionary actions. Neither did these conspiratorial organizations try to mobilize the peasantry in pursuit of their social, economic and political goals. Only with the crisis in the summer of 1794 did the possibility of a more far-reaching mobilization open up. Ernst Wangermann (1959: 141) describes pithily the political-military and socio-economic dislocations that led to the crisis:

> The failure of the (military) campaign of 1793 had shattered whatever hopes of a short war (with revolutionary France) had survived earlier disasters. The preparation of the 1794 campaign involved new financial burdens ... and a new drain of badly needed manpower from the land to re-form depleted regiments. The continued requirements of army provisions helped push up prices from the already high level prevailing since the Turkish War and jeopardized supplies for the capital. The attempts to suppress exports to Revolutionary France and, after April 1794, also to Revolutionary Poland inflicted considerable dislocation on Austrian commerce and industries. Everywhere an acute lack of money and men made itself felt. To crown all, the 1794 harvest in Hungary, the Monarchy's principal granary, was threatened by a severe drought. Inevitably, the brunt of all the hardship was borne by the non-privileged, who were still waiting for the concessions which had seemed at hand close of Leopold II's reign, but had been shelved in that of his son.

Peasant resistance to recruitment for war thus hardened in 1794, while sympathy for the French soldiers and for the ideas of the French Revolution as a whole took on force. This sympathy 'emerged in all the Habsburg provinces through which French prisoners of war had been transported, and even more in those where they finally settled' (Wangermann 1959: 142–3; Benda 1977: 278). The Jacobins tried to exploit this situation through revolutionary agitation (Reinalter 1988b; Grab 1978). As the state had been aware of the identity of the 'Jacobins' and had known about their activities since the summer of 1793, however, this challenge to the authority of the state could be dealt with without too much trouble, through police operations and the arrest, trial and execution of the 'ringleaders' in the 'Jacobin trials' of 1794 and 1795 (Schuh 1979; Schuh 1980; Wangermann 1959). The military and ideological threat from revolutionary France and the socio-political challenges to the Habsburg Monarchy from disillusioned members of the 'middle class', as well as large sections of the peasantry, spurred Crown and aristocracy to renew their cooperation.

Constitutionalism, parliamentarization and the struggle of the nationalities

The authoritarian police state that came to dominate the period between the Congress of Vienna in 1815 and the Revolution of March 1848, a period often described as *Vormärz*, arose out of the coalition between Crown and aristocracy in the crisis-ridden late 18th century. A central institution of this police state was the secret police, established already under Joseph II (Fournier 1912; Walter 1927). Under Joseph, the police increasingly lost its function as keeper of public welfare, that is, as fiscal-economic enforcer. Increasingly, its main task was defined as maintenance of public order. In the opinion of the head of the police, Count Pergen, it was the duty of the police to track down and punish, with all necessary means, 'those who stir up the gullible mass' and 'fool (the people) with regard to freedom' (Axtmann 1992). In 1801, within the context of these tasks, the 'Supreme Court Authority for Policing and Censorship' [*Polizei und Zensur-Hofstelle*] was set up – a kind of ministry of the police. Working closely together with other state bodies, such as the Central Information Committee founded in 1834, and the urban police headquarters [*Polizeidirektionen*], it supervised all police activities (Benna 1953).

The system of censorship played an important role in this until the revolutionary turbulence of 1848. The 'thaw' during the decade of the Josephine Enlightenment had led to a slackening of censorship (Bodi 1978; Bodi 1995; Sashegyi 1958). The state itself created a public sphere to accompany its reform project journalistically as it struggled against the opponents of reform. Many pamphlets were thus discretely supported by the state. Rapidly, however, a critical public sphere gathered steam which spared neither the Emperor nor his regime (Wangermann 1973: 130–47; Gnau 1911; Lettner 1988). To counter this critical public sphere, Leopold II began his propaganda war, in which he fell back on stricter censorship, a comprehensive system of propaganda, a network of informers and a reform of the school curriculum (Lettner 1988). Under Franz I the state made further efforts to bring the intellectual and cultural life of the monarchy under its control. As Oberhummer brings out in his study of the Viennese police (1938: I, 189–90), '(the state) was not content merely to take action to deal with newspapers and political criticism, but ... also launched a campaign against major writers and leading scientists. Professors were subjected to surveillance not only in their private life, but also in their lectures ... there was no freedom of teaching, learning or research in Austria.' Book auditing offices in Linz, Salzburg, Graz, Prague, Brünn, Lemberg, Milan, Venice, Zara, Ljubljana, Trieste and Innsbruck carried out censorship, and shortly before the Revolution of 1848, yet another agency overseeing censorship [*Zensur-Oberdirektion*] was established in Vienna. As early as 1834, the 'Central Information Committee' had been established under the ultimate authority of Prince Metternich. All reports by domestic and foreign authorities, officials and agents regarding publications and activities 'critical of the system' were channelled through this committee. In 1837 and 1838, special committees for Hungary, Siebenbürgen and Galicia were created and were incorporated into the Central Committee (Oberhummer 1936: 192; 197; Marx 1959).

Metternich's 'political' police 'were continually to observe and gather information in order to provide intelligence on potential sources of danger rapidly, reliably and seamlessly' (Höfer 1983: 51; Emerson 1968; Fournier 1913; Mayr 1940). How, though, was one to get hold of an opposition barred from the public sphere? 'How is one to learn about their intentions and plans, having banned political parties, prohibited journeymen from moving around, outlawed secret societies and imposed strict censorship?' (Adler 1977: 38) There was only one possible answer: through an extensive web of informers, agents and *agents provocateurs*. It was this network of informers that characterized the *Vormärz* era. The social-psychological effect of this police state has been described by Bibl (1927: 315–16):

> [It] led, as it must, to 'total apathy towards public affairs.' The 'quiet, policed atmosphere', the principle of calmness, was inevitably bound up with the dearth of any public spirit ... Now that the restraining policing ideology of the Restoration period had choked the *active* aspect of public-spiritedness, the urge to participate in the state through one's achievements, the *passive* aspect, the willingness to tolerate state-imposed restrictions, was also bound to wither. The sole component of this passive aspect of public-spiritedness that remained alive was the negative one, the right to criticize the necessity of such restrictions ... the Viennese, indeed, saw themselves as first-rate critics. (Original emphasis)

Political integration was thus to be enforced through policing measures. As in the past, however, the state bureaucracy was to be deployed as an integrating force (Hanisch 1986). As we have seen, Joseph II regarded the civil servant as a servant of the *bonum commune*, which he was encouraged actively to promote: 'He wished his officials to be priests of the state' (Heindl 1991: 22). After 1800, under

Emperor Franz, the ideal and ethos of public servants changed: 'As far as the ethos of officials was concerned, the ideal of the obedient, upright official, the recipient of orders, who did his duty and was willing to help the regime without question, could *not* be improved upon; the image of the responsible idealist who initiated reforms, for example, popular a few years before in the Josephine decade, had been dropped. Police control kept officials under surveillance, frightening the life out of them' (Heindl 1991: 47). The monarch's absolute right to issue directives and the official's strict obligation to follow orders made him an 'unscrupulous official' (Heindl 1991: 45). University studies of a legal and political nature became a prerequisite for a career in the upper echelons of the civil service. But it was not only specialist knowledge and performance that were expected, but also, above all, 'excellent morality' and 'piety' (Heindl 1991: 47). Nonetheless, the administrative system did not develop into a modern apparatus in the Weberian sense. In the 'Memoirs of an Austrian Civil Servant' [*Memoiren eines österreichischen Staatsbeamten*] from 1846, life within the Viennese bureaucracy, with its wickerwork of protectionism, patronage and clientelism, was mercilessly exposed. Byzantine organizational structures facilitated the efflorescence of a culture of intrigue and informers and allowed incompetence at all levels to be brushed under the carpet. Bureaucratic idleness and dawdling, and protectionism through doctored examinations, manipulation of job advertisements and job profiles, were as common as corruptibility and corruption among the poorly paid officials (Anonymous [A. Naske] 1846).

The American and French Revolutions in the last third of the 18th century had demonstrated a clear alternative to the bureaucratic-autocratic integration strategy: integration through constitutionalizing political rule and developing modern parliamentary representative bodies. The struggle over this integration strategy characterized the political history of the Habsburg Monarchy in the 19th century. Western 'revolutionary' constitutionalism was strongly linked with the concept of the nation-state. In the political dislocations of the French Revolution, the 'People' appointed itself the sovereign subject of history – and, consistently enough, beheaded the 'prince.' The legitimacy of the newly 'constituted' political order was rooted in the sovereignty of the People. The People understood itself as bearer of rights to political rule and formulated its demands for political autonomy and self-determination through the discourse of the 'nation.' The new state was understood as a 'nation' state; it was to be 'the state "of" and "for" a particular, distinctive, bounded nation', articulating the will of the nation and promoting its interests (Brubaker 1992: 28).

The metaphor of the 'nation' fused the plurality and antagonisms of class society into a political unity. The nation became a 'homogeneous' body endowed with sovereignty. How, though, should the 'nation' be defined, how to distinguish between 'us' and 'them'? Who or what constituted the nation? A nation could be understood as a community whose members were linked through descent and blood ties. Racial and/or ethnic-cultural commonalties are, on this view, the basis on which individuals can be integrated into the nation. Yet this idea of the 'nation' as a community of descent with a common culture and language would inevitably have implied the disintegration of the 'multi-national' Habsburg Monarchy. The French conceptualization of the 'nation-state', on the other hand, showed the potential for an understanding of the 'nation', which seemed more appropriate to the Habsburg 'multi-national state.' On the French view, the nation was understood as a unity made up of individuals, who consciously and freely banded together to form a political union and who enjoyed equal rights as citizens (Hanák 1978).

While the 'democratic' element of this concept of the nation was unacceptable even to the reformist members of the political class, the idea of the 'state-nation' allowed a discursive link to be made with the traditional 'Theresan-Josephine notion of the state'. The Austrian idea of the state in the second half of the 18th century was, after all, centred on a sense of mission, emphasizing welfare and civilizational progress. It was a state patriotism privileging the dynasty, the 'House Austria', which was simultaneously intolerant of national-particularistic crownland patriotism and of 'national' sentiment in general. As a consequence of the French Revolution, however, the concept of 'patriotism' was imbued with revolutionary tenor – with the result that Franz II (I) fell back on the revived notion of the divine right of kings and the maintenance of the power of the Imperial house, and thus placed emphasis on a supra-national and 'anti'-patriotic principle of legitimacy. The *Länder*, meanwhile, continued successfully to assert themselves in opposition to any strengthening of the Austrian state. This opposition in the *Länder* received ideological support from political romanticism, whose spiritual centre was Vienna. In the face of the omnipotent state, it privileged the individual person and individuality, hailing the cosmos of the Estates-based state rooted in pre-modern, medieval times and emphasizing universalistic Catholicism as preferable to modern, bourgeois-dominated society (Rumpler 1997: 77). The key political task was thus to maintain the Habsburg *Gesamtstaat* while recognizing the political-cultural heterogeneity of its constituent countries. Given that this emphasis on the *Gesamtstaat* inevitably entailed rejection of a Central European political order according to national(ist) principles, the issue of how best to institutionalize such political 'unity in diversity' became particularly pressing (Rumpler 1997: 135–6). The structure of the dynastic state, according to Metternich, rested on two pillars. First, it was vital to maintain the position of the 'parts' vis-à-vis the 'scourge of centralization', which reached a peak in the enlightened, rationalist welfare state, which was contrary to traditional law. Second, 'princely sovereignty' must be upheld, without which, according to Metternich, 'the Empire in its totality [*Gesammtreich*] is inconceivable, because national sovereignties cannot be positioned above one another, and the Empire, as the *Gesammtstaat*, is inconceivable under their aegis' (quoted in Rumpler 1997: 201).

One consequence of this point of view was the rejection of the notion of a representative constitution, as this would have 'brought bourgeois nationalism to power in the parliaments of the constitutive lands. Such parliaments would have plunged the unity of the state into crisis' (Rumpler 1997: 205). A further consequence was the problematic positioning of the Habsburg Monarchy within the European state system. This problem became particularly apparent in the 'German question' – as will become clearer as our account proceeds. As the disputes with Napoleon raged, the entire Austrian Monarchy was made a hereditary empire in 1804, thus transferring the idea of a supra-national locus of domination from the old Empire to Austria. The demise of the Holy Roman Imperial crown, following the founding of the Confederation of the Rhine [*Rheinbund*] in 1806, sealed the epochal shift in Austrian history: Austria parted company from Germany in full knowledge of the significance and consequences that this move entailed (Rumpler 1997: 68). Later on, Metternich made no attempt to revoke this parting of ways. As Rumpler shows, had Metternich pursued a more vigorous policy in Germany, Austria would almost certainly have become a German state and may even have led Germany:

> Such a course of action would, however, have meant a policy of privileging the German nation, an impossibility in multinational 'Austria.' Total separation from Germany (by leaving the German Confederation), meanwhile, would have driven the Germans in Austria to embrace nationalism. Austria could survive only if the Germans refrained from the obvious but dangerous path of national radicalization. Only in these circumstances could they retain their role as the key 'nation' holding up the state. This was also the prerequisite for a tense but non-violent maintenance of the Austrian *Gesammtstaat*. (Rumpler 1997: 208)

Thus, during the political and military disputes with France in the post-revolutionary era, no concept of the state took shape which might have formed the basis for the 'constitutionalization' of political domination. 'Through law and faith' [*Lege et Fide*] indeed became Franz II's (I's) credo, thus making law the foundation of the regime; but whenever the demand for freedom challenged traditional law, it was rapidly suppressed (Rumpler 1997: 30). For an extended period in the 19th century, however, ideas of a centralized constitutional state were linked with Josephine state patriotism. In the *Vormärz* period we find 'multiple layers of political ties to the dynasty, to the old *länder*, then to the peoples [*Völker*], which were gradually coming to the fore in these decades and becoming aware of themselves. There is no clear-cut and uniform orientation towards a particular "state" thought of as taking precedence over all other political entities' (Brunner 1962: 53). This background helps explain the connections between the central political conflicts that marked the 19th century Habsburg Monarchy: constitutionalism and parliamentarization on the one hand, and a federalist or an unitary-centralist approach to the struggle of nationalities on the other.

These conflicts rose to prominence in the revolutionary year of 1848. It is vital here to take into account the socio-economic aspect of the revolutionary upheaval within the Habsburg Monarchy. The state finances were a disaster. In the *Vormärz* era, national debt had risen to 1.131 billion guilders by 1847; in the same year, state expenditure was 208 million guilders, compared with a net state revenue of only 151million (Sandgruber 1995: 225). This acute fiscal crisis contributed to the erosion of the political system and led to calls for constitutional control of state finances. The economic dislocations can be traced to the total economic collapse of 1816. The depression that this triggered

> lasted until 1825/26. The half-decade following 1825 is frequently described as the real beginning of Austrian industrialization ... while growth rates slowed after 1830, recovery was apparent throughout Austria by the mid-1830s. The period between 1825 and 1844 represented a relatively lengthy period of progress ... Only from 1844 to 1848 did the serious depression, whose effects were still being felt in the 1850s, unfold. (Sandgruber 1995: 178–9)

The impoverishment of much of the labour force during the acute economic crisis radicalized the 'social question', already virulent in the preceding decades as an aspect of the class formation triggered by capitalist industrialization. We should however bear in mind that the 'social question' also applied to the peasantry, finding political expression in the call for reducing the financial and labour obligations of the peasants and the abolition of patrimonial jurisdiction.

The 'social question' was, however, marginalized by the 'constitutional question.' Neither the national problems of the Austrian *Gesamtstaat* nor the social problems of the workers and peasants were taken into account in the citizens' petition [*Bürgerpetition*] of 11 March 1848. Nonetheless, the constitutional demands, also made by students, were far-reaching. Freedom of the press, freedom of conscience, freedom of teaching and learning; the introduction of jury courts; reform of the *Länder* constitutions and the creation of autonomous municipal bodies; removal of the burdens borne by peasants and the legal status for Jews; but above all the call for all laws to be subject to parliamentary approval – measured by the political standards of the *Vormärz* period, these were revolutionary demands, largely put forward by members of the urban educated middle class and the business bourgeoisie (Kann 1974: 300; Rumpler 1997: 277). It had become possible to formulate these demands in the pre-revolutionary era because Metternich's police state had become permeable. Censorship had slackened and the first signs of a public sphere were beginning to appear in the network of associations and in publishing. Literature and journalism, primarily from Saxony and Hamburg, had gained currency, while publications, in particular by Austrian emigrants, had become accessible. Organizations such as the 'Legal and Political Reading Association' [*Juridisch-Politische Leseverein*], the 'Trade and Manufacturing Association' [*Gewerbeverein*] and the writers' organization 'Concordia' had become the first shapers of a new, liberal public opinion (Lutz 1985: 236).

The Pillersdorf Constitution of 25 April 1848 incorporated the central constitutional demand for parliamentary approval of all laws. By stipulating, however, that this approval must be obtained through the Senate, which represented the owners of the large estates, as well as the Parliament, whose members were to obtain their mandate through *Zensuswahlrecht* (limited franchise according to wealth), it ultimately contributed to further political radicalization. The liberals were dissatisfied because of the Senate's power of veto, and the radicals because of the restriction of suffrage to tax-payers: 'They demanded "general suffrage" for members of the petit-bourgeoisie who paid little tax, waged workers and the bulk of domestic servants and the unemployed' (Rumpler 1997: 280). Their 'Storm Petition' [*Sturmpetition*] of 15 May 1848 articulated the rise of the 'democrats' and caused the Emperor and the royal household to flee to Innsbruck. These constitutional disputes between the government, the bourgeois-liberals and the radical democrats coloured the discussions of the constitution in the Imperial Diet, established in July 1848. As late as early 1849, after the Imperial Diet had been relocated from Vienna to Kremsier and threatened with dissolution by the revived *ancien régime*, consideration was still given to 'linking the construction of ministerial responsibility while at the same denying any responsibility of the Emperor who, however, formally possessed executive power with the curtailment of the monarch's position in legislative matters to a mere power of delay' (Brandt 1985: 81). Nothing less than the parliamentarization of government was up for discussion.

To attain a comprehensive understanding of the Revolution of 1848, however, one must do more than link the constitutional question to the 'social question' (Häusler 1981). For it was the 'national question' that gave the revolution much of its flavour. The very survival of the Habsburg Monarchy as a multinational state was at stake. The year 1848 saw the 'springtime of peoples' [*Völkerfrühling*], the point in history when 'peoples' all over Europe defined themselves as 'nations' and clamoured for the right to live in the state in which their nation was located and to gain a state for their particular nation.

The nationalism of the *Vormärz* era had become emancipated from an 'Estates-based' consciousness of the unity of the 'country' – less so in Hungary, where the new national consciousness grew within the framework of the old Estates' constitution, but certainly in Bohemia and Moravia, and also in 'Slovenia' and of course strikingly in Italy and in the context of the 'German question'. The growing national consciousness now increasingly privileged the 'language community' and notions of cultural belonging and nourished nationalism as a political movement.

The 'national question' involved two key components. In connection with the revolutionary movement in Germany and the efforts of the political forces in the parliament in Frankfurt, the question of Austria's membership in any future German nation state came to the fore: 'Was Austria prepared to separate its territories situated in the future German state from the non-German ones and to limit its "umbrella statehood" [*Gesamtstaatlichkeit*] in favour of a mere personal union?' (Bruckmüller 1985: 353; Rumpler 1997: 310). The government at least failed to show such willingness. A declaration of April 1848 made it clear that

> Fully committed to a close union with Germany, Austria will happily grasp every opportunity which helps realize its devotion to the common German cause. It could, however, never agree to a complete abandonment of the special interests of its various

> territories belonging to the German Confederation, to an unconditional subordination to the federal assembly [*Bundesversammlung*], and to an abandonment of the independence of domestic administration ... (Quoted in Lutz 1985: 255)

In the German National Assembly in Frankfurt, however, the notion gained currency of a large, united and powerful Germany, whose political form would leave behind the 'German Confederation' and which would be turned into a federal state with a strong central government. In line with this, the Constitution of 27 October 1848 stipulated that no part of the German Empire could be united in a state with a non-German country. Where this was the case, the relationship between the German and non-German state should be reduced to a personal union. Membership of the 'Germanic nation-state' would have spelt the collapse of the Habsburg Monarchy and meant carving it up into the portion of the alpine lands and Sudetenland that would belong to the German state and the lands and territories of Hungary, Galicia and Lombardy-Venice, which were to be independent of the German Empire. Within the affiliated Habsburg lands, it would have meant privileging the 'German nation'; this would have entailed the risk of further fragmentation along ethno-cultural lines (Rumpler 1997: 310–13). The remaking of the German Confederation as a German national state thus involved an existential question for Austria. Austria's answer was the rejection of this idea for dynastic reasons and out of adherence to the idea of the *Gesamtstaat* and the responsibility for its multinational empire. This meant that the German-speaking groups in Austria either had to distance themselves from the Imperial house or throw in their lot with it (even) more decisively, if they were to hold their own in the struggle of the nationalities. This situation of the German speakers in Austria also explains their majority support for the unitary, centralized Austrian state.

The issue of union with Germany was just one aspect of the 'national question'. There was also the question of whether the dynastic Austrian Monarchy could continue to exist despite its internal conundrum of nationality. Would the 'association of states', constituted by the monarchy since 1526, be shattered by the national demands of its constitutive 'peoples'? Both aspects of the 'national question' could be fused, as evidenced by the development of Austroslavism in Bohemia and Moravia. The holding of elections to the German national parliament, demanded by Frankfurt and accepted by Vienna, met with resistance from Czech nationalism. For the Czechs, participation in the elections and incorporation in a German nation-state meant the loss of their national identity. Franz Palacky, the leader of the Czech nationalist movement, defined himself as 'a Bohemian of Slav ancestry' and developed an Austroslavic position, which embraced the retention of the Austrian Monarchy, the principle of the equality of all Austrian nationalities and religious groups, a warning of the danger of a Russian universal monarchy and a plea for a customs union between Germany and Austria (Lutz 1985: 256). With this standpoint, the Bohemian-Czech nation bid farewell to German history and committed itself to the idea of the multinational Habsburg Monarchy as protector of the smaller nations of Central Europe. Yet, the Bohemian Germans professed loyalty to the idea of German-Austrian unity, thus foreshadowing the nationality-based conflicts of the following decades (Rumpler 1997: 293–4).

The Imperial Diet was thus unable to avoid the 'national question.' The Kremsier constitutional committee settled on a federalization of the western half of the empire on the basis of historical and federalist principles: 'An ingenious compromise between federalism and centralism provided that the nationally mixed crownlands should be subdivided into homogeneous districts, whose representatives were added to the crownland delegations in the upper chamber. Thus the traditional political entities were preserved and yet a national organization on the lower administrative level was provided. It was to serve the interest of the national minorities in the multinational crownlands' (Kann 1974: 311; Rumpler 1997: 315). Through this construction, the problem of nationality was however ultimately conceived as a problem of regionalism: protection for nationalities was taken into account with the division of the larger districts into districts on ethnic grounds and the transfer of certain rights to autonomous administrative bodies, especially in matters of language. Equal status for all languages was also constitutionally anchored. The fact that the nationalities were no longer present at the level of the *Länder* and the *Gesamtstaat* was however to prove a disadvantage in the course of the following decades (Brandt 1985: 81).

The immediate reason for the defeat of the revolution was the state's military successes under Windisch-Grätz in Prague and Vienna, Jellacic in Hungary and Radetzky in Italy. The revolution, though, was not defeated through military might alone. After 'feudal' relations in the countryside had been abolished, the peasants lost their revolutionary élan. As soon as the working class had questioned private property, the bourgeoisie left the class coalition against the regime. The 'national question' became radicalized through the Hungarian Revolution, the uprising of Italians within the Empire and the Kingdom of Sardinia and the Congress of Slavs in Prague, thus threatening the unity and survival of the monarchy. The 'constitutional issue' was thus marginalized and the Viennese bourgeoisie, at least, gradually slotted itself back into the old regime: the Austrian *Gesamtstaat* was not to be given up (Rumpler 1997: 285).

Following dissolution of the Imperial Diet in Kremsier, the regime 'imposed' the March Constitution. This did not in fact take effect, but the Imperial Manifesto, which introduced the constitution, clearly summarized its intentions:

> to bring into harmony the unity of the whole with the autonomy and free development of its parts, a strong central power protecting law and order throughout the Reich with the freedom of the individual, the municipalities, the lands of our Crown and the diverse nationalities, the founding of a powerful administration, which keeps an equal distance from cramping centralization and fragmenting dissolution, while safeguarding sufficient room for manoeuvre for the noble forces of the country. (Quoted in Hantsch 1968: 340)

The Emperor's power was also secured through a comprehensive Imperial prerogative; executive power, indivisible and in its entirety, as it was expressed, lay in his hands. Rights to personal freedom, moreover, as conceived in the Kremsier draft constitution, were left untouched. Also as in that document, each 'descent group' [*Volksstamm*] was constitutionally guaranteed the 'inviolable right to keep and maintain its nationality and language' (Paragraph 6; cf. Hantsch 1968: 340–41).

The neo-absolutist regime, established after the putting down of the 1848 revolution, attempted institutionally to secure the centralist, hierarchical evolution of the state (Brandt 1978). The foundation of dynastic-centralist absolutism was the Sylvester or New Year's Eve Patent of 1851. It gave short shrift to the idea of representative government and national sentiments. While the crownlands remained a component of the Austrian Monarchy, the patent imposed a hierarchical administrative structure that established direct political control from Vienna. The autonomy of municipalities was removed, as was the separation of justice and administration at the lowest level. Jury courts were abolished, and judges were placed on a par with civil servants, removing their freedom from dismissal. The Emperor took over direct leadership of the government, which meant the tacit dismissal of the prime ministers and the removal of ministers' responsibility to Parliament. Pursuing a policy of 'dynastic centralization' (Mann 1993: 338) the regime also made efforts to develop a uniform administrative apparatus, whose officials were directly bound to the monarch and whose pledges of loyalty and oaths of office vis-à-vis the monarch took precedence over those to the state. The language of this bureaucracy was German: more than ever, the community of German speakers [*Deutschtum*] appeared to be the state's main support. On the other hand 'the other nations were averse not only to the government by officials, but also to *Deutschtum*' (Hantsch 1968: 346). Army and bureaucracy became the bearers *par excellence* of the political and cultural concept of the Austrian *Gesamtstaat*, while much was again made of the church's integrative significance: 'The Church was now not only in control of religious instruction but was empowered to see to it that teaching in any secular discipline (languages, history, science), must not be in conflict with the tenets of religious instruction. The Church also assumed the right of censorship of literature potentially dangerous to youth and the faithful altogether ... The new policy was backed largely by police informers ...' (Kann 1974: 322; cf. Hantsch 1968: 346–7). The Concordat agreed in 1855 between the Austrian Monarchy and the Roman Curia was intended ideologically to reinforce the hegemony of the Catholic House of Habsburg and lend strength to the monarchy as a major 'Catholic' power in its struggle to assert itself within Germany against Protestant Prussia and secular liberalism (Rumpler 1997: 347). The calculated development and instalment of the *Gendarmerie* as ancillary troops, whose task it was to support the bureaucracy, and the stationing of troops in Hungary to enforce its military subordination to the central government if need be, signalled the regime's readiness to ensure its continued existence by force, should this prove necessary.

The effort to achieve political integration through parliamentarization and federalization was thus abandoned once again, and the regime fell back on the old mechanisms of bureaucratic and military integration. As a 'bureaucratic modernizing dictatorship' (Brandt 1985) neo-absolutism was an attempt to catch up with the level of development in other Western states. The establishment of a unified customs system within the monarchy in 1850–51 was an early sign of the economic reforms measures and economic stimulation attempted within neo-absolutism. As Brandt (1988: 142) shows, this policy caused an 'industrial capitalist grand bourgeoisie, of German and German-Jewish provenance – with predominantly Austrian roots – to expand enormously or indeed to get off the ground in the first place'. Brandt, however, also points out that this class generally eschewed risk-taking. This attitude showed in economic terms in the desire for state protectionism; mentally, it meant 'a willingness to be integrated into Court culture through participation in the generous practice of ennoblement, hitherto mainly of benefit to the armed forces and the bureaucracy' and 'melting into the "second" Viennese society (high finance, bureaucracy and education) and its highly cultivated hedonism' (Brandt 1988: 142–3).

As so often in the history of the Habsburg Monarchy, the regime failed because of military defeats and fiscal crises. Defeat by the French in Solferino and the loss of Lombardy in 1859 clearly demonstrated the failure of neo-absolutism to secure Austria's position as a major European power. The crisis that hit the state finances – not least as a result of military expenditure – laid bare the monarchy's economic weakness: total national debt was 3 billion guilders, while annual state revenue came to 300 million; 140 million of this had to be used to service the debt (Sandgruber 1995: 243). Neo-absolutism was as incapable of meeting the fiscal demands made on it as the regime had been before the 1848 revolution. The regime was thus forced, after little more than a decade, 'to consider the legitimizing potential of a representative body and embrace the constitutionalism of 1848 and 1849' (Ucakar 1985: 551).

The bureaucracy and the grand bourgeoisie saw the military economy and permanent deficit as the state's most serious defects. They thus tried to secure the unitary state of 1849 by installing centralized parliamentary checks on the government. The strategy of political integration through constitutionalization and parliamentarization thus took centre stage once again. The neo-absolutist regime had however not only politically marginalized the bourgeoisie, but through the process of bureaucratization had also deprived the traditional feudal powers of their customary rights of domination. The crisis of neo-absolutism in 1859 now opened up the possibility, particularly for the Hungarian and Bohemian nobility, to intervene in the debate on reform of political institutions with a conservative, historicizing, federalist agenda. This agenda opened to the monarch the prospect 'both of gaining the Magyars' approval and securing comprehensive monarchical prerogatives, hindering real constitutionalization and securing the *Reich* the quality as a state, as achieved in 1849, by introducing partial administrative autonomy for the historic lands while re-establishing traditional noble leadership and consenting to modest semi-parliamentary budgetary control at the centre' (Brandt 1988: 143).

Tussles between 'federalists' and 'centralists' were thus disputes between aristocracy and bourgeoisie.

The options for political integration found constitutional expression. During the course of the political crisis, the large estates were first shown preference in the 'October Diploma' of 1860; it was then the grand bourgeoisie's turn in the 'February Patent' of 1861. The 'October Diploma' provided for 'participation' by the Imperial Council [*Reichsrat*] and the diets of the *Länder* in Imperial lawmaking. They possessed, however, no legislative initiative whatsoever and thus remained confined to the role of advisory bodies. While the Imperial Council gained the right to assent to the raising of new taxes and borrowing, it failed to achieve full rights to approve taxes or even comprehensive budgetary powers. Insofar as the Imperial Council was made up of representatives from the *Länder* assemblies, and was thus a de facto committee formed by the latter, the composition of the diets was of particular import to the question of political participation. As a matter of fact, nobility and clergy were again taken more fully into account, while the bourgeoisie and the class of civil servants received less attention (Brandt 1985: 90–91).

A construction of this nature was, however, incapable of tackling the real problem – the regime's dependence on the economic power of the bourgeoisie, which rendered the former unable entirely to disregard the latter's claim to rights of political participation. While the 'October Diploma' clearly attempted to take into account the autonomy of the crownlands, the 'February Patent' of 1861 was a centralizing-liberal constitution, which particularly emphasized the municipal autonomy – and thus opened up potential political space for the bourgeoisie. The central state institutions were also reformed. The Imperial Council was divided into a house of lords (composed of the Habsburg archdukes, high ecclesiastical figures and men nominated by the Monarch) and a parliament on the English model: 'The house of lords constituted ... a highly conservative element, an elite made up of men, who stood out through birth or office, service and spiritual achievements, an effective counterweight to any democratic tendencies in the parliament, whose 343 members ... were dispatched by the diets' (Hantsch 1968: 360). The Imperial Council had the right of legislative initiative; for a bill to become law, however, it required both the approval of a majority in both houses and the sanction of the Crown. The diets for their part consisted of four curia: large estates, chambers of commerce, towns and markets, and rural communities. The electoral system meant that alongside the traditional elite of large estates, finance, industry and bureaucracy, the urban bourgeoisie and wealthy peasants now also gained political representation. This constitutional change paved the way for bourgeois liberalism's entry into politics (Rumpler 1997: 378). At the same time, however, the electoral system favoured those social layers and institutions in which *Deutschtum* dominated. The new constitutional order ultimately 'aimed to consolidate the state by securing German supremacy politically' (Rumpler 1997: 378, 383–4). This paved the way for a further intensification of nationality-based discord.

A distinction was also introduced between the 'entire Imperial Council' (with the Hungarian Crown) and the 'narrower Imperial Council' (without Hungary). The 'entire Imperial Council' was to deal with all matters affecting the monarchy as a whole: the army, customs and trade, state budget, finance, credit and coinage, taxes and duties as well as with international treaties. Hungary, however, refused to send representatives to the Imperial Council. Politically, this meant that the government had the authority to pursue these matters in its own way. A further consequence was the dissolution of the Hungarian Diet; Hungary became again subject to absolutist rule. For the Western half of the empire, on the other hand, the construction of the 'narrow Imperial Council' entailed the establishment of a more coherent representative body. Yet, Hungary was not alone in refusing to send representatives to the Imperial Council (Rumpler 1997: 380–82). From 1863, the Czech National Party stayed away from it; and Poland, too, boycotted it for a time. In view of such resistance, which clearly demonstrated the failure of the constitution as a mechanism of political integration – particularly in the struggle of nationalities – it was suspended in September 1865.

Once again it was a military defeat that forced political reform. Austria's defeat in the war with Prussia at Königgrätz (Sadowa) in 1866 not only lost it Venetia, but finally excluded it from participating in the formation of the German national state. The Prussian notion that the German nation possessed a revolutionary right to a national state had prevailed over the Austrian-Habsburg idea that the state must take precedence over the nation, that Europe required a federative political structure and that Germany was best served by a 'federal' system. With the dissolution of the German Federation, Austria ceased to be a 'German power' (Nipperdey 1983: 768–93; Rumpler 1997: 386–401).

One consequence of the defeat was the restructuring of the empire as the Dual Monarchy of Austria-Hungary through the 'Compromise' [*Ausgleich*] of 1867. The two independent, constitutional monarchies were linked through personal union, but each had its own Imperial Diet. Only the army, foreign affairs and finances remained in common. To pass resolutions on these shared matters, delegations from both Imperial parliaments met for separate sessions, alternating annually between Vienna and Budapest. The important areas of foreign and security policy thus lay beyond the authority of each country's government and parliament. As far as top-level politics was concerned, the parliaments were thus unable to develop into centres of debate or to mould the public mood (Brandt 1985: 100). The costs of shared matters were split between the two halves of the Empire, though Hungary ('Transleithania') paid only 30 per cent, Austria ('Cisleithania') 70 per cent. Negotiations had to be held every ten years to adjust these quotas, which were later changed to 36.4:64.6. This 'adjustment' was always liable to become the focal point of political controversies (Rumpler 1997: 411–16). Anderson's (1974: 325) summary of the significance of the 'adjustment' is compelling:

> The Dualism which created 'Austria-Hungary' in 1867, gave the Magyar landowning class complete domestic power in Hungary, with its own government, budget, assembly,

> and bureaucracy ... While in Austria, civic equality, freedom of expression and secular education now had to be yielded by the Monarchy, in Hungary no such concessions were made by the gentry. The Hungarian nobility henceforward represented the militant and masterful wing of aristocratic reaction in the Empire .

This was thus the other outcome of the defeat at Königgrätz (Sadowa): another step towards a constitutional monarchy, on a parliamentary basis, in 'Cisleithania'. The December Laws of 1867 formed the constitutional foundation for this (Rumpler 1997: 416–19). They standardized a comprehensive constitutional package of basic rights and introduced a strict separation of judicial and executive powers. The creation of an Imperial Court was a further step in the direction of a 'constitutional state'. Attempts were made to solve the problem of ministerial responsibility through a judicial arrangement (impeachment of ministers), but this was not transferred to the parliamentary level (that is, by means of the parliamentary vote of confidence). Measures were also introduced to hinder the parliamentarization of government. There was thus no provision for binding government to Parliament's confidence; the government also continued to enjoy the authority to issue emergency decrees. Together with its unlimited right to dissolve or convene parliament and the establishment of immunity for key monarchical prerogatives in the military domain and in foreign policy, this significantly curtailed the parliament's sphere of activity.

The Parliament lost its character as a committee of *Länder* representatives in 1873 through the introduction of direct elections. The system of curia and the census-based electoral system were, however, retained. The electoral system ensured that only around 6 per cent of the adult male population were entitled to vote. Changes to the system in 1882 increased the number of voters in the cities by a third and in rural communities by one-quarter: 'From here on the question of electoral reforms tending in the direction of general, equal, male franchise came more to the attention of the public' (Kann 1974: 425; also: 346, 357–8). These reforms to the franchise, however, now led to a politicization of the masses with nationalism, anti-Semitism and the 'social question' being the most influential mobilizing factors (Rumpler 1997: 488–504).

Ucakar (1985: 554) points out that the success of 1873 was not achieved through a mass movement, but was rather a 'success of the centralism supported by the Austrian-German bourgeoisie.' As a consequence of the 1848 Revolution and the 'springtime of peoples' the bourgeoisie of the Habsburg Monarchy, which had previously spoken German as a 'class language', from now on evolved into a consciously 'German' bourgeoisie or one conscious of having its own national identity: 'From now on we can speak of "national" bourgeoisies, whose conscious core everywhere was the educated classes ... followed by the business bourgeoisie' (Bruckmüller 1991: 85). 'The German bourgeoisie now identified ever more clearly with the Habsburg state ... This identification ... no doubt grew to the extent that people felt threatened by the appearance of new, national, non-German bourgeois groupings' (Bruckmüller 1991: 86). Bruckmüller further states that, during the phase of 'liberal' centralism in the period following neo-absolutism, the bourgeoisie seized power

> not (thanks to) its own efforts ... but ... (because of) the weakness of the traditional power-holders, who obviously now allowed the German bourgeoisie a share of power not because it wished to cede power, but in order to retain it. The still high degree of Imperial power was acceptable to the old bourgeois elements as long as it helped maintain their own relatively privileged position. This liberalism thus remained very limited in nature; the unconditional state patriotism of large parts of this bourgeoisie is thus understandable. (Bruckmueller 1991: 87–8)

It was only after the definitive exclusion of Austria from the formation of the German national state after 1866 that radical German 'national' groups formed who no longer felt themselves to be 'German Austrians' but rather 'Austrian Germans.' These groups demanded that Austria be made into a German state and identified more with the German Empire than the Habsburg Monarchy. In such circumstances, a federalist solution to the cohabitation of Slavs and Germans was impossible. We must not, however, forget that any federation that would guarantee the Slavs equality or influence would have been rejected by the Magyars, both in their own Hungarian sphere of power, and in Cisleithania – Hungary's interest in the 'compromise' lay in the linking of Hungary with a German-led Austria, 'in order to secure Magyar rule in Hungary, especially over the Slavs. In brief, dualism rested on the supremacy of the Magyars and the Germans and the comprehensive exclusion of the Slavs from power on both sides' (Nipperdey 1983: 792–3).

Because of its privileged position within the state, German-Austrian liberalism could not be truly emancipatory. Any extension of rights to democratic participation would inevitably raise fears among the liberals and the *Deutschnationalen* that they might lose their supremacy: they risked being outvoted, above all by the Slavic nations (Ucakar 1985: 562–3; Bruckmüller 1984: 205). It was thus characteristic of – and ultimately fateful for – the political dynamics of the Habsburg Monarchy in the 19th century that processes of nation formation and democratization developed concurrently. At the level of the party system, this meant that parties could form only around a limited number of ideological or interest-specific cleavages; 'national' concerns and considerations remained paramount (Hanisch 1994: 230). There existed around 40 political parties. More important for the issue of representation, however, was the fact that national groups were represented by one or more deputies, 'who stood for different social and cultural interests, conservative, agrarian, clerical, liberal, later also socialist. These deputies of the nine Cisleithanian national groups were organized in loose organizations, such as the Czech or Polish club, the German United Left, or since 1910 the so-called German *Nationalverband*, which comprised about ten political parties' (Kann 1974: 430–31).

As a consequence, a fragile, regionally and nationally fragmented party system came into being, rather poorly organized at the central level, and above all undisciplined: 'As long as the parties and nationalities engaged in mutual obstruction, the prerogatives of the Crown and the dominance of the central bureaucracy remained untouched' (Hanisch 1994: 210). This was bound to have consequences for the political culture: 'It was not the democratic, but authoritarian element that was strengthened' (Hanisch 1994: 211). Above all, the simultaneity of constitutionalization, nation building and democratization, in a context in which one nation was privileged, meant that the struggle of nationalities was not dealt with as a constitutional issue. The failure to appreciate this constitutional point was also rooted in the fact that the struggle of nationalities was argued out politically 'in the form of conflicts over language and official languages, the problem of schools for minorities and national educational establishments' (Mommsen 1979: 155; Rumpler 1997: 504–14; Stourzh 1980). The famous Article 19 of the Constitution of December 1867 had fostered this kind of politicization of the struggle of nationalities. It recognized the equal status of all 'customary' languages in schools, official authorities and in public life, to be guaranteed by the state, and granted equality to all 'ethnic groups' [*Volksstämmen*]: each *Volksstamm* in the empire was granted 'an inviolable right to keep and maintain its nationality and language.' A constitutionally enshrined right to national affiliation was thus established. The *Volksstämme* were not, however, granted the status of legal entities with their own institutions. The treatment of national matters on the basis of individual rights was thus established. This failed to resolve the conundrum 'that the nationalities were striving for political influence and a share in the power to govern ... Already at the time of the Compromise with Hungary, mere national-cultural guarantees no longer (satisfied) the Austrian nationalities ... The key demand was to constitute the nationalities politically not as groups in need of protection from the state, but as groups seeking influence at the level of the state' (Mommsen 1979: 129).

Legally and politically, it was impossible constitutionally to accommodate the *Struggle of the Nations for the State* (Karl Renner) by means of parliamentary mediation. The Dual Monarchy disintegrated through its inability to solve the problem of political representation and participation and effectively to tackle the struggle of nationalities. The fact that this collapse occurred within the context of military defeats in the First World War once again lays bare the significance of geopolitical factors and military misfortune for the Habsburg Monarchy, throughout its history and until its bitter end.

Chapter 4

Feudal Patrimonialism and Ecclesiastical Coercion of Conscience in Austria

Literary examples from the end of the era

Even at the start of the 20th century, the Austrian habitus reflected the history of the centuries-old processes of state formation. We still find clear evidence of 'manorial absolutism' – despite today's fashionable talk of 'Viennese Modernity'. The same is true of 'confessional absolutism', in which the church functions as organ and instrument of state rule. And in a multiplicity of ways that hit home daily, one was reminded that scions of ancient warrior castes, along with their code of conduct, still set the social tone and impregnated attitudes with their mentality. How did this affect the Austrian habitus? What continued to shape the psychic life of the individual despite the social changes to the economy, (state) administration and family? Belletristic literature gives us graphic descriptions of how top-down relationships were actually experienced in those times.

Our first case shows how fathers and sons interrelate in an upper-class setting that is still semi-feudal and steeped in aristocratic ways. *Radetzkymarsch* [The Radetzky March], perhaps Joseph Roth's most famous novel, was published in 1932. Due no doubt to its airing on national television in two screen versions, Austrians are unlikely to forget the scene where Baron von Trotta greets his son at the start of the holiday season.

> He reserved the entire morning, from nine to twelve, for his son. Punctually at ten minutes to nine, a quarter hour after early mass, the boy stood in his Sunday uniform outside his father's door. At five minutes to nine, Jacques, in his gray butler's livery, came down the stairs and said, 'Young master, your Herr Papá is coming.' Carl Joseph gave his coat a last tug, adjusted the waist belt, took off the cap, and, as prescribed by regulations, propped it against his hip.
>
> The father arrived; the son clicked his heels; the noise snapped through the hushed old house. The old man opened the door and with a slight wave of his hand motioned for his son to precede him. The boy stood still; he did not respond to the invitation. So the father stepped through the door. Carl Joseph followed hut paused on the threshold. 'Make yourself comfortable!' said the district captain after a while. It was only now that Carl Joseph walked over to the large red-plush armchair and sat down opposite his father, his knees drawn up stiffly and the cap and white gloves upon them. (Roth 1995: 21)

This scene contains some familiar elements and, when we stop to reflect, very much that is weird. There is the hierarchic disparity we can certainly recognize even today in official and formal situations; there are also the concomitant feelings of uneasiness in the presence of overbearing authority (even if it would be hard to find anyone now who clicks their heels!). Father–son encounters these days look rather different – gone is the dramatic enactment of respect and obedience. Yet, exotic, too, would be the uniform. It reminds us that the military was once a pillar of state authority. We have before us members of a relatively new aristocratic family – Carl Joseph's grandfather, the 'Hero of Solferino', had only a short while before been raised to the nobility. As a ranking district captain, his father was a member of the monarchy's senior civil service and as such part of Austria's 'Second Society' (Bruckmüller/Stekl 1988: 173). At the same time, however, he was kept at arm's length by the ancient hereditary nobility. Yet this group remained under the 'feudal' thumb or was itself feudalized, as one can witness in the passage quoted above. Having been packed off to a military academy because of the social background of his family, the young von Trotta is socialized into military traditions and ways of life according to the code of the ancient warrior nobility. The military spirit also imbues domestic interaction with paternal authority. The warrior code, to be sure, is overlaid with no small number of elements stemming from the educated classes. Nevertheless, it forms a nucleus in terms of which the 'affective household' of the young baron is imprinted – a code of honour, a sense of fate, an insouciant attitude to money and women, but, first and foremost, a culture of command and obedience. All of these values are diametrically opposed to the ethos of the bourgeoisie and professional middle classes with their penchant for an arduously acquired education and for self-discovery, their compulsive need to take the initiative, and their commitment to self-regulation. Benign authority in the family that was based on command and obedience as well as benevolence (from above) and child-like love (from below), has also been typical of vertical relations of super- and subordination in the extra-familial domain, relations that are often, though simplistically, called 'patriarchal.'

In this study, we follow Max Weber's terminology as developed in his 'sociology of domination': 'patriarchal' means all forms of authority that are tied to paternal (and therefore male) domestic power exercised over women, children, servants and slaves in a peasant society. Weber uses the concept in the context of his analysis of Greek and Roman Antiquity and the agrarian Middle Ages. 'Patrimonial', in contrast, means protective custody in the sense of expanded power of coercion also over those not residing and living 'under one roof', the by-product of a process where the *oikos* of autarkic and unitary production, protection and maintenance has given way to differentiation and re-integration on a higher level. Patrimonial domination therefore applies primarily to serfs and copy-holders who are dependent on the lord of the manor. Weber understands Western feudalism as a special case in which prebendal elements mingle with vassalage. In the West, manorial lordship and military super- and subordination are articulated in ways different from China, for example, where the military aspects of vassalage or fealty were absent. Or, to take the Japanese case, vassalage at least in the late phase was dissociated from landownership (Arnason 1997). Weber (1978: II, 1106) argued that feudalism and patrimonialism are antithetical notions: 'Feudalism is always domination by the few who have military skills. Patriarchal patrimonialism is mass domination by one individual'. In the first case, the typically Western coupling of honour and fealty is characteristic, in the sense that faithful service cannot impugn honour (only Japan resembles Europe in this respect). In the second case, a 'patrimonial' figuration, while also based on fealty and sentiments of piety on the part of the weaker, does not recognize the subject who is being protected as a bearer of honour. These are, of course, ideal-typical distinctions. In the real world we find configurations that exhibit all three features: the household of aristocrat and peasant alike is patriarchically organized, the relationship between them patrimonial; while the nobleman's position in the overall social pyramid of power partly depends on his rank, his prestige as a member of an especially privileged group endowes him with a distinctive honour. These conceptual distinctions underpin the following considerations. 'Paternalism' is quite different from patrimonialism, signifying as it does a form of relationship in which the 'paternal' powers of domination only exist more metaphorically. In contrast to patrimonial Austria, this applies especially to the 'administration by notables' of the English gentry. According to Weber (1978: II, 1059–60), this group owes its genesis to the commercialization of agriculture and the concomitant acquisition of new administrative functions. As shown in a previous chapter, the unsalaried justice of the peace was emblematic of this rule of notables.

All these types of rule, however, stand in stark contrast to bureaucratic rule, with its familiar principles of impersonality and calculability, of adherence to law and statute, of going through the prescribed channels of appeal and keeping exact records. These 'ideal-typical', abstract and material, features of bureaucracy are married with the more personal features of patrimonialism in a 'patrimonial-bureaucratic' system.

The literature on the late monarchy provides many examples of just such a patrimonial order – often tending to idealize. It is in this context that Claudio Magris (1988) speaks of the 'Habsburg myth.' This myth was spawned chiefly by the backward-looking nostalgia of contemporaries, but was also in part due to their fear of the future. But it would be wrong not to acknowledge that this literature was often realistic and able to put its finger on the vulnerabilities of this order and to pinpoint its emerging adversaries. To take one case, Ferdinand von Saar depicted in a series of novellas and several major novels the feudal patriarchalism that still obtained in the early twentieth century. After all, we must not forget that even in the progressive western parts, bounded by the present-day borders of Austria, some 40 per cent of the active population worked on the land, as opposed to only 5 per cent in Britain (Bodzenta et al. 1985: 35; Taylor 1988: 437). Von Saar shows authority in an essentially benign guise – despite its being undermined by forces of commercialization (the aristocracy of money) and an intelligentsia keen to subvert public order. 'The dignity of decay', as C. Magris (1988) puts it, is written on the faces of von Saar's characters. In the novella Doctor Trojan (von Saar, 1980; first published in 1899) we find the narrator, who lives, as if nothing came more naturally, on the 'manor of R...' in Moravia, being addressed by the obsequious merchant Nezbada in respectful tones: 'May I be so bold, sir, as to assume that your excellency are the lord of the castle?' (von Saar 1980: 4). In another of von Saar's novellas, a high-ranking official displays benign authority when he ensures a favorable finding in the tragic case of the stone-breaker Georg (guilty, as it happens, of manslaughter) so that Georg can marry his faithful sweetheart (von Saar 1993; first published in 1874). Joseph Roth gives a list of all the things a count in Galicia could do for the common people should he be favourably disposed to them, as tradition prescribed:

> For by virtue of his natural authority, Count Morstin was able to secure tax reductions, to get the sickly sons of some Jews excused from military service, to forward petitions for clemency, to obtain reduced sentences for innocent or too harshly punished prisoners, to secure lower train fares for poor people, to get gendarmes, policemen, and officials who had gone beyond the limits to account for themselves, to get trainee teachers promoted to Gymnasium posts, to find retired NCOs a niche in civilian life as managers of Trafik stores, postmen, and telegraphists, and to obtain bursaries for the gifted sons of poor peasants and Jews. (Roth 2002: 250)

The extent to which the nobility retained power, despite having been stripped of its legal underpinnings (the formal-bureaucratic apparatus of state had by now, even in Galicia, long been up and running) is graphically shown by this passage. It is to Roth's merit that he shows benevolence and care as attributes of feudalism which are often denied by a historiographical argument that is traditionally skeptical of authority. To be sure, such patrimonial plenitude of power can be turned against the lower orders just as well. The extension of feudal rule into the domain of the menial family on the land could mean extremely hard living conditions, as the social history of the peasant family has copiously demonstrated (Sieder 1987).

Our second example refers to the peasant attitude to authority – more accurately, to familial authority amid the rural lower classes. Even as late as around the 1950s, such power relationships steeped in feudal traditions were still cropping up, largely intact, in the pages of Austrian literature. In the following case, Franz Innerhofer describes the thrashing that is being meted out to an illegitimate farm lad by his father:

> The Farmer took his time. He walked in just as Holl saw the Mauerer and Schneider children go by, outside, carrying bottles full of milk. The Farmer's face was more relaxed now. Holl had to let down his pants and say, 'Father, please, let's have the beating!' Then The Farmer grabbed his neck with his left hand, bent him over an extended knee and struck him, wielding the rope in his right, until the howling changed into a whine. Then Holl had to say, 'Thank you, Father, for the beating!' After these

> chastisements, Holl had to walk out with The Farmer; the latter even ordered him to mingle with the servants with a big grin on his face. (Innerhofer 1976: 20)

The lad's embittered alienation is reflected in the way in which he is even denied his Christian name; and his father is introduced simply as 'the farmer'. This scene, played out on a Salzburg farmstead, might give the impression that the father was a sadist. But the novel nowhere suggests that this is the case. The endless scenes of physical chastisement always have a cause – some inability or unwillingness on the part of Holl – and they take place as a matter of course and without any emotional involvement. When he is older, Holl develops violent phantasies of revenge, dreams of keeping a knife in the drawer to kill the farmer. It is only later that he realizes the illegitimacy of the violence he has absorbed. Cooperation is a key aspect of this relationship. It is not so much the body that is given a drubbing, but the will within. In the terminology of Elias, what is being set up is a form of self-constraint that is wholly dependent on massive external constraints. The farm and the menial family are still very much hierarchically organized along pre-industrial, patriarchal lines. What we get is 'subservience' and 'good behaviour' spanning the generations and which for the lower orders is the counter-pole to the aristocratic *gestus* of unquestioned dominance – a spill-over of the feudal system, although the latter had been dealt, by 1848 if not earlier, a severe body blow and had seen its economic power erode away by degrees ever since. The relationship between man and nature is characterized by a paucity of control over the latter and by miserable scarcity. The top-down relationships of those in service, expressed in commands whose volume ranges from raucous whisper to enraged bellow, are shaped by a general sense of hopelessness, a sense that though one might, perhaps, change one's master, one can never escape the basic fact of being dominated, the hallmark of which is long-term personal dependency. If, further up the social pyramid, the warrior's sword still, as ever, sets the tone, the peasants have long been disarmed; among them, however, it is the domestics on whom the entire edifice truly rests.

> It was a matter of getting through one day at a time. The servants and serfs were driven back into the darkness as soon as one of them dared stick his head out of the gloomy loft. Year after year, earning only their keep, they were driven across the glaring landscape, to work their way, day after day, closer and closer to the grave's edge, finally to cry out and fall in. They were raised on hunks of bread and stew, encouraged with kicks, to the point where eating and drinking were their prime activities, and with prayers and sermons they were shackled. There have been peasant uprisings, but no rebellions of servants .... (Innerhofer 1976: 15)

Their affective household is, above all else, marked by the heavy physical labour which was the lot of the menial family (composed of people who were not necessarily blood relations) that arose in Western feudalism. In addition, in the hierarchical structure of relationships it was rarely possible clearly to distinguish private and public life. Action chains are short; in this face-to-face world, it is the person in all its facets that is under scrutiny. The affects of the stronger, in this encounter, can be given freer rein than in a class-room or in the tranquil setting of an office. For the domestic it is a rough-and-ready world of being pushed around, a world in which great insecurity and great personal dependency meet. The enforced subservience is ambivalent: if the son is given a beating, he is even expected to thank his paternal chastiser. This means that he must control the aggression welling up in him, suppress all evidence of pain, and hide the shame he feels when the eyes of others are trained on him.

In addition to paternalism and patrimonialism we find the authority of the church as a further type of domination in a world shaped by feudalism. There are good reasons to regard the 'old European' agrarian order as a warrior–priest–peasant triangle. A central pillar of supra-local authority was undoubtedly the Church. In his novel *Schöne Tage* [Beautiful Days], Innerhofer reviews numerous instances of linkages between secular and church authority, as expressed in strategies of massive shaming, brachial physical punishment and unceasing indoctrination (for a systematic treatment of power sources see Gleichmann 1981).

The dark side of the ostentatious Catholicism of Salzburg-Baroque provenance, with its ceremonial processions and ritualized praying the rosaries, becomes manifest when Holl commits a minor infringement against the discipline of divine service:

> Holl stared at the side altar, the priest fell silent, and suddenly, as if she had been stamped out of the ground, the kindergarten sister stood in front of Holl. Now it was his turn. While the priest descended the creaky steps from the pulpit, Holl and his neighbour had to get out into the aisle. The faithful arose, in honour of the priest, and launched into a prayer. Holl felt the cold slate under his knees. With horror he thought of his father, standing farther back, in the pew of Farm 48. One pater noster after another Holl hurled toward the main altar-on one hand to create a distraction from this terrible situation, on the other to ask God to strike the congregation with blindness, at least until after the blessing. (Innerhofer 1976: 32)

If Holl forgets to make his confession, his father will see he gets a proper whipping. But his fear of being shamed is greater, one suspects, than his fear of the strap. Teacher and priest, farmer and village community form a cabal from which there is no escape. This is the dark underbelly of patrimonial benevolence. Operating hand in cahoots with the village grapevine is a tight-meshed code of surveillance, which, on pain of incurring a massive public shaming, makes individuals opt for rigid self-surveillance. Yet this too is a self-constraint which functions only when pressure from others is palpable, only when the transmitter of the norms is physically there. The climate of unending fear (even walking in the open, Holl cannot forget his last years of being whipped from pillar to post) is found also in other novels portraying rural Catholic Austria. We should think of books by Waltraud Mitgutsch and Thomas Bernhard. At the same time, the brakes on sexuality are extremely weak and rather threadbare – with familiar harsh consequences in the form of illegitimate births. The priest wields real power: his weapons of choice are the pulpit and the confessional. An 'internalized' religiosity is probably not to be expected from a product of this power set-up; what we get instead is the outer show of piety. Easy prey for any good caricaturist, we must imagine such a person to be unctuous and just a tad hypocritical, eyes rolling guilelessly upwards. How in a centuries-long osmosis he came to be fashioned, what he signifies for the Austrian affective household, are questions that will detain us below. Reversing the usual sequence, we first consider peasant reactions to feudal rule and then move on to the feudal warrior code as a whole.

Development of ecclesiastical authority and its imprint on the Austrian habitus

For those with an interest in Austrian psycho-history, there is no escaping the most eloquent chronicler of the 'struggle for the Austrian identity' (Heer 1981). Friedrich Heer's eponymous extensive study treats, in the first instance, Austrian commitment to the 'Austrian Idea', which blazes a trail, rough-and-ready to be sure and with any number of bifurcations, through the jungle of an extremely turbulent history, terminating finally in a republican statelet, initially (from 1918 to 1938) rejected by many, but latterly (since 1945) commanding virtually unanimous acceptance.

Only secondarily does Heer raise the issue of Austrian distinctiveness, of what makes the Austrian national character what it is. For Heer this is more or less self-evident, problematic only when exogenous forces by infiltrating the Austrian people jeopardize its identity. Thus the Protestant watchword, 'From Germany Salvation', is ranged against a Catholic-Baroque-Byzantine-Roman Austria, as universal as it is rooted in the soil. Thus Austrian idiosyncrasy is all about immense inner strife – small wonder since, as Heer points out, the massive steering from without of the historical-political edifice that is 'Austria' has been vented in two, at times even three or four, political religions. This has, he tells us, resulted in the formation of two nations – the one German-Lutheran, the other Austrian-Catholic – between the 16th and 20th centuries. These nations also fashioned finally their own cultures: a German-Lutheran cult of letters and the mind, and an Austrian-Catholic 'culture of the senses and sensuality' (Heer 1981: 22). This Austrian-Catholic culture is steeped in the Baroque of the Spanish-Latin-Counter-Reformation culture of the eye, in which theatre and processions, sermons and Jesuits, set the tone. Exogenous therefore are Reformation (Germany), Counter-Reformation (Spain and Italy), and civilizing Enlightenment (Western Europe). The latter, to be sure, entails for Heer a lamentable 'narrowing of horizons', away from the universalist humanism of the Austrian Baroque towards the mean-spirited civil wars fought over national and confessional issues – until German Protestant intellectual culture and Berlin and Budapest in political respects slowly but definitively throttle the universalist Austria of old. In this perspective, the history of Austrian 'identity' is simultaneously an inquest into the Austrian sickness: shame and self-hatred are intricately woven into the psycho-historical fabric of Austria.

Pondering the catastrophes of the last century, Heer unfurls his chequered and powerfully strung panorama of history. Behind the endless array of baffling historical details, we glimpse the contours of several major developments. The consolidating Habsburg power runs into a popular movement of bourgeois-peasant-feudal elements ranged against a centralist-hierarchical Rome. This is the great movement we know as the Reformation, a movement that stressed and bolstered national differences while giving revolutionary re-enforcement to the claims of peasants against nobility, of burgers against reigning princes, of the aristocratic orders against a (weak) central power. 'The Lutheran storm rages over Austria' – a youth movement of sorts, albeit one with lasting consequences (Heer 1981: 56). Driven into a corner, the Habsburgs respond with a series of bloody tribunals, by mobilizing foreign support, and by installing a finely meshed network of church–state surveillance. Even if they do not succeed in exterminating Protestantism in Austria and Bohemia (after all, Protestantism survives underground until religious pluralism is conceded at the end of the 18th century), nevertheless the success of the Counter-Reformation is as triumphant as it is disquieting. Many Protestants are murdered; many more have to emigrate; large segments of the nobility turn their backs on the land; books are burnt by the thousands; intellectual life suffers a perilous loss of substance with out-and-out destruction of cultural life as the result. Re-converts are driven at dagger point to the altar. Bavaria, Spain and Italy supply assistance with which, from its base in Graz, first Inner Austria and then Upper and Lower Austria can again be 'made Catholic'. Events take an even more dramatic turn in Bohemia: public executions of nobles, confiscation of property and the emigration of 30,000 families culminate in the installation of a 'Second Serfdom' nation-wide (Heer 1981: 73). With pacification having triumphed, the pompous and ostentatious Baroque of Austrian Catholicism can now get under way; but the consequences of subjugation, for Heer, are visible down to the present. A 'disguised soul' [*verdeckte Seele*] is a hallmark of the Austrian; '*Grüss Gott*' [God Bless], the signature greeting of the Counter-Reformation, its use then no mere matter of choice, is still in use even today. Black-and-yellow clerical Austria has triumphed; not castles or chateaus but churches will be its chief architectonic expression. Down to the times of Maria Theresa, protest is synonymous with emigration (or expulsion) – initially into territories beyond Habsburg rule; later into the remote provinces of the empire.

To understand the history of Catholic re-education, one could do worse than look at the numerous Jesuit dramas performed in Bavaria, Austria and other parts of the Holy Roman Empire that remained or became Catholic. These dramas are interesting in many respects for our purpose. Prominent among their themes are conversion, proselytizing, and the battle against heresy. At issue in these plays is the proclamation of the authority of the one true church as the sole dispenser of salvation. Some of the plays treat the extension of this authority into family life, to which end parents are generally enjoined to practice a code of unrelenting strictness towards their children (cf. Szarota 1983: III. 1, 32). Those summaries of individual scenes and acts that have come down to us do not describe explicitly the processes of re-education and re-anchoring of authority. They confine themselves to setting out what is desirable and expected. These plays are pitched less at the critical eye of the intellect than at the sensibilities of the psyche. Instilled are feelings of dread, of regret and contrition at the very instance of sinning, but also feelings of triumph at valorously seeing off falsehood and evil. Just like the countless processions and pilgrimages, the performance appealed less to reason than to the senses; the idea of accepting one's destiny as fixed and ineluctable, of piously accepting what was decreed from on high, counted for more in this ethos than the solitary striving of individuals to achieve insight and perfection.

For a memorable example, consider this drama first staged in Munich in the year 1597, where the Archangel Michael triumphs over the Devil (appearing in a variety of masks, one of them representing Heresy); over the tyrannical Roman emperors Nero and Decius; and over Julian the Apostate. The 'argument' of Act II proceeds as follows:

> Old Nick [i.e., the Devil] is tirelessly at work
> To make us bow and scrape before idols
> The Christian Church plies the other track
> Searches out and wins back many a Christian.
> [1] (Szarota 1983: 425; transl. B. A.)

Personified virtues such as Devotion, Modesty, Constancy and Conscience appear as helpers, while Lucifer, for his part, urges on the similarly personified vices of Avarice, Falsehood and Flattery. Pride, Indulgence and Gluttony – but also Liberty – practice their deceitful wiles. Church and Idolatry gather together their own, while the heretics have at their side a warring colonel [*Kriegsobristen*] and the Roman Emperor. Michael dispatches lightning, comforts the faithful, scatters the troops of the heretics, and celebrates – in the congregation of the martyrs – the final triumph of victory.

Thus heresy is vanquished by the sword and by *conscientia* and *cognitio sui* (self-knowledge). The fact that this play (and many like it) was performed in Bavaria, the state from where the Counter-Reformation was launched into Inner Austria by the later Emperor Ferdinand, is proto-typical, and does not diminish the value this source has for an understanding of the emerging Austrian habitus. Via the numerous Jesuit colleges, dramas of this type reached and influenced the aspiring educated classes of the monarchy. They propagated an ideal of harmonious unity between secular and spiritual authority; and appealed to those emotions that were considered to be consonant with this ideal. Disobedience and lack of piety were to be combated. For conflicts of authority within the family these Jesuit dramas propose solutions that are often barbaric and hard-hearted: far better for the child to die than disobey! Also revealing in this connection is the plot of one such play, staged in Muenster after the siege of Vienna by the Turks was lifted, whose sole purpose was to glorify the Habsburg Dynasty. In a manner familiar from historical accounts of ancient Byzantium (e.g., John Kaminiates' description of the capture of Thessalonica by the Arabs in AD 904; cf. Böhlig 1975), this incursion by the Turks is shown as just punishment for living a life of vice and pride, all of which is cast in an affect-laden and ritualized light. The Emperor absolves the sins of the faithful in a ceremony of divine service, whereupon God grants him sustenance so he can now defeat the Turks with the help of his pious field commanders. God's fame and triumph is at one with the Emperor's. Authority is mystically transfigured; God's grace from above matters more than individual valour in turning the tide of battle. In the terminology of Elias, the resultant social idea of order is, in large part, the product of affect-laden and poorly distanced thinking. The specifically Austrian variant is Habsburg *pietas*, whereby sacral elements are incorporated into the Imperial Throne.

The Counter-Reformation is followed by the triumphal progress of Austrian Baroque culture. This progress coincides with the only genuine period of expansion Austrian absolutism ever had which was founded on the hard-wrung victory over the Turks (amongst other things, brought about by Imperial troops) and the empire's successful containment of French power in the European theatre. Out of the Baroque-blessed wedlock of church and state, of art and science as the 'Restoration of Rome and Byzantium', 'Austrian man' [*Homo Austriacus*] is born (Acham 1992, for the historical development of European Baroque). Austria now turns away from the Western European, Protestant-bourgeois path. Instead of 'differentiating the various spheres of modernity' (politics, economy, religion, culture) it decides to fuse them: to unite the earthly with the heavenly, the spirit with the flesh, and reason with faith. Its architectonic symbols *par excellence* are grandiose cupolas, reflecting an Imperial architecture nothing if not global in its artistic reach; the *Karlskirche* in Vienna is to become the new *Hagia Sophia*, winged by Roman triumphal columns. The stylized greetings that can still be encountered today well articulate the various strands of 'Austrianness': the famous 'hand-kiss' has its roots in the courtly milieu (along with the Spanish-Catholic order of ceremonies, its true provenance is Burgundy); *Grüssgott*, the universal salutation already mentioned above, and the now-discarded 'Greeted Art Thou, Mary' [*Gegrüsst seist Du Maria*] both go back to the black-and-yellow Counter-Reformation launched by the Jesuits; nor must we forget 'At your service' [*Servus*], the salutation once pronounced by all Imperial officers to their Austrian fatherland, which has lost none of its popularity.

Such loyalty as Jesuits and Habsburgs could impose cast a long and depressing shadow, especially over intellectual life. To be sure, Austrian absolutism could point to an ever more resplendent courtly culture and social life. But it is a fair assumption that any 'bourgeois' culture centred on the middle orders remained inchoate at best, clearly in marked contrast to northern Germany, for example; and that it lay way behind the Spanish and Italian culture that was being imported so keenly. In richer France, which shared Austria's fate of Catholicization by violent means, evidence of bourgeois backwardness is much harder to find. But even the comparison with England turns up no unequivocal evidence. During the Restoration, there we find Protestants (Puritans) emigrating in massive numbers, and in the process settling North America by conquest. Although the blood-letting lasted a very long time indeed, neither the English nor the Scottish economies stagnated. There, as we have seen, incipient religious pluralism and the achievement of parliamentary rule, giving to all citizens basic civil liberties, were elements of a developmental trajectory wholly different to that of the Habsburg territories.

In the perspective of Elias, the fabricating of personality structures for which the peaceable balancing of interests, the sharing of power between government and opposition, was something normal and not hedged in by fears of courting the demise of one's own group, is a crucial developmental step. It was precisely this step that Austria did not take, or if it did, then only with such hesitancy that it could be reverted when circumstances changed. The religiously tolerant Maximilian II and the indecisive Rudolf were followed by Ferdinand, whose zest for enforced conversions was endless; after the Josephine 'thaw' came the repression of *Vormärz*. In sum, the Counter-Reformation ended in Austria with the total victory of Catholicism, driving all other elements into an opposition as impotent as it was surreptitious. Nothing better is likely to have resulted from a Protestant victory – as witness the Lutheran state churches in Germany after the Peace of Augsburg. Fear of the other side's triumphing was no less justified than the elation that followed victory for one's own cause. Compromises were only entered into when the central power felt its hand to be weak against the aristocratic orders; such weakness required much tacking and weaving, all of which led, in the fullness of time, to Austria choosing the track of the neo-corporatist 'social partnership'of the last decades.

How repressive, then, was the Catholic Counter-Reformation? How does it compare with other countries? Emigrations and executions took place in France as well. Nothing as dreadful as St. Bartholemew's Night can be found in the Habsburg hereditary lands, or in Bohemia and Hungary. Indeed this episode is highly reminiscent of modern 'totalitarian' forms of extermination, such as the 20th century has brought. A like talent for the synchronized dispatching of one's religious or political foes was, in any event, not evinced by the Habsburgs. The expulsion of the Huguenots into Protestant countries, many of which within Germany, seems to have blackened France's name less than Austria's; indeed, to date almost no one has dallied with the heady prospect that there might be a link between this episode and the emergence of an authoritarian national character in the French. ('Marianne' is still seen as saucy and cheeky, adding to her famed *coquetterie*.) If, therefore, the growing monopolization of force by the Habsburgs resulted in the Austrian populace becoming traumatized and succumbing to apathy, this should possibly be better linked to the ensuing period of attempts by state and church at disciplining the population. Given the growing importance of schooling, this last-ditch ideological battle waged by the Jesuits may finally have begun to reach the popular mind, to the point where suitable benchmarks of discipline were internalized.

Recall, if you will, Innerhofer's description of the incident in the church. As late as around 1950, the priest in the pulpit and the father within his four walls had effective weapons at their disposal for inculcating into adolescents the norms of proper conduct – massive public shaming or a good hiding, oral confession of one's sins or the rod. Innerhofer's novel paints a graphic image of the psychic cost exacted: the boy's dignity and pride are broken, a rich vocabulary rams home the extent of his degradation. The social field of personal dependency is as depressing as any resistance against internalized authority is hopeless. The faculty of conscience thus instilled is the product of extreme fear of punishment from above as well as loss of face before the other villagers. Holl's fate, to be sure, is that of a member of a very lowly group of social outsiders and we would be well advised to accept the possibility of a number of idiosyncrasies. But the social field is faithfully reproduced – the portrayal is such as to allow the context to be viewed in its complexity; and it can be checked in many of its details. Here literature has indeed become a form of sociological description.

The flowering of 'confessional absolutism' was followed, as we saw in a previous chapter, by the period known as 'reform absolutism'.

Against this backdrop and in reaction to the almost fatal outcome of the rivalry with Frederick II of Prussia (a figure, by the way, that Heer characterized as 'demonic'), the 'Josephine Revolution' saw the rise of a new sense of what it was to be Austrian: bureaucratic and bourgeois, worldly and relatively enlightened. At the same time, Heer detects in all these developments the same 'narrowing of horizons' that alienates Austrians from themselves: Prussia and the Protestant German North stake out an ever-larger niche in the Austrian psyche. An important waystation is the battle joined against Viennese popular comedy, decried as exuding heathen sensuality. Yet, for Heer, at the end of the road lie Austro-German nationalism and Austrian self-abandonment.

A landmark in the critical description of clerical authority is the literature of the Enlightenment, its first works dating from the end of the 18th century. Bodi's work on the Josephine *Tauwetter* ('period of thawing') (Bodi 1995a) reviews a series of influential early 'Enlightenment novels' which testify to the depth of penetration of bourgeois, secularized modes of thought and codes of conduct. Pezzl, Rautenstrauch, Richter and Friedel are the leading authors. When analyzing the rise of a professional officialdom, we will encounter them again as witnesses to, and prime movers of, the Bourgeois Enlightenment. A recurrent target of their shafts is the clerical orders, the *Pfaffen* or 'men of the cloth', all of whom they consider hypocrites; another target is monastic discipline, which they dismiss as 'stupefying'; finally they rage against the pressure imposed by rigid external surveillance of conscience, which they label despotic. In many of the novels, members of the ecclesiastical orders appear as begetters of children, brazen and cynical but talented in hiding their identity, while the mothers marry other men before delivery to avoid being disgraced. Thus it was that being Catholic was seen to be synonymous with double standards in sexual matters. The Josephine reforms tone down censorship and permit an urban-based literary audience to emerge. But the abolition of many monasteries and a sweeping bout of secularization are again partially reversed in the successive period of restoration. When Postl-Sealsfield (Sealsfield 1972; first published in 1828) – along with Pezzl and Richter, a former monastic pupil – describes in the midst of *Vormärz* the Austrian police state, his shafts are aimed also at the conscience control the clergy practice in the universities – where students, affirms Postl, undergo monitoring by their professors. Teachers of religion hear confession at least six times a year; leanings and traits of character are entered into ledgers, then forwarded to higher instances for inspection and filed away for possible later use (e.g., the Vienna-based Royal and Imperial Commission into Higher Education in the Dual Monarchy; the *Gubernium*; the School Archives). Their reading is closely monitored; their opinion of figures of classical antiquity – Brutus, Plato – no less so. The mere suspicion of liberal inclinations in those studying law or theology is enough to destroy all prospect of a career in the civil service, of ever being allowed to practice. Independent-minded professors like the theologian and philosopher Bolzano come in conflict not only with the church but the state authority as well. The phase of 'confessional absolutism' is now long past its zenith; but the bureaucratized state – mopping up after Joseph II's massive incursions into ecclesiastical life – still meshes closely with the church establishment. Abbots of the numerous monasteries, Postl tells us, are supervised by both prince-archbishop and the Imperial government. Bishops are appointed by the Emperor and play second fiddle to procurators and circle captains in many respects. The Imperial government watches over the training of theologians, and sometimes also decrees what processions will take place. As King of Hungary the Emperor is even Legate of the Roman See and can, by pulling the levers of this office, steer ecclesiastical policy in directions of his choosing.

Much later on, Herzmanovsky-Orlando, incomparably and gently, poked fun at the showy Austrian Catholicism of his boyhood years. The Baroque quality, even the touch of the heathen about it all, he evokes by telling of the 'court jester' who has learnt how to top up his income:

> … and on the side he must make a pretty penny with the Sufferings of Christ and the Seven Sorrows of Mary which he fashions out of wood, moss and such stuff and displays in little bottles for church festivals; and the figures of the apostles, too, molded out of genuine road-droppings from the Mount of Olives. (Herzmanovsky 1997: 5)

This slightly cynical, quasi-blasphemous linking of the Most Holy and the Most Vulgar (street dung) latches on to the preoccupation with mere outward show so central to Catholic piety in the Austrian Baroque. This 'ostentatious Catholicism' arguably represented a pillar of the hierarchical order, however far removed it was from Protestant inwardness. This Austrian superficiality was noted by many a visitor from the north and roundly damned. Austrian religiosity, for

Herzmanovsky, is in fact a late offshoot of heathen Antiquity, which he even suspects in the male busts adorning barber saloons ('mystical grand-nephews of ancient statues of Pan'). Even the incarnation of evil, the Devil himself, is transformed into 'His Satanic Counsellor Dr. Infern. Damianus Saperdibixi, Attaché to the Holy See') – that is to say, he is given a make-over as a Catholic bureaucrat – and so made an integral component, outwardly graspable in best Catholic tradition, of the Christian pantheon (in accord with the motto, 'First sin, then confess'). The outcome is a kind of conscience that is dominated by the fear of being found out. In such a fine-grained network of reciprocal surveillance, it is difficult to live out certain emotions. This applies, say, to displays of aggression in public. Habsburg *pietas* at times led to dissidents being ruthlessly dealt with, yet the clerical supervisory apparatus produced a habitus marked by peaceableness with regard to physical violence. It also produced good behaviour and a willingness to accept subordinate status. In addition, it produced taboos in the intellectual field that remained so exceedingly implict that they are still with us today.

Peasant attitudes to feudal-patrimonial authority: Some literary examples

A splendid example of the psychic experience of what Perry Anderson (1974) called 'eastern feudalism' is found in one of Marie Ebner-Eschenbach's short stories of manorial life in Polish Galicia. 'Jacob Szela' tells the story of the 1846 uprising against Austrian rule by Polish noblemen, including the surprising turn it took, occasioning great loss of blood, when the Polish peasantry spurned the call of their indigenous masters and remained loyal to the Emperor. The exact story-line need not detain us here. What is interesting, however, is the relation between a peasant – the later leader of the peasant revolt, Jacob Szela, who was a real historical figure – and an Austrian count.

> In the autumn of 1845 Szela one day went to the steward Sikorski and asked to see the count. Never before had Szela dared to make a similar request, and Sikorski, quite taken aback, said: 'I, ask for an audience for you? What are you thinking of? I would not even advise it with the count in a good humour, much less to-day when he is in his worst, because the rent collector has not brought him as much money as he wants for his journey to-morrow.' (Ebner-Eschenbach 1928: 63)

The social distance between the two is huge. Small wonder, since only a short while before a count could kill a peasant on his own estate with impunity and to do so on his neighbour's estate might set him back 15 guilders, according to Ebner-Eschenbach. Until quite recently, *robot* (forced labour) had still been common. But now the central state had begun to protect the peasants against the arbitrariness of their masters. The asymmetrical balance of power between the count and Szela, who, as it happens, is not *his* own bondsman but the neighbour's, is made clear even before they meet. The count's steward is extremely reluctant to admit Szela into the presence of an ill-tempered count:

> 'What do you want?' the count shouted, when he saw Szela. But when the latter stood still near the door and bowed low, bis demeanour seemed to pacify the count. Although he was small and thin, the old yeoman had indeed a venerable appearance. As it happened he was standing just below a portrait of the great emperor 'Theuerdank', and the resemblance between the two was striking, notwithstanding the emperor's being arrayed in a furlined velvet hunting coat, and the poor peasant wearing a smock.
> 'What do you want?' repeated the count.
> 'I humbly beg to be allowed to speak to thee without witnesses.'
> 'Without witnesses? ...You are insolent. I have no secrets with you. Speak before my steward or be off.'
> 'It is for thee to command, master,' Szela replied without moving a muscle. He had probably not expected a different reception. (Ebner-Eschenbach 1928: 64)

All the peasant wants to do is warn the count. He has come with good intentions. Although there is an appearance of equality between the two parties since they address each other by using an informal *Du* (the English 'thou' in the singular), their relationship is based on a vertical chain of command and obedience. The peasant's warning is not taken at all well (it concerns a close confidant of the count's, who has betrayed him).

> The count's eyes protruded from his head, his lips grew pale. He tore a riding whip from the stand, and a hail of lashes fell upon the peasant's head and shoulders. He stood still without wincing. Indescribable melancholy spoke from his deeply lined face. (Ebner-Eschenbach 1928: 65–6)

The count beats Szela until he is covered in blood. Yet his loyalty still shines through.

> Szela rubbed his aching shoulders. 'Poor master! I did not think he would be quite so blind. That wily Pole has quite bewitched him ...Pray to God, Pan steward, to turn away the mischief which this man will bring upon the poor count and his house.' (Ebner-Eschenbach 1928: 67)

We can fairly assume that Ebner-Eschenbach has realistically reproduced the power divide that manifests itself in seigneurial wilfulness.[2] Whether we should accept Ebner-Eschenbach's description of the peasant taking a beating in dignified silence, is less certain. In any event, this is a heroic tale complete with creative devices and effects. Later on in the story, Szela rescues the children of the ungrateful count from the pent-up rage of the peasants. When one of his fellow ring-leaders urges, 'The count is a severe master', he answers him in a way that illustrates the difference between Polish and Austrian domination:

> 'The devil take thee. …severe. …And if he is severe. …'; after a pause he continued: 'When he thrashes thee twice, think that a Polish master would have thrashed thee four times.' (Ebner-Eschenbach 1928: 79)

The enraged peasants slaughter their Polish lords. At Szela's bidding and out of loyalty to the Emperor, they spare only those of their masters who sympathize with Austria. When the count, the embodiment of legitimate authority, thanks the faithful Szela, he provokes an odd reaction:

> 'Szela,' he said with tears in his voice, 'you have saved my children's lives and I have never even come to thank you.'
> He held out his hand which the old man kissed…
> The old and yet a new man. He who had never betrayed any emotion either under the count's blows or when he heard his cry of ecstasy on seeing his children alive, was now almost beside himself. When he heard these simple words his lips trembled, his eyes overflowed with tears, he seemed ready to fall on his knees.
> 'What is the matter? What are you doing?' cried the count, and took hold of both his shoulders.
> 'Master, master,' stammered Szela, and looked into his face with passionate devotion, 'I never thought that anyone would say "thank you, Szela," to me before I died, and now thou hast come and said it.' (Ebner-Eschenbach 1928: 87–8)

Szela's emotional reaction is hefty and seemingly paradoxical. It flows from a deeply internalized attitude of awe in the presence of authority. The same authority that has often shown itself merciless and ungrateful awakens deep feelings of love and devotion the moment it is grateful and understanding. In Szela there is nothing that suggests proud distance or open rebellion. He may be heading a peasant uprising, but he is bound to the count by deep ties of sentiment despite everything that the count has done to him. Nor would it be accurate to call him 'servile', since this would imply a readiness to wheedle one's way to a tawdry favour or two in a manner that is both fawning and bereft of dignity. We may assume that the ambivalent social tie between peasant and master (between punishment and benevolence) has shaped Szela's character, exerting a constantly inhibiting force played out on many levels of action.

What does this model of patrimonial but comparatively direct personal authority imply for the emergence of an Austrian habitus? First of all, it describes very well a core facet of this habitus, namely an amalgamation of love and obedience. We do well, however, to appreciate the fact that such an extreme manifestation of this facet in the case of Szela was more likely to be found on the monarchy's eastern fringes and that the peasants in the Tyrol, for instance, were likely to have entertained quite different feelings. Furthermore, even in Galicia, the balance of power between peasantry and lords of the manor had already begun to shift under the inroads of state and market. Wherever the feudal burdens were heavy and *robot* obligations were onerous and prolonged, a habitus of this kind crystallized, at least in attenuated form. It is quite likely that the consolidating bureaucratic state could count on such submissive attitudes. They took a considerable psychic toll, in the form of inherited feelings of subordination and inferiority, a toll that continued to be exacted long after seigneurial authority had visibly crumbled. The bureaucratic state inherited from these feudal models two things: the idea of providential care and the idea of dependency and limited freedom of choice, both of these ideas going hand-in-glove under patrimonialism. In terms of political socialization, it is clear that peasant groupings with their characteristic 'mentalities' were always going to be hard to fit into a system of parliamentary rule and control. As soon as peasant interests form for the first time, they usually organize around a strong leader who can reckon on great loyalty. The likelihood of major fragmentation into numerous small parties is also considerable – as we have recently seen in the countries of the former Eastern Bloc. Former masters often remain in charge of organizing political interests on the land, something that happened with the passing of the monarchy. Above all, it is difficult to embrace political plurality in a system where hitherto only one authority had held sway. The same holds for the democratic readiness to tolerate, as a point of principle, divergences and political opposition and to confront them with arguments. Conflicts of loyalty become an insurmountable inner hurdle and trigger a deep sense of unease. Moreover, this attitude explains, at least in part, why the mobilization of Austria's and Russia's peasant armies in 1914 met no resistance: the feelings of devotion to the Emperor and the Czar were genuine and could be taken advantage of by the rulers. The Emperor's appeal – 'To My Peoples' [*An meine Völker*] – was not chosen lightly.

The feudal warrior code in Austria: Some reflections and a first comparison with England

If anything stands out about tiny, republican post-1945 Rump Austria, it is the virtual total absence of that feudal-militaristic spirit formerly (and probably until 1918) inseparable from the Dual Monarchy. This spirit was still palpable in the years between the wars when there were feuding private armies, one of which, the 'Home Guard' [*Heimwehr*], continued to be headed by aristocratic elements. The utter lack of enthusiasm for anything military in today's Austria doubtless reflects not just the experience of the heavy defeats inflicted on Austrian armies or those with Austrian participants in the last century but also a general trend in all advanced industrial societies. Yet it stands in crass contrast to an England far more ready to uphold military tradition and apply many war-related categories to a wide variety of social phenomena. This contrast is all the more surprising especially when one recalls how assiduously the heritage of the Dual Monarchy is kept up even today with its inexhaustible penchant for military brass bands. As a matter of fact, the Austrian mentality, even immediately before 1914, is hardly marked by anything like an unflinching and dauntless attacking spirit. All comparison with England in this respect is, and has always been, ludicrous. There is a certain paradox here: on the one hand, it cannot be doubted that Austria-Hungary, right up to its violent end, possessed and wielded considerable military might, the role of which in supporting and unifying the Dual Monarchy was recognized in practice by all parties (Deák 1991; Rauchensteiner 1993; Sked 2001). Equally clear is that this army was chiefly led by members of the nobility, whose mentality was that of a warrior caste in many respects. Neither should we forget that Austria, by declaring war on Serbia, almost suicidally began the blood-letting of 1914. Nor can we rule out that this decision was taken out of a sense that the warrior's code of honour was injured. On the other hand, many voices and witnesses demonstrate that Austria was not a militarized society. If Ernst Fischer (1945: 20–21) is to be believed, a distaste for drill and regimentation goes hand in hand with the Austrian propensity for 'muddling through' [*fortwursteln*]. This, of course, sets Austria apart from Prussia. Fischer claims that a career as an army officer was never thought the height of respectability.[3] In 1914 the army of the Dual Monarchy was manned by a much smaller percentage of the population than it was in France or Germany. In France one in 65 citizens was in uniform, in Germany the figure was one in 98; and in Austro-Hungary it was one in 128 (Rauchensteiner 1994: 42). Yet although the Habsburg Monarchy was clearly an 'under-achiever' in terms of demonstrated military prowess in the field, the army time and again – in 1859 and 1866 and again in 1914 – exhibited an impetuous, even suicidal, feudal *élan*. As Rauchensteiner has documented in depth, it was not an attacking spirit that the army lacked but rather the skills and expertise of a (bourgeois) career officer.

The dismissal of that army as nothing but an 'operetta army' was the privilege of the new media of film. Yet, in novels and plays, too, there we find representations of officers with little appetite for martial virtues: Musil's General Stumm von Bordwehr, to take one example, shows greater interest in his standing in 'good society' than in his military record. The army of the Dual Monarchy proved an easy target for gently teasing parody. A fine exemplar of this genre is the novellas of Herzmanovsky-Orlando which we shall discuss in later chapters. In which other literature would one find neologism of an ironic kind such as 'Military Beetle Collection' [*Militärkäfersammlung*]? In this respect, at least, the Austrian army was without rival in Europe. The contradictions dissolve to an extent if one keeps in mind that Austria-Hungary was still largely a feudal state under aristocratic rule which failed to impose its ethos on the rising middle-classes, which, for all their homogeneity as a class, remained divided among multiple nationalities. This ethos also suffered from the defeats of a great power in decline. The mentality of the ruling nobility continued to be focused on war and the martial virtues. For instance, the male members of the House of Windisch-Graetz lived by the ideals of courage and chivalry (Stekl/Wakounig 1992: 152–95). They would volunteer even in advanced years for military service and felt bound by a strict code of honour. Politically, the Windisch-Graetz family plotted a feudal-conservative course favourable to the ruling class – a policy pursued as much by the victor over the 1848–49 uprising as it was by the minister-president at the end of the 19th century. Their unswerving allegiance was to the Emperor; indeed, to rank as human, so a dictum attributed to Prince Alfred of Windisch-Graetz maintained, one must be at least a baron. Even three-year-olds in this family knew they were socially superior to nurses and servants (Stekl/Wakounig 1992: 24). The duel survived in Austria until the demise of the monarchy. We find celebrated literary witness to this form of self-justice, meted out in defiance of the state's monopoly of violence, in, for example, the pages of Joseph Roth (Roth 1995, *The Radetzky March* – the duel in question is between Count Tattenbach and Demant, the Jewish regimental doctor, who knows full well the archaic nature of this code of honour, but cannot, in the end, escape its clutches). There is also Schnitzler ('Lieutenant Gustl' [*Leutnant Gustl*]; here the duel does not actually take place, but in a silent monologue we are privy to Gustl's incapacitating fear at the imminent loss of honour; Schnitzler 1984; first published in 1901). We know that even in his final years, 'Ludwig Windisch-Graetz vigorously opposed the activities of the Anti-Duelling League, and pleaded – his esteem for the peace initiatives then underway notwithstanding – for the retaining of 'autonomous conflict-resolution mechanisms' in the Austrian army' (Stekl/Wakounig 1992: 179). Young nobles were originally educated in large part by private tutors, with cadet academies later growing in importance. In these places, iron discipline was the norm, and future leaders were expected to learn self-control. No especial sympathy for democracy was to be expected from these high-born youths. What they had in mind was some sort of aristocratic order, along the lines of the traditional *Ständeverfassung* (Weber 1978: II, 1086, calls it the 'polity of Estates'). Subordination to bourgeois-representative powers, as for example in the 1849 municipal legislation *Gemeindegesetz*, was considered intolerable by the Windisch-Graetz and their like (Stekl/Wakounig 1992: 222). The feudal-conservatives were the natural foes of the many nationalisms and would occasionally even form alliances with the working class. Despite such expediency, however, the Windisch-Graetz government of 1894 was not above taking harsh measures against the working-class movement (Stekl/Wakounig 1992: 231).

Norbert Elias has pointed to problems inevitable in Europe during transition from a 'dynastic territorial state' – that is, an authoritarian state ruled by descendants of the old warrior elites – to a comparatively democratic nation-state (Elias 1996: 121–70). He was particularly concerned to develop an adequate notion of conscience formation – or specific kind of self-constraint – in the transition from a predominantly hierarchical, Estates-based social order to one merely class-based and relatively democratic, a change he saw as giving rise to a novel type of affective bonding: national feeling or nationalism. In place of aristocratic group solidarity (underwritten by the warrior's canon of honour and bravery as manifested in a penchant for duelling) as well as in place of a feudal sense of attachment to one's 'lord and master', who was also one's supreme military commander, there emerges an attachment to the nation and so to self-created symbols of a specific collectivity. This collectivity now consisted of persons of unambiguously middle-class ('bourgeois') background, persons drawn less by a warrior code of honour than by bourgeois virtue. Whereas the personality structure of a civil servant in the dynastic state was chiefly shaped by constraints by others, democratic parliamentary rule requires a far more complex system of self-control, a much greater ability, that is, to withstand and resolve conflict and to make compromises. Multi-party parliamentarianism, taking over from the monarchical state with its autocratic leanings, legitimizes social conflict:

> Conflicts are not relegated to the category of the extraordinary, abnormal and irrational, but are instead treated as normal, indispensable aspects of social life. In this respect, one could say, democracy contradicts the laws of classical rationality, which equate order with harmony, that is, with lack of conflict. (Elias 1996: 292)

Nostalgia for a harmonious order, benevolent and paternal at once, is one of the central components of the 'Habsburg myth', as C. Magris described it. Class struggle and bickering between the nationalities menaced this essentially benign order without let-up. As Elias argues, this recourse to mythologizing stems from the fact that older personality structures (from the patrimonial-dynastic state with its autocratic, top-down command structure) lingered on in a rapid and non-unitary process of state formation requiring 'functional democratization'. For only by broadening the power base can the structural constraints of forced industrialization be met; emancipation of the middle and working classes is essential if economic productivity is to be raised. This process of evolving new personality structures is never without problems. At every turn, chasms of difference yawned between aristocratic and bourgeois codes and mentalities – between the imperatives of a 'Machiavellian warrior tradition', grounded in the use of violence, on command and obedience, and a 'humanist moral tradition of former subject classes (a process which obtained its impetus from the relatively high control of violence in *intra*-state relations)' (Elias 1996: 166).

Despite England having the most exclusive nobility in Europe (largely because titles traditionally passed by primogeniture), the merger of upper- and middle-class models of social intercourse was accomplished with relative ease. Accordingly, the English national character oscillates, as Max Weber (1976) pointed out, between 'two types of Englishness' – on the one hand, we have the gentleman; on the other, the puritanical-ascetic bourgeois (merchant, trader, skilled craftsman). Moreover, compared to Paris or Vienna, the influence of courtly society in London remained relatively modest. Though the English aristocracy (comprising the titled 'nobility' and the untitled 'gentry') participated in London courtly society (notably during 'the season', with its balls and assorted festivities), their life revolved, certainly as much, around their rural estates. Apart from a house in town, there was an ancestral seat in 'the country' to keep up, to which belonged a social round of hunting and socializing with one's peers. Whereas the Austrian national character in the most elevated ranks of society never fails to betray something of the courtier (suave and emollient ways, an impeccable bearing, a sense of occasion, obsequiousness and servility: all seamlessly blended), its counterpart across the Channel is indelibly marked by the 'sporting spirit' of the landowning classes. Moreover, the general mildness practiced by English landlords towards their tenants and all those under their authority as members of the village community in their capacity as justice of the peace or as vicar carries all the hallmarks, patronizing to be sure, of an indirect form of rule which is based less on subjugation than on respect. Since England at no time in its history maintained a standing army of any size, the social mode by which authority was exercised was based less on the sword – and even less on a culture of command and obedience than was the case in the absolutist states on the Continent. Rather, it was based on economic privileges and prerogatives of rank which grounded a culture of deference. Evidently, respect from social inferiors had to be earned. Exemplary behaviour was expected from those who would lead. These differences between Austria and England are pointed up time and again in the belletristic literature. The great importance that those bearing arms attached to honour as well as its potential undermining by bourgeois elements is emphasized by Schnitzler ('Lieutenant Gustl') and Roth (*The Radetzky March*) as well as others. Lieutenant Gustl seriously contemplates suicide, all because a baker has most reprehensibly threatened to break his sabre. The aristocratic duel was long passé in England, however. As Trollope (1982), writing in the mid-19th century, reports duelling was looked on as altogether atavistic and pathetic. In place of such 'dreary' Continental ways, the English public schools taught the noble art of boxing. The point of honour would be decided in a highly ritualized way and at relatively low risk to life and limb. In Austria ever more duelling fraternities were set up with a pan-German nationalist agenda which carried the aristocratic code of honour to the middle classes while at the same time excluding people perceived to lack honour such as Jews. Developments in England went in the opposite direction. Here, the public schools propagated the ideal of *muscular Christianity*. The use of physical force, though not forbidden, was constrained by a fine meshwork of moral rules in the form of 'fair play'. Books like *Tom Brown's Schooldays*, published already in 1857 (Hughes 1993), describe the world inhabited by pupils at elite schools in categories of coarse and plucky masculinity, kept in check by the Christian moralism of the middle classes. Yet this new masculinity confronts the unscrupulous aristocratic *bully* with a new republican spirit. This opens yet another chapter in the history of the malleable links between the gentlemanly ideal of the upper classes and the puritanical middle-class ethos of traders and merchants, a history that can be traced back as far as the Renaissance (Bristow 1991: 55). Thus this new gentlemanly ideal is at odds equally with older aristocratic and recent utilitarian models. This utilitarian competitive individualism in the economic sector had to be altered to accommodate virtues fitting their bearers for leadership positions in England and its global empire. One trait was a fondness for the classics; another was a focus on physical strength and stamina, just what an expanding colonial presence required of its explorers, rulers and administrators. Kathryn Tidrick (1992) has studied the close ties between the spirit of the public schools and the ethos of colonial rule. After Thomas Arnold's reforms, a new spirit lodged in these elite academies. These reforms were instrumental in inculcating a typically English system of discipline and self-discipline into the members of the ruling class, with its variegated benefits and (high) psychic costs. Especially prized was the ability to lead others, with its imperative of enormous self-control.[4] This ideal was embodied in the school prefect who was chosen from amongst the pupils. When pupils broke the rules or engaged in undisciplined behaviour, it was the role of the prefect (also known as *praepostor*) to restore order. This meant that older pupils were assigned responsibility over younger ones. This brought to the rigors of school discipline an injection of self-administration, so that playing by the rules became something deeply anchored – qua self-constraint – in the personality structure of the young Englishman. The price paid for this discipline are only too well known: the system of *fagging* and *flogging* could lead to sadistic excesses, while latent or flagrant homosexuality was as much a part of school life as it was repressed.

Where the Austrian *Internat* (or cadet academy), as depicted in Robert Musil's *Zögling Törless* [The Confusions of Young Törless, Musil 2003], differed from the English public school is not so much in any proclivity for sadistic practices (after all, no hierarchical system can quite escape this), but rather in the sort of counter-strategy devised by the school authority (in German: first published in 1906). The English system enforced compliance from below – the *headmaster* was only brought in as a higher authority, when all else failed and catastrophe was impending. Otherwise England, too, at turn of the 20th century, is gripped by that aggressive and unpitying Social Darwinism that Musil demonstrates in the behaviour of the two pupils, Reiting and Beineberg, who persecute and torture another boy. Rudyard Kipling's story 'Stalky and Co.', first published in 1899, is set in a public school where aggressive individualism and lack of respect for traditional authority are not only described but, one assumes, extolled (Kipling 1986). Such individualism is reflected – along with the notion that native peoples around the globe require enlightened leadership to guide them from heathen barbarism to the heights of English civilization – in a number of English novels from the turn of the century. Rider Haggard's hero Alan Quatermain (Haggard 1951; first published in 1887) is a 'typically' English blend of courage, fearlessness, Christian forbearance, manly thirst for adventure and overarching sense of fairness. Politically far to the right and much criticized in his time for his frequent descent into violence, Haggard exemplifies nevertheless just how close the ties were between public-school ideals and exigencies of empire (Tidrick 1992; Rich 1991; Holt 1989).

Tidrick has convincingly shown how these ideals underpinned the exercise of authority in the English colonies. It is worth emphasizing that the indirect rule of the English along the model of the gentleman-squire and on the basis of massive self-constraints that were caused by the expectation that they should lead by example may have been in many respects more benign and considerate than rule exercised by other European colonial powers. Recently, this is an argument that has also been put forward by Niall Ferguson (2004).

Authority in the dock: The experience of the Great War

And so we arrive at one of those great historical turning-points that divide epochs. To be sure, old hierarchical structures were being eroded and slowly undermined throughout the age of the bourgeois, as the rise of the market, industrialization, urbanization and democratization took their toll. Yet nowhere is the encroaching irrelevance of traditional notions of authority more clearly exemplified than in the social dynamics of what came to be called the Great War. At first thought by contemporaries not to be possible at all, this war, when the guns finally fell silent, made people doubt that the *status quo ante* could ever be restored. Reactions to the war in England and Austria differed widely even before its outcome, that would bring costly victory for England and total collapse for the Habsburg Monarchy. In the following analysis, we focus on that literature that was written to problematize the war rather than legitimize it. In the Austrian case, we must address the towering work and person of Karl Kraus, whose writings exhibit an almost photographic realism. Nor is it possible to overlook the autobiographical writings of Egon Erwin Kisch in which he reports on his experience of the campaign in Serbia (Kisch 1991). Robert Ranke-Graves's *Goodbye to All That* (Graves 1958; first published in 1929) is the English pendant to Germany's Erich Maria Remarque with his famous book *Im Westen Nichts Neues* [*All Quiet on the Western Front*]. No less celebrated in England was Siegfried Sassoon's trilogy on the war years. In the following analysis we shall concentrate on the first volume of his semi-autobiographical novel *Memoirs of a Fox-Hunting Man* (Sassoon 1986; first published in 1928).

Karl Kraus's monumental drama *Die letzten Tage der Menschheit* [*The Last Days of Mankind*]; abridged English version 1974 (Kraus 1986; first published in 1922), contains many critical angles on the war and on the society that waged it. In the context of our overall argument, we skip over Kraus's humanistic pacifism for which the blood-letting on both sides is far more terrible than it is for a late-feudal warrior caste for which courage, bravery and honourable death in battle evinces quite different emotions. Instead, we shall consider some passages in which Kraus treats relations of authority in wartime.

The scene is set in one of Vienna's barracks, the so-called *Deutschmeisterkaserne*.[5] We watch how an Austrian sergeant and an elegantly dressed citizen take each other's measure:

> Gentleman: Excuse me – Sergeant – could you – perhaps tell me – I have been standing here for three hours – and no-one has come – I have a C-Befund[6] you see – I registered voluntarily before the deadline for reporting for duty in order to be assigned a post in the orderly-room – and I was told I should – stay – but I have to –
>
> Sergeant: Shut up!
>
> Gentleman: Yes – please – but I would like – I have to – please, at least – let my family know – and I cannot, as I am now – I need of course – my things for washing – a toothbrush, a blanket and such like –

> Sergeant: Shut up!
> Gentleman: But – please – forgive me – I did register – I did not know – I have to –
> Sergeant: Listen you fat pig, you say one more word and I'll whack you one
> (The gentleman produces a ten Crown note from the pocket of his waistcoat and offers it to the sergeant.)
> Sergeant: well now – look Sir – I really can't let you go home, that's not possible, but if you want a blanket – I'll make sure you get one. (He leaves the room.) (Kraus 1986: 144–5 , transl. A. S.)

This scene shows very clearly what Elias (2000: 371) calls 'affect-moderating code of conduct as a result of monetarization': the sergeant gives free rein to the authority the state has vested in him, reducing the (evidently better-off) recruit to a stuttering wreck, until a bribe changes hands. Only then is the sergeant willing to change his tune and be (within limits!) accommodating. Another aspect is the corruption involved, for Kraus with his incorruptible sense of justice frequently a target in his writings. A third aspect is the evident loyalty that the better-off man shows towards the state, although this is likely to have taken a battering after exposure to the sergeant's rudeness. Many in Austria, after all, had wanted 'to fix it', as Kraus records on numerous occasions in his drama.

Siegfried Sassoon's book paints a rather different picture of national loyalty. The narrator's servant, Dixon, volunteers to go off and fight even before his master does.

> Dixon had gone away to join the Army Veterinary Corps. This had happened two days ago. He was forty-three, bur he hadn't a grey hair, and he had stated his age as thirty-five. The news had a bracing effect on me. It wasn't the first time that Tom Dixon had given me a quiet hint as to what was expected of me. (Sassoon 1986: 255)

The servant by his example puts gentle pressure on his young master to do his patriotic duty. Bad conscience soon causes him to join an infantry regiment. Although his reception by the army does not fully live up to his expectations, it nevertheless differs from that described in Kraus:

> When our luggage was unloaded we went to report ourselves at the orderly room. Everything was quiet and deserted, for the troops were drilling on a big fields a few hundred yards up the road which wentpast the camp. We entered the orderly room. The adjutant was sitting at a table strewn with documents. We saluted clumsily, bur he did not look up for a minute or two. When we deigned to do so his eyes alighted on Mansfield. During a prolonged scrutiny he adjusted an eyeglass. Finally he leant back in his chair and exclaimed, with unreproducible hauteur, 'Christ! who's your tailor?' This (with a reminder that his hair wanted cutting) was the regimental recognition which Mansfield received from his grateful country for having given up a good job in the woollen industry. My own reception was in accordance with the cut of my clothes and my credentials from Captain Huxtable. (Sassoon 1986: 261)

George Sherston's clothes are well-cut, clearly his uniform is the work of a bespoke tailor. Both literary passages provide the reader with atmospheric impressions that he or she would not get from other sources. It is clear that both Austria and England are equally far removed from a normatively elevated model of impartial bureaucratic rationality. Still, the minute or two the Englishman spends waiting is rather shorter than the three hours the Austrian sergeant exacts as his due. When this difference in the reception of the recruits, in the source of their loyalty and the response it elicits or fails to elicit, is systematically corroborated, we are somewhat wiser about the code of discipline in the two armies. Kraus in any event cites many examples of a brutal exercise of authority towards the lower ranks, such as the practice of pointless frontal attacks in battle, of countless executions of alleged spies (not causing the court-martial judges any pangs of conscience), and everywhere evidence that some were 'having a good war'. Witness this presumably classical example:

> Fallota: Guess what? Yesterday I pulled a nice Polish girl - hurrah! A pity she can't be in the group photograph we're sending to the *Muskete*[7].
> Beinsteller: Aha, a maiden! – Hey, the military priest is going to be photographed for the *Interessante*,[8] on horse-back, giving the last rites. That shouldn't be too difficult, could be set up if necessary, you know, a young man could lie down, and the editorial office asked for prayers at the grave of a soldier, that always works.
> Fallota: Hey, I took a very interesting picture for you yesterday. A dying Russian, a shot of his head, very natural, a classic of its kind. You know – he was still able to stare at the camera. You should have seen the way he looked at you, you know, it was like it was set up, first rate, do you think that might be something for the *Interessante*, do you think they'd take it?
> Beinsteller: Would they ever! And pay for it too. (Kraus 1986: 148–9, transl. A. S.)

Several things stand out about this passage. One is the nonchalance with which the officers converse: in choicest Viennese upper-class accent larded with self-distancing irony, they pass from the light-hearted to the appalling and then back again:

> Fallota: Really? Oh, you missed something good, the corporal fainted yesterday when he propped up the spy, you know the Ruthenian priest, for the Sascha film at the execution, a pity you weren't there.
> Beinsteller: What did you do with him?
> Fallota: Tied him up of course. We won't lock him up, we're not living in peace after all – lock him up, the boys would love that! (Kraus 1986: 148–9, transl. A. S.)

'Tying up' was anything but a light punishment. The victim's arms were tied shoulder-high to a tree-trunk, as if to a martyr's stake, which caused almost unbearable pain. No less appalling were the endless executions of 'spies' in Serbia but even more so in Galicia and the Bucovina. They were particularly frequent where the population was suspected of collaborating with the Russian or Serbian enemy. Especially after setbacks or defeats, a gulf opened between the waning loyalty of the local people and the increasing distrust of the military and civil authorities. Nor were their suspicions (prone to escalate into paranoia) without a rational core, since intercepted dossiers did show a network of informers in Russian pay. And yet, one should not overlook that it was the Emperor himself who, time and again, by specific written order or decree, intervened to spare the civil population and who spoke out against arbitrary practices of arrest and punishment. The war took on much the same character that Elias analyzed for the decivilizing tendencies of World War II. He argues that despite their martial ethos aristocracies are less likely to embrace a code of unrestricted violence than middle and lower classes, which used to be further removed from the use of force and encountered the bellicose ideal only when at war (Elias 1996: 181–2).

For the aristocracy it was self-evident that the enemy should be treated according to a gentlemanly canon, a sentiment that the middle and the lower classes would eventually cease to share. The specific problem of the monarchy was the highly multilayered loyalties of its more than 12 nations. Authority often cracks down hardest where, in reality, it is most powerless. Vis-à-vis the Czechs or Ruthenians with Russian sympathies this was indeed the case.

This aspect is virtually absent from accounts by English contemporaries. To be sure, nowhere were British troops in a comparable situation of having to face on their own soil a hostile population (possibly the closest approximation could be found in parts of the Ottoman Empire that had become colonies). In the Austrian case, Egon Kisch (who was radically opposed to the war, and a pacifist and Communist to boot) cites a whole raft of similar cases of a highly brutal occupation policy. The historian Manfred Rauchensteiner, in turn, offers the following judgement:

> Those hanged, strangled, mutilated and shot in Serbia and in even greater numbers in Bukovina and Galicia, contributed to making the war recognizable as something it had in fact been since the wars against the French Revolution: a war of People against People. (Rauchensteiner 1993: 178; transl. A. S.)

But authority would turn most brutal when it lost legitimacy. In the aftermath of Austria's first severe defeat at Serbian hands, Kisch jots in his war journal what his comrades on the front were thinking:

> 'A bunch of Redls! They're all the same, a bunch of corrupt bastards, a load of spies, a bunch of traitors.' This accusation was made again and again, even by the most intelligent of lads. Trust in the leadership had already been shaken in peacetime by the stupid way they dealt with the affair involving Chief of Staff Redl. (Kisch 1991: 60; transl. A. S.)

This first Serbian campaign was ill-prepared in terms of logistics and organization. Food and drink were hard to come by; stupendous feats of marching were exacted in the heat; and in the command structure chaos reigned. The defeat was as severe as unexpected; no one thought the Serbs would hold their ground so tenaciously. Where the Austrian conduct of war erred, as Kraus has classically shown, was in its poor organization. An Austrian general reasons pensively about his side's ineptitude:

> Each one of you should harbour the ambition to introduce organization. Look, gentlemen, say what you want about the Germans – you have to hand it to them, they are well organized – [...] We are certainly better than them in some respects, for example that certain something, that *je ne sais quoi*, *gemütlichkeit*, you have to grant us that – but when we're in a mess, along come the Germans with their organization and – (Kraus, 1986, p. 196; transl. A. S.)

Bluntly, Manfred Rauchensteiner needs 719 pages to arrive at the same verdict about the Habsburg Monarchy.

But what was the view from the English side? Here too we find reckless attacks with heavy losses (the casualties from General Haig's *big push* on the Somme were much higher – at least on some days of battle – than anything that the Habsburg Monarchy's armies had to face). Here too we find bungling and wanton miscalculation. Still, we do not find in Graves or Sassoon the same note of cynicism, of alienation from military authority. To be sure, the devastating battles on the Somme had an aftermath. Graves was wounded so severely he was first left for dead and then spent several months convalescing in England. There he first met Sassoon and both of them became opponents of the war. They had seen men being thrown into attacks that ended in senseless slaughter; witnessed shoddily planned actions in which just a few hundred machine-gunners on the German side killed or wounded in just a few minutes advancing British infantry by the thousands. For all that, both men were keen to uphold their reputation for personal bravery, and reported back to front duty as soon as they could. Their protest was directed at three things. They could not stand the knee-jerk patriotism ubiquitous on the 'home front', with its hollow phrases and jingoistic sentiments – any more than could Remarque's heroes, for whom returning to the bone-grinding horrors of the front was better than enduring one more day of *hurra-patriotismus*. The whole way the war was being run seemed inhumane, which hardly surprises; and they resolved, when they returned to the front, to become better officers, better in the sense of taking responsibility for the men under their command. Mindless bullying, the wanton throwing of men into attacks that had little chance of success, the incompetence of many inexperienced officers from the upper classes – all of this was an abomination to them. As Graves says at one point, the difference between a responsible commander and officer and one who wasn't could make all the difference to common soldiers. The severity of this critique made Sassoon even toy with becoming a conscientious objector and caused both men sarcastically to suggest that their war-enthused elders, not the youth of England, should be manning the trenches, as they were closer to the grave anyway. But despite this bitterness Graves did admire without any pathos the dogged heroism of whole regiments that stoically, as if it were a parade-ground exercise, went to their deaths. In the final analysis, Graves and Sassoon saw the basic structures of authority in their society in which soldiers were asked to die 'For King and Country' as legitimate. Thus there is hardly an English parallel to the despotism of a certain Austrian grocer who, at a time of extreme scarcity and soaring prices, knew only to treat his customers like dirt (viz. the figure of Chramousta, Kraus's *Viktualienhändler*[9]). Nor, for that matter, do we find a scene like the one Kisch reports:

> It is moreover well-known that everyone in the isolation clinic dies, which is why Frau H, the wife of a reservist, a very good woman and mother of three children, visited the regimental doctor St. and stayed with him for three hours. I met her that evening, she was quite agitated and confused. She asked me to keep it to myself, but her husband would be discharged from the clinic the next day. (Kisch 1991: 251; transl. A. S.)

Certainly, from this episode one should not squeeze far-reaching conclusions, but it does give pause for thought. The practice of doing deals to subvert the bureaucratic decision process is more typical of a pre-modern society than a modern one structured around the principles of impartial rationality. The English ruling classes achieved less in the way of formal rationalization of bureaucracy than one would assume. But they did develop a rather more effective defence against arbitrary interventions of the above kind: for their canon of gentlemanly fair play bore universalizing tendencies. Despite the just critiques of arrogated authority, of excessive demands for national loyalty linked to blood sacrifice, it was England rather than Austria that passed this – arguably – most difficult of tests, the legitimacy of demands for national loyalty.

Notes

1 In German:
Der Track bewirbet sich mit fleiß
Das man den Götzen Ehr beweiß
Die Christlich Kirch thuets widerspil
Suecht und gewuent der Christen vil. (Szarota 1983: 425)

2 Rossbacher correctly shows that Ebner-Eschenbach reproduced and interpreted the historical events *pro domo* (i.e., in light of the gathering conflict between the nationalities in Bohemia and Moravia) by taking up a conciliatory-legitimistic stance. In fact, she had not witnessed the events in question, but wrote at a later date and in another place. This is in no way to impugn her familiarity with how nobility and peasantry actually interacted. That she possessed this knowledge, as a highly observant member of an aristocratic order whose *modus vivendi* she is describing, can be fairly assumed (Rossbacher 1992: 458–9).

3 Still, the officer corps (a privileged group whose higher ranks, with few exceptions, were open only to those of noble birth) did enjoy considerable prestige – irrespective of its military feats.

4 Cf. the report of the Clarendon Commission on the condition of the English public schools, published in the 1860s. The benefits of such an education are explained thus: 'A second, and a greater still, is the creation of a system of government and discipline for boys, the excellence of which has been universally recognized, and which is admitted to have been most important in its effects on national character and social life. It is not easy to estimate the degree in which the English people are indebted to these schools for the qualities on which they pique themselves most – for their capacity to govern others and control themselves, their aptitude for combining freedom with order, their public spirit, their vigour and manliness of character, their strong but not slavish respect for public opinion, their love of healthy sports and exercise.' (Bristow 1991: 67)

5 Its name is linked to the famous traditional *Hoch- und Deutschmeister - Infanterieregiment* Nr. 4.

6 A 'C-Befund' means a medical statement on the health of drafted soldiers which indicates a limited fitness for use.

7 *Muskete* [musket] is the name of a military magazine.

8 *Das Interessante* means a column in a magazine that contains various articles of 'human interest.'

9 *Viktualienhändler* means victualler or grocer.

Chapter 5

Feudal Paternalism in England: Developments within the Gentleman Canon

A literary example from the end of the era

The canon of the English gentleman is taken from warrior traditions of earlier times, as passed through the sieve of Christian and patriarchal influences. In 1915 Ford Madox Ford characterized the English gentleman in a complex novel of love, jealousy, deception and even '"the black merciless things" which lie behind that façade' (Graham Greene), as follows:

> I could see his lips form a word of three syllables [...] – and immediately I knew that he must be Edward Ashburnham, Captain, Fourteenth Hussars, of Branshaw House, Branshaw Teleragh. [...] His face hitherto had, in the wonderful English fashion, expressed nothing whatever. Nothing. There was in it neither joy nor despair; neither hope nor fear; neither boredom nor satisfaction. He seemed to perceive no soul in that crowded room; he might have been walking in a jungle. I never came across such a perfect expression before and I never shall again. It was insolence and not insolence; it was modesty and not modesty. (Ford 1946: 29–30)

The gentleman in question is a good soldier from an old family; about him is that indefinable something, a quasi-mystical aura. Courage, trustworthiness, honour and steadfastness are as much a part of him as perfect control of his facial features – that vaunted English 'reserve'; in addition, he has a flair for living well – hunting, adventure, thoroughbred horses, good boots, the best soap, excellent cognac and so on. He is beloved of women, is in every way one of the *good people*. Moreover, to his poor tenants he is a benevolent and paternal landlord (or at least he seems to be, for later the narrator chips away at the impression initially conveyed: in reality Ashburnham is a romantic bankrupt, the true state of his affairs having been kept from him by his wife).

Turn-of-the-century English literature was teeming with gentlemen from the landowning classes. In his major study *The Decline and Fall of the English Aristocracy*, David Cannadine (1990) considers this to have begun around 1880. The decline of the nobility was caused by collapsing agricultural produce prices and the amassing of huge fortunes from industrial and speculative investment: each factor in turn was driven by the first wave of globalization and a growing tax burden. Prior to this decline political rule[1] was almost entirely the preserve of the English nobility, notwithstanding the Industrial Revolution and the rise of the middle classes.

While at the turn of the century the influence of estate owners was slowly on the wane, their influence would remain considerable in the run-up to 1914. Moreover, if one draws a comparison across European states, the English landowning classes must be considered fairly small and exclusive – even when compared with the Habsburg Monarchy. The latter practiced a more liberal approach to the ennobling of talented outsiders, so that a politically weaker 'nobility of merit' co-existed with the old land-based nobility. Authority relationships in this hierarchical England are cast rather differently from those in Austria: in England paternalism has a different meaning and the mode of exerting authority is somehow milder, less direct, less constrained by exclusive personal dependency. The English nobility had also hung up its sword long ago, which was certainly not the case with most Continental nobilities.

Elias describes how the English gentleman canon differs from its German counterpart:

> But in the course of centuries, the latter [here the former] had been gradually transmitted with recognizable shadings and variations from landowning, aristocratic groups to other classes; this migration and modification of what was originally an upper-class code through its absorption by wide sections of the population is indicative of the relatively high permeability of the boundaries between social strata typical of the development of British society. (Elias 1996: 50)

This difference also mirrors a different code of interaction between those not equal in society. Long before it was customary in Germany it was customary in English society for higher-ranked individuals not to be deferred to ostentatiously. Moreover, the gap between formal and ritualized situations where decorum and comportment were expected, and situations where strangers and casual acquaintances rubbed shoulders in unconstrained ambience, was narrower there than on the Continent. The English 'party' embodied an easy-going, non-committal tone, while an air of nonchalance eased social intercourse between strangers. In Germany, in contrast, formal socialization proceeded in line with quite unmistakable and mandatory rules – personal introductions, hand-shaking, topped off by the highly formal *Sie* (precluding any descent into intimacy). But in situations of great familiarity the formality–informality span (Elias 1996: 28) neatly reverses as one moves from Germany to England: Even relaxing with his close friends, the upper-class Englishman was expected to show great self-control, whereas in Germany (e.g., in the drinking sessions staged by the university fraternities) it was possible to unwind and give free rein to the emotions. For Elias a pronounced formal-informal divide therefore points to a society in which the balance of power between higher-ups and lower-downs (in the work-place, between the generations, in social standing generally, between the sexes) is relatively one-sided – in other words, a society with authoritarian leanings.

It is evident that the English character exhibits two chief (or at least pronounced and clearly apparent) syndromes. These correspond in their genesis to two different historical phases and point to distinct social bearer classes in which they were fashioned as 'social characters'. Gentlemen and Puritans have repeatedly left their mark on this social order (as well as being marked by it). Reflecting the gentleman strand is the top-down nature of English society. This aspect of English society not only stresses differences in rank and social standing (and class, naturally), but also – importantly – a readiness on the part of social inferiors to accept their subordinate status and defer to duly constituted authority. Reflecting the Puritan strand is the notion of egalitarian meritocracy and the contractual nature of relations between persons who legitimately value their own interests. The gentleman model permits those living within it to pick and choose their enjoyments from a whole range of items; the Puritan model, by contrast, restricts these enjoyments considerably and harnesses them, in the sense of a middle-class code of diligent go-getting, to the constraints of sober calculation in the work-place. The aristocratic principle of the 'gentleman' is, as many observers have noted, of pan-European provenance, that is, it is not an English invention; but the fact that it spread to broad swathes of society (the social type of the policeman not excepted) points to circumstances not found elsewhere, or at least not to the same extent. The *hidalgo* – also in possession of an ancestral claim to the land – may likewise have left traces in the Spanish national character, but has not fused as seamlessly with middle-class characteristics so as to resonate throughout society on remotely the same scale. Likewise, the Austrian top civil servant – or higher-ranking official – had something 'aristocratic' about him; but here the gap between him and the upwardly mobile lower and middle classes was too large for it to be bridged by acquiring the right syndrome (*Schönbrunn* in German, cool composure, the stress on honour, feudal attributes of life-style).

The gentleman code can be traced back to the Norman Conquest, when a French-speaking class imposed itself on the relatively egalitarian England of Anglo-Saxons and Danes and ruled them from its strongholds through a centralized bureaucracy. Another milestone on the long road to the formation of an English popular character was the finely differentiated rise of the *gentry*, or untitled members of the ruling class. They were able to penetrate the 'body politic' more deeply than was possible for their many Continental counterparts which exuded a caste-like exclusivity. A landowning, semi-aristocratic intermediary class of commercially successful landlords and estate owners still intent on emphasizing their feudal honour and distinction, sat relatively well with the rural peasant classes they controlled and directed, with the latter acknowledging their rank and deferring to them. A further – and possibly more seminal step – in the formation of the English character was the inception and transmission of gentlemanly traits despite the absence of an ancestral seat and hereditary title: by drawing on the 'symbolic capital' of *genteel manners* and a certain *savoir-vivre* (dashing and gallant ways, siding with the underdog) and by exhibiting an aversion to toiling away at a regular job, gentlemanly traits were cultivated. Initially appearing in the 18th century and gathering pace in the 19th, the image of the gentleman started to acquire moral and Christian overtones and bedecked itself with a number of bourgeois values (*muscular Christianity*) to further stem the tide of the working middle classes.

The second strand in the English social character is the Puritan, chiefly found in the working middle classes (though by no means confined to these). It is oriented to *Common Law*, hostile to the upper classes and suspicious of all conspicuous display. Pitted against the French-speaking Norman conquerors and their cavalier life-style was a native Anglo-Saxon insistence on a dry, pragmatic modesty and sobriety, in addition to an unwillingness to accept situations deemed to be unjust as the will of God.

Each syndrome has its specific relation to 'authority'. The gentleman chiefly inhabits a world of high-born others, with whom he consorts in a manner regulated by conventions, on an equal basis. While certain differences in internal ranking exist in this world these are negligible compared to the gap that divides the high-born few from the mass of commoners, from whom deference can be exacted. As to how one related to the 'people' and the extent to which dominant members of the landowning class could lord it over the rural low-born, was a matter for each European society to decide on its own. A variety of patterns emerged. The English variety was a specific kind of patronage. While the lord of the manor held sway in matters of jurisdiction and administration, he abstained from matters dealing with the many and varied prerogatives relating to 'underlings'. And so the gentleman (and his latter-day look-alike hailing from 'better' social circles) was vested with quite specific traits of authority – to convince by setting an example, rather than by recourse to coercion. A need for great self-discipline therefore existed as he who would rule others must first rule himself. There was also pressure to show consideration to inferiors and dependants (*noblesse oblige*). What was required from the low-born is not that they prostrate themselves, but that they should defer to their betters without forfeiting their dignity. While these elements remained formally unchanged for several centuries, their substance changed considerably in the same time. A primary cause was a massive revamping of several dimensions of social organization. One aspect was that of evolving technology and industrial markets which led first to an early and then to a fully developed mode of capitalist production. A second aspect was that of the institutions of the state monopoly of force. These facilitated the transformation from a still barely controllable rural society, based essentially on the land and given to warlike ways, to a state-society that was both peaceable and urban. A third dimension of change concerned the culturally available depositories of knowledge. In a barbarous warrior society with learned priests and monks, these depositories of knowledge were differently situated than in a professional society requiring lengthy periods of training by the young, where academies were accorded greater prestige.

In English society we repeatedly find aristocratic and Puritan canons amalgamating in specific ways, to the point where each could be said to pervade the other. Indeed they often co-existed in one person (Defoe in one passage in *Moll Flanders* talks of that 'amphibious creature', half *gentleman*, half *tradesman*; Defoe 1989: 104). This can be seen in the dimension of authority: although the thirst for freedom in the English Puritan was boundless, the virtues of restraint and self-effacement were also present. What sets aristocratic *understatement* apart from Puritan *sobriety* is not always easy to identify. And is Puritan self-effacement markedly different from aristocratic *deference*?

Based on *The Good Soldier*, a novel by Ford Madox Ford, we will sketch how the English gentleman looked close to the period under study, that is, on the eve of the Great War. This celebrated novel is set in a privileged social milieu and describes a lurid *ménage à trois* – or is it *à quatre*? – which although apparently Gallic in inspiration has a characteristically English palette, with fine pastel shades prevailing over bold primary colours. The plot revolves around a proto-typical English gentleman – or more exactly, certain aspects of one. In this case the protagonist exhibits an obscure, tragic proclivity for vice that lands him in a despair beyond either words or remedy and whose downfall spells catastrophe for others too. Captain Ashburnham, one of the central figures, is a notorious ladies' man with a sentimental streak; in financial matters, however, he is immature and must be watched at every turn. In addition to these qualities there is something of the wolf about him, which drags others down into misfortune. The plot itself need not detain us, except to say that we learn to what extent gentlemanly perfection – which Ashburnham seems to incarnate – can obscure the murkiness and blemishes of his 'true' character. But what exactly is it that makes him a gentleman? First is the matter of his birth. When the so tragically deceived narrator (an American from New England) first meets the Ashburnhams at a German spa in 1904, he instantly knows that he has fallen in with *quite good people*. Their family background alone proves this.

> They were descended, as you will probably expect, from the Ashburnham who accompanied Charles I to the scaffold, and, as you must also expect, you would never have noticed it. (Ford 1946: 12)

All aristocracy, it goes without saying, is synonymous with pedigree, a visible line of descent with a 'Lineage Charisma' (Weber 1978: vol. 2, 1135) all its own (expressed here by the sacral itself in the person of the martyred king, a mystery rendered the more impenetrable by the intervening centuries). But the same sentence that dwells on aristocracy of birth also refers to aristocracy as a quality of mind, or at least a matter of bearing: nothing in Ashburnham's appearance is so tactless as to reveal his family origins. His manner is not ostentatious, but unassuming; his *understatement* stems from a sense of higher worth that neither has to be shown nor has to be justified. This is the celebrated trait of *effortless superiority*. Each of the Ashburnhams represents (idiosyncratically and invisibly) rank, wealth and aristocracy – as borne out by manners and comportment.

> For I swear to you that they were the model couple. He was as devoted as it was possible to be without appearing fatuous. So well set up, with such honest blue eyes, such a touch of stupidity, such a warm goodheartedness! And she – so tall, so splendid in the saddle, so fair! Yes, Leonora was extraordinarily fair and so extraordinarily the real thing that she seemed too good to be true. You don't, I mean, as a rule, get it all so superlatively together. To be the county family, to look the county family, to be so appropriately and perfectly wealthy; to be so perfect in manner – even just to the saving touch of insolence that seems to be necessary. (Ford 1946: 15–16)

Several of the traits that Ford lists here are familiar currency: good manners, played-down affluence, being 'splendid in the saddle', even the 'saving touch of insolence' needed to avoid seeming too perfect. Add to this honesty, good-heartedness, the hint of naivety and perhaps even a dash of stupidity. But even these traits are an aristocratic privilege: *we* don't need to be cunning – cunningness, for example, is for those who have no other choice. Compare this picture with Defoe's or Fielding's. Here the gentleman is still ostentatious in his wealth and his high rank is flaunted openly: Moll Flanders's husband – an amphibious cross between *gentleman* and *tradesman* – drives an elegant coach, stops only at the best inns, and has access to every possible accoutrement definitive of a high social position. One constant is the horse. As in Fielding's day, the gentleman plays an important and powerful role in his county's affairs. Much like the character in Fielding's novel, *Tom Jones*, Ashburnham is cast as the defender of the poor and weak.

> Or again: Edward Ashburnham was the cleanest looking sort of chap; – an excellent magistrate, a first rate soldier, one of the best landlords, so they said, in Hampshire, England. To the poor and to hopeless drunkards, as I myself have witnessed, he was like a painstaking guardian. (Ford 1946: 18)

Ashburnham therefore conforms to the tradition of the venerable gentry. This, at least, is how it appears to the unwitting observer. For, in reality, a man of weak character lurks behind the solid image: a man who is both a philanderer and a spendthrift permanently in debt. The respectable couple are themselves deeply caught up in a hopeless 'clinch', robbing them of their dignity. Ashburnham is a local official in the tradition of the English gentry, a charitable patron and landlord. An important trait here and one that is aristocratic to the core, is that he is well-disposed towards the needy – a recurrent *leitmotiv* of English novels describing life on the land. The idea of *noblesse oblige* both co-existed with and transcended a middle-class culture of puritanical and utilitarian leanings. The latter derived from notions of self-improvement and the calculated pursuit of self-interest, while the former was to manifest in English social policies of a paternalistic state. The privileged wielders of authority also have duties to perform, an expectation that gained entry into English colonial practice. While colonials were never accorded equal standing with their white masters, they could, and did, lay claim to the latter's good will and benevolence. It is this kind of authority that the 'born gentleman' displays so inimitably and non-confrontationally, even though it is hardly called for in his capacity as a visitor at a German spa.

> And then, one evening, in the twilight, I saw Edward Ashburnham lounge round the screen into the room. The head waiter, a man with a face all grey – in what subterranean nooks or corners do people cultivate those absolutely grey complexions? – went with the timorous patronage of these creatures towards him and held out a grey ear to be whispered into. It was generally a disagreeable ordeal for newcomers but Edward Ashburnham bore it like an Englishman and a gentleman. (Ford 1946: 29)

Ashburnham tolerates the timidly patronizing manner of the head waiter and his body language reveals him to be very much the *Englishman* and *gentleman* who rises above the petty annoyances of everyday life. He doesn't seem to notice his surroundings, nor does he appear to need anything from anybody. Linked to this is his ability to control his facial expressions in a certain manner. With such mastery over one's facial expressions, controlling one's feelings comes easily. Not betraying how or what one feels is a skill good poker-players cultivate and excel at and hands to its possessor a considerable advantage over others in social interaction. It comes across as a strength and commands respect:

> His hair was fair, extraordinarily ordered in a wave, running from the left temple to the right; his face was a light brick– red, perfectly uniform in tint up to the roots of the hair itself; his yellow moustache was as stiff as a toothbrush and I verily believe that he had his black smoking jacket thickened a little over the shoulderblades so as to give himself the air of the slightest possible stoop. It would be like him to do that; that was the sort of thing he thought about. Martingales, Chiffney bits, boots; where you got the best soap, the best brandy, the name of the chap who rode a plater down the Khyber cliffs; the spreading power of number three shot before a charge of number four powder...by heavens, I hardly ever heard him talk of anything else. (Ford 1946: 30)

Projecting self-control in public requires prosaic virtues which are specifically male in their nature and revolve around hunting, warfare and various adventures. These are the tastes of the male ruling class and do not show any recourse to the feeble spheres of art and literature. Yet Ashburnham – like all good soldiers – is at root a man of sentiment. The words courage, fidelity, honour and dependability continue to hold great appeal for him.

The gentleman canon and Puritanism: Pathways to the English character

The example of Ashburnham, for which we are indebted to Ford, is an object lesson in the making of what we have called the 'gentleman canon' of conduct, or rather its latter-day manifestations. This canon is underpinned by highly complex social rules. No less complex are the ramifications for psychic experience or even 'affective control', in those guided by this canon. While undeniably rooted in the code of chivalry practiced by medieval warriors, it contains elements that take us farther afield. *Chivalry*, as understood in the Middle Ages, referred primarily to norms of warfare or courtly decorum, extended as a rule only to social equals. It was quite capable of co-existing with what, to us, seems incredible brutality and barbarity. Barbara Tuchman supplied numerous examples of this dichotomy in her *A Distant Mirror* which dealt with the Hundred Years War between 'England' and 'France' (both modern projections on to the past) (cf. Tuchman 1987). In contrast, Ashburnham's comportment and range of expressible emotion is in many ways restricted. His love of adventure is confined to clearly demarcated areas and he is otherwise peaceable in his ways. He does not duel and overbearing behaviour is avoided, as is any loudness or grossness of speech that might find outlet in some affect or other. Given that this novel is about a steamy relationship between three of the four principals, the hero's language is decidedly prudish. His behaviour – even towards those well below him on the social scale (described using terms like *timorous* and *creatures*) – is extremely controlled and reserved. Without regard to the person, he helps the poor and the marginalized and is evidently on good terms with the tenants of his manor in his capacity as landlord. Though the novel is poor in detail, our impression is that we are dealing with someone who wields power in a benevolent fashion and who views himself as an exemplary individual.

One of the peculiarities of English social development which is significant for wider European developments in general is its early transition to parliamentary rule and the early formation of the market. Both processes were heavily influenced by similar mentalities. It was Max Weber who attributed the rise of markets to a Protestant ethic centered on the middle classes and Norbert Elias who saw the emergence of parliamentary rule as going hand in hand with the 'sportization' of the English upper classes. For Elias, this constitutes something of a natural foil to the 'courtization' of the French warrior nobility – the English character having been indelibly marked in the process.

The rise of sport as a factor in English life affords insight into a specific civilizing process – namely, the curbing of physical violence and 'joy in attacking' (*Angriffslust* in Elias, usually translated only as 'aggressiveness'; cf. Elias 2000: 161–72; cf. also Mennell 1989: 249, who translates Elias's term – literally – as 'pleasure in attacking') under a precisely spelled-out code of *fairness*, which should be seen as a variant of the gentleman canon. Its rise, for Elias, ties in closely with English political power assuming the form it did. The histories of many pastimes indicate a certain pattern: as elements of traditional popular culture, we find an indeterminate number of wild events of a competitive nature involving bodily contact. Their rules are not written down anywhere, but nevertheless passed on through the generations. These spectacles either involved mass participation (whole villages, old and young, men and women) or were performed before spectators (ox-baiting, bear-baiting, cock fights, dog fights, bare-knuckle boxing, fencing duels). In all cases much blood was shed. In 1710, for instance, the German traveller von Uffenbach described such a spectacle in detail.

> They [the cocks] bleed most horribly from their combs and decapitate each other with their claws or tear each other's entrails out. Nothing provides more satisfaction than when one seems fatigued; then there are roars of triumph and horrific betting ... If someone bets but cannot pay up afterwards, he is punished by being made to sit in a basket; this is affixed to the ceiling and hoisted up, at which point great guffaws of laughter are heard. The people in their betting go at each other as hotly as do the cocks themselves. (von Uffenbach, in: Maurer (ed.) 1992: 56-7; transl. B. A.)

Von Uffenbach also reports on bull-baiting and fencing for prize money, in which opponents would often almost kill each other. These precursors of today's sporting fixtures were marked by two things: frequent outbursts of spontaneous (illegitimate) violence, as well as a generally high level of tolerated violence. This was also also true for games which were barely codified in form, often varied from county to county and served as precursors for present-day soccer and rugby. By the end of this trend that lasted well into the 19th century, violence and the impulsive expression of joy in watching the display of violence had been whittled away at and steered in certain directions by codes and rules. Uncouth working-class or popular spectacles gave way to relatively anodyne encounters, governed by rules of fair play and presided over by referees or umpires. These were encounters where self-restraint and the ability to get a handle on hatred and blind passion were central. A fruitless centuries-long struggle against popular sports subversive of the social order[2] finally yielded to the emergence of the team sports we know today. These sports emerged from *public schools* like Rugby or Winchester and demanded that a tight lid be kept on physical aggression. This became a model for the rest of the world. Another class of amusements was confined mostly to the landowning upper classes: tournaments and hunting had always dominated the life of the warrior castes that constituted Europe's nobility. (The Habsburgs too hunted as if the Lord's favour depended on it.) The tournament in courtly societies evolved into a chivalrous test of prowess for young noblemen at Court. In an England that from a certain period onwards associated martial leadership less with military skill than with command of the high seas, we find – according to Elias – an emerging refinement in the sense of a new notion of *fairness.* This notion was highly codified in its manifestations and even involved a certain degree of 'sublimation', as when the killing of the fox was left to the hounds (since the true excitement and point of the exercise lay in the chase rather than in its consummation).

Weber's study of the Protestant ethic's place in creating a mentality apt for a market economy (and for professionalization generally) is probably the most cited and commented on study in all of social science. Yet it has aspects that have been less well explored, one being the extent to which Weber describes the English national character. He does explicitly examine the *Volkscharakte*r of the English. One instance is when he casts casts doubt on its uniformity (Weber 1976: 88; the German expression *Volkscharakter* can be found in the German edition of Weber 1972: 81). In talking about Cavaliers and Roundheads in the 17th century, he notes that they were more than just the two contending parties in the Civil War and answered to 'radically different species of mankind'. He further contends that character logical differences between Hamburg and English merchants had barely existed 'beforehand'. Only after the rise of the religious movements had a new type formed in England. Weber talks of a still unfinished confrontation between two ways of being English. The pride the English took in their nation was, thanks to the Magna Carta, already present at the end of the Middle Ages. Also present was foreign recognition of the fetching ways of English maidenhood. And yet, according to Weber, the national character of all peoples with a Puritan past manifest a pessimistically tinged individualism devoid of illusion (Weber 1976: 105). The principal writers studied by him were English (Baxter and Wesley, first and foremost). In connection to this Weber cites warnings about trusting do-gooders, as well as the anti-authoritarian leanings of Puritans. To the latter he attributed the American objection to performing personal service, the democratic tradition and the immunity all puritanically inclined peoples show to Caesarism (in express contrast to Germany). According to Weber even English reserve (which is what is specifically English about the gentleman) stems from Puritanism (Weber 1976: 119). (The pendant in Weber to the ridiculous role Elias [2000: 404–5] assigns to the Duke of Montmorency, whose failure is due to his relish for attacking at the drop of a hat, is the sober Cromwell and his band of *Ironsides*. Cromwell is the father of modern military discipline: his Puritans ride, pistols drawn, right up to the enemy lines, holding their fire until the last. The ascetic principle of self-control proves its utility here!)

What we find in both Weber and in Elias – and this is true throughout their work – is a clear complementarity of substantive interests. These overlap repeatedly at points where the values and life-styles of the aristocratic ruling classes and predominantly bourgeois middle classes happen to meet. Citing the *Book of Sports*, Weber mentions the struggle of James I and Charles I against anti-authoritarian Puritans hostile to pleasure. Baxter's bourgeois code directly and indirectly offends the traditional ethos and life-style of the leisured nobility. In *The Civilizing Process* Elias paid more attention to these classes than to the citizenry as such. In Weber's work, on the other hand, the citizenry are always in the foreground, as they involve themselves in book-keeping and civil administration, religion and the division of labour, and find themselves even in discussions about ancient Rome, China or ancient Israel, In his studies on the rise of the seafaring vocations (Elias 1950), Elias contrasts the rank-conscious gentleman with the lower-class seaman ('tarpaulin'), while in his sociology of sport, Elias was chiefly concerned with depicting the gentleman in politics and at play. Similarly Weber's concern was to treat the working middle classes in terms of the economy, religion and the work-place. In the English character the theme underlying these perspectives is, firstly, a struggle between groups and, secondly, a struggle between character– forming life-styles, the latter involving a number of amalgamations, in which both elements, the aristocratic and the bourgeois, have a place.

A glance at Baxter's rules (Weber 1976: 155–83) reveals the bourgeois component:

- Striving for money and property is damned.
- Leisure and enjoyment must not be sought, action is mankind's goal.
- Wasting time is sinful.
- Gregariousness, luxury, bad language, even sleeping longer than six or seven hours, are to be eschewed. The result is the breaking of the spontaneity of life and enjoyment, engendering *melancholy* and *moroseness*.
- Constant reflection is called for, *watchfulness* is an imperative.
- Work is the royal road to ecstasy. Sexuality – unless for reproductive purposes – is condemned.
- Even the rich have to work. Working at a fixed trade is useful. Turning a profit is obligatory.
- Begging is a sin against charity. (As was the case earlier with the *Book of Sports*, here too the Stuarts sided with the old path of Christian charity and aristocratic *noblesse oblige*, favouring official relief for the poor as well as measures to get the jobless back into work, all of which drew an outraged outcry from Puritans.)
- God blesses sober-minded tradesmen and manufacturers; he does not condone seignorial ostentation (or the gentleman's focus on standing and rank).
- All forms of enjoyment are to be shunned – whether these be football, lyric poetry, singing, the theatre, nudity, fashion, idle speech; or (more generally) giving way to passion, pride, wealth; or taking any pleasure in material goods.
- What is practical and useful is to be preferred. Self-chastisement is unnecessary.
- Joylessness and diligently going about one's business is demanded, viewing sport not as a pleasurable pastime but as a disciplining of the body – these traits would outlive the expunging of their religious roots.

All these rules had, according to Weber, draped themselves like a frost over the life of *merry old England*. The different routes taken by Austria, with its manorial absolutism and its Counter-Reformation, and an England caught between the extremes of aristocratic privilege and the reforming zeal of the Puritans, the antithetical canons of the gentleman (cf. Macfarlane 1978) and the merchant, spring to mind. English literature is replete with examples of this stand-off (hard work vs. gentlemanly leisure), but it also reveals points of confluence (modesty, understatement, sobriety, mistrust of authority). Bunyan's *Pilgrim's Progress* (1678) to the Heavenly City will probably not be outdone in imaginative richness by the conversion dramas of the Jesuits, although by being a novel it may well speak less directly to the senses. The Puritan legacy crops up later on numerous occasions – in Defoe, for example, who can be seen to have written books both on the English gentleman and on the English tradesman (in *Moll Flanders* we encounter this polarity extensively). There are the Brontë sisters and Samuel

Butler's *The Way of All Flesh* (first published in 1903) and this polarity is also present in one of the giants of the 18th century, Henry Fielding.

Literary examples of how the gentleman canon evolved in the 18th century

Henry Fielding's novel *Tom Jones* (first published in 1749) sets out the gentleman canon as it stood in the first half of the 18th century in exemplary fashion. The canon is personified in the hero himself, though it must be said that here ideal traits (Fielding, we know, was much influenced by Cervantes and his Don Quixote; cf. Preston 1982) greatly overshadow realistic ones. This is very much the case with Squire Allworthy, the kindly and fair-minded estate owner and justice of the peace. He is, as the name implies, virtue personified. Squire Weston, however, is painted with a more realistic brush: a rollicking, hard-drinking member of the county gentry, whose passion for fox-hunting is boundless. No less realistic is the way Fielding sets out innumerable details of the social life of the time – from the peculiar ways in which masters and servants interact, to the risks of using public carriageways, to the vices and vanities of the clergy and the steamier side of London society.

If it is true that Tom Jones is the ideal-typical hero of a *Entwicklungsroman* in which moralism and satire vie equally for attention, then it is also true that the way in which the social values of the day are reproduced is nothing if not realistic. While it cannot be supposed that English gentlemen conform to this paradigm either broadly or narrowly, it is worth watching Tom as, in the following scene, he saves the lady of his heart from mortal danger:

> Tom Jones, who was at a little distance behind, saw this, and immediately galloped up to her assistance. As soon as he came up, he immediately leapt from his own horse, and caught hold of her's by the bridle. The unruly beast presently reared himself an end on his hindlegs, and threw his lovely burthen from his back, and Jones caught her in his arms.
>
> She was so affected with the fright, that she was not immediately able to satisfy Jones, who was very solicitous to know whether she had received any hurt. She soon after, however, recovered her spirits, assured him she was safe, and thanked him for the care he had taken of her. Jones answered, 'If I have preserved you, madam, I am sufficiently repaid; for I promise you, I would have secured you from the least harm, at the expense of a much greater misfortune to myself, than I have suffered on this occasion.' (Fielding 1985: 191–2)

What we are getting here, and in bold strokes too, is a code of chivalry handed down from medieval times. In a society dominated by feudal aristocracy, male strength and skill at arms were important status attributes. Also in high demand were devotion and fidelity to one's liege-lord, or to a high-born lady (celebrated as the unattainable object of higher love by wandering minstrels, also known as troubadours or *Minnesänger*). Equally indispensable were munificence, mildness of manner and a selfless commitment to aiding the weak.

At times, as will shortly be apparent, this code becomes a trifle overwrought:

> 'What misfortune', replied Sophia, eagerly, 'I hope you have come to no mischief?'
> 'Be not concerned, madam', answered Jones. 'Heaven be praised, you have escaped so well, considering the danger you was in. If I have broke my arm, I consider it as a trifle, in comparison of what I feared upon your account.'
> Sophia then screamed out, 'Broke your arm! Heaven forbid.'
> 'I am afraid I have, madam', says Jones, 'but I beg you will suffer
> me first to take care of you. I have a right-hand yet at your service, to help you into the next field, where we have but a very little walk to your father's house.' (Fielding 1985: 192)

The above passage structures chivalry, again, on two levels: there is the plot itself, where Tom in saving Sophia from falling manages to break his arm; and there is the ensuing exchange between them, where Tom downplays his injury to spare the damsel any qualms of conscience (he even begs her to consent to further ministrations on her behalf, taking care not to seem importuning). Fielding leaves us in the dark about as to whether or not he is drawing out this somewhat exalted gesture to the point of parody. Or is he simply playing to the sentimental urges of 18th century readers (as Richardson palpably does in *Clarissa*)?

But such altruism can be subsumed under more than the code of chivalry; there is also the aspect of romantic love. The natural counter-pole to this is the calculating and egotistical code of utility maximalization, as insisted upon elsewhere in market-minded England (see Defoe's *Moll Flanders*) and which is a very real presence. (The hypocrite and intriguer Master Blifil embodies this Puritan trait, as does Vicar Thwackum, Tom's teacher, with his unfeeling and heartless ways.) Here Fielding toys quite deliberately with the possibility that such altruistic urges, whether translated into action or confined to rhetoric, could be deployed as a decoy to attain goals closer to home, as is plainly the case in other passages.

Other than in the early 20th century, however, the world and the public space in which one moves is still far from peaceful.

Integral to the gentleman canon is the special stress placed on honour and rank (the higher the rank, the greater the honour) and this is not entirely surprising, given its origins within a warring aristocracy. The very mode of address – 'your worship' – exhibits this aspect. (Whereas *Euer Gnaden*, the form so dear to Austrians, articulates more strongly the idea of a horn of plenty, from which the addressee is presumed to be able, at his discretion, to dispense largesse – whether deserved or undeserved. Fielding too is well aware of the difference between *grace*, which is unearned, and *justice*, which is apportioned on the basis of merit, as he makes clear in Tom's relationship with Allworthy.) Of course, being a 'bastard', Tom can claim a gentleman's rank only insofar as the cultural capital of 'good breeding' and Allworthy's willingness to treat him as a member of his own family warrants this. Tom must fight for his honour, as when he finds himself (in defence of his Sophia's honour) trading blows with the churlish ensign Northerton (Fielding 1985: 342). In the 18th century their quarrel can only be resolved by violence; a century later this will largely have changed.

Here (and also in the duel of daggers with Fitzpatrick) Tom is instantly ready to challenge his man, contrasting oddly with the rational consideration he shows in other matters.

In Fielding's *Tom Jones*, as in Defoe's *Moll Flanders*, we find graphic descriptions of a high general willingness to resort to violence in everyday life. This would change with the establishment of a regular police force (only in 1829 did Sir Robert Peel turn his 'Bobbies' or 'Peelers' loose on the streets of London). Some indications are given as to how punishment was meted out, although these indications are few compared to what we find, for example, in the pages of Dickens. What stands out instantly is the number of occasions in which parties to a quarrel use their fists or even draw swords. Thus, for instance, a pitched battle takes place in the churchyard immediately after the Sunday service, '*where, amongst other mischief, the head of a travelling fiddler was very much braken*' (Fielding 1985: 181). Tom and Thwackum, the vicar, settle their differences in a boxing match, with Blifil and Squire Western being drawn in for good measure. We have already mentioned the spat between Tom and the ensign: it too ends bloodily. Jones and the jealous Fitzpatrick cross swords; and, time and again, we find the lady's maids (Fielding 1985: 326), the innkeeper's wife and the chambermaids (Fielding 1985: 569) exchanging blows. In London ne'er-do-wells incite and provoke brawls. On the whole the impression we get is one of a society with a decided taste for violence, in which *highway robbers* and *press gangs* are as much a part of the scene as the notorious proclivity for sporting with animals (bull-baiting, cock fights, dog fights). G. Gorer is therefore on to something when he finds it remarkable (Gorer 1955: 294–8) that one of Europe's more aggressive and unruly populaces changed into one of its most law-abiding and where the sight of the unarmed 'Bobby' on his beat soon acquired almost mythical force. The command of the state appears, therefore, in the shape of Allworthy, the local justice of the peace (JP); in the constable, who conducts Tom Jones to gaol (where Partridge, Jones's servant, visits him, knees trembling and heart pounding); in the regiment sent to crush the Jacobite Rebellion (the novel is set in 1746, the year of the Battle of Culloden); and in the cheery lock-up to which Jones is sent. The state's reach further manifests in the *press gangs*, who are quite taken with Tom's seafaring potential.

> It seems these fellows were employed by a lord, who is a rival of poor Mr. Jones, to have pressed him on board a ship. ...which he would never have done had he known Mr. Jones to have been a gentleman; but he was told that he was a common strolling vagabond. (Fielding 1985: 826)

That gentlemen were accorded different treatment emerges with even greater clarity when the constable extends the greatest courtesy to Tom who has (we can assume) just killed his opponent, as soon as it is plain that he has a man of that description before him.

> The constable seeing Mr. Jones very well drest, and hearing that the accident had happened in a duel, treated his prisoner with great civility, and, at his request, dispatched a messenger to enquire after the wounded gentleman, who was now at a tavern under the surgeon's hands. (Fielding 1985: 775)

To kill someone in a duel was classed in England as murder. However, convictions were hard to obtain from juries and remained so until the mid-19th century (cf. Pool 1994: 302–3). So while in terms of his 'joy in attacking' the 18th-century gentleman was not particularly given to peaceful ways and self-control (a fact related to the still flimsy controls placed on violence in public space), his *galanterie* and Christian charity had never been greater – his gentler virtues sitting uneasily with his harsher ones.

Now let us ask how the propertied gentleman, his authority semi-feudal in kind, related to those lower down the pecking order in house, municipality and society. Where did the authority of the landowning class reside? In contrast to much of the Continent (and so naturally in Central Europe) the landowning class exercised no direct control over a peasant class, as defined by the obligation of forced labour (a certain number of days of service a year on the landlord's estates) and by vocational immobility (only if the landlord allowed him, could the peasant switch to another trade). In *Tom Jones* we find many examples of this class's authority, shored up by clear legal title. Only members of the gentry (and grandees self-evidently too) have the right to hunt. Ownership of all game on their property is vested in them, not in their tenants. The gamekeeper is therefore a key figure. If he is careless, or himself does a bit of poaching on the side, he is sacked by Squire Allworthy (the fate of 'black George', of whom Tom is so fond). Allworthy keeps a watchful eye on his family and the domestics under his roof; for a misdeed Tom is flogged severely. As fathers, Squire Western and Squire Allworthy have the right (or rather the power) to marry their children off, even against their will, to whomsoever they choose. The chief consideration is that the match enhances both families' economic fortunes. Allworthy's 'authority' rests on many foundations: with respect to his family and the circle of domestics his 'patriarchal authority' is based on economic reality and ties of kinship. These are legally defined and constitute the remains of the function of violence control vested in him in earlier times and as yet not fully 'usurped' by the state. To his tenant farmers he is economic power personified, and as the local JP he has the final say in just about all legal and political matters bar the gravest (which have to be brought before a jury). His power reaches to all residents in his locality (requisite was a certain income and appointment to the post by a 'Lord Lieutenant', who disposed of the necessary executive power). 'Justices' (also known as magistrates) were the administrative lynchpins in that far-off England: they appointed the overseers of the poor, the constable, the inspector of highways; and they conferred regularly with other JPs of the county to discuss issues concerning society as a whole.

As late as 1883 English juries ruled against no more than 12,000 defendants; in the same year, local authorities locked up 80,000 persons without formal process (cf. Pool 1994: 196). To be sure, in the latter case there was a right of appeal (the King's Bench overturned two ill-considered verdicts by Squire Western, cautioning him that he would be stripped of office unless his performance improved), but it would seem that this was rarely invoked. Such stalwart privileges vested in the gentry (almost all magistrates and parish vicars were recruited from its ranks). This gave its members a position of strength and formed the basis for the respect and deference that was theirs, too, in a less formalized sense. Fielding affords us insights into how such authority was psychically processed by those lower down, as when he describes the actions of the female domestic who discovers the foundling Tom.

> Such was the discernment of Mrs. Wilkins, and such the respect she bore her master, under whom she enjoyed a most excellent place [...] and she took the child under her arms, without any apparent disgust at the illegality of its birth; and declaring it was a sweet little infant, walked off with it to her own chamber. (Fielding 1985: 57–8)

The respect Mrs Wilkins feels is so great that she is shocked at seeing her master on the fateful night standing there clad only in his night-shirt. Allworthy inspires the same or even greater respect in the young Tom, as when after he has been thrashed by Allworthy for stepping out of line, the latter mollifies him with a liberal present. Such mildness of manner on his chastiser's part brings Tom to the verge of confessing, which would have meant betraying his friend. This is a further indication that clemency rather than force brings forth that kind of self-constraint that we call 'conscience'. Threading its way through the entire novel is the theme of 'authority by example' – and to set an example to others, dignitaries must first work hard on themselves. When Fielding is describing something it is not easy to say what is being idealized and what is realistic. On the whole, however, we gain a sense of manorial authority, in which *charity*, active sympathy for the poor and internalized recognition of higher rank by lower-downs co-exists in tolerably harmonious asymmetry. Even into the 20th century, English colonial officials have, when practicing *indirect rule,* accepted this ideal of a life-style defined in distinctly moral terms, leading not by force alone but also by force of example. Tidrick has cited many examples of this (Tidrick 1992).

What Fielding is depicting here, long before it resurged in the *public schools* of the second half of the 19th century, is the ideal of *muscular Christianity*, to call it by its later name. He is thus promoting a sense of Christian compassion and charity; as in the case where Tom helps Mrs Miller find a high-born son-in-law for her daughter, allowing the woman to praise Tom as possessing '*one of the most humane tender honest hearts that ever man was blessed with*' (Fielding 1985: 780).

On his death-bed even Square, his hidebound old philosophy teacher, atones for his earlier misdeeds by describing Tom in the rosiest terms in a letter to Allworthy (*'your most obliged, obedient humble servant'*).

> Believe me, my friend, this young man hath the noblest generosity of heart, the most perfect capacity for friendship, the highest integrity, and indeed every virtue which can enoble a man. (Fielding 1985: 824)

We see here, however, how the specific virtues of the gentleman increasingly have to yield before a general human ideal – more is going on than meets the eye when, in a different passage and spoken of another gentleman, we read: *'he was so genteel, and had so much wit and good breeding'* (Fielding 1985: 835).

An oddity of the novel is that Tom has an abundance of the same Christian virtues of charity and selflessness that are so conspicuously absent in Master Blifil, his outwardly pious adoptive brother. Fielding has a sure feel for the discrepancy between formal (and therefore superficial) behaviour and the humanistic-cum-moral promptings of 'conscience', so much so that critics have fixed on this as something of a *leitmotiv* of *Tom Jones*.

This brings us to an important point. As already discussed in detail with respect to Max Weber, we can distinguish between 'two types of Englishness' – red-faced John Bull as the incarnation of 'merry old England' and the pale, thin-lipped Puritan, whose asceticism draped itself, 'like a hoar-frost', over all the merry-making. Tom Jones's sly and calculating foe is Master Blifil, aided and abetted by the bigoted vicar Thwackum, to whom, sadly, Allworthy has entrusted the task of educating young Tom. 'Sober and pious' the Puritan was supposed to be, as Weber treading in the footsteps of Baxter, Wesley and Franklin described him, and it is very much in these terms that Fielding describes the young Blifil:

> He was, indeed, a lad of a remarkable disposition; sober, discreet, and pious, beyond his age. (Fielding 1985: 123)

'Beyond his age' – thus encapsulated is Blifil's self-control, ruling out any sexual or other adventures. Blifil is devoid of the hallowed virtues of kindness, munificence and pity:

> Master Blifil fell very short of his companion in the amiable quality of mercy; but he as greatly exceeded him in one of a much higher kind, namely, in justice: in which he followed both the precepts and example of Thwackum and Square; ... (Fielding 1985: 147)

Fielding's ironic tone is unmistakable, indicating just where his sympathies lie. Such 'justice' is readily compatible with Thwackum wanting Tom to get the flogging he richly deserves. 'Justice' must at times turn its back on compassion, insists Thwackum.

> He said, in some instances, what the world called charity appeared to him to be opposing the will of the Almighty, which had marked some particular persons for destruction; and that... (Fielding 1985: 144)

We recognize here, readily enough, the Puritan doctrine of predestination to hell – fire. The whole novel in fact abounds with examples of Thwackum's and Blifil's treachery, leaving us in no two minds as to what hypocrites they both are. Or this, at least, is what Fielding intends – as to how much both are permeated perhaps by their conviction and stance, we will not even attempt to resolve. What we do note is that Fielding attaches (Thwackum is a Church of England man, but Blifil will later switch to the Methodists) a description of God-fearing business acumen to his account of Puritan piety, as may be seen in a scene (Fielding 1985: 144–5) where Blifil's facility with figures goes hand in hand with his plotting against Tom.

The contrast between this sober and ascetic trait of character, at once hypocritical and given to plotting and scheming, and the easy-going yet rather more upright life – style of the gentleman becomes clearer when we consider how Nimrod, who curses and drinks but feels genuine love for his daughter, captures the young Allworthy for Squire Weston:

> ...and many a wench have we two had together. As errant a whoremaster as any within five miles o'un. No, no. It will do'n no harm with he, assure yourself; nor with anybody else. Ask Sophy there – You have not the worse opinion of a young fellow for getting a bastard, have you, girl? No, no, the women will like un the better for't. (Fielding 1985: 182)

Allworthy's thoroughly loose sexual morals in his salad days were evidently no barrier to him becoming the epitome of goodness and fair-mindedness in later years.

We therefore do not err excessively in discerning a kind of show-down between two different codes of conduct in Fielding's novel. Honour is pitted against religion – not for nothing does Thwackum on one occasion ask: '*... or can any honour exist independent of religion?*' Here the vicar (who, as we have seen, was mostly appointed from the gentry) has the standing of one who carries authority with his flock.

So let us draw up a provisional balance of the gentleman canon and English attitudes to authority, such as these had developed by Fielding's day and find reflection in his work.

First, the canon is practiced by a leisured class, at a great distance from the 'common people'. *Manners, good breeding and wit* matter more than diligently plying a trade or demonstrating business acumen, qualities that are central to the Puritan canon. When Mrs Honour, the domestic, speaks of her master, she allows that '*to be sure gentle-folks are but flesh and blood no more than us servants*' (Fielding 1985: 196). But despite this shared humanity with their servants, run-of-the-mill work is quite out of the question (we find this attitude already in *Moll*

Flanders). Accordingly, from one's appearance much can be deduced – for instance, the handsome young Tom is described in the following terms:

> I am sure he is a very fine gentleman; and he hath one of the whitest hands in the world [...] one of the sweetest temperdest, best naturedest men in the world he is [...] all the servants and neighbours all round the country loves him. (Fielding 1985: 196)

An appropriate use for white hands would certainly not be physical work. His 'sweet' well-bred nature alerts us to another of the gentleman's distinguishing marks: he shows infinite restraint in expressing his feelings, to the point where 'gentle' acquires overtones of softness and considerateness. Here we see why Elias saw in the gentleman canon (and also in 'sportization' and the rise of parliamentary power) an English foil to the French code of courtly etiquette. The gentleman must not give offence by his manner; and this must be so much part of his make-up as to blur the line between *good breeding* and second nature.

> Allworthy could scarce refrain laughter at this; but he resolved to do a violence to himself: for he perfectly well knew mankind, and had too much good breeding and good nature to offend the squire in his present circumstances. (Fiedling 1985: 283)

Second, to laugh openly at someone would be insulting. The urge to do so must be restrained, whatever the effort. Here then (as in the preceding case) the ancient warrior canon has undergone significant refinement. The knightly sagas have already receded in the distance. Take, for example, the case of the court jester, whose wit traded openly on the platform of mockery and ridicule. What the landed English gentleman shares with the courtier is exquisite politeness to one's peers.[3] Moreover, Fielding's book is full of instances where social inferiors have a right to fair treatment. Excesses of the kind that Ebner-Eschenbach ascribes to the Galician count in her novella do not occur; farmers are free persons with well-defined rights as well.

Third, landlords to their tenants and masters to their servants must project themselves as moral examples. This imperative, if only as an ideal, is reiterated through the novel. From here it is but a small step to the schooling of character: there is no leadership without ethical credentials.

Fourth, to one's peers and the higher orders a ritualized modesty is generally expected. Even in the chivalry accorded women[4] the constraint of *understatement* applies. The danger Weber saw was a proneness to hypocrisy, for the semblance of chivalry is easier to achieve than the reality. As is known, both traits have been ascribed to the English character – with Germans and Austrians dilating more, until the caesura of 1945, on perfidious Albion and its predilection for 'cant' (cf. e.g., Friedell's *Kulturgeschichte der Neuzeit*, Friedell 1976; Stanzel 1988). However, it is primarily mercantile England that the character-trait of hypocrisy is ascribed to. On the other hand, aspects of the gentleman canon of downplaying oneself, as opposed to boastful self-aggrandizement (so large a part of the language of advertising!), and of facing fear or danger with a *stiff upper lip*, still feature in the English self-image, not to mention in how Continentals generally imagine the island race. An example is given by Hilde Spiel, an Austrian who describes the Blitz of 1940–41 in graphic terms (cf. Spiel 1991: 188–9). There is also the cult of the heroic loser, and an instinctive siding with the *underdog*, for each of which A. Glyn (1970) has cited a plethora of cases. Of particular interest is this notion of downplaying one's own role: *modesty* ranks among the 13 values of the Puritans and provides a centre around which a catalogue of norms which are otherwise so antithetical, gravitate. Here (as in the case of 'munificence') we glimpse the contrast with more recent American versions of modernity. As G. Mikes has illustrated to great effect, there is a no more unbridgeable gap than that between the in-your-face hype of Madison Avenue and venerable English understatement (Mikes 1986: 141–2) – for altruistic munificence and displays of open-heartedness are impossible in a milieu where success comes solely from positioning oneself well in the 'personality market'. But the gap is equally great to the pedantic Austrian civil servant, given to tormenting his underlings. Whatever may be said for officialdom straight from the pages of Herzmanovsky or Doderer, excessive zeal is displayed only when currying favour with superiors. Neither valour nor chivalry exactly characterize *Amtsrat* [office counselor] Zihal or *Hofrat* [court counselor] Sauerpfister when they insist on getting some bureaucratic regulation implemented down to the last little detail, to which end they expect no less than fawning compliance from their staff.

Fifth, although the gentleman still has a love of adventure and is not averse to a spot of competition, this trait is already obscured by others – the army, at least in Fielding, is hardly likely to inspire terror in the enemy.

How then does the gentleman canon evolve afterwards? The next case to be considered is a hundred years more recent. We discuss it in the context of parallel developments in English parliamentarianism.

The gentleman canon and parliamentarianism in Trollope's *Can You Forgive Her?*

In 1864 Trollope's first novel in the Palliser series appeared, entitled *Can You Forgive Her?* Trollope is the (almost unknown to a German-reading public) author of 47 novels and 16 other works. He is still highly thought of in the English-speaking world. (Harvie speaks of an American Trollope industry, which published some 90 volumes of his works between 1977 and 1982.) He represents, in Harvie's words, 'the Golden Age of the mid-Victorian political novel' (Harvie 1991: 83), a genre of which readers of German are equally ignorant. *Can You Forgive Her?* tells the story of a young woman who, having to decide between two rivals for her hand, first makes – in haste – the wrong choice (to the consternation and disapprobation of her higher-ranking, aristocratic relations), but manages to correct her blunder in the nick of time. John Grey, 'the worthy gentleman', who initially seemed to her to lack drive (and political designs), finally triumphs over the characterless George Vavasor with his egoistical and brutal ways. By the end of the novel, Alice, the high-minded heroine, has been forgiven not only by John and the author, but by the well-disposed reader too. This is assuming that he or she has not been overcome by the same sense of unease that Henry James was, who à propos of the title of the novel, opined that it was no trouble to forgive her, but it was even easier (and best) to forget her. Behind this leisurely-paced fable can be discerned a genre-image of the upper classes in Victorian England. It contains a portrait of society and politics that is both sociologically pertinent and attentively and acutely drawn. For purposes of this study, we focus on two aspects: the first concerns changes to the gentleman canon in the mid-19th century, as compared with the earlier part of that century and the preceding one. Here we deal with the form it then took, as manifested in several, in part highly divergent, varieties. We also analyze what this means, in sociological terms, for the forming of the English character, namely, a specific inhibiting of the affects. We show that this process can be linked to the formation of the British state, which followed a rather different path than its Austrian counterpart. The second aspect under which Trollope's novel is examined is English parliamentarianism, including how a constitutional monarchy is ruled. In particular, the novel follows the progress of young Plantagenet Palliser, presumptive 'Duke of Omnium' and heir to a fabulously wealthy magnate line, to the highest echelons in the political machinery of the greatest imperial power of the day. Here we table reflections on the English character and compare cross-Channel realities with the Habsburg Monarchy under Franz Joseph, the 'first gentleman of Europe' (in Sven Hedin's dictum). It goes without saying that any links between the gentleman canon and the Victorian political system have a claim on our attention.

The gentleman motif appears in *Can You Forgive Her?* in at least three variants. There is, on the one hand, John Grey, who represents the virtues of his time in the sense of an ideal with which Trollope seems to identify. He is a foil to the roguish and decidedly ungentlemanly George, who may come from a good family but is lacking in character. Then, as a second variant, we have Burgo Fitzgerald. Descended from the best families, he is rash, a pretty boy and devoid of self-control – a relic from an earlier age. The third is embodied by Plantagenet Palliser, the gentleman-politician, for whom politics has become a profession.

Changes in the gentleman canon vis-à-vis the 18th century

The most striking change we find is a greater commitment to peaceable and pacific ways. When gentlemen accompany higher-ranked women on travels, it is no longer their chivalrous duty to stand by them in instances of physical danger; rather they are there as 'absolute slaves' for their diversion and pleasure (cf. Trollope 1982: I, 21). The chief quality such a male companion must bring is patience and a watchful eye. Public space is now relatively free from danger (interestingly, however, in the expanses of the enormous colonial empire, the type of the gentleman-adventurer – the great white hunter – later makes a come-back and is elevated into an ideal for public schoolboys – in the sense of 'muscular Christianity'). We see this general pacification elsewhere as well – as, for example, when Grey and Vavasor have a physical show-down. Grey is very reluctant to get involved, and imposes on himself the utmost restraint in the use of force. He simply throws his adversary out of the house with a (desultory) shove, threatening to call the police (his rooms are in London, where Peel's Bobbies patrol the streets). If anyone can be said to be bloody-minded, it is the tailor Jones, his landlord. John, it goes without saying, takes no pleasure in his victory.

> But the reflection that he had been concerned in a row was in itself enough to make John Grey wretched for the time. Such a misfortune had never hitherto befallen him. In all his dealings with men words had been sufficient, and generally words of courtesy had sufficed. To have been personally engaged in a fighting scramble with such a man as George Vavasor was to him terrible. (Trollope 1982: II, 126)

Even after facing down his man, Grey is anything but relieved. His recourse to violence disgusts him to the core and sits ill with a strongly internalized principle. Later, John will decline a duel with pistols that the hothead George is set to fighting with him. Since duelling is now outlawed in England, George even proposes the duel to take place in France or somewhere else abroad. Here we witness a pivotal step on the path to fabricating a gentleman ideal in which civility and mild manners are prized. This is an ideal we today still associate with the English upper and middle classes, so that we, and Europeans generally, are amazed at the boorish ways of (admittedly) lower-class football fans fresh from 'the Island'. What happens when these very different codes – namely loutishness and gentlemanliness – rub shoulders has been neatly captured for mid-1980s England by Paul Theroux, who describes an incident in a train he once witnessed. A horde of loud-mouthed young men clearly looking for 'bother' got on and proceeded to terrorize, physically and mentally, the other passengers, respectable citizens all, whose response was simply to sit there in silence, not daring to intervene. This was until a small child broke the silence and asked in all innocence what was going on – which only led to another bout of silence (Theroux 1983: 22–4). Here the decencies of the middle-class canon – tact, sitting out attacks as if they were none of one's business – are no longer a matter of deliberate non-intervention, as is the case with Grey, who can of course still act differently should he choose to. Rather in Theroux's England these decencies have given way to a self-constraint born in and predicated on fear, and involving a massive sense of shame. Grey's self-control backed by scruples of conscience has been replaced by an automatic self-constraint, which chips away at one's defenses and exacts a considerable psychic toll.

Other elements of the gentleman canon remain in place. Riding to hounds and cutting a good figure still count. However, there is a world of difference between that self-destructive daredevil, Burgo Fitzgerald, related by birth to half of Britain's grandees but quite lacking in self-control, and a gentleman rider with a rational approach to the sport, who does not, like Fitzgerald, drive his horse to death. For all that, Burgo is a gentleman of the old school; the fact that he is incapable of planning anything beyond the moment or that he has spent his fortune in a spirit of utter indulgence cannot change that.

But Burgo, and George after him, define the fluid, increasingly redundant, world of 'gentlemanliness'. With George it is the dark forces of avarice. Using borrowed money he buys his way into politics, but with no intention of giving it his all – what drives him instead is blatant self-interest. Burgo's mistakes, however, have to do with his chivalrous habits being passé in a money-conscious bourgeois setting. Trollope dwells on the noble-but-stupid spontaneity that comes naturally to him. This leads to the following paradox: when the naive Burgo characterizes himself as naive, he displays slightly too much self-reflection for us to swallow his protestations of innocence. We see here, in ever clearer contours, the extent to which the English landowning ruling class had, by this point in time, discarded the warrior ethos. As with Jane Austen in *Pride and Prejudice*, all parties can put an exact financial tab on the fortunes of gentry and grandees alike. Speculating on a wealthy heiress takes up the time of younger sons. Rank does not reflect military service to the state, but the number of acres in one's estate and the size of one's income. A general style of calculating aforethought now prevails. Physical force and the willingness to use it have been banished to the rule-governed sporting pitch. Elsewhere the state's power clearly dominates. What remains is pride, honour, awareness of rank, and the idea of a commensurate life-style, sensed as binding on pain of social shame. To this may be added that for members of the politically empowered upper (and upper-middle) classes a clear-cut pecking order existed. It was so transparent that it could be discerned from face-to-face interactions. In shaping social differences modern plutocratic orders such as the United States, have to depend to an incomparably greater extent on money than was the case in Victorian England. Otherwise, in a relatively anonymous world, how can they justify disparities of rank? Money, however much it mattered in that distant England, was still largely dependent on holding land and on manners, neither of which was as easy to come by as wealth in a market economy.

But what does this 'pacifying' of the gentleman ideal, or of gentlemanly conduct per se (if we consider Trollope's depictions to be at all accurate), mean for our analysis of relationships to authority in mid-19th century England? There are at least two mechanisms by which attitudes prejudicial to the unbridled expression of physical force can trickle down to wider English society embodied in the middle and lower classes. The 19th century (the seminal years were 1829 and 1856) saw the creation of a modern, unarmed police force, modelled on the gentleman ideal: it played a large part in the pacifying of the formerly uncouth English people. At the same time modern sport arose in England, with violence being kept ever more under wraps. Here too the gentleman canon, mixed in with elements of middle-class thinking, supplied the rationale for banning older forms of violence. Gorer has given a fulsome account of the first stage of pacification (Gorer 1955: 294–8,

305–12), analyzing its formative effect on the English character. With the passing of Sir Robert Peel's Metropolitan Police Act in 1829, working-class criminality structurally linked to the enormous social costs of industrialization, was opposed by a new type of policeman. For the first time, policemen were recruited on the basis of 'character' – apart from having to be the right size and age, they had to meet the criterion of being, in the Minister of the Interior's opinion, *'of good character, physically and mentally fitted*' and *'sufficiently well educated.*' A Mr Mayne, Commissioner of the Metropolitan Police, was charged with seeing that these standards were met (cited by Gorer 1955: 296).

> The constable must remember that there is no qualification more indispensible to a police officer than a perfect command of temper, never suffering himself to be moved in the slightest degree by any language or threats which may be used: if he do his duty in a quiet and determined manner, such conduct will probably induce well-disposed bystanders to assist him should he require it.

Although Reiner (1985: 20–47), summing up a long debate, correctly points to the darker sides (the fostering of class rule, for example) of such pacification, he freely concedes that this new police body quickly gained the acceptance of the working class, even becoming an icon of national mythology (cf. here also Emsley 1992). That this could happen may largely be due to the English Bobby's dead-pan demeanour. He had to school himself in affective restraint and the non-display of aggression and dominance, much more than was ever the case with his colleagues on the Continent (including, of course, Austria). From the policeman was required a gentleman's self-control. Trollope's John Grey had internalized his repugnance of violence, and Mayne expected no less from officers in the new service. As the gentlemanly lord of the manor and village patron before him, so the policeman would lead by setting an example, thus ensuring popular support.

The English character therefore became *self-policing*. To gauge the special quality of this manner of relating to authority we compare it to what we find in the Prussian 'underling', Diederich Hessling (in Heinrich Mann's eponymous *Der Untertan*). His fear of the police and all authority has eaten its way into his system. For a bearer of a derivative position of authority not to shout or threaten, not to use his greater power to humiliate the other – some petitioner or miscreant – is for him to leave the latter with his dignity intact and no small portion of freedom to boot. Moreover, he assumes significantly greater accountability for the outcome of his intervention than if he were to nakedly display the state's power to intimidate, thus stamping citizens as mere underlings. In doing so, he appeals to the other's sense of fairness, or at least his willingness to comply, an appeal that extends to all third parties, involved or otherwise, who may be present. While there is certainly no doubting that the rules of interaction between police and the populace in 19th century England evolved in a more 'civilized' direction, that is, one characterized by greater self-control, this should not blind us to the paradox that England, in point of fact, was far readier to execute its citizens than was Austria as far back as

1840 or so (cf. for the relevant figures[5] Gatrell 1994: 616–19; Evans 1996: 228–31). Now what sense can we make of this paradox that an otherwise relatively liberal, even enlightened society could condone such a relatively inhumane penal practice? Evidently the patrimonial and bureaucratic control of a still much more heavily agrarian society was more effective than that wielded by the English ruling classes, who by then presided over a quite anonymous class society permeated by market dynamics and abstract, impersonal networks, in which the protecting of the property of the haves was deemed to outweigh compassion for the victims of market formation and unchecked population growth. The 'humanizing' of the English middle classes to which Elias refers evidently reached England at a later date, as far as curbing its barbaric enthusiasm for executions is concerned. In the case of Austria, with its more heavily patrimonial and personalized system of rule, a handful of reform-minded persons had considerably more success (after and during Josephinist times) in implanting Enlightenment principles than was the case across the Channel.

The second wave of civilizing, namely the tempering of spontaneous violence, occurred in England in the context of the invention of modern sport. Dunning and Sheard have shown that from the 1830s on, it was the public schools that encapsulated traditional football in a system of rules, the thrust of which was to demand greater self-control from players and curtail untoward brawling and other wild outbursts on the pitch (cf. Dunning and Sheard 1979). The old leisure pursuits and pastimes of the nobility (hunting, shooting and fishing), which were also practiced in these schools, were gradually phased out – for example, by Dr Arnold at Rugby – in favour of team sports of various kinds. Industrialization and the spread of civil society were instrumental in closing the power differential between grandees and gentry and the rest of the country. Crass *bullying* gave way to greater restraint in the orchestrating of dominance. Under the aegis of massive status competitions waged between schools fearful of their reputations, the relationship between *prefects* and *fags*, between *masters* and *boys*, was placed on a more formal footing, even as the rules of the different sports were codified in the name of 'fair play'. 'Indirect rule' as practiced by the *headmaster* by vesting 'controlled autonomy' in the pupils themselves; the principles of a 'manly education' in line with a modified gentleman canon; the essentially milder (vis-à-vis standard practice in the 18th century) 'civilized' intercourse between power-political unequals (and between older and younger persons too) – all played a part in creating the precursors of modern rugby and soccer (or 'football'). These were played according to rules that strike one now, as they did contemporaries then, as 'fair'. Thus the number of players on each side was fixed; permissible physical attacks on the opponent were distinguished from those that were not; and passing the ball to get it upfield was rated higher than the mere battle for possession. Skill and dexterity began to triumph over brute force (Dunning and Sheard 1979: 97). And so what started out as popular sports were given the gentlemanly status to which the boys themselves aspired. At the same time a civilizing offensive arose in England that drew down the curtain on the violent popular entertainments of earlier centuries (cock fights, dog fights, baiting bears or bulls, and the like): the year 1824 saw the founding of the Royal Society for the Prevention of Cruelty to Animals (RSPCA). This is undoubtedly a case of the civilizing process leaping ahead in a fairly brief span of time (cf. Holt 1989, for a detailed list of outlawed 'blood sports'), with the Victorian upper middle classes then mopping up any omissions. The threshold of legitimate affectivity was progressively raised, and infringements were ever more likely to incur moral censure. Squire Weston, obsessed by his passion for the chase, made way for the gentleman-amateur in an academic or public-school setting. For men of this sort a whole battery of claims on the English upper class, such as an ability to lead, health considerations and sexual abstinence, melded into a civilized canon, in which the sportsman must play by the book, possess stamina and a robust physique, and show a terrier's tenacity. In the distinction between rugby and 'football' (or soccer), and between professional cricket players of lower-class origin and their more gentlemanly peers, the class-bound nature of British sport also manifested itself (Dunning and Sheard 1979: 175–200). This time also saw a growing inclination by the old upper classes to make ever finer distinctions, in the light of an increasing uncertainty around their status. As bourgeois values gained ground in the ruling class, the thrusting new elites of industry and commerce entered the realm of aristocracy.

Gorer (1955) has read the resultant restraints on aggression in Freudian terms, as a taboo due to growing feelings of guilt. When all relevant forms of entertainment are outlawed; when the least sign of suffering must be hidden from others; when 'childish' aggression is punished and when cursing and abuse are branded as evidence of *bad temper*, then aggressions restrained across a lifetime turn inwards, where they continue to act in weird disguises: as English slowness or lethargy, even laziness or weak nerves. One then starts to fear one's own impulses. Until at least the 1950s great shyness was the product of an English middle-class education, as concluded by Gorer from thousands of questionnaires in a nation-wide survey. Relaxation and pleasure in childhood were possible only when the watchful parental eye was trained elsewhere, as encapsulated in the lapidary order, '*See what Johnny is doing and tell him to stop it*' (Gorer 1955: 288). Gorer likewise postulates a link with the Puritan value canon. When John Bull made way for John Citizen, the price, he tells us, was high.

We will now consider this process of transformation in the light of parliamentization as described by Trollope.

Parliamentary rule and character training

English embourgeoisement during the 19th century, the country's growing commercial focus and the rise of a professional class are reflected in the descriptions Trollope gives us of the political machinery of the English-styled 'Venetian aristocratic republic'. This is how he characterizes the English modus operandi, whose most representative mouthpiece was Parliament and the parliamentary political style. *Can You Forgive Her?* is, above all else, a political novel. Here we consider three aspects:

- What kind of character training and ideals does Trollope describe as essential to English parliamentary rule?
- How do they fit in with the institutional make-up of the latter, as compared to the political institutions of the Habsburg Monarchy?
- Commercialization, industrialization and bureaucratization also played a role, together with a massive leap-forward in the democratic process, in changing the nature of English parliamentarianism. What picture does Trollope paint of these changes in *Can You Forgive Her?* To what extent are wider changes in the relation to state authority evident?

Even in the 18th century England was perceived by Germanophone travellers (cf. Maurer 1992) as the land of freedom. They compared it to the relative despotism of their own states, where princelings and potentates ruled by decree and whim, imposing a crushing burden of taxation on their peasant subjects, and where freedom of movement was unheard of. To them the unique institution of the English Parliament seemed to epitomize freedom, so that for most of these visitors a trip to Westminster was imperative when visiting the English capital. They could only admire the ability of Parliament to set the political agenda in a happy collusion between government and opposition (with only one or two dissenting voices), possibly even against the will of the sovereign and in all autonomy of self-determination. In particular the *modus operandi* and the recruiting mechanisms of this system are described by Trollope in this novel, and in a brace of other political novels (the so-called Palliser series: *The Prime Minister*, 1876; *The Eustace Diamonds*, 1873; *The Duke's Children*, 1880; *Phineas Finn*, 1869; *Phineas Redux*, 1874).

One of the main questions, therefore, is this: does the type of politician – more generally, that of the politically interested, educated contemporary – which Trollope describes in several varieties represent an altogether new level of self-control and conscience formation? Does the latter differ from that achieved in the Habsburg Monarchy, its government and bureaucracy which has sworn allegiance to state and Emperor?

Anyone who has studied *Can You Forgive Her?* – the prototypical Victorian novel – will perhaps make a surprising discovery: the institution of the monarchy, or even the person of Queen Victoria, go practically unmentioned. What we have instead is a description of a rich yet patriotic and responsible oligarchy, which may in the reader evoke echoes of republican Rome or patrician (and republican) Venice, with the latter perhaps furnishing the closest model. Had it not in its time ruled the seas, driven by the spirit of commerce? In a chapter called 'Three Politicians' Trollope describes his hero Palliser in the following manner:

> Mr. Palliser was one of those politicians in possessing whom England has perhaps more reason to be proud than of any other of her resources, and who, as a body, give to her that exquisite combination of conservatism and progress which is her present strength and best security for the future. He could afford to learn to be a statesman, and had the industry wanted for such training. He was born in the purple, noble himself, and heir to the highest rank as well as one of the greatest fortunes of the country, already very rich, surrounded by all the temptations of luxury and pleasure; and yet he devoted himself to work with the grinding energy of a young penniless barrister labouring for a penniless wife, and did so without any motive more selfish than that of being counted in the roll of the public servants of England. (Trollope 1982: I, 246)

Pure altruism is rarely the whole story in human action, and as the novel progresses Trollope adds several other plausible motives for Palliser's selfless service to England. Still, the basic lay of the land is clear enough. Other than with the fawning courtiers and bureaucrats that we will shortly meet in Hermanovsky's caricature, all competing for the favour of His Supreme Highness in a bizarre display of pre-emptive obedience, here we have an impersonal dependency on something called 'England' (construed, if you will, as a quasi-metaphysical essence), in tandem with a high degree of self-determination (for which Palliser's personal wealth supplies a good fundament) and a highly abstract notion of duty. Trollope's belief was that a politician had to be wealthy – otherwise he would become entangled in a series of undignified dependencies. But wealth did not come without obligations, at least not in the case of the politician. Anyone like Palliser seriously interested in filling the highest offices of the land (when we first meet him, he is in contention for the position of the next chancellor of the exchequer, concerning which the Duke of St. Bungay, his high-born patron and facilitator, is in the course of paying him a visit) is already practicing politics as a profession. Palliser works hard, is colourless, even dull ('dull' is a predicate that was often used when John Major was in Downing Street – can it be a coincidence that Major, so we are told, is a Trollope enthusiast?), despises rhetorical excesses, loves figures and hard facts and wishes to shine by his expertise rather than by his wit or trenchant turns of phrase. He strives to be upright, predictable and to inspire trust.

'He had taught himself to believe that oratory, as oratory, was a sin against that honesty in politics by which he strove to guide himself' (Trollope 1982: I, 246–7). A long apprenticeship in self-possession, hard to accomplish in its own right, has left him with the knack – this above all else – of getting others to trust him. His work ethic, decency and patriotism show that they are not wrong in doing so. But in whom is this trust reposed? The Queen is not mentioned. Clearly his 'peers' are meant – those belonging to the ruling class: a broad church that reaches from the titled nobility and the gentry to the upper echelons of the middle classes, those who have risen through the ranks of industry and commerce.

But Palliser is not the only species of the English politician to be found in Trollope. The Duke of St. Bungay, also a prominent figure on the political scene, is sketched in rather different terms:

> The Duke was a statesman of a very different class, but he also had been eminently successful as an aristocratic pillar of the British Constitutional Republic. He was a minister of very many years' standing, being as used to cabinet sittings as other men are to their own arm-chairs; but he had never been a hard-working man. Though a constant politician, he had ever taken politics easy whether in office or out. [...] His voice in council was esteemed to be very great. [...] What he said in the House was generally short and pleasant, – with some slight, drolling undercurrent of uninjurious satire running through it. But he was a walking miracle of the wisdom of common sense. He never lost his temper. He never made mistakes. He never grew either hot or cold in a cause. He was never reckless in politics, and never cowardly. He snubbed no man, and took snubbings from no man. [...] All the world respected him, and he was a man to whom the respect of all the world was as the breath of his nostrils. (Trollope 1982: I, 251)

The character traits enumerated here seem closer to those we listed when describing the gentleman canon. Here too the broad thrust of self-improvement, of working on oneself, is towards toning down one's temperament in interpersonal relations. The Duke's success in containing his aggressive urges and of not admitting the error-prone passions of taking sides in political issues makes him the ideal and respected man when it comes to injecting a note of conciliation and compromise into a Commons' debate. Described here is a portion of political history that on the Continent generally, and in patrimonial and bureaucratic Austria especially, could scarcely ever prosper. Even today it is barely possible for Austrian politicians to allow their opponents finish their sentence. A simple explanation of why English parliamentarianism produced such features, while its Central European counterparts cut such a poor figure, might be that the former had begun at a much earlier date to debate serious matters without directions from 'above', that is, in all autonomy of responsibility. To this we might add that the English Parliament was spared – the situation in Ireland apart – national and class-based contrasts on a scale of virulence that turns men into bitter enemies. The ethos of imperial service of the likes of the Windisch-Graetz was quite above suspicion. No one of such a pedigree could be but the thoroughly loyal servant of dynasty and state. But members of this dynasty had to make numerous compromises and the imperial reach and power of the Austrian state, could not forever hold down Hungarians, Czechs and the rising middle classes. That said, it must be conceded that they and their kind, not to mention the countless groups of nationalist and class-based bourgeois parliamentarians in the *Reichstag*, lacked the centuries of experience in resolving conflicts of interest in a peaceful way that might have made the parties feel a commitment to compromise. Instead, passions in the *Reichstag* became so volatile that it had to be dissolved. The absurdity of this step was neatly captured by Musil: 'There was a Parliament, which asserted its freedom so forcefully that it was usually kept shut;…' (Musil 1996: 29).

But Trollope wrote at a time when this type of high-born politician was being displaced by the thrusting middle classes (even if, up to 1914, most British cabinet members were of aristocratic birth; cf. Cannadine 1990: 711, in his major treatment of the decline of the British aristocracy). The main plot of the novel turns on the efforts of the ambitious and unscrupulous George Vasavor to buy his way into the political limelight; had he succeeded, numerous companies and firms would have found in him a vigorous lobbyist on their behalf.

> Then there might be pickings in the way of a Member of Parliament of his calibre. Companies, – mercantile companies, – would be glad to have him as a director, paying him a guinea a day, or perhaps more, for his hour's attendance. Railways in want of vice-chairmen might try for his services; and in the City he might turn that 'M.P.' which belonged to him to good account in various ways. (Trollope 1982: II, 316)

This new type of politician is exposed to market forces – meaning the temptations of money – disproportionately more than to the promptings of honour and public-spiritedness, which had led an earlier generation of politicians to labour disinterestedly in the public interest. We should, however, not overlook the satisfaction of wielding power over others, a motive that Trollope has included in his list of Palliser's motives. In less morally bleak tones, Trollope describes Mr Bott, a political professional of rather obscure origins.

> Mr. Bott was a person who certainly had some success in life and who had won it for himself. He was not very young, being at this time only just on the right side of fifty. He was now enjoying his second session in Parliament, having been returned as a pledged disciple of the Manchester school. Nor had he apparently been false to his pledges. At St. Helens he was still held to be a good man and true. But they who sat on the same side with him in the House and watched his political manoeuvres, knew that he was striving hard to get his finger into the public pie. He was not a rich man though he had made calico and had got into Parliament. And though he claimed to be a thorough going Radical, he was a man who liked to live with aristocrats, and was fond of listening to the whispers of such as the Duke of St. Bungay or Mr. Palliser. (Trollope 1982: I, 253)

This hard-working and conscientious Member of Parliament may not be a rogue like George Vasavor, but he too has no manners to speak of and no superior ethos. And so three politicians meet in Palliser's castle, and although not a word is said as to the possibility of Palliser being earmarked as the next chancellor, all parties are perfectly content, inwardly and outwardly, with the tacit knowledge that this is what will happen – a reference to the implicit and informal nature of undertakings in political life, and indeed in social life generally (a trait shared, as it is happens, by English and Austrian social characters.)

At this point it may be helpful to learn something of Trollope's own background, which did not fail to shape his perceptions of English politics. Trollope (1815–82) belonged to the middle class – he was the son of an unsuccessful lawyer – and owed his rise to the highest position in the British Post Office to his own energy and ability. Yet all his life he was strongly taken by the landowning aristocracy. In his sketch of Trollope, Harvie has assembled much that gives the impression, on the whole, of a complex, even contradictory personality.

There is his early experience in the famine years of Catholic Ireland, which instilled in him a life-long sympathy for Ireland and Catholicism. This is significant when one recalls that only from 1829 could Catholics sit in Westminster (Jews had to wait even longer, until the 1860s).

Harvie sees Trollope as having been marked by Carlyle's Romantic cultural critique. In any event he can hardly be accused of excessive sympathy for the world of commerce and industry: his later works treat, among other things, the endangering of English political culture by unscrupulous plutocrats and democratic fantasies (in equal measure). His own failure to win a seat in the 1868 election may have played a part here. On the other hand, Trollope was an admirer of American democracy and worried that bureaucratic watchdogs in high places might throttle the life of the state, as witnessed in *The Three Clerks*, his novel on officialdom which came out in 1857. His description of himself as a (Venetian) republican is rather convincing. Few commentators today dispute that his depictions of British parliamentary life are authentic and cut close to the bone – as former Prime Minister Harold Macmillan put it: 'It's all in Trollope' (cited in Harvie 1991: 77).

In *Can You Forgive Her?* we therefore have an extremely live and sensitively observed account of the corridors of power in and around the 1860s. We are privy to the rhetorical performances of ministers and MPs, who dish out to the public (before assembled journalists from the broadsheets, who take notes) a decidedly different picture than their true stance or intentions would admit. They play up (or down) their enmities and amities in the crassest way, simulating emotions they barely feel: 'And men walked about the house in the most telling moments, – enemies shaking hand with enemies – in a way that showed an entire absence of all good, honest hatred among them' (Trollope 1982: II, 13).

Above all else, Trollope provides an in-depth description of the patterns of behaviour to which the ins and outs of daily political life drive MPs. These include a sudden switching of coalitions, so that yesterday's vilified opponent is today's esteemed friend (and vice versa) and a ritualized and mannered exchange of verbal (un)pleasantries, most of them aimed at the gallery. In all these cases political life is a constant masquerade, in which one's true feelings and intentions must on no account be shown.

> Then he touched lightly, and almost with grace to his opponents, on many subjects, promising support, and barely hinting that they were totally and manifestly wrong in all things. But – . Then the tone of his voice changed, and the well-known look of fury was assumed upon his countenance. Then great Jove (the PM of the day, authors' note) on the other side pulled his hat over his eyes, and smiled blandly. Then members put away the papers they had been reading for a moment, and men in the gallery began to listen. But – . (Trollope 1982: II, 12)

The MP, otherwise a good-natured man, works himself into an apparent fury of almost antique eloquence.

> The long and the short of it was this; that the existing Government had come into power on the cry of a reduction of taxation, and now they were going to shirk the responsibility of their own measures. They were going to shirk the responsibility of their own election cry, although it was known that their own Chancellor of the Exchequer was prepared to carry it out to the full. He was willing to carry it out to the full were he not restrained by the timidity, falsehood, and treachery of his colleagues, of whom, of course, the most timid, the most false, and the most treacherous was – the great god Jove, who sat blandly smiling on the other side. (Trollope 1982: II, 12)

Trollope makes clear in what follows that nobody, least of all the target of these choice barbs, is in any way consternated by what is happening. But the newspapers will be giving extensive coverage to the speech, which is half the point of the histrionics.

The typical English character that speaks through these lines – although it is a character that has, by now, gained entry in parliaments around the globe – is one that shares common values with other MPs which are sufficiently robust to withstand pounding from strong differences on matters of substance. At issue in this passage was the abolition of direct taxation, a central concern of liberals wedded to the famed 'Manchester School' who are today making something of a come-back, if only in an attenuated form. This is probably what Elias had in mind when he talked of 'sportization' and 'parliamentarization' as being both uniquely English and interlinked. In each domain freely chosen rules are observed, though such voluntary compliance is only possible in the absence of fear that the opposition, if it ever gained power, would exploit its new majority status to overturn everything and ruthlessly push through its interests.

That is what is special about English parliamentarianism, not the fact that it succeeded in drawing in all social classes at an early time. In fact, until 1838 only the few, namely those whose yearly income was £600 (for MPs representing counties) or £300 (for urban-based MPs), were entitled to sit at Westminster (Pool 1994: 102). Until 1872 there was no secret ballot. Broad-based popular representation was, all in all, achieved in England no earlier than in lands of the Habsburg Monarchy. And the extension of the franchise often went hand in hand with bribery, burough riots and other forms of nastiness we hardly associate with a 'mature democracy' in the modern sense. But the gradual expansion of political representation meshed – other than was the case in Austria – with already established structures and mechanisms. These gave rise to a singular 'political culture', one that could easily be passed between the generations. Thus Macmillan could in the 1950s rightly say that everything could already be found in Trollope. This would include the evolution of a critical public opinion, despite the fact that, even in Trollope's day, we see the first inroads of that fateful preponderance of the media that today has so much narrowed the scope (ominously, to be sure) for parliamentary manoeuvring. What havoc Rupert Murdoch can wreak with his tabloids and broadsheets in contemporary Britain can be matched, line for sensational line, by Austria's Hans Dichand with his *Kronen-Zeitung*. But on the whole Elias is right in stressing (the occasion was the two lectures he gave on British public opinion) its unique achievement – and on the national level too – in erecting a moral fence against the excesses of state power and the sheer Machiavellianism of politicians. The unhappy climate of confrontation which marked the First Austrian Republic had much to do with entrenched blocs sniping away at each other, with the popular press probably spouting this or that party line. As to how this came about, we need to consider previous developments in the round, namely a long defensive struggle by a state barely able to cope with the emotions and disparate interests of its citizenry. Bureaucrats and nobles were at the helm, torn by their loyalties but pledged to the Emperor.[6] By 1914, Austria had produced no democrats worthy of the name; all it could point to were authoritarian popular tribunes. Demagogic haranguing rather than civil virtues marked the political life of the Danube Monarchy, while the reins of power remained, as ever, with a nobility owing personal allegiance to the Emperor. If in Austria it was the social character of the bureaucrat that cast a long shadow, then in England it was the idea of the gentleman.

Notes

1 In economic terms, large estates (defined as anything with more than 1000 acres of land) covered some 56 per cent of the English landscape; for Scotland and Ireland the respective figures were 93 per cent and 78 per cent. For the whole of Great Britain, two-thirds of the country was owned by some 11,000 individuals, at the head of which stood some 250 grandees (cf. Cannadine 1990: 9, for an exact breakdown). Measured in political terms, the aristocratic grip was even greater – principally concentrated in the still powerful Upper House, in administration and government, and in broad swathes of the House of Commons (cf. Cannadine 1990: 13–14).

2 Sheriffs and Kings alike sought between 1315 and 1615 no less than 23 times to ban by edict football – all to no avail (cf. Elias/Dunning 1986: 118).

3 German travellers during the 18th century noted the difference between politeness *à la française*, with its easy descent into servility, and the somewhat prouder English variety.

4 In *Tom Jones* of course we find any number of instances where this code of chivalry, its troubadour underpinnings of Romantic provenance long gone, counts for very little, especially in how men relate to their wives:

> She scarce indeed ever saw him but at meals; where she had the pleasure of carving those dishes which she had before attended at the dressing. From these meals she retired about five minutes after the other servants, having only stayed to drink the King over the Water. (Fielding 1985: 309)

'The King over the Water' is a Jacobite lay, which Western, an embittered anti-Hanoverian, is wont to strike up at the slightest pretext.

5 For England and Wales in the period 1816–37 Evans (1996: 228–31) puts the average number of death sentences handed down each year at 1,137 (the population was then

around 16 million); in Austria over a comparable period (1803–48) the annual rate was, by contrast, a lowly 28 (for a population of about 22 million – as of the year 1789, omitting Belgium and Milan; cf. Bruckmüller 1985: 288). Even allowing for the frequency (90 per cent in England; 60 per cent–90 per cent in Austria) with which the death penalty was commuted, we still have a glaring disparity, with Austria only executing 10 persons a year during the period in question.

6 Thus Prince Alfred von Windisch-Graetz, minister-president between 1893 and 1895, had a standard response whenever the Emperor asked a question: *'Wie Eure Majestät befehlen!'* [As Your Majesty Commands!] (Stekl and Wakounig 1992: 235). Generally speaking, Austrian nobles were reluctant to enter politics, a point which is noted by Stekl and Wakounig (1992).

Chapter 6

The Courtly Element in the Austrian Character: Authority, Pretence and Servility

An example from the end of the era

Fin-de-siècle Vienna, Prague and Budapest were metropolises in which social, intellectual and cultural life was still strongly cast in a courtly-aristocratic mould. 'The Aristocracy and the Aristocratization of the Bourgeoisie' – not for nothing did Rossbacher so title a chapter in his book on literary culture during the *Ringstrasse* era (Rossbacher 1992: 117–14). If the Habsburg Monarchy did not produce courtly society on quite the French scale, the imperial court at least outshone its English counterpart, and even more its Prussian one. 'Viennese Modernism' (cf. the eponymous anthology, ed. by Wunberg 1984) is full of pieces in which a strongly aristocratic culture with psychologizing tendencies, with a faiblesse for ornamental aestheticism and music, rubs shoulders with a scientific and philosophical culture rooted in middle-class expertise and working-bourgeois professionalism. A world of salons and other venues for prestigious self-display now beckons. Schnitzler's *Reigen* [*Hands Around*, also: *La Ronde*], Broch's *fröhliche Apokalypse* [gay apocalypse] shed light on this milieu, as do Vienna's many operettas (cf. Csáky 1996). Then there is Doderer's *Strudlhofstiege* [*The Strudlhof Steps*][1] or Musil's *Mann ohne Eigenschaften* [*The Man without Qualities*], whose much-touted 'Parallel Campaign' takes place mainly in or around the salons, each one presided over by a female luminary of stately beauty, wit and taste. If we accept Lhotsky's ideas (Lhotsky 1974) on the rise of Austrian man – his yardstick is 1526, the year which saw the first origins in the creation of a single aristocratic class spanning Austria, Bohemia and Hungary – we can readily postulate diffusion processes that shaped the corresponding affective structures. Here it is imperative to analyze, in terms of its psychic effects, the phenomenon of courtly aristocracy (as opposed to military-related feudal aristocracy, which was already treated above).

Courtly authority, as opposed to authority based on working bourgeois, middle-class expertise, is based on proximity to the supremely radiant sun of the Imperial Presence; also on the rank and prestige of a class of former warriors, now devoted to peaceful pursuits, prominent among which is profligate consumption and living non-productive lives as rentiers. While the personal happiness and good fortune of people with a working-bourgeois background chiefly flow from success or failure in a work-place partitioned off from the private or public domains, that is, flow from their ability to acquire or skillfully deploy capital or expert knowledge, in the case of courtiers (of both sexes) success or failure depends on quite different resources. These can be actuated in face-to-face communication, in what may be called a ritually organized dominance unit whose chief point is representation (cf. Kuzmics 1989: 279–80, for an enumeration of all points of difference between courtly and professional life). Beyond a doubt, these resources include gratifications arising from some real social functions which the grand nobility fulfills: Duindam (1997) has shown that the role of such gratifications should not be under-estimated. But the court and the social opinion moulded in its environs take on as well a life of their own. Between similarly ranked individuals, as Elias (1983) has pointed out, there is a structured competition for monopolististically controlled status chances; diplomatic caution, tact and flattery now become more central, while physical prowess and demonstrative displays are tabooed. To one's social inferiors, though, no especial consideration is required; servants are downgraded into 'non-persons', to speak with Goffman (cf. Goffman 1959: 150). Virtue (bourgeois by nature) and hard-headed expertise (ditto) are socially recognized values; what count are not manners, wit, taste and refinement. 'Superficial' qualities trump 'inward' ones; individual self-control is vented, or tends to be, in strategic self-mastery for purposes of improving one's rank, not in conscience formation proceeding from any strong identification with the weaker.

Indeed, several of Hofmannsthal's points of comparison between Prussians and Austrians turn on courtly traits (cf. Hofmannsthal 1957: 615–16). Emollient ways, lack of principle, fondness for the merely decorative – all of which seem so very Austrian – are not lacking either in courtly milieus. To which add the 'femininity' of the Austrian character, so diametrically opposed to earnest Prussian manliness. Neither on the barrack-grounds (of which Berlin always reminds one more than a little) nor, for that matter, in the accounts department do we find women of good society being adulated and waited upon to quite the same extent; hence, Vienna danced to a different tune than cool and herb Albion.

All the above traits can be recognized, without difficulty, in passages of Musil's novel treating the social setting where the 'Parallel Campaign' has its origin. At the house of 'Diotima', wife of the bourgeois-born senior official Tuzzi, have congregated – at Count Leinsdorf's behest – an unclearly delineated circle of senior figures from the administration, clergy, economy and art, and (even) from the military; their aim: to promote the 'great patriotic campaign'. Although the heads of science, in particular, are generally from the middle classes, all take their cue from the manners and proprieties of the courtly aristocracy. There now develops a lively 'competition as a cultural phenomenon', to use Mannheim's phrase (Mannheim 1952: 191–229). Such is the stubbornness of the bourgeois Diotima, however, that to the opening session of this so very Austrian fixture she must bring along the Prussian Arnheim:

> Count Leinsdorf found himself ambushed; it was the first time since he had known her that his middle-class friend had surprised him by committing an indiscretion. Arnheim, too, felt taken aback, like a sovereign whose entrance has not been staged with the proper fanfare; he had of course been certain that Count Leinsdorf had known and approved his being invited. (Musil 1996: 178)

How then is the Count to react to this *coup de main*? What we get is one of many manifestations of his very Austrian sense of tact.

> [A]nd His Grace was basically too fond of his friend Diotima to show his surprise beyond his first, involuntary, recoil. He met Diotima's explanation with silence and after an awkward little pause amiably held out his hand to Arnheim, assuring him in the most civil and complimentary terms that he was welcome, as in fact he was. Most of the others present had probably noticed the little scene and wondered about Arnheim's presence insofar as they knew who he was; but among well-bred people it is generally assumed that there is a sufficient reason for everything, and it is considered poor taste to ask too many prying questions. (Musil 1996: 179)

Count Leinsdorf manages (but only just) to tone down his comments on 1866 and Austria's fateful defeat at Prussia's hands. We have cited this passage, as proxy for many others in the novel, for its wider relevance to Austrian life. Tact springs from the constraint of having to allow for the powerful interests of individuals or groups of individuals. Otherwise one could follow one's impulses and coarsely set to rights the object of one's ire or irritation (imagine, for example, how a gang of Hells Angels would deal with an interloper discovered in their midst). Such consideration is extended by Leinsdorf, in one instance, to a woman of some consequence – as measured by her social standing, her beauty, her somewhat cloudy intellect – and in another, to a powerful representative of a powerful, friendly country. Both situations are such as to render diplomacy incumbent – with Musil, here and in several other passages, leaving no doubt that this has long since become second nature for Leinsdorf and is practiced by him also when confronted by the many curious articulations or diverse groups wishing to participate in the Parallel Campaign. They can be characterized to contain a certain 'corporatist' element, and the subtle balance between the societal forces within this Parallel Campaign have to be treated with patience, tact and a sense for compromise. (To be sure, this second kind of tact differs from the first in that sharing a room with flesh-and-blood persons differs from dealing with an institutional tangle of unions and associations.)

In 1900 there was no shortage of channels and institutional receptacles in which courtly aristocratic models could trickle down to bourgeois circles, though, to be sure, this process was hardly new. Not for nothing did one of the classical formulaic greetings in the Austria of old – *Kuess die Hand* – originate in a courtly setting (contrast this with the Counter-Reformation's *Gruess Gott* and the military's *Servus*). One of the institutions in which senior officials could count on finding a quasi-courtly ambience was the café (Roth's Herr von Trotta was known to hobnob there between 5pm and 7pm). Doderer depicts the 'meditative' atmosphere of the café as follows:

> Around the columns of dark marble wafted the traditional atmosphere of a Viennese café, the aromas of mocha and cigarette smoke, and that absolute innocence of any cooking odor or smell of frying, since one could have coffee prepared and served in any of six varieties but could not order more to eat than a little ham sandwich or a couple of eggs at the very most. There were always plenty of empty tables, and everyone who came in to take a seat tried to get as far away as possible from the ones already occupied, which is in itself enough to show the reticent and well-nigh meditative demeanor of the patrons in a Viennese café expressing itself.
>
> 'Has the lieutenant placed his order yet?' the waiter asked, knowing full well that Meltzer had just walked in; avoiding any head-on manner of address, though, was counted as one of the ceremonial prerequisites for service here. (Doderer 1985: 74, transl. by Vincent Kling)

Bureaucratic self-control combined with aristocratic distance, the nasal pitch of *Schönbrunn* German – thus the Austrian variant of 'reserve', whereby the upper class set itself apart from the patrimonial devotion expected from their inferiors.

> 'How is Frau Nechwal?' Herr von Trotta would inquire regularly. He had been asking that question for years. He had never seen her, nor did he wish ever to meet the wife 'from a simple background.' Whenever Herr Nechwal would be leaving, the baron would always say to him, 'My verybest to Frau Nechwal, whom I do not know!' And Herr Nechwal promised to give her the message and assured the baron that his wife would be delighted.
>
> 'And how are your children?' asked Herr von Trotta, who could never remember whether they were sons or daughters.
>
> 'The eldest boy is doing well at school,' said the kapellmeister.
>
> 'So he'll be a musician too?' asked Herr von Trotta und Sipolje with a smidgen of condescension.
>
> 'No,' replied Herr Nechwal, 'another year and he'll be entering military school.'
>
> 'Ah, an officer!' said the district captain. 'That's good. Infantry?'
>
> Herr Nechwal smiled. 'Of course! He's capable. Maybe someday he'll join the general staff.'
>
> 'Certainly, certainly!' said the district captain. 'Such things have happened.'
>
> A week later, he had forgotten everything. One did not recall the bandmaster's children. (Roth 1995: 28)

Many senior officials were nobles by birth or else had been ennobled by the Emperor. As ennobled officials (in France called *noblesse de robe*), they long remained – even after 1918 – a key instance in all matters of taste and etiquette in 'good society': these top bureaucrats, as Roth noted, made a point of wearing the same moustache as Franz Joseph. The diffusion of the courtly model under the Habsburg Monarchy occurred mostly, it would seem, in social environments where a nobility steeped in courtly norms, impacted with their life-style in growing reciprocal dependency on ordinary citizens. Employing numerous servants and domestics, they also interacted with bureaucrats and other professionals including urban-based craftsmen and merchants – who then proceeded to take over from these courtly structures and to develop patterns of their own, chiefly those relating to consumption. Courtly psychology and the art of observing one's fellow man may, in this diffusion process, have undergone a deal of cross-pollination from the urbane wit of ordinary citizens, including that of the petty bourgeois – of points of contact there was no shortage in a city like Vienna with its specific public space of theatre, popular entertainments, spectacles, processions and the like. Public life then, we should remember, was far less screened off from private life than is the case today, or was even then in contemporaneous England – where the anonymous fragmentation of the market had destroyed those forms of public life which, according to Sennett (1977), gave rise to a 'public person' in earlier times.

In the next section we will plot the psychic habituations that resulted from transfer of courtly norms to Austria's urban-based classes, especially petty bourgeois and bureaucrats.

The Austrian mode of interaction with authority as exemplified by Viennese popular comedy

Any attempt to isolate the chief qualities of the Austrian character from that country's literature, and then say where the differences lie with England, runs into a stumbling-block: in 18th century Austria very few novels were written. But there *is* Viennese popular comedy – and what initially seems to pose a technical difficulty for comparative purposes, takes on strategic importance for purposes of sociological description and explanation. Vienna – in Napoleon's time home to somewhere between 300,000 and 350,000 inhabitants and the third-largest city in Europe, only outstripped by London (one million) and Paris (800,000; cf. Rommel 1952: 596) – lacked the individualized readership of certain other metropolises in Western Europe. What it did possess was vitality, in the form of a populace given to thronging the streets and squares, filling the taverns and cafés and, above all else, the theatres, which night after night were sold out, despite the fact that almost no district lacked one – to name some names, there was a *Theater an der Wien*, a *Theater beim Kärntnertor*, a *Theater in der Leopoldstadt*. Rommel's seminal account (1,096 large pages of detailed knowledge assembled in 40 years of collecting activity!) of Viennese popular comedy furnishes a plastic image of the life and theatrical passions of this ancient imperial city – which had evolved a social life in public space quite unlike the bourgeois retreat into private life that was to come. In dialogue with the audience were shaped those juicy and meaty scenes whose influence in Vienna extended down the centuries, which even now cast a long shadow, as in an ongoing Viennese uneasiness with recondite abstraction and a preference, now as then, for concrete detail over airy speculation. Thus there is a double civilizational trajectory: one top-down, the other bottom-up.

In the first the aristocratic model prevails, influencing indirectly the bureaucrat of bourgeois provenance; in the 18th century it was not uncommon for an Austrian nobleman, though, to be more at home in French than in German, the literature he read often enough classicist in spirit and imbued with pan-European humanism. A good example is the diary of Count Karl von Zinzendorf, an émigré from Saxony, where he had been raised at strictly Pietist lines, who succumbed joyfully to erotically tolerant Viennese society; his restless frequenting of the theatre (each visit documented in flawless French) embraced both aristocratic amateur acting at houses like those of the *Thun* and *Starhemberg*, *Lubomirski* and *Lobkowitz*, as well as visits at the newly renovated *Burgtheater* and that of Schikaneder *an der Wien* (cf. Wagner, ed. 1972: 99–107). His preferences also ran to concerts and operas, of which an abundance are documented in his diary. In the public life of courtly Vienna, nobles of high standing appear in the guise of patrons – Vienna's reputation as a musical city still owes a lot, as it did then, to this courtly aristocratic public. The second civilizational trajectory is from the bottom up: this aristocratic culture of self-display is not walled off from the 'little people', who, within the limits of their means, were swayed by the same passions. As for the theatre of the 18th century: its very best patrons were the 'little people', attracted by the frank hedonism, the relatively unrestrained play of affects, that went with a society with a low degree of individualism. This can be seen in the burlesque figure of *Hans Wurst*; in the renaissance of baroque phantasmagoria, with its magical effects wrought by behind-the-scenes machinery; and in its figures of Kasperl, Bernardon, Thaddädl and Staberl, all portrayed by actors of legendary renown. This bottom-up trajectory begins in the classical period of Viennese theatre with Raimund, Nestroy and Grillparzer. It then takes off in the bourgeois novel in which the 'Habsburg myth' is mirrored – a world which, for all its lingering hedonistic excesses, is already succumbing to order – of which one symptom, among others, is that Emperor Franz has now taken to wearing bourgeois clothes whenever he can. A station in the slow transformation of the Austrian character or 'habitus' (a multi-track notion, to be sure, for nobility, bourgeoisie and peasantry have by now evolved in different directions) may be discerned in the polemical writings of the Enlightenment critic, Sonnenfels (in his *Briefen über die Wienerische Schaubühne* [*Letters on the Viennese Stage*]), for whom the popular comedies were too uncivilized – for him the drolleries were excessively drastic, the endless ad-libbing in the impromptu acts played too obviously to the gallery, while the whole attitude of catering to mass sentimentality, with its stunted sense of decency and decorum, was an affront to his aesthetic sensibility (cf. Sonnenfels 1988: 312–13; cf. also Acham 1994). Later, as popular comedy acquired greater intellectual depth, impromptu performances died out.

We noted earlier that what was specifically Austrian only really crystallized during the absolutism of the 18th century, largely by way of the nobility and the bureaucratic class. Yet we must not omit the melting-pot of Vienna, Imperial seat and largest city in the realm, with its fabulous multi-national diversity. Influences on the Viennese stage were disparate and many: there was the figure of Hans

Wurst, with its antecedents in English stage comedy [*Pickelhäring*]; also the Italian *commedia dell'arte*, performed originally at the court itself; then too, a number of elements were lifted from the great Baroque dramas with their classical plots and spectacular magical effects, including the plays about the Roman emperors put on by the Jesuits. Indeed, these elements lived on in the *Maschinenkomödie* (which used machines for the creation of various visual or acoustical illusions, e.g., in Philipp Hafner's *Mägera, die förchterliche Hexe oder das bezauberte Schloß des Herrn von Einhorn* [*Megera: The Ghastly Witch or the Enchanted Castle of Lord Unicorn*]) as well as in the fairy and ghost plays of the time – all part of a tradition that is still at work in Raimund's phantasmagoria and in Nestroy's satires. Although courtly theatre developed ever more in bourgeois directions, its audiences remained as supremely colourful as ever. The inhabitants of Vienna dressed up, regional costumes vying with uniforms of rank and standing, in a feast of polychrome eclecticism. Pezzl reports as follows:

> You often come across...the Hungarian striding along stiffly with the fur-lined jacket, tightly fitting trousers reaching down to his ankles and great long pony-tail, the round-headed Pole with his monk-like haircut and flailing cuffs; both nations are inseparable from their boots. The Armenians, Walachians, Moldavians with their semi-oriental clothing are a far from unusual sight. The Serbs with their handlebar moustaches inhabit an entire street all of their own. Troops of Greeks in their clumsy wide clothing puff away at their long pipes in the coffee houses at the Leopold Bridge. The bearded Muslims, their broad daggers in their belts, walk lumbering along the mucky streets in their yellow slippers. (Pezzl, nach Rommel 1952: 598; transl. A. S.)

The nationalities thronging Vienna's theatres, streets and salons were, even before the Industrial Revolution, a factor of no small relevance in the concoction of a specific mindset – a plethora of encounters in public space with 'ethnic others' supplied all the ingredients. That public life had lost none of its exoticism by the first half of the 19th century can be discerned from Huizinga's *The Waning of the Middle Ages* (Huizinga [1919]1924).

> In the 'city' one could still make out the messenger, the armchair-bearer, the innkeeper, the man-servant, the chambermaid, the washer girl and of course the wedding herald, the announcer of funeral processions and the well-wishers during the various festivals. (Rommel 1952; 598; transl. A. S.)

A semi-private, semi-public lifestyle would remain Vienna's hallmark down to the second half of the 19th century. It was in the theatre that a panoply of distinct human types – service staff of all kinds and degrees, the artisans, the rich baron – came to be typologized and given names, the very mention of which would spark instant recognition, to the extent their bearers had not already given themselves away by stock gestures, tricks of speech and a swag of other mannerisms. Thus, names lifted from the *commedia dell'arte* (Odoardo, Colombine, etc.) become code for character types that, in the perennial relationship between playwrights, actors and audience acquire ever more 'realistic' elements.

The theatre is harder to interpret than the novel. Much that matters on stage has little to do with spoken dialogue – movements and gestures are left unspecified in the script. While the novel is essentially descriptive, theatrical scenes consist of speech *acts*, alongside other histrionic elements. Further, the plays themselves have been handed down, as a canon, if you will, for centuries – even impromptu comedy feeds from a store of accreted tradition. Italian motifs, some reaching back to antiquity, turn up in 18th century Vienna. That said, the theatre is nevertheless well able to illuminate sociological issues.

The fact that a theatre so little encumbered by intellectual baggage, so heavily predisposed to coarse affects, managed to appeal not only to 'the masses' but also to more elite circles (the upper ranks of the bourgeoisie, the nobility), is informative in its own right. The scenes are boisterous, the language over the top and devoid of subtlety (something to which Sonnenfels, doubtless representing a different civilization 'level', takes exception). In Hafner's posthumously performed play, *Evakathel und Schnudi*, there is a prince who weeps because he fails to win his beloved's hand, who, shortly thereafter, in a fit of pique, lops off the head of the man who was to have been his father-in-law. Thence follows a scene with his beloved, in which he hands over the decapitated head (she still cannot bring herself to declare her true feelings for her rejected suitor, and kills herself with, of all things, a pocket-knife). Today we would call such scenes surrealistic, but in the culture of exaggeration then they were nothing out of the ordinary. Hans Wurst exhibits a blunt earthiness which far outstrips anything in *Tom Jones*.

One constellation is of especial interest, namely, how authority is portrayed in the bulk of plays. Superiors are addressed by their titles (with Nestroy, indeed, we detect a certain titular inflation creeping in, with anyone outranking a mere servant being addressed as His Lordship This (e.g., 'His Lordship Weinberl') or as Her Ladyship That. Exchanges between menials and masters are jocular, even intimate; and Vienna's well-known fondness for titles, which goes back to the Baroque, lasts well into the modern era. Servants keep a weather eye out for their advantage, while the toffs they serve, the great and good of Viennese society, alternate between avarice and benevolent fatherliness. Such relationships dance to a tune of their own, and it is certainly not the sober-minded, contractual self-interest of an English society that, even then, was heavily commercialized. In the face of all-powerful circumstances barely amenable to change, least of all by the 'little man', we encounter the voluntary diminution and self-ironizing of the servant who holds the weaker cards and knows it – let the great affect a jargon of stilted pathos, the Hans Wurst is human and pokes fun at the toffs in whose service he stands, owning up freely to his own weaknesses (his terrible trembling pushed to the point of exaggeration).[2]

Several generations on – by the time of the classical writers Raimund and Nestroy – the popular comedy has been *reformed*, that is, characters trading in pure spontaneity have been sidelined; plays are now vehicles for thought, their themes more realistic, more 'bourgeois'. What still remained – acclaimed by the whole of Europe – was the actor-centred theatre; many character types of the 18th century lived on, and even the miraculous effects so dear to the Baroque stage are still (or once again) present in the plays of the day. The fairy Lacrimosa, the evil spirit Lumpacivagabundus, the fairy Cheristane – the very names testify to this ongoing influence. The Vienna of the first half of the 19th century, for all its back-to-the-wall, *Biedermeier* mentality and espousal of absolutist restoration, had become a highly turbulent showground where rapid careers and precipitous falls from grace were equally possible. The turn of fortune's wheel, stardom or the gutter, is largely beyond the individual's power to influence, being decided by fairies and spirits, those seeming arbiters of fate. Raimund's character, Fortunatus Wurzel, in *Der Bauer als Millionär* [*The Peasant Millionnaire*] (first performed in 1826) turns from forest peasant into millionaire thanks to the world of spirits; he then passes through a phase of arrogance and folly, which incurs the retribution of the fairies – only after learning that 'Contentment' comes from making do with little does he achieve 'happiness'. Note that 'Contentment' (like Youth, Age and Envy) appears in personified form from the land of the fairies.

Wurzel's final lyric runs thus:

> Hier ist der Zufriedenheit herrlichste Perl,
> Ich habs bei der Falten, ich glücklicher Kerl;
> Doch kommt's mir allein nicht zu, glücklich zu sein,
> Wir nehmen's in d'Mitten und schließen sie ein. (Raimund 1990: 77)
>
> ['Here is Contentment's noblest pearl,
> I have it by its folds, I, luckiest of men;
> Yet it will not yield happiness for me alone,
> We embrace it and enclose it in our midst.'] (transl. by B. A.)

Imbedded as Viennese man (and woman) is in a largely patrimonial world, caught up as s/he is in personal networks structured along the lines of kinship lineages, in which s/he needs to keep in (and hobnob!) with a large number of others to have any chance of attaining his goals, it is apparent that neither individual drive nor education nor manners alone can yield success. Formulaic greetings reflect the balance of power – if the weak must learn to accept submissiveness, while the strong can afford to be as brusque and condescending as they wish, the former at least have the weight of numbers on their side in this service-slanted society. In the battle for a place in the sun, social space in the Habsburg metropolis is hard to come by – and envy waits in every wing. Not surprisingly, therefore, we find resignation and despondency being laid on by the trowelful (as in *Der Arme Spielmann* [Poor Fiddler] of Grillparzer); melancholy too is never far away (especially in Raimund), as when *Brüderlein fein* [Brotherkin Fine] sounds forth thus in his *Hobellied* [Milling Song]. Magris (1988) has attributed these features to the 'Habsburg myth' – renunciation and resignation will indeed characterize

Austrian literature into the 20th century. And it is probably fair to say that envy is a central plank, still today, in the Austrian character.

The courtly pattern and Vienna's urban middle classes in Nestroy's reception

Nestroy's work resists simple or realistic interpretation for a number of reasons. One is that, being a writer of comedies, he had to submit to the constraints of his genre. For audiences to be able to laugh, plays must end on a more or less positive note, which rules out certain outcomes; moreover, the action, that is, the interactive dynamic between the characters, is subject to manifold constraints. Generally speaking, it is harder to interpret theatre realistically than it is to extract sociology from narrative prose. This is so because characters on stage have only their words and actions through which to communicate – setting aside the scant instructions heading each scene, the author has no narrative role to play. Another reason is that Nestroy was a satirist, which always makes for a highly complex relationship between image and reality – in parody and satire many traits are exaggerated, sometimes grotesquely so, while others are entirely omitted – at the cost of nuance and subtlety, neither of which is likely to have loomed large in the satirist's mind anyway.

Yet, for all that, Nestroy's plays fairly abound with life. He tenders, in dialogues and in twists and turns uniquely crafted for the stage, an iridescent picture of Viennese mores and society from the time of *Vormärz* to the decade following the 1848 Revolution, which lets us study the unfolding of the Austrian habitus at first hand. Discounting, for interpretive purposes, a certain skewing effect due to genre and depictive mode, Nestroy's plays lend themselves, in a variety of ways, to describing and explaining the Austrian character. We will allude, in what follows, to several intermeshing levels.

Nestroy's works could hardly be bettered for depicting the infinite grades of subordination and superordination practiced in sundry Viennese milieus. He draws a lively picture of how authority is discharged between master craftsman, journeyman and apprentice in the trades and in commerce – indeed, for social scientists studying the era he is the *fons et origo* to which they must repair. He rams home the power disparities separating craftsmen and traders (victuallers, master tailors and the like) from their more or less well-heeled and noble customers. Old money, pillars of the establishment, nouveau-riches: all these recognizable types have the mirror held up to them, showing how they behave in the presence of fawners or when confronted by the suspicious or envy – and this in a world where success and failure, as we see in Raimund, frequently hang in the balance. The strategies of go-getters, those determined to rise in society, range from bare-knuckled impudence, devoid of pretence, all the way to benevolence and solicitude towards those entrusted to their care. The weaker too are not without their options: they can plumb the depths of servility or resort to a combination of cheek and guile. Not infrequently a mélange of both strategies marks how women relate to male authority – the Austrian character is indeed, as one judge has pronounced (Hofmannsthal 1957), larded with elements that are nothing if not feminine, of which the genesis is perhaps best described by Nestroy. Viennese society as received by Nestroy is not the so-called 'first' tier of the nobility, nor even the 'second' tier, consisting of the upper bourgeoisie, in the main bureaucrats now elevated to the nobility (for an appraisal of the extent to which 'suburban society' is realistically drawn by the playwright cf. Yates 1981). Society in Nestroy means the classical, sturdy craftsman and the upwardly mobile nouveau-riche; the inflationary use of the lowest aristocratic title (e.g., 'von' Zwirn) attests to the revolutionary dynamic informing the social realities of Vienna – ancient capital, Imperial seat, showcase of the monarchy. The recurring arrogance of high rank is standard fare; its risibility when exposed as such no less.

Thus we may discern several typical facets of the Austrian character (assuming, as we may, that that country's habitus is set in a Viennese mould, which is not to deny the presence of a certain tension with the 'Alpine' segments in what is, after all, a composite mindset, a tension kept alive, to this day, in the mutual antipathy between Vienna and province). What Nestroy well renders is the tug-of-war between masters and servants, as played out in a courtly aristocratic, or bourgeois, or even petty-bourgeois setting. For those bent on learning how far down the social pyramid the courtly aristocratic structures reached in Nestroy's day, the dramatist has assembled a rich arsenal of types and figures. On the other hand, there are the patriarchal structures of old, with craftsmen and tradesmen living under one roof. Similar social structures can be found elsewhere (the courtly syndrome in Paris, the artisan-patriarchal syndrome in Europe as a whole), but not the uniquely coloured emotive worlds of Vienna and, by extension, Austria. In what does this singularity consist? And how do Austrian realities differ from English ones here? How too, in cross-comparison, is the state (and the state's influence) manifested?

Nor are Nestroy's works lacking in facets that address general attitudes to authority, order, coercion – or, for that matter, their contraries: liberty, for example. A typically Austrian syndrome is to accept what has been handed down from 'on high', a stance in which clear-minded fatalism co-exists with a lack of illusions and a determination to keep a low profile, in which bitter reality is kept at bay by a pinch of irony. If it is true that Nestroy's humour stands in a long tradition, running from the Viennese popular comedy of the beginning of the 18th century (to set a *terminus a quo*) to its latter-day offshoots in 20th-century cabaret, then it is all that more appropriate to subject it to close sociological analysis. It seems that Nestroy's humour typifies what Bodi (1985), referring to the Enlightenment literature of the Josephine era and the long shadow this cast over later times, has dubbed the 'comic ambivalence' of the Austrian mind. Bodi traces this stance back to the contradictory demands to which reforming bureaucrats in the *Tauwetter* [The Thaw] and restoration periods were exposed. In the case of Nestroy, we associate this stance with the patrimonial-courtly syndrome, though we freely concede that the transition to the state-bureaucratic type is a seamless one. Nestroy was certainly one of the great mockers of Austria; we hope, by examining him closely, to elucidate something of Austria's make-up.

Traditional 'patriarchal' authority in Nestroy

Hierarchical relationships of a certain kind between masters and servants are commonplace in Nestroy's works: there is a strong tendency for social inequality to be expressed in luridly personal terms. Take, for example, the following milieu, which the dramatist depicts with not the slightest attempt at comedy – young Kathi, god-child of the 'confused' ([Der Zerrissene]; English translation: The Man Full of Nothing) Herr Lips (in a play first performed in 1844) has come to settle a debt with the man she calls her 'Göd' (god-father).

> ...When we reached the end of our rope, and mother was sick, I took heart and went to my godfather for a loan of a hundred thalers. He handed it to me right away and just laughed when I talked about paying it back. But I promised Mother before she died not to forget our debt. So I went to work for Uncle Kraut, and I worked and I saved, and I saved and I worked, and now after three years of scraping and scrimping I have the money, and I've come to pay it. (Nestroy1967: 36)

Patriarchal structures like this can be encountered at every turn in Nestroy: as witness the just and well-meaning but strict master craftsman, Hobelmann, Leim's future father-in-law in *Lumpacivagabundus*, or Principal Zangler in *Einen Jux will er sich machen* (in Thornton Wilder's English version, *Play the Matchmaker*; see also Tom Stoppard's *On the Razzle*, both based on Nestroy), to cite just two of many instances. Although in Nestroy's day a new industrial working class was fast springing up, the most common form of dependency was to be in service, either in a household or on an estate.[3] Domestics, apprentices, journeymen and rural workers, following time-honoured European tradition, were part of the family. Lips may be an estate owner, but he belonged to a class whose land holdings are of no great antiquity. Bruckmüller sees him essentially as a parvenu, one of a class 'who lord it over others simply to underline their new social status' (Bruckmüller 1985: 301). Such parvenus he contrasts with the old order of aristocratic estate owners, whose attitude to agriculture was unsentimental: it had to pay its way. Lips represents therefore, Bruckmüller suggests, a case of a nouveau-riche seeking to gain admission to a feudal-aristocratic caste by the classical ploy of land acquisition. The case shows how the traditional, personal dependency of an indentured menial class (the master, in a simulation of kinship, is godfather to any children born under his roof) has become infused with the anonymous, market-based, contractual dynamic of bourgeois capitalism. Life in the lower orders (the milieu of those in service) revolves around solidity, parsimony; its watchwords are conscientiousness and a sense of honour; Nestroy loves nothing more than caricaturing the fortune-hunters, the social climbers, the flatterers: those who long ago turned their backs on working-class solidity to become unprincipled, opportunistic windbags. Such was the fate of the 'friends', for example, of the 'confused' Herr von Lips, who suffers himself from the fashionable *malheur* of a diffuse distaste for life, ennui having driven out all sense of direction. Something similar holds – in *Lumpacivagabundus*, which was first performed in 1833 – for Zwirn's friends Windwachel and Lüftig, despite the fact that these opportunists converse in High German, not in the rough tones of the 'solid' figures drawn from the lower orders. (Nestroy also puts High German into the mouths of his 'serious' figures, more at home in the world of the reformed stage than in popular comedy.)

For the traditional fundament of hierarchy (a fundament to which the Windwachels and the Lüftigs are foils) we must turn to urban and rural models of the menial family.

The disparity in power and authority between master and servant, parent and child, man and wife – if we are to believe the socio-historical literature on the peasant and petty-bourgeois family (cf. Sieder 1987) – was great, with harsh treatment, psychic abuse and moralizing ways feeding into a repressive disciplinarianism. A careful reading of Nestroy turns up no shortage of instances of this, most of them exploited for comic effect (no surprise this, given the genre) or in some way having their fangs drawn. Thus, for example, Leim, the joiner's apprentice, catches in mid-air the chisel the irate Master Hobelmann has just hurled at his daughter; Gluthammer in *Der Zerrissene* [The Man Full of Nothing] is shown as a choleric with a fondness for brawling; while the leaseholder Krautkopf is no less of a bully to his labourers – to name a couple of instances. But this is not the full story. Inferiors (servants, labourers, apprentices, etc.) can – more or less with impunity – answer back and in the verbal exchanges give as good as they get, nor is there much their masters can do about this; faced with such insolence from 'below', they do best to look the other way. In *Einen Jux will er sich machen* we find just such a situation – Principal Zangler is conversing with his man-servant to be – albeit presented in ideal-typical form. Melchior is trying to worm his way into a job:

> Melchior (entering shyly, centre stage): Excuse me, is Your Grace the spice peddler?
> Zangler: The first is too much, the second too little. I am not Your Grace, just Herr Zangler: but I am not a peddler but a trader of a range of goods.
> Melchior; I heard that Mr trader of a range of goods had a servant who was a downright rogue. (Nestroy 1986a: 9; trans. A.S.)

A trace of impudence on Melchior's part is already apparent in this exchange; but to learn just what a high opinion the new domestic has of himself, we must pass to the following scene, in which the matter of board and lodging is taken up:

> Zangler: Six guilders a month, food, lodgings, clothes washed.
> Melchior: Well now, clothes washed and lodgings, that's the least I'd expect, but the food where I was before was first-class.

Zangler: No-one in my household goes hungry either. – Soups, beef, side dishes and more besides.
Melchior: Much more besides though. And about breakfast – I always had coffee there.
Zangler: It wasn't normal in my household for the servant to drink coffee –
Melchior: You see, I'm sure you have a Rosolio among your range of goods.
Zangler: Oh yes, but –
Melchior: There, you see, then it is to both our advantage for you to give me coffee, otherwise you would be bound to tempt me with alcohol! (Nestroy 1986a: 10; trans. A.S.)

From the dynamics of this exchange (Melchior's mixture of obsequiousness and saucy repartee is brazen enough to actually be funny) we gain insight into how deeply ingrained this trait of the Austrian character was in the domestic milieu of Nestroy's day. Through gossip, the sharpest weapon in what was an otherwise limited arsenal, domestics in the menial family of old could, and did, bargain their way to fuller access to their master's larder, not that, come next Candlemas, after serving out their 12 months, many a serving man wouldn't think twice about changing his master, if he thought he might thus improve his lot. Yet it remains true that relationships of this kind were not measured entirely in monetary terms; they were not contractual (in the full-fledged market sense); the economy of which they were part was still an organic one, giving to such relationships a tacitly personal dimension. Farmers who fed their labourers and servants scraps from their table soon found themselves the butt of the neighbourhood; as a result, they found it hard to attract or hold good personnel. Presumably not all menials had the impertinence of a Melchior, who, as we see from this passage, doesn't hesitate to bombard his master with unsolicited advice, poking fun at him all the while (one of his specialities is rolling his eyes to heaven in mock devotion). But this canon, affording servants the right to cheek their masters albeit in the nicest possible way, is exemplified again and again; and it is very much a stock-in-trade of Nestroy's. At every turn, we find authority being held up to scorn. Transporting his audience into the exotic milieu of South Seas cannibalism, Nestroy soon has the daughter of the grim-faced *Häuptling Abendwind* ([Chief Evening Breeze]; the play was first performed in 1862) heaping ridicule on her father in choicest Viennese argot. Papa holds a speech expressing all the right sentiments – at least that is his intention, it is just that the playwright, through the daughter, won't let him get away with it: cut down to size by her interjections, he is soon rightly exposed as a repetitious boor.

Atala (to herself): What torture Father goes through to compose a speech!
Abendwind (continues): This white bear, which brings me luck as the son of the Sun and is in a way my ancestor – I also wish – (again losing the thread of the speech) Damn! I don't know what I want now – (goes on) since he is in a way my ancestor –
Atala: Father, that is the second time you have said that – 'is in a way my ancestor.' (Nestroy 1988: 38; trans. A.S.)

Often indeed it is the women – daughters or wives – who are able to challenge male authority with impunity. Such dexterity in turning the tables, to be sure, has been mistaken by several non-Austrian observers of the Austrian soul for perfidy, which it is not. 'Comic ambivalence' (Bodi 1985) is alive and well too in Qualtinger/Merz's *Herr Karl* (Qualtinger/Merz 1991), who signals to the mistress (she is the boss of a grocer's store) in whose service he stands that 'there are enough olives' – she has just questioned him on this point – only to proceed then, without skipping a beat, to plunder her larder and help himself to her best cognac, all this behind the woman's back (but in seeming complicity with a silent dialogue partner). And, in another instance of brazenness, he suggests to his mistress that she might care to provide her own cigarettes, instead of expecting him to perform this office. Since Master Karl, or rather the eponymous play, is a portrait of a Nazi supporter and demonic 'doer of one's duty', the wounding edge of the clichés Karl drops at every turn has been taken by many commentators to signal an especially insidious mindset, putting him beyond the pale – which is rather unfair, since Karl merely embodies a centuries-old servant ethos.

We are similarly transported into an exotic milieu in Nestroy's parody of Hebbel's *Judith und Holofernes* (first performed in 1849). We encounter here another sending-up of authority. In the following scene, we discover the Ambassador of Mesopotamia grovelling before the powerful Holofernes.

> Emissary: Mesopotamia surrenders unconditionally, at your pleasure or displeasure; even your displeasure is our pleasure.
> Holofernes: Why so late? You are as slow as molasses! Is Mesopotamia so far from here? Why didn't you make up a special train?
> Emissary: I take the liberty in the name of my king to tremble before your wrath.
> Holofernes: I swore the nation that surrendered last would be burnt out like cockroaches.
> Emissary: But we are only the next to last, and we pray your mercy ever so nicely, while the obstinate Hebrews still hold out. They entrench themselves in their city and slam their insolent gates in the heroic face of Holofernes. (Nestroy 1986b: 99)

Apart from the parodying nature of this exchange, to which we will return in a moment, we again note that even when the power differential is one-sided, as it is here, the weaker can count on his wit partly to redress the balance, if only his sallies are brash enough. While there is no mistaking the element of servility, the wheedling tone in which the stronger is asked to show understanding, generosity of spirit and forbearance, what is equally evident is the touch of impertinence that the Ambassador injects into his remarks. If we add these elements together, we get something not far removed from Bodi's 'comic ambivalence'.

The courtly element – flattery and servility

In interacting with persons of consequence, the degree of flattery resorted to is inversely proportional to the strength of the weaker party's cards. Thus the rise of a culture of flattery is also a mark of patrimonial dependency, in which the weaker (at least for the duration of the interaction) is ready to set aside all thoughts of personal dignity. The social setting in which, traditionally, flattery is most at home is the Court and its environs; not for nothing is this culture of obsequiousness often described, in German, as *byzantinisch* [sycophantic] – the palaces in the 'Rome of the East', with their endless chambers (to which only the eunuchs had access), with their interminable appetite for intrigue, with their excessive (by Western standards) predilection for courtly protocol, were famed for producing such fawning ways. One cannot, of course, identify the absolutist courts in Western Europe with Byzantium – egalitarian traditions efficacious even in an order dominated by feudal castes always kept such proclivities in check, so much so that Louis XIV himself was still, in a certain sense a *primus inter pares*. Still, one does not err too much in ascribing servility, Austrian-style, to the preponderance of courtly aristocratic relationships, still more the plethora of appropriate settings, in the urban capital and Imperial seat that was old Vienna. Nestroy grappled with the propriety of these servile ways in several couplets:

> One talks to a man, who can help or hinder,
> To make an enemy of him would be a great error,
> His behaviour is proud, his statements stupid,
> To call him an ass, what one wouldn't give for that chance! –
> But wait – one would pay a high price for this ass,
> It is better to lie at his feet like a subject:
> 'Your Grace, Your wisdom and great understanding
> Always go hand in hand with your great nobility,
> Your Grace is a shining example to us all!
> [Pretence of this kind is no mean feat.] (Nestroy 1987: 53; trans. A.S.)

The need for diplomatic caution can easily slide over into unbridled flattery; a stock theme in Nestroy is the frequency with which opportunistic rhetoric of this kind has the rug pulled from under it by what the fawners and grovellers actually do the moment diplomatic constraints are relaxed (or are believed by them to have been). In *Der Zerrissene* [A Man Full of Nothing], for example, we find Stifler, Wixer and the absurdly Anglophile Sporner quickly dancing to another tune as soon as they think their friend Lips is dead; and in *Lumpacivagabundus*, Zwirn's friends Windwachel and Lüftig constantly amaze the audience with their limitless cynicism.

Now, many of Nestroy's figures are sited in a transitional zone where courtly and commercial-capitalist norms rub shoulders, where market elements co-exist with institutions of 'good society' (the latter by its very nature interpersonal). This brings us to a further type of internalized attitude, one used in circumstances of unequal power. Authority is *arrogated*, rendering it worthless (through inflationary use) and ridiculous. This attitude is typical of the parvenu.

> First servant (from the middle door): Your Grace, a customer is here!
> Zwirn: I am no longer available today.
> First servant: Very good Your Grace (exit)
> Zwirn: People think a tailor exists only to serve them.
> First journeyman (from the side door on the left): Mr von Zwirn!
> Zwirn: What is it?
> First journeyman: Mr von Fidibus has paid his bill. (Tries to give him money.)
> Zwirn (refusing with pride): That is a matter for the book-keeper. (Nestroy 1991: 37; trans. A.S.)

This humble tailor, through a chain of unlikely events come into possession of a winning lottery ticket, feels no longer bound to his clientele, so urgent is his desire for admission to 'better circles'. In an instant, his servility gives way to overreaching pride.

> Second journeyman (also from the left): Master –
> Zwirn: Boor! Does he not know my title?
> First journeyman (to the second, quietly): You have to say 'Mr von Zwirn.'
> Zwirn: If you say 'master' once more, you've had it.
> Second journeyman: Mr. von Zwirn, this account has been blocked.
> Zwirn: Take it to the book-keeper again as quickly as possible and inform the Kanzlei staff of my anger. (Journeymen exeunt.) (Nestroy 1991: 37; trans. A.S.)

Evincing a fine eye, Nestroy calls the journeyman here a 'ruffian' for addressing Zwirn by what, after all, is his proper title. The gist of this passage would seem to be this: aspiring to a loftier rank than is one's due culminates in a loss of reality, followed at not too many turns by certain ruin. It is only against a background of habitual bourgeois-craftsman solidity that such outrageous self-aggrandizement stands out. The moralist and social critic in Nestroy, acute student of human nature that he was, cannot, it goes without saying, hide his ulterior motive in depicting such cases. But the tension he reveals between traditional solidarity and nouveau-riche thrusting for advancement can also be documented in works by other authors: for example, in Raimund's *The Peasant as Millionaire* [*Der Bauer als Millionär*] and *The Spendthrift* [*Der Verschwender*], nor should we overlook the evidence of social-historical studies of economic life in *Vormärz* Vienna. Bruckmüller, for instance, has taught us of the constant displacement from highly regulated so-called *Polizeigewerben* (from trades supervised by the authorities) to *Kommerzialgewerben* (less regulated commerce in the area of supra-local supply and demand); but he cautions us against perceiving in this a harbinger of industrial expansion, since it amounted to no more than a growing concentration of 'factories equipped with permission from the provincial authority' [*kleine oder große Landesbefugnisse*] (Bruckmüller 1985: 307). But at least we have here a counterpiece to the servility of old, namely the crudeness with which parvenus exploited their newly acquired position of power, with Nestroy lampooning the inappropriate character of this strategy. In similar vein, he parodies a woman who has married above her station, only to find her new status impugned when she finds herself a widow:

> Madame Schleyer (with great elegance to Kathi): Herr von Lips is thus your *Göd* or in fact godfather, as we nobles express it.
> Kathi (shyly): Yes, Your Grace. (Nestroy 1987: 24; trans. A.S.)

Nestroy never tires of chipping away at borrowed airs and graces; the very fact that Frau Schleyer, formerly the milliner Mathilde, is here addressed as 'Madame' is a dig at the Viennese bourgeoisie, with its penchant for French-courtly models, including its insistence on a life-style, thus conceived, as a mark of distinction from the lower orders. Nestroy reveals himself a master of parody, nowhere more, indeed, than when he has the butt of his scorn, Frau Schleyer, instantly set about parading her new-found nobility, something no true aristocrat – or, for that matter, non-aristocrat – would ever do. But more than in the solidly Protestant bloc of bourgeois countries, there was in Austria, and indeed still is, a readiness to parade one's rank by means of a life-style of conspicuous consumption, with the productive virtues being kept on a short leash. In this respect, Austria resembles France more than, say, Switzerland, England or Scandinavia, where luxury tends to keep a low profile. This could never be said of an Austria addicted to ceremonial sparring for status of members of the higher-ranking estates. One of the diffusion channels of this courtly code of conspicuous consumption, enabling it to achieve mass dissemination, was the increased incidence of upward mobility, as ever more parvenus integrated into the upper middle classes.

Now the same code of addressing people Kathi uses in the presence of her creditor and master is also available for use on unknown (higher-ranking) individuals, as soon as she has cause to believe they inhabit the same plane as her master and patron. We see this when Kathi approaches the malicious Madame Schleyer, who turns out to be Lips's Chosen One:

> Kathi (gradually gaining courage, approaches Madame Schleyer): Your Grace is so generous as to talk to me, you will allow me a question; it is perhaps a stupid question – (somewhat anxiously) am I right, it seemed to me as if my Herr *Göd* would like to marry?
> Madame Schleyer: He is projecting something of that kind.
> Kathi (somewhat taken aback): He is to marry? – And who is he going to marry?
> Madame Schleyer (proudly and curtly): Me!
> Kathi (hiding her inner feelings): You! – You like him very much, do you not? He is so nice – such a good-hearted gentleman – he deserves it, and he lacks nothing in his happiness but a true heart – oh, Your Grace will surely make him very happy.
> Madame Schleyer (brusquely): I rather think you wish to lecture me on how to make a man happy? (Nestroy 1987: 24–5; trans. A.S.)

The obverse of social submissiveness, indeed implicit in every hierarchical relationship, is the haughtiness of the higher-ranked. (Pip in Dickens's *Great*

Expectations has to imbibe liberal doses of this from Estella, his ill-bred, blasé 'lady' – which shows that in England too this gathering dynamic of an indiscriminate (and therefore inflationary) readiness to ascribe genteel status in dubious quarters was not unknown.) Another diffusion channel for this code of top-down servility is the relationship between merchant and customer. It is important (and of great interest) to note how this canon of personalized-hierarchical relationships is extended ever further, in the wake of growing commercialization and consumerism, to social outsiders, sending it into an inflationary spiral. This is well exemplified in *Mussi Weinberl* by the journeyman victualler working in Zangler's general merchandise shop.

> Weinberl (to Christopherl). Keep up a nice steady flow of 'Your Grace' and 'Madam', hand over the goods politely, address every little rascal as 'love', hand over change gracefully with index finger and thumb, the other three fingers are to be used only for shaking hands with [women] cooks. (Nestroy 1986a: 19; transl. A. S.)

While the apprenticed lad instinctively reaches for his shock of hair – fully aware it is liable to be yanked at any time, so junior is his status – he must keep at the ready, in order to ingratiate himself with his customers, a repertoire of polite formulaic greetings (and other accoutrements of devotion). Even now, whenever Austrian women enter a shop they can expect to be addressed as *Gnädige Frau* [Gracious Lady] or *Frau Doktor* [Madam Doctor] – in the latter case, even when it is the husband, not the customer, that is the doctor or academic. Accordingly, such passages in Nestroy's plays strike us as rather less outlandish than would any listing of the terms then in use (exotic-sounding though they now are) for the various victuals, none of which can be expected to mean much to today's audiences. This raises an interesting question: by what means and modalities was the social reproduction of this code effected, given that it took place at a time when changes nothing less than dramatic were coming about in other social domains? In terms of the code then prevailing, to be sure, the room for manoeuvre enjoyed by the higher-placed was considerable. Superiors can afford to be gross, if they so choose – of this Nestroy supplies plentiful examples. The higher-ranked have, thanks to their superior spending power (tips, bribes) and status, little trouble in hitching to their bandwagon, whenever they see fit, even the coercive power of the state. Among them are the likes of Principal Zangler, a readily recognized Viennese figure who runs a general merchandise shop, assisted by a journeyman and a young apprentice (cf. Bruckmüller 1985: 308, for the relevant figures: in the Vienna of 1837, for example, for every commercial trader there were some 1.3 persons in his employ). Zangler, for example, sends the constable off on a mission: without bothering with elaborate explanations, he instructs him to apprehend the presumptive lovers (his daughter and her beau, in stead of whom, however, he discovers Weinberl and Christopherl). Provided one was not oneself from the lower orders, it was not hard to enlist a constable in one's cause, the likelihood of negative fall-out, in the event of compliance, being slight.

Bruckmüller, attempting to clarify the class structure of Vienna's urban populace, cites an ordinance listing groups of persons who were exempted from the requirement of a magistrate's approval to marry: '1. the nobility; 2. all civil servants (national, urban, territorial); 3. doctors, magisters [i.e., university graduates], professors and teachers in public schools and other educational facilities; 4. lawyers and agents; 5. all citizens; 6. all house and estate owners; 7. qualified master craftsmen and all persons possessing national factory, factory or so-called government authorization (decree of protection)' (Bruckmüller 1985: 305). Situated below these classes were servants and menials generally, workers employed in manufactories and cottage industries, craft journeymen and the like. Vienna in Nestroy's day and age, spanning some four decades, was a city caught up in tumultuous change. It now wore more of a bourgeois face than before, and it was rapidly industrializing; that said, it had managed to retain its character as a metropolis of aristocrats and aristocratic ways, where personal dependency for commoners was the norm. If in the first half of the century it was still possible to encounter the 'gentleman's courier' [*herrschaftlicher Läufer*] and a gallery of other types (none to today's sensibilities less than exotic) of a traditional service society, then it is also true that many patterns of personal relationship had, by then, been transferred to more 'modern', more abstract figurations, thus ensuring cultural reproduction of a specific habitus that is still extant.

The inflationary use of honorifics like *Euer Gnaden* (equivalent to 'Your Honour', literally 'Your Grace') and the practice of hand-kissing (thus the apprentice Christopherl expresses his gratitude to the principal) attest, therefore, to the cultural reproduction of a social code long standing. (Jane Eyre, a contemporary of Christopherl's but living in a stately home in the north of England, simply addresses her 'master' as 'Mr Rochester'; and for him she is simply 'Miss Eyre', although her status as governess is infinitely lower than that of the true 'blue-blood' that he is). Kathi addresses her master in the third-person plural, not by more personal, second-person *Sie*; and Lips uses the third-person singular on her (at least he does prior to recognising she is his god-child, at which point he switches to the familiar *Du*). None of this has any equivalent in the former case, where both Jane and Rochester address each other as *you*, an appellation that is rather more egalitarian.

The courtly element in Habsburg bureaucracy parodied: the case of Herzmanovsky-Orlando

If in this inquiry Nestroy chiefly matters for his depiction of courtly influences on the (petty-) bourgeoisie, that is, the class of traders, merchants and household servants, then Herzmanovsky-Orlando, who lived well into the 20th century, is memorable for his mildly teasing analysis of the courtly origins and make-up of Austrian bureaucracy. As to how closely Herzmanovsky-Orlando's satire is rooted in reality and rates serious mention in the literary communicative process, this will detain us in some detail below, as will a number of his representations concerning bureaucrats and the Austrian mentality.

The unreal – or surreal – ambience of *Kakanien* [Kakania] or (to speak with the author himself) *Tarockanien* [Tarockania; *Tarock* is the name of a favourite card-game] is enunciated in the opening image of his short story *The Tragic Demise of a Faithful Court Official* (Herzmanovsky-Orlando 1997, first published in 1928).[4] A 'wondrous train from the Theatre at *Kärntnertor* [one of Vienna's city gates]' accompanies Zephyses Zumpi, the Imperial Dwarf (retired), and his beanpole of a wife. The very contrast between the dignity of occupying an official position at court and the incongruity of his tiny stature which cannot fail to provoke either embarrassment or open laughter, paves the way for realism of a higher order. Paraded before us in all transparency is the high dignity of a court official, to which even unruly nature can find nothing substantial to object. Here too – as in many other names and metaphors – is rendered visible the courtly origin of all bureaucracy in Austria. All offices in the Habsburg Empire are founded on proximity to court, the source of all preferment being His Imperial Majesty – hence the patrimonial genesis of bureaucracy. Since the functions of the 'Dwarves-of-Court' remain rather obscure, indeed indeterminate (we later learn that the Royal Ear at times hearkens to his advice in this matter or that), the advent of the Imperial Dwarf as an institution marks the *terminus a quo* for the principal ceremonial-decorative aspect of all offices. This applies no less to the spirit of unreality, which some of Austria's contemporary observers even have associated with the 'modern' state (they are thinking of the Second Republic) and the provisions it makes for its vital interests (cf. Bassett 1988: 37, 66; Menasse 1992: 65–6). In how he names his characters (or, more accurately, persons) Herzmanovsky-Orlando expresses much, as it happens, that bears on his deepest beliefs about the historical roots, and the true meaning of the idea of 'Austrianness'. Hence his choice here of the figure of 'Zephyses', just one of many bold concoctions of his in which Bohemian, Polish, Alpine, Italian and Greek influences rub shoulders with roles, characters and institutions nailing down what 'Austria' is and has historically been. A final point: the institution of the Imperial Dwarf expresses, it is clear, the harmless side of the Austrian character – a culture cannot be all that aggressive, cannot be all that nasty or bent on prevailing, come what may, if it can accommodate something as bizarre as court dwarves, or create a post the sole *raison d'être* of which is to dust down the 'Military Beetles' Collection.' The tendency to make oneself smaller, therefore more harmless and in need of protection, is exhibited in many cultures. The Dutch, for example, are given to tacking on to personal names a diminutive; and the English culture of 'understatement' avoids, at the least, openly articulating a desire to dominate, though in neither case do we find the same appetite for risibility as in Austria. For self-irony to become part of the national habitus is, if we may believe Elias, one index of a culture's maturity, an accolade he is willing to bestow on the English (cf. Elias 1960); whereas aggressive, ambitious nations, those that are determined to dominate the stage, have little use for self-irony – of which more later. In Austria, this tendency is not unconnected with the fact that making oneself smaller, diminishing one's stature, helps keeps at bay the demands, the admonitions and threats, of the authorities – as in the couplet: *Ich bin klein / Mein Herz ist rein* [Tiny me / My heart spot-free]. This goes also with the fact that no initiative, scheme or aspiration emanating from 'below' is liable to get very far, or, if it does succeed in going the distance, then only because it has been 'co-opted' by 'those above' or given their 'blessing'. So what is self-irony? – a sign of maturity or a gesture of humility? The answer would seem to be that the former does not rule out the latter. It is perfectly possible to build self-irony into an admission of weakness, and one can even make this part of the national self-image.

The Austrian bureaucrat, as we have come to know him through the centuries, legitimizes his status as sanctioned 'on high' – by which he has in mind the monarchical order and perhaps even the divine one too, just as Herzmanovsky-Orlando has Secretary-of-Court von Eynhuf say of himself:

> One should never question the hierarchy of officialdom, I always say, and it's all due to the subversive fomentations of the damned Freemasons that court dwarfs have lost their position. They were all loyal supporters of throne and altar and averse to any revolutionary movement. (Herzmanovsky-Orlando 1997: 3–4)

Sonnenfels, an émigré from the north, and the freemasons already constitute between them a threat to the old order. The duty of a true Habsburg bureaucrat is to stand at the Emperor's side.

> Many a Roman emperor' – he made a slight bow at the thought – 'gladly lent a Supreme Ear to the worthy little people. Those must have been marvellous gentlemen! How often I used to hear my dearly-departed grandfather speak of them. Long lists of glorious names!' He counted to himself on his fingers: 'There were first of all: Einoehrl, Wimhoelzl, Zirps, and Tschwertschkarsch – he's the one who got trampled by August the Strong at an evening outdoor concert – then there were Hirnwimmerl, the brothers Zirm, Domhopf, Kipfeltanz, Krschiwoprd, Schuschniak – not to mention the unforgettable Krschisch. Word has it that he was the inventor of the Bohemian language – supposedly thought it up for a melancholic prince of the House of Habsburg! It cured the melancholia and since then, so goes the story, there's been a certain preference at Court for … stop it!' Nervously he looked all around. (Herzmanovsky-Orlando 1997: 4)

Aside from dazzling us with this list of slightly ludicrous Austrian names, illustrating the multi-national make-up of the empire, this passage reveals much about the psychic structures laid down by power differentials within the bureaucracy. The very tone Eynhuf adopts articulates the loyalty that is writ so large in his person. He 'bows inwardly' at the mention of the Supreme Authority; were he ever to catch himself entertaining a non-conformist impulse of his own, no matter how insignificant, he would look around nervously (in case some eavesdropper might denounce him for his unspoken thoughts). The 'subaltern' official bows and scrapes; his subservience is deeply internalized, as is the reflexive fear that any false step his superiors get wind of may cost him his job. A loyal official knows his place, but does not, however, conceal his awareness of outranking all those situated further from the all-warming sun of the Imperial Presence. The power disparity between Emperor and Court Dwarf is such that the latter can (perhaps unintentionally) be trampled on without this conferring any right of protest. To satisfy the Princely Whim, even the Bohemian language was invented. But for a lifetime of loyalty the rewards were not inconsiderable; the Court Dwarf could look forward, upon retirement, to a handsome pension and to a dignified title, such as 'Court Dwarf 1st Class' ('holding a major's rank' – no matter that this epithet exposed the military hierarchy to a certain risibility) or even 'Lord High Dwarf' (Herzmanovsky-Orlando 1997: 5).

For the newly ennobled bureaucrat of bourgeois provenance (Eynhuf, in any event, is *Edler von*) there are other ways of winning higher honours. One of these is the pivot on which the whole story turns – a subject's attempt to recommend himself to His Imperial Majesty by pleasing Him in something dear to His heart. It must however be said that, by the close, one is no wiser about Eynhuf's motives: does he act as he does from pure altruism or from loving devotion? In a manner reminiscent of Robert Musil's 'Parallel Campaign', it is Eynhuf's intention, nurtured across many years, to make the Emperor a present to mark the anniversary of His accession to the Throne – this without the Emperor knowing or in any way signalling He was disposed to receive such a present. But what in Musil is a bizarre concentration of driving social forces remains, in this case, the deeply felt, considered strategy of one person:

> But Eynhuf's greatest joy could not be found in these books; rather, he became immersed in thrills of delight whenever he thought (in the purest and most chaste manner, of course) about his private pride and joy: his baby tooth collection, the largest and most complete in the entire Empire – all the experts had assured him of that. What could be more pristine than these pearls of innocence, this jewelbox of humility? Each time the little treasure chest was opened he imagined seeing pink clouds and hearing little lambs in blue ribbons tenderly chiming out a concert on crystal triangles under the direction and watchful eye of a senior lamb. And it was certainly not on account of selfish greed or private avarice that he expended so much effort on the collection. No! It was for his Kaiser! To Him were dedicated the fruits of all of these many years of searching and collecting. For Him these tiny teeth, pleasingly arranged in an attractive tableau, would one day shine forth with their smile at the anniversary celebration of His Majesty's ascension to the throne. (Herzmanovsky-Orlando 1997: 11–12)

The present-to-be is a collection of milk teeth in pristine condition – true, anything less useful and more absurd would be hard to imagine, yet it is also true that nothing could be more difficult to collect. Here again we glimpse a characteristic trait of Habsburg Austrian authority and how it is dispensed. In the Imperial Presence one need feel no fear – the love one feels is not born of anything as crude as physical coercion (indeed, recourse to the latter normally signals the absence of the former). The aura surrounding the Emperor's person is that of good-natured, affable superiority, drawing on the celebrated Habsburg *clementia*, that benevolent mildness of tone which, according to F. Heer, constitutes a core difference between Prussia and Austria. What we get is the difference between the 'male' and 'female' principles (cf. Heer 1981: 123–34, on the contrast between the Habsburg *clementia* of Maria Theresa and the harsh childhood of Frederick the Great, whose father seems to have been determined to humiliate him before all Europe). One often gains a sense that authority in Austria exhibits more than a whiff of this female 'element' – difficult though it is to prove this for the social history of the Austrian family. (Of some interest here would be a close analysis of Elizabeth I's reign, as compared with Maria Theresa's, from the perspective of how aristocratic males came to terms with being ruled over by a woman. Elizabeth's carefully nurtured image as the 'Virgin Queen' is well known; but it could not have differed more from that of the Austrian empress, mother to 16 children and the very incarnation of fertility and 'motherliness.') What does surprise, though, is that in the whole long line of Habsburg rulers it is hard to find a single despot – which cannot be said of Prussia, or Russia either. It would probably be fair to say that although the House of Austria produced no geniuses, no downright scoundrel ever sat on the Imperial Throne.

But even such vaguely 'feminine' – at any event not harshly punitive – authority weighed heavily on the psyche of those subject to it – in Eynhuf's case, so much so that even his digestive system fails him when he is casting around for a way of inducing in his Imperial Master the quintessence of pleasure. Finally, saving inspiration comes his way:

> Joyously he danced on his black-clad stork legs around and around the green diplomat's desk, oblivious to the fact that he had bumped into and tipped over the huge wastebasket fashioned in the style of an ordinary pail. To his misfortune the door opened at that moment and Privy councillor Sauerpfister strode in and observed with a critical eye the untoward antics of his subordinate. 'Pardon me,' Eynhuf murmured, 'I was merely expressing most submissively my joy at having just read in the Official Gazette that His Majesty the King of Portugal has successfully recovered from sheep's rot.' (Herzmanovsky-Orlando 1997: 12)

Submissest, as the term suggests, is the *non plus ultra* of complete submission – and it is with an equally rote, complaisant excuse that Eynhuf, in this passage, reacts to his superior's reproof, conveyed by a mere glance. Note that the 'untoward antics' have a perfectly innocent explanation, in the form of: Eynhuf's boundless jubilation at the brain-wave he has just had: he will obtain the missing milk tooth from Höllteufel, an actress famed for her beauty. It is just that he can't come out with this revelation. The only excuse that will wash is to invoke higher authority, in this case the King of Portugal and that unimpeachable source of legitimate information, the official gazette.

This whole bureaucratic culture with its penchant for ridiculous titles (Deputy Examiner of Ancestral Testing, Second Class, at the Imperial Stud Depot, Herzmanovsky-Orlando 1997: 8) is imbedded in a world of salons where hedonism is celebrated in a Baroque-courtly setting. Coffee parties are notorious affairs, so much so that the word for such gatherings, *Jause*, which normally translates as a rather simple meal offered between breakfast and lunch or lunch and dinner, now stands for unbridled gluttony. An eccentric sensuality all its own, quite incompatible with Victorian prudishness, envelops the 'night stool' [*Leibstuhl*] in a rhetoric of anal-eroticism, in which matronly old ladies set the tone. Nor is the courtly milieu alone grist to Herzmanovsky-Orlando's mill; he is good at reconstructing (e.g., in *Kaiser Joseph und die Bahnwärterstochter* [Emperor Joseph and the Stationmaster's Daughter]) an anachronistic (or pseudo-anachronistic) feudal social order (Herzmanovsky-Orlando 1995: 293–328). Deserving officials of the railway (no matter that it hasn't yet been invented, it is, however, 'anticipated' – never in clever Austria a problem) are personally ennobled by the Emperor; in return, tolls from sections of the railway line-to-be are made over to His Majesty as feudal dues. At one point in this stage spectacle, some 'Britishers' get up and forbid this anticipation – the railway, after all, is *their* invention – whereupon they arrogantly storm from the stage without so much as a by-your-leave.

Authoritarianism and self-irony in the Austrian habitus: Some remarks on the literary examples in Herzmanovsky-Orlando and Nestroy

By no later than the Counter-Reformation, Habsburg 'Austria' seems to have acquired a reputation as repressive and authoritarian, at least when measured against other Western societies, a reputation that has stuck, in one form or another, down to the present day. Almost as far back can be traced, too, a rather different take: that of a vivacious, easy-going Vienna enamoured of the life of the senses, as exemplified nowhere better than in the figure of *Lieber Augustin*, who is quite capable of falling asleep, after one of his binges, in a pit dug for victims of the plague; such figures can be counted on, even as the Apocalypse looms – the 'joyful Apocalypse that was 1880s Vienna' (Bloch 1975: 145–6) – never to lose their cool, an attitude best expressed by the old adage: *Die Lage ist hoffnungslos, aber nicht ernst* [The situation is hopeless, but not serious] (the Prussians of course have their own version: *Die Lage ist ernst, aber nicht hoffnungslos* [The situation is serious, but not hopeless]). Numerous observers of the Austrian temperament have noted not only this almost suicidal lightness of being, co-existing with – not that it is at all the same – a highly developed sense of self-irony (see, e.g., James, L. 1994: 44–5). It is tempting to postulate a link between these traits. The courtly patrimonial exercise of authority and its reception both in Austrian literature and on an Austrian stage (we are thinking of Viennese popular comedy down to Nestroy and, at a later date, cabaret) with a long tradition of parody and satire can perhaps be taken together for analytic purposes. This will, hopefully, illuminate key facets of how Austrians interact with authority.

Certain idiosyncrasies in the structuring and wielding of authority can be correlated with certain strategies for venting one's helplessness in humour. An (in its extreme form) almost pathological self-irony protects the weaker from the arbitrary reach of Janus-faced inscrutable authority – the latter's benign face makes protection possible, its menacing face renders it necessary. 'Making oneself smaller' than one really is goes hand in hand with a sarcasm verging on nihilism, which manages to thrive in the shadow of duly constituted authority, without in any way threatening it (or even wishing to do so). Since powerlessness absolves the weaker from accountability in how s/he responds, there flourishes a culture of innocuous idiocy, of anodyne barminess, in which reflexivity and association work overtime (pulling no punches) with one aim: to turn the sublime into the ridiculous. Nowhere is this attitude deployed to more devastating effect than in Nestroy (cf. Hannemann 1977). A relatively civilized outlet for impotence is when excessive self-irony and purposeless, nihilistic sarcasm result in an affective household marked by massive self-restraint, or else impose a considerable burden of affective control. That this represents a great cultural achievement is equally apparent. To study more closely the causes of this constellation, we again repair to the person of Nestroy, whose wit can take a far nastier turn than that of the essentially good-natured and considerate Herzmanovsky-Orlando.

Herzmanovsky-Orlando's oeuvre was one long exercise, it is no exaggeration to say, in exploring the Austrian temperament. If we may believe the reminiscences of his widow Carmen (cf. Herzmanovsky-Orlando 1995: 288–9), this was a task to which he brought some theoretical bearings of his own. It was plain to him that Austria was the chief (perhaps the sole) heir to the Hellenistic heritage of pagan antiquity, with the Crusades and the Italian Renaissance in the role of intermediaries. Its latter-day manifestation was Catholic-Baroque sensuality, unfolding a languid (yet perfectly vacuous) culture of ostentation with courtly and Christian echoes – in which it sometimes seemed there was nothing, not even the most useful items, that the painter's brush could not turn into coy decoration. Herzmanovsky-Orlando was, at the time of the monarchy's demise, already into his forties, and would outlive it, in Meran/Southern Tyrol (belonging to Italy since 1918), by another 30 years. That suffices, as rule, to deeply imprint in someone all a culture has to offer – in his patterns of thought, certainly, but perhaps even more in the reaches of his personality, his affective make-up, that are fashioned after what we have learned, since Freud, to call the 'unconscious'. This imprinting with all and everything Austrian went so deep, in the person of Herzmanovsky-Orlando, that, if we may credit his wife's testimony, he took himself to be simply stating the literal truth (though, he would surely allow, a truth eluding superficial inspection). In contrast we, the reader or the theatre-goer, think what we are getting is a phantasmagoria of ludicrously over-drawn effects, a collage where image is piled on image in a display of associative virtuosity, the prolific outpouring of a 'freakish' mind. We are confronted with a question to which there is no easy answer: how are we, faced with such a free-floating style – where one drollery gives way to the next (and in no apparent order), where the author seems prepared to take poetic license to new limits in holding up the mirror to reality – how are we, then, to get at the underlying sociology? One way is to construe such 'ironic' jumping between over- and understatement as we might a newspaper caricature. There too features are coarsened or distorted; sometimes colour, nuance and perspective are omitted, and yet we normally have no trouble in discerning likeness to the original – think of de Gaulle's long nose and his imperious gestures. Apart from the performative aspects of corresponding speech-acts, the resultant construction (or distillation) is not too many steps removed from the celebrated 'ideal types' of Max Weber, or even the synthesizing cognitive model of Norbert Elias. Herzmanovsky certainly aimed at getting the audience to laugh, although, as already stated, the situation with Herzmanovsky-Orlando is not so simple, for in this playwright the exuberance is latent in the objects themselves, necessary though his helping hand is to liberate it. In both cases, understanding is achieved other than in a naively inductive, empirical approach, which is not to say the latter is dispensable – quite the contrary. Similar considerations apply to Nestroy's satire. If we treated Nestroy earlier chiefly as a sociological realist (albeit one who inspected reality through a satirical prism and nursed a predilection for ideal types), it is time now to take stock of him as parodist and self-ironist. This dimension can be studied in his play *Judith und Holofernes*.

What we find in this play (his third after the March Revolution, the first being *Freiheit in Krähwinkel*[5] [Freedom in Krähwinkel], followed by *Lady und Schneider* [Lady and Tailor]) is scepticism and absence of illusions about human nature (and, it is fair to assume, the society of his day), a stance he conveys with great economy of means. This work repays closest attention, given the array of sociological insights it contains into the Austrian character.

Judith und Holofernes is modelled on Hebbel's *Judith*, which itself draws on the biblical narrative. We know that Nestroy initially concealed his authorship; the shy, inhibited Austrian had met in Vienna the rather more worldly North German Hebbel. Nestroy's travesty can be described as a parody playing on two levels and in (at least) four dimensions. On one level, it caricatures Hebbel's pathos in scathing tones, which did not go down at all well with his erstwhile admirer.[6] On the other level, it parodies in no uncertain terms the virtues his characters stand for, twisting them into unrecognizability.

That the play parodies Hebbel's pathos and holds it up to ridicule (partly by exaggeration, partly by the device of tying the grand passions to other, rather earthier (and certainly more trivial) passions, is prefigured in the play's overall structuration. Of the heroic, self-sacrificing figure of Judith – who has been twice violated (once by being raped, once by having her patriotism impugned), turning her into a 'virginal widow', who for a multiplicity of reasons must kill Holophernes – there is no trace in Nestroy's version. What he gives us instead is her brother Joab, who dresses up in drag so as to play his sister, which lets the dramatist exploit a suite of well-known theatrical effects. Nor does Joab-Judith really, in Nestroy's play, behead the hapless Holophernes: the 'head' in question turns out to be a paper-maché requisite – a device taken over from popular comedy (already in the 18th century we find it, for instance, in Philipp Hafner). Nor, for that matter, does Holophernes seem capable of anything remotely like rape, which prompts Judith (i.e., Joab) to a flight of wit: 'Not too much for a woman to fear here...' Holophernes himself, apart from his terrible cruelties, which even parody cannot disguise, turns out a thoroughly good-natured specimen of Viennese manhood (Judith: 'Great Holophernes eats frugally, ... Just a chicken with salad and a schnitzel, veal if you please'). Thus ancient Hebrews are recast as Jews from downtown Vienna, who were not known for their martial virtues or warlike ways.

But Nestroy does not just reserve his barbs for Hebbel: a whole raft of grand passions and virtues are parodied, which goes a considerable way to explaining why this play has lost none of its power to delight. As for the four dimensions of Nestroy's parody, referred to above, the first takes issue with the powerful, titanic heroism Hebbel has injected into his rendering of Holophernes; what Nestroy gives us instead is a highly agreeable blood-sucker.

> Judith (Joab) (coquettishly): I've been told of the terrible things that you do –
> Never sparing men's lives – you naughty man, you.
> And I've also been told – though I simply refuse
> To believe it of a man like yourself – you eat Jews.
>
> Holophernes: I'm not as bad as all that. I am merely in the habit of laying things waste. Sit down and dine with me. (Reclines in the Greek manner on the sofa.)
> (Nestroy 1986b: 116)

Monstrosities are passed off as run-of-the-mill peccadillos, barely worth the mention. Holophernes shows himself to be a philistine, who wants from Judith 'the first kiss' [*das erste Bussi*]; he listens with interest and sympathy to Judith's tale of her disastrous wedding-night with the deceased Manasses. Nestroy's parody allows us to catch a glimpse of his own, somewhat gentler values; almost all critics have picked up on this, perceiving a linkage to Austrian realities in that year of revolution (thus Hein 1988: 78; also Hein 1970: 114–15, concerning the pacifism of the Hebrews; Mautner 1974: 293; Kahl 1970: 273; for a contrasting view see Hannemann 1977: 76–7, who considers Nestroy to be tilting simultaneously at the Titanism of German *Sturm und Drang*).

Here Nestroy, whose sympathies were bourgeois – at any rate, not feudal-aristocratic – is at one with contemporary audiences, most of whom fancy themselves enlightened enough to have rejected bellicose ways. But there is a second dimension to note: the raillery and derision Nestroy heaps on the Bethulian brokers who, even with catastrophe looming, can think only of their 'cut' (here Nestroy is caricaturing, and none too subtly either, the Jews of Leopoldstadt). Although one of the themes Nestroy never tires of is the corrupting effect of money, he does not, by and large, see it as specifically Jewish; rather, it is a 'general human' failing. A third dimension is the scant courage of the Hebrews, also their forced nature of their heroism.

But Nestroy's choicest bolts of satire are reserved for religion – or rather, priests and prophets.

> Joacim (entering from the side): Vey, vey! Three times vey!
> Ammon: This is all the solace the priesthood has to offer us?
> Joacim: When you all perish by the sword of the foe, remember you brought it upon yourselves with your sins.
> Hosea: How about this man? Off our taxes he lives, he's the one we must tithe to. (Nestroy 1986b: 101–2)

The rationalist Nestroy, child of the Enlightenment that he is, has little time for religion, and none at all for its remarkable consolations. One of his best sardonic flashes comes when he has the blind and dumb prophet, Daniel, appear on stage ('Why didn't he say he was blind? – Because he's struck dumb, that's the whole problem'). The prophet is liable to order someone to be stoned whenever his own monetary interests are at stake. For Nestroy not even the noble virtue of compassion is sacred, not when he has religion in his sights. Thus Nestroy's wit is cast in the mould of a bloody-minded (if playful) reckoning-up (cf. Hannemann 1977: 136) with practically every vice there is, plus its opposing virtues – with tyranny and oppression, but also with organized resistance; with courage on the battlefield, but also with the prevalence of self-serving cowardice; with the pathos of the defenders, but also with their religiously grounded quiescence and fatalism. Certainly, in Nestroy we encounter at every turn the cognitive and emotive universe of the reason-affirming Enlightenment, whose values were largely his own – but each time this supreme mocker executes a volte-face, we feel the needle of our moral compass spinning wildly. This has led to Nestroy being classified as a nihilist; he was accused – by Hannemann, for example – with using his wit to almost completely negate the 'positive side' of human nature, with only knowing the evil side of people (or their times). His wit, it has been said, was a stylistic conduit for the non-committal, the overflow of an illusion-free, nihilistic mind. Even by his contemporaries (Speidel, for example, according to Hannemann 1977: 136), Nestroy's humour was seen as proof of a certain lack of principle, and linked to the general political passivity of Viennese youth during *Vormärz*. Young people, according to the Liberal, von Bauernfeld (who was a friend of Grillparzer's), 'dined at the time on raucous Nestroyian slogans, thin gruel indeed; albeit outwardly encouraged by the police, it was hardly likely to breed on its own warriors for freedom' (Bauernfeld, cited by Hannemann 1977: 136).

Nestroy as actor and playwright was deeply immersed in the venerable traditions of Viennese popular comedy, and played easily on all the stylistic stops in this genre.[7] He achieved comic effect, in the drastic manner of his theatrical forebears, dishing up the standard fare of requisites. He wrote comedies of errors [*Verwechslungslustspiele*] 'antics with choral accompaniments' [*Possen mit Gesang*] , magic plays [*Zauberspiele*]; but his greatest talent lay, it can be fairly said, in the domain of parody (cf. Mautner, 1974, p. 24f.), where he excelled through witty asides of (at times) boggling complexity. Even now in Austria it is parody that is still a prime conduit for the nation's humour. This means a wide-ranging facility for imitation, often ensconced in (to outsiders) impenetrable dialect, using the means of subtle (or not-so-subtle) exaggeration, or downright distortion, to chip away at some hapless victim from what is sensed to be his or her weakest angle. But not just any kind of parody: it must stand in the Austrian tradition of 'comic ambivalence', in which the ridicule detaches itself from the 'more authentic' objects, seemingly turning against those very figures whose claim on our sympathy is greatest, only then to engulf author and audience alike in a (more or less) grotesque turning of the tables. In the end, all seems to dissolve in a value relativism – call it 'nihilism' – wearing demonic features; and if the audience had been hoping for a homily or two (popular comedy, let us recall, was partly rooted in the edificatory dramas of the Jesuits) they were courting disappointment. Not that such total parody started with Nestroy, any more than it ends with him: Karl Kraus's *Letzte Tage der Menschheit* [The Last Days of Mankind] and Qualtinger's *Herr Karl* abound in passages where one catches oneself feeling sympathy for characters who, even at their malicious, unreflecting worst, are not without colour, wit or a human sentiment, to the point where the moral ground we had taken for granted begins to slip away.

In both Nestroy and Herzmanovsky-Orlando, it is not difficult for modern audiences (and here they do not differ from past ones) to see the weapon of irony as directed at themselves, not at some more or less distant outside party. Thus this kind of humour is a plank in the collective Austrian identity, an 'identity marker', to use Bodi's phrase (Bodi 1985), and it draws on the means of satire, parody, buffoonery to achieve its grotesque effects, to dabble in 'comic ambivalence'.

'Ambivalence' may be taken as wobbling in evaluating properties that are the objects of irony (and self-irony), so that these come to express approbation and disapprobation alike. 'Ambivalence' can therefore also intimate waiting, inhibition, a broken relation to action. Under certain circumstances, contends Bodi, this aspect of the culture of a people – an ethnic group, a nation, or simply a language group segment displaced culturally from the rest – can be deployed to mark it off from others, thereby staking out identity. The factors impelling to such collective self-stylization can be many and varied: sometimes, too, degradation from without can be neatly inverted into an ironizing element of social self-labelling, a case in point being Jewish humour. Perhaps it is not so different with the object of our present enquiry, Austria, which saw itself as confronting a twofold problem: how to mark itself off from the other German-speaking countries with (in part) Protestant bourgeoisies, and as well from the non-German-speaking nationalities under Habsburg sway. Self-irony became a conspicuous part of Austrian self-image. But perhaps this is just self-stylization of a rather superficial kind? Or might it be that self-irony has trickled deeper, and become part of the Austrian habitus or an aspect thereof?

For this last interpretation speaks the fact that Viennese popular comedy has a long history of resonating broadly across class lines, in crass contrast to the

Protestant countries with their bookish traditions; indeed, it seems deeply imbedded in the social structure of a Habsburg Monarchy wedded, as it was, to Catholic universalism. Bodi specifically links the zenith of this theatre of parody to the bourgeois Enlightenment having played out in an absolutist setting. During the Josephine reforms (which inaugurated a 'thaw' [*Tauwetter*] in that there was now a critical public, with consequences after 1781 not unlike those we saw in the post-Stalinist Soviet Union) a typical 'intelligentsia' sprang up that would last throughout the 19th century. This found its voice in musical theatre and complex comedies, instead of venting itself, as it did in metropolises elsewhere, in verbal or book-based exchanges on a literary marketplace. Evading the censor's reach – expanded again in the shocking wake of the French Revolution – became something of a national sport; parodying official announcements by reading out choice tidbits (in which the government's stupidity was more than usually apparent) was now standard practice. Thus was born the linguistic sensibility (and with it, a talent for psychologising) that still flourishes on the nation's stage and in its prose literature.

If we are to relate such complex cultural attainments as irony and self-irony to social habitus, we must first achieve some clarity on the various levels and layers of social personality, including the formative institutions (or figurations) in which they are imbedded. Talk of habitus is only justified, as argued above in some detail, when irony and self-irony are reproduced in everyday life and this with such regularity as to imprint, lastingly and consequentially, the 'affective household' of the members of that society, becoming a kind of 'second nature'. This presupposes that the forms of institutionalized humour vented on stage or in prose literature do not stand alone, but indicate a wider use in countless interactions of everyday life. Not only is here no getting past this postulate from the sociology of knowledge, but it has, we submit, the force of reason on its side. Popular comedies could only attract, we will assume, mass audiences savouring the witty exchanges and verbal repartee if they first understood them – implying, in turn, that audiences had discursive knowledge at their fingertips from everyday life.

To understand how the use of humour in everyday life can give rise to habituations, to social characters, we must analyze the emotions that are triggered by or accompany humour – which again raises the question of how emotions relate to human cognition. Koestler (1994) is probably right in construing humour – or wit – as a specific type of stimulation of the laughter reflex (stimulated otherwise, spontaneous or involuntary laughter may result instead); here we can, in the case of laughter and expressions of other human emotions, distinguish between processes that are biologically derived (unlearnt, but specifically human, i.e., species-specific) and processes or structures that are socially derived (learnt). Following Elias (1987), we can analyze all emotions not only in terms of the role they play in communication between members of human groups (drawing on phylogenetically older structures of behavioural control, i.e., structures not located in the neo-cortex), but also in terms of how the emotion is structured for the individual group member himself. As is the case with other emotions (e.g., tearful grief), in amusement spilling into laughter we have a *somatic component* (e.g. a motor reflex, i.e., breathing with a specific rhythmicity), a *behavioural component* (changes to the musculature controlling the mimetics of the laughing face) and a *feeling component*. Note in this connection that the joke was already analyzed by Freud as a psychic motion aiming at maximizing pleasure under particular circumstances, as a compromise between conscious and unconscious stimuli (cf. Freud 1974). Severely depressed persons or persons gripped by overwhelming anxieties are known not to laugh. Besides the affective, biologically fixed components, there is in laughter too, as with the other affects, a component of learning-based cognitive control, or dirigibility, this being particularly evident in the complex cultural phenomenon of humour. When analyzing the social role of humour, it is important to recognize the existence of two levels: we all know how readily laughter can spread within a group, to the point where it may be hard to stop, no matter how hard one tries (which testifies to the comparatively rigid, stabilizing, stimulus-reinforcing role the affects play in behavioural control). On the other hand, there are subtle forms of humour (to which irony and self-irony may certainly be reckoned), in which the urge to laugh stops short of its goal and elicits only wry pensiveness. Phylogenetically speaking, laughing and smiling would seem to correspond to two highly disparate symbolic functions (and needs). Laughter in primates is associated with 'the play face' (cf. Argyle 1989: 40) that individuals regularly adopt when playing with companions (i.e., this facial expression is typical of tension-free situations). Smiling, on the other hand, may have evolved from intentional motor acts of a defensive nature (i.e., appeasement gestures and the like), and is used, in the higher primates, to signal friendliness or a desire to placate (van Hoff, cited by Argyle 1989: 48; in tandem with affiliative needs, as when infants smile instinctively upon seeing their mother's face; Argyle 1972: 48). It can be said of the affects generally that they are significantly more rigid than cognitive-based forms of behavioural control (among their somatic components is the chemistry of signal communication via messenger substances like noradrenalin, acetylcholine, dopamine and serotonin). That said, the sheer extent to which human affects are cognitively permeated is well exemplified in laughter – whether it be an obsequious grin, or a bitter grimace, or a disdainful hoot at somebody else's expense, the bandwidth of mimetic expression is broad indeed; and the sheer plasticity of the enabling facial musculature ensures that cultural mimetics finds many and varied expressions. Whether to fend off embarrassment or deliberately incite it in another, humour is at all times a ready tool, closely related to the experience of power and powerlessness in social situations – for so we must construe it. (All theoreticians of the joke have picked up on its aggressive component, always waiting in the wings: it can preponderate as with East Frisian jokes – the German equivalent of English jokes targetting the Irish – or with jokes in a less politically correct era against dumb blondes; or else it can be vestigial as with jokes of childlike naivety.) In this sense it is hardly new to observe that mockers and self-ironists alike often are highly vulnerable individuals, shame-ridden and with something of an inferiority complex; at any rate, this characterization fits Nestroy to a tee, if we are to lend credence to his contemporaries.[8] Now the cognitive, that is, 'self-directing' or 'self-controlling' component, at work in the imprinting of the affective household, does not exist in a vacuum; rather it feeds into the fact that humour, meaning here irony and self-irony, can be harnessed in a variety of ways to confer pleasure, foster joie de vivre and bolster the ego. The core element in humour is the achieving of 'comic contrast', that is, in which the tables are deftly turned to induce sudden release. This basic pattern can be deliberately induced by a single device or by many: a flash of insight might do the trick, though long years of training may have gone into its making; practitioners of self-irony trade on its having a disarming effect – perhaps too they are betting that the self-detachment implied by turning one's wit on oneself will call forth admiration. Moreover, a pact can be inaugurated, as in the case of English understatement, which plainly has a contractual aspect: in return for humbling oneself (or exercising a degree of self-restraint) the other undertakes to honour this show of self-effacement on the plane of symbolic elevation. Indeed, this is all part of the gentleman canon. Humour can also take the form of good-natured (or even slightly edgy) banter in a group situation, with all competing for the joker's crown – once again, the pleasurable relaxation induced by a good joke, or a clever remark, is mixed with a need to triumph in tilting the power balance in the group the joke-tellers's way. (Even co-operate needs, considerable though they may be, must at such times play second fiddle to the imperative of trumping the others.)

What 'figurations', therefore, explain the rise of Austrian humour? One answer might be that there were, in Habsburg society generally and in the Viennese society of the 18th and 19th centuries particularly, very specific forces at work, which gave rise to an equally specific brand of humour. For the weaker, in a world where power was asymmetrically distributed, it was a source of power, a way of turning the tables on the great and mighty; yet, at the end of the day, when the laughter had faded away, little or nothing was found to have changed in the situation's overall structuration. Of course, humour is not *just* a way of reacting to social impotence; even highly egalitarian societies have valued it as a cultivated attainment, at once giving pleasure and dissipating tensions. Here loss of face is forever waiting in the wings, in line with deeply internalized standards, and humour is a device for heading this off; Goffman (1967) ranks the telling of jokes among the prime (co-operative) strategies for avoiding embarrassment in social interactions. But humour, let us not forget, often asserts itself in highly distressing situations, even when not obviously triggered by some wielder of authority – a sense of powerlessness may alone do the trick: in figurations of this kind, there is no need for the powerful to be 'personally' present, as there might be in a face-to-face society. In the complex, multi-tiered society that was the Vienna of Old, both factors were at work; nor should we omit to mention the climate of unfreedom, which added its own flavour. This was very possibly a property already of the basic structure of Austrian society, in which confessional absolutism and courtly patrimonialism (the courtier, too, is obliged by the weak cards he holds to learn diplomatic ways) amalgamated to create a climate where 'open' expression of conflict, anything that smacked of 'aggression', was tabooed from earliest years in word and (physical) deed. A root cause may be suspected, to be sure, in how authority and dependency played out in the middling and lower orders, cocooned as these orders were in a domestic economy (an *oikos*). Here, the stark facts of subordination and servility could be offset, every so often, provided one did not make a habit of it, by a touch of rebelliousness, by giving as good as one got in a verbal exchange, or by making a snide remark behind the master's back, if not to his face. The courtly setting certainly refined the art of observing one's fellow man, even as it honed a talent for psychologizing, for uncovering endless nuances and shades of behaviour in all and sundry (including oneself). Humour also enabled one to interact with others in a spirit of play, this a consequence of the 'trickle-down effect', whereby the norms of polite society, of the environs of court, found ready imitators in the petty bourgeois, urbanized classes (their worlds converging to a degree anyway) – amounting to a downward diffusion of cultivated ways. In this sense both irony (offensive) and self-irony (defensive) have common cultural roots. On the other hand, humour has much to do also with the need to dissipate tension in tight situations, to achieve inner distance from role-assigned constraints – it can unite groups faced with stresses from without, welding discrete individuals into a 'band of brothers'.

But authority can sometimes be so high-handed, so unrelenting, as to throttle laughter. Is not the Austrian variant of irony and self-irony a kind of reaction to manifestly imperfect authority – in which nemesis, though never entirely absent, has its edge often blunted by poor execution? This could indeed be called the 'anomie model', and it makes good sense of certain forms of humour. Absolutism, even when attenuated by sloppiness (*Absolutismus, gemildert durch Schlamperei*, a dictum by Viktor Adler) was in many respects anything but effective; even today Austrians put their faith less in the letter of the law, in the orderly grinding of the bureaucratic mill; they resort rather to personal intervention, known to open a 'backdoor' or two. A culture of joking can also be a reaction to lack of transparency and predictability in circumstances that are rarely less than mildly chaotic. In the absence of duly constituted strong authority, there are no clear rules. Indeed, remove such father figures and persons inured to hierarchy and coercion from earliest years find it hard to take responsibility for themselves and get on with their lives, as they might in more horizontal or individualistic societies. (Not for nothing do cultures of an activist bent suffer from a deficit of wit.) Nestroy's 'nihilism' reflects, to boot, a loss of bearings in the absence of clear – legitimate and time-sanctioned – rules. A case in point is *Freiheit in Krähwinkel*, where the futility and effeteness of the revolution have already fostered a self-deprecating wit. Humour also thrives where more active outlets are blocked off, especially in situations of indecision and lack of conviction that goals are achievable by word and deed. Thus self-irony is frequently observed in the wake of catastrophes, self- or other-inflicted. Cases in point are Austria's heavy defeats by Prussia in the 18th century; by Napoleon, who in 1809, under particularly humiliating conditions, even installed himself in Schönbrunn and had his men exercise in the courtyard. Then there was the threat of self-dissolution of the Austrian state in 1848, and the fateful Battle of Königsgrätz in 1866 – all of which made self-disparagement into something of a national pastime, to which we find no parallel in an England used to carrying the field.

The Viennese popular comedy of old dealt in a none-too-subtle, earthy brand of humour, in which blows were freely traded; for an audience of today, the fecal expletives and salacious allusions would be only embarrassing. Beyond a doubt, institutionalized humour in the interval between Stranitzky and Nestroy learnt rather more civilized ways. This was a time in which Austrians were exposed to new levels of discipline; sent to school, they imbibed morality and civilization. However, in the social milieus of today's mass political parties and bureaucracies, mechanisms seem to have carried over that our forebears would have no difficulty in recognizing, just as Nestroy's wit and Karl Kraus's satire are significantly closer to us than we might have expected from a whole suite of other characteristics of that world of yesteryear, now beyond recall.

A rewarding task – one whose call we shall resist in these pages – would be to write a history of Austrian humour from the civilizational perspective.

Notes

1 This is the title of the only translation which has ever been produced (by Vincent Kling; see <http:\\www.doderer-gesellschaft.org/english/pdf/The_Strudlhof_Steps.pdf>; it is a translation of the first 80 pages and we will use it also for the English version of examples from this book that form part of our argumentation).

2 The prototype of all such figures may well have been the Hans Wurst created by Stranitzky; in his play *Türckisch-bestraffter Hochmuth oder das Anno 1683. Von denen Türcken belagerte und von den Christen entsetzte Wienn und Hans Wurst* [Turkish Pride Rebuked or Vienna, Invested by the Turks and Relieved by the Christians, and Hans Wurst] (in Rösler, ed. 1991: 33–6). Stranitzky pulls out all the stops, ranging in dramatic effect from in-your-face cheek to juicy anal allusions to comic bowing and scraping.

3 For Vienna and its environs at the end of the 18th century, Bruckmüller puts the number of persons in service at around 40,000 (approx. 15 per cent of the population); by the 1820s, in what would later become the 1st District, domestics comprised around 45 per cent of the total population (cf. Bruckmüller 1985: 314).

4 All subsequent excerpts are from this special edition.

5 *Krähwinkel* [Crow's-nest] is a fictitious location remotely resembling Vienna.

6 So great was Hebbel's disgust that he pronounced, famously, that even a rose would begin to stink after Nestroy had smelt it.

7 According to Mautner, there are four styles that Nestroy puts into the mouths of his characters: 1) a natural and realistic style, in keeping with the character's social rank, 2) a forced and stilted style, reflecting the character's line of work, 3) Nestroy's own personal style, a mixture of concrete observation and abstraction with a pronounced relish for wordplay, 4) stylistic parodies, set off for effect from natural speech patterns (cf. Mautner 1974: 38).

8 Nestroy is often described as awkward and easily embarrassed: for example, in his local tavern he is said to have been too shy even to call the waiter, preferring to entrust this office to others; reports of his meeting with Hebbel insist that he was, on that occasion, inhibited in the extreme, etc. (cf. Kahl 1970; Hannemann 1977: 152).

Chapter 7

Proud Detachment as an Element of English Authority Relationships: 'Indirect Rule'

An example from the end of the era

The last chapter surveyed the full spectrum of courtliness imbuing the Austrian character, from Baroque, pompous frivolity to the encouragement of flattery and obsequiousness (interspersed, however, with irony and self-irony). In this chapter this Austrian personality regime is contrasted with the very different English model characterized by 'proud detachment'. An aspect of the habitus of subordinates as well as that of their superiors, proud detachment is the opposite of subservience. Pride runs like a thread through English history, frequently in the form of English group pride; other European countries often acknowledged that England indeed had grounds for such sentiment (cf. Maurer 1992). It is probably no accident that this model is bound up with the practice of 'indirect rule', the roots of which, as we showed in detail in our analysis of the political and administrative position of the English gentry, reach back at least to the – still very direct – rule of honoratiores (rule of notables; cf. Weber 1978: vol. 2, 1059–64) of the 18th century (as embodied in the institution of 'justices of the peace'). 'Indirect rule' as an explicit concept of English colonial rule, meanwhile, first emerged, according to Tidrick (1992: 195), in northern Nigeria in the first decade of the 20th century. She attributes the idea to Sir Frederick Lugard and his writings. It involves leading and administering the indigenous population through delegation, leaving largely intact indigenous judicial and administrative authorities. A key factor in this mode of practicing colonial authority 'behind the scenes' is the relationship between the British 'resident' and the diverse tribal chiefs and other indigenous dignitaries, conceived as a personal relationship of trust, featuring a great deal of tact on the part of the British and safeguarding of the local population's honour.

This chapter traces the development of such authority relationships and probes their psychological, habitual effects. This contrast is of course not meant to imply that Austria as a system knew nothing of pride and honour. This would be as dubious as portraying England as a society free of all courtly flattery and subservience: Christopher Sykes has produced an impressive portrait of his uncle, who had the misfortune to be helpless in the face of the 'practical jokes'[1] of his merciless master Edward (heir to the throne and later King Edward VIII of

England) (cf. Sykes 1986: 27–8). The English code of proud detachment is, however, more deeply and broadly diffused throughout English society than was the aristocratic and Estates-based concept of honour in middle- and lower-class Austria.

K. Tidrick has also treated the system of 'indirect rule', first formulated explicitly and intellectually as an ideal order by Lugard and consistently advocated by others (such as Temple in his book: *Native Races and their Rulers*, 1918), as a kind of ideological sleight of hand, because the real power largely rested with the British, not with the various local princes. The white man's tone of patronizing civilizational authority is anathema to many today – Tidrick is right to underline the military violence and economic ruthlessness which brought about the asymmetric power relationships pertaining between the colonialists and members of the indigenous elites. Yet there is something unique and unmistakable about relations between the British and African or Indian dignitaries. A finely spun web of protocol marked the treatment of princes and chiefs during meetings in person (cf. Tidrick 1992: 197): the politeness to be shown to a particular guest was to be measured precisely in line with his rank. A high-ranking chief was offered a carpet to sit on, rather than a mere blanket. The 'resident' had to stand up when greeting and saying good-bye. When making contact with a highly placed indigene, one had to take into consideration the demands made on his time, and assume this to be, more or less, as valuable as one's own. Important indigenes were informed in detail of impending visits. A similar practice was usual in English high society (the servant delivered his master's calling card to announce his visit; cf. Curtin 1987). The language in which such official relations between colonial master and the conquered were clothed was that of personal friendship: 'I am very pleased with my visit to Kano', wrote Lugard to his emir (Tidrick 1992: 197), 'and I am glad to have seen you again, for I regard you as my personal friend, in whom I place entire confidence and trust.' We shall again meet this language in Defoe's portrayal of Robinson and his servant Friday. It is however astonishing, in light of the history of brutal violence and economic cunning with which the British elites for a time subjugated half the globe (as we have seen in the history of the English monopoly of taxation, they were mainly financed in this endeavour by the lower and middle classes).

Honour, respectability and love, as well as friendship, became entwined not only in the vast world of colonial relations, but in the socializing nucleus of the 'public school'. As Tidrick correctly points out, when requests for and offers of love are bound up with requests for and offers of an honour that establishes superiority, the psychological outcome is highly ambivalent. In this way, the colonial relation could take particularly interesting forms. By demonstrating proud inner independence, colonized peoples seemed to the British richly to deserve the recognition of honour and mutual respect. This applied above all to two peoples: the Arab Bedouin and the African Masai. Bravery in battle, and a demeanour that privileged detachment, were the key elements provoking an almost immediate admiration in most British colonial officials – a willingness to support and even to love them. (In the Second World War, an English officer allowed a courageous if foolhardy Masai to keep the Samurai sword he had taken from a captured Japanese: 'Please do not take this sword away from this soldier [...] He is a Masai.' (Tidrick 1992: 174). The British valued the Masai's classical warrior-stature, stoical courage, consciousness of their own superiority, and tact, which meant that they rarely requested anything.

> They were never importunate, never servile; they never tried to lure Europeans into the kind of patron-client relationship which is often assumed to be vital to the functioning of the colonial psyche but which many Englishmen in fact found more annoying than gratifying. (Tidrick 1992: 175)

The unbroken Masai – like the proud desert sheikhs – stood out pleasingly from the 'coolie' mentality of many other peoples. They made it easier to exercise an authority which aimed at self-control and self-management rather than slavish compliance with oppressive regimes in the ruled. In the English public school – an elite forge whose task it was to produce leaders – the moral demand to engage with authority openly and proudly was linked with the unconditional recognition of authority. Kipling's story 'Stalky and Co', mentioned above, provides a compelling picture of how these two elements could be fused. It depicts three lads devoting themselves to all kinds of manly, adventurous games, viewed by the school as illegitimate; the reaction to these activities by competent as well as incompetent authority figures (teachers); and the linkage between the hierarchical principle of the prefect and 'fag' system, embedded in the hierarchy of the school leadership, and the open, egalitarian, gentleman codex of the English elites. When the three boys break the rules and enter the property of Colonel Dabney, a man of Irish origin, in order to steal eggs from bird's nests, they are taken to task by the furious Colonel. M'Turk, one of the pupils, and also of Irish birth, talks to him:

> 'Do you know who I am?' he gurgled at last; Stalky and Beetle quaking.
> 'No, sorr, nor do I care if ye belonged to the Castle itself. Answer me now, as one gentleman to another. Do ye shoot foxes or do ye not?'
> And four years before Stalky and Beetle had carefully kicked M'Turk out of his Irish dialect! Assuredly he had gone mad or taken sunstroke, and as assuredly he would be slain – once by an old gentleman and once by the Head. A public licking of the three was the least they could expect. Yet – if their eyes and ears were to be trusted – the old gentleman had collapsed. It might be a lull before the storm, but –
> 'I do not.' He was still gurgling.
> 'Then you must sack your keeper. He's not fit to live in the same country with a God-fearin' fox. An' a vixen, too – at this time o' year!'
> 'Did ye come up on purpose to tell me this?'
> 'Of course I did, ye silly man', with a stamp of the foot. 'Would you not have done as much for me if you'd seen that thing happen on my land, now?'
> Forgotten – forgotten was the college and the decency due to elders! M'Turk was treading again the barren purple mountains of the rainy West Coast, where in his holidays he was viceroy of four thousand naked acres, only son of a three-hundred-

> years-old house, lord of a crazy fishing-boat, and the idol of his father's shiftless tenantry. It was the landed man speaking to his equal – deep calling to deep – and the old gentleman acknowledged the cry. (Kipling 1986: 10)

M'Turk has noticed that Dabney's game-keeper shoots foxes out of season – a truly sacrilegious act. While he, as a youth, is clearly subordinate in the relationship of authority, and, moreover, has himself an offence to answer for, he is able to call upon his quality as a gentleman by class and education. As such, he is heir to a huge estate and thus on an equal footing with the Colonel. His unrestrained, equal bearing is appropriate to this status. In this story, the teachers are for the most part incapable of practicing authority by example; only the head of the school[2] has the intelligence and generosity – not a superior class position - to overlook the pupils' refractory behaviour in light of their status as gentlemen and future leaders, and warriors of the empire, and thus to punish them more symbolically than actually. This casts some light on this peculiar institution of upper-class education: the school is, on the one hand, a harsh, indeed backbreaking regime (public beatings and merciless persecution by older pupils were part and parcel of the system); on the other hand, it is precisely the upper-class background of the pupils that prevents them from slipping into servility, and allows them to retain their honour – if often as psychologically battered human beings, who, after bitter years of persecution and disparagement by older boys, at last get the chance to tyrannize others, though they are then also subject to the egalitarian group pressure that characterizes the community of school-boys.

Bristow has commented upon the same episode from Kipling's tale (Bristow 1991: 74–80). He places it above all in the context of Social Darwinism and individualist resistance to the authority of the school – within the broader context of developments stretching back centuries. However, the astonishing stability of the 'proud detachment' model is no less striking. It requires a comparatively large degree of self-control at both ends of an authority relationship: the weaker must suppress his or her fear and avoid doing anything that might be interpreted as weakness, whilst the stronger must be willing to acknowledge this evidence of courage and greatness with magnanimity. We now scrutinize the development of this model more closely.

Defoe's Robinson and his servant Friday

Probably the most famous master-servant relationship in world literature (that between Don Quijote and Sancho Pansa being perhaps the only possible rival) begins, on the part of the savage Friday, with dramatic gestures of total submission:

> At last he lays his head flat upon the ground, close to my foot, and sets my other foot upon his head, as he had done before; and after this, made all the signs to me of

> subjection, servitude, and submission imaginable, to let me know how he would serve me as long as he lived. (Defoe 1985: 209)

Now slavery was in Defoe's time (and for long afterwards) a normal practice, in which English businessmen participated (as had Robinson long before) and from which they greatly profited. It is therefore no surprise that Defoe describes here the proskynesis found in Oriental societies as well as Byzantium and among Malinowski's harmless Trobrianders. The offer of submission is quickly accepted by Robinson:

> ...and first, I made him know his name should be Friday, which was the day I saved his life; I called him so for the memory of the time; I likewise taught him to say Master, and then let him know, that was to be my name;.... (Defoe 1985: 209)

Defoe's novel, published in 1719, is today considered a classic description of *homo oeconomicus*, who mulls over his goal-oriented rational [*zweckrationale*] options in solitude and acts accordingly. Commentators (Watt 1982 is representative) have also noted his secularized Puritanism. Rather like Bunyan's *Pilgrim's Progress*, *Robinson Crusoe* also involves a story of the Fall and of moral purification through conversion, although in a diluted form as far as the religious aspect of Robinson's feelings are concerned. During his life, Defoe himself was active as a non-conformist and a principled advocate of business interests. He led an extremely adventurous life featuring bankruptcy, repeated stints in jail (he was once placed in the pillory), and worked as a secret agent and journalist. In the sense that his own circumstances were quite unmanageable and he was tossed hither and thither by dramatic developments, his life was rather 'uncivilized' – his adventure novel is thus 'realistic', although Defoe attributed to his tale more autobiographical authenticity than the state of his knowledge justified. When we consider how realistic his description of the master-servant relationship is, we must take into account all these factors: it is certainly more an embodiment of normative notions of how this relationship should be from the point of view of the reformed Christian and English merchant, than it is a mere picture of reality. This is exemplified in the description of how Robinson civilizes Friday by dissuading him from the practice of cannibalism:

> ...he pointed exactly to the place, and shewed me the marks that he had made to find them again, making signs to me that we should dig them up again, and eat them; at this I appeared very angry, expressed my abhorrence of it, made as if I would vomit at the thoughts of it, and beckoned with my hand to him to come away, which he did immediately, with great submission. (Defoe 1985: 209)

Robinson also converts Friday to (a Protestantly imbued) Christianity, while the savage proves an apt, naive but intelligent dialectician. The relationship between the two is characteristic of the further development of the theme of 'contact between savages and civilized' as a whole within English literature; ceaseless instruction goes hand in hand with teaching by example, which brings forth the most delightful results in Friday's case. A similarly teachable, proud savage appears in the jungle stories of Rider Haggard. Here as well the human lives of the savages are worth little as soon as they oppose the whites: Robinson carries out a massacre with his rifle on the beach (after which, in a puritanical, businesslike manner, he compiles a precise list of the fallen), not unlike Allan Quatermain's dispatching of 250 savage Masai, most of whom fall victim to English repeating rifles (cf. Haggard 1951: 473) in a 'slaughter grim and great'.

The final result of all his educational efforts is plain to see. Again and again Robinson feels distrustful, yet Friday never disappoints him:

> But I needed none of all this precaution; for never man had a more faithful, loving, sincere servant, than Friday was to me; without passions, sullenness, or designs, perfectly obliged and engaged; his very affections were ty'd to me, like those of a child to a father; and I dare say he would have sacrificed his life for the saving mine upon any occasion whatsoever; the many testimonies he gave me of this, put it out of doubt, and soon convinced me that I needed to use no precautions as to my safety on his account. (Defoe 1985: 211–12)

The difference in rank, however, always remains clear: Friday remains forever a poor, honest fellow, his joy naive and innocent, and never fails to show his 'Master' the respect which is his due. He is the first of his 'subjects' on the island, later joined by several others; Robinson then practices religious tolerance:

> My man Friday was a Protestant, his father was a pagan and a cannibal, and the Spaniard was a Papist: however, I allowed liberty of conscience throughout my dominions. But this is by the way. (Defoe 1985: 241)

Friday, though not an out-and-out warrior like Quatermain's Zulu friend Umslopogaas, is also brave and resolute in battle; what he lacks in comparison with the latter, however, is the boundless pride of the warrior. The relationship between Robinson and Friday as a whole is thus different in nature from that between proud, independent gentlemen. It is, rather, paternalistic on the Austrian model – the response to superiority is grateful love. Friday is the only person that Robinson has no need to fear. The power balance between the two is such that Friday owes almost everything to Robinson; he pays this debt in love. We must bear in mind that Defoe, if we take into account his background as a whole, was moulded by the business-oriented, Puritan ethos of the middle classes. Appeals to the Christian conscience appear far more frequently in his work than, for example, in that of Kipling or Haggard. Despite the exotic, adventurous background to the meeting between 'savage' and 'civilized' (though civilization itself was in this case quite savage at times), the relationship between Robinson and Friday is characterized less by the warrior codex than by the codex of the Christian businessman and his practical reason. As K. Tidrick has shown – in the figure of the colonial official Lugard for example – this puritanical, scruple-laden middle-class code was later combined with that of gentlemanly honour. Both strands led to the development of a system of 'indirect rule'. The next section investigates the erection of the second pillar by looking at an example apparently far removed from the above discussion: Jane Austen's depiction, which appeared shortly after 1800, of the scheming and manoeuvres through which young ladies made sure of a 'good match' while still managing to retain their self-respect.

Authority, proud reserve and English character in Jane Austen's *Pride and Prejudice*

Authority and power differentials saturate the entire edifice of a society. They accompany or are the essence of social layering. They become manifest in the organization of the family, kinship, work and state power. The vertical organization of a society features many forms and intermediate stages – at one end is organization by caste, which creates a group of the socially disdained and ritually impure, and brands contact with its members shameful and infectious in the sense of sharing in group shame. At the other end lie aristocratic formations which, while not free of rank-based gradations, feature an equality that is, in some respects, more than an empty delusion – whatever the differences in power, rank and prestige, in all aristocratic associations (Weber called one of their key traits 'genteel charisma'), the pride and honour of its members are left intact. One of the main theses that run through this book locates the genesis of significant elements of the English character in the evolution of the English aristocracy's potential to shape it. Almost all European peoples, nations and societies have featured an aristocracy; but they were moulded to very different degrees by the way of life, point of view and mentalities of this group.[3] The nations with which one most often associates the attribute of 'pride' – England, Hungary, Spain – were also very clearly marked by a multi-layered aristocracy: decisive in this process was the emergence of a large landed gentry that penetrated deeply into society as a whole and was able to mould the behaviour and perception of the urban artisanal and commercial classes that later arose. The English gentry, an 'untitled nobility', resembles the Hungarian landed minor nobility in this respect or the Spanish *hidalgo*, which tended to be poor but proud.

The various, heterogeneous parts of the Habsburg conglomeration of countries, duchies, counties and kingdoms also contributed to varying degrees to the diffusion of an aristocratic warrior code among the lower classes. What united and characterized the Habsburg territories, however, was the originally rather weak central power, which later attempted to stretch a kind of Chinese bureaucratic state over all classes. One result of this patrimonial bureaucracy was the development of that code of uprightness and willing subservience found in ironic, over-the-top form in Herzmanovsky-Orlando. Pre-emptive compliance, and capricious and arbitrary acts of mercy became central elements in the Austrian character, which thus corresponded to the semi-modern bureaucratic hierarchy of the increasingly sophisticated state apparatus. Preventing descent into an endless Byzantinism, however, was the old symmetry of lordly duties and subjects' rights, which, in a less clearly defined form, curbed the arbitrary rule by lords that marked feudal society – and which characterized bureaucratic society even more. The course of events in England was often quite different. The differentiation between the aristocratic gentlemanly code and the police-state character of absolutist law enforcement – police as the guarantee of the monopoly of violence – never became as extensive as in Habsburg Central Europe.

Analyses of the English character written in the 1950s and 1960s by English scholars have dealt thoroughly with the peculiarly English way of dealing with and exercising authority. A. Glyn has pointed out, as an analytical opener, how deeply the hierarchical principle is anchored in English society – as a result of the instalment of a foreign elite in Anglo-Saxon England. French-speaking lords, as late as 1346 at the battle of Crécy, failed to make themselves understood to the English archers (Glyn 1970: 17–18). Even the Civil War in the 17th century, Glyn suggests, may be viewed as a tardy Saxon revenge on the Normans, and Cromwell as avenger of the defeat at Hastings. He also refers, however, to the English trait of erecting a cult around the heroic loser, battling alone against a superior power. The losers of battles have, he states, always been the ones to attract England's sympathy – from Boudicca, the legendary British princess, to Bonnie Prince Charlie, the last, unfortunate Stuart prince. Rebels too are said to have received an empathetic response – Thomas Beckett and the Catholic Guy Fawkes being prime examples.

Heroic retreats are claimed to offer further examples – Dunkirk, and Auchinleck's retreat during the initial stages of the Africa campaign in the Second World War, were, Glyn states, celebrated more than some victories. In sport too the sympathies of the English public – Wimbledon epitomizes this – apparently tend to lie with the loser. Not the American admiration for the victor, but steadfastness in defeat, is said to form a key aspect of the English character. Glyn, like Kipling ('If you can meet with triumph and disaster/and treat those two impostors just the same') – not without a certain narcissistic coquetry – assumes that the English cult of understatement, of ritual modesty, is something quite unique, in that empathy with the defeated hinders the savouring of triumph. This strength, Glyn asserts, comes from not having been conquered for 900 years. England has, moreover, in Glyn's view, always stood on the side of the weaker party and opposed the victors within the European concert of power-politics. Admiration for the brave enemy, whether Joan of Arc, Smuts, Rommel, Ghandi or Washington is said to constitute the same kind of phenomenon. In light of this noble restraint on a grand scale, one may wonder how the British could possibly have acquired such a great empire – and Glyn, with mild self-irony, answers by mentioning blind chance and the willingness of the subject peoples to entrust themselves to a particularly beneficent hegemony.

What Glyn highlights so strongly here, Elias has also viewed as an English trait in several of his works (Elias/Dunning 1986; Elias 1960; Elias 1996): situations which cry out for the savouring of superiority, for making use of one's dominant position, are in fact often marked by restraint, brought about through establishment of a code of 'fairness', which includes the demands of inferiors. Elias links this form of reining in aggressive emotions – triumph, rage, revenge – historically with the rise of peaceful parliamentarism and their sublimation in sport. (Glyn too devotes an entire chapter to 'fairness'.) Elias, however, also mentions the humanism of the English middle classes in the 19th and 20th centuries, which tamed the small-minded nationalistic canon ('jingoism') to such an extent (more, above all, than in Germany), that it became possible to pursue a realistic foreign policy in wartime and to give up the colonies in a comparatively painless, flexible manner. Glyn and Elias both place humour within the same class of cultural institutions – or, more precisely, the capacity for self-irony, of putting oneself down, rendering the offence to others caused by one's own claims to superiority far less distressing. (This includes the recalling of famous 'last words', such as, for example, those of Thomas Morus, condemned to death by beheading: 'I pray you, Master Lieutenant, see me safely up. For my coming down I will shift for myself' (Glyn 1970: 170).

It is plain that the English way of exercising authority – even if Glyn paints a somewhat idealistic picture – makes it difficult to realize superiority over those who are in principle of equal rank. The ritual modesty of 'understatement' has its well-spring in an extremely strong social norm, a clear group pressure, which functions both from without and from 'within': 'to get above oneself' and announce to the world one's elevated status is perceived as inadmissible and forbidden on pain of intense feelings of shame. This does not necessarily mean raising children in a loving, gentle atmosphere – on the contrary, Glyn's chapter on the education of children is the most incriminating in the entire book: the English (upper-class) child-raising ideal is marked by particular cruelty and harshness. For all the cold severity and early training in self-reliance (a clear difference from patrimonial Austria), however, the recognition and exercise of authority, even in the notorious 'fagging' system, is always sharply limited by group norms and requires reciprocity and role changes (everyone can become a prefect).

Jane Austen's *Pride and Prejudice* appears at first sight to have little to do with such issues. The fate of the Bennet sisters in rural gentry-based England just after the turn of the century revolves around such harmless matters as a ball at Netherfield, whose well-situated young master attracts the interest of all daughters willing to get married in the neighbourhood; unkept promises of marriage; good and bad manners within the frame of self-presentation in this 'marriage market'; the choice of an appropriate strategy for achieving one's aims; and the more or less dramatic mishaps on the way to a satisfactory solution to all these problems, which involves the ultimately happy union of both heroines with young men of social standing. In English literary criticism, Jane Austen's novels have, justifiably, the status of classics (cf. Trilling 1982; Bradbury 1982); their relaxed air of cheerfulness and ironic, detached art of people-watching are indeed particularly apparent in this book, which has always been one of her most read. The following pages do not aim to add to the countless, profound literary analyses of this novel. They instead turn the spotlight on a sociologically interesting constellation, which points beyond the harmless themes mentioned above. Jane Austen obviously saw herself as a kind of painter of miniatures,[4] and her work does in fact recall the patient composition of colourful still lives of entirely quotidian items. The French Revolution, the Napoleonic wars, the emerging dramatic upheaval of the Industrial Revolution, the destitution of the poor and the life of the metropolis of London, all are absent from this rural environment of lovely manors in a neighbourhood of three or four gentry families. Yet it is precisely the sociological perspective that has justifiably – and at times unjustifiably – underlined the significance of the entirely everyday in producing and securing a social reality of huge significance, and in this sense the study of the patterns of partner choice, marriage and family is of course highly significant. Choice of partner and the decision to start a family, moreover, also determine future social position to a significant degree; in societies that offered women no market in which they could pursue their own economic advancement independent of the intentions and actions of their husbands, this applied to almost all women. If girls from better families wished to avoid gaining the permanent status of 'spinster' or that of 'governess', a subaltern in an alien household (Jane Austen was in the first category until her death at 41), they were forced to channel their entire personality towards acquiring a suitable husband. The family, however, particularly the mother, played a vigorous role in the formation of their personality, as the status and respectability of the family of origin depended indirectly on the opportunities provided by the 'good match'. English society, immediately before and during the intensifying Industrial Revolution, was unique in that it already featured a relatively finely graded transitional zone between the upper and middle classes, with far more social mobility and mutual adoption of lifestyles, than, for example, in Germany. Rank and social distance remained nonetheless important, but the gradations became ever finer and more differentiated through competition and social mixing. Jane Austen describes an important constellation in *Pride and Prejudice* – the striving for upward mobility through marriage, from the perspective of the weaker party within an unequal power balance: the daughters of the Bennet family are of lower status than the desirable bachelors available on this local marriage market, men who might yield rich pickings. How does one deal with this inferiority? Which resources can one tap to even things out and maintain one's dignity? The Austrian model, apparent in Nestroy or Raimund, involves a great deal of servile coquetry on the part of the (at times cheeky) chambermaids or daughters of upright master craftsmen. Austrian authority relationships are not generally marked by great emphasis on pride and honour on the part of the weaker party. If one of this book's central theses is correct, attempts to maintain proud reserve, and to distinguish oneself from social superiors in a hierarchically structured world, are key features of the English character, which can, for example, also be found in the behaviour of the working classes (in this case, though, in the form of a rough, masculine ideal of authenticity) towards representatives of the employers. The insistence upon ritual teabreaks, the legendary struggle over the stoker on the electric locomotive, were of the same character. As in a laboratory, we now find in the upper-middle-class marriage market of the early 19th century, under quasi-microscopic analytical conditions, a quite analogous situation: a social divide and the pursuit of dignity and self-respect among the socially inferior. How is the field of power, which imbued the strategies of all participants, created? What do these strategies look like individually? How do the pressures to plan one's own behaviour influence the psyche and personality of the participants? To what extent do they influence emotional life and 'affective household'? To what extent do these social fields reproduce a mentality different from the Austrian, as a product of a more general 'Englishness'? Is the assumption that these structures still have an effect in the present-day correct? 'Authority relationship' here means three things: it refers to a specific form of the division of power between the sexes and in the family, between classes and ranks, and to their 'inner' reflection in the English 'national habitus'. It is crucial here to take into account that Jane Austen's 'miniature' portrays an event that must itself be seen as a component of long-term social processes – processes of social closure or opening, increasing foresight in dealing with one's own needs and those of others, the necessary planning of feelings and affects, the production of sentimentalities and sublimations, all as a result of a rampant, though not unreflected upon, dynamic. (Jane Austen's world-view is indeed already characterized by great sensitivity. However, in comparison to the subsequent romantic works of the Brontë sisters, it is still 'classical'.) The development of emotional complexes such as those found in Romanticism (the 'gothic novel', a horror novel with a background of sinister and bizarre nature, is an example) is itself a fact in need of explication in terms of the sociology of knowledge. Elias has elucidated this through the example of the emergence of the courtly romanticism that marks the pastoral novel (Elias 1983): certain experiences of alienation (taking leave of the rural environment of childhood, experienced as more simple, and the transition to the complex, polyvalent relational structure of the court), can lead people to endow the past with sentiment. The English equivalent (partly nourished by German motifs) may have represented a reaction to the threat posed to the rural gentry lifestyle by growing commercialization, mechanization and urbanization. In any event, it reflected a sense of loss in view of the increased potential to merely consume nature through travel; the emerging age of travel itself is a byword for the transformation of certain more tangible desires into the pleasure of the gaze. The triumphant advance of the revivalist religious movement also represents a transformation of affective structures in Jane Austen's time, another development that led to the Victorian tightening of sexual self-constraint and which itself cries out for explanation. We come across a great deal of sexual prudery in Jane Austen – a clear difference from the more drastic language of Defoe and Fielding. The feminization of literature itself may have contributed substantially to this development of a more strongly euphemistic code.

All these points should be born in mind as we now adopt a quite differently conceived approach to the analysis of the sociological content of *Pride and*

Prejudice. We here treat Jane Austen fundamentally as a sociologist of the English family, or to be more precise, of the upper-class English family during a phase of growing individualization. Like all sociologists of the family, she probes in detail the determinants of partner choice, the institution of an unofficial 'marriage market' under the aegis of characteristic economic constraints. Jane Austen's family is not yet, as it is today, largely an appendage of bureaucracy and state, but rather, with all its revenue from traditional property rights, still a very strong, semi-autarkic economic entity and effective fulcrum of communal living. Certain traditional characteristics of society (parents and relatives have a say in, or indeed largely decide, the choice of partner) persist, though young women are gradually permitted ever-increasing scope for individual decision-making. This, and a certain change in the power balance between the sexes, is not only seen and straightforwardly reported by Jane Austen, sociologist of the family and marriage guidance counsellor, but also encouraged: she wishes to convince us of the merits of the new rules and sensibilities (much like many contemporary sociologists of a socially critical bent, whether in Austria or England). She analyzes in great detail the strategies and room for manoeuvre of the key players in this process: her subject is the most careful calculation of young women's chances of achieving a satisfactory marriage, which implies a precise estimation and assessment of the prospective partner's traits. The outcome, in *Pride and Prejudice*, is a kind of compromise between feelings and reason, which may vary somewhat from case to case (in Jane's case emotion is privileged, in that of the heroine Elizabeth, who certainly embodies the author, it is reason that holds sway). The novel is also a sociology of the relations between a (rising) middle class and the old aristocracy, and entails a minutely detailed analysis of power resources and power relationships between representatives of these groups: how do they deal with the social chasm within the realm of 'connubium' and its *preparatory stages*? What difference does this divide make, and how can the weaker party compensate for it? How do all participants handle pride and shame, honour and disgrace, detachment and closeness?

The first sentence of the novel, which appeared in 1813, introduces this soberly analytical, in fact 'sociological' stance, in the guise of an ironic, mildly mocking observation:

> It is a truth universally acknowledged, that a single man in possession of a good fortune, must be in want of a wife.
>
> However little known the feelings or views of such a man may be on his first entering a neighbourhood, this truth is so well fixed in the minds of the surrounding families, that he is considered as the rightful property of some one or other of their daughters. (Austen 1988: 3)

One hundred years after Defoe's *Moll Flanders*, this basic fact of the power balance between the sexes in the 'marriage market' has changed little or not at all. Women have to strive to ensure that they are provided for, and the initiative lies with them (or more accurately with Mrs Bennet, mother of Jane, Elizabeth and Lydia):

> 'My dear Mr. Bennet,' said his lady to him one day, 'have you heard that Netherfield Park is let at last?' (Austen 1988: 3)

The young Mr Bingley is a very wealthy single man; the rather foolish and immoderate mother immediately thinks about the possibility that one of her daughters could marry this entirely unknown man; she already suspects, however, that he will in fact 'fall in love' with one of them.

It is the world of the manor houses and parks, of worthy, venerable families, that is described here, as experienced by Jane Austen, daughter of a rector from the gentry milieu, who herself had several sisters, but also brothers who later rose to high office.[5] Neighbourhood remains very important: one knows one's neighbours and invites them to one's home on a regular basis. The 'marriage market' too is far from anonymous: it is a component of a 'high society' consisting of people personally acquainted with one another. This also explains why the good opinion others (should) have of one is so important. The network of the English 'landed classes', an extensive class of leaders, sharply differentiated internally and represented by two parties – 'Whigs' and 'Tories' – in Parliament, was (and still is to a certain extent) a 'face-to-face' society. This makes England, to this day, a shame society – the opposite of social respectability is social disgrace, to be avoided at all costs. The ball, as an institution enabling the sexes to meet, is a significant pillar of the marriage market and its physical, spatial frame. Here, the social value and respectability of the potential future spouse is ascertained and made visible. Elizabeth experiences this at the first ball held by the new owner of Netherfield as follows:

> When the dancing recommenced, however, and Darcy approached to claim her hand, Charlotte could not help cautioning her, in a whisper, not to be a simpleton and allow her fancy for Wickham to make her appear unpleasant in the eyes of a man of ten times his consequence. Elizabeth made no answer, and took her place in the set, amazed at the dignity to which she was arrived in being allowed to stand opposite to Mr. Darcy, and reading in her neighbours' looks their equal amazement in beholding it. (Austen 1988: 90)

Now, this observation is far from sensational. It could probably have been made at the splendid balls of imperial Vienna and in Scarlett O'Hara's South. More interesting, however, is the fact that the constellation depicted above immediately triggers a brief, intense struggle over self-worth within the heroine Elizabeth:

> They stood for some time without speaking a word; and she began to imagine that their silence was to last through the two dances, and at first was resolved not to break it; till suddenly fancying that it would be the greater punishment to her partner to oblige him to

> talk, she made some slight observation on the dance. He replied, and was again silent. After a pause of some minutes she addressed him a second time with
> 'It is *your* turn to say something now, Mr. Darcy. – *I* talked about the dance, and *you* ought to make some kind of remark on the size of the room, or the number of couples.'
> He smiled, and assured her that whatever she wished him to say should be said. (Austen 1988: 91)

The determinants of the power balance within this relationship are diverse (not all are made explicit by the author; the physical attractiveness of Darcy or Elizabeth, for instance, presumably plays a major role). In this description, in any event, Darcy, related to high-level aristocrats, is initially the stronger party. He can afford the luxury of holding his tongue; Elizabeth has to initiate the conversation. He smiles and demonstrates that he is in no rush to answer. Elizabeth, though, comes out of it nicely thanks to her quick-wittedness and by making a joke; her self-respect, briefly destroyed, is redeemed.

The process of self-control, aimed at achieving honour in the eyes of others and respect for oneself, is one of the dominant themes of Austen's book. This is, moreover, not simply a matter of controlling oneself, but also entails attempts to control others: Elizabeth has her hands full ensuring that others have a particular kind of positive opinion of her. Goffman's (1959: 208–9) term 'impression management' seems to capture this well, though it is very important to the heroine that a certain type of expression makes an impression on her high-ranking friends: not content to appear as a beauty or as the ideal future wife, ready and willing to kow-tow, she wishes to impress by dint of her cleverness, restraint and organizational competence. She thus endows herself with entirely 'masculine' virtues within this social field and counters Darcy's authority, and that of his high-ranking relatives, anchored in birth and education, with her own skills. Elizabeth's striving for pride and detachment, moreover, inevitably involves other people – two counter-examples of heavy-handed, undignified sharing of confidences make this issue of detachment, within her social psychological analysis, far more general in nature: her pushy cousin Mr Collins and her own mother.

> Her mother's thoughts she plainly saw were bent the same way, and she determined not to venture near her, lest she might hear too much. When they sat down to supper, therefore, she considered it a most unlucky perverseness which placed them within one of each other; and deeply was she vexed to find that her mother was talking to that one person (Lady Lucas) freely, openly, and of nothing else but of her expectation that Jane would be soon married to Mr. Bingley. – It was an animating subject, and Mrs. Bennet seemed incapable of fatigue while enumerating the advantages of the match. His being such a charming young man, and so rich, and living but three miles from them, were the first points of self-gratulation; and then it was such a comfort to think how fond the two sisters were of Jane, and to be certain that they must desire the connection as much as she could do. (Austen 1988: 98–9)

None other than Bingley's sisters prove to be snooty schemers as the story progresses, and the mother's judgement could hardly be more wrong; her lack of self-control in fact comes close to wrecking Jane's marriage and causes Darcy to disrespect the Bennets.

> In vain did Elizabeth endeavour to check the rapidity of her mother's words, or persuade her to describe her felicity in a less audible whisper; for to her inexpressible vexation, she could perceive that the chief of it was overheard by Mr. Darcy, who sat opposite to them. Her mother only scolded her for being nonsensical. [...]
> Her mother would talk of her views in the same intelligible tone. Elizabeth blushed and blushed again with shame and vexation. She could not help frequently glancing her eye at Mr. Darcy, though every glance convinced her of what she dreaded; ... (Austen 1988: 99–100)

Jane Austen's observations are finely tuned. The key capital that the Bennet sisters have at their disposal – apart from their attractiveness – is their 'social' capital. This entails the practice and appreciation of art and music, good manners and a certain degree of self-control, which must match the improved social standing they hope to achieve through marriage. This art of examining motives, which at times recalls Proust, also reflects the objective pressure to plan and steer emotions and their expression when interacting with others. Such women certainly have some freedom of action; their relatives intervene, but it is ultimately for the women themselves to decide. Given the central significance of marriage and family within society, a painstaking calculation of their conduct before they plunge into dependency on a man is all the more important. Because they are social climbers (or have to be, since their father Mr Bennet is unable to leave them much in the way of inheritance), it is vital that they as individuals act to correct the power gulf between the classes (Elizabeth, in conversation with Lady de Bourgh, emphasizes that she herself is the daughter of a gentleman). Elizabeth does all she can to redeem her family's honour and her sister's happiness, after the proud Mr Darcy has torpedoed Jane's union with his friend Mr Bingley. She accuses Darcy of unfeeling arrogance; during the course of several meetings, she makes a strong impression on him – one which has little to do with her physical, sexual attractiveness, and seems rather to be the result of the beauty and boldness of her soul or spirit.

Darcy's letter, motivated by his affection for Elizabeth, shows her that she too had been prejudiced and that his accusations were not unjustified. Reeling from his criticism, she struggles despairingly to maintain her inner balance: she recognizes that she herself is unable to live up to the ideal of unprejudiced, impassive reason, and that her conceitedness was thus inappropriate. His justification for his accusations relating to her family (that they were interested only in a 'good match', which they had pursued in an importunate manner, adding to their low social rank a matching lowness of mentality) hits home even more sharply:

> When she came to that part of the letter in which her family were mentioned, in terms of such mortifying, yet merited reproach, her sense of shame was severe. The justice of the charge struck her too forcibly for denial, and the circumstances to which he particularly alluded, as having passed at the Netherfield ball, and as confirming all her first disapprobation, could not have made a stronger impression on his mind than on hers.
> The compliment to herself and her sister, was not unfelt. It soothed, but it could not console her for the contempt which had been thus self-attracted by the rest of her family; – and as she considered that Jane's disappointment had in fact been the work of her nearest relations, and reflected how materially the credit of both must be hurt by such impropriety of conduct, she felt depressed beyond any thing she had ever known before. (Austen 1988: 208–9)

We here see very clearly how the mechanism of 'class marriage' functions. First, Elizabeth identifies spontaneously and entirely and without further rational evaluation with the honour or disgrace of her family – she, whom Darcy had expressly excluded from his comments, feels nonetheless affected, just as if she herself had been humiliated. Whatever one might say about the individualization, the 'affective individualism' (Stone 1977) of the English family on the threshold of modernity, this is the point where it stops: this disgrace is a group disgrace, just as family honour is shared by all its members. Second, the heroine shares the standards of the evaluation; theoretically, she could have been immune to Darcy's criticism (either distancing herself from her foolish mother or doubting the right of this man of higher standing to prescribe his benchmark as valid). It is typical for a relatively stable, vertically organized society, that the inferiors consent to a yardstick that makes them inferior. At the same time, it is characteristic of Austen's discursive world that by no means all social foundations of inequality are accepted; it is indisputable that aristocrats such as Lady de Bourgh can be heavy-handed, presumptuous, tactless and banal, and this pulls the rug decisively from under their claims to recognition of their social superiority. Noble birth must – in the eyes of the more middle-class, educated members of the gentry – be accompanied by nobility of the soul and the spirit. Nonetheless, within this framework, inherited rank and hierarchy determined by birth was, again and again, broadly acknowledged in England; no chasm gaped between nobility and bourgeoisie; views, manners and lifestyles were rather marked by a multiplicity of blurred borderlines, and this cushioned the impact of increasing social mobility and the social energies that it unleashed. Class marriage in Viennese 'good society' (including the old nobility, and the just recently nobilitated or grand-bourgeois members of the 'second' society or *zweite Wiener Gesellschaft*) was certainly no less developed, but this group was numerically far smaller. This pertained at least until industrialization took off – social fluidity was ultimately to increase here too.

The 'English' element of the model recognizable in Jane Austen is precisely the consciousness of rank and proud detachment on both sides. The fact that this model is also transferred to conduct between the sexes is another distinctly English peculiarity. In Austria – that is, in Viennese high society – the discursive tone between the sexes was far less marked by respect and mutual regard for spirit and character. Lady Montagu wrote in 1716 of her visit to Vienna that it was good for a woman's reputation to have a lover as well as a husband; possession of a lover is almost a social obligation, which can also increase the husband's status (cf. Bruckmüller 1985: 280). This was the kind of 'right' enjoyed by the ladies of Viennese high society – something that puritanical Elizabeth would have found extremely unseemly. Anyone familiar with the atmosphere of Schnitzler's *Reigen*, or who passes in revue the many other affairs and flings described in Austrian literature (from Nestroy's eager-to-please mistresses and chambermaids to Musil's Diotima), knows that the bracing erotic climate is bound up with jocular coquetry and courtly gallantry. It shows no sign of the puritanical, emancipated earnestness with which English women register their need for spiritual equality and recognition of their depth of character – in a gentry milieu marked by 'embourgeoisement', whose sexual asceticism contrasts so sharply with Austrian Catholic permissiveness.

Jane Austen reserves her harshest criticism, however, not for sexual libertines or loose women, but for women who, like her mother, are uneducated and foolish. They make marriage into a nightmare for the man as well – something of which Elizabeth, identifying with her father, is convinced. The following excerpt is interesting because it makes clear what was (or ought to have been) regarded as the ideal of marriage and partnership in this milieu. This in turn illuminates an important motif of the model: the extreme importance, before marriage, of gaining a reliable picture of the candidate's character. This can be achieved through a detailed and probing 'character test'.

> Had Elizabeth's opinion been all drawn from her own family, she could not have formed a very pleasing picture of conjugal felicity or domestic comfort. Her father captivated by youth and beauty, and that appearance of good humour, which youth and beauty generally give, had married a woman whose weak understanding and illiberal mind, had very early in their marriage put an end to all real affection for her. Respect, esteem, and confidence, had vanished for ever; and all his views of domestic happiness were overthrown. (Austen 1988: 236)

The woman writing here is one who very much identifies with the world of men (in the shape of her father). Respect and deference – concepts that sound old-fashioned today – are here feelings shown to women who prove themselves worthy of them through their reason and virtue. The division of power between husband and wife is almost equally balanced – the quotation above provides a hint of the extensive gender equality within marriage, that is, in private; in public, in the worlds of work and politics, this certainly did not pertain, but Jane Austen's novel reveals the English wife's astonishing freedom of action within the family. Austen's marriage ideal thus requires both sexes to consistently show reason, that is, the capacity for rational self-control and self-constraint; the issue of sexual compatibility does not arise (as the depiction of Elizabeth's 'love scene' with Darcy makes abundantly clear: both speak, but Austen fails to intimate even the slightest touch, much less a kiss). The most important element in a successful (lifelong) union is spiritual harmony, which Elizabeth also demonstrates ex negativo:

> Elizabeth, however, had never been blind to the impropriety of her father's behaviour as a husband. She had always seen it with pain; but respecting his abilities, and grateful for his affectionate treatment of herself, she endeavoured to forget what she could not overlook, and to banish from her thoughts that continual breach of conjugal obligation and decorum which, in exposing his wife to the contempt of her own children, was so highly reprehensible. But she had never felt so strongly as now, the disadvantages which must attend the children of so unsuitable a marriage, nor ever been so fully aware of the evils arising from so ill-judged a direction of talents; talents which rightly used, might at least have preserved the respectability of his daughters, even if incapable of enlarging the mind of his wife. (Austen 1988: 237)

What Elizabeth calls 'so unsuitable a marriage', clearly cannot be measured by contemporary standards. Nowadays, in the industrialized West, every third or even second marriage ends in divorce and we tend not to view a marriage, particularly if it ends in a reasonably civilized manner, as 'unsuitable'. Since marriages in the past ended almost exclusively with the death of a spouse, the quality of these long relationships was imbued with a different significance than applies today. This is what made the detailed prenuptial character test so important: it is nowadays a commonplace that the 'romantic ideal of love' developed within the 'bourgeois' marriage. Study of the reconciliation scene between Darcy and Elizabeth, in which they admit to each other their misunderstandings and misjudgements, reveals a marriage ideal which is not particularly romantic in nature. The 'lovers' seem like respectable accountants of the soul, who now, through beautiful reciprocity, bid farewell to their pride and prejudices. Darcy opens this contest in virtue:

> 'What did you say of me, that I did not deserve? for, though your accusations were ill-founded, formed on mistaken premises, my behaviour to you at the time, had merited the severest reproof. It was unpardonable. I cannot think of it without abhorrence.'
>
> 'We will not quarrel for the greater share of blame annexed to that evening,' said Elizabeth. 'The conduct of neither, if strictly examined, will be irreproachable; but since then, we have both, I hope, improved in civility.'
>
> 'I cannot be so easily reconciled to myself. The recollection of what I then said, of my conduct, my manners, my expressions during the whole of it, is now, and has been many months, inexpressibly painful to me. Your reproof, so well applied, I shall never forget: 'had you behaved in a more gentleman-like manner." Those were your words. You know not, you can scarcely conceive, how they have tortured me; – though it was some time, I confess, before I was reasonable enough to allow their justice.' (Austen 1988: 367–8)

So it goes on, back and forth. We are presented with the astonishing picture of a rich man of high social rank falling over himself to show remorse, although he was largely in the right, judged by the standards of the time. The image of the 'gentleman' is decisively moralized – in a manner typical of the middle classes.

Elizabeth's pride and honour are redeemed. She can enjoy lasting marital happiness on an equal footing at this man's side.

Digression: Ships, discipline and English character as exemplified in the Hornblower novels of C. S. Forester

Britain is an island, *a Kingdom by the Sea*[6] inspiring numerous hypotheses about the connection between this geographical fact and the mentality of its inhabitants. Whatever one might think of such notions – England was long exposed to a strikingly large number of invasions with serious consequences, despite forming part of an island – from around the middle of the 16th century, one English institution undoubtedly developed particularly strongly thanks to this geography: seafaring, which made a strong fleet essential. The navy held the same significance for England as did the standing army for the continental powers, though it is important to bear in mind that the navy fused civil – above all mercantile – and military functions. Trade and war were often meshed together to such an extent that one of the most well-known continental (above all German) clichés brands England the land of the pirates. English armies were not, in contrast to those of France, Austria and Prussia for example, particularly impressive outfits – mercenaries from the Continent were not infrequently sent in to quell rebellions (peasant uprisings and the American War of Independence being examples); even in the Civil War, the English army proved less capable than the experienced, efficient European armies. As a sea power, however, England knew no equals. After overcoming the Armada and defeating Holland, it was *the* guarantee of England's success in the competitive struggle between European states until the eve of the Second World War; sheer size – huge numbers were recruited to serve at sea – justifies describing the navy as one of the pillars holding up England, rather as Prussia is always defined by the spirit of its Junker classes. England had the navy to thank for securing its territorial integrity at least three times – in the struggle against the Armada, against Napoleon and against Germany from 1914 to 1918.

The English fleet's importance as a military tool in disputes with other states was matched by its significance as the leading social site of authority and discipline. In the first place, discipline was crucial to the management of large ships, in times of peace as well as war. Sailing ships, manned by several hundred sailors, were, even without a war going on, extremely complex and hierarchically organized social structures. As a result of the pressures of war, when split-second decisions and daring manoeuvres were the order of the day – and drowning or imprisonment were an ever-present threat – they were forced to transform themselves into precisely functioning machines, which had to be ready to follow orders from a central 'brain', if they were to prevail under the most taxing of conditions. Many conventions, which the English themselves ascribe to their national character, are connected directly or indirectly with naval warfare:

boldness, decisiveness, unbending, stoical calmness in the face of danger – all values that are scarcely explicable on the basis of Jane Austen's peaceful world of the English gentry.

Elias too underlined the significance of the English navy for the English 'habitus' on several occasions. Borrowing from Hintze, for example, he remarks that a fleet can never be deployed against the native population (as were certain infantry and mounted regiments, used to hunt down vagabonds in Lower Austria). In this sense, a naval force is more compatible with the political freedom of a 'civil society' than a standing army, which is funded by the country and controls it (trade and naval war, in contrast, often financed themselves and generated profit, helping keep the tax burden low; even in wartime, lucky captains could become rich by seizing the prize bounty of captured ships). Elias illuminates another aspect of the English navy through the example of the naval officer as career: these complex, bureaucratic systems could only be managed by 'professional seafarers', not in an amateurish way by 'gentlemen' who lacked the specific skills involved (cf. Elias, 1950). For a time, competent, well-trained, lower-class seafarers, who lacked fine manners, *savoir vivre* and social refinement, co-existed with the 'born leaders' of noble blood, education and distinction, who were, however, totally devoid of nautical knowledge. This unsatisfactory situation was slowly overcome through the mutual rapprochement of both groups and codes – until the 19th century, when the educated, socially competent and professional naval officer came into being, a figure who united within himself all the qualities necessary for success (this is anything but self-evident; it did not yet apply to the English or old Austrian army in 1914: all too often, all that distinguished the officers from the lower ranks was fine manners and the capacity for drills, often leading to rapid decimation of the higher-ranking soldiers in wartime. Ample evidence attests to this and to the incompetence of aristocratic officers in both armies).

It is thus worthwhile investigating English structures of authority, psychological qualifications and characteristics at sea, in a word, 'discipline'. It is also revealing to compare this with the corresponding structures in the Habsburg monarchy – those of a land power – which as a whole can hardly be said to have led to a energetic, consistent, bold, decisive and reliable mentality.

As the author of numerous adventure novels at sea – 12 'Hornblower' novels from 1937 on – Forester has enriched a genre in an almost ideal-typical way, a genre almost non-existent in Austrian literature. (Anyone in Austria wishing to read adventure novels has little choice but to turn to Germany's Karl May and English writers.) For our purposes, Forester is an exception – a 20th century writer, who does not know the early 19th century world about which he writes from first hand experience. Nonetheless, few have grappled so intensively with the historical sources and striven to achieve an empathetic understanding, ranging across centuries, of this past. (Nonetheless, his statements on inner psychological events must be judged with a certain degree of scepticism.) Forester is a writer of adventures, and certain omissions in his work reflect the conventions and thus the limits of his genre. It is, for example, clear that the hero, Hornblower, is in fact a hero – while he is thoughtful, shy and extremely concerned with duty, when push comes to shove he takes quick, decisive action, is unafraid of danger and successful against powerful foes. The stories, moreover, always have a happy – that is, successful – ending, which is not unusual for English novels in general and which says something about the English national habitus. If we look beyond the formulaic, however, we find many realistic scenes in the Hornblower novels. These include many facets of authority and rank-based relationships, both at sea and in society. Hornblower is introduced to the reader as a young ensign from a lower-class background (he was never to be entirely free of his social insecurity when interacting with people of noble or at least gentry background). He rises rapidly through the ranks as a result of his professional competence. Forester depicts with great empathy the problem of the professional climber, quite unable to afford the clothing appropriate to his rank and not particularly well endowed with the qualities of a good conversationalist, as required by the conventions of the salon, whose education is in general limited to professional skills, and which certainly did not help him make sound judgements in matters of taste. Far more blatant in this regard are the deficits of his subordinates, particularly crews that had been rounded up (a large proportion of seafarers were recruited by 'press-gangs', as an alternative to prison following serious offences). Hornblower is almost always portrayed as solitary decision-maker; his strength is not physical in nature, and he is not especially skilled in the practical matters of life at sea – others are quicker on their feet and less often seasick than he is. His authority vis-à-vis officers and crew rests on two pillars. First, his indisputable professional competence (no-one understands nautical matters, and the engineering arts central to steering the sailing ship, that unique machine, better than he). Second, his position: the captain of a ship at high sea is an almost absolute master of life and death – it was often a long time until formal legal procedures could be carried out, and, particularly at times of war, the captain enjoys almost unlimited power of sanction (he can, for instance, sentence a man to 500 lashes, leading either to infirmity or death). Although Hornblower's authority thus rests on two strong pillars, he goes out of his way to appear ritually superior in the eyes of his subordinates as well. He surrounds himself intentionally, and even more often unintentionally, with a certain aura – the most important precondition for this is the painstaking maintenance of detachment. Forester's novels teach us much about forms of address and rules of dialogue; these are primarily intended to anchor the functionally necessary distance so firmly in the heads of subordinates that they never dare to challenge the authority of their superiors. Hornblower sometimes achieves this aura through the success of his daring operations, sometimes by means of the sense of isolation he radiates. Not infrequently, the crew themselves have a strong need to idolize. A high degree of self-discipline is, however, always necessary on both sides of the authority relationship: the man in a position of responsibility required a specific form of self-control. He must never appear uncertain when making decisions, fearful or weak; equally, no-one would forgive him for moody behaviour that made him seem unfair or arbitrary in dealing with the crew. In this respect, Forester conceived of

Hornblower as an unqualified paragon of virtue; looking beyond these dramatic components, however, we can perceive a more general pattern of authority successfully upheld and defended. The sailors and non-commissioned officers must display absolute self-control and subordination when addressing their superiors; in many situations they are expected to rid themselves of feelings of fear as well as any unjustified tendency towards arrogance. They were also required to demonstrate, in moments of danger (when struggling against forces of nature or battling an opponent), great presence of mind and skill in sailing the ship and using military equipment. This in turn could only be achieved through training – through drills that led to a perfection of which Spanish or French seafarers could only dream.

Spaniards and Frenchmen are the most frequent opponents – most Hornblower novels are set in the Napoleonic wars. England is facing the overmighty dictator of Europe quite alone; only English sea power stands in the way of his victory, helping convey money and other resources to allies. In this life and death battle against a dangerous opponent of freedom and the English way of life (many of Forester's motifs can easily be transferred to the struggle against Germany), the more professionally competent but also the more decisive and pro-active party wins. Here, authority is always viewed as functional: clear hierarchical structures, clear division of authority and decisive action are the key to success. Herzmanovsky-Orlando's depiction of Habsburg officials is a very different matter: indecisiveness, Baroque illusion, lack of a clear distinction between realms of superior and inferior authority, a failure to sufficiently separate official office and private affairs – these were the key traits of Austrian authority. Forester of course overeggs the pudding, but anyone with a fine ear can, to this day, pick up numerous metaphors in English news reports on sport or politics redolent of martial decisiveness, stoical acceptance of adversity and military success. The 'right attitude' and battle-readiness are still much more important than – technical or tactical – finesse as a player. To complain about bad decisions by the referee is greatly looked down upon.

How does our captain impose his authority? The following dialogue between Hornblower and an individual questioning his authority casts much light on this. The man involved is the minister of the young reigning prince of a minor German state – both fleeing Napoleon, the prince himself is nothing less than grand-nephew of the King of England. The (somewhat doltish) German minister attacks Captain Hornblower (currently in charge of a small warship), because he (correctly) believes that Hornblower has injured the honour of his master:

> 'I trust you will make amends, then. And may I remind you that you are sitting in the presence of royalty?'
> 'You call me "sir",' snapped Hornblower. 'And you will address me as my subordinate should.'
> [...]
> 'As Secretary of State I am addressed as "Your Excellency",' he said.

'But as surgeon in this ship you are addressed as "Doctor". And that is the last time I shall overlook the omission of the word 'sir". Now. Your qualifications?'
'I am a surgeon – sir.'
The last word came out with a jerk as Hornblower's eyebrows rose.
'You have been in practice recently?'
'Until a few months ago – sir. I was surgeon to the Court of Seitz-Bunau. But now I am –'
'Now you are surgeon in H.M.S. *Atropos*, and we can leave off the farce of your being Secretary of State.'
'Sir –'
'Silence, if you please, Doctor. Mr. Horrocks!'
'Sir!'
'My compliments to Mr. Still. I'll have these two gentlemen's baggage swayed up.' (Forester 1985: 100–101)

This battle between two people, both of whom lay claim to high rank, illuminates authority in general and in England in particular in a number of ways.

Pecking orders are a general feature of human relations and appear in many, if not all, cultures. The ritual subordination that goes hand in hand with this likely involves even more explicit elements in many societies than in this example (the Byzantine emperors for example insisted that foreign envoys prostrate themselves. They had to lie prone while the emperor moved his throne heavenwards with the help of a hydraulic mechanism hidden from visitors). A symbolic barrier must always be erected that emotionally hinders the subordinate from questioning this relationship and reversing the relations of power. In our case, this entails the consistent use by one party of the term 'sir', which must be used in every sentence, even when a statement has little to do with the personal character of the interaction. The language surrounding commands in the armed forces features ritual repetition of the command; the subordinate, who must carry out the command, repeats it, which is to a degree useful, since uncertainties can always arise and these must be avoided as much as possible in emergencies. Repeatedly addressing those of higher rank by their title also serves to make obedience second nature within the armed forces. It is, however, an English peculiarity that the foreign title is viewed as a triviality, that the captain's authority extends to *everyone* aboard (a norm is laid down of a very general, universalistic character) and that this is intended to produce appropriate character traits. The symbolic reinforcement of Hornblower's authority (along with his competence and position, this constitutes another source of 'ritual' elevation) means a special kind of reining in and steering of affect. Every sentence he speaks rams home to the subordinate that he must accept the will of his superior. The gesture of submission reinforces the sense of subjugation. The bodily postures learnt in drills have a similar function – chest out, stomach in, arms at one's sides, standing to attention: all make it very difficult for the subordinate to take the initiative, in other words, to take the first step towards challenging authority and ultimately toppling it.

Superior officers meanwhile must display almost as much self-control. Forester describes this vividly in a scene in which the captain finds himself in a near-hopeless situation:

> It took every ounce of his moral strength to conceal his despair and dismay – from Turner as well as from the Mudir – and as it was he sat silent for a while, shaken, like a boxer in the ring trying to rally after a blow had slipped through his guard. Like a boxer, he needed time to recover.
>
> 'Very well,' he said at length, 'tell him I must think over all this. Tell him it is too important for me to make up my mind now.' (Forester 1985: 267)

Again and again, Hornblower faces the dramaturgical problem of 'information control', controlling how one expresses oneself in order to optimize the impression one makes on others (for the most part one's inferiors). (Goffman called such manoeuvres techniques of 'impression management'.) It is not, however, the relaxed attitude of the professional actor that lies behind this, as one might think from reading Goffman, but rather concealment and suppression of one's own fear and despair. (Arlie R. Hochschild 1983, is clearly barking up the wrong tree in ascribing such acting of emotions mainly to female professional roles. Forester depicts numerous cases that prove the opposite.) The famous English 'stiff upper lip', emphasized for instance by many Continental refugees in London during the Blitz, probably evolved from a similar social pattern – anyone wishing to make decisions and lead others can ill afford the luxury of a certain self-pity, of indulgence in one's own fears. Authority would dissolve; the situation would spin out of control. The English 'stoical composure', entailing a refusal to allow oneself to be overly impressed by one's own inequality and to loudly complain to those (supposedly) to blame, has, moreover, become a general feature of the English character.

The flipside of these virtues was, however, for a long time, a ruthless harshness both towards subordinates and as exercised by such towards themselves. On board ships that were often completely out of touch with civilization for months at a time, draconian discipline by means of corporal punishment was the order of the day. Hornblower even has the young German prince, grand-nephew of the king, beaten in the above-mentioned novel, because he exposes the crew to danger through his ineptitude. It would be interesting to link the practice of punishment so characteristic of the public schools (which represent the self-enslavement of the upper class: no-one *has to* attend these schools) to the relevant practice at sea. Forester explains the logic of punishment by referring to that dealt out to the young German prince:

> Humanitarians had much to say against corporal punishment, but in their arguments, while pointing out the harm it might do to the one punished, they omitted to allow for the satisfaction other people derived from it. And it was some further training for the blood royal to display his acquired British imperturbability, to bite off the howl that a well-applied cane tended to draw forth, and to stand straight afterwards with hardly a

> skip to betray his discomfort, with hardly a rub at the smarting royal posterior, and with the tears blinked manfully back. Satisfaction or not, Hornblower was a little sorry afterwards. (Forester 1985: 292)

The practice of authority at sea is thus also linked with massive physical violence. Yet punishment is fair; exceptions are made for no-one. This form of corporal violence corresponds to a certain civilizational standard – from that point on, beatings became substantially less common and were even formally abolished. To beat someone senseless or kill them by doing so would be viewed nowadays as a case for Amnesty International and be considered extremely barbaric. People, during the period considered here, thought and felt differently – although this form of punishment was not as a rule an expression of individual sadism, but was ordered independently of affect. The victim could demonstrate his pride while the punishment was being meted out through self-control – although we cannot, of course, come to any firm conclusions about the quantitative distribution of such acts of heroism on the basis of Forester's work.

Forester endowed his heroes with a peculiar inner asceticism. Hornblower nonetheless silently enjoys achieving success and demonstrating competence. His professional abilities ultimately make him an admiral – though he still lacks social talents and influential friends and benefactors. His entire life is marked by Protestant frugality – but this leads, after sober *contemplation* and sober self-examination, to certain success, achieved through steadfastness, tenacity and self-discipline. A comparison with sensuous Austria once again suggests itself. Scarcely any other European state was more often compelled to send its armies into battle than Habsburg Austria. Its enemies were the best and most experienced fighters in Europe: the fearful Ottomans, the ambitious French, well used to war, the haughty Prussians. All in all, the Habsburg armies did not too badly – they inflicted upon Napoleon his first defeat, came close to robbing Prussia's Frederick of his kingdom and liberated southeast Europe from Turkish rule. Yet we are unaware of a single book patriotically reminding young people of the many battles fought and victories achieved by Austrian armies. Austrian literature is lacking entirely in that sober confidence of victory which makes success a matter of calculation and eschews an aura of the miraculous. It indeed appears that Austrian structures of authority, in peacetime but above all in times of war, function quite differently than their English counterparts – they were in any event able to mobilize less enthusiasm and devotion than appears to have been the case for England.

Reflections on the examples dealt with thus far, and on comparison with Austria's courtly model

We have pursued a line of argument in this chapter which may perhaps surprise many. The 'proud detachment' model was first identified in the attitudinal framework of high-ranking English colonial officials. The case of English esteem for the proud Masai brought to light a style of authority less partial to servile submission than to self-confident interpretation of the authority relationship, including the interpretive efforts of the weaker party. This marks a clear difference from the Austrian model, which we label 'courtly'. This entails flattery and submission, which we have traced by reference to Nestroy and Herzmanovsky-Orlando; it appears in the latter in caricatured form. We have not derived this 'courtly' model solely from the Court – the dependence on domestic authority found among the rural and urban lower classes is also related to its patrimonial order. 'Feminine' cunning and dissimulation also represent a side-effect not only of the courtly aristocratic world, but also of the family set-up described by Nestroy. In the other corner we have the English model, involving the demand for dignified detachment (or the struggle to attain such detachment) transferred after a certain point to the socializing institution of the English upper classes: the 'public school' – an (almost) entirely masculine institution. By examining Jane Austen's *Pride and Prejudice*, we shifted the gender of the key actors as well as the main object of their interest: a good marriage does indeed enhance the rank of the family, as does sending the son to a good school, but the skills and manoeuvres involved are rather different. Assuming that we can interpret Jane Austen here as realistic (the only argument against doing so perhaps being that her discourse on social superiority and inferiority is highly conscious and constructed with specific interests in mind – which could lead to distortions), it is striking that both situations are underpinned by a common model: a situation of inferiority is transformed under certain circumstances into one of equality. This also constitutes the difference from the relationship between Robinson and Friday: though Robinson refrains from ever deliberately attacking Friday's self-respect, the asymmetry here is incurable.

How can we explain the fact that proud detachment was obviously more highly valued in England than in Austria? The explanation is in fact relatively straightforward. The English aristocracy and gentry were never entirely deprived of their thirst for adventure and their wildness – the instalment of a warlike Norman over-class generated embryonic models of proud, independent behaviour. Supervision by a centralized Court played a far less significant role than independence from the Crown, later supported by political and economic resources. This proud attitude thus spread to a different milieu as noblemen 'domesticated' themselves, becoming members of a broad oligarchy and sharing in responsibility: even without physical bravery, it was possible to defend one's rank. English aristocratic society was for a long time characterized more by wildness than anything else: there is no Habsburg equivalent of the hundreds of rebels, or those treated as such, laid to rest in the Tower of London, themselves often members of the royal family. The pacification of this class – money replaced the sword with increasing frequency – did not make them obedient. This model spread downwards, through lively social exchange with the middle, professional and commercial classes, relatively easily and became widely diffused. This also created situations – via marketization – in which freedom of choice took on particular meaning. Situations of enduring, personal, relatively one-sided dependency were comparatively rare. The Austrian civilizing process meanwhile adheres far more strongly to the French model of courtization. The Court as social environment fused security with dependence; it also caused one to glance nervously at the value of one's person on the stock market of public opinion. This model was passed on downwards via the mechanisms of (patrimonial) bureaucracy and (via large households) by servants; there existed comparatively few self-confident (professional) bourgeois groupings. Insofar as the model of proud detachment spread to the gender relations prevalent in English society, in the shape of a certain puritanical seriousness, the English habitus also lacked that element of coquetry and femininity inherent in its Austrian counterpart.

Another example casts yet more light on this. Charlotte Brontë's novel *Jane Eyre* (1847), written a little more than a generation after Jane Austen's work appeared, revolves around the relationship between an educated but orphaned and penniless governess with her master, Mr Rochester, who is much older and is, as lord of the castle, of higher social rank. Mutual affection develops – the power resources of each and thus the power balance between them are thus determined from two poles. Here too one observes the young governess's seriousness and struggle for dignity, apparent in the following dialogue:

> 'I am disposed to be gregarious and communicative to-night', he repeated, 'and that is why I sent for you: the fire and the chandelier were not sufficient company for me; [...] It would please me now to draw you out – to learn more of you – therefore speak.'
> Instead of speaking, I smiled; and not a very complacent or submissive smile either.
> 'Speak', he urged.
> 'What about, Sir?'
> 'Whatever you like. I leave both the choice of subject and the manner of treating it entirely to yourself.'
> Accordingly I sat and said nothing: 'If he expects me to talk for the mere sake of talking and showing off, he will find he has addressed himself to the wrong person', I thought.
> 'You are dumb, Miss Eyre.' (Brontë 1985: 164)

Rochester's tone is uncouth and direct. He makes his need for conversation quite clear and demands submission. Jane Eyre, however, has no intention of fulfilling his wish and sees her self-respect as a valuable commodity.

> She finally replies:
> I don't think, Sir, you have the right to command me, merely because you are older than I, or because you have seen more of the world than I have; your claim to superiority depends on the use you have made of your time and experience.

Rochester then softens his tone; this new attitudinal timbre continues to characterize their entire relationship, increasingly one of love. We have here a case of a multi-dimensional authority relationship.

The first dimension is the formal authority of the employer, who is entitled to demand respect from his employee. The extent of this power divide of course still depends, beyond the nature of the working contract itself, on the strength within society of the classes to which both belong. This divide is expressed, among other things, in the asymmetry of forms of address ('Sir', 'Miss Eyre'). (This contrasts with Austria – Nestroy features a number of examples of this – where the subordinate is often addressed in the third person singular. Addressing others in the third person, though, is still standard in the British House of Commons, where it surely expresses something other than contempt.)

The second dimension is that of age and experience, which Jane Eyre herself touches upon. Seniors demand and receive more respect than juniors, although only if they are not discredited by poverty or lowly social background.

The third dimension is that of gender relations – as it was in Jane Austen, here too emancipation from male superiority is an explicit discursive theme. The English model of respect, which demands authority in exchange for respect, to which the subordinate also lays claim, thus straddles all three dimensions – such that it is near-impossible to decide which is decisive in this case. This fact is of key significance to how effectively 'social character' and (national) habitus are shaped. It means that models can spread from one social location to others; that even when far-reaching changes occur, such as the rise of 'bourgeois' and 'working class' groupings, the behaviour of such 'new' groups is pressed into the same mould. This casts light on why the late-courtly tone, which also imbues gender relations in, for example, Schnitzler (*Reigen*) or Musil (in Ulrich's relationship with Bonadea or Diotima) – centred on feminine coquetry, masculine gallantry, though often directed at loveable 'fools' not taken entirely seriously – demonstrates such a different hue even from Oscar Wilde's salon comedies in England (*Bunbury*, *The Importance of Being Earnest*). An aura of cool masculine austerity and a certain sexual prudery marks English gender relations, at least among the middle and upper classes, around 1900 – the novels of the Brontë sisters, generically close to the 'Gothic novel', provide an insight into the accelerating tendency towards the suppression of drives corresponding to this particular aura (perhaps explicable in part through their close involvement with Wesleyan Methodism; cf. Hodge 1990: 55–6 for an analysis of the social background and genre-specific elements of their novels). In any event, a clear overall difference – ultimately rooted in the quite different position of the aristocracy vis-à-vis state, crown and the lower classes – emerges between aspects of Austrian authority relations and their English counterparts. The former are marked by arbitrary dispensation of mercy, subjugation, overbearing authority, flattery and pretence, the latter by a fusion of the demand for deference and respect on the part of those of higher social rank with a certain restraint, proud detachment and autonomy among subordinates. This does not, of course, mean that the English working classes were able to maintain their dignity and self-respect during the industrial revolution, which shook society like a force of nature. It does, however, mean that they were able to win back some of their self-respect in the wake of the gradual power shift that unfolded during the course of the 19th century, from which they benefited; and if they succeeded in doing so, they utilized the English culture of respect and proud detachment that we have here portrayed in detail.

Notes

1 The whole affair began in a club, when the prince poured a glass of brandy over the head of his 'friend' Christopher as a lark, to which he could only reply: 'As your Royal Highness pleases' (Sykes 1986: 28). Everyone present burst out laughing, and from then on and until the end of his days Sykes was the butt of an unbroken chain of humiliating jokes, against which he was unable to defend himself.

2 The school in question was the United Services College, which Kipling himself attended; he thus experienced the life of the school at firsthand.

3 There are of course some well-known exceptions: the Irish, and to a much lesser extent the Czechs, had their indigenous aristocracy removed by an outside force and replaced with a foreign one. Some peoples remain, like the Norwegians, peasant peoples, whose nobles never left the village; some, like the Swiss-Germans, developed their identity through struggles with a feudal nobility perceived as 'foreign'. One can, however, point to a great deal of evidence proving that European feudalism was anything but unimportant to these peoples.

4 For Vladimir Nabokov it was 'fine needle work'; it was none other than Nabokov, who refused to accept that the novel in general is 'realistic', who scrupulously reconstructed Austen's descriptions of the interior of manor houses (cf. Nabokov 1980). Cf. also Pool 1994, for a detailed analysis of everyday English life at the time.

5 Two of them became admirals; one was adopted by a nobleman. J. Austen's family also produced a good number of clergy, who belonged to the High Church and who had a pastorate at their disposal as a means of making a 'living' (although formally assigned by the church, a benefice of this kind often remained the property of one family for several generations). The 'ascriptive' element of social status – through association of birth – is still very strong.

6 See the book of the same name by Paul Theroux, who approached the English national character at the time of the Falklands War via a land journey along the coast of Britain; he met Jonathan Raban, carrying out a similar undertaking in a boat travelling in the opposite direction (cf. Theroux 1983; Raban 1987).

Chapter 8

Bureaucratization as an Austrian Civilizing Process

Examples from the end of the era

The bureaucratic outlook which has come to characterize Austrian society is apparent in an almost classic excerpt from Doderer who depicts his *Amtsrat Zihal* (literally, office councilor) engaging in an activity far removed in principle from his official duties. Zihal slips into a bureaucratic argot, typical of officials and expressive of their innermost being when he writes:

> Accordingly, what presented itself for consideration was the necessity of procuring a table that offered sufficient space for the observer's chair on its surface, as well as a small end-table that could be placed in front as support for the short tripod. In that regard, the little smoking table could be considered suitable, even if there was a certain amount of distrust toward that piece of furniture because of the noise it caused a bit ago. The smoking accoutrements located on top would have to be removed and locked up ahead of time a) because of their complete superfluity, and b) because of the commotion caused previously, which, in the event of a repetition or relapse respectively, would be subject to prosecution. Perhaps that was the way to proceed, combined with the immediate withdrawal of Herr Wänzrich's permit, for which, in view of the new arrangements that had to be made, there appeared to be a clear indication. (Doderer 2000: 90)

Doderer skilfully captures here the essence of official language. German legalese, which avoids designating a concrete, acting subject (reflecting adherence to impersonal norms; on the evolution of Austrian administrative language see Bodi 1995b) expresses in a suggestive manner Zihal's bureaucratic super-ego. It liberates him from moral constraints in a taken-for-granted way. No one reading such a text would guess that it describes the preparations of a voyeur who is watching women undress in the lit windows opposite and who has to fend off an attempt at blackmail by Wänzrich.

The quotation above demonstrates not only Doderer's precise knowledge of Austrian officialese, but also its spread to the private, everyday realm and thus its contribution to the formation of the Austrian habitus. These qualities, however, originate in the office – to be precise, the Central Office for Calculation of Taxation and Tolls [*Zentral-Tax und Gebühren-Bemessungsamt*]. Julius Zihal retired as the *Amtsrat* of this body in 1913. Such environments were the breeding ground for the

> Zihalesque virtues (virtutes et facultates): scrupulous punctuality, appearing at the right time, even if no one has called or sent for one, and if sent for, then emerging exactly on time like the revolving figurines on old town hall clocks, melting entirely into the background whenever one's presence is undesirable (echoes of those with an exceptionally sensitive nose, able to sniff out the fact from under the door of a superior's office that this is not the right moment to enter and who thus, already standing in front of the high double-doors, turn on their heels and disappear smoothly and soundlessly back to their own desk); the almost absolute order and reliability, pushing the limits of the humanly possible in all matters, the glassy stare and closed ears vis-à-vis petitioners, who are viewed as powerless; otherwise, friendly behaviour with everyone, an inscrutable smile and a steady flow of unctuous phrases – now, [...] all these virtues were consciously possessed, nurtured and mastered; [...] (Doderer 1985: 402; trans. A.S.).

This quotation from the *Strudlhofstiege* describes a Mr Scheichsbeutel who, as a 'Zihaloid', lacks a solid inner core but closely resembles Zihal, at least in his outer behaviour. Doderer is here trying to illuminate a 'type' featuring a bundle of qualities such as punctuality, orderliness and reliability, without which there could be no bureaucratic rationality: they lend the running of this human machine a degree of calculability achievable only through the precise interlocking of its individual components. These very bourgeois virtues require a significant effort to steer affect, and a considerable degree of self-constraint, which has to be drummed into people from a young age. This version of the 'methodically rational conduct of life' (after Max Weber) imposes a far from negligible psychological cost. These virtues are joined by the social skills that people of bureaucratically imbued character must develop if they are to satisfy those above them in the hierarchy (who, after all, also have their moods). Their dominant position makes social exchange structurally asymmetric. Dealings with clients are marked by general disregard of the individual person, the 'petitioner' – the official develops a keen sense for the degree of social power a particular subject has at his disposal. The Habsburg official, however, never raises his voice. He is merely inaccessible, and most people receive a polite smile – along with a 'flow of unctuous phrases'. The courtly and bureaucratic models intersect here once again.

Doderer wrote both his novels, *Die erleuchteten Fenster* [published in English as *The Lighted Windows or The Humanization of the Bureaucrat Julius Zihal*, Doderer 2000] and the *Strudlhofstiege*, after the period we have been examining (they were completed in 1939 and 1951, respectively), yet they still largely reflect the vanished Habsburg world, which, according to Magris (1988), ended up as a 'Habsburg myth'. Doderer was certainly no straightforward naturalist or realist in his descriptions and, similar to Herzmanovsky-Orlando, worked with ideal types and used a great deal of irony and parody[1] with highly theoretical intentions. Conservative in his politics and world-view, he was rather more favourably disposed towards the beings he observed and created than Heinrich Mann in his famous *Untertan*, set in Wilhelmine Germany. In a certain sense, Zihal becomes a Viennese equivalent, portrayed more sympathetically, of Diederich Heßling, who identified with his more dynamic emperor:

> He, Zihal, had served loyally, for a lifetime, and hadn't attained his higher salary levels – and thus retirement benefits – by merely piling up extra time credits. However, regulations are regulations. He was sitting where he was by the power of precept. To bow before it imparts greatness. His gaze fell upon the picture of the Monarch, actually right through it; in his mind, he was taking in the Double Eagle over the door of the office building. He, Zihal, was in harmony with it all. His work had not – never – been found less than satisfactory. There was a slight degree of moistness around his eyes as he went out to warm up the leftover morning coffee, because it was time for some refreshment. (Doderer 2000: 18)

Loyalty (with its feudal overtones and which had originated, historically and socio-genetically, in feudalism), obedience, and longing for harmony determine the Austrian bureaucratic mentality towards the end of the monarchy and for some time afterwards. Correctness is also a dominant ideal (though one cannot of course assume that Doderer's characterization of Amtsrat Zihal automatically applies to all officials in the monarchy); above all, however, it means the absence of 'complaints' – from 'above', as a rule. Zihal's self-esteem, his pride, is grounded in his hegemonic position. This is not based on military strength, courage or bravery, nor on land or capital. Neither is it anchored in Zihal's manners – although these are probably far from poor. The core reason for Zihal's pride and 'dignity' is his position within the bureaucracy, an organization that embodies hegemony and is bound up with laws and 'regulations'. Behind this, though only dimly perceptible, lies the state's monopoly of violence. If push comes to shove, the state can secure taxes, for the collection of which Zihal shares responsibility, through violence. Zihal's position within society is thus grounded in these 'sovereign' functions.

The machine-like rationality of the Austrian bureaucracy is, however, only one of its aspects. As we have seen in the analysis of the socio-cultural dynamics of state formation in Austria and through literary examples, the upper echelons of the bureaucracy were still mainly reserved for aristocrats or consisted of older networks of kinship and acquaintance (similar to the English *old boys' network*) and which were thus in conflict with the 'impersonal' norms (according to Max Weber) and procedures of this machine of state.

The following realistic scene shows how this can function from below:

> Third, the place was filled with a heavy intimation that here one was expected to wait, without asking any questions. His policeman, after stating the grounds of the arrest, stood beside Ulrich like a column. Ulrich immediately tried to give some sort of explanation. The sergeant in command of this fortress raised an eye from the form he had been filling in when the convoy arrived, looked Ulrich up and down, then dropped his eye again and without a word went on filling in his form. Ulrich had a sense of

> infinity. Then the sergeant pushed the form aside, took a volume from the shelf, made an entry, sprinkled sand on it, put the book back, took down another, made an entry, sprinkled sand, pulled a file out of a bundle of similar files, and continued as before. Ulrich felt a second infinity unfolding during which the constellations moved in their predetermined orbits and he did not exist. (Musil 1996: 167–8)

If one replaces 'Ulrich' with the initial 'K', we are not far away from Kafka's *Trial*. The gloomy, paranoid apathy of the wrongly accused main character who has been brought to trial for reasons that remain opaque, is the flipside of the 'modern' objectivity of bureaucratic procedure, carried out in this case without regard for the individual involved. The officials commit no transgression. They do not shout. They do not abuse their victim. They simply make him feel that he is no longer truly part of this world. English literature (the detective novel, for example) contains no equivalent of this orientalistic fatalism, the outcome of a machine of state which was in itself constructed on a 'rational' basis. Austria has for long been a police state in comparison to England, considering the continuity of, for instance, compulsory registration from the early modern period to the present day (cf. Axtmann 1992). To this day, the individual in England is under no obligation to legitimize and justify his or her existence from birth onwards.

The quotation from Musil shows that the bureaucratic rationality at work here is relative in nature; it would in fact be better to employ a comparative concept of 'rationalization': if one includes, for example, an economic (costs-based) perspective or the viewpoint of those (such as Ulrich) affected by this machine, many less rational traits become apparent. The present-day state bureaucracy probably retains this Janus-face; Kafka tells us about this in drastic fashion in his suffocating 'trial'. Here, the boundary between the formal, or public, and the private, is repeatedly crossed. Co-defendants are in cahoots with the court or friends and acquaintances turn into accomplices of the prosecution. Goffman's 'total institution' functions in a similar way: the dividing line between public and private vanishes here, too (cf. Goffman 1961: 17). At the same time, commentators have claimed that Kafka's bureaucracies were terrible not because of their despotism, but because of their anonymity and dreadful precision (cf. Hermsdorf, drawing on Obschernitzki 1977: 45). Which was worse: soulless modernity or ancient despotism?

The two guards, in any event, find the hierarchy in which they are ensnared quite confusing:

> We are humble subordinates who can scarcely find our way through a legal document and have nothing to do with your case except to stand guard over you for ten hours a day and draw our pay for it. That's all we are, but we're quite capable of grasping the fact that the high authorities we serve, before they would order such an arrest as this, must be quite well informed about the reasons for the arrest and the person of the prisoner. There can be no mistake about that. (Kafka 1992: 6)

Now, the veil of ignorance affects not only these two subaltern officials, but – in line with the book's core motif – also K himself. From start to finish, the nightmarish fog never clears. Psychoanalytic interpretations may link this ceaseless obscurity to K's equally endless and diffuse sense of having to repay a debt, and ascribe the surreal elements of the situation to the *conditio humana*. Yet as a comparison with Doderer makes plain, much in Kafka's text points to the officialese of the Habsburg Monarchy:

> The great privilege, then, of absolving from guilt our Judges do not possess, but they do have the right to take the burden of the charge off your shoulders. That is to say, when you are acquitted in this fashion the charge is lifted from your shoulders for the time being, but it continues to hover above you and can, as soon as an order comes from on high, be laid upon you again. As my connection with the Court is such a close one, I can also tell you how in the regulations of the Law Court offices the distinction between definite and ostensible acquittal is made manifest. In definite acquittal the documents relating to the case are said to be completely annulled, they simply vanish from sight, not only the charge but also the records of the case and even the acquittal are destroyed, everything is destroyed. That's not the case with ostensible acquittal. The documents remain as they were, except the affidavit is added to them and a record of the acquittal and the grounds for granting it. (Kafka 1992: 158)

Here, law and legal terminology are deployed in a manner very similar to their use by Amtsrat Zihal. Subtle (pseudo-)distinctions occur here and there; the person seems little more than a marionette of bureaucratic forces. Just as the inmates of Goffman's 'asylums' react to the permanent exposure and destruction of the private sphere with strong feelings of fear and shame, K becomes exhausted, apathetic and is plagued by feelings of shame and guilt: '"Like a dog!" he said, it was as if the shame of it should outlive him.' (Kafka 1992: 232)

K's fear is also Kafka's fear of his father. In 'Letter to Father' he writes:

> I had lost my self-confidence in your presence and exchanged it for a boundless sense of guilt. (Recalling this boundlessness, I once went so far as to write of someone: 'He fears that his shame will survive him.') (Kafka 1975: 43; trans. A.S.)

As we shall see later, Grillparzer's experience of bureaucracy (first at school, then in an office) is also combined with great fear of fatherly authority. Kafka informed Brod of his intention to call his complete works 'Attempts to break out of the paternal domain' (cf. Garaudy 1981: 127). Kafka's own experiences were garnered in old Austria – as a German-speaking Jew in Prague; as a member of the education-focused Jewish middle class; in his law studies and as an official of the semi-state 'Workers' Accident Insurance Institute' [*Arbeiter-Unfall-Versicherungsanstalt*], for which he worked almost his entire adult life. As a writer, he was certainly no straightforward realist, and his interpreters can choose between the Jewish experience, the gloomy dreamworld of psychoanalysis, the *conditio humana*, the horrors of totalitarian bureaucracies and the Habsburg, specifically Austrian, officialdom. If one chooses the last of these perspectives, one should not ignore the others. Persons, as Elias compellingly shows (Elias 1991: 153–238), are structured like the skin of an onion in their we – I balance: family, village or town, ethnic group and the state all act to mould people; conflicts and clashes of loyalty often exist between various attachment groups. Kafka, who considered himself a 'restless western Jew', was also deeply affected by the state society in which he lived.

We again have Musil to thank for illuminating another dimension of Austrian bureaucratization wich had consequences for the development of a corresponding habitus.

The entire 'Parallel Campaign'[2] itself – as literary invention – is a manifestation of enlightened absolutism:

> 'What has brought us together', Count Leinsdorf said, 'is the shared conviction that a great testimonial arising from the midst of the people themselves must not be left to chance but needs guidance by an influence that sees far into the future from a place with a broad perspective – in other words, from the top.' (Musil 1996: 179)

On another occasion,

> [A] resolution was being passed in the conference room after Count Leinsdorf had thanked the General for his important and valuable suggestions, though the time had not yet come for examining proposals on their merits, as the organizational groundwork must be laid first. To this end, all that was needed now – apart from suiting the plan to the realities as represented by the ministries – was a final resolution to the effect that those present had unanimously agreed to submit the wishes of the people, as soon as these could be determined by the Parallel Campaign, to His Majesty, with the most humble petition to be allowed to dispose freely of the means for their material fulfilment (which would have to be raised by then) if such were His Majesty's most gracious pleasure. (Musil 1996: 193–4)

In ironic fashion, these two excerpts express very well the continued existence of an authoritarian state structure; the central importance of harmony, agreement and love vis-à-vis the highest authority; the co-existence of the feudal-aristocratic element of unconditional loyalty with a bourgeois-bureaucratic element of professional specialization, expressed in a perfectly parodied officialese. The spirit of bureaucratic dithering, the ponderousness of the decision making process, is crystal clear in this language. This is another example of the Austrian opacity and unreality so perfectly expressed by Herzmanovsky-Orlando and somehow still familiar to contemporary Austrians from their dealings with the state bureaucracy.

Lhotsky (1974) is surely right to trace the development of the 'Austrian person' from the nobility through the armed forces to the official. Courtly and bureaucratic traits can be discerned here as typically Austrian. Austria's state-centred social history could hardly be more different from the English tradition of relying on the unplanned, rampant dynamics of economic (market liberalism) and political parliamentary development. English 'civil society' (cf. Keane 1988) stands in sharp contrast to Austria's enlightened absolutism. There is broad agreement that the bureaucratization of Austria was the result of the reformist absolutism of the18th century. When modernization was pursued from above (in response to the wars with Prussia, which saw the Habsburg dynasty engaged in a genuine struggle for survival), the result was generally *somewhat* more repressive, and its effects were more uncertain, conflict-ridden and contradictory, than would have been the case with a broad movement anchored in the middle strata of society (in this case, the bourgeoisie).

The result was the bureaucratic colouring of the Austrian national character. Magris has made the oldish, pedantic official, programmed for renunciation, one of the key figures of the Habsburg myth: from Grillparzer's *Der arme Spielmann, Ein treuer Diener seines Herrn*, through the self-denying figures found in Stifter and Saar, to the types of officials in Musil, Roth, Kafka, Herzmanovsky and Doderer, a winding trail extends through Austrian literary history. The higher these officials are located within the hierarchy, the more noble, aristocratic and feudal their images are; the lower they are located, the more sullen they are, the more slavishly they carry out orders, and the more obsessively pedantic they become. Examples of this developmental thread are ubiquitous – from Postl-Sealsfield's *Austria, As It Is* (1828) to Kafka's hopeless nightmare in *The Trial* und Karl Kraus's critique of mindless exercise of power and bureaucratic corruption of subalterns.

We have outlined how the state's predominance in the development of Austrian society influenced the development of a corresponding habitus. We shall now trace the genesis of this habitus. We shall highlight the evolution of the bureaucratic habitus as a process of rationalization in a narrow sense, particularly against the background of gradual, though never entirely completed, decoupling from its patrimonial origin. The theme of bourgeois freedoms and their fluctuating importance in the process of Austrian state formation, with consequences for the development of a particular political culture, was another key factor here. Finally, this topic requires us to look at those peculiarities of the evolution of state and society in Austria that led to dithering, hesitation and the tendency to muddle through. As we have shown in detail above, their roots clearly lie in the 'struggle of nationalities', the dilemma faced by an old monarchical state trying to modernize. For this state, in the age of the nation state, each step forward seemed like a step into the abyss.

From Josephinist officialdom to the *Vormärz* police state: Reflections in bourgeois literature

An old stereotype of the Austrian character is that of the hedonist. The Viennese zest for life, Vienna as the 'Falstaff' of German cities, 'fat old Vienna', (Bauernfeld, drawing on Magris 1988: 34) inspired the German Protestant Nicolai to claim that the common man in Vienna was no friend of steady work; always on the lookout for distraction, he was as devoted to fried chicken, fireworks and pilgrimages (that is, performative Roman Catholicism) as he was to constant waltzes (cf. Magris 1988: 36). This cliché is very old – it was expressed in the late middle ages by the Italian humanist Aeneas Sylvius Piccolomini, in Schiller's description of the 'city of hedonists' [*Stadt der Phäaken*], and survives to this day, painstakingly preserved by the tourist industry, along with the Austrian passion for music. The Austrian mix of peoples, according to Ernst Fischer (Fischer 1945), who makes use of a well-known image, has had a particular influence on the development of an Austrian national character – which has also led other observers to attribute to it a certain conciliatory quality and flexibility (cf. Lhotsky 1974). How could the apparently contradictory models, ascribed by Magris to a thoroughly bureaucratic mentality in the following quotation, have arisen?

> A sense of order and hierarchy, aversion to all titanic greatness and avoidance of all attempts to actively transform things are sublimated in the bureaucratic being; this being crops up again and again throughout Austrian literature, from Grillparzer to Musil, and even finds expression in the 'official, slow, slightly nasal language' of Herr von Trotta. The political immobilism that forms the foundation for this being is transferred to the nuances of human behaviour: maturity, the preferred age for characters in Austrian literature, methodical and meticulous pedantry, the near-religious sacrificing of one's own person for the sake of formal order. (Magris 1988: 17; trans. A.S.)

Lhotsky, in a 1967 lecture on the 'Problem of the Austrian Person', attempted to pin down the historical genesis and scope of this personality type. The 'Austrian Person' was, Lhotsky argued, created through the emergence of an Austrian supranational nobility which arose as a consequence of the unification of the Bohemian, Hungarian and 'Austrian' lands in 1526 through intermarriage, and because the Habsburg sovereign retained the right to adjoin foreign aristocrats to the native nobility [*Indigenat*] – that is, Hungarian nobles became Austrian ones and vice versa. The establishment of a supranational Austrian nobility did not entirely succeed, but, according to Lhotsky:

> The fact that national differences came to the fore later, in the wake of other developments, did not prevent the Austrian-Bohemian-Hungarian aristocracy from retaining certain lasting characteristics of mentality and behaviour which clearly marked them out from others. (Lhotsky 1974: 314; trans. A.S.)

The nobility long held the most important posts within the administrative apparatus (and thus, as Elias puts it, dominated the crucial monopolies of taxation and violence). The reforms under Maria Theresa created a class of officials to serve the new centralized state, and this class, according to Lhotsky, did more than anything else to generate an 'Austrian people': '(this) is the result of a particular kind of education, which required transferral of responsibility for the ideology of the state from the nobility to the class of officials and then to the army' (Lhotsky 1974: 316). 'Austrian Personhood' was thus produced, and this defines the scope and limits of our observations: Austria's medieval foundations consisted of a plethora of lands and cultures, and, to a certain extent, it has remained heterogeneous. From Trieste to Galicia, however, there were homogenizing influences – which declined markedly though not entirely in 1918 and which, together with the new economic and political order, shaped the reality of Central Europe in the successor states. For today's 'young nation' of Austria it is a heritage whose influence continues to be felt, though it is one influence among several. The official was, according to Lhotsky, the product of a new ideal of education (emanating from France): 'No longer the chivalrous virtues of the middle ages, no longer the courtier, the Renaissance *cortigiano*, nor the gentleman that had recently risen to prominence in England, but simply the *citoyen*, the citizen' (Lhotsky 1974: 316). Piarist monks loyal to the state and secular priests loyal to Joseph II raised the generation of bureaucrats, who then served under Franz I. They were required to uphold the law faithfully and display a deep-seated loyalty to the state; they had to love the monarch as a child loves his father. The overall picture that emerges is of a hierarchical, patrimonial vision of the world. The Austrian Person is imbued with it to this day – and it has produced a structure of feeling largely alien to the English.

What brought about this apparently surprising shift from hedonist to meticulous pedant? Or did both aspects come to co-exist? From conciliatory diplomat to rigid ritualist? In fact, these partially contradictory qualities continued to exist in Austria; but in a significant way they also express a civilizing process, more particularly in the sense of an enduring structural shift towards firmer, more regular affect controls. As we elaborated earlier, the massive development and expansion of the Austrian bureaucracy was due to the drive to reform that marked Habsburg absolutism; the corresponding civilizing thrust entailed embourgeoisement and was never again free of the Janus-face of progress and repression. Insofar as reformist absolutism opposed the conservative forces of the landowning nobility and the church, improved the position of burghers and strengthened that of the peasants, it was certain to meet with the approval of advocates of the Enlightenment; insofar as it made the state stronger and almost invulnerable and – through the coalition between the monarch and the aristocracy – established a tight-knit apparatus of surveillance, it clashed with the goals of Enlightenment supporters, who, moreover, not infrequently belonged to the very bureaucratic apparatus that was supposed to promote progress.

In his pathbreaking work on the literature of this 'period of thaw' (when censorship was slackened, a broader public opinion arose and opponents' subsequent reaction to far-reaching 'bourgeois' freedoms proved unable to end them), Bodi (1995a) has laid bare the huge ambivalence of this process. An Austrian 'Enlightenment novel' was in fact emerging at the time. It provides rich insights into this process. It also reveals, however, the development towards a professionalized bureaucracy, in which the virtues of the official, from their crude beginnings, were increasingly refined. We shall now investigate this process, which was also a civilizing one.

The class of officials itself had its source in the fusing of elements of feudal law with those of absolutism. Vassalage was feudal; the feudal tenure of offices [*Amtslehenschaft*] was a transitional form on the way to the emergence of the official class (cf. Armanski 1983: 19–20). Mutual obligations of loyalty linking lords and vassals survived in the 'oath of service' [*Diensteid*]. In the long transition from the 14th to the 18th century, the higher offices were largely held by nobles, such that one can speak of a new form of aristocratic rule. It was one, however, which featured greater openness to the bureaucratic bourgeois patriciate from town or country. The depersonalization and codification of relations of subordination which had formerly privileged the personal bond betweeen the official and the sovereign, corresponded to the absolutist state with its bounded territory, the unity of its subjects, its interest in mercantile ventures and thus calculable relations, its standing armies and consequently great need for increased tax revenue. The relationship of service was established publicly and legally and by means of a sovereign act; the official's duties and rights were stipulated ever more meticulously; guidelines on education, promotion, welfare and maintenance of discipline were specified ever more precisely. While many feudal elements were thus retained (the oath of service, personal loyalty to the monarch, trust and lifelong dependency), others were thoroughly objectivized – in contrast to older kinship networks. Max Weber, of course, emphasized professionalism and qualification for a particular office, attachment to regulations and laws, the depersonalization of authority and the weeding out of arbitrary personal elements. The personal obligation of loyalty was thus joined by the official's obligation to the state (along with the obligation of subjects, which already existed). Protection from dismissal, financial support to ensure the welfare of the official's entire family, taking possession of the 'entire person', the principle of securing adequate accommodation [*Alimentation*] instead of a salary, the impossibility of changing one's job (employment for life), and membership of a group with its own code, detached from the society around it, were old-fashioned features that complemented compulsory loyalty. This 'conviction-based profession' [*Gesinnungsberuf*] was secured by its own group language ('officialese') and, as we have already stressed, through the non-market criterion of lifelong employment. In these characteristic features we can already begin to discern the key dimensions of a 'civilizing thrust' of a particular kind, which began to imbue the official as a 'whole person'.

Let us first consider the consequences that a long-term relationship of service per se brings with it. It forces the employee himself to calculate, on a long-term basis, his opportunities, needs, risks and any actions that might have negative consequences for his chances of promotion. This is exactly why the Austrian administration developed the tight-knit system of surveillance with the help of personal records containing information about the conduct of its officials known as the *Conduite-Listen*, as shown above. The result is a strong inner dependency on the authority of superiors and a general caution which forces civil servants to suppress all aggressive emotions: officials are peaceful. They are not necessarily peaceful as a result of elevated moral insight acquired through their own efforts, though. Rather, automatic-reactive self-constraint occurs on the basis of a certain anxiety, as does instrumentally motivated, conscious self-control. In any event, it is small wonder that several generations of character training and habituation to a peaceful environment changed the perception and values of a significant chunk of the Austrian elites; it was most likely no accident that 'reformist officialdom' with an Austrian hue became the proponents of the Enlightenment in the administration of justice and the execution of sentences and advocated a pacifism opposed to the warlike spirit of the aristocracy.

Moreover, it usually took several generations until the new spirit of reliability, punctuality, hard work and general awareness of duty took concrete form in appropriate behaviour. Since most people are neither particularly reliable nor hard-working without external pressure (the palette of preferred distractions ranges from simple gossip to the more tangible temptations of the flesh), a close-knit apparatus of external constraints developed in Austria, to which people became accustomed in the course of time, as apparent in Doderer's descriptions of the Zihalesque personality. Pedantry, or to be more neutral, a sense of order – the tendency towards formalism or ritualism – is a character trait acquired at a high psychological cost. The corresponding affective restraint can indeed become a person's so-called 'second nature', yet this type of transformation of external into internal constraint presumably involves excessive tension between 'super-ego' and 'the unconscious'. If socialization, laying the groundwork for such restraint, is already underway within the bureaucratic bourgeois family, then the civilizing process may have undesirable results, as Elias explains:

> Particular branches of drives are as it were anaesthetized in such cases by the specific structure of the social framework in which the child grows up. Under the pressure of the dangers that their expression incurs in the child's social space, they become surrounded with automatic fears to such an extent that they can remain deaf and unresponsive throughout a whole lifetime. In other cases certain branches of drives may be so diverted by the heavy conflicts which the rough-hewn, affective and passionate nature of the small human being unavoidably encounters on its way to being moulded into a 'civilized' being, that their energies can find only an unwanted release through bypasses, in compulsive actions and other symptoms of disturbance. In other cases again, these energies are so transformed that they flow into uncontrollable and eccentric attachments and repulsions, in predilections for this or that peculiar hobby-horse. (Elias 2000: vol. 2, 376)

Both Grillparzer's 'Poor Fiddler' and Herzmanovsky-Orlando's Secretary Eynhuf have paid this price of civilization, as we shall see below. Persistent external control from above under these circumstances is more likely to lead to a reactive, automatic form of self that makes one defenceless than to flexible internalization on the model of 'reflexive civilizing' (cf. Waldhoff 1995: 315–16); Waldhoff contrasts an external constraint/super-ego axis with a super-ego/ego axis of behavioural steering). Persons formed in this way tend to become peaceful but dependent. Their mode of living is calculable and rarely features physical violence, yet their conscience is far from the demanding normative concept of radical, solitary self-steering. The same applies also to the official's emotional identification with his office and the corpus of laws, decrees and the spirit of correctness that imbues them. From this point of view, deviance is not simply immoral. It offends, so to speak, one's aesthetic reflexes.

The bureaucratic conscience did not, however, develop overnight. And as we shall see, it was in fact comparatively undeveloped in the early stages. One can nonetheless also assume that, within a vertical, hierarchical structure there would have been ample opportunities for the inhibition of aggression when dealing with those above which would have been balanced out by the relatively free flow of affect towards those lower down in the hierarchy (subordinates, 'petitioners' from the general public). The potential for balancing things out was, however, strictly limited by laws and regulations – according to Weber, weighing things up 'sine ira et studio' and disregarding the personal circumstances of the subjects of administration are key characteristics of bureaucracy, and establish its modern objectivity. This route to the 'steely stare' and 'closed ears' surely also required a certain amount of self-control on the part of the official – particularly when high-ranking personalities intervened. The Austrian Enlightenment novel during the Josephinist thaw contains numerous examples showing how laborious was the production of the model official. Joseph Richter, born in 1749 and known above all for his *Briefe eines Eipeldauers* [from 1787; 'letters from a citizen of Eipeldau = a small fictitious location'] dealt satirically with the sloppy work and ignorance of the state official in his '*Wienerische Musterkarte*' [Viennese collection – or map – of exemplars]; his critique also tackles the network of police informers, already massively expanding under Joseph II. In other words, lack of freedom was the flipside of modernization. An excerpt from Richter's novel *Herr Kaspar. A Novel against Hypochondria* (1787) casts light on the as yet rather limited work ethic of officials:

> Now, however, he suddenly found himself in his true element. He saw around him nothing but friendly, merry faces: rather than working, his colleagues gathered together in a circle, took snuff, conversed about the latest happenings in town or even played a game of Piket [a card game]. He often saw nothing of his superiors for weeks at a time, and when the weather was particularly pleasant, the entire chancellery went to play bowls ... (Richter, in Bodi 1995a: 206–7; trans. A.S.)

Even if such portrayals are somewhat over the top (around 20 years later, for instance, Mme. de Staël praised the Austrian administration as exemplary; cf. de Staël 1962: 77), they nonetheless suggest that things were as yet a long way from 'pedantry'. They also imply that the emerging Austrian police state was unable completely to smother cheerfulness. On the contrary, here and in numerous other novels a certain species of erotic permissiveness prevailed. Johann Pezzl, an immigrant from Bavaria who had previously attended a monastic school, also describes in his 'sketch of Vienna' both the surveillance of subjects by the police and their network of informers and the impact of bureaucratization:

> The soft character of the Viennese yields no heroic virtues. But what is the point of heroic sentiment nowadays, in present conditions? Our machines of state are organized so mechanically, even our normal, domestic life is arranged so methodically, that large, extraordinary explosions of the head and heart cause more confusion and havoc than benefits and blessings. (Pezzl, in Bodi 1995a: 226; trans. A.S.)

Nonetheless, embourgeoisement on the model of bureaucratic rationality had advanced far enough that the great passions – at least in Pezzl's eyes – appeared tamed. In his novel *Mr Schlendrian or the Judge According to the New Laws* [*Herr Schlendrian oder der Richter nach den neuen Gesetzen*] (1787), F.X. Huber provided a satirical take on the juxtaposition of old and new forms of subjection, of the will to progress of the highest, imperial authority and its failure as a result of unintended consequences, adversities, in-built contradictions and simple inconsistencies. This book (so successful that it was followed by two more) deals with the contradictions arising from the modernization of penal law and the enforcement of sentences, which stemmed from sloppiness, poorly thought out laws and the surprisingly atrocious consequences of humanization through 'rational' measures in general. The French Enlightenment thinkers were the inspiration for these writings; their Austrian kindred spirits, though, obtained their material from their own society, before this window for the formation of public opinion closed once again. Friedel was another who lamented the snail's pace of the bureaucracy ('the more servants (officials) there are, the worse the service'). Alongside sharp attacks on the clergy (Ignaz von Born's *Monachologie* (1783) stands out from the crowd in this regard, with its absurd, Linneaen mania for classification of monks in various orders), the Josephinist state, greeted with jubilation by the Enlightenment thinkers not long before, soon became the target of mockery and satire. This also applied to J. v. Eybel's satire *The Island of the Bullfinches* [*Die Gimpelinsel*, 1783], in which a critique of officials or 'Nikowitzes' as they are called here (birds, in this fable), was expressed in an exotic manner.

Bodi succeeded in bringing out the ambivalence of the Austrian Enlightenment authors who originally helped carry out Joseph II's reforms and often worked as officials themselves. An example was Paul Weidmann in the novel *The conqueror* [*Der Eroberer* 1786; new edition 1997] – and who spoke out, as did Huber and Richter, against bureaucratization, militarization and the despotism that they saw coming. However, they, like many Austrian intellectuals after them, were biting the hand that fed them. This paradoxical climate (which often generated 'obedient rebels', see Heindl 1991) was certainly partly responsible for the Austrian attitude of 'comical ambivalence' which we analyzed earlier as a trait of patrimonial dependency. Joseph II was in fact far from a leading light of the Enlightenment, if we consider his campaign against the Turks (Huber devoted a parody – which recalls Kraus – to this failure and how it was represented in semi-official language) or the harsh punishments that sent people to serve on galleys, which replaced older forms of corporal punishment. The policing apparatus, later deployed within the context of the 'reaction', was also developed under him. A large number of authors predicted this. Moravian ex-novitiate Karl Postl's famous polemic demonstrates how this presented itself to a critical observer in the middle of the *Vormärz* (the pre-revolutionary period that ended with March 1848).

Karl Postl's (Charles Sealsfield's) *Austria, As It Is* as an analysis of the *Vormärz* authoritarian state: Authority and Austrian national character in the early 19th century

This debut publication by the Austrian Karl Postl, a young man from a Moravian peasant family who fled from a monastery in Prague, was printed in London in 1828. It can in many ways be regarded as a treasure trove for the study of the Austrian character, particularly its relationship to authority. Postl was, of course, later to turn into Sealsfield, a writer straddling two hemispheres – his depictions of the world of the American pioneers, frontiersmen and Indians even attained the character of much-read children's books. Postl was under 30 when he wrote his 'pamphlet'. It depicts a semi-fictitious travel report which, while it reflected biographical experience with Austria, was only partly based on the exile's 1826 journey across Europe, from Le Havre to Vienna. Fictional travel writing[3] had already helped produce numerous works of social criticism, and this certainly applies in this case, in which the author remained anonymous, understandably enough given the political situation in Austria and the character of the work.

When the travellers crossed the borders of Austria, they were immediately confronted with a quite specific bureaucratic bearing. Before the black and yellow barrier, the guard-house with the double eagle, they come across a customs official, a sergeant and two Austrian soldiers:

> A custom-officer, with a serjeant and two soldiers, stepped out of a door surmounted with the double eagle. My friend had thought proper to place my books and writing under his immediate protection; but this precaution was almost superfluous. The custom-officer, with many bows to my companion, asked only who the other gentleman was. Being satisfied upon this point, cap in hand, he inquired after foreign books, and was going to open my trunks; when my companion signified, with a sneer, at the same time indifferent and haughty, 'We will deliver the gentleman's passport ourselves. He is my friend, and you may send down to E— for a haunch of venison and a barrel of beer.' The officer expressed his satisfaction by respectfully kissing the hand of my gracious C—, the soldiers by a grim smile; … (Sealsfield 1972: 25–6)

Much in this scene strikes the modern reader as alien – one cannot expect the customs officers of today, dealing with huge numbers of cars, to deliver too many bows. Nor are they likely to kiss one's hand. These gestures of subservience, of servility,[4] no longer fit our matter-of-fact and more democratic habits when dealing with authorities. Moreover, ritualized, servile behaviour of this kind is not found in 'normal' social manners. The code appropriate to the great power imbalance that typifies societies sculpted by aristocratic-courtly norms no longer exists. The spectrum between formality and informality in social interaction has become far smaller throughout the industrial societies of the West and thus also in Austria. The fact that the courtly kiss of the hand was still a bureaucratic norm at the beginning of the 19th century is also worth mentioning. It points to the multiple roots from which the behavioural repertoire of the authoritarian state grew in encounters with imperial subjects.

Again and again, Sealsfield points to the flipside of an authority he felt to be boundless: the unrestrained servility of the Austrians. He bases this on concrete experience of the police state under Franz I and Metternich, but touches repeatedly upon character traits and institutional particularities that predated the *Vormärz*. He describes in detail the system of spies and informers, from high officials to people from the lower ranks of society, who inform on their bosses for money; and the meticulous surveillance of students and professors, though the professors (of theology or jurisprudence) themselves became spies as a consequence of office. This is the particular achievement of the restoration period that followed the Josephinist reformist zeal – it is the era of the Jacobin trials, the aristocracy's great fear of losing its dominant position through revolution, a time of ideological spying and the cultivation of a compliant, mediocre professional bureaucracy in which the privilege to make decisions on promotion became a powerful weapon in the hands of superiors, used to battle against professional competence and the capacity for critical judgement, insofar as these were not coupled with boundless devotion and loyalty.

Yet Austrian authoritarianism did not first arise under Franz I, but had its precursors in the patrimonial-feudal relationship between subject and sovereign: the *Innerösterreicher*[5] loved his emperor, in the same way that the German tribes generally loved their princes (Sealsfield 1972: 125). This was a venerable heritage that even Franz was unable to wreck entirely.[6] Love, devotion and loyalty thus characterized the relationship between the Habsburgs and the peoples subject to their rule. The development of a 'surveillance state', however, endangered this relationship. It alienated, according to Postl-Sealsfield, the subject from his sovereign. Postl's description of the stages in the bureaucratizing thrust that turned Austria from a feudal-patrimonial structure into a modern state is a key element in the appeal of *Austria, As It Is*.

Bureaucratization had now shifted the power balance towards the central government – the pendulum, as it were, had firmly swung the other way – and the bourgeois, sober official (who the emperor was keen to keep sober and disciplined, unlike his aristocrats, who were permitted to lead a far more extravagant lifestyle) was selected to be the loyal, dependent, 'sincere and devoted' tool of imperial power.

Austria, As It Is describes how all this played out in Austria in astonishing detail. Lack of education and ignorance triumphed within the bureaucracy, since loyalty and dependency came to have priority over specialist knowledge and competence: the emperor himself passed over an outstanding official when making appointments to the Court Chamber [the *Hofkammer*, the finance ministry], because his views on import duty were too liberal (Sealsfield 1972: 80–81). Superiors as a rule acted as moral watchdogs when dealing with candidates, even in cases where the post itself was unwaged; if the slightest suspicion arose that the candidate may have lacked loyalty, promotion and his position itself may have been at risk and the superior himself may easily have been suspected of being partly to blame. Every department was said to include two spies reporting to what we may call the Ministry of Police and Censorship [the *k.k. oberste Polizei- und Zensurhofstelle*] or to the emperor himself. Sealsfield showed how seniority replaced expert knowledge, with catastrophic consequences for the efficiency of administration and the army. Fewer than 50 officials in the entire empire had a solid grasp of the state finances, fewer than 50 captains out of 1000 had an understanding of tactics, since colonels and generals were appointed merely on the basis of length of service.

Authority, Sealsfield claimed, leads to servility ('sincere devotion') and incompetence. The army of 60,000 was said to be exceptionally ineffective. The Austrian administration worked slowly. The superior department had to take care of every detail itself, nothing was dealt with independently by the lower offices. Climbing the ladder of authority was a drawn-out business. From district leader [*Kreishauptmann*] via provincial authority [the *Landesstelle*] to the Imperial Ministry [*Hofstelle*], State Council [*Staatsrat*] and emperor; even details were decided from above with enormous expenditure of effort. This was matched by a mentality of subservience and anxiety (Sealsfield 1972: 128), of obedience, rather than a sense of honour and awareness of justice. This mentality is thus seen as part of the explanation for Austrian bureaucratic ineffectiveness. However, we ought to maintain at all times a certain critical distance from Postl-Sealsfield's statements on this subject. He was certainly familiar with the situation in Austria, but not with that abroad. As we shall see in Trollope's novel *The Three Clerks*, the English 'civil service' was not always a model of efficiency.

When Sealsfield was young, Austria was already a well-organized country in which 'a foreigner whose papers are in order' (Sealsfield 1972: 32) could travel relatively unhindered and count on the honesty of landlords and tremendous hospitality. The price paid for this in the Metternich era, however, was far from negligible. An army of spies and informers controlled the population, even in the upper echelons of the nobility, and thus continued with bureaucratic means the authoritarian, patrimonial exercise of dominance that had for centuries suppressed with comparative severity the peasant subjects in Austria, Bohemia and Hungary (though Postl also saw significant differences between Tyrol, Lower Austria, Bohemia and Hungary – between free peasants, those who were as good as free, the personally free but economically oppressed as found in Bohemia and serfs as in

Hungary). 'Policing pressure' constituted a heavy burden, above all for the 'lower orders'. The upper classes tended to be affected only if they carried the 'stigma of the revolutionary' (under which circumstances high officials would send even their friends to prison). What kind of animal was an Austrian spy?

At the well-known spa of Teplitz, distinguished people never chatted about politics because:

> One of these persons, however, deserves your attention. He has a smiling face, speaks fluently French, English, and German, – a sort of weathercock, of whose character you are quite uncertain; but if you are a new-comer you may be sure of having him *vis-à-vis* at the table. While the Russian count treats him with a great deal of civility, the Pole darts furious looks at him; the Austrian general looks up to him with a sort of humility, and his aid-de-camp, the young, rich Count N—, treats him decidedly *en bagatelle*; but this personage is quite unconcerned. He is a close observer; and, if you are a stranger, you may be sure of being attentively watched. He is the counsellor of the Bohemian Government, B— C—, the Imperial spy, who at the expense of his Majesty spends the season here, and lives in very high style, known to every body in the company, on familiar terms with all, and terrible to none except to the unwary. You will find this personage every where, even in the private circles of the nobility; for, in order to show their loyalty, and how '*hand and glove*' they are with the Imperial interest, they think it necessary to have the good opinion of B— C—, or of his colleagues in other bathing-places. (Sealsfield 1972: 31–2)

This excerpt repays careful reading. It is generally hard for us today to imagine what it meant in the times of *Vormärz* to live in a 'police state'. We have here an example of how state control functioned: very straightforwardly, far removed from the perfectionism of an Orwellian Big Brother deploying electronic technologies. Personal acquaintance between strangers is still possible (in contrast, often, to contemporary mass tourism); manners are obviously good and of courtly provenience (Metternich too, according to Postl, was a courtier through and through); it was moreover far from difficult to avoid danger, since the strange 'spy' practically rings a bell to announce his presence and is anything but anonymous and concealed. Nonetheless, this species of control could be so effective that fear of authority and good behaviour in public arose. It probably did nothing to prevent 'double think' (Bodi 1985), however, in which one's private, secret thoughts differ from one's public statements – a 'schizophrenic' bearing, which probably continues to characterize contemporary Austrian national character and which makes open resistance to authority very difficult. It leads rapidly to joking, to a sense that matters to be decided are irrelevant, and to apathy towards the 'higher' levels where decisions are made.

The traditional subservience of the people, long a feature of Austrian history, is a prerequisite for the network of informers itself. Postl again sketches a psychogram of the Austrian character, and the resulting picture is far from pleasing:

> In a country where the lower classes are servile and ignorant, the feeling of honour, of course, very precarious, it requires little pains for the agents of the police to induce servants to betray their masters. For every information the former carry to the police, they obtain one or two ducats. (Sealsfield 1972: 84)

Censorship and a small-minded, conformist press, moreover, generated a suffocating climate of intellectual repression:

> A more fettered being than an Austrian author surely never existed. A writer in Austria must not offend against any Government; nor against any minister; nor against any hierarchy, if its members be influential; nor against the aristocracy. He must not be liberal – nor philosophical – nor humorous – in short, he must be nothing at all. Under the catalogue of offences, are comprehended not only satires, and witticisms; – nay, he must not explain things at all, because they might lead to serious thoughts. If he venture to say any thing upon these subjects, it must be done in that devout and reverential tone which befits an Austrian subject, who presumes to lift the veil from these *ticklish secrets*! (Sealsfield 1972: 209–10)

The Austrian variant of the surveillance state (with all its loopholes and premodern incompleteness), particularly of course during the repressive period, contrasts strikingly with the policing powers found in England. Common Law, the Bill of Rights and Habeas Corpus Acts put an effective stop to the arbitrary exercise of state power in England, at least for the property-owning classes. The sanctity of the private sphere in parliamentary England was – in part through an incomparably livelier press, which watched over 'bourgeois' freedoms with eagle eyes – significantly better guaranteed (despite the temporary suspension of some of these freedoms in the post-Napoleonic period). It is at first sight hard to tally this with the fact that England meted out some of the most severe punishments for crimes against property in all of Europe. The brutal executions of children who had twice stolen a spoon, until around 1830, are almost without parallel, and entirely alien to Austria. It is legitimate to speak here of a war waged by the upper classes against the lower ranks. Literary examples suggest how sinister – before the reforms that created a modern police force in line with the gentleman code (Sir Robert Peel's Metropolitan Police) – an encounter with the English constables, prison officers and judges, all too quick and casual in their sentencing, could be. Defoe's *Moll Flanders*, who spent some time in 'Newgate' for thieving, is a prime example. As illiberal as English economic liberalism was as far as defending property was concerned, however, the system of 'checks and balances', which hindered misuse of state control and democratic freedoms in the political domain, was indeed liberal and balanced.

The 'blind obedience' and servility of the Austrians therefore have, according to Postl-Sealsfield, solid foundations in *Biedermeier* Austria.[7] Yet even he cannot help mentioning the good-natured patrimonial traits of the Austrian system of domination, even in the phase of absolutist reaction. A certain affable good-naturedness prevailed amid the repression, emanating from the ruling house, which has become typical of the Austrian character when dealing with authority. For many Austrians, Emperor Franz I was *der Franzl*; and in the verbal utterances handed down by Postl (this is not the right place to investigate their authenticity) a characteristic is apparent for which one would search in vain in England: in an address to an enthusiastic voluntary corps of noble students, *der Franzl* is supposed to have said:

> 'Oh! you look very handsome; I could not have believed it: but I am glad I don't want you. We have now peace, and you may go home again. (Sealsfield 1972: 115)

Harmless good-naturedness but also a lack of interest in the feelings of his subjects emerges from these words. No inspiring pathos, no acknowledgement of their willingness to make sacrifices, but rather straightforward, naive stoicism, which he also expressed during the battle of Deutsch-Wagram which went badly:

> 'Have I not told you', said the Emperor to his Aid-de-camp, B—n D—, rising at the same time, 'that John will leave us to fight our battle alone, and that we shall have again to pay the reckoning? Now we may look for the hole which the carpenter has left open!' (Sealsfield 1972: 116–17)

Emperor Franz's (good old Franz's) affability was proverbial, as was his simple loden coat, which he wore when riding in his coach in the Prater. Here, authority does not appear (a curious contrast with the extremely formal courtly ceremonial typical of the Habsburgs in Spain) as a cold, hostile, proud or oppressive power, merely insisting upon obedience, but is rather imbued with the Austrian-Habsburg 'clementia', mildness, which in turn assumed the love and devotion of the subjects. The monarch demands this loyalty and dependency, following the expansion and development of an army of officials, above all from the 'public servants', who are at the same time his quite personal subjects. Sealsfield describes this particular relationship of authority as follows:

> Theirs characters tally so exactly with that of the Emperor, that from this affinity of thinking there cannot but exist the greatest harmony between the Austrian and his Emperor. [...]
>
> Our landlord, an honest and wealthy wine cultivator of Rotzbach, had a lawsuit against the lord of the domain, respecting a ward, to whom the former was guardian. Determined not to have the suit procrastinated, he went forthwith to see the Emperor Francis. He was of course received, and stated his case. 'Have you got the cognisance?' demanded the Emperor. – 'Yes, I have,' replied the farmer. – 'Then I will tell you what,' resumed the Emperor; 'you had better go to the Aulic counsellor S—z, and let him see it.' – 'But would it not be better,' said the frank Austrian, 'if your Majesty would command M. Schwarzin to do it?' – 'No, my child,' said the Emperor, 'you don't understand; that business must have its way; I cannot do any thing beforehand; go, go, and you will hear what he says, and then come and tell me.' (Sealsfield 1972: 94–5)

This curious manner of exercising and recognizing authority (love mixed with respect) deserves closer analysis. It is hard to deny the effectiveness of this aspect of the exercise of authority in Austria for several centuries. Even in the modern welfare state, we can still find elements of this relationship, now couched in terms of legal guarantees and made independent of the arbitrary imperial dispensation of mercy. The contemporary Austrian, too, is on the one hand well-behaved and prepared to love his 'sovereigns'; while on the other, thoroughly spoiled and with guileless impertinence, he makes numerous demands on the welfare state. He accepts what the state offers him happily and with a clear conscience, and just as willingly subjugates himself to the numerous bureaucratic rules developed by a close-knit surveillance state – insofar as these rules cannot be escaped. If this is possible, though, he or she thinks nothing of deceiving the state guilelessly and with a good conscience. For Austrians, 'morals' are in such cases strongly orientated towards pressure from outside or from above – if this is lacking, no particular guilt exerts pressure from within.

This, however, applies above all to a public sphere, in which one acts outside of close, enduring blood relations and friendship. The formula: authority = love and respect has a quite different meaning within the family and with other kin than within broader social and political spaces. 'Love' is a feeling which tends in principle to occur in the realm of interpersonal relationships in a narrower sense – and less so in the more abstract network embracing the members of society writ large (even when, and this certainly applied to Austria, political authority demanded family-style love). One would, moreover, have to distinguish between spontaneous, vigorous, 'charismatic' love and the far weaker permanent variety which must be free of emotional fluctuations. Authority as respect mixed with love, or as affection mixed with respectful fear, however, even in the specific case of parental authority, leaves room for numerous empirical means of making a child acknowledge this authority, from infancy to the establishment of an independent adult existence (according to the law: a full position as head of a peasant or master craftsman's household is equal to a new family; when marriage occurs at a relatively mature age, following a long period of sexual asceticism, in the so-called European marriage pattern; cf. Laslett 1989). We cannot expect Sealsfield to furnish us with the insights gleaned from the contemporary Austrian novel and numerous autobiographical depictions from 'oral history', which provide an overview of the entire spectrum of parental instruments of power, ranging from harsh beating to the bad conscience reinforced from the Catholic pulpit (here, the child must express gratitude for corporal punishment). The end result of such training, if it works, is not a fear of authority based on mistrust and rebelliousness, but rather heartfelt consent in the existing division of power. We shall not explore here how 'love' is inculcated and thus banishes open resistance on pain of a serious inner conflict, such that massive feelings of guilt and shame limit freedom of action. We shall, however, scrutinize this inculcation by reference to the work and life of the ultimate Austrian classical figure: the official and writer Grillparzer.

Grillparzer: Patrimonial authority and bureaucratic timidity as Austrian character traits

If Sealsfield, the ardent admirer of English freedom, was also the sharpest critic of the Austrian bureaucracy, Franz Grillparzer in his later years was a highly ambivalent commentator on the system in which he lived. He broke with an England that had disappointed him, abusing its freedom to pursue a narrowly national *Realpolitik* and displaying indifference towards the Irish famine (cf. Lengauer 1996). He was, moreover, a part of the Austrian system in a way that Postl-Sealsfield never was – a long-serving official. He can at the same time be considered an excellent source of information on the effect of this bureaucratic, state-heavy regime, insofar as it affected him and his psyche. Those of his literary works scrutinized here also shed light on the roots, in the family and school, of those patrimonial and bureaucratic constraints which are essential for grasping the evolution of the social character traits of the Austrian official during this historical period.

Claudio Magris sees Grillparzer as the writer who has contributed most and most consistently to the creation of a 'Habsburg myth'. This 'myth' is in part a construction which idealizes Austrian circumstances and character traits or exaggerates them in other ways, but a good deal of its content can in fact be found – perceived and thought through at a profound level – in the Habsburg reality. Grillparzer's characterizations of Habsburg indecisiveness in his plays have become famous: his portrayal of procrastination, at times tragic, at times wise (in *Ein Bruderzwist* [Fraternal Strife] *in Habsburg*) and his famous formulation of Austrian modesty in comparison with the other German lands (in *König Ottokars Glück und Ende* [King Ottokar's Fortune and Misfortunes, 1824]), which has the Austrian step forward quietly and determinedly, only to remain silent and let the others speak. Famous, too, are his Austrian patriotism (despite all his difficulties with the censors he quickly became the 'Austrian national writer') and his eulogy to the faithful pursuit of one's duty and devoted loyalty (*Der treue Diener seines Herrn* [The Loyal Servant of His Master, 1826]; 1848 in a poem on the Austrian commander *Radetzky*: *In deinem Lager ist Österreich* [Austria Is in Your Camp]). It has been said of Grillparzer that he embodies the essence of the Austrian soul itself (Baumann, in Magris 1988: 97–8). Grillparzer, suffused with the Josephinist Enlightenment spirit and inclined towards anticlericalism and freedom, has at the same time become the classical advocate and champion of moderation and order, which he mixed with a 'paternalistic patriotism' (Magris 1988: 104). Magnificent mediocrity, calmness, respect and order were for him the building blocks of the Austrian personality – partly in contrast to the noisy, fashionable Germany, poisoned by nationalism. If the claim that the official has penetrated the Austrian character more than any other social type is correct, then Grillparzer is the most authentic observer of the Austrian personality one could hope to find and *Bancbanus* (*Der treue Diener seines Herrn*) the epitome of the official's virtues and the bureaucratic sense of duty.

Grillparzer was a dramatist above all. Analysis of his 'classical' plays, particularly those dealing with Habsburg Austria, would surely enrich a study of the Austrian habitus. Such analysis would, however, also be problematic: a certain form of distortion would be difficult to eliminate – one which arises from pursuit of a higher, noble, morally elevated poetic truth in both expression and form. His prose works are closer to reality: *Der arme Spielmann* [The Poor Fiddler]; begun in 1831 and published in 1847 and his *Selbstbiographie* (abandoned in 1853). For Magris *Der arme Spielmann* is a paradigmatic analysis of the Austrian personality – its particular realism and descriptive richness are anchored in the novella's obviously strongly autobiographical elements, as parallel reading of his autobiography, written upon official request of the 'Academy', reveals (see Träger 1990: XXXVI for the same evaluation). Comparative interpretation of both sources allows us to penetrate Grillparzer's emotional world – childhood, the formative parental home, youth and the world of the burgeoning bourgeoisie (Grillparzer was the son of a respected lawyer) and its behavioural imperatives – and plumb its emotional depths. Parental, above all paternal, authority is portrayed clearly and caustically in *Der arme Spielmann*; as is feudal, courtly and bureaucratic authority in pre-1848 *Vormärz* Austria. In many ways, Grillparzer was a child of a transitional period – almost all high-level dignitaries were aristocratic, but the bureaucratic milieu was predominantly the reserve of the 'educated classes'. While Grillparzer could write for an anonymous market and a wide public (which, however, he later opted out of), his key supporters were a few high-ranking dignitaries, upon whose good-will he was always to remain personally dependent. The state to which he was deeply loyal was still, above all, dynastic but nationalisms had already made their presence keenly felt and by the end of his life it had lost its great power status. The young Grillparzer had seen Napoleon carrying out military exercises in Schönbrunn; as an old man he experienced the defeat of Königgrätz. Despite all the apparent solidity of Habsburg state power, the creaking foundations of the Imperial house were clearly audible. Grillparzer was only too aware of this. The 'most vain nations' on God's earth, the Czechs and Hungarians, had already imitated the romantic, aggressive nationalism of the young Germany, which Grillparzer perceived as somewhat childish. The economy in particular was in the throws of a dramatic transformation; indeed, the most dramatic of all – guild-based crafts and state factories were, in Austria, too, being replaced by dynamic industrial capitalism. Yet until 1918, the monarchy remained largely a political entity in which aristocrats were still firmly in the driving seat. The interesting thing about all these changes is the persistence of certain models, which can be described as clearly and typically Austrian and which helped to determine the 'national' habitus of today. The work and life of Grillparzer contain rich material for describing and explaining the role of authority, impersonal and personal power, and the social fields which constantly reproduce them. Grillparzer elaborates the elements peculiar to the Austrian relationship to authority more clearly than many other authors, that paralyzing fear and deeply felt guilt, which lead to an inability to defend oneself against those of higher social rank (who may be women), because what one fears most is that someone may withdraw his or her favour. This fear, once acquired in childhood and later reinforced time and again, can, in fact, determine one's whole life. It can make one wary of decisions and poor at implementing them. It is probably the background of a good deal of the 'Austrian fate' and may explain many suicides. *Der arme Spielmann* tells just such a sad story. It is the story of a life in which the 'things not done' count for more than those done, in which that which usually constitutes happiness is missing and is coped with only through the quiet heroism of self-denial. The street musician, now old, who the first-person narrator has noticed, cannot even play. He also fails, as it turns out, to get the woman he loves, is disowned by his own family and fails to build one of his own. He serves his great love selflessly and altruistically his whole life. He finally goes to rack and ruin after sacrificing himself for the sake of others. He is humiliated, made fun of and pushed around, yet he nonetheless retains – his only capital – a certain dignity. When the narrator calls on the fiddler's old flame after his death in order to buy the often abused violin from her, the old, now unsightly woman refuses to cooperate, turns away and is overcome with tears. A lifetime of restraint determined their relationship. She chose the butcher over the dreamer with his head in the clouds, yet he himself still taught the son of his successful rival to play violin.

The story is not our most important theme; we should focus on the motif of a self-denial that blinds one with tears, and a humiliation followed merely by a secret, posthumous status elevation: it is lacking in England, but common in Austria. The English novel can, as Dickens shows, tell stories that are just as sad, but at the end of the day things work out rather well. The heroes – Oliver Twist, David Copperfield or Pip – experience their adversities, resolve their conflicts, ultimately reap a tremendous spiritual profit, save whatever they have left and head for a thoroughly positive ending. This 'dictatorship of the happy ending' indeed seems to us typical of the English novel. Whatever misfortune may befall the heroes and heroines (in Charlotte Brontës' *Jane Eyre* for example): they ultimately furnish themselves with a tolerable life through their initiative and talent. The English reader probably has little time for failures, lacks sympathy for them and steers clear of misfortune by avoiding such books. In Austria there are countless examples of the hopelessly tragic – Ferdinand von Saar's *Tambi*, Stifter's *Hochwald*, Joseph Roth's *Radetzkymarsch*, in the plays from Arthur Schnitzler and Ödön von Horvath, and also in the contemporary work of Bernhard. This fact is as striking as it is hard to explain.

In any event, the poor fiddler is such a character and his appearance fits that of the central Austrian figure, the bureaucrat. Grillparzer's first-person narrator first sees him at a festival in Vienna:

> His bald head was uncovered; following the custom of itinerant musicians he had put his hat open on the ground. He stood, belabouring an old, cracking violin, beating time not only with his foot, but by swaying his bent body to and fro. This, however, did not help in giving one an idea of the rhythm; what he played were merely disconnected notes

> without tune or time. His heart and soul were in his performance, his lips were twitching, his eyes riveted to the sheet of music … yes! he was actually playing from music. (Grillparzer 1928: 6)

This is clearly the description of a failure – a person who, while he does his ‘job’ devotedly, is utterly lacking in talent and success. While the street musicians around him play cheerful waltzes by heart, the ‘poor fiddler’ is entirely dependent on his sheet of music:

> He turned over the leaves and I saw enormously difficult compositions by great masters, black with passages and harmonies. It looked like a careful copy in a stiff hand. So that was what the old man’s clumsy fingers had been trying to play! (Grillparzer 1928: 11)

What makes this fiddler special is the ‘method in the madness’ of his playing – he is totally devoid of creativity, a respectable, bureaucratic pedant scoffed at and merely tolerated by those around him, who receives almost nothing from his public, yet is nonetheless somehow content, convinced that, in all things, a person must stick to a certain kind of order without which he or she would descend into savagery. When the narrator, now curious, gets to know him better, the mendicant musician turns out to be a quasi-official with a methodical approach, living his life according to an ambitious goal, without of course managing to achieve anything at all. The fiddler’s conscience, his super-ego, betrays his bourgeois origins, which he is unable to deny even by living with disorderly journeymen:

> A broad chalk mark divided the room into equal halves. The contrast between the two small worlds on either side of this equator could not have been greater. (Grillparzer 1928: 15)

The fiddler’s biography is soon revealed to the astonished visitor. Grillparzer has obviously transformed his own biography – as the editor of the German edition states in his introduction (Gräber 1990). Transformed, since Grillparzer was of course neither a musician nor without the trappings of success. Alongside astonishing parallels in outward details (here and there we come across a strict, unapproachable, demanding father, several brothers, poorly passed school examinations – ‘cachinnum’, the very word that neither Grillparzer nor the fiddler recalls occurs twice in the exam) it is above all the inner parallels that invite closer analysis. Grillparzer was long plagued by agonizing self-doubt and fear of failure; his external success was not matched by inner certainty. He was unable to ‘enjoy’ such success, as the performance of some of his works, because he lacked an inner conviction of their value. For Weigel, his ‘neurotic’ attitude prevented him from producing first-rate work; he denies Grillparzer the status of classic and considers his life a particularly glaring case of Austrian ‘flight from greatness’ (Weigel 1978). Grillparzer was, in any event, plagued by agonizing shyness in the presence of the great and good. In contrast to the ‘poor fiddler’, however, Grillparzer’s struggle with creativity and inner freedom was far more successful. The distorted image presented in the novel certainly features the heightened reality of nightmarish fears:

> My father was ambitious and quick-tempered. My brothers gave him complete satisfaction, I was the dull one of the family, he said, and certainly I was slow. [...] My brother leapt like chamois from subject to subject. I could not do that. I was never able to leave out anything; if I missed a single word I had to start again from the beginning. My teachers were always hurrying me on, piling new subjects on top of the unassimilated old. This made me stubborn. For instance, music which is now the joy and staff of my life, was made positively hateful to me. (Grillparzer 1928: 18–19)

Grillparzer may also have had the fate of his brothers in mind here. They died young and were rather unsuccessful, and he seems to have fused his fate with theirs in the novella. We can certainly state, on the basis of his autobiography, that he felt similarly pressurized and rejected by his father. Here, though, Grillparzer also tries to come to terms with a problem which resonates to this day. The key here is the complex relationship between pressures from without (external constraints) and the inner willingness (self-steering) of the adolescent learner, essential to bringing about a learning process which can be experienced as 'meaningful'. In his autobiography, Grillparzer graphically describes his own struggles with this dynamic. In arithmetic, for example, he remained, on his own admission, permanently deficient; his teachers were frequently dissatisfied with him even in those areas in which he later achieved so much as a writer and polymath. And Grillparzer himself often found his achievements less than inspiring in retrospect. Many aspects of education at the time revolved around rote learning, a kind of mental dressage, which contrasts sharply with what we today refer to as 'creativity'. It would be worth examining the development of this art of memory training in more detail through a devoted socio-historical study. As is well known, non-literate societies – to this day in parts of Africa – produce a kind of bardic culture in which myths and rituals central to the culture overall are learned by heart and passed down in a largely fixed form from one generation to the next. Literacy means that one can cease making people into living libraries, for now one can archive cultural knowledge and make it accessible to readers at any time. Books only became accessible and obtainable in vast abundance with the rise of printing. Ample evidence from the sociology of literature attests to the rapid expansion of non-theological book-based knowledge beyond the bible, alongside the development of a bourgeois public, as it arose from the late 18th century until the flowering of the bourgeois novel in the mid-19th century. Natural scientific knowledge also increased rapidly in parallel, and a situation soon arose not unlike that which pertains today – namely the possibility of transforming this 'objective culture' into a meaningful 'subjective participation' (Simmel). The more open the 'pictures of the world' transmitted by education are, the more space the individual pupil needs to appropriate these in an independent fashion or to force his way through this 'jungle'. This applies even more to the creative domains of music, painting and writing. In 'The Poor Fiddler', Grillparzer thus underlines both the problem of pushing children too hard through authoritarian instructions in the, as we would say today, 'cognitive' sense – the tale's unhappy hero is stuck within a vicious circle of underdevelopment – but also 'creatively', for he is quickly put off music and the fine arts by the repressive nature of his upbringing. It is questionable whether this failed attempt at good, bourgeois education was truly typical of Austria in contrast to other places – at the end of the 19th century, in his largely autobiographical novel *The Way of All Flesh* (Butler 1994), Samuel Butler described very similar problems in an Anglican clerical milieu using very similar words. In Victorian England, too, a child might well be helpless in the face of the authority of parents and teachers. The father's coldness may have been yet more frightful than that found in Grillparzer's novella. Those institutions beyond the family in which the adolescent, then the young adult, finds himself are therefore more likely to be typical of the particular society under examination. Here, the specific combination of a general attitude towards paternal authority and the demands of a particular culture take shape: in Austria, these were mainly personal domination and dependence, with only a highly diffuse distribution of duties and rights. In England, in which marketization and individualization took hold early, the steering of the affective household was much more strongly connected among the educated classes with the utilitarian pursuit of self-interest, and also with the canon of the 'gentleman ethos', which meant group pressure in support of altruistic values – self-restraint of a gallant, chivalrous or Christian variety under the watchful eyes of one's 'peers'. English society thus necessarily allowed the individual more potential for later development and self-correction – and tied the individual far less tightly to the favour or disfavour of individuals of high rank.

In *Der arme Spielmann*, the ensuing catastrophe is sealed in a specific situation – an examination, which the unloved son must pass in front of his father and for his father:

> All went well until I missed a word in a verse of Horace which I had to recite. My master, all smiles to me and obsequiousness to my father, whispered the word to me. but I did not hear him as I was searching for the word in its context in my own brain. He repeated it several times, but it did not help me. At last my father lost patience. 'Cachinnum' (that was the word), he shouted at me. Now I knew I was lost. For the one word that I was told I had forgotten all the others, every effort to steer me back into a safe course was vain. I had to stand down, and when I went to kiss my father's hand as usual, he pushed me away, got up, bowed stiffly to the assembly, and went out. He called me 'ce gueux,' which I was not at that time, but am now. Parents often unconsciously predict their children's future. You understand, my father was really kind at heart, but quick-tempered and ambitious.
>
> After that day he never spoke to me again. He sent me his orders through some member of the household. (Grillparzer 1928: 19–20)

As the son of a high-ranking official, the examinee was treated significantly better by the teachers than by his own father. The exam was in fact a set-up intended to curry favour with the father. In the novella, Grillparzer transformed his own final school exam, which he had to sit as one of the five best pupils in his school, in the sense that it became, as often happens in nightmares and in contrast to reality, an examination in face of his father. As in the autobiography, here, too, the father is 'a good man' – the terrible, icy rejection of the child, the annihilation of his existence by rejecting all his expressions of love, the deep shame which can never be shaken off – these things affect a person unable to defend himself, who is condemned to love the one who has caused him such pain. These points constitute a key to understanding some of the problems that plagued Grillparzer throughout his life. '*Cachinnum*' [*cachinnus*]; loud laughter – this was the word which, in real life too, he failed to remember during his exam, but he says nothing about his father being there. Grillparzer did, however, write, in a quite distant tone, of his father's negative reaction to his artistic efforts:

> My own aesthetic creations came up against a formidable barrier in the shape of my father. He was, whenever I showed him one of my poems or such like, initially unable to conceal a certain joy, which, however, soon turned into increasingly severe criticism, always concluding with the stock phrase, 'You'll end up dead in the gutter'. (Grillparzer 1990: 122; trans. A.S.)

Threatening authority, even dressed up as good-naturedness, produces massive fear of shame in the dependent child. Norbert Elias, in his theory of civilizing processes (Elias 2000) and recently Thomas Scheff (Scheff/Retzinger 1991; Scheff 1993; Scheff 1994) in a series of contributions to the sociology of the emotions, have shown how central feelings of shame are to human self-steering and self-perception. For Elias, it is a characteristic of feelings of shame that they render the individual defenceless in the face of the demands of the stronger, higher-ranking party, because the subordinate, when he or she feels ashamed, recognizes these as demands which he or she makes of himself. This is, of course, a generally unconscious process. The person feeling shame acknowledges his or her subordinate status (Elias 2000: 414–15). The feelings are automatic in nature and render one defenceless. While attacks on one's person can otherwise be neutralized through flight or attack, situations of extreme embarrassment appear hopeless. As Goffman mentions in his analysis of embarrassment, the detachment of the 'actor' breaks down. After the voice cracks, one begins to blush and one's hands shake; one can often do nothing other than express a new, deeper emotional rhythm characteristic of fundamental human experiences, such as sobbing, holding one's head in one's hands: a kind of 'implosion of the self' may result (cf. Goffman 1967: 97–112). Elias saw the specific form of feelings of shame, their strength, frequency and linkage to social norms as the result and a component of so-called civilizing processes – enduring structural changes in society and personality. The eruption of affect and the 'expression of instinctual drives' could be steered by specific social constraints (and situations of constraint) such that individuals got used to restraining their 'affective' impulses apparently of their own volition and on pain of feelings of shame. Societies were able to evolve, for example, in which sexual needs were punished with tremendous fear of shame, such that highly ambivalent emotions made it impossible for the individual to meet his needs spontaneously. Similarly, social norms could develop that placed taboos on the settling of conflicts by means of physical violence: an automatic inhibition threshold was established that punished spontaneous surges of aggression, still in embryonic form, with feelings of fear and aversion. Here, Elias – drawing on a corresponding concept in Freud – posits a correspondence between the great parental power over the little, growing human being, a power that forces him to learn a socially required 'apparatus of self-constraint', in the context of which his embryonic human existence is largely at the mercy of others, with the great vertical distance between 'id' and 'super-ego' within the adolescent's personality and psyche. Outer hierarchy reflects inner hierarchy – the super-ego is above all punitive in its effects, as in the well-known image of the occupying troops of a hostile power in a captured stronghold. For Elias, the outer hierarchy includes the family but above all the state, that is, the developing monopoly of violence, and pacification from above and outside. In his self-steering, the individual is orientated primarily to those 'above' – those higher in rank in court society, the monarchical authority's expressions of intent, and the super-human parents, particularly the father. Yet Elias avoids lapsing into the reductionism of a vulgar psychoanalysis, instead reconstructing the institutional events (from the knightly to the royal court, the rise of the bourgeoisie) in great empirical detail. Fear of shame typical of the standards of shame and embarrassment at a certain level of social development are, at least for him, part and parcel of the typical social habitus of an era and can also influence the shape of a particular 'national habitus'. This helps to explain, for instance, the frequently observable fact that Germans and also Austrians seem far more inhibited when appearing in public than English people do – their body language as a whole betrays the far greater level of social fear in the face of a public that is also perceived as an authority.[8] Elias also views it as important to recognize that these standards come into being in a socially unplanned way, without individual people being aware of them. His theory of shame accentuates the vertical dimension, the aspect of power in social relations, in which shame is perceived above all as inferiority, much more than two other components of shame recently emphasized by Scheff and Retzinger (1991): feelings of shame are the counterpart of a sense of pride, and thus indicate – also at the horizontal level of social encounters between equals or in respect to the situation of the individual in the group – alienation, rejection or the (temporary or relatively enduring) absence of social bonds that are essential prerequisites for social cooperation. Shame feelings can thus be best understood as 'key emotions' that regulate an individual's relationship to the group and which form the foundation of his self-steering in that context. Elias thus conceives of shame above all in terms of psychological costs within social interaction, and as a weapon (often, of course, deployed without conscious awareness) wielded by those of higher rank against those lower down on the social ladder (those of equal rank treat each other, according to this model, as superiors), in the face of which one must 'restrain' oneself. For Scheff shame is an integral element of the human being's group nature. Scheff's theoretical limits vis-à-vis Elias involve a failure to take into account the historical development of standards of shame. They are also seen, perhaps, in a model of community in an overly 'positive' light. In one important respect, though, he has added something that is missing in Elias – the fact that 'shame' and 'disgrace' must be analyzed not only from the vantage-point of vertical relations between group members but also from that of horizontal relations. These feelings can arise not only as a consequence of the demonstration of power by the stronger, but also through rejection by those of equal status. One can thus, in fact, view shame as one of the key components of human emotional equipment. This is also true in the sense that these feelings are part of an older system of human self-steering, developmentally speaking, than 'reason' and 'conscience' which can be located in the neo-cortex.

If we now analyze the humiliating experience of the 'Poor Fiddler' using these concepts, assuming that Grillparzer's own experience was much the same, we can follow Elias and turn the spotlight on the typical features of the power divide between father and son among the burgeoning educated class, and the production of the massive fears that was bound up with it, closely entwined with a requirement of central importance to the educated member of the middle class, namely the acquisition and proof of an education essential to a professional career; the 'affective household' is geared towards 'learning', while 'stupidity' or 'laziness' become something particularly looked down upon, rather as 'cowardice' must have seemed in the knightly world. Elias also helps us to cast light on the precursors of the Central European-Habsburg variant of these power relations and the societal demand for qualifications that they involved; becoming a career official was the best way to advance socially for citizens in an aristocratic-feudal context, within the particular framework of a late but enduring and very strong bureaucratization, which reflected the Habsburgs difficult struggle to obtain absolute power – especially the monopoly of taxation. This framework was absent in England or at least differed greatly from that in Austria.

The necessity for adolescents to kiss their father's hand was a distinctive feature of Austrian relations of authority in Grillparzer's day.[9] The element of inferiority visible here (and collaboration in this inferiority) was a quite drastic aspect of the great power divide within the family and between generations. The traumatizing situation of the examination depicted by Grillparzer, however, also had other consequences. The social tie linking father and son was visibly cut. The child felt humiliated and experienced this condition as hopeless; it undermined his sense of self-worth in the long-term and led to isolation. According to Scheff, following humiliating or disgracing experiences, the participants may deal with each other in one of two possible ways: the first leads one out of the 'implosion of the self' with its typical verbal and non-verbal concomitants in language, facial expressions and gestures, to re-establishment of the interpersonal link, as the humiliated party's isolation by the other parties is overcome through re-integrating gestures, words and other signs that the affected party's value has been re-established (this occurs more easily if the type of shame involved is visible and consciously acknowledged, such that the humiliated party can himself take the appropriate steps, which are again (to use Goffman's phrase) 'ratified' by the other party). If the humiliated party is quite unaware of his shame, if he 'fails to admit' to it ('by-passed shame', as Helen B. Lewis puts it – Lewis found this type of shame to be a frequent concomitant of psychotherapeutic situations) it becomes difficult to re-establish the community in the usual way. 'By-passed shame' is almost impossible to repair and may form, if experienced early and persistently, a lifelong disposition: an enduring sense of inferiority, scarcely visible in verbal or non-verbal habitus, which is expressed in a given situation by, for example, rapid, superficial speech. This type of shame is viewed by Scheff and Retzinger as particularly destructive to the manner in which interactions proceed (between spouses for example) in case of repeated conflict – the normal course of a relationship. The normal repairing of the bond and reintegration have become impossible, and a shame–rage spiral can arise as a result of the isolation on both sides. Through the case of Hitler, who displayed both open and by-passed shame, Scheff has lent plausibility to this interpretation – 'humiliated fury' was Hitler's reaction to the incessant insults by his violent father, a feeling that matched that of the Germans after the First World War had been lost. Grillparzer's case was less extreme, yet it is striking how strongly the rest of his biography, his 'character', was imbued with tremendous feelings of shame. He felt constant doubts about his own talent, which shook him to the core, leading to extensive withdrawal from society (Grillparzer clearly established this connection in his funeral oration to Beethoven, by depicting Beethoven's 'difficulty' and seclusion not as an expression of lack of social involvement, but as a result of excessive sensitivity). And Grillparzer fled indeed from the society of tremendous relevance to him. He avoided high-ranking patrons as he did theatre productions of his own works; he also stayed away from Goethe, whom he greatly admired, failing to turn up when Goethe invited him. This shyness crops up again in his portrayal of the Austrian's character traits. The eulogy to service in *Der treuen Diener seines Herrn* and numerous comments on the German-Austrian relationship, in which a not very eloquent naturalness is contrasted with a rather pompous, fashionable German erudition, are in the same category.

The poor fiddler, in any event, never recovered from the savage insults meted out by his father, Hofrat and confidant of ministers. He would never amount to much now:

> I was industrious, but I worried too much. Doubtful punctuation, an illegible or omitted word in the original, even where it could easily be supplied, gave me hours of misery. Hesitating whether I was entitled to add of my own or ought to follow the original, I wasted my time in painful scruples, and was blamed for neglect when I was really taking

> my work much more seriously than my colleagues. For several years I worked without pay, for when I had been on the point of promotion, my father had given his vote at the board meeting to another. (Grillparzer 1928: 21)

He became a failure, an eternal ditherer, an indecisive bureaucratic ritualist, unable to exist without guidance from without and who felt a vague sense of fear if this was missing, a fear that bound him slavishly to the prescribed order. Even in his working life, his father represented an ill-intentioned authority – as if it was not enough that he found this authority within himself as a punitive, denying, prohibiting force. It was surely no accident that Grillparzer, despite all his Enlightenment-inspired criticism of lack of freedom and censorship repeatedly invoked order, respect and authority in his dramatic works, as well as persistence and wise procrastination, as Magris brings out in his analysis of *Ein Bruderzwist in Habsburg*. Grillparzer's turn towards the camp of authority, visible in 1848, and siding with those opposed to the revolution (which also mobilized him to oppose nationalist tendencies in Bohemia and Hungary) may be rooted in insight, but may just as well be linked to the motivational landscape of his psyche.

In any case, *Der arme Spielmann* provides an insight into the instruments of paternal-bourgeois authority, still anchored in the tradition of the 'house as a whole' and the dependency of children and servants on domestic authority. These instruments resulted in the total degradation of the son:

> While I was still in my father's house, where none of the inmates took any notice of me, I occupied a small back room which looked out upon a yard. At first I still had my meals with my family, but no one spoke to me. My mother had been dead many years. When my brothers had left the home and my father dined out constantly, he thought it inconvenient to keep meals going for me. The servants and I were put on board-wages, mine were not paid to me, but to a boarding house where I took my meals. I was therefore rarely in my room except at night, for my father expected me to be home punctually half an hour after the office closed. (Grillparzer 1928: 22)

To punish him, the son was placed on a more or less equal footing with the servants. The father's power was still extensive enough for him to tell his unloved offspring where and how he was to spend his free time – at home. This kind of control is a de facto incapacitation. It is again useful to take a look at Butler's story *The Way of All Flesh*, set in England at almost the same time: here, paternal power to control consisted – as long as the son attended school – in the capacity of Theobald Pontifex, father of Ernest, to send his son to a public school, where he enjoyed a certain influence through personal contacts from his student days. Discipline in this school was described as very harsh, and young Ernest suffered from this just as he did from the coldness of his Victorian, clerical parental home. In a sense, he also came to grief as a result of his father's demands, above all moral in nature. Pontifex senior steered his son's studies through skilful manipulation and by altering the boy's environment, and thus tried to determine his choice of career; he is to become a cleric. Yet in this story, the son is able to escape his father's clutches. He freed himself from the parental home, from the prescribed religiosity, abandoning his clerical career. London seemed to offer numerous opportunities to make an independent living. Along with a generous inheritance from his aunt, which rendered him independent of his father, these employment opportunities gave him the chance to find himself. As in Vienna at the time, in London, too, the influence of the family and its control over educational and career path was still very strong; in contrast to the 'Poor Fiddler', there existed a broad, anonymous market, which offered career opportunities and enhanced mobility. In England too, internal dependence on a repressive 'super-ego' stood in the way of outward emancipation; only when he had attained inner autonomy could Ernest Pontifex leave his clerical post and become a writer. Unlike in Austria, however, numerous models of citizenship were available which meant liberal-mindedness, individual initiative, and political pluralism – above all, there was a broad-based economic bourgeoisie. (The young Pontifex, it should be said, followed a baneful path in this regard and even involved himself in speculative business ventures.) Novella and novel show another interesting parallel: both 'heroes' were offered the chance early on to liberate themselves from the ruinous influence of their fathers, which could determine their fate, through inheritance. Both failed as a result of exploitation and betrayal by acquaintances. While Ernest, however, got a second chance and took it – and the story thus ended on a satisfying note – the 'poor fiddler' received no further chances of this kind and missed out on professional fulfilment a well as love.

He was unable to make use of the benefits of his background, although this certainly offered significant resources in a Viennese society still suffused with the influence of the Estates:

> 'I am his son,' I said timidly, as though I were telling a lie. I have seen many sudden changes in people, but never one so complete as came over this man's whole bearing. Having already opened his mouth for abuse, his jaw dropped, and while his eyes had not yet lost their fierce expression, a smile began to spread upwards. […] 'The Privy Councillor's son?' at last exclaimed the old man, of whose face the smile had now taken entire possession; 'please sir, be seated. Barbara, a chair.' The girl unwillingly moved a fraction on hers. 'Wait, you idle hussy, […]' he said, taking a basket off a chair and wiping it. 'It is a great honour for us. Your Honour the Councillor … I mean Your Honour the Councillor's son, are an amateur of music? (Grillparzer 1928: 33–4)

This excerpt entailed an encounter which featured an astonishing switch in relationships of rank – a still despised and reluctantly tolerated individual experienced a dramatic improvement in social standing. This miracle was triggered by mention of the title 'Hofrat'. Facial expressions, gestures and practical actions showed reverence to the visitor's high rank – all became expressions of servility. The daughter, of lowest status within this interaction, was demonstratively pushed around and humiliated. The father's status was automatically transferred to the son – as if an inherited title was involved. Dickens provides an example in *Great*

Expectations (written in 1860–61; Dickens 1985) that is in many ways similar. The young smithy's apprentice, Pip, suddenly gained financial means through an unknown benefactor, which allowed him to lead the life of a 'gentleman' with 'great expectations'. With both his uncle and at the tailor's, he experienced the same astounding transformation – here again we see examples of servility towards those of higher rank. At the tailor's, an apprentice was demonstratively humiliated. The key difference is the underpinning of high social rank: the gentleman as opposed to the official (or official's son).

The writer, Grillparzer, also had to become an official. In his *Selbstbiographie* he identifies precisely the circumstances (above all hindrances) that marked his dual professional career path – as writer and public servant. In both fields of action, patrimonial and modern features were combined. Both circles, moreover, constantly overlapped. Both as official and literary figure, he was dependent on the favours of high-ranking benefactors. In Austria, the formal rationality of the bureaucracy repeatedly clashed with the personal world of the feudal nobility. As a dramatist, he was only ever partially involved in what one might call a literary market – a small number of people accumulated a disproportionate amount of power in their hands, and on top of all this were the difficulties with the *Zensur*, the thought-policing element of the late-absolutist surveillance state, which, while certainly a system, nonetheless offered the emperor and individuals of high rank a good deal of space for patrimonial arbitrariness. Grillparzer depicted with precision the web of dependency in which he struggled. It made him unhappy, hindered his productivity and often brought him close to resigning. He no longer published in his later years. Major plays, such as *Bruderzwist* and *Libussa* ended up on the shelf. (*Weh dem, der lügt* [Woe Betide the Liar], which appeared in 1838, was the last play premièred during his lifetime.)

Grillparzer, who gave literary expression to the Austrian character, the essence of the Austrian soul, as no-one else has, can also be considered as the prototype of the so-called Austrian fate. Underestimated during his lifetime, a creative genius, but victim of much scheming and intrigue, officially honoured but with little material success, he shared the fate of innumerable composers, writers, scientists and inventors, who have come to see their own country as their greatest foe. This can be illuminated through an exploration of the social web in which this creative, highly gifted man was caught. Sociological reconstruction shows that it was not simply a matter of his being tightly bound by outer dependencies (on authority and authorities, which did not, of course, entirely succeed in thus binding him), but that these were effective only because they took hold simultaneously 'within' his character.

After his father's early death, Grillparzer was forced, as the eldest son, to work to maintain his family (mother and brother) – first as *Hofmeister* (a kind of teacher) in the family of a count, and then as an official. The patronage of a high-ranking nobleman helped secure him a position:

> At the same time, one of my uncles, through his business activities, had come into contact with the then executive vice-president of the Finanzhofkammer, Count Herberstein. Herberstein had known and respected my father; he asked about his family, learned of our situation and that the eldest son was working in the Court Library without pay. This practical man was taken aback. He found this last, given the lack of future prospects, irresponsible, and demanded to speak to me. (Grillparzer 1990: 155; trans. A.S.)

This introduces a motif which was as central to Grillparzer's later life as it is to Austrian social structure to this day: personal contacts and kinship ties facilitate recruitment in a system of formal bureaucracy which is, in fact, supposed to employ people according to the criteria of formal rationality – taking on anyone with specified qualifications, according to the availability of the positions involved. This was a system that was meant to proceed objectively and impersonally, but which instead privileged people with influential fathers or at least uncles (the upper echelons often, in fact almost always, consisted of men of noble origin), a system run in line with principles typical of pre-industrial, 'agro-literate' societies. 'Reciprocal exchange', favours on the basis of a hazy notion of give-and-take, preferences and aversions informed by friendship, mere acquaintance, recommendation and ties of kinship formed a complex system of 'patronage'. Rather than responding to legitimate, verifiable demands, high-ranking patrons conferred favours or 'mercy'. Grillparzer, as an official and (later a celebrated) writer was repeatedly forced to make use of such favours. Herberstein was one patron, later the finance minister Graf Stadion, who moved the perfect bureaucrat [*vollendeten Kameralisten*] Grillparzer from the Lower Austrian customs administration to an office, where he was to deal primarily with matters pertaining to theatre. Graf Wurmbrand, the empress's Lord High Chamberlain [*Obersthofmeister*], introduced him to courtly circles during a trip to Italy, yet all this patronage failed to prevent Grillparzer from being swindled out of promotion by rival authorities and individuals, promotion which he thought was his due given his length of service and qualifications: he fell 'victim to inter-authority friction'. This involved:

> At last, much later, a fourth person, who, when I entered into competition with the protégé of another statesman of far higher rank by applying for a position, had indicated that he was well-disposed towards me in writing and orally, confirmed, when asked his opinion of me officially, my usefulness and meritoriousness in the warmest terms, but added – in order to leave the way clear for the protégé of the powerful patron – that I was indispensable in my post as archival director of the Court Chamber. Indispensable as archival director of the Court Chamber? A third party may well have found that highly amusing. (Grillparzer 1990: 191; trans. A.S.)

For the influence of those well-disposed towards him (such as Baron Pillersdorf) was as a rule insufficient to protect Grillparzer from ill-intentioned or at least unsympathetic superiors; Grillparzer lost authority over certain areas. The 'impish and low character' of his boss who lacked all understanding of art got him a reputation for negligence. Some sponsorship from on high proved almost damaging, because those in lower positions managed to undermine it. Grillparzer came close to enjoying the favour of the Court (on which he was already significantly less dependent than Mozart had been two generations before him; cf. Elias 1993; close, because he himself ultimately refrained from taking advantage of it), because his cousin as secretary to the Empress was able to open up contacts to him. Yet this elevation (Grillparzer himself was erroneously treated as secretary to the Empress and enjoyed the protection and company of Count Wurmbrand during the Court trip to Italy) did not prevent him – having returned – from once again being passed over for promotion. During this phase of his life – his first theatrical successes had already materialized – the writer and official moved frequently in aristocratic circles, yet this forced him to struggle for creative autonomy, and inspired him to abstain from the Empress's favours:

> The Empress, one of the most excellent and most educated of women, was also known for the strictness of her religious convictions, whereas my own religiosity had little to do with the conventions of the Church. Any approach or obvious favour would have forced me to consider, in my future work, whether I was offending the views of high-ranking patrons. (Grillparzer 1990: 184; trans. A.S.)

This quotation lays bare how difficult it was for an artist to live with the web of personal dependencies. Caution and thoughtful consideration become second nature under such circumstances. The citizen, eager for authenticity and truth, clashed with the courtier. Grillparzer was caught in a net of never-ending gratitude and felt unfree. He was frequently the recipient of an act of mercy. This stifled aggressiveness and damaged self-worth, even if Grillparzer had been convinced of his objective value, his vocation, from an early stage. Until his retirement at 65 and conferment of the title *Hofrat*, he was passed over again and again – with precisely the same lack of transparency that marked favours from benefactors. He sums up:

> At the same time, the ceaseless slights, and that insolence of office through which wretched people all too eagerly asserted their authority against me, embittered my soul. (Grillparzer 1990: 201; trans. A.S.)

While Grillparzer thus became the most significant definer of the Austrian soul, his own soul developed in the fraught context of this patrimonial-bureaucratic system in precisely the way he described: procrastination, anxiety, caution rather than spontaneity, aggressiveness and sturdy self-belief. It appeared again and again in his dealings with this often beneficent, disarming authority, which made him – already appropriately primed by his relationship with his father – dependent and ashamed:

> I do not find it difficult to be cheerful, indeed even to joke around, under such circumstances, only it mustn't last too long or happen too often; when the situation has been enjoyed to the full, it loses its appeal. The essential condition, however, is that I am able to let myself go naturally and unhindered; should considerations arise that constrain this freedom of movement, the situation becomes intolerable. [...] If, however, those involved are good and benevolent, people, for example, whom I owe a debt of gratitude, I reach a state of exhaustion that differs from sleep only through the voluntary nature of the external movements. Because I am ashamed of this lack of mastery over my own moods, ashamed of myself rather than concerned with others' opinions, I get even more carried away, a mental gloom envelops me, and I am no longer truly aware of what I am doing or saying. (Grillparzer 1990: 210; trans. A.S.)

His struggle to achieve dignity and autonomy was moulded by two elements – the external matrix of power, which forced him to be grateful, and his own emotional matrix, in which contradictory emotions paralyzed one another, to the point that he was no longer truly his own master and was beset by 'spiritual gloom'. This is a hypothesis about his paralysis, but probably not a terribly daring one, if one takes into consideration how Grillparzer's childhood was shaped by his strict but 'good' father and the consequences of this for his feelings of self-worth. It seems likely that a Grillparzer free of fear of authority would also have had to reach a compromise with the constraints imposed by his higher-ranking surroundings. More than a few courtiers were compelled to wear masks, which they were then able cheerfully to shake off. Grillparzer's emotional heaviness, tinged with the desire to advance socially, and his melancholy resignation betray something different – the narrow confines of the social space of a member of the 'educated classes' and the great anxiety which he felt.

There is a good institutional reason why Grillparzer was so frequently dependent upon the personal favours of individuals. Theatre and writing were not yet merely market-based phenomena, open to the talented and yielding a good income, freeing one from obligations to anyone other than the anonymous public. Two institutional factors stood in the way: translocal monetary rewards for talent came to grief due to lack of copyright, which imposed no costs on copying; only in Vienna could one make money. Then there was censorship – the peculiar thought police of the late-absolutist surveillance state, born of the fear of revolutionary bourgeois emancipation. This was not merely restricted to the *Zensurhofstelle* in a narrow sense, but also informed the overall climate, underpinning a general public taboo on all non-conventional ways of thinking and feeling. Censorship could lead to the banning of even the most loyal of plays, not because they truly entailed offensive elements but because one could never be sure whether something might provoke offence.

All of this ultimately inspired Grillparzer to refrain from having his later work performed; he thus gave up the chance to see the characters of his imagination in flesh and blood – thus failing to truly bring them to life. He likewise did without fame, success and honour.

It has often been stated that censorship was ultimately unable to prevent the diffusion of critical, revolutionary, or at least Enlightenment texts. Not infrequently, it may have had the paradoxical effect of arousing interest in thought-provoking texts by the very act of banning them. Censorship was, no doubt, incapable of sparing the Habsburg Monarchy from Western European-style bourgeois political emancipation in the long term. It was, however, probably capable, as a component of a long tradition which included the Catholic Counter-Reformation, of warping the personality in a certain sense, of establishing taboos that hindered attempts to come to terms with present and past in a spiritual sense, taboos that probably still exist today, by creating a 'spirit of legitimacy'. Anyone offending this spirit was and is punished by a diffuse sense of fear, wrongness and inner turmoil.

Let us return to Grillparzer and censorship. Almost all his plays caused him problems. The harmless *Ahnfrau* [Ancestor], which would never have seen the light of day if it had not been for the advice and encouragement of the patron Schreyvogel, which indicates the limits of artistic autonomy, was banned before and after being performed. The basically loyal *König Ottokars Glück und Ende* was even pointlessly delayed by the censors for two years. *Ein treuer Diener seines Herrn* is said to have been bought, after its first performance, on the express wish of the Emperor with a one-off payment, thus banishing it from the world. And Grillparzer was particularly damaged by a poem which he wrote on the occasion of his stay in Rome at the 'Campo Vaccino' and which was interpreted as being anti-church. The censor (in the shape of his friend and patron Schreyvogel) had, in fact, approved this poem, but it met with the disapproval of the Bavarian crown prince and thus put Grillparzer in the Emperor's bad books as well as causing him to be summoned before the chief of police. Until 1848, Grillparzer was thus considered a 'semi-Jacobin'. The peculiarity of this system was its partly anonymous-bureaucratic, partly personal, small-group orientated character. As in the matter of his career as an official – promotion and transfer – he came into personal contact with some of the highest placed representatives of the state, such as Metternich, Gentz, Sedlnitzky, as well as archdukes. The performance of *Ottokar* was even made possible by the personal request of the Empress, causing the Emperor to intervene. The Empress herself saw 'nothing but good and praising' elements in the play. Much later, Grillparzer learned why it had been left on the shelf for so long. A friendly top official revealed the truth:

> 'When your "Ottokar" was left on the shelf for two years, you probably believed that an embittered enemy prevented its performance. Do you know who withheld it? I did, and I am not, God knows, your enemy.' '– But, Herr Hofrat' I retorted, 'what was it about the play that you thought dangerous?' – 'Nothing at all' he said, 'but I thought: you never can tell – !' (Grillparzer 1990: 218; trans. A.S.)

This quotation is interesting for two reasons: first, it is easily possible to meet the fateful, intervening 'opponent' in person (Austria seemed organized more like a compact club than a complex modern society; an impression one might also have of the multi-pillared, 'neo-corporatist' Austria of today); and second, the presence of fear and caution, which had taken on systemic form and which arose *independently* of individual actors. The bureaucratic ponderousness and slowness often attributed to Austria was also a result of this systematically built-in fear of overstepping the mark, a fear that initiative was more likely to be punished than rewarded. In this case, censorship ultimately failed to *prevent* performance of the play (although it is impossible to know how many other plays it strangled at birth), but it delayed, slowed down and blocked, eventually inspiring reaction such as: 'That there was, under such circumstances, no place for a writer in Austria at the time, became ever more apparent to me' (Grillparzer 1990: 218; trans. A.S.).

The person speaking here was not a resigned old man but someone bursting with creative energy. Again and again, his encounters with authority were marked not by their spitefulness or frightfulness, but by a friendly, beneficent attitude, as in his audience with Archduke Ludwig, the quasi-deputy of Emperor Ferdinand 'the Benignant' (whose mental deficiencies rendered him incapable of performing the normal duties of office). The archduke met Grillparzer kindly, quite out of keeping with the rumours about him, which portrayed him as taciturn and abrupt:

> I did not, however, obtain the position itself, which, despite this friendliness that raised my hopes, went instead to a mean clerk in the Court Library, who had served for about half as long as me and earned half as much, but who was recommended by one of his superiors, who himself would have required a recommendation in order to recommend someone else. This same director, incidentally, was one of my most enthusiastic friends and admirers. In general, a kind of idiocy prevailed in respect to myself, by dint of which people believed they had fully compensated me through praise and esteem. (Grillparzer 1990: 269; trans. A.S.)

It was thus not the case that Grillparzer achieved no recognition for his talents within Austrian society (that is, Viennese high society). Yet even this loyal servant of the Crown suffered a series of disappointments at the hands of well-wishers (quite apart from his bullying, ill-intentioned superiors and spiteful critics), which further paralysed and weakened him, plagued as he was by self-doubt, a sense of inferiority and indecisiveness. Nonetheless, Grillparzer never failed to carry out his duties as official, thinker and scholar stoically. Ample evidence testifies to his indecisiveness in the arena of love. He resembled the 'poor fiddler' in his lifelong bachelorhood. To what extent was Grillparzer's fate, his 'habitus' (mirrored in the figure of the 'poor fiddler') typical and representative of the contemporary Austrian character? He contrasted sharply with a much-loved stereotype that rose to world-wide popularity via the 'spirit of the operetta' and the films of the 1930s. This evoked the Austrian as an eternally cheerful, happy-go-lucky dancer of waltzes and breaker of hearts – a figure of male gender – or as a charmingly naive, buxom simpleton – so to speak, of female gender. The wine flows as the gentleman flutters his eyelashes disarmingly at his beloved, gently patting her hand, and urging: 'But my dear lady, let's not talk about me. Tell me about yourself.' (Hans Moser, playing an adorably cantankerous old official or porter, is a standard feature of these films.) There is nothing light-hearted about Grillparzer and the poor fiddler, though they did find themselves in environments marked by frivolity from time to time, among aristocrats or journeymen. Their habitus contrasted with that of bourgeois officials struggling for social advancement and recognition; nations, or societies in which the state is the key organizing principle, generate more than one form of 'habitus'. The interpretation presented here applies above all to those milieux or social fields rooted in the particular constellation created by the bureaucratic apparatus of the Austrian state: a strong feudal aristocracy, which fell under the dominion of the crown at a historically late juncture; a rising bourgeois society which, however, found its ascent hindered by feudal prerogatives and as yet lacked the strength to replace these with its own norms and interdictions; an angst-ridden central power which needed the citizen as much as it wished to avoid offending the aristocracy, the church, and later the nations, and which thus feared all changes other than the purely economic or technological; an authoritarian, patrimonial order that pervaded society as a whole, imbuing peasant and artisan families and the educated classes alike, an order marked by acute economic scarcity and the frequent deployment of brute force; and the recent experience of the Habsburg Monarchy's state system, which came close to witnessing the erasure of its very identity (Napoleonic rule temporarily downgraded Austria to the status of satellite state; it thus saw its existence threatened for a second time, Prussia providing its first taste of such treatment in 1740). It was neither expansion, procurement of great employment and thus life opportunities, nor the spirit of freedom based on ownership of property, that held sway in Austria. Financial collapse, over-taxation, the necessity for extreme frugality and an army and state apparatus of repression, in much need of replenishment as a result of Austria's reinstatement as a great power, constituted the distributive framework that determined the life chances of citizens. The bureaucratic sector was excessively large – the state, and thus the monarch, was for many the sole guarantee of income and life chances. As anxious and endangered as it was, it demanded far-reaching loyalty from its subjects – a loyalty that extended not only to the external world, but also to the citizen's inner psychological structures.

Many of this system's characteristics seem familiar to modern Austrians as well. An authoritarian, benevolent welfare state remains excessively strong in relation to the free market world of private commerce based on exchange and initiative. Many Austrians – in their schooling, as citizens directly or indirectly dependent on the state, associations and parties, as users of social services and as pensioners – remain embedded in a system of well-behaved subservience, which rewards loyalty with modest rewards. There is nothing mythical about the 'national habitus': as long as the environments which produce a particular character are themselves reproduced, this character itself remains identifiable and stable.

To summarize: Grillparzer has furnished us with a great deal of evidence testifying to the burgeoning within Austrian society of a behavioural model anchored in the bureaucratic bourgeoisie. While this does not provide a precise picture of officials' activities and relationships within their professional domain, it did include important information on the formation of corresponding models in the family and on the consequences of such formation for lifestyle in general. A code privileging duty predominated; material incentives, appeals to individual self-interest, taken for granted in a society determined by business and commerce, were rare indeed. Grillparzer also provided penetrating insights into the psychological costs of survival within a social environment of this kind. Passivity, resignation, shameful dependency were the possible consequences of bureaucratic relations of authority, particularly if they stand in the way of freedom of choice, and professional and political initiative, as a result of older, patrimonial dependencies. Compared with the Josephinist professional bureaucracy in its early days, a certain shift towards objectification and qualification had probably already taken hold; but 'pre-modern' forms of nepotism and patronage persisted. They ensured that Austrian bureaucratic domination retained a certain element of the arbitrary dispensation of favours. The repressive police state of the *Vormärz* era demonstrated a similar trait, and reinforced a mentality which has long survived it. We shall now probe more closely the inner world of the bureaucracy and the relations between superiors and inferiors. A second look at the world of the Austrian official, as found in Herzmanovsky-Orlando, will help us to do so.

The official through parody: Herzmanovsky-Orlando

The portrayal of the lot of the Austrian official in Herzmanovsky-Orlando, whom we have met twice already (in the analysis of Habsburg Catholicism and of the bureaucracy's courtly elements) is less bitter and sad than in the 'Poor Fiddler'.

The Austrian tendency to regard things as given only when they have been given the official seal of approval, is well illustrated in the following example. In a conversation between two individuals taking a stroll, a dancer is labelled the 'prince of gracefulness':

> 'Not justified in the least,' interjected Eynhuf, 'a) as far as I know he has not been granted official permission to use this sobriquet, and b) the man has flat feet that look like cymbals. ... If his brother weren't the Royal and Imperial Supreme Candle-Snuffer Cleaner, I assure you he would never be permitted a place in the Chamber Ballet. I'm sorry to have to topple him from his pedestal....' (Herzmanovsky-Orlando 1997: 2)

Herzmanovsky, of course, treated this trait ironically here and exaggerated it. Like Doderer (in his bureaucratic epic *Die erleuchteten Fenster*) he caricatured the bureaucratic habitus in an attempt to bring the unruly abundance of everyday reality into ordered, logical form, in the shape of legal language (a, b, ...) (cf. also Bodi 1995b). In contrast to England with its tradition of 'Common Law', in Austria 'legal' usually meant 'administratively legal'. Furthermore, this example did not only introduce a remarkably original title (*k.k. Oberhoflöschhornputzer*, translated here as 'Royal and Imperial Supreme Candle-Snuffer Cleaner'), but referred to the quasi-legal status of the all-embracing favouritism. 'Nepotism' and 'patronage' constituted a model that arises when older – family or other local – loyalties collide with more formal, bureaucratized procedures and mechanisms (which are extended to a larger area, for example through the process of state formation), which in turn necessitate new loyalties to people at a 'higher level'. From the viewpoint of the older, simpler system, nepotism was normal and socially approved; from the point of view of the newer, more complex system, it was illegitimate. From the reign of Maria Theresa and Joseph II onwards, Austria found itself an intriguing intermediate form of empire, which has persisted to some extent in the shape of the contemporary alpine successor state's Second Republic. Anyone who finds the title *Oberhoflöschhornputzer* strange, ought to peruse the titles of academic staff at modern Austrian universities. The need to differentiate titles and thus rank as much as possible always arises when something good (a post leading to a desirable position) has to be restricted and managed precisely because it is sought after. As Hirsch has shown in his theory of positional goods, a range of goods exists which loses value merely because it has proved impossible to deny them to others (cf. Hirsch 1976). Should it prove impossible to divert the clamour for such goods – such as status positions, whose value primarily depends upon their remaining scarce – into other channels, the good involved will undergo inflationary devaluation. New ranks and ranking categories are created, which provide a differentiating buffer, until this, too, is overwhelmed by the number of applicants. 'Austria' was and is a system that provides many examples of this practice: the first imperial councils, the advisory bodies which assisted Charles V and Ferdinand I, were soon so overfull with envoys that they became useless as decision-making bodies and had to be replaced by smaller, 'privy' councils. The Habsburg process of state formation involved the establishment of new bodies; the same fate soon befell these, too. 'Privy' court councils had to be differentiated from visible ones, 'real' court councils from titular ones, etc. Similarly inflationary is the Austrian approach to the title of 'Professor' – not only has it been applied even to secondary school teachers for many years, it is also an instrument available to the Austrian federal president to honour personalities from almost all realms of cultural life. Popular theatre and film actors thus end up adorned with this title – a state of affairs to which Ephraim Kishon (under the guidance of Friedrich Torberg) has devoted a brief, delightful satire (Kishon 1987: 129–32).

Officials have their own special god, the *hl. Ärarius, Blutzeuge und Märtyrer, erstickt in glühendem Streusand* (Herzmanovsky-Orlando 1995: 22; he invented here a saint of the exchequers, a martyr suffocated in glowing blotting-sand). In this cosmos it is entirely acceptable for one to use the opportunity provided by the 'suffering of Christ' to earn a bit of cash, thus linking the sacred with the profane (money), as has occurred in the major Catholic sites of pilgrimage since time immemorial (where, of course, the trade in *Devotionalien*, venerable objects of worship, flourishes). Austrian officials would, moreover, always be well-advised to make a bit of money on the side, since they cannot expect a generous wage, given the state's cash-strapped predicament. A fair number of this so-called *Extrabene* therefore end up being rather degrading: such as authorization to sell leftovers from the *Court table* (Herzmanovsky-Orlando 1995: 20).

Through an outpouring of names, Herzmanovsky characterizes the peculiarities of the Austrian administrative system. The following *single* high-ranking officials live, like Eynhuf, in the *Kleines Querulantenhaus* [literally: the little house of the grumblers]:

> For example, there was Privy Councillor Unklar von Dobblworth, the Court Calligraphist Futzler, the Senior Government Auditor Kreibenzahl, the Secretaries Zweifelschuetz and Muechtelmann, and finally the Captains of the Bodyguard for the Gentlemen-at-Arms Stojesbal von Standschlaf and Quapil Edler von Sumpfritt. (Herzmanovsky-Orlando 1997: 8)

These vivid names express some of the qualities of administrative culture that Karl Postl (Charles Sealsfield) has already compellingly highlighted – authority relationships generate lack of initiative, indecisiveness, opaqueness, ritualism and plain inactivity. These qualities are found in concentrated parodic form in the sad lot of a *Ahnenprobenexaminatorstellvertreters II. Klasse im K. Hofhengstendepot* (a title that refers to a second-in-command examiner second class in the royal stud who has to inquire about the ancestry of stallions), whose life is snuffed out while at work by an unexpected kick from a horse. This official, who has more or less nothing to do, is portrayed as zealous, meritorious and showing good promise [*zu den schönsten Hoffnungen berechtigend*]. Herzmanovsky uses the dynamic term 'hope' in an ironic way to characterize the snail's pace of the passive bureaucratic world. One can only guess at what this upright official's duties in fact involved. For inactivity is here linked with uprightness. This is also apparent when Herzmanovsky enumerates the despicable qualities of the *Bubenzopfmädel* – the sole contrast to the general picture of good behaviour. These free and easy girls commit one atrocious deed after another. They spit in the saucepan of a half-blind old woman and make unconventional use of rolling pins, riding around on them demonically. The ascetic Secretary Eynhuf, meanwhile, goes to bed early to build up his strength, the better to perform the duties of office:

> Eynhuf could never set foot in the Ministry without feelings of joyful pride tempered with appropriate awe and reverence. In the office of Privy Councillor Sauerpfister, his austere superior, there hung a beautiful painting consisting of many small figures: 'Pilgrimage of the Entire Hereditary Aristocracy to Maria-Taferl on the Danube'; it was Eynhuf's daily responsibility to dust off this picture since Sauerpfister did not trust such a delicate task to the custodial staff. (Herzmanovsky-Orlando 1997: 10)

Respect and pride characterized Eynhuf's complaisant acceptance of the relationship of authority. His superior, Sauerpfister, was strict but apparently fair; dusting the painting appeared to be Eynhuf's most important duty (the post was, as

Herzmanovsky tends to put it, largely *ressortlos* [without any describable function]). This duty consisted of a special act of loyalty, which those of lower rank were obviously incapable of carrying out (were they too sloppy? Did they fail to display the appropriately respectful bearing?).

> Carefully he removed all freshly-deposited flyspecks, particularly when these might be obscuring honorary medals or other insignia of distinction; he utilized only a spezial polish of moistened bread crumbs, the used portion of which he regularly saved and passed on to Secretary Wanzenhengst, Sauerpfister's second-in-command and a passionate siskin breeder, for the maintenance of the birds' mealworm sustenance. (Herzmanovsky-Orlando 1997: 10)

We are once again confronted with the frugality necessitated by the particular historical context – exemplified in this case by the re-use of *Semmelschmolle* [the soft, inner parts of rolls of bread]. It is also revealing that Eynhuf displayed reverence for his superior's private passion while at work. In this sense, his 'duties of office' were defined very liberally and broadmindedly.

> Eynhuf never gazed at the painting without a deep sense of respect and even a slight shudder, for he was well aware that anyone related to those discovered missing from that celebratory procession was henceforth barred from ever holding a ministerial position in Austria. (Herzmanovsky-Orlando 1997: 10)

Once the Catholic Counter-Reformation had been implemented successfully, the Habsburgs' main aim was to render their nobility malleable and Catholic. Maria Theresa herself, of course, drove out Protestants from the hereditary lands, and Herzmanovsky's image of the pilgrimage of the hereditary landed nobility stands on firm historical ground. It also points to a venerable Austrian instrument of power, which, over the course of centuries, made it comparatively easy to make the ruled conform – rendering loyalty visible. This was achieved by creating places in which all loyal subjects could be assembled in a clear arrangement (the 'Court' of course existed in all other absolutist societies; the Austrian variety, as F. Heer has brought out, came to involve pilgrimages and processions from an early stage – a 'confessional' element of Austrian Catholicism). Furthermore, this practical test of mentality was linked with the hereditary principle: the loyal nobility 'leased' government posts to be passed on to their grandsons and great-grandsons. Loyalty was more important than work performance.

> This loyalty reflected in Eynhuf's reaction to this news visibly mollified the severe Sauerpfister and caused him to forget why he had come. With measured strides he returned to the privacy of his sanctum and the third *petit déjeuner* of the morning. As he made his way through the outer office, the journal scribes Kuscher and Schluckentritt quickly resumed scrawling busily over paper: due to the fact that their department was assigned virtually no sphere of responsibility, they had been charged with the task of

> recopying all available documents in green ink with initial capital letters in black and gold. (Herzmanovsky-Orlando 1997: 12–13)

Sauerpfister's authority was *measured*, that is, he, too, had to go to considerable lengths to control his emotions. He had a *Sanctissimum* at his disposal, a space to which normal subordinates (let alone the general population) had difficulty in gaining access. As the names of the *Diurnisten* [clerks] in this roving department betray, they had at times to accept treatment of an even more brutal nature. The work itself was entirely ritualized and devoid of meaning; it recalled the extra work given to school pupils for bad behaviour rather than 'professional' work as understood within the bourgeois conception of employment. Officials often feigned zealousness as a result.

The English-style 'civil servant' is in many, though as we shall see not all, respects far removed from the Austrian official. The terms themselves clarify the difference: while the *Beamte* has received his post from 'above', the 'civil servant' has obligations to a 'civil society' and its norms.

The great difference between the Central European and British model, however, is that the English 'civil servant' is polite, friendly and liberal even when dealing with the broad mass of people (if very non-committal; he is a servant, but not the slave of the people, as George Mikes, the ex-Hungarian satirist, has shown through a clever comparison between England and the continent; Mikes 1986: 86–7). Austrian Baroque servility extended only to relations with those of higher rank. The more powerless the 'administered' party was, however, the cruder and more officious the lower officials tended to be.

A comparison with England: The 'civil servant' in Trollope

The looming presence of the official in Austrian society and the Austrian novel is matched by his insignificance in England and the English novel. This is not, of course, because the country produced no officials; as early as the Tudor period, England saw a bureaucratizing spurt, which was not, however, followed by further development on a Josephinist scale. The difference lies in the social position of officialdom, as one of the few novels to have made officials into heroes immediately lays bare.

A. Trollope's *The Three Clerks* in fact involves not only one official, but as is indicated by the title, three. This amusing tale of the changeable fate of three young public servants was first published in 1858 and obviously contains numerous autobiographical elements: young Charley Tudor was an easygoing, far from zealous official at the fictional 'Internal Navigation', a shipping authority of no great renown (Trollope changed this to 'Infernal Navigation' because the young men were to be seen far more often in rough taverns than at their posts; Hall 1992: X). Charley Tudor, like Trollope, became a writer. Trollope was himself also an official – and ultimately became head of the English postal service. The 'infernal navvies' were a wild bunch, the (real) department of 'Weights and Measures', where the other two protagonists worked, was more important and more respectable. Even the name of this department recalls Zihal's workplace; Grillparzer, too, was a writer and official. Yet when one compares the Austrian and English bureaucracy it is the differences that predominate and the commonalities that fade into the background.

Why? The frameworks themselves were different. The English official is not the pride of creation. He lacks the status that marked out his Habsburg counterpart as quite different from a run-of-the-mill (educated or business bourgeois) subject. If Elias attributes to top officials in Wilhelmine Germany between 1871 und 1918 greater prestige than wealthy businessmen, entrepreneurs and bankers (cf. Elias 1996: 57), this applies at least as much to the Habsburg Monarchy (cf. Bruckmüller/Stekl 1988, for a similar appraisal). In England things were different. No aura of sovereign secrecy surrounds the English 'civil servant', although he, too, is in the 'service of the Queen' and citizens are no less 'subjects of the Crown' than in Habsburg Austria. Instead, the English public has a very low opinion of officials and their work. Trollope devoted an entire chapter in journalistic style to such public criticism (Trollope 1992: 308–9). Under the title 'The Civil Service', he investigated the reasons for the low public esteem in which the official was held and for his many enemies. These range from landowners through businessmen to the newspapers, as the mouthpiece of the public. Officials were considered stupid, disrespectable, lazy and incompetent skivers.

The work of the official was considered mind-numbing, dull and mechanical (making written copies of documents was thought to take up most of their time). In this chapter – something of a departure from the framework of the story, it presents, so to speak, Trollope's overall view of the topic 'officials' – the author also explored the widespread patronage in England (posts served as sinecures for the younger sons of aristocrats) and officials' insufficient education in comparison with France, whose officials he considered excellent. Trollope located the causes of this multifaceted malaise in the lack of performance incentives (a poor salary, but also insufficient punishment for misdemeanours). This argument could surely also have been applied to Austrian officials. What Trollope views as the greatest failure of the English political system could not, however, have been said of Austrian politics, namely that officials were more or less barred from pursuing a political career. He thought this damaged politics, which thus missed a chance to benefit from professional expertise:

> But a Chancellor of the Exchequer must be a politician, and have a fixed line of politics. He must have a seat in parliament. He must go in and out with a certain party. He must therefore be a man of fortune, he must possess influence in the country, and on all these accounts cannot be selected from the office clerks. (Trollope 1992: 314)

This was certainly not the case in Austria, as we have shown in some detail. Trollope was of the opinion that the appeal and value of a career as an official would be decisively enhanced if an incumbent could see a seat in Parliament or in government at the end of the bureaucratic tunnel. To simplify somewhat, England was well governed but badly administered, while Austria was badly governed but well administered. Trollope, in any event, thought that the career of an official, which he ultimately viewed as 'the noblest employment of mankind' (Trollope 1992: 316), would greatly benefit from the expanded pool of energy and talent that less restrictive recruiting practices would bring about:

> It is so in no other country. In no other country is it now necessary that state power and private wealth should go hand in hand together. In Venice such usage existed, but Venice has fallen. (Trollope 1992: 316)

The book is devoid of any mention of a special, authoritative status within society to which an official might be entitled. One of the story's motif's, however, is the temptation for the official to make use of his position in a dishonourable way for purposes of personal financial enrichment (through speculation on the stock market; commercialization and corruption of the bureaucratic ethos also loom). The difference between a bright, gifted and a dull, mediocre, limited official is portrayed through the examples of Alaric Tudor, a man far from morally flawless, and the 'Zihalesque', uncompromising Neverbend. The first is flexible, shows initiative, makes up his own mind, is capable of writing a concise yet informative report; the latter ossifies in dull, stupid routine. Trollope's theme throughout is thus improving bureaucratic efficiency and not, as in Austria, selfless devotion to duty and godlike correctness. Yet English officials also have to work and fulfil their duties in a methodical manner: the official in 'Weights and Measures' has such duties, in humorous contrast to the 'infernal navvy', whose examinations are a farce and who is scarcely overtaxed by lounging around in the office for five hours:

> It behoves him that his life should be grave and his pursuits laborious, if he intends to live up to the tone of those around him. And as, sitting there at his early desk, his eyes already dim with figures, he sees a jaunty dandy saunter round the opposite corner to the Council Office at eleven o'clock, he cannot but yearn after the pleasures of idleness. (Trollope 1992: 2)

Yet Trollope's subsequent, ironic paragraph makes it clear that the great mass of officials not working in 'Weights and Measures' tended to regard its denizens as ambitious pedants unsuitable for emulation. Trollope's rendering of the recently introduced entrance examinations for public service, which oscillated between unworldly rigour (demanding knowledge of hydraulics, differential equations and other similarly forbidding topics) and farce (as exemplified, of course, by the infernal navvies) slots into the same framework.

In any case, we certainly do not come away from this 'novel of officialdom', written by a commentator with firsthand knowledge of the subject, with the overall sense of having been privy to the development of one of the key factors shaping

English society. One of the young officials, Henry Norman, leaves his post to accept an inheritance after the death of his father, a gentleman. Gentlemanly virtues remained significantly more important than those of the bureaucratic bourgeoisie; insofar as there was any demand for bourgeois character traits, history favoured those of the increasingly powerful business bourgeoisie. As mentioned above, officials in the crucially important colonial service retained a pre-bureaucratic, charismatic air. This means that both patrimonial and bureaucratic authority were absent in England, or were present to a far lesser degree than was typical in Austria until at least 1918. Patronage, nepotism and sponsorship displayed a less clear-cut pattern: the English ruling classes also failed to respect the absolute objectivity ('without regard for the person', selection based on qualification only) attributed by Max Weber to the ideal-typical bureaucracy. Trollope provided numerous examples of this. One difference between England and Austria, however, appears to be that the networks of kinship and acquaintance which had been and which remained important in England were not straightforwardly patrimonial in character. Above all, individuals had a number of options to choose from, options frequently unavailable to their counterparts in Austria. The Austrian state often determined the distribution of career and life chances monopolistically. Its role in shaping character was correspondingly greater than in England.

Notes

1 Doderer's writing style has sometimes been categorized as 'late realism' (cf. Weber 1963: 7), while this kind of humour has been designated as typically Austrian and 'self-mutilating' by Magris (Magris 1988: 186–7). Doderer's own theory of writing assumed 'two realities', the second of which was cleansed of concrete details, restricted to certain holistic principles of form, and highly conceptual in nature. Cf. Doderer 1959, for his theory of the novel, and the article by Magris 1976, in the volume resulting from the symposium marking Doderer's 80th birthday; cf. also Weber 1987 for a biography of Doderer. Both quotes from Doderer are based on an art of observing people, which does not attempt to reproduce specific situations and interactions but to grasp that which is typical of a series of situations and personalities.

2 The 'Parallel Campaign' is meant to celebrate the 70 years of rule of the Austrian Emperor Franz Joseph (expected to take place in 1918) in order to overshadow the simultaneously expected celebration of 30 years of rule of the German Kaiser.

3 The description of society can certainly be regarded as realistic, even if the grotesque distortion of place-names and personal names in the London edition and the errors of research rapidly pointed out by his biographers have to be taken into account (see R.F. Arnold and G. Winter in an edition combining both the German and the English version, Sealsfield 1972). It is hard to say which elements of Postl-Sealsfield's perceptions of Austria should be attributed to his youthful experiences and which to the detachment acquired by the traveller across America. One must certainly take into account his liberal political attitude, modelled on Western constitutionalism and English freedom, the French Revolution (he had very positive things to say about Napoleon) and the already perceptible American spirit, all of which he used as a yardstick to appraise Austrian

despotism – during a period in which Austria was still almost omnipotent within Germany. Sealsfield's text was frequently described as a 'pamphlet' by contemporaries and also by later critics – as a firebrand against absolutism and the arbitrary exercise of sovereign power. He leaves his readers in little doubt about where his sympathies lie.

4 When Christoph Mylius, a German travelling to England around 1753, experienced English customs officials, they were certainly both brutal and pedantic ('The inspectors now came on board and inspected us all in a barbaric fashion, feeling under our waistcoats and scarfs, our armpits, in our pockets and even in our trousers.' Mylius in: Maurer (ed.) 1992: 135; tans. A.S.), but there is no mention here, nor in any other part of his report, of courtly behavioural forms.

5 *Innerösterreich* means literally Inner Austria, that is the provinces of Styria, Carinthia, and Craniola (forming a duchy between 1564 and 1619), but it seems that Sealsfield used the term in the wider sense that embraces all German-speaking Austrians east of the Tyrol.

6 The Tyrolese – a venerable privilege – are allowed to use the informal version of 'you' (*du*) when addressing their Emperor, and Franz's response to their demands, presented by a delegation, while caustic in content, is plain in form. He also intervenes on behalf of a Lower Austrian wine grower (to whom he had granted an audience) instructing his own officials to take appropriate action (Sealsfield 1972: 91), though the bureaucratic machinery also limits the Emperor's room for manoeuvre to some extent.

7 The term *Biedermeier* has come to denote the pre-revolutionary period between 1815 and 1848.

8 For a comparison of the Swiss habitus with its southern German-Swabian counterpart, see Parin/Parin-Matthèy 1976, who links a certain Swiss linguistic awkwardness with family and early socialization.

9 The history of hand-kissing in Austria would be worth examining in more detail. The greeting 'Kiss your hand, Madam' [*Küß' die Hand, gnä Frau*] is more or less all that remains of this practice today, and this is almost entirely restricted to a small number of upper class Austrians. Actual kissing of the hand is rare indeed. This custom is very likely of courtly origin and was not limited to male gallantry towards women. Of particular interest is its development into a gallant ritual and its importance in Austria and Hungary – an indication of women's considerable power within courtly-aristocratic society, which then rubbed off on bourgeois salon culture. While *Grüß Gott* preserves the Catholic Counter-Reformation in an everyday greeting, 'Kiss your hand' is clearly a legacy of the Court.

Chapter 9

Puritanism, Book-Keeping and the Moralization of Authority in the English Habitus

Examples from the end of the era

In Samuel Butler's aforementioned largely autobiographical novel, *The Way of All Flesh*[1] (first published in 1903, but in fact written in the 1870s), the hero Ernest Pontifex suffers the bitter fate of being robbed of his entire fortune by a faithless friend and, as a result, even being sent to prison. Butler reflects on the importance of such economic disasters, comparing them with other types of woe:

> Granted, then, that the three most serious losses which a man can suffer are those affecting money, health and reputation. Loss of money is far the worst, then comes ill-health, and then loss of reputation; loss of reputation is a bad third, for, if a man keeps health and money unimpaired, it will be generally found that his loss of reputation is due to breaches of parvenu convention only, and not to violations of those older, better established canons whose authority is unquestionable. In this case a man may grow a new reputation as easily as a lobster grows a new claw, or, if he have health and money, may thrive in great peace of mind without any reputation at all. (Butler 1994: 239)

These sentences express perfectly the perception of social classes whose position primarily depends rather on private property and the market than on reputation. In contrast, to members of the old warrior caste, nothing seemed more important than honour. Butler explicitly places reputation third; for him (and the large number of others in Victorian England whose opinion he represents), loss of money hits people significantly harder than serious surgery, incurable illness or being hanged – even this fate was dealt with coolly and calmly by many. Suicide, meanwhile, was a common consequence of loss of money: this was not only in itself the most painful affliction, but also the cause of all the others.

Victorian England was indeed the most bourgeois of all nations, if this be judged by the importance of the business bourgeoisie. It did not, however, become so all of a sudden: one of the most striking features of English social history is the almost linear decline of the peasant population from the late 17th century. All other countries, including the United States, experienced this change far more suddenly, later and more dramatically. It is thus little wonder that the bourgeois affective household, more strikingly in Victorian England than anywhere else, revolved around securing a constant money income, and that behavioural models reflecting this stretch back far into the past. A cautious, calculating lifestyle is, naturally enough, central to Butler's novel:

> Midland stock at the end of August, 1850, when I sold out Miss Pontifex's debentures, stood at £ 32 per £ 100. I invested the whole of Ernest's £ 15.000 at this price, and did not change the investment till a few months before the time of which I have been writing lately – that is to say until September, 1861. I then sold at £ 129 per share and invested in London and North Western Ordinary stock, which I was advised was more likely to rise than Midlands now were. I bought the London and North Western stock at £ 93 per £ 100, and my godson now, in 1882, still holds it. (Butler 1994: 289)

The capital that Ernest's godfather has invested for him thus increases almost by a factor of five. Here, security comes solely from invested capital; the bourgeois living is not grounded economically on state social insurance or the official's pension. Christopher Lasch underlines that during this era the family represented 'a safe haven in a heartless world', and was strikingly different from its present-day counterpart, a mere appendage of private and state bureaucracies (cf. Lasch 1977; Lasch 1980). The economics of Victorian England – during the golden age of capitalism (Hobsbawm 1994) – thus also meant freedom from personal dependence on patrimonial authority or the contemporary form of state authority: dependence on the anonymous capital market of the stock exchange is something rather different. This relative freedom makes it possible for young Ernest to work as a writer. The economic framework, however, also forces people to adopt an economic mentality as a key principle as they go about their lives:

> I wished him to understand book-keeping by double entry. I had myself as a young man been compelled to master this not very difficult art; having acquired it, I have become enamoured of it, and consider it the most necessary branch of any young man's education after reading and writing. I was determined, therefore, that Ernest should master it, and proposed that he should become my steward, book-keeper, and the manager of my hoarding, ... (Butler 1994: 289)

Here we meet with a deep-rooted feature of the habitus of the English property-owning classes (book-keeping would have of course been superfluous for the *working poor*) which caused Continental European, including Austrian, commentators to attach to England the label of nation of traders or shopkeepers; a tendency which was of course reinforced by rivalry in major wars. 'Perfidious Albion'[2] was also claimed to exhibit a latent tendency towards puritanical hypocrisy; Egon Friedell, for example, in his *Kulturgeschichte der Neuzeit* [English edition: *A Cultural History of the Modern Age*, 1927–31], makes several references to English 'cant', as well as the genesis of English capitalism in piracy ('under the ultimate authority of the state, which took a share of the profits', Friedell 1976: vol. 1, 380) and 'robber barons'. He suggests that 'smuggling, piracy and the slave trade' were entwined with 'English and modern capitalism as a whole from the very beginning' (Friedell 1976: vol. 1, 380). For Friedell, and probably for many others in an Austria moulded by the peasantry, feudalism and guilds, 'almost all trade and money-making is nothing but swindle in civilized and ordered form' (Friedell 1976: vol. 1, 380). This statement contains an important insight, namely that civilization does not automatically lead to pleasant or desirable consequences; one could also mention that the outcomes of entirely legal, legitimate and peaceful inequality may be so brutal in nature that mere acts of physical violence pale in comparison – as demonstrated by the Irish famine and the destitution of English industrial workers in the heyday of the Industrial Revolution. Taking people's wealth from them in a peaceful fashion can, moreover, lead to mobilization of physical violence, such that some forms of civilizing almost unavoidably provoke direct regression into barbarism. On the other hand, Friedell, an Austrian Jew and admirer of Frederick II and Bismarck, also demonstrates a typical affective predicament – typical, that is, of identification with a habitus with little time for the spirit of calculability (Friedell also prefers the Christ-like God of love to the vengeful Old Testament variety) – which can ultimately be explained by reference to the quite different context of Austrian feudal and bureaucratic society. Friedell writes:

> What is cant? Cant is not 'lying', 'hypocrisy' or anything of that kind, but something far more complicated. Cant is a talent, namely the talent of believing that everything which brings one practical advantages is good and true. When the Englishman finds something unpleasant for some reason, he decides (in his unconscious of course), to declare it sinful or untrue. He thus has the peculiar ability to behave in a perfidious manner, not only towards others, but also towards himself, and he puts this ability into practice with a clear conscience, quite naturally, for he is acting instinctively. Cant is what you might call 'honest lying' or 'the gift of deceiving oneself'. (Friedell 1976: vol. 1, 377; transl. A. S.)

The high point of English cant, however, was reached among the Puritans in the post-Civil War period. Their twanging, cheek-turning bigotry, their slow walk and measured movements, their constant sniffing out of sin in every corner are anathema to Friedell. Like Max Weber, he sees a great deal of intolerance in the Puritanical attitude (Weber indeed wrote of the Calvinists' 'ethic of unbrotherliness' given their lack of sympathy with the poor and aversion to alms-giving). For Friedell, they are cruel, militant servants of Jehova rather than Christians.

The first half of the nineteenth century, as we have discussed in some detail, saw a tremendous growth of Puritan evangelicalism within British society. These are the values and emotional complexes found among the middle and lower classes, that K. Tidrick, in her study of *Empire and the English Character*, identifies as at least partly responsible for the emergence of the governmental ethos of 'indirect rule' over the diverse colonial peoples – alongside gentlemanly paternalism. For her, one of its well-springs was the evangelical cult of the personal role model as a form of legitimate authority. The contrast with Friedell is obvious. The key questions in her study are: what did Englishmen's ideal self-image as the ruling race look like within the context of colonial service? Elias speaks of the we-image and the we-ideal of the members of a national state society (cf. Elias 1996: 148–54). How was this ideal expressed practically? And finally: how did the leading English political figures in the colonies deal with the clash between the practical exigencies of colonial rule, which tended to require straightforward violence, and a wish to fuse this with their Christian conscience? The result was clearly a moral dilemma; the British stance on the issue was marked by ambivalence.

Tidrick sees a good example of what one might call the 'moralization of authority' vis-à-vis colonial peoples in Hugh Clifford, one of the most renowned colonial governors of his age. His service began in 1883 in the jungles of Malaysia and ended in 1929 following a psychological breakdown, which he experienced there during the summer of the previous year. Clifford was not only a practitioner of colonial administration, and a very knowledgeable one at that, but also a theoretician of such administration – he wrote numerous stories and even novels dealing with the encounter between the English and the natives. His depictions were considerably more empathetic and complex than those of big-game hunters and other adventurers, whose Social Darwinist theories of everyday life assumed the superiority of the White Man and felt no need to justify it. He was aware that raw violence had dangerous consequences:

> If the matter were left in the hands of the frontier-man, the expansion of the empire would proceed at a rate positively terrific, and England would have more little wars on her hands than she owns men to fight them. (Clifford, cited by Tidrick 1992: 98)

Crucially, Clifford was always convinced that English colonial rule must be grounded morally and that it must bring advantages to the ruled, that their life would become better, more decent and happier than without it. In his stories, this often resulted in him overstating the bloody and violent character of the indigenes – the unambiguous moral was that English rule was legitimate because it brought about peace. His depictions of native life, however, also express his great fascination with this 'wild', primal violence; and, despite omnipresent filth and base desires, which often inspired disgust and caused him to despise the natives, he showed enduring enthusiasm for the long history of their civilizations. Clifford did not hesitate to resolutely defend African farmers for their seemingly backward, but ecologically sound agriculture and to protect them against ignorant attacks. At the end of the day, Clifford himself demanded that colonial officials display good character and sharply criticized the French and Dutch for their cruelty and lack of empathy. While he was no fan of nationalist movements aimed at gaining a degree of political power, he went to great lengths to see things from the native point of view, identified with the ruled and produced a sophisticated concept of moral authority, which he felt must accompany the political and military might of the English. Elias ascribed this 'belief in their traditional egalitarian and humanistic code of norms – in the moral code which excluded and implied a fundamental identification with all human beings – ' (Elias 1996: 143) primarily to the non-aristocratic industrial or business-based middle classes. He analyzes the difference between this codex and that of the old European warrior classes, particularly by connecting it with the 'nationalization' of Europe, and draws attention to its influence on inter-state relations within the European system of states. For Elias, the old aristocratic values of honour and uninhibited pursuit of dynastic self-interest (the 18th century was indeed notorious for its innumerable *Kabinettskriege*, wars of the princely cabinets) were – in England more than Prussia – replaced by the new (one might say, though Elias avoids the term, 'Christian') code of conscience, though the continuing belief, now more nationalist in tenor, that it was right for the state to ruthlessly pursue its self-interest, limited the impact of the new middle-class canon. We can see here a similar conflict between differing moral standards, not in the domain of inter-state relations, but of interethnic and intercultural relations, between an 'imperialist' country and those under its rule. The middle-class code that Elias mentions clearly has Christian, Puritanical traits, though some of its representatives, such as Clifford, were of a Catholic background. Others, like the missionary brothers Henry and John Lawrence in Punjab, were deeply influenced by Evangelicalism (this did not however stop them, in 1857, from brutally quelling the Indian Mutiny).

The catalogue of Puritanical virtues was however as critical of authority, emphasizing the value of humility before all, as it was beneficial to economic activity. It formed the basis of the tritest utilitarianism and most patient pacifism. The fusion of both motifs and justification of their compatibility was certainly the element most likely to inspire charges of hypocrisy among Continental Europeans. England's Protestant nature – as L. Colley has convincingly shown – was in fact central to the English national self-image ('popery' almost always seemed the greatest enemy of English freedom) and was invoked repeatedly during crises: it bolstered English resistance to Napoleon, reinterpreted even disasters such as Dunkirk in 1940 as temporary setbacks within a 'Pilgrim's Progress' à la Bunyan, and helped Londoners survive the 'Blitz' in stoical fashion (cf. Colley 1992: 29).

These examples point to the central importance of three aspects of the relation between authority, money and Puritanism in particular. The first relates to the relative egalitarianism of the Puritans, which constituted a consistent alternative to the hierarchical character of the gentlemen's code and the class structure that defined it within English history. The Catholic Counter-Reformation in Austria is strikingly different – still perceptible to this day in aesthetic appreciation of architecture and painting: as proud as the Austrians may be of their rich Baroque world, overflowing with red and gold and dominated by *trompe l'oeil* ornamentation, the English find it repulsive, preferring its pastel tones and pointed-arch Gothicism (cf., e.g., Bassett 1988: 74, 86, for a downright spiteful expression of such disdain). Legalized regicide is not the only element that corresponds to this egalitarianism; so does the contractual, exchange-based, sober character of an already far more anonymous, marketized society, which contrasts with Austrian emphasis on social bonds and personal hierarchical dependence. The second facet of the Protestantism–Utilitarianism complex is the economic morality of pitilessness, which took concrete form during the golden age of economic liberalism in the institution of the workhouse. This morality also became part of the English habitus; but it faced more opposition than in the United States, moulded primarily by the middle-class section of the Anglo-Scottish settlers. The 19th century, thus, also bore witness to an English assault on this utilitarianism (Ruskin and Carlyle are the names most frequently mentioned in this regard), which ultimately led the English welfare state to display features quite similar to the patrimonial cameralism of Austria. The third aspect of the Puritanism–book-keeping complex is the moralization of political and economic power to which we have already referred, which frequently resulted in an unsatisfactory compromise. Yet it expressed a type of civilizing that tied the English we-ideal to adherence to certain moral principles (cf. Elias 1996: 324). Fervent patriot and melancholy obituarist of the Habsburg Monarchy, Joseph Roth, was left only with a commitment to the sublime person of the Emperor. We conclude the present study by bringing out this contrast.

Defoe's *Moll Flanders* and the anonymous authority of the market

Defoe's novel *Moll Flanders*, one of the first ever English 'novels', appeared in 1722, three years after the famous *Robinson Crusoe*. It is the story of a woman who, as a result of unfortunate circumstances and her own actions, becomes caught up in a life of vice, in which she becomes ever more deeply ensnared, practicing 'whoredom' and involving herself in professional thievery; she comes to regret her behaviour and ultimately achieves bourgeois prosperity and religious and moral purification. Beyond its somewhat ritual form, which has much to do with the author's puritanical self-understanding, the novel also provides information about a fascinating period of English social history. We find a society in which human relations are already very closely bound up with money (including, strikingly, sexual relations or those between the sexes). The world described here is breathtakingly 'modern' in some respects – characterized by a high degree of social mobility, a desire for social advancement, calculation and calculability. Yet we also find very 'traditional' elements of older agrarian societies – the streets are dangerous places, justice is barbaric (minor offences against property lead, if one is caught, to rapid execution on the gallows), and the gentleman carries his weapon at all times. Poverty can be a bitter business; many children (including Moll Flanders) are orphans, people often die young and suddenly; young children are given away to nurses, who take poor care of them, beat them and allow them to go hungry. 'Nature' (a nature insufficiently subject to social control) thus imposes numerous separations; human relationships often take a highly unpredictable course in comparison with modern day relationships. Hopes of a better life are wiped out by unexpected turns of events. All the caution in the world cannot prevent one from plunging back into poverty from the best of circumstances.

The social context is the city – more precisely, London at the end of the 17th century, which was very familiar to the journalist and chronicler Defoe, as was the life of its bourgeoisie. The social models of the aristocracy (Defoe also wrote a book on the *Compleat English Gentleman*) and of the business bourgeoisie (another of his works deals with the *English Tradesman*) both appear in his portrayals: Moll is constantly moving through a social space based on hopes of advancing – through marriage – into the milieu of the gentleman of leisure, but she mostly ends up with bourgeois professionals, who have to work to pay for her upkeep. At one point she attains a husband who, 'amphibious creature, this land-water thing called a gentleman' that he is, combines the qualities of a tradesman (a *linnen-draper*) with those of a gentleman (with sword) (Defoe 1989: 104).

Moll's astonishing geographical mobility, however, extends to large parts of England, Ireland and even the New World – she twice makes it to Virginia. She often moves around with the complete anonymity made possible by a public space that permits fleeting relationships. This movement is facilitated by as yet very crude administrative practices, which enable her to marry several times, in bigamy, change her name almost at will and thus conceal her background. A curious individualism becomes possible – with astonishing frequency, Moll is able, though also compelled, to make decisions that change her life; she is fundamentally 'alone in the world' (we shall later look at what this means in more detail), and time and again she acts on the basis of the most painstaking calculations, suppressing both more noble and less noble feelings. One pole of this world is an egotistical utilitarianism marked by the logic of commerce, another is made up of the remnants of a more generous, more spontaneous altruism (in the guise, on one occasion, of selfless love).

One can thus interpret *Moll Flanders* in a whole range of different ways. The development of the market and individualization lead to a very particular species of affect modulation. This includes the development of very specific – new – forms of self-steering. Special new forms of power relations form in the context of the market, which have far less to do with older forms of personal dependency. These relations – growing commercialization, anonymization and increasing mobility – go hand in hand with new emotional predicaments and types of 'inner' experience arising between traditional society and modernity, which also involve the 'price of civilization'.

Moll grows up an orphan; her mother gave birth to her in prison, and she was handed over to a 'Child-Taker' arranged by the authorities (the city) to bring her up. This institution frequently led to the death of children – cynical nurses pocketed the money and let the children starve. Such practices seem extremely barbaric nowadays. At three Moll was placed in the care of a 'nurse'; these children usually had to start working at the age of eight. By this point, Moll had already learnt to sew and *weave:* '...so as to be well able to provide for themselves by an honest industrious behaviour' (Defoe *1989: 44).* Moll was responsible for paying her own way from an early age: she works, in exchange for clothing and food, for her nurse, (who runs a small school and supervises the children's work, frequently striking them) from the age of eight. It is a hard, merciless world, which also forces Moll's foster mother to play by its rules: she too weeps frequently and is full of sympathy, but the context leaves little room for compassion. 'Charity' is certainly practiced by the young ladies, the daughters of the mayor, when, for example, Moll's foster mother dies and her daughter, laughing and merciless, consigns Moll to the street (Defoe 1989: 58–9). This happens to Moll at 14; at 10, she is already the right hand of the 'nurse' in the school and helps teach the other children; at 12 she earns enough to pay entirely for her own needs. Many people are thus responsible for themselves at an early age in this society – both success and failure are attributed to the individual. Fear of poverty (which Moll got to know early on) comes to imbue her behaviour throughout her life: she gets through five husbands, always for fear of being left unprovided for and of poverty, factors that drive her into 'matrimonial whoredom', which Defoe criticized in detail in another text. The market as institution later appears above all as 'marriage market', though men hold the better cards and only girls with money have a good prospect of landing a husband. Without a dowry, marriage is impossible. Defoe later has his heroine say:

> The Case was alter'd with me, I had Money in my Pocket, and had nothing to say to them [suitors]: I had been trick'd once by that Cheat call'd LOVE, but the Game was over; I was resolv'd now to be Married or Nothing, and to be well Married or not at all. (Defoe 1989: 103)

Moll, though, first acquires this cool, instrumentally calculating approach after she – at a very young age – falls victim to romantic love. After this initial fall, however (she loses her virginity to a gentleman with no intention of marrying her), she becomes cautious – she steers clear of passionate love (with one exception, when she meets her later Lancashire husband – he is also a perfect gentleman, whom she forgives for betraying and robbing her). Moll learns and uses a specific form of instrumental rationality which, while made all but impossible by the profound backwardness of economy, transport (security here was particularly poor: her journeys to Virginia are dangerous to life, limb and worldly goods), technology and medicine, can be deployed whenever situations of psychological or social malleability arise: Defoe's heroine develops a keen eye for her own advantage, instrumentalizes others, manipulates them through subtle manoeuvres, and also steers her own feelings, needs and interests such that these do not stand in the way of her getting what she wants.

Defoe's Moll is a utility-maximizing, female Robinson Crusoe, not on a desert island, but in the middle of social relations, which degrade sexual love to a kind of 'prostitution'. (Defoe's concept of *whoredom*[3] should be understood metaphorically rather than literally.) But it is not only sexual love, but also feelings of friendship, a willingness to help others, and generous altruism that are affected by the chaotic competitive individualism of early bourgeois society. Our analysis of *Moll Flanders* now attempts to explain the individual calculations, experiences and feelings dependent on the social constraints of this specific context.

Moll soon finds out about the circumstances under which she must present herself: '*On the other Hand, as the Market ran very unhappily on the Mens side, I found the Women had lost the Privilege of saying No...*' (Defoe 1989: 112).

Defoe's excellent knowledge of market logic (he himself was a businessman for a time and was moreover a precise and knowledgeable chronicler of English business) is here ascribed to the heroine. When she becomes intimate with her first lover, who does not become her husband, she takes steps to protect herself from financial risk:

> It is true, and I have confess'd it before, that from the first hour I began to converse with him, I resolv'd to let him lye with me if he offer'd it; but it was because I wanted his help and assistance, and I knew no other way of securing him than that: But when we were that Night together, and, as I have said, had gone such a length, I found my Weakness, the Inclination was not to be resisted, but I was oblig'd to yield up all even before he ask'd it. (Defoe 1989: 172)

The ease with which Moll can be bribed, however, is fundamentally linked to her fear of poverty and hunger: here, Defoe portrays with great precision the situation of a person who considers all parameters in advance, but is nonetheless overwhelmed by the momentum of a particular event. Rational planning meets the spontaneity of the need for tenderness and devotion – her 'weakness' and 'affection' prove stronger than the self-control of calculation. She repeatedly emphasizes that she is alone in the world. Every manoeuvre she makes to land a man, and her later moral descent into thievery, is a consequence of this fear of decline and 'poverty'. Defoe probably knew Moll King, a notorious thief, from visits to Newgate prison; 'Moll Cut-Purse', a character well-known from the theatre of the early 17th century, is likely to have been a literary inspiration; the reputation of Flemish prostitutes ('Flanders') had, moreover, persisted in London for several centuries. 'Poverty' itself is however not clearly defined in the book. Her first and second marriage render her (the latter to a 'linnen-draper') prosperous; she travels in a liveried coach and only stays in guesthouses; she herself later employs two serving girls – even for the Puritan Defoe (cf. Watt 1982) a gentlemanly lifestyle is seen as legitimate.

Again and again Moll emerges as meticulous chronicler of her own financial situation, each time she begins a new relationship, or, as a result of despicable circumstance, is catapulted from a protective bond into unwelcome solitude:

> Including this Recruit, and before I got the last 50 £. I found my strength to amount, put all together, to about 400 £. so that with that I had above 450 £. I had sav'd above 100 £. more, but I met with a Disaster with that, which was this; that a Goldsmith in whose

> Hands I had trusted it, broke, so I lost 70 £. of my Money, the Man's Composition not making above 30 £. out of his 100 £. I had a little Plate, but not much, and was well enough stock'd with Cloaths and Linnen. (Defoe 1989: 180)

Whatever vicissitudes befall her – death and financially ruined husbands, having to bid farewell to her children (she always has a few more, most of them die, others she leaves behind without much of a guilty conscience whenever she finds something new to focus on) – only Moll's calculating behaviour remains stable. Many of the situations found in Defoe's biography and in that of his heroine seem extremely adventurous: Defoe, as a Dissenter, had to flee for a time following the failed rebellion led by the Duke of Monmouth, and he was later a supporter of William III of Orange, a secret agent and had several stints in jail because of his satires and political enemies; he also suffered several bankruptcies. Moll lives incestuously with her brother for a time, risks her life on dangerous sea voyages and becomes a wanted thief and 'whore'. Yet her life is nonetheless characterized by her calm maintenance of equilibrium:

> When I came he made several Proposals for my placing my Money in the Bank, in order to my having Interest for it; but still some difficulty or other came in the way, which he objected as not safe; and I found such a sincere disinterested Honesty in him, that I began to muse with my self, that I had certainly found the honest Man I wanted; and that I could never put my self into better Hands; so I told him with a great deal of frankness that I had never met with Man or Woman yet that I could trust, or in whom I cou'd think my self safe, but that I saw he was so disinterestedly concern'd for my safety that I said I would freely trust him with the management of that little I had, if he would accept to be Steward for a poor Widow that could give him no Salary. (Defoe 1989: 187–8)

Moll thus gets to know husband number five (now a bigamist or polyandrist), and the economic principle is ranked, with the utmost clarity, alongside love and marriage. 'Trust' and 'security' are sought-after goods in a thoroughly anomic society. She was previously betrayed by husband number four, while she herself had been intending to betray him; her fear of being cheated is certainly justified. In the case of her third husband, cunning and betrayal again come into play – on Moll's side – and her search for him is preceded by precise market analysis:

> ...and I found nothing present, except two or three Boatswains, or such Fellows, but as for the Commanders they were generally of two Sorts. 1. Such as having good Business, that is to say, a good Ship, resolv'd not to Marry but with Advantage, that is, with a good Fortune. 2. Such as being out of Employ, wanted a Wife to help them to a Ship, I mean. (1). A Wife, who having some Money could enable them to hold, as they call it, a good part of a Ship themselves, so to encourage Owners to come in; Or. (2). A Wife who if she had not Money, had Friends who were concern'd in Shipping, and so could help to put the young Man into a good Ship, which to them is as good as a Portion, and neither of these was my Case; so I look'd like one that was to lye on Hand. (Defoe 1989: 111)

Defoe is here describing the male demand curve on the English marriage market (at least in the country; in London things were rather different). The female supply curve is shaped by the following components:

> That as my Sister in Law at Colchester had said, Beauty, Wit, Manners, Sence, good Humour, good Behaviour, Education, Virtue, Piety, or any other Qualification, whether of Body or Mind, had no power to recommend: That Money only made a Woman agreeable: That Men chose Mistresses indeed by the gust of their Affection, and it was requisite to a Whore to be Handsome, well shap'd, have a good Mien, and a graceful Behaviour; but that for a Wife, no Deformity would shock the Fancy, no ill Qualities, the Judgment; the Money was the thing; the Portion was neither crooked or Monstrous, but the Money was always agreeable, whatever the Wife was. (Defoe 1989: 112)

This listing of qualifications (which also represent power resources in an unequal exchange) is exhaustive, a rational market analysis, as precise as any in the world of business. Moll sets up, with the help of her newly acquired friend, a deceitful manoeuvre, feigning her way around her negligible financial resources (rumours of her supposed wealth begin to spread) – just as a deceitful businessman would do.

Moll sets to work with yet greater cunning when she is forced, after the wedding, to gradually admit the bitter truth to her husband. In a step-by-step process, she brings him to regard what little she in fact has as sufficient and to consider her particularly honest and generous. In almost all Moll's sexual relationships, calculation, self-interest, contractuality, and efforts to inform oneself precisely of the financial circumstances of the prospective partner play a central role. Businesslike rationality also holds sway when things go wrong – as in the case of unwelcome pregnancy. Here, Defoe describes a special, ingenious institution – the 'Midwife' business, whose practitioners offer single women board and lodgings during the final three months of pregnancy, look after them during the birth and organize the christening (their service includes dealing with the problems that an unmarried mother new to the area tends to suffer at the hands of the parish authorities). A quote from a 'Midwife', who earns her money mainly by looking after pregnant prostitutes, includes a precise itemization of the three levels of service she provides: luxury, quality and (minimal) standard (Defoe 1989: 223–4).

Alongside calculability, early modern England featured a complex social field of action, a high degree of mobility of people and capital, anonymity and privacy. Not one of Moll's marriages is 'arranged' by relatives or the authorities; she herself is always master of her decisions and has great freedom of choice, limited only by the laws of the market (above all the marriage market). In most of the settings in which she seeks to make her fortune, she is a stranger without acquaintances or friends. Her ability to travel around England[4] so freely and uninhibitedly is astonishing; this mobility – particularly for women, if Defoe's descriptions here can be believed – is in any event very unusual in so-called traditional societies, in a word, something modern. In line with this, Moll is able to leave others with comparative ease – even, repeatedly, her own children: 'My two children were indeed taken happily off of my Hands by my Husband's Father and Mother, and that by the way was all they got by Mrs. Betty' (Defoe 1989: 102).

Mrs Betty is her name from her serving girl days – when she married the younger brother of her first seducer, she did not yet call herself 'Moll Flanders'. Ian Watt does not view these carefree, calmly accepted farewells from her own children, which she was to experience again and again, as an indicator of Moll's heartlessness, but as an element of Defoe's narrative technique: he quickly dropped certain characters in order to progress from episode to episode (Watt 1982: 163). Even if this is correct, one could not so easily fob off a modern public: accusations of heartlessness would be so overwhelming that no storyteller could afford to ignore them. It seems likely that it is not Moll's individual cruelty that emerges from this and other parts of the text, but the callousness of the society in which she lived, where children counted for far less than in the subsequent, emotionalized, romanticized world of bourgeois pedagogy and family.

The relationship between lack of social ties, privacy, anonymity and the older 'pre-modern' relational forms of hospitality and charity is particularly interesting. As F. Heal has demonstrated in her detailed examination (Heal 1990), the capacity for aristocratic households to run a boundlessly open, hospitable house had become much reduced even in early modern England. A 'gentleman' defined himself (and *Moll Flanders* includes many good examples of this) mainly through his manners, which had to be 'civil', through his right to idleness (he disdained bourgeois employment), his pride and his core of gallantry, but no longer through a great house. 'Hospitality' and 'charity' had already been rent asunder – while in the Middle Ages the poor were often able to sit at table, they were later dealt with at the gate or at the back door and later still were handed over to institutions, which were financed by the wealthy, who were no longer directly confronted with the poor. Marketization not only involved a culture of heartlessness (about which both Marx, in Chapter 24 of the first volume of *Capital* (Marx 1972) and Weber – with the concept of 'unbrotherliness' – in the *Protestant Ethic* have written), but 'charity' was placed on a more objective, almost 'businesslike' basis.

There are many examples of the relationship between 'self-interest', 'privacy', 'hospitality' and 'charity' in *Moll Flanders*. It is the sympathy shown by the socially superior neighbours (the mayor's family), which provides the young Moll with membership of a family and an upbringing aimed at the production of a 'gentlewoman' (including dancing, French, writing and music); on the other hand, the daughter of Moll's nurse simply turns her out onto the street on the basis of economic calculation. She never becomes a full member of the family and later, following her first husband's early death, she has no right to their support. Macfarlane views this individualization as a key feature of the English family (Macfarlane 1978) from the very beginning, in contrast to the Polish peasant family which ideally featured joint property. When Moll travels, she does not usually appeal to someone's hospitality, but visits inns and rents rooms from strangers. These are, however, often quite flexible with regard to payment, allow her to stay for a while free of charge, and make friends with her, as did her landlady in Bath, who, as a stranger, becomes a confidante and even helps her obtain a lover:

> [H]owever she used to tell me that she thought I ought to expect some Gratification from him for my Company, ... she told me she would take that part upon her, and she did so, and manag'd it so dextrously, that the first time we were together alone, after she had talk'd with him, he began to enquire a little into my Circumstances, as how I had subsisted my self since I came on shore? and whether I did not want Money? (Defoe 1989: 160)

This help is not, however, entirely altruistic: the money enables Moll to pay the rent. Her privacy, and her withdrawal from society, is again apparent in the following quotation:

> [I] kept no Company but in the Family where I Lodg'd, and with a Clergyman's Lady at next Door; so that when he was absent I visited no Body, nor did he ever find me out of my Chamber or Parlor whenever he came down; if I went any where to take the Air it was always with him. (Defoe 1989: 171)

Although she already bears the 'unmusical, harsh-sounding title of whore' at this point in time (the initiation of sexual relations marks the switch from 'friend' to 'whore'), Moll is practically living the ideal of bourgeois privacy.

Defoe is not describing a world devoid of all compassion. Even her accomplice, the woman who instigated the theft, visits her in Newgate prison and supports her for reasons other than mere calculation. And despite the book's heavy load of utilitarianism, Moll also listens to the voice of love, of uncalculated generosity, when she gets to know her husband in Lancashire and then finds him again, old and ruined, in prison. The business-savvy 'Midwife', on the other hand, expresses utter heartlessness towards children when she informs Moll that her prices are lower in cases of still-birth: '...then there is the Minister's Article saved' (Defoe 1989: 225). Moll, torn between self-interest and motherly love, is later gripped by intense inner conflict: she gives her child up for adoption, although she knows about the harsh practices of the nurses; she separates from her child in tears but quickly silences the voice of conscience. This process, in which self-deception also plays a certain role, takes place in stages. Moll, surprisingly, even expresses an awareness, redolent of modern developmental psychology, of the dangers of a loveless childhood; this too she suppresses in order to save the little money she has left. This moral 'degeneracy' is depicted by Defoe with great realism[5] and subtlety – sociologists rarely devote such careful attention to the actual, 'subjective' meaning of social norms and market relations.

Defoe is describing here a stage in the development of business bourgeois conceptions of rationality with a specific, national cultural (English) tenor. In Elias' terms, this involves a particular variant of the 'compulsion to develop foresight and self-constraint' (Elias 2000: 379–81). This is of course a type of foresight different in some respects from courtly rationality, the central theme of *The Court Society* (Elias 1983) and *The Civilizing Process*. The civilizing of the worldly upper classes of the West led to the refinement, pacification and increasing restraint of emotional and bodily expression in a face-to-face society in which the maintenance of prestige was paramount; absolutism, Court and aristocratic palaces constitute the key settings of this society. Part of this process also influenced the modulation of the 'affective household' (Elias's version of Freud's 'economy of drives') of bourgeois modernity insofar as it constitutes a historical background relevant to bourgeois models. But as Elias himself has already clearly stated, the world of the professional bourgeoisie differed significantly from its aristocratic, courtly counterpart – manners are of less importance, since the social survival of the individual is far less dependent on his position within the matrix of prestige. The constant work of self-constraint and self-control helps construct a socially acceptable self, which must assert itself within a world of bourgeois competition typified by career, money and goods. Many of the social relations on which the individual depends are anonymous in nature – or numerous contacts arise with strangers who only become enduring acquaintances as the relationship proceeds. The modulation of affect tends above all towards greater restriction of sexual behaviour and frugality (in contrast to courtly extravagance), that is, the core patterns involved with career and money-making or which contribute to these imperatives. Some fears, which evolve into self-constraints, are significantly stronger than among the nobility; the resulting 'apparatus of self-constraint' also often appears – above all in the early stage of bourgeois advance, when the bourgeois as yet displays no behavioural standards of his own with pride and self-confidence – less uniform and crude in comparison to the code of the aristocrats.

Moll Flanders contains an abundance of examples showing all the elements involved in this new type of affect modulation. In contrast to the concretized concepts of economic rationality, it is apparent how inseparably the realms of feelings, bodily expression and cognition ('reason') are bound up with one another, and that this new type of 'foresight' can only be explained by reference to the social field in which it occurs (in Elias's terms: the 'figuration').

It is apparent that Moll's reason, her cognition, is bound up with strong emotions; it is in fact a result of such emotions. Above all, this means fear: fear of destitution and poverty forms one of her strongest motivations. This is the key reason for her calculating approach. Another type of fear accompanies the constant suspicion of being taken advantage of by others, which also forces her into solitude. Defoe himself was harassed almost half his life – as a consequence of his economic misfortunes (repeated bankruptcy) and political persecution; we can assume that he knew what he was writing about. Rationality is also present in the midwife's cynical, businesslike heartlessness, specifying her charges for a still-birth. The scene with the banking advisor, meanwhile, shows how important a sense of trust is for Moll when she involves herself in 'business'. Nowhere do we see boundless utilitarianism – Defoe shows with great realism that even the best intentions count for nothing when the spontaneous violence of emotions comes into play (Moll concedes more to her lover than she had intended). Alongside crude avarice, we frequently find sympathy and spontaneous altruism. These emotions are joined by several forms of bodily expression of affect. Frequent slaps mark children's experience of school, while people many times break down in tears, especially in prison, where Moll falls apart in the face of her punishment and experiences purification. This represents a ritual element of religiously motivated literature: conversion forms a high point and turning point in the narrative. She has to cope with numerous experiences of separation – the increased mobility of market society repeatedly leads to solitude. Moll's cynicism and distrust, reinforced by numerous setbacks and terrible loneliness, are hard to separate from Robinson Crusoe's economic rationality. Ian Watt quotes a passage from *Robinson Crusoe* in which he sighs deeply and expresses a sentiment probably stemming from the depths of Defoe's heart:

> [I]t seems to me that life in general is, or ought to be, but one universal act of solitude. Everything revolves in our minds by innumerable circular motions, all centering in ourselves....we love, we hate, we covet, we enjoy, all in privacy and solitude. (Defoe, cited by Watt 1982: 158)

Dickens's *Oliver Twist* and the morality of pitilessness

More than one hundred years after Defoe's *Moll Flanders*, English society had indeed changed economically and socio-culturally in many ways. Dickens' *Oliver Twist*, however, which attained the status of classic children's book and was first published under a pseudonym in 1837, shows astonishing continuities in the mentality and emotional structure of significant sections of this English society. It was not only *the* book, which helped more than any other to change the utilitarian, merciless attitude towards poverty and childhood; the famous opening chapters paint a gloomy picture of human avarice and heartlessness, which strongly recalls the darkest pages of *Moll Flanders*.

The authorities place the orphan Oliver, still an infant, in the care of a woman whose 'system' ends in the death of eight out of ten children; they either fall ill through lack of food or warmth or fall in the fire or meet with some other fatal misfortune as a result of negligence:

> Sevenpence – halfpenny's worth per week is a good round diet for a child; a great deal may be got for sevenpence – halfpenny: quite enough to overload its stomach, and make it uncomfortable. The elderly female was a woman of wisdom and experience; she knew what was good for children: and she had a very accurate perception of what was good for herself. (Dickens 1992: 5–6)

Defoe has already furnished us with plentiful examples of the ruthless pursuit of one's own advantage, coupled with strategic or thoughtless heartlessness. The advance of urbanization, industrialization and uncontrolled population growth led to the collapse of the old Poor Law; the 'New Poor Law' was implemented and civilizational standards, to the best of our knowledge, fell far behind those of the 18th century (on the introduction of the 'New Poor Law' see Taylor 1988: 238–52; on life expectancy around 1839–40: Taylor 1988: 307). In Dickens, the elected guardian who sets Oliver to pick oakum at the age of nine in the workhouse is also under the sway of a 'philosophically' elevated form of pitilessness:

> 'Boy,' said the gentleman in the high chair, 'listen to me. You know you're an orphan, I suppose?'
> 'What's that, sir?' inquired poor Oliver.
> 'The boy is a fool – I thought he was,' said the gentleman in the white waistcoat. (Dickens 1992: 10)

Dickens sums up the view of the elected 'Board of Guardians' who, according to the New Poor Law, are to control the workhouses and administer the law:

> The member of the board were very sage, deep, philosophical men; and when they came to turn their attention to the workhouse, they found out at once what ordinary folks would never have discovered – the poor people liked it! It was a regular place of public entertainment for the poorer classes; a tavern where there was nothing to pay; a public breakfast, dinner, tea, and supper all the year round; a brick and mortar elysium, where it was all play and no work. 'Oho!' said the board, looking very knowing, 'we are the fellows to set this to rights; we'll stop it all, in no time.' (Dickens 1992: 11)

Dickens here provides a concise summary of the discussion that led to an intensified work ethic for all and made the workhouse so unattractive that economic freedom of choice meant little more than gradual or rapid starvation. Christian prayers and thin gruel, families torn apart against their will, forced labour in a prison-like environment were the reality of this unique institution, in which all kinds of poor people were thrown together – the insane, children, the old, and invalids made up the dregs of English society administered in this particular way. Keeping costs down was the prime necessity; this explains the reaction of disbelieving horror when Oliver stands up at table and asks for more food.

> 'For more!' said Mr. Limbkins. 'Compose yourself, Bumble, and answer me directly. Do I understand that he asked for more, after he had eaten the supper allotted by the dietary?'
> 'He did, sir', replied Bumble.
> 'That boy will be hung', said the gentleman in the white waistcoat. 'I know that boy will be hung'. (Dickens 1992: 13)

While it is not certain that Dickens himself experienced such a scene, the moral conviction that it expresses, with its callousness towards human misery, was something with which he was well familiar. *Oliver Twist* and *David Copperfield* contain a great deal of autobiographical material. It is well known that Dickens was traumatized by his father's bankruptcy and stint in prison, events which forced him to work in a warehouse at the age of 12. He studied his material, moreover, with journalistic meticulousness and proclaimed that his characters would say nothing that he had not himself heard. Dickens's realism is, however, questionable in one respect: he endows his hero Oliver exclusively with noble characteristics that invite identification; the villains too are thoroughly villainous, in line with Dickens's moral discourse, through which he intended to bring about change by depicting certain relationships. Dickens belongs to that category of authors who have made a significant contribution to changing the image of childhood (cf. Kümmel 1997: 44; Coveney 1967: 127). His humanism, moreover, his ready sympathy for the fate of the victims of market society or the utilitarian ideology that went with it, can be placed in the same category as statements by other intellectuals, who envisioned better worlds as alternatives to base materialism – such as Carlyle and Ruskin, who imagined an idealistically elevated Middle Ages. Dickens thus played a significant role in the further development of a humanistic middle class canon (a departure from utilitarianism and narrow-minded Evangelicalism).

This movement should of course itself be seen as sociologically meaningful and explicable. It can best be understood within the broader context of the changes in the power balance between the classes within the state, which Elias terms 'functional democratization' (Elias 1978): within the industrializing nation state, the aristocratic upper classes are increasingly dependent on the middle classes, who in turn depend ever more on the working classes. Increasing sympathetic identification with the fate of working people or the poor is also connected with their improved power base: one can simply no longer afford to ignore the needs of these groups. The moralization of the concept of childhood (with the attributes of innocence, need for protection, genuineness, etc.) is rooted in a very similar motivational matrix: fear of underclass criminality, insights into the economic wastage increasingly perceived as the social cost of neglecting children, and the fear of a 'degeneration' of the English nation as a result of urbanization and pauperization, were real motives underlying the discourse of reform. The 'degeneracy scare' in particular, reinforced by English fears of being overtaken militarily and economically by other imperialist powers if it failed to produce a healthy and educated population, seemed all too justified: members of the urban lower class became smaller, weaker and sicker (cf. Kümmel 1997, for a collection of statements by contemporaries on this subject).

Humanization was of course not only a matter of the rational self-interest of the upper and middle classes, but also played itself out – perhaps predominantly – in a changed emotional predicament. People began to feel ashamed of the wretchedness of the working classes. The capacity to place oneself in the position of others, or the willingness to remove the emotional armour plating which kept the destitution of others at a safe distance, forms the foundation of this particular civilizational thrust. The Evangelicalism of the early nineteenth century had far-reaching consequences. The fact that the Christian notion of sympathy managed to become socially meaningful, however (Puritanism in fact hardened hearts for a time), can hardly be put down to an autonomous 'religious sphere', but was the result of the change in the whole context of relationships between rising and established classes, far more extensive than in the past. This is also the underpinning of what is known as 'Victorian sentimentality' (cf. Churchill 1982: 119–20); like the equally perplexing 'hardening of hearts' which marks certain eras (of, for example, increased market and professional competition), it is a product of the largely unconscious dynamics of human interaction. (One cannot always afford the luxury of tender feelings.) The numerous figures, now of proverbial renown, produced by Dickens's imagination, are thus also a result of Dickens's affects and attitudes, which enabled him to portray situations, interactions and persons in accordance with his feelings.

The 'workhouse' chapters thus contain, for the first time in English literature, a view of society from the perspective of the child; his feelings of loneliness, his predicament at the mercy of rough and brutal people far stronger than he is, are described in detail from the perspective of the narrator, which invites readers' identification (there is probably a certain amount of self-pity in this, which may contribute to the impression of sentimentality). Dickens compellingly describes the blunt arrogance of subaltern officials, the asymmetric interactions in which they involve themselves as they wield their positional power, and precise architectural details of the workhouse and other depressing environments. His realism though, is always anchored in his emotional structure; its individual character does not prevent his narrative from connecting firmly with reality, but makes it crucial to relate it to a sociology-of-knowledge perspective.[6]

This certainly applies to the description of the treacherous and hypocritical Mr Pecksniff in *Martin Chuzzlewit*, a prototype of the utilitarian but sanctimonious social character. Pecksniff is the epitome of selfishness shot through with hypocrisy, which – as in Thackeray's *Vanity Fair* (1848) – takes the form of personified habitus. Dickens describes dialogues in which certain intentions and interests are concealed, as well as the gestures and postures through which they unwittingly betray themselves; these constitute a person's 'second nature'.

Evangelicalism and the rise of a new middle-class morality: Jane Eyre and St John Rivers

Protestant ethic and economic utilitarianism are closely entwined through a multiplicity of threads, but Dickens's indictment of society is evidence that they may also be kept quite separate. The paradox, underlined by Weber, that it was none other than the ascetic virtues that led to very worldly riches – such that the socio-cultural dynamics facilitated simple avarice in order to maintain the structure of capitalist bondage – is also the foundation of Dickens's social criticism. Yet Puritanism, as a living and felt religiosity, had not yet completely disappeared; on the contrary, it was famously revived by John Wesley in the 18th century, its impact far from negligible. Its significance for the emergence of an ethic of modesty, engagement in support of the weak and the linking of authority to moral yardsticks, an ethic that was the polar opposite of the gentleman code (in the shape of a code of honour and now gallant warrior code), is incalculable. Before it again became imbricated, as part of the ideology of 'muscular Christianity', with the aristocratic code of gallantry (its roots in the middle ages, after all, are also partly Christian), it developed in specifically pure form in diverse missionary activities.

Charlotte Brontë's *Jane Eyre*, which we have referred to already in another connection, provides a compelling picture of the strong emotions that underpinned and imbued this missionary Christianity. It portrays these emotions through numerous examples, but nowhere more clearly than in the case of St John Rivers, who wishes to make Jane his wife and carry her off to a hard missionary life in India: he thus becomes the antithesis of Mr Rochester, though he has no real chance of coming out on top. Jane's experience of his preaching is captured in the following quotation:

> It began calm – and indeed, as far as delivery and pitch of voice went, it was calm to the end: an earnestly felt, yet strictly restrained zeal breathed soon in the distinct accents, and prompted the nervous language. This grew to force – compressed, condensed, controlled. The heart was thrilled, the mind astonished, by the power of the preacher: neither were softened. Throughout there was a strange bitterness; an absence of consolatory gentleness; stern allusions to Calvinistic doctrines – election, predestination, reprobation – were frequent; and each reference to these points sounded like a sentence pronounced for doom. (Brontë 1985: 378)

Jane shrewdly notices that this sermon merely makes her feel sad, that this eloquence is rooted in dark, unfulfilled wishes and longings, in disappointments and insatiable demands that make one restless. Yet the methodically controlled emotions beneath the surface, tamed by self-constraint of a particularly inexorable kind, reveal great strength.

St John has no interest in worldly profit. He is poor, and he wishes to remain so. His familial bonds are weak; he regards himself as a stranger in his own land. He is modest: his help is that given by the blind to the lame. The concerns of the flesh mean little to him; but he is ready to answer the call of heaven. When he offers Jane a position teaching in a village school for the poor, he states his reasons with the following words:

> And since I am myself poor and obscure, I can offer you but a service of poverty and obscurity. You may even think it degrading – for I see now your habits have been what the world calls refined: your tastes lean to the ideal, and your society has at least been amongst the educated; but I consider that no service degrades which can better our race. I hold that the more arid and unreclaimed the soil where the Christian labourer's task of tillage is appointed him – the scantier the meed his toil brings – the higher the honour.

> His, under such circumstances, is the destiny of the pioneer; and the first pioneers of the Gospel were the Apostles – their captain was Jesus, the Redeemer, Himself. (Brontë 1985: 380)

This quotation lays bare the break with the morals and conventions of the educated and refined 'good' society. No similar radical-ascetic middle-class movement exists in contemporary Austria; especially when one considers the heavy emphasis on 'work' and the extreme seriousness and demand for moral consistency that were the hallmarks of this movement. This chapter of English social history is all the more exciting since it demonstrates one of the possible routes of so-called cultural reproduction, which ensure that there exist identifiable continuities in the social or national habitus of a state society. The reproduction of the puritanical code can only be grasped by taking into account how the many analytically separable levels and dimensions are woven together in the particular network of social relations. The element of people's stock of knowledge is just one, and probably not the most important, of these levels: excerpts from the Old and New Testament, the Common Prayer Book, religious songs, the building plans for churches, etc. Another level is what is often referred to as 'values', whose existence and cultural reproduction are sometimes treated as if the values of the 'Protestant ethic' had an almost metaphysical life of their own and (because they come from God?) as if they could be dealt with independently of the socio-cultural circumstances. (The structural-functionalist modernization theory of American provenience of the 1950s and 1960s creates this impression; cf. for example Parsons 1979: 517–18). Weber's famous study also leaves one with the feeling that a causal relationship exists between religious economic ethic and capitalist acquisitiveness. Weber did attempt to qualify this by using the expression 'affinity', yet the notion of two independent 'spheres', the economic and the religious, is central to his thought (cf. Kuzmics 1993, for a detailed analysis). Instead, we assume that a comprehensive explanation must show why someone adopted such dramatic religious views. This can succeed only if we consider the affects involved in this and 'rational' actions and understand them as responses to a given social context; the influences from this social field all come together in and impact upon the individual person, within his or her 'affective household'; these influences may be economic or political constraints, dependence on others in the form of deep-seated needs to overcome fear and insecurity, or a need for redemption, which can be satisfied socially through religious communities. The cult of humility, of modesty, is thus central to our discussion of authority – humility, of course, is unthinkable in the world of the warrior or a world of extravagant, ostentatious splendour. We must thus consider how this social space can be reproduced over several generations, a space which creates the fears, scarcities and constraints which are then expressed in strict self-constraint, including the willingness to sacrifice oneself and refrain from sexual indulgence and numerous other pleasures, a self-constraint that crops up again and again throughout the book. St John, for example, attempts to persuade Jane to commit to missionary work in India:

> 'Humility, Jane,' said he, 'is the groundwork of Christian virtues: you say right that you are not fit for the work. Who is fit for it? Or who, that ever was truly called, believed himself worthy of the summons? I, for instance, am but dust and ashes.' (Brontë 1985: 428)

It is this humility that is most sharply opposed to the claims to dominance of worldly authority and which can be deployed to bolster the moralization of authority. Yet this humility must be combined with a number of other virtues if it is to bear fruit:

> In the village school I found you could perform well, punctually, uprightly, labour uncongenial to your habits and inclinations; I saw you could perform it with capacity and tact: you could win while you controlled [...] (L)ucre had no undue power over you. In the resolute readiness with which you cut your wealth into four shares, keeping but one to yourself, and relinquishing the three others to the claim of abstract justice, I recognized a soul that revelled in the flame and excitement of sacrifice. (Brontë 1985: 429)

St John also commends Jane's selflessness, indefatigable tenacity and unshakeable equanimity, her courage and loyalty, and her diligence. All in all, he feels, she would make the ideal head of an Indian school and helper of Indian women. Jane immediately sees the advantages of such an arrangement: it is very meaningful and satisfying because all the this-worldly sacrifices it involves remove one's fear of the next world. Yet this seemingly satisfying arrangement comes to nothing because Jane does not want to become St John's wife:

> 'I have a woman's heart, but not where you are concerned; for you I have only a comrade's constancy; a fellow-soldier's frankness, fidelity, fraternity, if you like; a neophyte's respect and submission to his hierophant: nothing more – don't fear.' 'It is what I want', he said, speaking to himself; 'it is just what I want.' (Brontë 1985: 433)

Jane's romantic protest – she is unable to love him – completely baffles the future missionary. Soldiery loyalty and brotherliness are enough for him: many such couples were to enter the colonial service, the women without ornamentation but with a great deal of resolute vigour. The English colonial empire was not won solely through a piratical urge to steal and a big-game hunting thirst for adventure, but also through a far from negligible portion of missionary spirit and considerable asceticism. Keen observer Charlotte Brontë (there were clearly models for St John Rivers in her own life, cf. Leavis 1985: 28), however, also sees the despotism of this way of thinking, its intolerance, rigidity and failure to include warm-hearted love. It is thus no surprise that qualities of domination also emerge when St John's image of his missionary work with the Indians is described:

> As to St. John Rivers, he left England: he went to India. He entered on the path he had marked for himself; he pursues it still. A more resolute, indefatigable pioneer never

> wrought amidst rocks and dangers. Firm, faithful, and devoted, full of mercy and zeal, and truth, he labours for his race; he clears their painful way to improvement; he hews down like a giant the prejudices of creed and caste that encumber it. He may be stern; he may be exacting; he may be ambitious yet; but his is the sternness of the warrior greatheart, who guards his pilgrim convoy from the onslaught of Apollyon. [...] St. John is unmarried: he will never marry now. [...] his glorious sun hastens to its setting. The last letter I received from him drew from my eyes human tears and yet filled my heart with divine joy: he anticipated his sure reward, his uncorruptible crown. (Brontë 1985: 477)

A comparison with Austria: Nation and patrimonial authority in Joseph Roth

While the distance between the English gentleman canon and the Austrian officials' code is fairly large, so are the differences arising from England's early development as a Protestant, market-oriented society and Austria's Counter-Reformation Catholicism and rejection of the market. England's turn towards Protestantism, of course, resulted not only from economic forces but from the pursuit of political independence; Hungarian Calvinism was also inspired by non-economic factors, the aristocrats flocking to embrace the option least appealing to the Habsburgs. The 'Protestant ethic' and its accompanying habitus nonetheless had something to do with the advance of the market. For the purposes of comparison, three questions – or question clusters – are of key import:

(1) What was the Habsburg Monarchy's equivalent of the puritanical behavioural model, its species of self-constraint, its conception of authority, its model of political and religious freedom?

(2) What were the consequences of delayed market development and the long predominance of personal ties for the Austrian habitus? The subdual and regulation of affect through the web of monetary relations is quite distinct from the affect management anchored in the constraints of a warrior code and the power of domination rooted in one's position within the bureaucracy. Insofar as the expansion of mutual dependencies through the web of monetary relations may undermine feudal or state authority, to what extent does this find expression in 'habitus'? Which habitual reactions produced the dynamics of economic competition in Austria, which arrived late but then took hold with tremendous force? What was the equivalent of the utilitarian morality of pitilessness?

(3) What was the Austrian equivalent of that moralization of authority which can be conveyed by the catchword 'humanization'? Was there an Austrian equivalent of this taming of power and making it 'responsible' within a) the intra-societal, internal state framework, b) inter-state or inter-ethnic relations? What did the Austrian counterpart of the English national state we-ideal look like, if such existed at all? We take a final, close look at literary evidence in the shape of Joseph Roth, the Austrian with multiple loyalties, and his *Radetzkymarsch*.

The fact that England saw itself as a haven of freedom was, as L. Colley (1992) convincingly shows, connected with its Protestantism, whose significance to English identity arose above all from struggles against Catholicism from outside (Spain, France) and within its borders (the church's para-state authority, particularly when supported by kings – such as some of the Stuarts). The notion of a 'chosen people', freedom from popery, pride in the ability to read the Bible oneself without mediation by a priest, placed above one in a hierarchy, were connected with this; significant too were pride in parliamentary freedom and the privileging of the individual conscience. This conscience itself may have been merciless and tyrannical, but the English (and as Colley shows, Protestant Scots and Welshmen too) felt free. Austria was something like the natural antithesis to Protestant England (which also frequently showed solidarity for the victims of the Counter-Reformation and attacked Austria or the Habsburgs by mentioning the *legenda negra*). Recatholicization shaped mentality, as the Jesuit dramas and prose literature of the Austrian Enlightenment show, by helping to maintain fear of authority and deeply internalized inhibitions against any development of non-conformist opinions and habits, and bolstering thought taboos and an 'uprightness' that corresponded to the universalistic demand for harmony, that is, the Baroque unity of worldly and spiritual authority. Instead of a discourse pursued by means of argument and reference to texts (including the Bible), there was 'persuasion', an appeal to all the senses. In many ways, the formation of the English conscience was more consistent, complete and tight-knit, because it was underpinned by egalitarian relations, including those between the sexes (the example of *Jane Eyre* shows a seriousness and asexual timbre missing in Catholic, Baroque, sensual Austria); there is practically no English equivalent of the erotic scenes and images of women found in the *Volkskomödie* [the people's comedy], the Josephine Enlightenment novel, in Nestroy or later in Musil and Schnitzler. Austrian cynicism and a scarcely concealed double standard contrast with Puritan earnestness, which can however degenerate into bigotry. In place of the comparatively egalitarian code that marked relations between the sexes, in Austria one often finds male authority and female flattery and cunning. In relations between those of unequal rank, the Puritan concept of humility contrasts sharply with the ostentatious emphasizing of rank; Nestroy bristles with examples of the arrogation of authority. In England, puritanical humility met the gentleman's consciousness of rank; the relative strength of each model reflected the fluctuating distribution of power between landowners and the commercial middle classes, though the borderline between them was blurred.

2) The formation of the habitus through the market and money was strikingly different in Austria and England. This is particularly apparent in the stylized punctuation which Doderer's official Zihal and Defoe's Moll Flanders deploy. Abstract administrative language fused with the authority of the state in one case, and with the logic of book-keeping and rational market analysis in the other. Exaggerating slightly, one could state that the main source of external constraints leading to self-constraint is the state in Austria and the market in England.

Earnestness dominates contrasting realms. Another important dimension is the very different importance of *money* in relation to the *honour* of the warrior: death in a duel in order to re-establish injured honour (as in Roth's *Radetzkymarsch* for example) contrasts with the far from spectacular resolution of the conflict between two rivals in Trollope. Money makes people peaceful. A further consequence of marketization is increasing freedom of choice, the possibility of escape from long-term personal dependency. Herzmanovsky-Orlando's bizarre and Grillparzer's tragic relationship to patrimonial, bureaucratic authority, leading to resigned submission in the case of the latter, are unthinkable in the world of *Moll Flanders*, and remain so until the end of the period considered in the present work. The early, conflict-ridden development of the English market system had one decisive consequence, however, especially during the Industrial Revolution: the constant threat of de-civilizing tendencies that could lead to the morality of pitilessness and heartlessness. Austria developed from the state-led protection for the peasants under Maria Theresa to paternalistic state interventionism of an Austrian hue. A good example of the knee-jerk appeal to paternalistic authority in view of the 'social question' (a kind of counterpart to *Oliver Twist*) is provided by von Saar in his novella *Die Steinklopfer* [stone-cutters; Saar 1993; first published in 1874]: the setting is the gigantic building site of the *Semmeringbahn*; the dismal, depressing working conditions are made worse by a mean foreman, yet the fairness of a paternalistic military judge who cares about people's welfare ultimately saves the day. The killer and his loving companion, two of the poorest people in society, receive a piece of land and thus remove themselves from proletarian circumstances. The reaction to the *Bauernlegen* – the enforced selling of arable farm land in a process of marketisation of Austrian agriculture – in Rosegger's *Jakob der Letzte* [James the Last], Rosegger 1979; first published in 1887–88) is similar. Urban landlords acquire peasant land, and the response to the anonymous, violent and unstoppable advance of the market is the romanticization of a paternalistic peasant world. The response to the unbounded utilitarianism of the market was thus quite different in Austria and England – including the fact that trade unions in competition with one another developed in England, while Austria saw the rise of monocratic, unified unions. Older structures and structural differences were reproduced in the development of professional associations and mass parties.

There is no doubt that the Habsburg Monarchy was in many respects in step with the Enlightenment tendencies of the European middle-class elites. From the Josephinist Enlightenment novel to Karl Kraus, a clear thread of 'humanization' is to be found, which held up a 'bourgeois', 'civilized' mirror to the repression and cruelties of the late feudal, 'Machiavellian' code of the subsequent dynastic state, which led to constant embroilment in wars. The differences from England are nonetheless clear: the social background of the Enlightenment was narrower in Austria, the urban bourgeoisie numerically far smaller, the surrounding agrarian society far more significant and 'backward', the aristocracy which loomed over all was more clearly separate and less 'commercialized', while the church, which functioned as an organization of dominance, was more clearly opposed to the Enlightenment-oriented bourgeoisie than in England. Two further differences are also significant: the long tradition of keeping bourgeois groups from participating in state power in Austria and the multiethnic or multi-national character of the empire. The first produced – under the particular Austrian circumstances of heavy bureaucratization within the context of reform absolutism – an apathetic, cynical and ambivalent attitude, that of the 'obedient rebel' (Heindl 1991), towards the state and the exercise of dominance. The second was responsible for the middle class humanization movement's inability to simply lead the Austrians to an ideal we-image as a nation, as Elias has plausibly argued in the case of England and Colley for 'Protestant Britain' (cf. Elias 1996; Colley 1992). Instead, at the close of the Habsburg monarchy, there were several options: ranging from the Grillparzer dictum 'from humanity through nationality to bestiality', in which humanism was linked to the Habsburgs, via the strongly nationalizing, narrower code of the established national groupings and those catching up with them, to the final fleeting internationalism of those who claimed to speak for the workers, as expressed, for instance, by Kisch in his indictment of war.

Linda Colley's emphasis on the Protestant role in the development of British national identity since the union of England and Scotland, with its deeply internalized urge for freedom and its mistrust of unregulated royal power, must be contrasted with the unusual fragmentation of the Catholic Habsburg Monarchy, its multiplicity of political cultures and religions (see Heer 1981). Here, humanization was often anti-Catholic and thus anti-state. In the case of England, it is reasonably easy to distinguish between the intra-state, intra-society relations of power and authority and their inter-state, international counterparts; relations with the colonies being the third key element. In Austria, intra-state also means inter-ethnic; in both the Austrian and Hungarian parts of the monarchy numerically small ethnic groups claimed dominance over a majority.

A final look at the literary production of Joseph Roth brings out the complexity of the Austrian mixture of loyalties, ties and attitudes and mentalities relating to political authority. Within the Habsburg Monarchy, Roth might identify with his home city – Brody in Galicia; with the Crown land of Galicia itself; with Jewishness, an early influence within family and community to which he always remained bound; with Germanness, mediated through the language and culture of his schooling; and with the umbrella state, represented in the person of the emperor and related bodies, whose presence was felt in the farthest corners of the empire. Later, when he emigrated, Roth experienced intensely another realm of identification – humanity as a whole, to which he also felt a commitment – in emotional and conscious contrast to the narrow nationalism which was to dominate the first half of the twentieth century in such tragic fashion.

The important thing about all these loyalties is that they do not always seamlessly complement one another, but often conflict; even if one feels a particular loyalty, very ambivalent feelings may co-exist with it. Competing loyalties mean a conflictual balance between various 'we-feelings' within the person, behind which conflicting reference groups or units of social organization ultimately stand. Yet ambivalent feelings can also exist towards one and the same 'we' – as in the case of Jewish 'self-hatred', the structural basis of which often appears to be the frequently contradictory evaluation by the surrounding Christian community. Roth furnishes us with examples of all these phenomena, which also tell us much about the reality of the Habsburg Monarchy. Imperial patriotism, loyalty to the Habsburgs and nationalism often collide – an empire, which according to Musil, disintegrated because of an error of language.

The Radetzky March and *Kapuzinergruft* [*The Emperor's Tomb*; Roth 2002] are the most Austrian of Roth's novels. The story of the Trotta family is one of decline, of descent from heroic greatness to despairing then resigned weakness – in the *Kapuzinergruft* this weakness becomes a paralyzing, lonely fate in a world gone to pieces in the wake of a terrible war. The young Carl Joseph, son of the district commissioner [*Bezirkshauptmann*] and grandson of the hero of Solferino, is – in *Radetzky March* – filled with childlike love for the ruling house:

> Only now did his vacation begin. Another quarter hour, and he heard the first rattling drumroll from the band leaving the barracks. Every Sunday at noontime it played outside the official residence of the district captain, who, in this little town, represented no lesser personage than His Majesty the Emperor. Carl Joseph, concealed behind the dense foliage of the vines on the balcony, received the playing of the military band as a tribute. He felt slightly related to the Hapsburgs, whose might his father represented and defended here and for whom he himself would some day go off to war and death. He knew the names of all the members of the Imperial Royal House. He loved them all sincerely, with a child's devoted heart – more than anyone else the Kaiser, who was kind and great, sublime and just, infinitely remote and very close, and particularly fond of the officers in the army. It would be best to die for him amid military music, easiest with 'The Radetzky March'. The swift bullets whistled in cadence around Carl Joseph's ears, his naked saber flashed, and, his heart and head brimming with the lovely briskness of the march, he sank into the drumming intoxication of the music, and his blood oozed out in a thin dark-red trickle upon the glistening gold of the trumpets, the deep black of the drums, and the victorious silver of the cymbals. (Roth 1995: 23–4)

The 15-year-old Trotta attends a cadet school. Like his grandfather he represents one of the three pillars of the monarchy, the armed forces. His father represents the second, officialdom; and Roth himself, apologist for the monarchy, became a Catholic because he saw the church as one of the throne's main supports (Bronsen 1981: 548–9).

The strength of this feeling is connected to the size of the sacrifice demanded of the soldier; he must be willing to give his life if the supreme commander so wishes. It is not the social construction of the 'nation' that represents this highest of values; the relationship to the survival unit of the 'state' is also one of personal loyalty to the paternal monarch. The 'cold Habsburg sun' shines in the furthest reaches of the empire. The Radetzky marching music referred to in the title of the book conveys this feeling, while rhythm and the frenzy of colours transmit deep feelings of devotion.

The intense identification which Roth has the young Trotta display is far from sociologically self-evident. It certainly mirrored Roth's own identification.

Yet soldiers in the sovereign states of Europe were for a long time press-ganged mercenaries whose officers, descendants of the noble knights of old, were the only ones to deeply internalize their loyalty. 'Patriotism' – in the form of an Imperial patriotism, love of fatherland and emperor – first took hold in Austria during Maria Theresa's wars with Frederick's Prussia, and was a fleeting side-effect of the wars of liberation against Napoleon. It first became a mass feeling, perhaps, in 1914; as an accompaniment to the mass mobilization of modernity and promoted by schools, which did a tremendous amount to incorporate the lower classes into the state. But in contrast to bourgeois Western Europe the Imperial patriotism of the Habsburg Monarchy was supra-national, the Habsburg God was no German or Hungarian, but was truly universal:

> King of Jerusalem: that was the highest rank God could award a majesty. And Franz Joseph was already King of Jerusalem. Too bad, the Kaiser mused. Someone whispered to him that the Jews were waiting for him outside in the village. They had forgotten all about the Jews. Ah, now those Jews too! the Kaiser thought, distressed. Fine! Let them come. But they had to step on it! Otherwise they'd be late for the fighting.
> [...] Like a field of strange black stalks in the wind, the congregation of Jews bowed to the Kaiser. (Roth 1995: 221–2)

Franz Joseph was a beneficent protector of the Jews; of all the peoples of the monarchy it is perhaps among the Jews that we find the greatest Austrian patriots: Roth demonstrated this within his own person when he distanced himself from his earlier socialism and became a tireless apologist for the Habsburgs in exile, presenting the monarchy as saving Austria from fascism. Several authors (Bronsen 1981; Beller 1993; Heer 1981) have drawn attention to the fact that the Viennese Jewry (whether assimilated, Westernized or Jews from the Galician east) identified with the monarchy in a special way: despite or perhaps because of the antisemitism on the increase from the 1880s, from which many thought only the emperor could save them. The characters in Roth's novel with which he most identified, according to his biographers, were young Baron Trotta, of Slovenian origin, and the Polish Count Chojnicki. Roth is also known to have harboured a strong aversion for the 'Sudeten' and 'Alpine' Germans; he has Count Chojnicki state that the Alpine idiots have destroyed the monarchy (in *The Emperor's Tomb*). Roth was only too aware of how poorly the Galician Jews were regarded in Vienna; and like many others, his aversion for the intolerant native occasionally turned into Jewish self-hate.

The Trotta family's loyalty to state and dynasty is one of the dominant themes of the *Radetzky March*. It shares, however, the unhappy fate of the monarchy as a whole. The death of the representatives of the old order – of the servant Jacques, the emperor himself, the old baron, without hope after the death of his only son, is symbolic of the death of the monarchy. This announces itself long before, when Count Chojnicki opens the old baron's eyes:

> This era no longer wants us! This era wants to create independent nation-states! People no longer believe in God. The new religion is nationalism. … The German Kaiser still rules even when God abandons him; perhaps by the grace of the nation. The Emperor of Austria-Hungary must not be abandoned by God. But God *has* abandoned him!
> The district captain rose to his feet. … All processes in nature and all events of everyday life suddenly achieved an ominous and incomprehensible meaning. (Roth 1995: 161–2)

Many of the characters in the novel demonstrate a lack of faith in Austria. The soldier son of bandmaster Nechwal does not believe in the army; booze-ups in the garrisons are laden with anomie and fatalism;[7] even the baron's chess partner, Skowronnek, an official, no longer trusts in the future of the monarchy.

Both *The Radetzky March* and *The Emperor's Tomb* contain numerous depictions of the nationality issue.

> And the army, in the district captain's opinion, was the only force that you could still rely on in the monarchy.
> The district captain felt as if the whole world were suddenly made up of Czechs – a people he viewed as unruly, hardheaded, and stupid and as the inventors of the very concept of 'nation'. A lot of peoples might exist, but no nations. And besides, the governor's office kept sending him various barely comprehensible decrees and orders detailing a gentler treatment of 'national minorities' – one of the terms that Herr von Trotta hated most, for by his lights 'national minorities' were nothing but large communities of 'revolutionary individuals' (Roth 1995: 228).

From the standpoint of high-level bureaucrats loyal to the state nationalism must indeed have seemed a revolutionary, anti-state ideology. It is not however only officials to whom nationalism seems disloyal, but also the characters with whom Roth himself most clearly identified: Count Chojnicki and Carl Joseph, officer in the dying army. An air of divine twilight dominates the famous scene in *The Radetzky March* when news of the heir to the throne's murder arrives and the Hungarians present 'can be glad that the bastard is gone!' (Roth 1995: 297). The anti-semitism widespread in the army is apparent in the lead-up to the fatal duel in which the Jewish regimental doctor takes part. *The Emperor's Tomb,* set in impoverished, absurdly diminished alpine Austria, becomes a symbol of the destruction of everything worth living for; Roth portrays the oppressive consequences of the shift away from the universalistic, spacious, multi-hued Austria in the cramped, small-minded, unwanted successor state. The lives of all the people in this novel, who find themselves living in a run-down boarding-house, have been robbed of meaning, devalued; they have been put out to pasture. The central figure here is Count Chojnicki – the Trottas live on in the shape of a distant cousin of Carl Joseph. The fate of this Franz Ferdinand von Trotta means, like that of Roth himself, incurable nostalgia and endless flight.

Roth's loyalties were multi-layered and, as Bronsen makes clear in his biography, they also changed over the course of his life. He was fundamentally moulded by the social environment of Brody in Galicia – with a large Jewish population, though the German language and culture exercised a great pull on Roth (and many of his fellow Jewish gymnasium pupils). The young Roth attended a German gymnasium, but the teaching staff and pupils were multinational: a good half of the pupils were Jews, the language of instruction German, but Polish language was on the advance. The eastern Jewry – Roth was, however, according to Bronsen, never very religious – gained a particular opportunity to access the German Enlightenment movement (in opposition to the mysticism of *Chassidism*). Roth seems to have opted for assimilation at an early stage; he was obviously something of an outsider, who had little to do with his Jewish or Catholic schoolfellows. He also privileged Austrian over Polish assimilation early on; the Poles of course formed a privileged upper class in Galicia, who enjoyed a superior social status vis-à-vis the Ukrainian peasantry. The bond to the emperor was not only mediated by the school; the Galician Jews generally regarded him as their protector; unsurprisingly, in light of the then still contemporary experience of pogroms in Tsarist Russia. The emotional bond to the more humane of the three conservative powers of Prussia, Russia and Austria could also be found among the Poles; most of the minorities needed the monarchy to protect them from the hegemonic strivings of the 'stronger' peoples for an extended period.

On the eve of the First World War, we thus find in Austria and England very different mentalities and group feelings, shaped by the specifics of state and societal development.

The English (or, since 1707, also British) we-feeling, or the last stage it reached within the process of state formation, is habitually informed by the bond with the nation (in the 'Empire' too) and Protestantism; its Habsburg equivalent by state, dynasty and a universalistic Catholicism. Colley (1992) points out that this trait is found in the most popular English hymns, and in *Rule Britannia* (1740), in which Britain rises out of the sea on divine command and even the guardian angels sing that Britons shall never be slaves. In *God Save the King* too, God helps the king to dispel his enemies, though he is urged to defend English laws. He is, moreover, only worthy of support as long as he justified this. The picture is quite different in Roth, who declares his unconditional love for Franz Joseph:

> I felt at the time I was an Austrian: an old-style Austrian...All Austrian emperors are my emperors, but Emperor Franz Joseph I is my special Emperor, the Emperor of my childhood and youth...This is why I make the pilgrimage, when I am fortunate enough to be able to return to Austria, to greet my Emperor. [...]
>
> 'Dear Emperor! I have served you, I have buried you, I perhaps tried once, high-spiritedly, to influence you – and I have survived you. Yet you are stronger than me even in death. Forgive me my high spirits! I love all Austrian emperors: the one who

> succeeded you and all of those to come. But you, my Emperor Franz Joseph, I seek out because you are my childhood and youth. I greet you, Emperor of my childhood days. I buried you: for me, you never died.
> Your Joseph Roth' (nach Bronsen 1981: 483–4, trans. A.S.)

While this quotation reflects a sentimentality fed by emigration and alcoholism, it is not related to the nation – how, indeed, could it be? There are plenty of examples of English sentimentality – yet their subject is England or Britain, not the queen. The English we-feeling, shortly before the Great War, is self-confident and triumphant: 'We don't want to fight, but, by Jingo, if we do, we've got the men, we've got the ships, we've got the money too.' Its Habsburg counterpart has little of its Counter-Reformation triumphalism left.

How representative is Habsburg loyalism in Roth of the feelings of the members of the major social groups in the monarchy as a whole? Most commentators believe that the bureaucratic bourgeoisie was most loyal to the state.[8] The upper echelons of the armed forces, career officers in the second loyal institution of the monarchy, were also few in number.[9] Roth's Austrian novels thus deal with a milieu that was particularly loyal to the state and was linked to this state in a patrimonial fashion. But even officials of German nationality or members of the many other nationalities could have multiple loyalties, which may have conflicted with one another to some extent. They might be anticlerical and opponents of political Catholicism; they might also feel affiliation to the 'black-yellow' Habsburg-loyalist camp. While this problem also existed in Britain, it did so within far narrower parameters: in the case of the Irish there was a denominational conflict, still having an impact in the present day, in the case of the Scots the nostalgic myth of a 'stateless nation'. On the whole, though, a far more unquestioned national identity developed on the island than was the case in Austria. Above all though, it proved possible there to attach humanization to the national self-image – and it thus significantly shaped relations with other states. Within British state society it was comparatively easy to extend participation in political power (parliamentarization), to turn from an aristocratic into a bourgeois nation. In Austria-Hungary this was complicated by the struggle of nationalities; the universalist, Catholic ideal of harmony contrasted with the reality of emotion-laden conflicts, for which the Austrian 'political culture', with its dependence on patrimonial authority, was insufficiently prepared. This feature of the Austrian habitus was never overcome, despite the formation of class- and nation-based camps: in this sense, the 'Habsburg myth', with its insistence on order and longing for strong, beneficent authority, was an Austrian reality. It is also no surprise that the disaster of imperial collapse and national hatreds often resulted in a nostalgic turn towards 'Habsburg humanity': rather than being integrated into the Austrian we-image, it became something mythical, which remained tied to the person of the emperor, to official posts and the army – something which ultimately came from above.

Notes

1 Here, Butler himself appears split between the older, experienced first-person narrator Overton, and the young, unfortunate Ernest Pontifex, his godson, who liberates himself from the influence of his coldly calculating and bigoted father Theobald Pontifex, which he experiences as suffocating, and from his clerical milieu (cf. Churchill 1982: 349).

2 The concept of 'perfidious Albion' goes back to French opposition to England since the Hundred Years War and has a good deal to do with the capacity of English diplomacy to form coalitions (cf. Stanzel 1998, for evidence of this).

3 Defoe wrote a critical text (*Conjugal Lewdness: Or Matrimonial Whoredom*) on this in 1727, in which he is damning about marriages for the sake of money (cf. Blewett, D., Introduction, in: Defoe 1989: 6).

4 Defoe, however, mentions (1989: 140) that the husband's approval was required; without this, Moll was unable to travel.

5 Ian Watt's assessment of the 'realism' of Defoe's writing is interesting: 'Defoe's most important innovation in fiction was his unprecedentedly complete narrative realism. There is little doubt that it springs directly out of his long practice of journalism' (Watt 1982: 153).

6 The autobiographies of former inmates of such institutions are testimony to the realism of Dickens' descriptions of the inner worlds of childhood. Cf. Steel 1939; Steedman 1990

7 One must however take into account that the depiction of this carouse is in fact a vehicle of Roth's style, which he deploys to illustrate the inevitability of degeneration. One cannot therefore speak (in this case) of a realistic, empirically 'correct' description of the Austrian army. Suicides were in fact far more common in the Habsburg army than in others (six times as many as in the British army, for example, according to Deák), but this had been the case for a long time. And booze-ups are a common feature of perhaps all armies. It is vital to make Roth's distortions explicit, particularly if one wishes to interpret him 'realistically' (cf. Deák, I., 1991: 131).

8 According to a contemporary estimation, there were 40,000 state officials as opposed to 24,000 officers and military officials in Austria in 1857 (which still included northern Italy) which thus made up only a small percentage of the middle classes as a whole (around 1,600,000; Bruckmüller/Stekl assume, on the basis of their own corrections, including dependants, a middle class of around 3 millions, around 7.5 per cent of total population. Bruckmüller/Stekl 1988: 168–70). In 1910 only 6.6 per cent of Austrian households had servants; this too points to the meagre extent of the Austrian bourgeoisie.

9 In 1910 there were around 18,000 career officers, as opposed to 1.5 million troops; in 1900, according to official statistics, 80 per cent of officers were German, 7.6 per cent Hungarian, 5.3 per cent Czech and 2.8 per cent Croatian. Deák's own estimation reduces the German portion to 55 per cent. For these groups, however, as Deák agrees, national sentiment was equal to treachery (cf. Deák 1991: 221–3).

Bibliography

Abrams, Philip, *Historical Sociology* (London: Open Books, 1982).

Acham, Karl, 'Barock heute. Zur Wirkungsgeschichte einer Epoche', in *Lust und Leid. Barocke Kunst – barocker Alltag: Steirische Landesausstellung 1992* (Graz: Verlag für Sammler, 1992), pp. 391–416.

——, 'Nachwort: Sonnenfels und seine Zeit – eine Vergegenwärtigung', in Joseph von Sonnenfels, *Aufklärung als Sozialpolitik. Ausgewählte Schriften aus den Jahren 1764–1798*, ed. and introd. by H. Kremers, with an afterword by Karl Acham (Vienna: Böhlau, 1994), pp. 227–247.

Adler, Hans (ed.), *Literarische Geheimberichte. Protokolle der Metternich-Agenten*, vol. 1: 1840–43; vol. 2: 1844–1848 (Cologne: Leske, 1977/1981).

Almond, Gabriel A., 'The Study of Political Culture', in Dirk Berg-Schlosser and Ralf Rytlewski (eds), *Political Culture in Germany* (Basingstoke: Macmillan, 1993), pp. 13–26.

Anderson, Perry, *Lineages of the Absolutist State* (London: Verso, 1974).

Anon. [Naske, A.], *Wiener Kanzlei-Zustände. Aus den Memoiren eines österreichischen Staatsbeamten* (Leipzig: Johann Friedrich Hartknoch, 1846).

Arendt, W.A., 'Die brabantische Revolution 1789–1790', *Historisches Taschenbuch*, N.F. 4 (1843): 239–412.

Arens, Franz, *Das Tiroler Volk in seinen Weistümern* (Gotha: Friedrich Andreas Perthes, 1904).

Argyle, Michael, *Soziale Interaktion* (Cologne: Kiepenheuer und Witsch, 1972).

——, 'Personality and Social Behaviour', in Rom Harré (ed.), *Personality* (Oxford: Blackwell, 1976), pp. 145–88.

——, *Körpersprache und Kommunikation* (Paderborn: Junfernmann, 1989).

Ariés, Philippe and Duby, Georges (eds), *Geschichte des privaten Lebens* (5 vols, Frankfurt/Main: S. Fischer, 1993).

Armanski, Gerhard, *Das gewöhnliche Auge der Macht. Sozialgeschichte der Beamten* (Berlin: Transit-Verlag, 1983).

Arnason, Johann P., *Social Theory and Japanese Experience: The Dual Civilization* (London: Kegan Paul International, 1997).

Asch, Ronald G., 'Krone, Hof und Adel in den Ländern der Stuart Dynastie im frühen 17. Jahrhundert', *Zeitschrift für historische Forschung*, 16 (1989): 183–220.

Asch, Ronald G. and Birke, Adolf M. (eds), *Princes, Patronage, and the Nobility. The Court at the Beginning of the Modern Age, c. 1450–1650* (Oxford: Oxford University Press, 1991).

Austen, Jane, *Pride and Prejudice* (Oxford: Oxford University Press, 1988).

Axtmann, Roland, '"Police" and the Formation of the Modern State. Legal and Ideological Assumptions on State Capacity in the Austrian Lands of the Habsburg Empire, 1500–1800', *German History*, 10 (1992): 39–61.

—, 'State formation, discipline and the constitution of society in early modern Europe', *Australian Journal of Politics and History*, 42 (1996): 173–91.

Balázs, Éva H., 'Die Lage der Bauernschaft und der Bauernbewegungen (1780–1787). Zur Bauernpolitik des Aufgeklärten Absolutismus', *Acta Historica Academiae Scientiarum Hungaricae*, 3 (1956): 293–327.

Baltl, Hermann, 'Die österreichischen Weistümer', *Mitteilungen des Instituts für österreichische Geschichte*, 59 (1951): 365–410, 61 (1953): 38–78.

Baltl, Hermann and Kocher, Gernot, *Österreichische Rechtsgeschichte: unter Einschluß sozial- und wirtschaftsgeschichtlicher Grundzüge, von den Anfängen bis zur Gegenwart.* 7th edn (Graz: Leykam, 1993).

Barker-Benfield, G.J., *The Culture of Sensibility. Sex and Society in Eighteenth-Century Britain* (Chicago: Chicago University Press, 1992).

Barton, Peter F. (ed.), *Im Zeichen der Toleranz – Im Lichte der Toleranz. Aufsätze zur Toleranzgesetzgebung des 18. Jahrhundert in den Reichen Josephs II., ihren Voraussetzungen und ihren Folgen* (2 vols, Vienna: Institut für Protestantische Kirchengeschichte, 1981).

Bassett, Richard, *Waldheim and Austria* (Harmondsworth, Middlesex: Viking, 1988).

Bauman, Zygmunt, *Modernity and the Holocaust* (Ithaca, N.Y.: Cornell University Press 1989).

Beattie, John, *The English Court in the Reign of George I* (Cambridge: Cambridge University Press, 1967).

Beckett, J.V., 'Land Tax or Excise: The Surging of Taxation in Seventeenth-Century England', *English Historical Review*, 100 (1985): 285–308.

—, *The Aristocracy in England, 1660–1914* (Oxford: Blackwell, 1988).

Beidtel, Ignaz, *Über österreichische Zustände in den Jahren 1740–1792.* (Sitzungsberichte der Akademie der Wissenschaften, VII und VIII) (Vienna: Akademie der Wissenschaften, 1851).

—, *Geschichte der österreichischen Staatsverwaltung, 1740–1848,* vol. 1 (Innsbruck (1898)/Frankfurt a. M. (1968 [reprint]): Sauer und Auvermann).

Beller, Steven, *Wien und die Juden 1867–1938* (Vienna, Cologne, Weimar: Böhlau, 1993).

Benda, Kálmán, 'Nationalgefühl und Nationalitätenkämpfe in Ungarn am Ende des 18. Jahrhunderts', *Anzeiger der österreichischen Akademie der Wissenschaften, phil.-hist. Klasse*, 108 (1972): 43–56.

——, 'Probleme des Josephinismus und des Jakobinertums in der Habsburgischen Monarchie', in Helmut Reinalter (ed.), *Jakobiner in Mitteleuropa* (Innsbruck: Innsbrucker Verlag, 1977), p. 38.

——, (1979) 'Der nationale Gedanke und die ungarischen Jakobiner', in Julius H. Schoeps and Immanuel Geiss (eds), *Revolution und Demokratie in Geschichte und Literatur.* (Duisburger Hochschulbeiträge, vol. 12) (Duisburg: Walter Braun Verlag, 1979), pp. 197–203.

Benna, Anna Hedwig, 'Organisierung und Personalstand der Polizeihofstelle, 1793–1848', *Mitteilungen des österreichischen Staatsarchivs*, 6 (1953): 197–239.

Bérenger, Jean, *A History of the Habsburg Empire, 1273–1700* (London: Longman, 1994).

Berghoff, Hartmut, 'Adel und Bürgertum in England 1770–1850. Ergebnisse der neueren Elitenforschung', in Elisabeth Fehrenbach (ed.), *Adel und Bürgertum in Deutschland 1770–1848* (Munich: Oldenbourg, 1994), pp. 95–127.

Bibl, Viktor, 'Die niederösterreichischen Stände und die Französische Revolution', *Jahrbuch des Vereins für Landeskunde von Niederösterreich*, 2 (1904): 77–97.

——, *Die Wiener Polizei. Eine kulturhistorische Studie* (Leipzig, Vienna: 1927).

Bireley, Robert, 'Ferdinand II: Founder of the Habsburg Monarchy', in R.W.J. Evans and T.V. Thomas (eds), *Crown, Church and Estates. Central European Politics in the Sixteenth and Seventeenth Centuries* (Basingstoke: Macmillan, 1991), pp. 226–43.

——, 'Confessional Absolutism in the Habsburg Lands in the Seventeenth Century', in Charles Ingrao (ed.), *State and Society in Early Modern Austria* (West Lafayette, Ind.: Purdue University Press, 1994), pp. 36–53.

Blewett, David, 'Introduction', in Daniel Defoe, *Moll Flanders* (Harmondsworth, Middlesex: Penguin Books, 1989), pp. 1–24.

Bodi, Leslie, 'System und Bewegung: Funktion und Folgen des josephinischen Tauwetters', *Wiener Europagespräch 1977* (1978): 37–53.

——, 'Comic Ambivalence as an Identity Marker: The Austrian Model', in Pavel Petr et al. (eds), *Comic Relations. Studies in the Comic, Satire and Parody* (Frankfurt/M.: Peter Lang, 1985), pp. 67–77.

——, *Tauwetter in Wien: Zur Prosa der österreichischen Aufklärung, 1781–1795* (Vienna: Böhlau, 1995a).

——, 'Traditionen des österreichischen Deutsch im Schnittpunkt von Staatsräson und Sprachnation. (Vom Reformabsolutismus bis zur Gegenwart)', in Rudolf Muhr, Richard Schrodt and Peter Wiesinger (eds), *Österreichisches Deutsch: Linguistische, sozialpsychologische und sprachpolitische Aspekte einer nationalen Variante des Deutschen* (Vienna: Hölder-Pichler-Tempsky, 1995b), pp. 17–37.

Bödy, Paul, 'The Hungarian Conspiracy of 1794–1795', *Journal of Central European Affairs*, 22 (1962): 3–26.

Bodzenta, Erich, 'Entwicklung und Struktur der österreichischen Gesellschaft', in Erich Bodzenta, Hans Seidel and Karl Stiglbauer, *Österreich im Wandel: Gesellschaft-Wirtschaft-Raum* (Vienna: Springer, 1985), pp. 1–76.

Böhlig, Gertrud (ed.), *Johannes Kaminiates: Die Einnahme Thessalonikes durch die Araber im Jahre 904*. trans. and introd. Gertrud Böhlig (Graz: Styria, 1975).

Born, Ignaz von, *Monachologie. Nach Linnäischer Methode* (Frankfurt, Leipzig: [no publisher], 1802).

Borsay, Peter, *The English Urban Renaissance. Culture and Society in the Provincial Town 1660–1770* (Oxford: Clarendon Press, 1989).

Bradbury, Malcolm, 'Jane Austen's Emma', in Boris Ford (ed.), *The New Pelican Guide to English Literature*, vol. 5: *From Blake to Byron* (Harmondsworth, Middlesex: Penguin Books, 1982), pp. 172–86.

Braddick, Michael J., *The Nerves of State. Taxation and the Financing of the English State, 1558–1714* (Manchester: Manchester University Press, 1996).

Bradler-Rottmann, E., *Die Reformen Kaiser Josephs II* (Göppingen: Kümmerle, 1976).

Bradley, Ian, *The Call to Seriousness. The Evangelical Impact on the Victorians* (London: Jonathan Cape, 1976).

Brandt, Harm-Hinrich, *Der österreichische Neoabsolutismus: Staatsfinanzen und Politik, 1848–1860* (2 vols, Göttingen: Vandenhoeck & Ruprecht, 1978).

—, 'Parlamentarismus als staatliches Integrationsproblem: Die Habsburger-Monarchie', in Adolf M. Birke and Kurt Kluxen (eds), *Deutscher und Britischer Parlamentarismus* (Munich: Saur, 1985), pp. 69–105.

—, 'Liberalismus in Österreich zwischen Revolution und Großer Depression', in Dieter Langewiesche (ed.), *Liberalismus im 19. Jahrhundert* (Göttingen: Vandenhoeck & Ruprecht, 1988), pp. 136–60.

Brauneder, Wilhelm and Lackmeyer, Friedrich, *Österreichische Verfassungsgeschichte*. 6th edn (Vienna: Manz, 1992).

Brewer, John, 'English Radicalism in the Age of George III', in J.G.A. Pocock (ed.), *Three British Revolutions: 1641, 1688, 1776* (Princeton: Princeton University Press, 1980), pp. 323–67.

—, 'Commercialization and Politics', in Neil McKendrick, John Brewer and J.H. Plumb, *The Birth of a Consumer Society. The Commercialization of Eighteenth-Century England* (London: Europa Publications, 1982), pp. 197–262.

—, *The Sinews of Power. War, Money and the English State, 1688–1783* (London: Unwin Hyman, 1989).

Briggs, John et al., *Crime and Punishment in England. An Introductory History* (London: UCL Press, 1996).

Bristow, Joseph, *Empire Boys: Adventures in a Man's World* (London: Harper Collins, 1991).

Broch, Hermann, 'Hofmannsthal und seine Zeit', in Hermann Broch, *Kommentierte Werksausgabe* (ed. P.M. Lützeler), 9/1, Schriften zur Literatur, 1. Kritik (Frankfurt/Main: Suhrkamp, 1975), pp. 111–284.

Bronsen, David, *Joseph Roth. Eine Biographie* (Munich: Deutscher Taschenbuch Verlag, 1981).

Brontë, Charlotte, *Jane Eyre* (Harmondsworth, Middlesex: Penguin Books, 1985).

Brubaker, W. Rogers, *Citizenship and Nationhood in France and Germany* (Cambridge, Mass.: Harvard University Press, 1992).

Bruckmüller, Ernst, *Nation Österreich. Sozialhistorische Aspekte ihrer Entwicklung* (Vienna: Hermann Böhlaus Nachfolger, 1984).

—, *Sozialgeschichte Österreichs* (Vienna: Herold, 1985).

—, 'Die Strafmaßnahmen nach den bäuerlichen Erhebungen des 15. bis 17. Jahrhunderts', in Erich Zöllner (ed.), *Wellen der Verfolgung* (Vienna: Österreichischer Bundesverlag, 1986), pp. 95–117.

—, 'Ein begrenzter Aufstieg. Das österreichische Bürgertum zwischen Biedermeier und Liberalismus', in Helmut Rumpler (ed.), *Innere Staatsbildung* (Vienna: Verlag für Geschichte und Politik, 1991), pp. 69–90.

—, *Nation Österreich: Kulturelles Bewußtsein und gesellschaftlich-politische Prozesse*. 2nd edn (Vienna: Böhlau, 1996).

Bruckmüller, Ernst and Stekl, Hannes, 'Zur Geschichte des Bürgertums', in Jürgen Kocka (ed.), *Bürgertum im 19. Jahrhundert. Deutschland im europäischen Vergleich* (3 vols, Munich: Deutscher Taschenbuch Verlag, 1988), vol. 1, pp. 160–92.

Brunner, Otto, 'Staat und Gesellschaft im vormärzlichen Österreich im Spiegel von I. Beidtels Geschichte der österreichischen Staatsverwaltung, 1740–1848', in Werner Conze (ed.), *Staat und Gesellschaft im deutschen Vormärz, 1815–1848* (Stuttgart: Klett Verlag, 1962), pp. 38–78.

—, *Land und Herrschaft. Grundfragen der territorialen Verfassungsgeschichte Österreichs im Mittelalter*. 5th edn (Darmstadt: Wissenschaftliche Buchgesellschaft, 1973).

Brusatti, Alois, 'Die Stellung des herrschaftlichen Beamten in Österreich in der Zeit von 1780 bis 1848', *Vierteljahreshefte für Sozial- und Wirtschaftsgeschichte*, 45 (1958): 505–16.

Bucholz, R.O., '"Nothing but Ceremony": Queen Anne and the Limitations of Royal Ritual', *Journal of British Studies*, 30 (1991): 288–323.

Burgess, Glenn, *The Politics of the Ancient Constitution. An Introduction to English Political Thought, 1603–1642* (London: Macmillan, 1992).

—, *Absolute Monarchy and the Stuart Constitution* (New Haven: Yale University Press, 1996).

Burrell, Sidney, 'The Apocalyptic Vision of the Early Covenanters', *Scottish Historical Review*, 63 (1964): 1–24.

Butler, Samuel, *The Way of all Flesh* (Ware, Hertfordshire: Wordsworth, 1994).

Cannadine, David, *The Decline and Fall of the British Aristocracy* (New Haven: Yale University Press, 1990).

Cannon, John (ed.), *The Whig Ascendancy. Colloquies on Hanoverian England* (London: Edward Arnold, 1981).

Cannon, John, *Aristocratic Century. The Peerage of Eighteenth-Century England* (Cambridge: Cambridge University Press, 1984).

Christianson, Paul, *Reformers and Babylon: English Apocalyptic Visions from the Reformation to the Eve of the Civil War* (Toronto: University of Toronto Press, 1978).

Churchill, R.C., 'Three Autobiographical Novelists', in Boris Ford (ed.), *The New Pelican Guide to English Literature*, vol. 6: *From Dickens to Hardy* (Harmondsworth, Middlesex: Penguin Books, 1982), pp. 341–52.

Cockburn, J.A., *A History of English Assizes 1558–1714* (Cambridge: Cambridge University Press, 1972).

Colley, Linda, *Britons: Forging the Nation 1707–1837* (New Haven: Yale University Press, 1992).

—, *Britons. Forging the Nation, 1707–1837* (London: Pimlico, 1994).

Collini, Stefan, *Public Moralists. Political Thought and Intellectual Life in Britain, 1850–1930* (Oxford: Clarendon Press, 1991).

Corrigan, Philip and Sayer, Derek, *The Great Arch. English State Formation as Cultural Revolution* (Oxford: Blackwell, 1985).

Cragg, G.R., *From Puritanism to the Age of Reason* (Cambridge: Cambridge University Press, 1950).

Crane, R.S., 'Suggestions Toward a Genealogy of the "Man of Feeling"', in R.S. Crane, *The Idea of the Humanities and other Essays Critical and Historical* (Chicago: Chicago University Press, 1967), pp. 188–213.

Csáky, Moritz, *Von der Aufklärung zum Liberalismus. Studien zum Frühliberalismus in Ungarn* (Vienna: Österreichische Akademie der Wissenschaften, 1981).

—, *Ideologie der Operette und Wiener Moderne: ein kulturhistorischer Essay* (Vienna: Böhlau, 1996).

Curtin, Michael, *Propriety and Position* (New York: Garland, 1987).

Dahrendorf, Ralf, *Society and Democracy in Germany* (New York: Doubleday, 1969).

—, *On Britain* (London: British Broadcasting Corporation, 1982).

Dann, Otto (ed.), *Lesegesellschaften und bürgerliche Emanzipation* (Munich: C. H. Beck, 1981).

Davis, Walter W., *Joseph II. An Imperial Reformer for the Austrian Netherlands* (The Hague: Martinus Nijhoff, 1974).

Deák, Istvan, *Der k. (u.) k. Offizier: 1848–1918* (Vienna, Cologne, Weimar: Böhlau, 1991).

Defoe, Daniel, *Robinson Crusoe* (Harmondsworth, Middlesex: Penguin Books, 1985).

—, *Moll Flanders* (Harmondsworth, Middlesex: Penguin Books, 1989).

Dickens, Charles, *Great Expectations* (Harmondsworth, Middlesex: Penguin Books, 1985).

—, *Oliver Twist* (Ware, Hertfordshire: Wordsworth, 1992).

Dickson, Peter G.M., *Finance and Government under Maria Theresa, 1740–1780* (2 vols, Oxford: Oxford University Press, 1987).

—, 'Monarchy and Bureaucracy in Late Eighteenth-Century Austria', *English Historical Review*, 110 (1995): 323–67.

Doderer Heimito von, *Grundlagen und Funktion des Romans* (Nürnberg: Glock and Lutz, 1959).

—, *Strudlhofstiege* (Munich: Biederstein [45.–61.Tsd.], 1985).

—, *The Lighted Windows or The Humanization of the Bureaucrat Julius Zihal*. Transl. and with a foreword by John S. Barrett (Riverside, Calif.: Ariadne Press, 2000).

Donaldson, Ian, 'Cato in Tears: Stoical Guises of the "Man of Feeling"', in R.F. Brissenden (ed.), *Studies in the Eighteenth Century* (Toronto: University of Toronto Press, 1973), pp. 377–95.

Duindam, Jeroen, 'Style and Power: a Reappraisal of Court Culture', in Eva Barlösius et al. (eds), *Distanzierte Verstrickungen: die ambivalente Bindung soziologisch Forschender an ihren Gegenstand* (Berlin: Edition Sigma, 1997).

Dunning, Eric and Mennell, Stephen, 'Preface', in Norbert Elias, *The Germans. Power Struggles and the Development of Habitus in the Nineteenth and Twentieth Centuries*, ed. by Michael Schröter. Translated from the German and with a preface by Eric Dunning and Stephen Mennell (Cambridge: Polity Press, VII–XVI, 1996).

Dunning, Eric and Sheard, Kenneth, *Barbarians, Gentlemen and Players. A Sociological Study of the Development of Rugby Football* (Oxford: Martin Robertson & Co., 1979).

Eagleton, Terry, *Literary Theory. An Introduction* (Oxford: Blackwell, 1983).

Ebner-Eschenbach, Marie von, 'Jakob Szela', in *Selected Austrian Short Stories* (The World's Classics), transl. by Marie Busch (London: Humphrey Milford, 1928), pp. 59–93.

Ehalt, Hubert Ch., *Ausdrucksformen absolutistischer Herrschaft. Der Wiener Hof im 17. und 18. Jahrhundert* (Vienna: Verlag für Geschichte und Politik, 1980).

Elias, Norbert, 'Studies in the Genesis of the Naval Profession', *British Journal of Sociology*, 1/4 (1950): 291–309.

—, *Nationale Eigentümlichkeiten der englischen öffentlichen Meinung*. Vortrag gehalten in Bad Wildungen (Bad Homburg: Verlag Dr. Max Gehlen, 1960).

—, *What Is Sociology?* Translation from German by Stephen Mennell and Grace Morissey, with a foreword by Reinhard Bendix (London: Hutchinson, 1978).

—, *The Court Society* (Oxford, Basil Blackwell, 1983).

—, 'On Human Beings and their Emotions: a Process-Sociological Essay', *Theory, Culture and Society*, 4/2–3 (1987): 339–61.

—, *The Symbol Theory*. Ed. by Richard Kilminster (London: Sage, 1991a).

—, *The Society of Individuals*. Translation from German by Edmund Jephcott (Oxford: Basil Blackwell, 1991b).

—, *Mozart. Portrait of a Genius*. Translation from German by Edmund Jephcott (Cambridge: Polity Press, 1993).

—, *The Germans. Power Struggles and the Development of Habitus in the Nineteenth and Twentieth Centuries*. Translation from the German by Eric Dunning and Stephen Mennell and with a preface by the translators (Cambridge: Polity Press, 1996), pp. vii–xvi.

—, *The Civilizing Process*. Translation from German by Edmund Jephcott (Oxford: Blackwell, 2000).

Elias, Norbert and Dunning, Eric, *Quest for Excitement: Sport and Leisure in the Civilizing Process* (Oxford: Blackwell, 1986).

Ellis, Markman, *The Politics of Sensibility. Race, Gender and Commerce in the Sentimental Novel* (Cambridge: Cambridge University Press, 1996).

Elton, Geoffrey R. (ed.), *The Tudor Constitution* (Cambridge: Cambridge University Press, 1960).

Emsley, Clive, 'The English Bobby: An Indulgent Tradition', in Roy Porter (ed.), *Myths of the English* (Cambridge: Polity Press, 1992), pp. 114–35.

Evans, Richard, *Rituals of Retribution: Capital Punishment in Germany. 1600–1987* (Oxford: Oxford University Press, 1996).

Evans, Robert J.W., 'The Austrian Habsburgs. The Dynasty as a Political Institution', in A.G. Dickens (ed.), *The Courts of Europe. Politics, Patronage, and Royalty, 1400–1800* (London: Thames and Hudson, 1977), pp. 121–45.

—, *The Making of the Habsburg Monarchy, 1550–1700. An Interpretation* (Oxford: Clarendon Press, 1979).

Evans, Robert J.W. and Thomas, T.V. (eds), *Crown, Church and Estates. Central European Politics in the Sixteenth and Seventeenth Centuries* (Basingstoke: Macmillan, 1991).

Eybel, J. von, *Die Gimpelinsel* (lacking publishing date and publisher, 1783).

Feigl, Helmuth, *Die niederösterreichische Grundherrschaft vom ausgehenden Mittelalter bis zu den theresianisch-josefinischen Reformen* (Vienna: Verein für Landeskunde von Niederösterreich und Wien, 1964).

—, *Rechtsentwicklung und Gerichtswesen Oberösterreichs im Spiegel der Weistümer* (Vienna: Österreichische Akademie der Wissenschaften, 1974) (Archiv für österreichische Geschichte, vol. 130).

—, 'Die Auswirkungen der theresianisch-josephinischen Reformgesetzgebung auf die ländliche Sozialstruktur Österreichs', in Richard G. Plaschka et al. (eds), *Österreich im Europa der Aufklärung* (2 vols, Vienna: Österreichische Akademie der Wissenschaften, 1985), vol. 1, pp. 45–66.

— (ed.), *Die Auswirkungen der theresianisch-josephinischen Reformen auf die Landwirtschaft und die ländliche Sozialstruktur Niederösterreichs* (Vienna: Selbstverlag des Niederösterreichischen Instituts für Landeskunde, 1982).

Ferguson, Niall, *Empire: How Britain Made the Modern World* (Harmondsworth, Middlesex: Penguin Books, 2004).

Fielding, Henry, *The History of Tom Jones* (Harmondsworth, Middlesex: Penguin Books, 1985).

Fiering, Norman, 'Irresistible Compassion. An Aspect of Eighteenth-Century Sympathy and Humanitarianism', *Journal of the History of Ideas*, 37 (1976): 195–218.

Firth, Katharine R., *The Apocalyptic Tradition in Reformation Britain, 1530–1645* (Oxford: Oxford University Press, 1979).

Fischer, Ernst, *Die Entstehung des österreichischen Volkscharakters* (Vienna: 'Neues Österreich' Zeitungs- und Verlagsgesellschaft, 1945).

Fletcher, Anthony, *Gender, Sex and Subordination in England 1500–1800* (New Haven: Yale University Press, 1995).

Fletcher, Jonathan, *Violence and Civilization. An Introduction to the Work of Norbert Elias* (Cambridge: Polity Press, 1997).

Fodor, Heinrich, 'Der Jakobinismus in Ungarn', *Archiv für Kulturgeschichte*, 37 (1955): 234–43.

Ford, Ford Madox, *The Good Soldier. A Tale of Passion* (Harmondsworth, Middlesex: Penguin Books, 1946).

Forester, Cecil Scott, *Hornblower and the Atropos* (Boston: Little, Brown & Company, 1985).

Fournier, August, 'Kaiser Josef II. und der geheime Dienst. Ein Beitrag zur Geschichte der österreichischen Polizei', *Historische Studien und Skizzen*, 3 (1912): p. 1

Friedell, Egon, *A Cultural History of the Modern Age: The Crisis of the European Soul from the Black Death to the World War* (3 vols, New York: Knopf, 1927–31).

—–, *Kulturgeschichte der Neuzeit* (2 vols, München: Deutscher Taschenbuch Verlag, 1976).

Gampl, Inge, *Staat – Kirche – Individuum in der Rechtsgeschichte Österreichs zwischen Reformation und Revolution* (Wien: Böhlau, 1984).

Garaudy, Roger, *Für einen Realismus ohne Scheuklappen – Picasso, Saint John – Perse, Kafka* (Vienna, Munich, Zürich: Europa Verlag, 1981).

Gatrell, V.A., *The Hanging Tree: Execution and the English People 1770–1868* (Oxford: Oxford University Press, 1994).

Gerhard, Dietrich (ed.), *Ständische Vertretungen in Europa im 17. und 18. Jahrhundert*. (Veröffentlichungen des Max-Planck-Instituts für Geschichte, vol. 27). (Göttingen: Vandenhoeck & Ruprecht, 1969).

Giddens, Anthony, *The Consequences of Modernity* (Cambridge: Polity Press, 1990).

Girouard, Mark, *The Return to Camelot. Chivalry and the English Gentleman* (New Haven: Yale University Press, 1981).

Gleichmann, Peter R., 'Zum Entstehen einer Machttheorie. Referat in der Ad-hoc-Gruppe "Zivilisationssoziologie"', in W. Schulte (ed.) *Soziologie in der Gesellschaft*. Tagungsberichte Nr. 3 beim 20. Deutschen Soziologentag Bremen 1980 (University of Bremen, 1981).

Glyn, A., *The Blood of a Britishman* (London: Hutchinson, 1970).

Gnau, Hermann, *Die Zensur unter Joseph II.* Straßburg (Leipzig: Verlag der Hofbuchhandlung Singer, 1911).

Goffman, Erving, *The Presentation of Self in Everyday Life* (New York: Doubleday Anchor, 1959).

—, *Asylums: Essays on the Social Situation of Mental Patients and Other Immates* (New York: Doubleday Anchor, 1961).

—, *Interaction Ritual: Essays on Face-to-Face Behavior* (New York: Doubleday Anchor, 1967).

Goldberg, Rita, *Sex and Enlightenment. Women in Richardson and Diderot* (Cambridge: Cambridge University Press, 1984).

Gorer, Geoffrey, *Exploring English Character* (London: Cresset Press, 1955).

Grab, Walter, 'Demokratische Freiheitskämpfer Österreichs im Zeitalter der Französischen Revolution', *Wiener Europagespräche 1977* (1978): 54–71.

Graves, Robert, *Goodbye to All That* (New York: Doubleday, 1958).

Greyerz, Kaspar von, *England im Jahrhundert der Revolutionen, 1603–1714* (Stuttgart: Eugen Ulmer, 1994).

Grillparzer, Franz, 'The Poor Fiddler', in *Selected Austrian Short Stories* (The World's Classics), transl. by Marie Busch (London: Humphrey Milford, 1928), pp. 1–58.

—, 'Der arme Spielmann. Selbstbiographie', in *Grillparzers Werke in drei Bänden* (3 vols, Berlin, Weimar: Aufbau-Verlag, 1990), vol. 1, pp. 47–270.

Grüll, Georg, *Der Robot in Oberösterreich* (Linz: Oberösterreichisches Landesarchiv, 1952).

—, *Bauer, Herr und Landesfürst. Sozialrevolutionäre Bestrebungen der oberösterreichischen Bauern, 1650–1848* (Linz: Oberösterreichisches Landesarchiv, 1963).

Grünberg, Karl, *Die Bauernbefreiung und die Auflösung des gutsherrlich-bäuerlichen Verhältnisses in Böhmen, Mähren und Schlesien* (2 vols, Leipzig, 1893/94).

Guy, John, *Tudor England* (Oxford: Oxford University Press, 1990).

Haggard, H. Rider, *Three Adventure Novels: She – King Solomon's Mines – Allan Quatermain* (New York: Dover Publications, 1951).

Haley, Bruce, *The Healthy Body and Victorian Culture* (Cambridge, Mass.: Harvard University Press, 1978).

Hall, N. John, 'Introduction', in Anthony Trollope, *The Three Clerks* (London: The Trollope Society, 1992), pp. VII–XIV.

Haller, William, *Foxe's Book of Martyrs and the Elect Nation* (London: Jonathan Cape, 1963).

Hanák, Peter, 'Österreichischer Staatspatriotismus im Zeitalter des aufsteigenden Nationalismus', *Wiener Europagespräche 1977*, (1978): 315–30.

Hanisch, Ernst, 'Beobachtungen zur Geschichte der österreichischen Bürokratie', *Zeitgeschichte*, 14 (1986): 1–18.

—, *Der lange Schatten des Staates. Österreichische Gesellschaftsgeschichte im 20. Jahrhundert* (Vienna: Ueberreuter, 1994).

Hanke, Gerhard, 'Das Zeitalter des Zentralismus, 1740–1848', in Karl Bosl (ed.), *Handbuch der Geschichte der Böhmischen Länder* (Stuttgart: Anton Heisemann, 1973/74), pp. 413–645.

Hannemann, Bruno, *Johann Nestroy. Nihilistisches Welttheater und verflixter Kerl: Zum Ende der Wiener Komödie* (Bonn: Bouvier, 1977).

Hantsch, Hugo, *Die Geschichte Österreichs*, vol. 2: *1648–1918* (Graz: Styria, 1968).

Harth, Friedrich, 'Die patrimoniale Gerichtsbarkeit in Österreich unter der Enns nach dem Stand der heutigen Forschung', *Monatsblatt des Vereins für Landeskunde von Niederösterreich*, 9 (1910): 120–36, 146–57.

Harvie, Christopher, *The Centre of Things. Political Fiction in Britain from Disraeli to the Present* (London: Unwin Hyman, 1991).

Haselsteiner, Horst, *Josef II. und die Komitate Ungarns: Herrscherrecht und Ständischer Konstitutionalismus* (Veröffentlichungen des österreichischen Ost- und Südosteuropäischen Instituts, vol. 11) (Vienna: Böhlau, 1983).

Hassinger, Herbert, 'Die Landstände der österreichischen Länder. Zusammensetzung, Organisation und Leistung im 16.–18. Jahrhundert', *Jahrbuch des Vereins für Landeskunde von Niederösterreich*, NF 36 (1964): 989–1035.

——, 'Ständische Vertretungen in den althabsburgischen Ländern und in Salzburg', in Dietrich Gerhard (ed.), *Ständische Vertretungen* (1969), pp. 247–85.

Hayton, David, 'Moral Reform and Country Politics in the Late Seventeenth-Century House of Commons', *Past and Present*, 128 (1990): 48–91.

Heal, Felicity, 'The Crown, the Gentry and London: The Enforcement of Proclamation, 1596–1640', in C. Cross et al. (eds), *Law and Government under the Tudors* (Cambridge: Cambridge University Press, 1988), pp. 211–26.

——, *Hospitality in Early Modern England* (Oxford: Clarendon Press, 1990)

Heal, Felicity and Holmes, Clive, *The Gentry in England and Wales, 1500–1700* (Basingstoke: Macmillan, 1994).

Heckenast, Gusztáv, 'Die Habsburger und Ungarn im 18. Jahrhundert', *Acta Historica Academiae Scientiarum Hungaricae*, 31 (1985): 113–28.

Heer, Friedrich, *Der Kampf um die österreichische Identität* (Vienna: Böhlau, 1981).

Hein, Jürgen, *Spiel und Satire in der Komödie Johann Nestroys* (Bad Homburg: Gehlen, 1970).

——, 'Nachwort', in Johann Nestroy, *Judith und Holofernes. Häuptling Abendwind* (Stuttgart: Reclam, 1988), pp. 77–84.

Heindl, Waltraud, 'Gehorsam und Herrschaft – Zur Entwicklung des Beamtendienstrechts (1780–1815)', in *Bericht über den 16. österreichischen Historikertag in Krems an der Donau.* (Veröffentlichungen des Verbandes österreichischer Geschichtsvereine, vol. 25). (Vienna: Verband der österreichischen Geschichtsvereine, 1985), pp. 328–41.

——, *Gehorsame Rebellen. Bürokratie und Beamte in Österreich, 1780 bis 1848* (Vienna: Böhlau, 1991).

Heiss, Gernot, 'Princes, Jesuits and the Origins of Counter-Reformation in the Habsburg Lands', in Robert J.W. Evans and T.V. Thomas (eds), *Crown, Church, and Estates* (Basingstoke: Macmillan, 1991), pp. 92–109.

Hellbling, Ernst, *Österreichische Verfassungs- und Verwaltungsgeschichte.* 2nd edn (Vienna: Springer, 1974).

Hellmuth, Eckhart (ed.), *The Transformation of Political Culture* (Oxford: Oxford University Press, 1990).

Herzmanovsky-Orlando, Fritz, *Das Beste von Herzmanovsky-Orlando.* Ed. by F. Torberg (München: Langen-Müller, 1995).

——, *The Tragic Demise of a Faithful Court Official.* Transl. and with an afterword by David A. Veeder (Riverside, Calif.: Ariadne Press, 1997).

Hirsch, Fred, *Social Limits to Growth* (Cambridge, Mass.: Harvard University Press, 1976).

Hobsbawm, Eric, *Nations and Nationalism since 1780: Programme, Myth, Reality* (Cambridge: Cambridge University Press, 1990).

——, *The Age of Extremes: The Short Twentieth Century* (Harmondsworth, Middlesex: Penguin, 1994).

Hochschild, Arlie Russell, *The Managed Heart: Commercialization of Human Feeling* (Berkeley: University of California Press, 1983).

Hodge, Robert, *Literature as Discourse. Textual Strategies in English and History* (Cambridge: Polity Press, 1990).

Hoefer, Frank Thomas, *Pressepolitik und Polizeistaat Metternichs. Die Überwachung von Presse und politischer Öffentlichkeit in Deutschland und den Nachbarstaaten durch das Mainzer Informationsbüro (1833–1848)* (Munich: K.G. Saur Verlag, 1983).

Hofmannsthal, Hugo von, 'Preuße und Österreicher', in Hugo von Hofmannsthal, *Ausgewählte Werke, Erzählungen und Aufsätze* (Frankfurt/M.: S. Fischer, 1957), pp. 615–16.

Holmes, Geoffrey, 'The Achievement of Stability: the Social Context of Politics from the 1680s to the Age of Walpole', in John Cannon (ed.), *Whig Ascendancy* (London: Edward Arnold, 1981), pp. 1–22.

Holt, Richard, *Sport and the British: A Modern History* (Oxford: Oxford University Press, 1989).

Hont, Istvan and Ignatieff, Michael (eds), *Wealth and Virtue: The Shaping of Political Economy in the Scottish Enlightenment* (Cambridge: Cambridge University Press, 1983).

Huber, Franz X., *Herr Schlendrian oder der Richter nach den neuen Gesetzen* (Berlin: [no publisher], 1787).

Hughes, Thomas, *Tom Brown's Schooldays* (Ware, Hertfordshire: Wordsworth, 1993).

Huizinga, Johan, *The waning of the Middle Ages: A Study of the Forms of Life, Thought, and Art in France and the Netherlands in the 14th and 15th Centuries.* Translated by F. Hopman (London: E. Arnold, 1924).

Ingrao, Charles W. (ed.), *State and Society in Early Modern Austria* (West Lafayette, Ind.: Purdue University Press, 1994).

Inkeles, Alex, *National Character. A Psycho-Social Perspective*. With contributions by D.J. Levinson et al. (New Brunswick: Transaction Publishers, 1997).

Innerhofer, Franz, *Beautiful Days* (New York: Urizen Books, 1976).

Innes, Joanna M., 'Politics and Morals: The Reformation of Manners Movement in Later Eighteenth-Century England', in Eckhart Hellmuth (ed.), *Transformation* (Oxford: Oxford University Press, 1990), pp. 57–118.

Isaacs, Tina, 'The Anglican Hierarchy and the Reformation of Manners, 1688–1738', *Journal of Ecclesiastical History,* 33 (1982): 391–411.

James, Louis, *The Xenophobe's Guide to the Austrians* (Horsham, West Sussex: Ravette Books, 1994).

James, Mervyn, 'English Politics and the Concept of Honour, 1485–1642', in Mervyn James, *Society, Politics and Culture. Studies in Early Modern England* (Cambridge: Cambridge University Press, 1986), pp. 308–415.

Jones, M.G., *The Charity School Movement. A Study of Eighteenth–Century Puritanism in Action* (London: Frank Cass, 1964).

Kafka, Franz, *Brief an den Vater* (Frankfurt/M.: S. Fischer, 1975).

——, *The Trial.* Introduction by George Steiner. Transl. from the German by Willa and Edwin Muir (New York: Schocken Books, 1992).

Kahl, Kurt, *Johann Nestroy oder Der wienerische Shakespeare* (Vienna: Molden, 1970).

Kann, Robert A., *A History of the Habsburg Empire, 1526–1918* (Berkeley: University of California Press, 1974).

Kavke, Frantisek, 'Die Habsburger und der böhmische Staat bis zur Mitte des 18. Jahrhunderts', *Historica,* 8 (1964): 35–64.

Keane, John (ed.), *Civil Society and the State. New European Perspectives* (London: Verso, 1988).

Kenyon, John (ed.), *The Stuart Constitution, 1603–1688* (Cambridge: Cambridge University Press, 1966).

Kipling, Rudyard, *Stalky & Co.* (London: Pan, 1986).

Király, Béla K., 'Peasant Movement in Hungary in 1790', *Südost-Forschungen,* 26 (1967): 140–56.

——, *Hungary in the Late Eighteenth Century. The Decline of Enlightened Despotism* (New York: Columbia University Press: 1969).

Kisch, Egon Erwin, *Schreib das auf, Kisch!* Das Kriegstagebuch von Egon Erwin Kisch (Berlin: Aufbau-Verlag, 1991).

Kishlansky, Mark, *A Monarchy Transformed: Britain 1603–1714* (London: Lane, 1996).

Kishon, Ephraim, *Wie unfair, David! und andere israelische Satiren* (Frankfurt/M.: Ullstein, 1987).

Klein, Lawrence E., *Shaftesbury and the Culture of Politeness* (Cambridge: Cambridge University Press, 1994).

Klima, Arnost, 'Mercantilism in the Habsburg Monarchy – With Special Reference to the Bohemian Lands', *Historica*, 11 (1965): 95–119.

—, 'The Role of Rural Domestic Industry in Bohemia in the 18th Century', *Economic History Review*, 27 (1974): 48–56.

—, 'Agrarian Class Structure and Economic Development in Pre-Industrial Bohemia', in T.H. Aston and C.H.E. Philpin (eds), *The Brenner Debate. Agrarian Class Structure and Economic Development in Pre-Industrial Europe* (Cambridge: Cambridge University Press, 1985), pp. 192–212.

Klingenstein, Grete, *Staatsverwaltung und kirchliche Autorität. Das Problem der Zensur in der theresianischen Reform* (Vienna: Böhlau, 1970).

Klueting, Harm, 'Deutschland und der Josephinismus. Wirkungen und Ausstrahlungen der theresianisch-josephinischen Reformen auf die außerösterreichischen deutschen Territorien', in Helmut Reinalter (ed.), *Josephinismus* (Frankfurt/M.: Lang, 1993a), pp. 63–102.

Kluxen, Kurt, *Geschichte und Problematik des Parlamentarismus* (Frankfurt/M.: Suhrkamp, 1983).

—, *Englische Verfassungsgeschichte. Mittelalter* (Darmstadt: Wissenschaftliche Buchgesellschaft, 1987).

Körner, Alfred (ed.), *Die Wiener Jakobiner* (Stuttgart: Metzler, 1972).

Koestler, Arthur, 'Humour', in *The New Encyclopaedia Britannica.* 15th edn (Chicago: Brittanica, 1994).

Kraus, Karl, *The Last Days of Mankind.* Abridged and edited by Frederick Ungar (New York: Frederick Ungar Publishing, 1974).

—, *Die letzten Tage der Menschheit* (Frankfurt/M.: Suhrkamp, 1986).

Kümmel, Ruth, *The Foster Child in Nineteenth-Century England. State Policy and the Emergence of a New Awareness in Reform Debates.* M.A. thesis (Graz, 1997).

Kuzmics, Helmut, *Der Preis der Zivilisation. Die Zwänge der Moderne im theoretischen Vergleich* (Frankfurt: Campus, 1989).

—, 'Weber and Elias on Civilization: Protestant Ethics and Sport in England', *Arena Journal*, 1 (1993): 195–220.

Lamont, William M., *Godly Rule. Politics and Religion, 1603–60* (London: Macmillan, 1969).

Landau, Norma, *The Justices of the Peace, 1679–1760* (Berkeley et al.: University of California Press, 1984).

Langford, Paul, *Englishness Identified. Manners and Character, 1650–1850* (Oxford: Oxford University Press, 2000).

Laqueur, Thomas Walter, *Religion and Respectability. Sunday Schools and Working-Class Culture, 1780–1850* (New Haven: Yale University Press, 1976).

Lasch, Christopher, *Haven in a Heartless World: The Family Besieged* (New York: Norton, 1977).

—, *The Culture of Narcissism. American Life in an Age of Diminishing Expectations* (London: Abacus, 1980).

Laslett, Peter, 'The Wrong Way through the Telescope: A Note on Literary Evidence in Sociology and in Historical Sociology', *British Journal of Sociology*, 27/3 (1976): 319–42.

—, *The World We Have Lost* (London: Routledge, 1989).

Leavis, Queenie D., 'Introduction', in Charlotte Brontë, *Jane Eyre* (Harmondsworth, Middlesex: Penguin Books, 1985), pp. 7–29.

Lengauer, Hubert, 'Von eurer Freiheit habt ihr nichts behalten, Als das ungewaschne Maul: Grillparzer und England', in Helmut Koopmann and Martina Lauster (eds), *Vormärzliteratur in europäischer Perspektive: Öffentlichkeit und nationale Identität* (Bielefeld: Aisthesis, 1996).

Lepenies, Wolf, *Die drei Kulturen. Soziologie zwischen Literatur und Wissenschaft* (Reinbek bei Hamburg: Rowohlt, 1988).

Lettner, Gerda, *Das Rückzugsgefecht der Aufklärung in Wien, 1790–1792* (Frankfurt: Campus Verlag, 1988).

Levy, Miriam, 'Leopold II, Joseph von Aschauer, and the Role of the Estates in the Habsburg Monarchy', *Mitteilungen des österreichischen Staatsarchivs*, 38 (1985): 197–222.

Lhotsky, Alphons, 'Das Problem des österreichischen Menschen', in Alphons Lhotsky, *Der österreichische Mensch.* Aufsätze und Vorträge, edn H. Wagner and H. Koller, vol. 4. (Vienna: Verlag für Geschichte und Politik, 1974), pp. 225–331.

Liebel-Weckowicz, Helen, 'Auf der Suche nach neuer Autorität: Raison d'Etat in den Verwaltungs- und Rechtsreformen Maria Theresias und Josephs II.', in Richard Plaschka et al. (eds), *Österreich* (2 vols, Vienna: Österreichische Akademie der Wissenschaften, 1985), vol. 1, pp. 339–64.

Link, Christoph, 'Die Habsburgischen Erblande, die böhmischen Länder und Salzburg', in Kurt G. A. Jeserich et al. (eds), *Deutsche Verwaltungsgeschichte,* vol. 1: *Vom Spätmittelalter bis zum Ende des Reichs* (Stuttgart: Klett Verlag, 1983), pp. 468–552.

Link, Edith Murr, *The Emancipation of the Austrian Peasant 1740–1798* (New York: Columbia University Press, 1949).

Loades, David, *The Tudor Court* (London: B.T. Batsford, 1986).

Loewenstein, Karl, *Staatsrecht und Staatspraxis von Großbritannien*, vol. 1: *Parlament – Regierung – Parteien* (Berlin: Springer Verlag, 1967).

Lorenz, Ottokar, *Joseph II. und die belgische Revolution. Nach den Papieren des General-Gouverneurs Grafen Murray 1787* (Vienna: Wilhelm Braunmüller, 1862).

Lütge, Friedrich, 'Das 14./15. Jahrhundert in der Sozial- und Wirtschaftsgeschichte', *Jahrbücher für Nationalökonomie und Statistik*, 162 (1950): 161–213.

Lutz, Heinrich, *Zwischen Habsburg und Preußen. Deutschland 1815–1866* (Berlin: Propyläen, 1985).

MacCaffrey, Wallace T., 'Place and Patronage in Elizabethan Politics', in S.T. Bindhoff (ed.), *Elizabethan Government and Society* (London: Athlone Press, 1961), pp. 95–126.

MacDonagh, Oliver, *Early Victorian Government, 1830–1870* (London: Weidenfeld and Nicolson, 1977).

Macfarlane, Alan, *The Origins of English Individualism* (Oxford: Blackwell, 1978).

Magris, Claudio, 'Doderers erste Wirklichkeit', in Wendelin Schmidt-Dengler (ed.), *Heimito von Doderer 1896–1966.* Symposium anlässlich des 80. Geburtstages des Dichters, Vienna 1976. (Salzburg: Neugebauer, 1976), pp. 41–60.

—, *Der habsburgische Mythos in der österreichischen Literatur.* 2nd edn (Salzburg: Otto Müller, 1988).

Mann, Michael, *The Sources of Social Power,* vol. 1: *A History of Power from the Beginning to AD 1760* (Cambridge: Cambridge University Press, 1986).

—, *States, War and Capitalism* (Oxford: Blackwell, 1988).

—, *The Sources of Social Power,* vol. 2: *The Rise of Classes and Nation-States, 1760–1914* (Cambridge: Cambridge University Press, 1993).

Marx, Julius, *Die österreichische Zensur im Vormärz* (Vienna: Verlag für Geschichte und Politik, 1959)

Marx, Karl, *Das Kapital*, vol. 1 (Berlin: Dietz, 1972).

Matis, Herbert, 'Staatswerdungsprozeß und Ausbildung der Volkswirtschaft', in Herbert Matis (ed.), *Glückseligkeit* (Berlin: Duncker & Humblot, 1981a), pp. 15–27.

—, 'Die Rolle der Landwirtschaft im Merkantilsystem – Produktionsstruktur und gesellschaftliche Verhältnisse im Agrarbereich', in Herbert Matis (ed.), *Glückseligkeit* (Berlin: Duncker & Humblot, 1981b), pp. 269–93.

—, (ed.), *Von der Glückseligkeit des Staates. Staat, Wirtschaft und Gesellschaft in Österreich im Zeitalter des aufgeklärten Absolutismus* (Berlin: Duncker & Humblot, 1981).

Maurer, Michael (ed.), *O Britannien, von deiner Freiheit einen Hut voll: deutsche Reiseberichte des 18. Jahrhunderts* (Munich: C.H. Beck; Leipzig, Weimar: Kiepenheuer, 1992).

Mautner, Franz, H., *Nestroy* (Heidelberg: Carl Winter, 1974).

Melton, James Van Horn, 'The Nobility in the Bohemian and Austrian Lands, 1620–1780', in H.M. Scott (ed.), *Enlightened Absolutism* (Basingstoke: Macmillan, 1995), pp. 110–43.

Menasse, Robert, *Das Land ohne Eigenschaften. Essay zur österreichischen Identität* (Vienna: Sonderzahl, 1992).

Mennell, Stephen, *Norbert Elias: Civilization and the Human Self-Image* (Oxford: Basil Blackwell, 1989).

Merz, Carl and Qualtinger, Helmut, 'Der Herr Karl', in Walter Rösler (ed.), *Geh'n ma halt a bisserl unter: Kabarett in Wien von den Anfängen bis heute* (Berlin: Henschel, 1991), pp. 345–367.

Mikes, George, *How to Be a Brit* (Harmondsworth, Middlesex: Penguin Books, 1986).

Mikoletzky, Lorenz, 'Der Versuch einer Steuer- und Urbarialregulierung unter Kaiser Josef II.', *Mitteilungen des österreichischen Staatsarchivs*, 24 (1971): 310–46.

Mill, John Stuart, *A System of Logic Ratioactive and Inductive. Being a Connected View of the Principles of Evidence and the Methods of Scientific Inquiry.* Collected Works, vol. VIII. Ed. J.M. Robson (Toronto and London: University of Toronto Press and Routldege & Kegan Paul, 1974).

Mommsen, Hans, 'Die Rückwirkungen des Ausgleichs mit Ungarn auf die zisleithanische Verfassungsfrage', in Hans Mommsen, *Arbeiterbewegung und nationale Frage. Ausgewählte Aufsätze* (Göttingen: Vandenhoeck&Ruprecht, 1979), pp. 147–65.

Musil, Robert, *The Man without Qualities.* Transl. from the German by Sophie Wilkins and Burton Pike (New York: Vintage Books, 1996).

—–, *The Confusions of Young Torless.* Transl. from the German by Shaun Whiteside (Harmondsworth, Middlesex: Penguin 20th Century Classics, 2003).

Nabokov, Vladimir, *Lectures on Literature* (San Diego et al.: Harvest Books, 1980).

Nathanson, Donald L., *Shame and Pride: Affect, Sex, and the Birth of the Self* (New York: Norton, 1992).

Neale, John, *Essays in Elizabethan History* (London: Jonathan Cape, 1958).

Nestroy, Johann, 'A Man Full of Nothing' in *Three Comedies by Johann Nestroy.* Transl. by Max Knight and Joseph Fabry. Foreword by Thornton Wilder (New York: Frederick Ungar Publishing, 1967).

—–, *Einen Jux will er sich machen* (Stuttgart: Reclam, 1986a).

—–, 'Judith and Holophernes', in *Three Viennese Comedies by Johann Nepomuk Nestroy.* Transl. and with an introduction by Robert Harrison and Katharina Wilson (Columbia, South Carolina: Camden House, 1986b), pp. 93-122.

—–, *Der Zerrissene* (Stuttgart: Reclam, 1987).

—–, *Judith und Holofernes. Häuptling Abendwind* (Stuttgart: Reclam, 1988).

—–, *Der böse Geist Lumpazivagabundus oder Das liederliche Kleeblatt* (Stuttgart: Reclam, 1991).

Newman, Gerald, *The Rise of English Nationalism: A Cultural History, 1740–1830* (New York: St. Martin's Press, 1987).

Nipperdey, Thomas, *Deutsche Geschichte, 1800–1866: Bürgerwelt und starker Staat* (Munich: Beck, 1983).

O'Brien, Patrick, 'The Political Economy of British Taxation, 1660–1815', *Economic History Review*, 61 (1988): 1–32.

O'Brien, Patrick and Hunt, P.A., 'The Rise of a Fiscal State in England, 1485–1815', *Historical Research*, 66 (1993): 129–76.

Oberhummer, Hermann, *Die Wiener Polizei. Neue Beiträge zur Geschichte des Sicherheitswesens in den Ländern der ehemaligen österreichisch-ungarischen Monarchie* (2 vols, Vienna: Gerold, 1938).

Obschernitzky, Doris, *Franz Kafka, Das 'Schloß'. Poetische Irrealität und gesellschaftliche Wirklichkeit. Ein Beitrag zum Streit um Kafkas Realismus und zum Wirklichkeitsgehalt des Schloß-Romans*. Diss. phil. Berlin, 1977.

Ogris, Werner, 'Joseph II.: Staats- und Rechtsreformer', in Peter F. Barton (ed.), *Toleranz* (Vienna: Institut für Protestantische Kirchengeschichte, 1981), pp. 109–51.

Osterloh, Karl–Heinz, *Joseph von Sonnenfels und die österreichische Reformbewegung im Zeitalter des aufgeklärten Absolutismus* (Lübeck: Matthiesen Verlag, 1970).

Österreichische Zentralverwaltung (OEZ), *Von der Vereinigung der österreichischen und böhmischen Hofkanzlei bis zur Errichtung der Ministerialverfassung, 1749–1848*. (Veröffentlichungen der Kommission für Neuere Geschichte Österreichs, vols 18, 29, 32, 35, 36, 42, 43) (Vienna: Österreichische Akademie der Wissenschaften).

Otruba, Gustav, 'Anfänge und Vorbereitung der böhmischen Manufakturen bis zum Beginn des 19. Jahrhunderts (1820)', *Bohemia Jahrbuch*, 6 (1965): 230–331.

Palmer, Robert R. and Kenéz, Peter, 'Two Documents of the Hungarian Revolutionary Movement of 1794', *Journal of Central European Affairs*, 20 (1961): 423–42.

Palmer, Stanley H., *Police and Protest in England and Ireland, 1780–1850* (Cambridge: Cambridge University Press, 1988).

Pánek, Jaroslav, 'The Religious Question and the Political System of Bohemia before and after the Battle of the White Mountain', in R.J.W. Evans and T.V. Thomas (eds), *Crown, Church, and Estates* (Basingstoke: Macmillan, 1991), pp. 129–48.

Parin, Paul and Parin-Matthéy, Goldy, 'Typische Unterschiede zwischen Schweizern und Süddeutschen aus dem gebildeten Kleinbürgertum: Ein methodischer Versuch mit der vergleichenden Psychoanalyse (Ethnopsychoanalyse)', *Psyche*, 30 (1976): 1028–48.

Parsons, Talcott, *Das System moderner Gesellschaften* (Munich: Juventa, 1970).

—, 'Evolutionäre Universalien der Gesellschaft', in Wolfgang Zapf (ed.), *Theorien des sozialen Wandels*. 4th edn (Königstein/Ts.: Athenäum et al., 1979), pp. 55–74.

Patrouch, Joseph F., *A Negotiated Settlement. The Counter-Reformation in Upper Austria under the Habsburgs* (Boston-Leiden-Cologne: Humanities Press, 2000).

Patzelt, Erna, 'Bauernschutz in Österreich vor 1848', *Mitteilungen des Instituts für österreichische Geschichtsforschung*, 58 (1950): 637–55.

Peabody, Dean, *National Characteristics* (Cambridge: Cambridge University Press, 1985).

Peck, Linda Levy, '"For a king not to be bountiful were a fault". Perspectives on Court Patronage in Early Stuart England', *Journal of British Studies*, 25 (1986): 31–61.

Plaschka, Richard Georg et al. (eds), *Österreich im Europa der Aufklärung. Kontinuität und Zäsur in Europa zur Zeit Maria Theresias und Josephs II* (2 vols, Vienna: Österreichische Akademie der Wissenschaften, 1985).

Pocock, J.G.A., 'Cambridge Paradigms and Scotch Philosophers: A Study of the Relations between the Civic Humanist and the Civil Jurisprudential Interpretation of Eighteenth-Century Social Thought', in Istvan Hont and Michael Ignatieffl (eds), *Wealth and Virtue* (Cambridge: Cambridge University Press, 1983), pp. 235–52.

—, *Virtue, Commerce, and History. Essays on Political Thought and History, Chiefly in the Eighteenth Century* (Cambridge: Cambridge University Press, 1985).

Polasky, Janet L., *Revolution in Brussels, 1787–1793* (Brussels: Académie Royale de Belgique, 1987).

Pool, Daniel, *What Jane Austen Ate and Charles Dickens Knew: From Fox-Hunting to Whist – The Facts of Daily Life in Nineteenth-Century England* (New York: Simon & Schuster, 1994).

Porter, Roy, 'The Enlightenment in England', in Roy Porter and M. Teich (eds), *The Enlightenment in National Context* (Cambridge: Cambridge University Press, 1981).

Press, Volker, 'Adel in den österreichisch-böhmischen Erblanden und im Reich zwischen dem 15. und dem 17. Jahrhundert', in Herbert Knittler et al. (eds), *Adel im Wandel. Politik, Kultur, Konfession, 1500–1700* (Vienna: Amt des niederösterreichischen Landesmuseums, 1990), pp. 19–31.

—, 'The System of Estates in the Austrian Hereditary Lands and in the Holy Roman Empire: A Comparison', in R.J.W. Evans and T.V. Thomas (eds), *Crown, Church, and Estates* (Basingstoke, Macmillan, 1991), pp. 1–22.

—, 'The Imperial Court of the Habsburgs: From Maximilian I to Ferdinand III, 1493–1657', in Ronald G. Asch and Adolf M. Birke (eds), *Princes, Patronage, and the Nobility* (Oxford: Oxford University Press, 1991), pp. 289–312.

Preston, John, 'Fielding and Smollett', in Boris Ford (ed.) *The New Pelican Guide to English Literature*, vol. 4: *From Dryden to Johnson* (Harmondsworth, Middlesex: Penguin, 1982), pp. 305–22.

Quinlan, Maurice J., *Victorian Prelude. A History of English Manners, 1700–1830* (New York: Columbia University Press, 1941).

Raban, Jonathan, *Coasting* (London: Pan Books, 1987).

Raimund, Friedrich, *Das Mädchen aus der Feenwelt oder der Bauer als Millionär* (Stuttgart: Reclam, 1990).

Rauchensteiner, Manfried, *Der Tod des Doppeladlers. Österreich-Ungarn und der Erste Weltkrieg* (Graz: Styria, 1993).

Rebel, Hermann, *Peasant Classes: The Bureaucratization of Property and Family Relations under Early Habsburg Absolutism* (Princeton, N.J.: Princeton University Press, 1983).

Reinalter, Helmut (ed.), *Jakobiner in Mitteleuropa* (Innsbruck: Innsbrucker Verlag, 1977).

—, *Aufgeklärter Absolutismus und Revolution. Zur Geschichte des Jakobinertums und der frühdemokratischen Bestrebungen in der Habsburgermonarchie* (Vienna: Böhlau, 1980).

—, *Der Jakobinismus in Mitteleuropa. Eine Einführung* (Stuttgart: Kohlhammer, 1981).

—, *Die Französische Revolution und Mitteleuropa* (Frankfurt/M.: Suhrkamp, 1988).

—, 'Soziale Unruhen in Österreich im Einflußfeld der Französischen Revolution', in Helmut Berding (ed.), *Soziale Unruhen in Deutschland während der Französischen Revolution* (Göttingen: Vandenhoeck und Ruprecht, 1988), pp. 189–201.

—, (ed.), *Der Josephinismus. Bedeutung, Einflüsse und Wirkungen* (Frankfurt/M.: Lang, 1993a).

—, (ed.), *Aufklärungsgesellschaften* (Frankfurt/M.: Lang, 1993b).

Reiner, Robert, *The Politics of the Police* (New York: Harvester Wheatsheaf, 1985).

Rich, Paul J., *Chains of Empire: English Public Schools, Masonic Cabbalism, Historical Causality, and Imperial Clubdom* (London: Regency Press, 1991).

Ritter, Gerhard A., *Parlament und Demokratie in Großbritannien* (Göttingen: Vandenhoeck und Ruprecht, 1972).

Roberts, Clayton, 'The Constitutional Significance of the Financial Settlement of 1690', *Historical Journal*, 20 (1977): 59–76.

Roberts, James Deotis, *From Puritanism to Platonism in Seventeenth-Century England* (The Hague: Martinus Nijhoff, 1968).

Robson–Scott, W.D., *German Travellers in England: 1400–1800* (Oxford: Blackwell, 1953).

Romani, Robert, *National Character and Public Spirit in Britain and France, 1750–1914* (Cambridge: Cambridge University Press, 2002).

Rommel, Otto, *Die Alt-Wiener Volkskomödie. Ihre Geschichte vom barocken Welttheater bis zum Tode Nestroys* (Vienna: Schroll, 1952).

Rosegger, Peter, *Jakob der Letzte* (Munich: Staackmann, 1979).

Rosenstrauch–Königsberg, Edith, *Zirkel und Zentren. Aufsätze zur Aufklärung in Österreich am Ende des 18. Jahrhunderts* (Vienna: Deuticke, 1992).

Rösler, Walter (ed.), *Geh'n ma halt a bisserl unter: Kabarett in Wien von den Anfängen bis heute* (Berlin: Henschel, 1991).

Rossbacher, Karlheinz, *Literatur und Liberalismus. Zur Kultur der Ringstraßenzeit in Wien* (Vienna: Jugend und Volk, 1992).

Roth, Joseph, *The Radetzky March.* Transl. from German by Joachim Neugroschel (Woodstock, N.Y.: The Overlook Press, 1995).

—, 'The Bust of the Emperor' in *The Collected Stories of Joseph Roth* (New York: W. W. Norton & Company, 2002), pp. 227–47.

—, *The Emperor's Tomb* Woodstock (New York: The Overlook Press, 2002).

Rozdolski, Roman, *Die große Steuer- und Agrarreform Josephs II* (Warsaw: Pánstwowe Wydawnictwo Naukowe, 1961).

Rule, John, *Albion's People: English Society, 1714–1815* (London: Longman, 1992).

Rumpler, Helmut, *Eine Chance für Mitteleuropa. Bürgerliche Emanzipation und Staatsverfall in der Habsburgermonarchie* (Vienna: Ueberreuter, 1997).

—, (ed.), *Innere Staatsbildung und gesellschaftliche Modernisierung in Österreich und Deutschland 1867/71 bis 1914* (Vienna: Verlag für Geschichte und Politik, 1991).

Rupp, Gordon, *Religion in England, 1688–1791* (Oxford: Clarendon Press, 1986).

Saar, Ferdinand von, *Doktor Trojan. Sappho* (Stuttgart: Reclam, 1980).

—, *Die Steinklopfer. Tambi* (Stuttgart: Reclam, 1993).

Sashegyi, Oskar, *Zensur und Geistesfreiheit unter Joseph II. Beitrag zur Kulturgeschichte der Habsburgischen Länder* (Budapest: Studia Historica Academiae Scientiarum Hungaricae, 1958).

Sammlung aller k.k. Verordnungen und Gesetze vom Jahre 1740 bis 1780, die unter der Regierung des Kaiser Joseph II. theils noch ganz bestehen, theils zum Theile abgeändert sind ... 8 Bände und ein Registerband, 2nd edn (Vienna: Mößle, 1787).

Sandgruber, Roman, *Ökonomie und Politik. Österreichische Wirtschaftsgeschichte vom Mittelalter bis zur Gegenwart* (Vienna: Ueberreuter, 1995).

Sassoon, Siegfried, *Memoirs of a Fox-Hunting Man* (London: Faber and Faber, 1986).

Sayles, George O., *The Medieval Foundation of England.* 2nd edn (London: Methuen, 1950).

—, *The King's Parliament of England* (London: Edward Arnold, 1975).

Scheff, Thomas J., *Violent Emotions: Shame and Rage in Destructive Conflicts* (Lexington: Lexington Books, 1993).

—, *Bloody Revenge: Emotions, Nationalism and War* (Boulder: Westview Press, 1994).

Scheff, Thomas J. and Retzinger, Suzanne M., *Emotions and Violence* (Lexington: Lexington Books, 1991).

Schindler, Norbert and Bonß, Wolfgang, 'Praktische Aufklärung – Ökonomische Sozietäten in Süddeutschland und Österreich im 18. Jahrhundert', in Rudolf Vierhaus (ed.), *Deutsche patriotische und gemeinnützige Gesellschaften* (Munich: Kraus International Publications, 1980), pp. 255–353.

Schindling, Anton, 'Delayed Confessionalization. Retarding Factors and Religious Minorities in the Territories of the Holy Roman Empire, 1555–1648', in Charles Ingrao (ed.), *State and Society* (West Lafayette, Ind.: Purdue University Press, 1994), pp. 54–70.

Schnitzler, Arthur, 'Leutnant Gustl', in Gotthart Wunberg (ed), *Die Wiener Moderne* (Stuttgart: Reclam, 1984), pp. 407–15.

Schramm, Gottfried, 'Armed Conflict in East-Central Europe: Protestant Noble Opposition and Catholic Royalist Factions, 1604–20', in R.J.W. Evans and T.V. Thomas (eds), *Crown, Church, and Estates* (Basingstoke: Macmillan, 1991), pp. 176–95.

Schremmer, Eckart, *Steuern und Staatsfinanzen während der Industrialisierung Europas. England, Frankreich, Preußen und das Deutsche Reich, 1800 bis 1914* (Berlin: Springer, 1994).

Schröder, Hans-Christoph, 'Der englische Adel', in Armgard von Reden-Dohna and Ralph Melville (eds), *Der Adel an der Schwelle des bürgerlichen Zeitalters, 1780–1860* (Stuttgart: Franz Steiner Verlag, 1988), pp. 21–88.

Schuh, Franzjosef, 'Analyse von Verhörsprotokollen und Prozeßakten der Wiener Jakobinerprozesse 1794–98', in Otto Büsch and Walter Grab (eds), *Die demokratische Bewegung in Mitteleuropa im ausgehenden 18. und frühen 19. Jahrhundert* (Berlin: Colloquium Verlag, 1980), pp. 115–29.

—, 'Einige Beobachtungen über Rechtsstaat und aufgeklärten Absolutismus im Österreich der Jakobiner-Prozesse', in *Revolution und Demokratie in Geschichte und Literatur. Zum 60. Geburtstag von Walter Grab*. Duisburger Hochschulbeiträge, vol. 12 (Duisburg, 1979), pp. 171–84.

—, 'Die Wiener Jakobiner — Reformer oder Revolutionäre?', *Jahrbuch des Instituts für Deutsche Geschichte* [Tel Aviv, Israel], 12 (1983): 75–121.

Schulze, Hagen, *States, Nations and Nationalism. From the Middle Ages to the Present* (Oxford: Blackwell, 1994).

Schulze, Winfried, 'Das Ständewesen in den Erblanden der Habsburger Monarchie bis 1740: Vom dualistischen Ständestaat zum organisch-föderativen Absolutismus', in Peter Baumgart (ed.), *Ständetum und Staatsbildung in Brandenburg-Preußen* (Berlin: Veröffentlichungen der Historischen Kommission zu Berlin 55, 1983), pp. 263–79.

Scott, H.M., 'Reform in the Habsburg Monarchy, 1740–90', in H.M. Scott (ed.), *Enlightened Absolutism* (Basingstoke: Macmillan, 1990), pp. 145–88.

—, (ed.), *Enlightened Absolutism. Reform and Reformers in Later Eighteenth-Century Europe* (Basingstoke: Macmillan, 1990).

—, (ed.), *The European Nobilities in the Seventeenth and Eighteenth Centuries*, vol. 2: *Northern, Central and Eastern Europe* (London: Longman, 1995).

Scruton, Roger, *England. An Elegy* (London: Pimlico, 2001).

Sealsfield, Charles (Karl Postl), *Austria, as it is or Sketches of Continental Courts by an Eye Witness. Österreich, wie es ist.* Zwei Bände in einem Band. Ed. K.J.R. Arndt (Hildesheim, New York: Olms, 1972).

Sennett, Richard, *The Fall of Public Man* (New York: Alfred A. Knopf, 1977).

Sharpe, J.A., *Crime in Early Modern England 1550–1750* (London: Longman, 1984).

Sharpe, Kevin, 'Crown, Parliament and Locality: Government and Communication in Early Stuart England', *English Historical Review*, 101 (1986): 321–50.

—, *The Personal Rule of Charles I* (New Haven: Yale University Press, 1992).

Sieder, Reinhard, *Sozialgeschichte der Familie* (Frankfurt/M.: Suhrkamp, 1987).

Sked, Alan, *The Decline and Fall of the Habsburg Empire 1815–1918*. 2nd edn (Burnt Mill, Harlow, Essex: Longman, 2001).

Smith, Anthony D., *The Ethnic Origins of Nations* (Oxford: Basil Blackwell, 1986).

Smith, Dennis, *The Rise of Historical Sociology* (Cambridge: Polity Press, 1991).

Smuts, R. Malcolm, *Court Culture and the Origins of a Royalist Tradition in Early Stuart England* (Philadelphia: University of Philadelphia Press, 1987).

Sonnenfels, Joseph von, *Briefe über die Wiener Schaubühne*. Ed. H. Haider-Pregler (Graz: Akademische Druck- und Verlagsanstalt, 1988).

Speck, William A., *Stability and Strife. England 1714–1760* (London: Edward Arnold, 1977).

Spiel, Hilde, *Die hellen und die finsteren Zeiten. Erinnerungen 1911–1946* (Reinbek b. Hamburg: Rowohlt, 1991).

Staël, Germaine de, *Über Deutschland* (Stuttgart: Reclam, 1962).

Stanzel, Franz K., *Europäer. Ein imagologischer Essay*. 2nd edn (Heidelberg: C. Winter, 1998).

Stark, Werner, 'Die Abhängigkeitsverhältnisse der gutsherrlichen Bauern Böhmens im 17. und 18. Jahrhundert', *Jahrbücher für Nationalökonomie und Statistik*, 164 (1952): 270–92, 348–74, 440–53.

Steedman, Carolyn, *Childhood, Culture and Class in Britain: Margaret McMillan, 1860–1931* (New Brunswick: Rutgers University Press, 1990).

Stekl, Hannes and Wakounig, Marija, *Windisch-Graetz. Ein Fürstenhaus im 19. und 20. Jahrhundert* (Vienna: Böhlau, 1992).

Stone, Lawrence, *The Crisis of the Aristocracy, 1558–1641* (Oxford: Clarendon Press, 1965).

—, *The Family, Sex and Marriage in England, 1500–1800* (London: Weidenfeld and Nicolson, 1977).

—, 'The Results of the English Revolutions of the Seventeenth Century', in J.G.A. Pocock (ed.), *Three British Revolutions: 1641, 1688, 1776* (Princeton, N.J.: Princeton University Press1980), pp. 23–108.

Stourzh, Gerald, 'Die Gleichberechtigung der Volkstämme als Verfassungsprinzip 1848–1918', in Adam Wandruszka and Peter Urbanitsch (eds), *Die Völker des Reiches*, vol. 3: Die Habsburgermonarchie 1848–1918 (Vienna: Verlag der österreichischen Akademie der Wissenschaften, 1980), pp. 975–1206.

Stradal, Helmut, 'Die brabantische Revolution des Jahres 1789 aus Wiener Sicht', in *Standen en Landen*, vol. 47: Anciens Pays et assemblées d'État (Brussels, 1968), pp. 271–317.

Stundner, Franz, 'Die Kreisämter als Vorläufer der politischen Behörden I. Instanz', in Johannes Gründler (ed.), *100 Jahre Bezirkshauptmannschaften in Österreich* (Vienna: Selbstverlag, 1970).

Sturmberger, Hans, *Die Entwicklung der Verfassung Österreichs* (Graz, 1963).

—, 'Der absolutistische Staat und die Länder in Österreich', in Institut für Österreichkunde (ed.), *Der österreichische Föderalismus und seine historischen Grundlagen* (Vienna: Ferdinand Hirt, 1969), pp. 67–104.

Sugar, Peter F., 'The Influence of the Enlightenment and the French Revolution in Eighteenth Century Hungary', *Journal of Central European Affairs*, 17 (1958): 331–55.

Sykes, Christopher, *Four Studies in Loyalty* (London: Century Hutchinson, 1986).

Szarota, Elida Maria (1983) *Das Jesuitendrama im deutschen Sprachgebiet. Eine Periochen-Edition: Texte und Kommentare*, vol. 3: *Konfrontationen*, part 1 (München: Wilhelm Fink, 1983).

Taylor, David, *Mastering Economic and Social History* (Houndmills, Basingstoke: Macmillan, 1988).

Temple C.L., *Native Races and their Rulers. Sketches and Studies of Official Life and Administrative Problems in Nigeria* (Cape Town, 1918).

Thane, Pat, 'Government and Society in England and Wales, 1750–1914', in F.M.L. Thompson (ed.), *The Cambridge Social History of Britain, 1750–1950*, vol. 3: *Social Agencies and Institutions* (Cambridge: Cambridge University Press, 1990), pp. 1–61.

Theroux, Paul, *The Kingdom by the Sea* (Harmondsworth, Middlesex: Penguin Books, 1983).

Thompson, Edward P., 'The Moral Economy of the English Crowd in the Eighteenth Century', *Past and Present*, 50 (1971): 76–136.

Thompson, F.M.L., 'Britain', in David Spring (ed.), *European Landed Elites in the Nineteenth Century* (Baltimore, London: Johns Hopkins University Press, 1977), pp. 22–44.

Tidrick, Kathryn, *Empire and the English Character* (London: Tauris, 1992).

Tilly, Charles, *Popular Contention in Great Britain, 1758–1834* (Cambridge, Mass.: Harvard University Press, 1995).

Todd, Janet, *Sensibility. An Introduction* (London: Methuen, 1986).

Tosh, John, 'Was soll die Geschichtswissenschaft mit Männlichkeit anfangen? Betrachtungen zum 19. Jahrhundert in Großbritannien', in Christoph Conrad and Martina Kessel (eds), *Kultur und Geschichte. Neue Einblicke in eine alte Beziehung* (Stuttgart: Reclam, 1998), pp. 160–206.

Träger, Claus, 'Einleitung', in *Grillparzers Werke in drei Bänden*, vol. 1 (3 vols: Berlin: Aufbau-Verlag, 1990) pp. V–XL.

Trilling, Lionel, 'Jane Austen: Mansfield Park', in Boris Ford (ed.), *The New Pelican Guide to English Literature*, vol. 5: *From Blake to Byron* (Harmondsworth, Middlesex: Penguin Books, 1982), pp. 154–171.

Trollope, Anthony, *Can You Forgive Her?* (Oxford: Oxford University Press, 1982).

——, *The Three Clerks* (London: The Trollope Society [Omnium Publishing], 1992).

Tuchman, Barbara, *A Distant Mirror: The Calamitous 14th Century* (New York: Ballantine Books, 1987).

Tull, Stephan, *Die politischen Zielvorstellungen der Wiener Freimaurer und Wiener Jakobiner im 18. Jahrhundert* (Frankfurt/M.: Lang, 1994).

Tyacke, Nicholas, *Anti-Calvinists. The Rise of English Arminianism, c. 1590 to 1640* (Oxford: Clarendon Press, 1987).

Ucakar, Karl, *Demokratie und Wahlrecht in Österreich. Zur Entwicklung von politischer Partizipation und staatlicher Legitimationspolitik* (Vienna: Verlag für Gesellschaftskritik, 1985).

Varouxakis, Georgios, 'National Character in John Stuart Mill's Thought', *History of European Ideas*, 24/6 (1998): 375–91.

Varouxakis, Georgios, *Mill on Nationality* (London: Routledge, 2002).

Wagner, Hans (ed.), *Wien von Maria Theresia bis zur Franzosenzeit. Aus den Tagebüchern des Grafen Karl von Zinzendorf* (Vienna: Jahresgabe der Wiener Bibliophilen Gesellschaft, 1972).

Waldhoff, Hans-Peter, *Fremde und Zivilisierung: wissenssoziologische Studien über das Verarbeiten von Gefühlen der Fremdheit* (Frankfurt/M.: Suhrkamp, 1995).

Walter, Friedrich, 'Die Organisierung der staatlichen Polizei unter Kaiser Joseph II.', *Mitteilungen des Vereins für Geschichte der Stadt Wien*, 7 (1927): 22–53.

——, *Österreichische Verfassungs- und Verwaltungsgeschichte von 1500–1955* (Vienna: Böhlau, 1972).

Wangermann, Ernst, *From Joseph II to the Jacobins Trials. Government Policy and Public Opinion in the Habsburg Dominions in the Period of the French Revolution* (Oxford: Oxford University Press, 1969).

——, *The Austrian Achievement, 1700–1800* (London: Thames and Hudson, 1973).

——, 'The Austrian Enlightenment and the French Revolution', in Kinley Brauer and William E. Wright (eds), *Austria in the Age of the French Revolution, 1789–1815* (Minneapolis: Centre for Austrian Studies, 1990), pp. 1–10.

Watt, Ian, 'Defoe as Novelist', in Boris Ford (ed.) *The New Pelican Guide to Englisch Literature*, vol. 4: *From Dryden to Johnson* (Harmondsworth, Middlesex: Penguin Books, 1982), pp. 151–64.

Weber, Dietrich, *Heimito von Doderer. Studien zu seinem Romanwerk* (Diss. phil., Hamburg: 1963).

——, *Heimito von Doderer* (Munich: C.H. Beck, 1987).

Weber, Max, *Gesammelte Aufsätze zur Religionssoziologie*, vol. 1 (Tübingen: J.C.B. Mohr [Paul Siebeck], 1972).

Weber, Max, *The Protestant Ethic and the Spirit of Capitalism*, transl. by Talcott Parsons, 2nd edn (London: Allen & Unwin, 1976).

——, *Economy and Society*. Ed. Guenther Roth and Klaus Wittich (Berkeley, Los Angeles: University of California Press, 1978).

Weidmann, Paul, *Der Eroberer. Eine Parodie der Macht*. Ed. L. Bodi and F. Voit (Heidelberg: Carl Winter, 1997).

Weigel, Hans, *Flucht vor der Größe* (Graz: Styria, 1978).

Wende, Peter, 'Revisionismus als neue Orthodoxie? Parlament und Revolution in der modernen englischen Historiographie', *Historische Zeitschrift*, 246 (1988): 89–106.

Whigham, Frank, *Ambition and Privilege* (Berkeley: University of California Press, 1984).

Wiener Europagespräche 1977, *Wien und Europa zwischen den Revolutionen (1789–1848)* (Wiener Schriften, vol. 39) (Vienna: Jugend und Volk, 1978).

Wiener, Martin J., *English Culture and the Decline of the Industrial Spirit, 1850–1980* (Cambridge: Cambridge University Press, 1981).

Williams, Penry, *The Tudor Regime* (Oxford: Clarendon Press, 1979).

Wilson, Kathleen, *The Sense of the People: Politics, Culture and Imperialism in England, 1715–1785* (Cambridge: Cambridge University Press, 1995).

Winkelbauer, Thomas, 'Sozialdisziplinierung und Konfessionalisierung durch Grundherren in den österreichischen und böhmischen Ländern im 16. und 17. Jahrhundert', *Zeitschrift für historische Forschung*, 19 (1992a): 317–40.

—, '"Und sollen sich die Parteien gütlich miteinander vertragen". Zur Behandlung von Streitigkeiten und von "Injurien" vor den Patrimonialgerichten in Österreich und Niederösterreich in der frühen Neuzeit', *Zeitschrift der Savigny-Stiftung für Rechtsgeschichte* (Germanische Abteilung), 109 (1992b): 129–58.

Winter, Gustav, 'Das niederösterreichische Banntaidingwesen in Umrissen', *Jahrbuch für Landeskunde Niederösterreichs*, N.F. 12 (1913): 196–235.

Wolffe, John, *The Protestant Crusade in Great Britain, 1829–1860* (Oxford: Clarendon Press, 1991).

Wouters, Cas, 'Informalisierung und der Prozeß der Zivilisation', in Peter R. Gleichmann, Johann Goudsblom and Hermann Korte (eds), *Materialien zu Norbert Elias' Zivilisationstheorie* (Frankfurt/M.: Suhrkamp, 1979), pp. 279–98.

Wright, William E., *Serf, Seigneur, and Sovereign. Agrarian Reform in Eighteenth Century Bohemia* (Minneapolis: University of Minnesota Press, 1966).

Wunberg, Gotthart (ed.), *Die Wiener Moderne: Literatur, Kunst und Musik zwischen 1890 und 1910* (Stuttgart: Reclam, 1984).

Wunder, Bernd, 'Die Institutionalisierung der Invaliden-, Alters- und Hinterbliebenenversorgung der Staatsbediensteten in Österreich (1748–1790)', *Mitteilungen des Instituts für österreichische Geschichte*, 92 (1984): 341–406.

Yang, Kuo-shu, 'Will Societal Modernization Eventually Eliminate Cross-Cultural Psychological Difference?' in M.H. Bond (ed.), *The Cross-Cultural Challenge to Social Psychology* (Newbury Park: SAGE, 1988), pp. 67–85.

Yates, W. Edgar (1981) 'Zur Wirklichkeitsbezogenheit der Satire in Nestroys Posse "Eine Wohnung ist zu vermiethen"', in *Maske und Kothurn.* Internationale Beiträge zur Theaterwissenschaft, 27 (1981): 147–54.

Young, George M., *Victorian England. Portrait of an Age* (London: Oxford University Press, 1966).

Zagorin, Perez, *The Court and the Country. The Beginning of the English Revolution* (London: Routledge and Kegan Paul, 1969).

Zöllner, Erich (ed.), *Wellen der Verfolgung in der österreichischen Geschichte* (Vienna: Österreichischer Bundesverlag, 1986).

Index

Abrams, Philip 9
absolutism 15–17, 26, 76, 83–4, 107, 115, 124, 126, 184–5, 211–12, 250–51, 254, 291–2, 306, 317
Acham, Karl 124,184
Adler, Hans 99
affect 5, 10, 46, 237, 246, 271–2, 306, 314
regulation of 314
affective 10–11, 14, 17, 151, 170, 204, 230
affective control 46, 151
affective household 4–6, 11–12, 116, 119–21, 204, 209, 294, 306, 312
affect-modelling 1, 6, 9, 25–6, 306
affects 2, 5, 11, 14, 20, 45, 49, 119–20, 127, 153, 164, 184, 210, 223, 254, 256, 310, 312, 322
Albion 3
Almond, Gabriel 19, 20
altruism 157, 172, 201, 299–301, 307
amateur 170
Anderson, Perry 2, 110, 128
Anne (Queen of England) 40, 47, 51
antisemitism 111, 319–21
apathy 15, 248, 261
Arendt, W.A. 94
Arens, Franz 75
Argyle, Michael 6, 210
aristocracy 26–8, 41, 48, 55–6, 70, 72, 79–83, 91, 93, 95–8, 145, 147, 169, 173–4, 179, 183, 221, 226, 240, 242–3, 252, 255, 286, 299, 316–17
aristocratization 169
Armanski, Gerhard 254
Arminius, Jakob 34
Arnason, Johann P. 117
Arnold, R.R. 291
Arnold, Thomas 135, 169
Asch, Roland G. 48, 52
Ascham, Roger 49
Auchinleck, Sir Claude 222
Auersperg 80
Austen, Jane 167, 223, 225–32, 240–42
Austria-Hungary 131–2, 265–6,
Austrian humour 213
Austrian identity 121–2
Austrian mentality 131
Austrian national character 16, 121, 258–65, 277
Austrian Netherlands 94–5
Austrian patriotism 265
Austrian police 262
Austrian upper class(es) 139, 255
Austroslavism 105
authoritarianism 203, 259
authority 1, 2, 12, 14–20, 25–6, 28–9, 33, 69, 75, 79, 87, 109, 116–18, 120, 123, 130, 136–40, 148, 150, 155, 159–60, 162, 168, 179, 183, 188–90, 192, 194, 202–3, 211–12, 215–18, 221–3, 228, 233, 235–8, 242, 250, 254, 258–66, 270–71, 274–5, 279–82, 288, 293, 295–8, 311–12, 314–15, 317, 322
  feudal-patrimonial 18, 128
  paternalistic 53, 150, 316
  patriarchal 116
Axtmann, Roland 34, 77, 98, 248

Bacon, Francis 49
Balázs, Eva 92
Baltl, Hermann 70, 75
Barker-Benfield, G.J. 46
Baroque 21, 84, 120–21, 121, 124, 127, 186–7, 315
Barton, Peter F. 86
Bassett, Richard 14, 199, 297
Bauernfeld, Eduard von 207, 251
Bauman, Zygmunt 11

Bavaria 7, 122–3, 256–7
Bavarians 7
Baxter, Richard 154, 161
Beattie, John 47
Becket, Thomas 222
Beckett, J.V. 38, 41–2, 52, 62
Beethoven, Ludwig van 274
Behavioural models 294
Beidtel, Ignaz 87
Beller, Steven 319
Benda, Kalman 95, 97–8
Benna, Anna H. 98
Bérenger, Jean 79, 81–3
Berghoff, Hartmut 53
Bernhard, Thomas 120
Bibl, Viktor 96, 99
Bireley, Robert 81–2
Birke, Adolf M. 48
Bismarck, Otto Fuerst von 295
Blewett, David 323
Bodi, Lesli 15, 98, 126, 189, 193, 208–9, 245, 253, 256–7, 261, 284
Bödy, Paul 97
Bodzenta, Erich 117
Bohemia 69, 78–81, 92, 95, 104, 122, 125, 142, 260–61, 275
Bohemian 69, 79, 80–82, 88, 90, 105, 108
Bohemian Estates 79
Böhlig, Gertrud 124
Böhm, Stefan 143
Bolzano, Bernhard 127
Bonnie Prince Charlie 222
Bonß, Wolfgang 97
book-keeping 294, 315
Borsay, Peter 45
Boudicce 222
bourgeoisie 3, 14, 17, 55–6, 59, 83, 89, 92, 97, 106, 108–9, 111–12, 124, 126, 132–3, 135, 137, 148, 154–5, 167, 250, 254, 291, 316–17
Bradbury, Malcolm 223
Braddick, Michael J. 60–63
Bradler-Rottmann, Elisabeth 87
Bradley, Ian 56, 58
Brandt, Harm-Hinrich 104, 106–10
Brauneder, Wilhelm 70
Brewer, John 38, 40, 44, 47, 62, 64
Bristow, Joseph 135, 143, 218
British Empire 1, 46, 63,
Broch, Hermann 203
Brod, Max 249
Bronsen, David 318–22
Brontë, Charlotte 241, 311–14
Brubaker, W. Rogers 100
Bruckmüller, Ernst 3, 15, 74, 76, 78–80, 83, 89, 91, 93, 104, 111–12, 116, 178, 190, 195, 197, 213, 231, 289, 323
Brunner, Otto 70, 73–4, 103
Brusatti, Alois 89
Brutus, Marcus Julius 127
Bucholz, R.O. 47
Buckingham, George Villiers 30, 51
Bucquoy 80
Bunyan, John 297
bureaucracy 1, 7, 15–16, 38, 42–3, 107–9, 117, 142, 164, 198–9, 226, 240–41, 253, 256, 265, 277, 284, 289,
bureaucratic authority 291
bureaucratic habitus 284
bureaucratic rule 117
bureaucratization 108, 171, 250–51, 256–7, 259, 273, 316
Burgess, Glenn 32–4
Burnet, Gilbert 43
Burrell, Gilbert 34–5
Butler, Samuel 270, 293–4
Byzantine 70
Byzantium 124, 194, 219

Calvinism 43, 78, 314
Calvinist 79, 295
Cambridge Platonists 43
cameralism 298
Cannadine, David 146, 173–4, 177
Cannon, John 41–2
cant 163, 295
capitalism 190, 294–5
Carlyle, Thomas 298, 309
Castiglione, Baldassare 49
Catholic Church 17, 76–7, 79, 82
Cavalier Parliament 35,
censorship 98–9, 103, 107, 209, 253, 262, 275, 277, 280–82
character 2, 6, 8–9, 13, 19, 27, 46, 50, 53, 57, 59, 75, 111, 130, 140, 147, 163, 165, 168, 174, 188, 192, 215, 221, 231, 246, 251, 257, 263, 265, 271, 274, 277–9, 281–4, 291, 296–7

social 2, 5, 176–8, 245
see also national character
charity 58, 155, 160, 304
charity school 58
Charles I Stuart 30–33, 35, 37, 61, 149, 154
Charles II Stuart 15, 35–6, 40
Charles V Holy Roman Emperor 78
Charles VI Holy Roman Emperor 84
China 116–17, 154
Chivalry 18, 56, 152, 156–7, 163
Christianson, Paul 35
Church of England 30, 35–6
Churchill, R.C. 309–10, 323
Cicero, Marcus Tullius 50
citizen 92, 132, 283
civil servant 63, 81, 94, 109, 147, 288–9
civil society 15, 47
civil war 54, 61, 84, 95, 154, 222
civilization 10, 22, 295, 299
civilization theory 22, 25
civilizing process 12, 14, 17–19, 22, 25, 46, 169, 255, 305–6
civilizing thrust 26–7
Clifford, Hugh 296–7
Cockburn, J.A. 53
code of honour 19, 49, 132, 135
Colley, Linda 41, 48, 297, 315, 317, 321
Collini, Stefan 13
colonial rule 216, 296
comic ambivalence 193, 208
commercialization 1, 26, 46–7, 55, 75, 92, 177–8, 171, 197, 225, 299
commercial classes 240
Common Law 30–3
Commons 27–8, 30, 33, 38, 242
compromise(s) 59, 125, 134, 173, 181
Conduite-Listen 254
confessional absolutism 15–6
conscience 123, 133, 139, 157, 161, 220, 256, 264, 268, 295
constitution 31, 33–4, 70, 96, 98–113
constraints 4, 10, 14, 17–18, 134, 147, 181, 194
constraints by others 4, 255
see also self–constraint
Contentment 187
Corporatist 346
Corrigan, Philip 59
corruption 44, 138
Counter-Reformation 16–17, 76–7, 82–3, 85, 121–3, 125, 155, 322
Courage 133–4, 137, 206–7, 240, 246
court 17, 29–30, 40, 47, 49–52, 82
Court and Country 50–51
Court Chamber [Hofkammer] 71, 73–4, 87, 260, 278
courtier 2, 49
courtization 82, 152, 241
courtly 26, 152, 179, 184, 239, 246
Courts of High Commission 31
Cragg, G.R. 43
Crane, R.S. 43
cricket 53, 170
Cromwell, Oliver 35, 154, 222
Csáky, Moritz 96, 179
Cudworth, Ralph 43
cuius regio eius religio 78
cura religionis 77
Curtin, Michael 216
cynicism 141, 306, 315
Czechs 105, 112, 140,
Czernin 80

Dahrendorf, Ralf 15
Dann, Otto 97
Davis, Walter W. 94
De Gaulle, Charles 205
Deák, Istvan 131–2, 323
Decius 123
decivilization 10
deconstructionism 21
deference 19, 135, 149, 160
Defoe, Daniel 14, 22, 148–150, 155, 218–21, 226–7, 298–307, 315, 323
democratization 5, 16, 58, 112–13, 134, 137, 309
dependability 151
Desfours 80
despotism 248, 257, 291–2, 313

Dichand, Hans 176–7
Dickens, Charles 22, 158, 196–7, 267, 276–7, 307–10, 323
Dickson, Peter G.M. 87, 90
Dietrichstein 78, 104, 109–10,
dignity 118, 126, 150, 199, 225, 227–8, 241, 242, 247, 267, 280
Directorium in publicis et cameralibus 87

Discipline 37, 77, 120, 139, 233–5, 238, 254, 275
Disgrace, social 227
Dissenters 37–9
divine right of kings 32, 35
Doderer, Heimito von 22, 164, 182, 246–9, 255, 284, 291, 315
dominance 41, 48, 112–13, 119, 152, 168–9, 237, 317
domination 27
Donaldson, Ian 43
double think 261
Dual Monarchy 2, 113, 131–2
duel 127, 133, 135, 159, 315–16, 320
Duindam, Eric 6, 9, 15, 25–6, 46, 153, 169, 222–3
dungeon of the peoples 3
Dunning, Eric 6, 9, 15, 25–6, 46, 169

Eagleton, Terry 21
Ebner-Eschenbach, Maria von 128–30, 142, 163
ecclesiastical authority 121
economy of drives 4
Edward I 27
Edward VIII 215–16
effortless superiority 149
egalitarianism 297
Ehalt, Hubert Ch 83
Elias, Norbert 1–15, 20, 25–7, 40–2, 44–6, 59, 119, 124, 133–5, 138, 140, 146, 152–4, 163, 169, 176–7, 180, 199, 205, 222–3, 305–6, 309, 317
Elisabeth I 29, 49, 59–60, 202
Ellis, Markman 45
Elton, Geoffrey 29, 33
Elyot, Sir Thomas 49
embourgeoisement 170, 253, 257
Emerson, Donald 99
emotion 35, 130, 152, 226
emotions 1, 6, 8, 11, 14, 20, 43, 45, 50, 175, 306
Emsley, Clive 168
English humour
English identity 13
English national character 13–4, 27, 46, 153–4, 243
English national 12, 243
English upper class(es) 16, 26
Englishness 1, 13, 134, 161
Enlightenment 45, 126, 316
Episcopal constitution 31, 33–4
Estates 72–4, 78–82, 87–8, 93, 95, 101, 104, 146
Evangelical Revival 53
Evangelicalism 55–6, 295, 297, 309–10
Evans, Robert J.W. 73, 82–3
external constraints 4–5, 11, 17, 119, 269
Eybel, J.v. 257

fagging 136
fairness 8, 15
fascism 10, 318
fatalism 189, 248, 319
Fawkes, Guy 34
Feigl, Helmut 74, 91–2
feminization 46
Ferdinand 'the Benignant' (Austrian Emperor) 282
Ferdinand I (Holy Roman Emperor) 69–71, 83
Ferdinand II (Holy Roman Emperor) 79–81, 123–5
Ferdinand III (Holy Roman Emperor) 82
Ferguson, Niall 136
Fernes, John 49
feudalism 15–16, 117, 119–20, 128, 243, 247
Fielding, Henry 150, 156–64, 177
Fiering, Norman 45
financial administration 63, 72, 87–8, 90, 93
First World War 1–2, 59, 67, 82, 133
Firth, Kathrine R. 34–5
fiscal monopoly 61
Fischer, Ernst 132, 252
flattery 123, 193–4, 215, 242
Fletcher, Anthony 49–50
Fletcher, Jonathan 10
flogging 136
Fodor, Heinrich 97
football 155, 166, 169
Ford, Ford Madox 146, 149–51
foresight 5, 225, 306
Forester, Cecil Scott 233–9
Formality-informality span 146
Fournier, August 98–9
foxhunt 137, 156
France 2, 5, 17, 26–8, 30–31, 36–7, 42, 47, 50, 58, 62, 76–7, 84, 96–8,

102, 124–5, 131, 152, 166, 196, 253, 289, 315
franchise 111
Franz I, (Holy Roman Emperor) 253, 9
Franz II, (Holy Roman Emperor)
  as Austrian Emperor Franz I 98, 100–101
Franz Joseph I, (Austrian Emperor) 165
fraternities, duelling 135
Frederick II of Prussia 126, 202, 239, 295, 319
Frederick, son-in-law of James I 30, 79–80
Freedom of action 229, 231, 264
French national character 5, 125
French Revolution 46, 100, 140, 224
Freud, Siegmund 3, 204, 210, 272
Friedel, Johann 163
Friedell, Egon 126, 257, 294–5
functional democratization 5, 309

Galicia 94, 99, 105, 118, 128, 130, 139–40, 142, 253, 317, 321
Gampl, Inge 78, 83, 85–6
Gandhi, Mohandas Karatschand 222
Garaudy, Roger 249
Gatrell, V.A. 168–9
gender relations 242
genteel charisma 221
gentleman 23, 26, 49–51, 57, 141, 145–51, 155–6, 159, 161, 163–5
gentleman canon 17, 56, 140, 145, 151, 156–7, 163–5, 175
gentlemanly code 217, 311
Gentry 49, 51, 147, 159–63, 167, 215, 221, 234, 240
Gentz, Friedrich von 281
George I 40, 42, 47–8
George II 40
George III 61, 63
German 8, 10, 16–7, 22, 69, 80, 86, 104, 105, 107–8, 110, 112, 126, 136, 141, 142, 149, 151, 153, 164
German nationalism 126
German nationalism in Austria 7, 126
Germans 7, 11, 22, 105–6, 112, 291–2, 319
Germany 2, 22, 102, 105, 121, 125, 132, 137, 141, 146, 163, 236, 289, 291–2
Giddens, Anthony 9
Girouard, Mark 56–7
Gleichmann, Peter 120
Glorious Revolution 28, 37–9, 54, 61–2
Glyn, Arthur 164, 222–3
Gnau, Hermann 98
Goethe, Johann Wolfgang von 274
Goffman, Erving 180, 211, 228, 238, 248, 271, 274
Goldberg, Rita 46
Gorer, Geoffrey 158, 167, 170
Gothic novel 225–6, 242
government 30, 33, 176
Grab, Walter 98
Graves, Robert 141–2
Great War 137, 322
Greyerz,Kaspar 32, 34, 36–7, 39
Grillparzer, Franz 184, 187–8, 264–5, 268–84
group shame 221, 230
Grüll, Georg 92
Grünberg, Karl 92
Guy, John 29

habitualization 18
habitus 1, 6–12, 17–9, 26, 115, 128, 130–31, 170, 198, 209, 242, 250, 266, 274, 292, 294, 314–15
  Austrian 115, 121, 130, 188, 203, 245, 266, 314, 322
  English 9, 22, 241, 293–5, 298
    proud detachment 216, 218, 242–3
  see also national habitus; national character
Habsburg 1–3, 7, 16, 19, 25, 30, 70–73, 76, 81, 83, 87, 96, 98, 100–102, 104–5, 108, 111–13, 122, 132, 171, 176, 289, 314, 316–18
Habsburg clementia 201–2, 263
Habsburg Monarchy 1–2, 7, 19, 25, 30, 70–73, 76, 81, 83, 87, 96, 98, 100–102, 104–5, 108, 111–13, 132, 137, 141, 146, 165, 171, 176, 289, 314, 316–18
  multi-ethnic character 7, 17, 100–101, 104–5
Habsburg myth 117, 187–8, 246, 251, 322,
Hafner, Philipp 205–6
Haggard, H. Rider 136
Haig, Douglas 141

Haley, Bruce 57
Hall, N. John 288
Haller, William 50
Hanák, Peter 101
hand-kiss 124, 258, 292
Hanisch, Ernst 112–13
Hanke, Gerhard 92, 101
Hannemann, Bruno 204, 206–7, 213
Hans Wurst 186–7
Hantsch, Hugo 107, 109
harmony 18–19, 134, 231, 250
Harth, Friedrich 74
Harvie, Christoph 164, 174–5
Haselsteiner, Horst 95
Hassinger, Herbert 72–3
Haugwitz, Frierdich Wilhelm, Graf 87
Hayton, David 58
Heal, Felicity 52, 304
heartlessness 118, 304–7
Hebbel, Friedrich 205–6, 213
Heckenast, Gustav 95
Hedin, Sven 165
Heer, Friedrich 3, 121–2, 126, 317–19
Hein, Juergen 206
Heindl, Waltraud 91, 99–100, 257, 317
Heiss, Gernot 78
Hellbling, Ernst 70, 88
Henrietta Maria 34
Henry VI 28
Henry VII 28
Henry VIII 29
Herberstein 278
Herzmanovsky–Orlando 22, 127–8, 132, 164, 284–8
Hintze, Otto 234
Hirsch, Fred 285
Hitler, Adolf 274
Hobsbawm, Eric 8, 294
Hochschild, Arlie R. 238
Hodge, Robert 21, 242
Hoefer, Frank Thomas 99
Hofmannsthal, Hugo von 14, 180, 189
Holmes, Geoffrey 43, 52
Holt, Richard 136
Holy Roman Empire 122
homo oeconomicus 219
honour 260–61
Horvath, Ödön von 267
hospitality 304–5
House of Commons 33, 41
Huber, Franz X 256–8
Hughes, Thomas 57, 135
Huizinga, Johan 185
humanism 49, 121, 184, 223, 309, 317
humanization 15, 169, 257, 310, 314, 316–17
humour 203, 208–13, 223
Hundred Years War 27–8
Hungary 8, 16, 69, 79, 94–7, 99, 104–6, 112–13, 125, 221, 266, 275
Hunt, P.A. 61–2
Hypocrisy 162–63, 295, 297

identity 12–13, 43, 84–5, 98, 105, 121, 208, 243, 283
ideology 44, 51, 252–3
immunity 72, 80, 154
Imperial Aulic Council [Reichshofratsordnung] 71
Imperial Chancellery [Reichskanzlei] 71
Imperial Council [Reichsrat] 109–10
Imperial Diet [Reichstag] 104, 106, 110
Impromptu performances [Stegreifkomödie] 184
indirect rule 17, 136, 160, 169, 215–16, 295–6
individualization 6, 12, 137, 152, 229–30, 299
Ingrao, Charles W. 70
Inkeles, Alex 9
Inner Austria 69, 122–3
Innerhofer, Franz 118–20, 126
interdependence 5–6
irony 208–12, 215, 286
Isaacs, Tina 58

Jacobin 98, 281
James I 30, 32, 34, 50, 154
James II 36–8
Japan 116
Jellacic, Josip 106
Jesuit dramas 122–4
Jesuits 112, 122–6, 185
Jews 317–19
John (Archduke) 263
Jones, Mary G. 58
Joseph II (Holy Roman Emperor) 15, 83, 85–7, 89–90, 94–5, 98–100, 127, 256–7, 285
Josephine 100–2, 125–7
Josephinism 127, 169, 256

Josephinist 96–7, 259, 316
Josephinist Thaw 125, 189
Julian 123
jury 159
Justice of the Peace 53

Kafka, Franz 22, 80, 248–9
Kahl, Kurt 206, 215
Kaminiates, Johann 124
Kann, Robert 69, 103, 106, 111–12
Kaunitz, Wenzel Anton Fuerst von 87
Kavke, Frantisek 80
Keane, John 251
Kenéz, Peter 97
Kenyon, John 30–32, 34, 36–7
Khevenhueller 78
Kinsky 80
Kipling, Rudyard 136, 217–18, 220, 222
Király, Bela K 95–6
Kisch, Egon 140, 142–5,
Kishlansky, Mark 32–3, 35, 37
Kishon, Ephraim 285
Klein, Lawrence 45
Klíma, Arnost 92
Klingenstein, Grete 87
Klueting, Harm 84, 86
Kluxen, Karl 27–30, 35, 37
Kocher, Gernot 70
Königgrätz (Sadowa), Battle of 110–11
Körner, Alfred 96–7
Köstler, Arthur 209
Kraus, Karl 137, 139, 141–2, 213, 251, 316,
Kümmel, Ruth 309

Lachmayer, Friedrich 70
Lamont, William M. 35
Lancaster 28
Landau, Norman 54
landed interest 42–3
Laqueur, Thomas Walter 59
Lasch, Christopher 19, 294
Laslett, Peter 15, 21–2, 264
Latitudinarians 43–4
Lawrence, Henyr 297
Lawrence, John 297
Leavis, Queenie 313
Lengauer, Hubert 265
Leopold II 95–8
Lepenies, Wolf 20
Lettner, Gerda 20, 98
Levy, Miriam 96
Lewis, Helen B. 274
Lhotsky, Alphons 14, 180, 250, 252–3
liberalism 107, 110, 112, 250
Liebel-Weckowicz, Helen 89–90
Lineage Charisma 149
Link, Christoph 70, 78, 85–6, 93
literature of the Enlightenment 126, 189, 281
Loades, David 48–9
Loewenstein, Karl 28
London 1, 42, 46, 48, 50, 52–3, 58, 134, 158, 164–6, 183, 224, 238, 258, 294, 299, 302–3
Long Parliament 35
Lord Lieutenants 31, 52, 159–60
lords of the manor 53, 72–8, 89–95, 130, 148, 316
Lorenz, Ottokar 94
Louis XIV French King 36
Low-Church 39
Lower Austria 69, 82, 122, 234, 260–61
lower class 53, 58, 166, 196–97, 240, 319
loyalty 11, 15, 28, 35, 39–40, 121, 125, 131, 133, 138, 253–4, 259–60, 317, 287–8, 319
Lubomirski 184
Ludwig, archduke of Austria 36, 194
Lugard, Frederick Sir 215–16, 221
Lutz, Heinrich 103–5
luxury 155, 196–7, 228, 238, 303, 310

MacCaffrey, Wallace T 49
MacDonagh, Oliver 67
Macfarlane, Alan 155
MacHardy, Karin 80
Machiavellism 316
Macmillan, Harold 175–6
Magna Carta 27, 154
Magris, Claudip 14, 117–18, 246, 251, 265–6, 275, 291
Malinowski, Bronislaw 219
man of feeling 43–5
Manchester liberalism 176
Mann, Michael 2, 16, 60, 64–5, 107
manners 46–7, 58, 147–8, 150, 162, 167, 174, 180, 224, 229, 230, 234, 247, 304, 306
Mannheim, Karl 180
manorial absolutism 15–16, 76, 78,

March Revolution (1848) 205
Maria Theresa, Empress 15, 71–2, 85, 87–90, 93, 122, 202
market 240, 316
marketization 17, 136, 152–3, 169, 240, 304, 316
marriage market 223, 226–7, 300, 302
Marx, Karl 59, 304
Masai 216, 220, 239–40
Matis, Herbert 85, 89, 91–2
Matthias (Holy Roman Emperor) 79
Maurer, Michael 118–19, 153
Mautner, Franz 206–8, 213
Maximilian I Holy Roman Emperor 69, 83
Maximilian II Holy Roman Emperor 83, 125
May, Karl 234
Mayr, Josef K. 99
Melton, James van Horn 82
Menasse, Robert 199
menial family 118–19, 191
Mennell, Stephen 6, 10
mentality 2, 115, 131–3, 153, 185, 225, 233–4, 252, 260, 284, 307
Merz, Carl 193
Metropolitan Police 168, 262
Metternich, Clemens, Fuerst von 99, 101, 166, 260–62, 281
middle-class 6, 14–16, 18, 59, 98, 148, 232
middle-class morality 228, 309
Mikes, George 164, 288
Mikoletzky, Lorenz 93
military (Austria) 1, 94–6, 107, 318
military (Britain) 1, 27, 31, 37–8, 237
military expenditures (Austria) 108
military expenditures (Britain) 38, 65
military state (Austria as) 93
Mill, John Stuart 12
Mitgutsch, Waltraud 120
modernization 9, 16, 56, 256–7
Mohács, Battle of 84
Mommsen, Hans 113
money 116, 128, 167, 150, 153–5, 167, 197, 236, 240, 259, 280, 285, 294, 297, 300, 303–6, 316
monetarization 138
monied interest 42
Monmouth, James Scott, Herzog von 302
monopoly of force 15, 125, 148
monopoly of taxation 15–16, 26–8, 59, 72, 74
monopoly of violence 247, 272
Montagu, Lady Mary Wortley 231
moralization 17, 293, 295–6, 298, 309, 312–14
moralization of authority 17
More, Hannah 56
More, Henry 43
Morus, Thomas 223
Moser, Hans 1, 283
Mozart, Wolfgang A. 279
Murdock, Rupert 176–7
muscular Christianity 57, 135, 160, 166, 311
Musil, Robert 22, 136, 173, 181, 201, 242, 247–8, 250, 252, 315, 317
Mylius, Christoph 292

Nabokov, Vladimir 243
Napoleon 102, 212, 239, 262, 266, 291, 297, 319
Naske, A. 100
nation 7–8, 12, 29, 37, 43–4, 47, 104, 208, 252–3, 309, 314, 316–21
nation formation 7, 112–13
nation state 8, 12, 100–101, 110
national character 2, 5, 7–8, 10–14, 19, 46, 147
see also Austrian national character; English national character
national habitus 5–14, 19, 199, 225, 235, 272, 283, 312
national pride 12
national question 98, 102–6, 113,
nationalities, struggle of 98, 102, 110, 113, 134, 142
navvy 290
Neale, John 49
Neo-absolutism 111–12
Neo-absolutist regime in Austria 107–8
nepotism 39, 283–4, 291
Nero 123
Nestroy, Johann 22, 184–98, 203–8, 210–14, 224, 240, 242, 315
Newman, Gerald 46
Nicolai, Friedrich 251–2
nihilism as Austrian attitude (Nestroy) 204, 212
Nipperdey, Thomas 110, 112

nobility 15–17, 28, 31, 53, 55, 73, 78–80, 95, 97, 108, 110, 116, 122, 132, 145–6, 153, 252
noblesse oblige 150
nonconformists 36

obedience 19, 116, 129, 247, 262–3
Oberhummer, Hermann 99
Oberste Justizstelle [supreme legal authority in Austria] 87, 96
O'Brien, Patrick 62–3
Obschernitzki, Doris 248
official 100, 116, 199, 202, 251, 254, 259
officialdom 17, 200, 255, 290
officials 90–91, 99–100, 182, 247, 254, 257, 289
Ogris, Werner 87
Orwell, George 261
Osterloh 88
Otruba, Gustav 92
Ottoman Empire 2, 69–73, 79, 94–5, 140

pacification 26, 42
Palacky, Franz 105
Palmer, Robert R. 97
Palmer, Stanley 59
Pánek, Jaroslav 80
Parallel Campaign
Parin, Paul 392
Parin-Matthey, Goldy 392
Parliament, English 26–42, 49
parliamentarism 15, 26, 29, 134, 164–5, 171
parliamentarization 26, 37, 42, 98–113, 322
parody 3, 15, 18–20, 26–8, 132, 186–7, 192, 195–6, 198, 203, 205, 207–8, 259, 284
Parsons, Tacott 2, 312, 323
paternalism 53, 117, 146, 211, 295–6
  feudal 16, 145
patriarchal 116–17, 190
Patrick, Simon 43, 134
patrimonial 15, 74, 89, 116–17, 130
patrimonial authority 15, 74, 314
patrimonial bureaucracy 15, 316
patrimonial courts 74, 89, 189
patrimonial domination 116
patrimonialism 115, 117, 131, 295–6
feudal 15–16, 116–19, 128–9, 247
patriotism 12, 101, 141, 265, 318
patronage 38, 41, 49, 100, 148, 277–8, 288–9, 291
Patzelt, Erna 92
Peabody, Dean 14
peasant rebellions 130
Peck, Linda, Levy 49
pedantry 252, 255–6
Peel, Robert Sir 158
peers 18, 32, 40–41, 49, 163
perfidious Albion 3, 294, 323
Pergen, Graf 98
Permanent Conference [Ständige Konferenz] 71
Pezzl, Johann 126–7, 185, 294–5
Piccolomini Äneas Sylvius 80, 25
pietas Austriaca 83
Pillersdorf, Franz, Freiherr von 103, 278
pitilessness 307
Pius V 34
Plaschka, Richard Georg 87
Plato 127
Pocock, J.G.A. 45
Polasky, Janet L. 94–5
police 1, 76, 89, 98–9, 167–8, 195, 207, 222, 257, 260, 262
politeness 45–6, 50, 163
political socialization 15, 20, 131
Pool, David 159–60, 176, 243
Porter, Roy 45
Postl, Karl 127, 258–263, 286
power 1–3, 7, 15–17, 19–20, 22, 26–8, 30–33, 37–8, 40–41, 49–50, 52, 54–5, 59, 61, 70, 72, 74, 75, 78, 81, 84–5, 87–92, 96, 105, 108, 110–13, 117, 122, 128–9, 132–3, 136, 167, 173–4, 176, 226, 231, 259, 264, 266, 275, 277, 296–8, 310, 314, 316–18, 322
power balance 16, 26–8, 30, 38, 70, 84, 128–9, 187, 259
  between the sexes 225–6, 231
power differentials 221
power resources 211, 226, 241, 303
Presbyterian constitution 34
Press, Volker 82
Preston, John 156
pride 12, 123, 126, 155, 167, 195, 215, 220–21, 224–8, 228, 232, 239, 240, 247, 272, 286, 303–4, 306, 315

privacy 14, 305
Privy Conference [Geheime Konferenz] 71
Privy Council [Geheimer Rat] 38, 52, 71, 202
property 33, 35, 37, 42, 51–2, 55, 74, 94
Protestant Ethic 153, 312, 314
Protestant sects 35
Protestantism 34, 50, 76, 78, 122, 125, 314–15, 321–2
Proust, Marcel 229
Prussia 2, 87, 95, 126, 132, 179–81, 202, 212–3, 233, 239, 251, 283, 297, 319, 321
psychic habitus 5
Public Schools 56–7, 135, 142–3, 153, 238–9
Puritanism 14, 17, 33, 151, 154, 219, 293, 297
Puritan 44, 55, 59, 147–9, 154–5, 157, 161–2, 164, 170, 297, 309–10

Qualtinger, Helmut 193
Quinlan, Maurice J. 58

Raban, Jonathan 243
Radetzky 106, 115, 133, 135, 318–19
Raimund, Ferdinand 184, 186–9, 224
rationality 5, 9, 15, 18, 134, 139, 142, 246, 247–8, 257, 277–8, 303, 305–7
rationalization 15, 142, 248
Rauchensteiner, Manfried 131–2, 140–41
Rautenstrauch, Johann 126
reason vs. sentiment 226
Rebel, Hermann 75
reform absolutism 16, 83–4, 90–93, 126, 251, 253, 317
Reformation 29, 34–5, 50, 82, 121–2
Reinalter, Helmut 96–8
Reiner, Robert 168
religious pluralism 125, 128
Remarque, Erich Maria 137, 141
Representationen und Cammern 87
reserve 51, 145, 154, 221, 224
respect 53, 128, 134–6, 146, 151, 160, 220, 230, 232, 242, 263–4, 287
restoration (English) 15, 43, 125
restoration period (English) 99
Retzinger, Suzanne M. 20, 271, 274
Rich, Paul J. 136
Richardson, Samuel 14
Richter, Joseph 126–7, 256–7
Roberts, Clayton 38
Roberts, James Deotis 43
Robson-Scott, W.D. 12
Romani, Robert 13
Romantik 101, 225
Rommel, Otto 183, 185, 222
Rosegger, Peter 316
Rosenstrauch-Königsberg, Edith 97
Rossbacher, Karlheinz 142, 179
Roth, Joseph 115, 118, 133, 135, 181–3, 298, 314, 317–22
Roundheads 153
Rozdolski, Roman 94
Rudolf II (Holy Roman Emperor) 79, 83, 125
rugby 153, 169
rule 15–19, 22, 31, 36, 67, 81, 86, 117, 125, 134, 153, 168
Rule, John 41, 321–2
Rule Britannia 321–2
Rumpler, Helmut 96, 101–7, 109–10, 113
Rupp, Gordon 58
Ruskin, John 298, 309
Russia 2, 84, 131, 139, 202
Ruthenians 139
Ruttenham, Georg 49

Saar, Ferdinand von 117–18, 316
Sandgruber, Roman 72, 75–6, 78, 102–3
Sashegyi, Oskar 98
Sassoon, Siegfried 22, 137–8, 141–2
Sayer 59
Sayles, G.O. 27–8
Scheff, Thomas 20, 271, 274
Schikaneder, Emanuel 184
Schiller, Friedrich 252
Schindler, Norbert 97
Schindling, Anton 82
Schnitzler, Arthur 133–4, 242, 267, 315
Schönbrunn German 147, 182
Schramm, Gottfried 79
Schremmer, Eckart 62–9
Schreyvogel, Joseph 281
Schröder, Hans-Christoph 53, 55–6
Schuh, Franzjosef 96–8
Schulze, Hagen 29
Schulze, Winfried 72
Schwarzenberg 80

Scotland 28, 31, 42, 177, 317
Scott, H.M. 87
Scruton, Roger 13
Sealsfield, Charles 127, 259–64, 291–2
Second World War 140, 217, 222, 233
secularization 127

Sedlnitzky, Josef, Graf von Choltitz 281
seigneurial authority [Grundherrschaft] 74, 117, 128–9, 190
self-constraint 4, 10–11, 120, 133, 136, 160, 231, 246, 255, 305, 311–12, 315–16
self-constraint, apparatus of 4, 272, 306
self-control 4, 14, 56, 133, 135–6, 146, 151, 166–7, 218, 229, 231, 238–9, 255, 306
self-interest 167, 186, 309
self-irony 18, 186, 208–12, 222
self-reliance
self-respect 227, 247, 279–80
self-restraint 4–5, 10, 120
Sennett, Richard 183
sentimentality, culture of 225, 310
Serbia 84–5, 132, 139–41
serfdom 51, 92, 173, 205–6, 257, 262, 296
seriousness 56
servants 40, 100, 177, 186–92, 198, 212–13, 262
servility 177–9, 193–5, 212, 218, 259, 261–2, 276, 288
sexual self-constraints 231
Shaftesbury, Anthony Ashley Cooper 56
shame 4, 18, 120, 126, 166, 212, 227, 229, 274, 271–4
Sharpe, Kevin 51–2, 54
Sheard, Kenneth 169–170
shyness 170, 268, 274
Sieder, Reinhard 118, 191
Simmel, Georg 269
Sked, Alan 131
slavery 218–19
Slavs 17
Smith, Anthony 7–8
Smith, David 9
Smollett, Tobias 14
Smuts, Jan Christian 51–2, 222
Social Darwinism 136, 218
social habitus 6–7, 10, 209, 272
social partnership (Austrian institution) 19, 125
social question 103, 111
sociogenesis 17–18, 25, 27
Sonnenfels, Joseph 184, 186, 200
Sophia, Electoress of Hanover 39
Spain 29–31, 50, 122
Speck, William A. 39–40, 44
Spiel, Hilde 164
spoils system 40
Stadion, Johann Philipp, Graf von 278
Staël, Germaine de 256
Stanzel, Franz 163
Star Chamber 31
Starhemberg 78, 184
Stark, Werner 92
state character 2, 7–8
state competition 134–5, 233
state formation
  Austrian 2, 7, 12, 16–17, 19, 25, 77
  English 2, 7, 12, 17, 19, 25–7, 59, 77
state revenues
  Austrian 93, 108
  English 38, 61–2, 67
Steedman, Carolyn 323
Stekl, Hannes 116, 132–3, 289
stereotypes, national 9
Stifter, Adalbert 251, 267
Stillingfleet, Edward 43
Stone, Lawrence 43, 49, 230
Stourzh, Gerald 113
Stradal, Helmut 94–5
Stranitzkys, Josef Anton 213
structuralism 21
Stuart Monarchy 40, 43, 50
Stundner, Franz 88
Sturmberger, Hans 72, 89
Sugar, Peter F. 97
Sunday School 58
super-ego 3–4, 255
surveillance state (Austria as) 263–4
survival-units (states as) 7
Sykes, Christopher 217, 243
Symbol Theory 8
Szarota, Elida Maria 122–3

Taaffe, Eduard Graf 80
tact 56, 163, 166, 180–81, 215, 267–8, 318
tax reform 93–4

taxation, burden of 93–4
taxation, England 27–9, 31, 38, 40, 67
taxation, right of 72, 80, 87, 93, 109
Taylor, David 117, 307
Teplitz 261
Thackerays, William Maepeace 310
Thane, Pat 67
Theroux, Paul 166, 243
Thompson, Edward P. 59
Thompson, F.M.L. 55
Thun-Hohenstain, Leo Graf 187
Tidrick, Kathryn 135, 160, 215–17, 221, 295–6
Tillotson, John 43
Tilly, Charles 63
Todd, Janetz 45
Torberg, Friedrich 213, 285
Tories 46–8, 50, 221
Träger, Claus 266
Trautmannsdorff, Grafen von 80
Trieste 69, 88, 99, 253
Trilling, Lionel 223
Trollope, Anthony 164–6, 172–6, 288–91
Tuchman, Barbara 152
Tudor 28, 49, 288, 290
Tudor Monarchy 49
Tull, Stefan 96–7
Turks 79, 84–5, 95, 122–3
Tyacke 34
Tyrol 69, 72, 260–61
Tyroleans 131, 189, 291

Ucakar, Karl 108, 111–12
Uffenbach, Zacharias Conard von 153–4
unbrotherliness 304
understatement 149–50, 155, 163, 199, 210, 222–3
upper class(es) 10, 16, 25–6, 59, 139, 321
urbanization 55, 77–8, 137, 225, 307–8
utilitarianism 297–9, 304, 306, 309–10, 316

Varouxakis, Georgios 13
Vereinigte Hofstelle 88
Victoria, Queen 171
Vienna 79, 82, 98–9, 101, 104, 106–7, 110, 123–4, 137, 179–180, 183–9, 194–5, 197, 203, 205, 211, 256
Viennese Modernity 115, 179
Viennese popular comedy 14, 126, 183, 207
Viktorian age 164
Vladislav II. 69
Vormärz 99, 102–4, 125, 188, 207, 258–9, 260, 284

Wagner, Hans 184
Wakounig, Marija 132–3, 178
Waldhoff, Hans Peter 255
Walpole, Sir Robert 40
Walter, Friedrich 70, 98
Wangermann, Ernst 85, 87, 95–8
warrior code 116, 121, 131, 220–21, 311, 314
Watt, Isaac 58
Weber, Max 46, 100, 116–17, 133–4, 149, 152–5, 163, 295
We-feeling 321
We-I-balance 250
We-ideal 296
We-identity 12
Weidmann, Paul 257
Weigel, Hans 268
We-image 322
Weistümer 75
welfare state 67, 264, 298
Wenceslaus 69
Wesley, John 154, 161
Westminster 171
Whichcote, Benjamin 43
Whigham, Frank 49
Whigs 40, 44, 47, 227
White Mountain, Battle of the 30, 80
Wiener, Martin 56–7
Wilde, Oscar 219, 242, 268
William III 37–40, 58
William the Conqueror 27
Williams, Penry 28
Wilson, Thomas 46
Windisch-Graetz 106, 132–3
Winkelbauer, Thomas 75–6
Winter, Gustav 75, 291
Wolffe, John 55
working class 17, 58–9, 106, 224–5
Wright, William E. 92
Wunberg, Gotthart 179
Wunder, Bernard 91,
Wurmbrand, Graf 278–9

Yates, Edgar 189
York 28

Zagorin, Perez 50
Zensurhofstelle 260, 280
Zinzendorf, Karl Graf von 78, 184